Mastering Elixir

Build and scale concurrent, distributed, and fault-tolerant applications

André Albuquerque
Daniel Caixinha

BIRMINGHAM - MUMBAI

Mastering Elixir

Commissioning Editor: Richa Tripathi
Acquisition Editor: Sandeep Mishra
Content Development Editor: Anugraha Arunagiri
Technical Editor: Jash Bavishi
Copy Editor: Muktikant Garimella
Project Coordinator: Ulhas Kambali
Proofreader: Safis Editing
Indexer: Pratik Shirodkar
Graphics: Tania Dutta
Production Coordinator: Shantanu Zagade

First published: July 2018

Production reference: 1280718

Published by Packt Publishing Ltd.
Livery Place
35 Livery Street
Birmingham
B3 2PB, UK.

ISBN 978-1-78847-267-8

www.packtpub.com

To Ana and José

–André Albuquerque

To Raquel and Gabriel

–Daniel Caixinha

`mapt.io`

Mapt is an online digital library that gives you full access to over 5,000 books and videos, as well as industry leading tools to help you plan your personal development and advance your career. For more information, please visit our website.

Why subscribe?

- Spend less time learning and more time coding with practical eBooks and Videos from over 4,000 industry professionals

- Improve your learning with Skill Plans built especially for you

- Get a free eBook or video every month

- Mapt is fully searchable

- Copy and paste, print, and bookmark content

PacktPub.com

Did you know that Packt offers eBook versions of every book published, with PDF and ePub files available? You can upgrade to the eBook version at `www.PacktPub.com` and as a print book customer, you are entitled to a discount on the eBook copy. Get in touch with us at `service@packtpub.com` for more details.

At `www.PacktPub.com`, you can also read a collection of free technical articles, sign up for a range of free newsletters, and receive exclusive discounts and offers on Packt books and eBooks.

Contributors

About the authors

André Albuquerque is a software engineer at Onfido, after working in the banking industry for seven years. He has a master's degree from Instituto Superior Técnico in distributed systems and software engineering, and, during his banking detour, he obtained a master's degree in economics. He is currently developing Onfido's microservices using Elixir and Ruby, learning every day about how applications can score and scale if we apply the correct tools and sound coding practices from the get-go. In his time off, he loves to build his own keyboards, play basketball, and spend time with his wife and son.

Thank you, Caixinha, for being crazy enough to embark on this journey with me, and thank you Paulo, for being the kind of mentor that I could only hope to find one day. To all my Onfido colleagues, it's a pleasure to grow with you everyday.

This book wouldn't have been possible without the love and support of my family and friends.

Ana and José, I am blessed to have you in my life.

Daniel Caixinha is a software engineer at Onfido, where he is using Elixir to build resilient systems that can also handle the high growth of the business. After graduating from Instituto Superior Técnico, he joined the startup world, mainly using Ruby, but also got the chance to play around with Elixir. Upon joining Onfido, he got the chance to take Elixir more seriously, which made him fall in love with functional programming in general, and Elixir in particular. Besides building Elixir applications, he is fostering the use of Elixir, being also a member of the Lisbon Elixir meetup.

First and foremost, this book is dedicated to my soulmate, Raquel, and my son, Gabriel. Without your love, this book wouldn't have been possible. I would also like to thank Onfido in general, but two individuals in particular: André, for being in the trenches with me, and Paulo, who fooled me well into believing I could write a book. Last, but definitely not least, I want to thank my parents for always supporting me to be better.

About the reviewer

Paulo A Pereira is a senior software engineer. He fell in love with Elixir and has a passion for exploring new technologies and keeping himself up to date with the industry's developments.

He previously worked as a consultant and lead developer for Mediadigital, implementing Grails and Rails solutions, and is currently working at Onfido Background Checks, a London-based tech start-up that is proving to be a key player in the background checking industry

Packt is searching for authors like you

If you're interested in becoming an author for Packt, please visit `authors.packtpub.com` and apply today. We have worked with thousands of developers and tech professionals, just like you, to help them share their insight with the global tech community. You can make a general application, apply for a specific hot topic that we are recruiting an author for, or submit your own idea.

Table of Contents

Preface

Running scalable, concurrent, and fault-tolerant applications is a demanding endeavor. After learning the abstractions that Elixir offers, developers are able to build such applications effortlessly. That being said, there is a big gap between playing around with Elixir and running it in production and serving live requests. Mastering Elixir helps you to fill this very gap, and it not only goes into detail about how Elixir works, but also guides you to put the learned concepts to good use with the help of concrete examples.

In this book, you will learn how to build a rock solid application, beginning by using Mix to create a new project. You will then explore how to use Erlang's OTP as well as the Elixir abstractions that are built on top of it, allowing you to build applications that are easy to parallelize and distribute. Having got to grips with the basics, you will master Supervisors and comprehend how they are the basis for building fault-tolerant applications. In addition to this, you will understand how to use Phoenix in order to create a web interface for your application.

Upon finishing implementation, you will study how to thoroughly test and monitor the developed file server. Toward the end, you will learn how to take this application to the cloud, using Kubernetes to automatically deploy, scale, and manage it.

Who this book is for

Mastering Elixir is for you if you're a programmer who has some experience in using Elixir and want to take it to the next level. This comprehensive guide shows you how to build, deploy, and maintain robust applications, allowing you to go from tinkering with Elixir on side projects to using it in a live environment. However, no prior knowledge of Elixir is required to enjoy the complex topics covered in the book.

What this book covers

Chapter 1, *Preparing for the Journey Ahead*, starts our odyssey by introducing Elixir. It starts by covering the data types of Elixir and how pattern matching works, moving on to then explore how to create modules and functions, while also seeing, among other things, how to work with collections and use control flow in Elixir. After reading this chapter, you will be familiar with Elixir's syntax, and how to use it to write some simple functions.

Chapter 2, *Innards of an Elixir Project*, kicks off by analyzing what makes an Elixir application and what an Elixir project is. It then examines how to use the Mix tool to create projects and manage their dependencies. It's here that we'll create an umbrella project for the ElixirDrip application that will be developed throughout this book.

Chapter 3, *Processes – The Bedrock for Concurrency and Fault-tolerance*, starts by exploring how the BEAM VM works and its concurrency model, the actor model. Then, it shows how to create and work with processes in Elixir, building a piece of the ElixirDrip application as an example. This chapter also explores how to link and monitor processes, and how Supervisors build on top of this to detect crashing processes. Finally, this chapter explores how we can group Supervisors to create supervision trees, which enable the creation of fault-tolerant applications.

Chapter 4, *Powered by Erlang/OTP*, introduces OTP and examines both the battle-tested OTP abstractions that Elixir inherited from Erlang, such as GenServer and Erlang Term Storage, and the new Agent, Task and Registry abstractions that Elixir brought to life. Each abstraction is put to good use by implementing a media cache, a text search function, and a search results cache.

Chapter 5, *Demand-Driven Processing*, goes a long way to explain how the GenStage and Flow abstractions introduced by Elixir let the developer process data using a demand-driven paradigm. Instead of processing data as fast as possible to match the rate at which data is produced, this approach turns the problem on its head and forces the producer to inject new data into the pipeline at a rate controlled by the data consumers. It's in this chapter that the upload and download pipelines of the ElixirDrip application are developed.

Chapter 6, *Metaprogramming–Code that Writes Itself*, unveils the constructs that allow the developer to easily control what happens in compile time, by writing regular Elixir code that produces more code. The chapter starts by iterating on a macro whose purpose is to measure the time a function takes to execute, and ends by implementing a Domain-Specific language which significantly simplifies the media upload and download pipelines defined in the previous chapter.

Chapter 7, *Persisting Data Using Ecto*, explores how to work with databases. It starts by explaining how to connect an application to a database and how database structure changes can be applied as migrations. It then examines how to create and enforce table relations and how to use changesets to persist and update data. In the end, different ways to query the database are analyzed.

Chapter 8, *Phoenix: A Flying Web Framework*, introduces the Phoenix framework and explains how to use it to add a web layer to our ElixirDrip application. The chapter begins by the conventional topics, such as routers, controllers, and views, but toward the end, also explores more progressive concepts, such as building a JSON API or using Phoenix Channels.

Chapter 9, *Find Zen through Testing*, dives into different kinds of testing. It begins with unit and integration testing, and goes on to explore more elaborate topics, such as how to test macros and Phoenix components, and also how to write property tests.

Chapter 10, *Deploy on the Cloud*, takes the ElixirDrip application running to its live environment, storing media from real users. This chapter starts by explaining how to use Distillery to package the application in an efficient way and then introduces the concept of application containerization and how it suits the development and deployment phases of our application. The last half of the chapter examines how to deploy the application to a Kubernetes cluster and,ultimately, how to automate this process by using a continuous integration service.

Chapter 11, *Keeping an Eye on Your Processes*, teaches you how to monitor your application so that you can ensure that your application is working as it should. You will begin by learning how to collect metrics from your application. Then, we will teach you how to use an Erlang tool, called Observer, which allows us to tap into what is going on inside the BEAM virtual machine. You will learn how to get statistics from the BEAM (such as CPU and memory utilization), as well as from the state of each process inside your application. Lastly, we'll look at how to inspect our application and check what's happening under the hood. You will learn how to investigate a bottleneck by profiling our ElixirDrip application, while also checking how to use Erlang's standard library to trace calls to a certain process.

To get the most out of this book

As mentioned earlier, no prior knowledge of Elixir is required to read this book. In the initial chapters, we provide an introduction to Elixir, covering all the necessary concepts to be able to follow the more advanced topics explored later in the book.

To get the most out of this book we recommend that you follow along each chapter, by building and running the application we will develop in this book. To build this application, we have used free and open source software as much as possible. When this was not possible, we have used software with long trial periods, so that you can build and run the application on your own.

Download the example code files

You can download the example code files for this book from your account at
`www.packtpub.com`. If you purchased this book elsewhere, you can visit
`www.packtpub.com/support` and register to have the files emailed directly to you.

You can download the code files by following these steps:

1. Log in or register at `www.packtpub.com`.
2. Select the **SUPPORT** tab.
3. Click on **Code Downloads & Errata**.
4. Enter the name of the book in the **Search** box and follow the onscreen instructions.

Once the file is downloaded, please make sure that you unzip or extract the folder using the latest version of:

- WinRAR/7-Zip for Windows
- Zipeg/iZip/UnRarX for Mac
- 7-Zip/PeaZip for Linux

The code bundle for the book is also hosted on GitHub at `https://github.com/PacktPublishing/Mastering-Elixir`. In case there's an update to the code, it will be updated on the existing GitHub repository.

We also have other code bundles from our rich catalog of books and videos available at `https://github.com/PacktPublishing/`. Check them out!

Conventions used

There are a number of text conventions used throughout this book.

`CodeInText`: Indicates code words in text, database table names, folder names, filenames, file extensions, pathnames, dummy URLs, user input, and Twitter handles. Here is an example: "In Elixir, you create a process by calling the `Kernel.spawn/1` function".

A block of code is set as follows:

```
IO.puts("Hello, World!")
```

Any command-line input or output is written as follows:

```
$ touch hello_world.ex
```

Bold: Indicates a new term, an important word, or words that you see on screen. For example, words in menus or dialog boxes appear in the text like this. Here is an example: "Select **elixir** from the **Processes** tab."

Warnings or important notes appear like this.

Tips and tricks appear like this.

Get in touch

Feedback from our readers is always welcome.

General feedback: Email feedback@packtpub.com and mention the book title in the subject of your message. If you have questions about any aspect of this book, please email us at questions@packtpub.com.

Errata: Although we have taken every care to ensure the accuracy of our content, mistakes do happen. If you have found a mistake in this book, we would be grateful if you would report this to us. Please visit www.packtpub.com/submit-errata, selecting your book, clicking on the Errata Submission Form link, and entering the details.

Piracy: If you come across any illegal copies of our works in any form on the internet, we would be grateful if you would provide us with the location address or website name. Please contact us at copyright@packtpub.com with a link to the material.

If you are interested in becoming an author: If there is a topic that you have expertise in and you are interested in either writing or contributing to a book, please visit authors.packtpub.com.

Reviews

Please leave a review. Once you have read and used this book, why not leave a review on the site that you purchased it from? Potential readers can then see and use your unbiased opinion to make purchase decisions, we at Packt can understand what you think about our products, and our authors can see your feedback on their book. Thank you!

For more information about Packt, please visit `packtpub.com`.

Preparing for the Journey Ahead

1

Welcome to this incredible journey! This is the beginning of an odyssey that will take you through the many features of Elixir, and how to use them to build, test, deploy, and maintain applications. This journey may require some shifting of your mindset and how you think about programming (and problem-solving in general) if you're not already familiar with functional programming.

Before diving into this book, we want to point out that this introductory chapter is deliberately short. Although we'll be introducing the language, its tooling, and its ecosystem, this won't be a complete reference guide. Elixir treats documentation as a first-class citizen, and this is shown in the incredible documentation of its modules and functions. Hence, we decided to teach you how to search for what you need, and target on the core concept of book–building an Elixir application. We think that this pragmatic approach is the one that delivers the most value to you, as you'll be able to follow an application right from its inception and into its production, including its deployment and monitoring, which are sometimes overlooked.

In this chapter, we will cover the following topics:

- Data types in Elixir
- Working with pattern matching and how to apply it to various types
- Working with functions and bundling them in modules
- Working with collections
- Using classic control-flow constructs (such as `case`)
- Using typespecs on your functions
- Creating behaviours, and adopting them in other modules
- Using protocols to make our functions polymorphic

- Some of the most useful tools that ship with Elixir
- Calling Erlang libraries directly
- Interacting with operating system processes through ports

Why functional programming?

Coming from an object-oriented background ourselves, we can't emphasize enough how valuable this shift is. Adopting the functional programming paradigm brings along some benefits, such as the following:

- The data-transformation flow becomes more evident. This is in contrast with what usually happens in object-oriented programming, where objects strive to encapsulate the data; in functional programming, we mutate data using functions. This makes the transformations that are applied to the data explicit, which in turn makes the applications written this way easier to understand.
- Functions are (mostly) side-effect-free. With immutable data, you can be sure that the value of a certain variable you hold a reference to will remain the same, since if another function or process wants to change it, it has to create a copy first—and operate on that copy. This makes code much easier to analyze and comprehend, since you can rest assured that your variables will remain as you expect. However, note that since Elixir isn't a pure functional language, your code can still have side effects. For instance, if a function writes to a file, it creates a side effect.
- Programs can be parallelized easily. Coming out as an added bonus of immutability, it's usually very simple to parallelize this type of program, since there is no shared state.

One possible disadvantage of having immutable data is that you can incur a performance penalty, as each time you need to change something, you must make a copy of it. This greatly depends on the implementation, and while this concern is generally valid, Elixir employs clever techniques when compiling your code to minimize this effect. For instance, in certain conditions, Elixir can just point to existing variables when creating new ones, as it knows all variables are immutable and will never change.

If you're overwhelmed with all this functional programming jargon, lie down and relax, as we will explore these concepts in greater detail throughout this book.

Elixir and Erlang

Elixir, created by José Valim, runs on the **Erlang VM** (also known as **BEAM**). Erlang, developed at Ericsson more than 30 years ago, was created to improve the reliability and scalability of the company's telecom systems. Nowadays, it is used in a number of different settings, from database systems to chat applications. Erlang has fault-tolerance and distribution baked into its design, and is famous for running systems with nine nines of reliability.

Erlang's runtime is natively distributed, given that it was designed to be deployed on multiple telecom switches simultaneously. Programs running on the Erlang VM can take advantage of this by easily distributing an application across multiple nodes, but also across multiple CPUs—since multiple cores is just a specific case of a distributed system. This is an incredible selling point of the Erlang VM (and thus of Elixir), since in today's setting CPUs are not getting much faster, and we're instead seeing CPUs with an increasing number of cores coming out.

In this opening chapter, we will be introducing Elixir. Beginning with its data types, we will also look at pattern matching, anonymous and named functions, modules, and some control-flow constructs. Then, we will see how to work with collections, and then we will briefly touch on behaviours and protocols. The chapter will end with an overview of the incredible tooling Elixir provides, along with some ways to exploit the existing interoperability between Elixir and Erlang.

Elixir's data types

We will now describe Elixir's data types, which extend upon Erlang's data types. Elixir is a dynamic programming language. Consequently, you don't declare the type of each variable—it depends on the value it holds at each moment.

To improve the learning experience, we'll be providing some examples along the way. For now, we'll just use Elixir's REPL, **IEx** (short for **Interactive Elixir**). To start an IEx session, you must have Elixir installed on your machine. Elixir has an official page with instructions on how to do this if you don't have it installed, whether using package managers, the precompiled version, or compiling from the source yourself:

```
http://elixir-lang.github.io/install.html
```

We will not dive into the memory usage of each type in Elixir. If you're curious about this, the official Erlang documentation contains detailed information: http://erlang.org/doc/efficiency_guide/advanced.html.

Provided that you have Elixir already installed on your machine, type `iex` on your terminal to start a new IEx session. With this, you can run the examples present in this chapter in your machine. Note that your default `iex` prompt contains a number in between parenthesis, which represents the number of expressions you've entered in the current session, such as `iex> (1)`. To declutter the output, in our examples, we've removed this number.

We'll be exploring IEx in greater detail toward the end of this chapter, in the *Tooling and ecosystems* section. Throughout the following subsections, we'll be mentioning some built-in modules in Elixir. We'll explore what modules are in the *Functions and modules* section—for now, it's enough to know that a module is a collection of functions.

Whenever you're done with your IEx session, you can either press *Ctrl + C* twice or *Ctrl + \ *. This will kill the operating system process that's running the Erlang runtime (along with all background jobs). Alternatively, you can stop the system in a more polite way by entering `System.halt` in the shell.

Integers

This type contains, as you would expect, numbers that can be written without a fractional component. The size of integers adjusts dynamically according to its magnitude—you don't have to worry about this: an integer will simply occupy more words in memory as it grows. Here's some basic arithmetic with integers:

```
iex> 25 + 8
33
```

To improve the readability of the code, you can also use underscores in between the digits of an integer, as shown here:

```
iex> 1_000_000 - 500_000
500000
```

Besides decimal, Elixir also supports integers written in binary, octal, and hexadecimal (using 0b, 0o, and 0x, respectively):

```
iex> 0b10001
17
iex> 0o21
17
iex> 0x11
17
```

Floats

In Elixir, *floats* are written with a decimal point, with digits before and after it, meaning that .1 is not a valid float in Elixir (as it is, for instance, in JavaScript). In Elixir, you have to be explicit and write the leading 0—so in this case, you'd write 0.1. Here's an example of the multiplication of two floats:

```
iex> 0.1 * 0.5
0.05
```

You can also write floats using the exponent notation, as shown:

```
iex> 0.1e3
100.0
```

Floats are represented in IEEE 754 double precision, which yields between 15 to 17 significant decimal digits. As usual, you should take care when comparing floats for equality.

Beware that the division operator (/) always returns a float, even if the result of the division could be an integer:

```
iex> 4/2
2.0
```

If you want to circumvent this behavior, use the auto-imported div function from the Kernel module. Also, if you want to get the remainder of a division, use the rem function.

Atoms

Atoms are a constant, whose value is its own name. They are always prefixed with a leading colon (:), followed by alphanumeric characters (and possibly _ or @). They may terminate with an exclamation or a question mark. Atoms are similar to enumerations in C and symbols in Ruby. Here are some examples of atoms:

```
iex> :ok
:ok
iex> :error
:error
iex> :some_descriptive_name!
:some_descriptive_name!
iex> :value@start
:value@start
```

You can create atoms with arbitrary characters with the following syntax:

```
iex> :"Atom name with arbitrary characters#$%^"
:"Atom name with arbitrary characters#$%^"
```

As with all data structures in Elixir, atoms can't be modified after their creation. Furthermore, they are not garbage-collected. Atoms are kept in the *atom table,* and upon compilation, their value is replaced by a reference to their entry on this table. This makes comparing atoms very efficient. As you'll learn throughout this book, this is one of the major use cases for atoms in Elixir, as we are constantly matching the return of a function against a certain expected atom.

 Since atoms are not garbage collected, don't create atoms dynamically from sources you can't control, as you can very easily use up all of the space allocated for the atom table. For instance, if you're parsing a JSON response and creating a map out of it, don't use atoms for its keys—use strings instead (both of these types, maps and strings, will be described later in this chapter).

Booleans

Elixir has three values related to Boolean operations: true, false, and nil (where nil represents the absence of value—similar to null in most other languages). However, those are just some syntatic sugar, as internally they are represented as atoms of the same name, as you can see in the following example:

```
iex> true == :true
```

```
true
iex> false == :false
true
iex> nil == :nil
true
```

You have the common Boolean operators, `or`, `and`, and `not`:

```
iex> true or false
true
iex> true and false
false
iex> not false
true
```

However, these operators are type-strict in their first argument: they only accept `true` or `false`. If you pass anything else as an argument, you'll get `BadBooleanError`.

This is where the concept of *truthiness* and *falseness* enters. Similar to what happens in Ruby or C, `false` and `nil` are treated as *falsey* values, and everything else is considered to be *truthy*. The operators that work with *falsey* and *truthy* values are `&&` (and), `||` (or), and `!` (not):

```
iex> "a value" || false
"a value"
iex> "a value" && false
false
iex> nil && "a value"
nil
iex> !"a value"
false
```

Notice how these operators short circuit depending on the arguments. With `||`, it returns the first value that's *truthy*, whereas with `&&`, it returns the first *falsey* value (in both cases, in the event those conditions never happen, they return the last value).

You also have the other normal comparison operators, such as greater than (`>`) and inequality (`!=`)—you can find the full list at `https://hexdocs.pm/elixir/operators.html`. The one that's worth pointing out is the *strict equality* operator, which, besides comparing values, compares types:

```
iex> 3 == 3.0
true
iex> 3 === 3.0
false
```

Tuples

Tuples are used to group a fixed number of elements together. They can hold any value—even other tuples. They are stored contiguously in memory, which provides constant access time to elements inside a tuple. You create a tuple surrounding the elements with curly brackets ({ and }), and separate the elements with commas:

```
iex> {:ok, 3.14}
{:ok, 3.14}
```

A common usage of tuples in Elixir is to pattern-match on the result of a function to ensure its success (usually with an :ok atom) or deal with an error. We will be looking to pattern matching and functions later in this chapter.

To access an element inside a tuple, we use the elem function (from the Kernel module), providing the tuple and a zero-based index:

```
iex> result = {:ok, 3.14}
{:ok, 3.14}
iex> elem(result, 1)
3.14
```

> Functions from the Kernel module are auto-imported. Thus, we don't need to prefix them with the module name.

To change the elements on a tuple, you can use the put_elem function. The arguments are similar to the elem function, but you also provide the new value for that position of the tuple:

```
iex> put_elem(result, 1, 1.61)
{:ok, 1.61}
iex> result
{:ok, 3.14}
```

Notice how the result variable hasn't changed. As we discussed in the beginning of this chapter, data in Elixir is immutable. As such, although we've updated the tuple with a new value, the original tuple hasn't changed—Elixir updated the value on a copy of the original tuple. This way our code is side-effect free, and any other function holding a reference to the result variable won't have any surprises.

The general recommendation in Elixir is that tuples should hold up to four elements—anything more than that and you probably should be using another type.

Lists

Lists are created by wrapping the elements we want inside it with square brackets ([and]), separating the values with commas. Internally, lists are implemented as singly linked lists, meaning that accessing the elements of a list is a O(n) operation. Lists aren't stored contiguously in memory as arrays in other languages. As with tuples, list elements can be of any type:

```
iex> [1, :an_atom, 0.5]
[1, :an_atom, 0.5]
```

We have the ++ and -- operators that are exclusive to lists, and serve to concatenate and subtract lists, respectively:

```
iex> [0, 1, 1] ++ [2, 3, 5]
[0, 1, 1, 2, 3, 5]
iex> [0, 1, 1] -- [1, 2, 3]
[0, 1]
```

To check whether a certain element is present in a list, you can use the in operator:

```
iex> 1 in [0, 1, 1, 2, 3, 5]
true
iex> 99 in [0, 1, 1, 2, 3, 5]
false
```

To get the head of a list, we use the hd function, whereas to get the tail of a list, we use the tl function:

```
iex> hd([0, 1, 1, 2, 3, 5])
0
iex> tl([0, 1, 1, 2, 3, 5])
[1, 1, 2, 3, 5]
```

Notice that the semantic of *tail* here is the list without its head (which is also a list), and not the last element of a list. We'll be exploring this concept in more depth, along with some more examples on how to work with lists, in the *Working with collections* section. For reference, you can find a detailed list of operations you can make on lists at https://hexdocs.pm/elixir/List.html.

Appending to a list is a O(n) operation, as we need to traverse the whole list. Prepending to a list is O(1). To prepend an element to a list, you can use the following syntax: [new_element | list].

Maps

Maps are key-value data structures, where both the key and the value can be of any type. They're similar to hashes in Ruby and dictionaries in Python. To create a map, you enclose your key-value pairs in `%{}`, and put a `=>` between the key and the value, as we can see in the following snippet:

```
iex> %{:name => "Gabriel", :age => 1}
%{age: 1, name: "Gabriel"}
```

In this case, the keys are both of the same type, but this isn't required. If your keys are atoms, you can use the following syntax to make the map declaration simpler:

```
iex> %{name: "Gabriel", age: 1}
%{age: 1, name: "Gabriel"}
```

To access the value associated with a certain key, put the key inside square brackets in front of the map:

```
iex> map = %{name: "Gabriel", age: 1}
%{age: 1, name: "Gabriel"}
iex> map[:name]
"Gabriel"
```

As with the map declaration, when the key is an atom, we have some syntatic sugar on top of it:

```
iex> map.name
"Gabriel"
```

 When you try to fetch a key that doesn't exist in the map, a `KeyError` error will be raised when using the `map.key` syntax–unlike the `map[key]` syntax, which will return `nil`.

To update a key in a map, you can use `%{map | key => new_value}`. If the key is an atom, we can use the same notation described previously:

```
iex> %{map | age: 2}
%{age: 2, name: "Gabriel"}
```

 If you're coming from an object-oriented programming background, you may instinctively use the following syntax to change the value of a key: `map[key] = new_value`. Remember that in Elixir all types are immutable and you never operate on the data structure itself but always on a copy of it.

This will only work for keys that already exist in the map—this constraint allows Elixir to optimize and reuse the fields list when updating a map. If you want to insert a new key, use the `put` function from the `Map` module:

```
iex> Map.put(map, :gender, "Male")
%{age: 1, gender: "Male", name: "Gabriel"}
```

As with all other types, in the official documentation, at `https://hexdocs.pm/elixir/Map.html`, you can find a pretty detailed reference on what you can do with maps.

Binaries

A *binary* is group of consecutive bytes. You create them by surrounding the byte sequence with << and >>. Here we are creating a two-byte binary:

```
iex> <<5, 10>>
<<5, 10>>
```

In the decimal base, a byte can only contain values up to 255 (otherwise it overflows). If we want to store values greater that 255, we need to tell the runtime to use more space to store this binary:

```
iex> <<5, 256>>
<<5, 0>>
iex> <<5, 256::16>>
<<5, 1, 0>>
```

As you can see, when we specify the size (16 bits in this case) we can see that the output as an extra byte and the overflow didn't occur. The size doesn't have to be a multiple of 8. In that case, a binary is usually called a *bitstring*.

Most programmers will not handle data at such a low level, so your use of binaries may not be that frequent. However, they're extremely useful in certain scenarios, such as processing the header of a file to find a magic number and identify the file type, or even when dealing with network packets by hand.

Strings and charlists

Strings are binaries with UTF-8 codepoints in them. You create a string with the usual double-quote syntax:

```
iex> "hey, a string"
"hey, a string"
```

Charlists are, as the name implies, lists of character codes. You create them using the single-quote syntax:

```
iex> 'hey, a charlist'
'hey, a charlist'
```

Since this is just a list, you can use the hd function to get the code for the first character:

```
iex> hd('hey, a charlist')
104
```

You can find out the code of a certain character with the ? operator. For instance, to find out the character code of a lowercase d, you'd use ?d.

Both representations support string interpolation:

```
iex> "two plus two is: #{2+2}"
"two plus two is: 4"
iex> 'four minus one is: #{4-1}'
'four minus one is: 3'
```

Both representations also support the heredoc notation, which is most commonly used to write documentation. To create it, use three single or double quotes:

```
iex> """
...> a string with heredoc notation
...> """
"a string with heredoc notation\n"
iex> '''
...> a charlist with heredoc notation
...> '''
'a charlist with heredoc notation\n'
```

The closing delimiter of a heredoc string/charlist must be on its own line.

Elixir provides *sigils* as another syntax to declare strings or charlists, which can be handy if you want to include quotes inside your string. You can use ~s to create a string and ~c to create a charlist (their uppercase versions, ~S and ~C, are similar but don't interpolate or escape characters):

```
iex> ~s(a string created by a sigil)
"a string created by a sigil"
```

```
iex> ~c(a charlist created by a sigil)
'a charlist created by a sigil'
```

There's another sigil that's worth mentioning: ~r, which is used for regular expressions. In the next snippet, we're using the run function from the Regex module to exemplify the usage of the ~r sigil:

```
iex> Regex.run(~r{str}, "a string")
["str"]
iex> Regex.run(~r{123}, "a string")
nil
```

You can find the list of supported sigils (and also how to create your own!) at http://elixir-lang.github.io/getting-started/sigils.html.

The convention in the Elixir community is to only use the term string when referring to the double-quote format. This distinction is important, since their implementation is very different. Functions from the String module will only work on the double-quote format. You should always use the double-quote format, unless you're required to use a charlist—which is the case, for instance, when you're using Erlang libraries. You can use the following functions to convert between the two formats:

```
iex> String.to_charlist("converting to charlist")
'converting to charlist'
iex> List.to_string('converting to string')
"converting to string"
```

Other types

We'll now succinctly describe some other types. We'll begin with the types that build upon some types we've already described: keyword lists, ranges, mapsets, and IO lists.

Keyword lists

A *keyword list* is a list in which its elements have a specific format: they are tuples where the first element is an atom (the second element can be of any type), as demonstrated in the following example:

```
iex> [name: "Gabriel", age: 1] = [{:name, "Gabriel"}, {:age, 1}]
[name: "Gabriel", age: 1]
```

We can create keyword lists using the following syntax:

```
iex> keyword_list = [name: "Gabriel", age: 1]
[name: "Gabriel", age: 1]
iex> keyword_list[:name]
"Gabriel"
```

As you can see from the previous snippet, a keyword list is indeed a list of tuples, with an atom; you can access values in a keyword list using the same syntax as you would in maps. As an alternative, you can use the `get` function from the `Keyword` module. Note that this way of declaring a keyword list is just syntatic sugar, as internally this still is a list of tuples–which means that searching for an item in a keyword list is `O(n)`, and not `O(1)` as in maps.

In a keyword list, contrary to what happens in maps, you can have more than one value for a given key. Also, you can control the order of its elements. Usually, keyword lists are used to allow functions to receive an arbitrary number of optional arguments. We'll be showing an example of this when we look at named functions later in this chapter. You can find all the operations you can do on a keyword list at `https://hexdocs.pm/elixir/Keyword.html`.

Ranges

Ranges, again, similar to what happens in Ruby, represent an interval between two integers. To create a range, we use this:

```
iex> 17..21
17..21
iex> 19 in 17..21
true
```

Similar to what we do with a list, we can use the `in` operator to check whether a number is between the start and the end of a range.

MapSets

If you're looking for an implementation of a set in Elixir, you're looking for `MapSet`. You create and manipulate them with the functions from the `MapSet` module. Here are some examples:

```
iex> set = MapSet.new
#MapSet<[]>
iex> set = MapSet.put(set, 1)
#MapSet<[1]>
```

```
iex> set = MapSet.put(set, 2)
#MapSet<[1, 2]>
iex> set = MapSet.put(set, 1)
#MapSet<[1, 2]>
```

Sets, by definition, can't contain duplicates. So, inserting a value that's already there has no effect. You can find the documentation for the `MapSet` module at `https://hexdocs.pm/elixir/MapSet.html`.

There are three types, related to the underlying Erlang VM, that we have to mention before closing this section. They are as following:

- **Reference:** A reference is a type created by the `Kernel.make_ref` function. This functions creates an almost-unique reference, which gets repeated around every 2^{82} calls. We will not use references in this book.
- **Port:** A port is a reference to a resource. The Erlang VM uses it to interact with external resources, such as an operating system process. We will talk a bit more about ports later in this chapter, when we discuss the interoperability between Elixir and Erlang.
- **PID:** A PID is the type used to identify processes in the Erlang VM. You'll see PIDs in action later in this book, when we start working with Erlang VM processes.

To complete this section, there's a function that we want to highlight: the `i` function, which is auto-imported from the `Kernel` module. You can use it to find out more information about a data type. It will print information about the data type of the term you pass as an argument. Here is an example with a string:

```
iex> i("a string")
Term
  "a string"
Data type
  BitString
Byte size
  8
Description
  This is a string: a UTF-8 encoded binary. It's printed surrounded by
  "double quotes" because all UTF-8 encoded codepoints in it are printable.
Raw representation
  <<97, 32, 115, 116, 114, 105, 110, 103>>
Reference modules
  String, :binary
Implemented protocols
  IEx.Info, Collectable, List.Chars, String.Chars, Inspect
```

And, with this, we've finished our tour of the data types in Elixir! We didn't go into much detail, but with the links we left throughout this section, you'll see how incredible the documentation in Elixir is, and how easy it is to figure out what a certain function does or the purpose of a certain argument.

We will now jump into one of the most prominent features of Elixir (and also one that will definitely change how you write programs): pattern matching.

Pattern matching

When we were describing Elixir's data types, we used the = operator to bind a value of a certain type to a variable. We didn't stop there to explain what was actually going on, as the syntax is very similar to most dynamic programming languages. In fact, it is so similar that, at first glance, we assume it works the same way.

If you don't have a functional programming background, your first instinct would be to call the = operator, the *assignment* operator. However, in Elixir, it is called the *match* operator. Let's see the reason for this difference in nomenclature with some examples:

```
iex> x = 3
3
iex> x * 3
9
iex> 3 = x
3
iex> 2 = x
** (MatchError) no match of right hand side value: 3
```

 We've seen our first exception being raised on our IEx session. We'll discuss them later in this chapter, when we talk about control flow.

The first two statements are analogous to what you'd see with an assignment operator—we just set the x variable to 3, and then multiply that variable by 3, giving us the expected result of 9. Now, notice what happens on the following lines. We have an integer literal on the left-hand side of the = operator, and that is a valid expression, returning a value of 3. You're seeing the match operator in action.

Similar to what you do with equations in algebra, this operator tries to match the pattern on the left-hand side to the term on the right-hand side. On the first line of the preceding snippet, this means matching the x variable on the left to the 3 term on the right.

Elixir can make this match succeed by binding the x variable to the 3 term. On the third line, we're again matching the left and right sides, and it succeeds because x has the 3 value, so both sides are equal. On the next line, we're trying to match the 2 literal to the x variable. Elixir can't find a way to make this match work, which results in an error being raised. It's important to point out that binding to variables only happens when they are on the left-hand side of the = operator—when they're at the right-hand side, the variable is simply replaced by its value.

From this snippet, we can also notice that we always have a return value—even when doing a pattern match. This is the expected behavior, since everything in Elixir is an expression–there are no statements. Every operation you can do will always return a value, whether you're printing something to the console or making an HTTP request. While you can achieve the same things with expressions and statements, always having a return value is very useful because you can chain functions together and define the program flow according to the values being returned. In the case of pattern matching, when it is successful, we always get back the term that was matched on the right-hand side.

The match operator is not confined to bind variables to simple values–it's actually a very powerful operator that is able to destructure complex data types (and make your code ridiculously simple to read). We will now show how you can use this operator on several of the types we've presented in the previous section, while also demonstrating other aspects of the pattern matching process.

Pattern matching on tuples

The following snippet shows how pattern matching can be done on tuples:

```
iex> {number, representation} = {3.1415, "π"}
{3.1415, "π"}
iex> number
3.1415
iex> representation
"π"
```

The process here is the same as we have described in the preceding snippet. By setting the {number, description} pattern on the left-hand side, we're stating that we expect a tuple with two values—again, if that's not the case, a MatchError will be raised. In this case, the match succeeds, and we can see that the variables number and representation are bound to the expected values.

Unlike Erlang, Elixir allows you to rebind a variable, which is why the following works:

```
iex> a = 1
1
iex> a = 7
7
```

However, a variable can only bind once per match:

```
iex> {a, a} = {3, 3}
{3, 3}
iex> {a, a} = {2, 3}
** (MatchError) no match of right hand side value: {2, 3}
```

On the first line, the match succeeds because each a is binding to the same value, 3. On the second line, we get a MatchError because we're binding a to two different values on the same match. Later in this chapter, we'll see how we can make Elixir behave like Erlang in this regard, by using the *pin* operator.

We can set our expectations even further, using literals on the left-hand side:

```
iex> {3.1415, representation} = {3.1415, "π"}
{3.1415, "π"}
iex> representation
"π"
```

Now our expectation is a tuple with two elements, where the first one is the 3.1415 float literal. We can use this on other Elixir types as well, such as lists or maps. This technique becomes even more fruitful when we apply it to functions, as we will see in the next section.

Pattern matching on lists

Matching on lists is akin to matching on tuples. Here's a simple example:

```
iex> [first, second, third] = ["α", "β", "γ"]
["α", "β", "γ"]
iex> first
"α"
iex> second
"β"
```

```
iex> third
"γ"
```

There's nothing new here. What if, for instance, we don't care about the second element of the list? That's where the _ (underscore) *anonymous* variable is convenient:

```
iex> [first, _, third] = ["δ", "ε", "ζ"]
["δ", "ε", "ζ"]
iex> first
"δ"
iex> third
"ζ"
```

We're again matching a list with three elements, but now bind the second element to the _ variable, which means that we accept anything in that position and we won't use its value.

> The _ variable can never be read from–if you do so, you will get a `CompileError`:
>
> ```
> iex> _
> ** (CompileError) iex:83: unbound variable _
> ```
>
> This way, Elixir is protecting you from inadvertently reading from this variable, which could easily cause unexpected behaviors in your application.

As we've mentioned on the data types section, you can use the hd and tl functions from the Kernel module to get the head and the tail of a list. You can do the same with pattern matching:

```
iex> [first | rest_of_list] = ["α", "β", "γ"]
["α", "β", "γ"]
iex> first
"α"
iex> rest_of_list
["β", "γ"]
```

While in this contrived example, this approach yields no benefit, this technique is a fundamental piece to operate on a list using recursion. We'll look at this in greater detail in the *Working with collections* section.

Pattern matching on maps

To use pattern matching on a map, we set our pattern with the key-value pairs we want to match on, as you can see in the following example:

```
iex> %{"name" => name, "age" => age} = %{"name" => "Gabriel", "age" => 1}
%{"age" => 1, "name" => "Gabriel"}
iex> name
"Gabriel"
iex> age
1
```

Note that in this case we're matching on all keys of the map, but this isn't necessary–we could just match on `age`, for instance. However, your pattern may only contain keys that exist on the map that's being matched on, otherwise `MatchError` will be raised.

Sometimes, you may want to match on the value of a variable, instead of rebinding it to a new value. To this end, you can use the *pin* operator, represented by the ^ character:

```
iex> name = "Gabriel"
"Gabriel"
iex> %{name: ^name, age: age} = %{name: "Gabriel", age: 1}
%{age: 1, name: "Gabriel"}
iex> %{name: ^name, age: age} = %{name: "Jose", age: 1}
** (MatchError) no match of right hand side value: %{age: 1, name: "Jose"}
```

As we can see in the preceding snippet, we have the `name` variable bound to `"Gabriel"`. We then match a map as we did previously in this section, this time using the contents of the `name` variable. This is equivalent to using the `"Gabriel"` literal on the left-hand side. When we're trying to match against a map that has a value different than that of the pinned variable, we get a `MatchError`, as expected.

 When working with the pin operator, the variable you're using must already be bound, as it will not bind the variable in case it doesn't exist. If you use the pin operator on a non-existent variable, you'll get a `CompileError` stating that the variable you're trying to use is unbound.

Pattern matching on binaries and strings

The following example shows how you can use pattern matching on binaries:

```
iex> <<first_byte, second_byte>> = <<100, 200>>
<<100, 200>>
iex> first_byte
```

```
100
iex> second_byte
200
```

As previously stated when describing binaries, this can be incredibly helpful when you're dealing with bytes directly, such as parsing a packet from a given network protocol. By applying pattern matching to binaries, you can extract bits or bytes as necessary, while your code remains extremely expressive.

Since strings are just binaries underneath, we can use the same strategy as we did in the preceding snippet:

```
iex> <<first_byte, second_byte>> = "YZ"
"YZ"
iex> first_byte
89
iex> second_byte
90
```

However, this isn't very helpful when dealing with strings, as you're getting the decimal code of the characters in UTF-8 (also, as UTF-8 is a variable width encoding, a code point may take more than one byte). To match on strings, the best approach is to use the functions from the `String` module, such as `starts_with?`, `ends_with?`, or `contains?`.

> As we've explained in the beginning of this section, everything in Elixir is an expression, and in pattern matching, when the match succeeds, the right-hand side of the expression is returned. Due to this behavior and taking into account that Elixir rebinds the variables on the left-hand side, we can write expressions such as the following one, binding multiple variables to the same value:
>
> ```
> iex> x = y = 100
> 100
> iex> x
> 100
> iex> y
> 100
> ```

Functions and Modules

Despite not being mentioned in the data types section, functions in Elixir are a type as well–in fact, they are a first-class citizen, as they can be assigned to a variable and passed as arguments to other functions.

As with most functional programming languages, functions are an important type, hence they justify having their own section, away from other built-in types.

We will start by exploring anonymous functions, followed by an explanation of modules and named functions, and then we'll end this section with a quick tour of module attributes and directives.

Anonymous functions

Anonymous functions, usually called *lambdas*, are created with the `fn` keyword, as we can see in the following example:

```
iex> plus_one = fn (x) -> x + 1 end
#Function<6.99386804/1 in :erl_eval.expr/5>
iex> plus_one.(10)
11
```

Here, we are defining a function that takes one argument, which we've named `x`, and simply adds one to the provided argument. We then bind this anonymous function to a variable named `plus_one`, and execute it with 10 as the argument, using the syntax we can see in the preceding snippet. As expected, we get `11` back.

 There is no `return` keyword in Elixir–the return value of a function is the value returned by its last expression.

An anonymous function can also have multiple implementations, depending on the value and/or type of the arguments provided. Let's see this in action with an example:

```
iex> division = fn
...>    (_dividend, 0)       -> :infinity
...>    (dividend, divisor) -> dividend / divisor
...> end
#Function<12.99386804/2 in :erl_eval.expr/5>
iex> division.(10, 2)
5.0
iex> division.(10, 0)
:infinity
```

Imagine that we want a special division function, that, instead of raising `ArithmeticError` when dividing by 0, would just return the `:infinity` atom. This is what the anonymous function we see here achieves. Using pattern matching, we say that when the second argument (the divisor) is 0, we simply return `:infinity`. Otherwise, we just use the `/` arithmetic operator to perform a normal division.

Aside from the lambda with multiple bodies, notice that we prefix the unused variable with an underscore (_), as in `_dividend`. Besides increasing the readability of your code, following this practice will make the Elixir compiler warn you when you use a supposedly unused variable. Conversely, if you don't use a certain variable but don't prefix it with an underscore, the compiler will also warn you.

> Parentheses around arguments of an anonymous function are optional. You could write the `plus_one` function we introduced earlier as `fn x ->` `x + 1 end`.

Beyond accepting arguments, anonymous functions can also access variables from the outer scope:

```
iex> x = 3
3
iex> some_fun = fn -> "variable x is #{x}" end
#Function<20.99386804/0 in :erl_eval.expr/5>
iex> some_fun.()
"variable x is 3"
iex> x = 5
5
iex> some_fun.()
"variable x is 3"
```

As you can see, our anonymous function can access variables from the outer scope. Furthermore, the variable can be bound to another value, and our function will still hold a reference to the value that the variable had when the anonymous function was defined. This is usually called a *closure*: the function captures the memory locations of all variables used within it. Since every type in Elixir is immutable, that value residing on each memory reference will not change. However, this also means that these memory locations can't be immediately garbage-collected, as the lambda is still holding references to them.

We'll end this section on anonymous functions by introducing a new operator–the *capture* operator (represented by &).

This operator allows you to define lambdas in a more compact way:

```
iex> plus_one = &(&1 + 1)
#Function<6.99386804/1 in :erl_eval.expr/5>
iex> plus_one.(10)
11
```

This syntax is equivalent to the one presented before for the `plus_one` function. `&1` represents the first argument of this lambda function—and, more generally, `&n` will represent the nth argument of the function. Similar to what happens in the `fn` notation, the parentheses are optional. However, it's better to use them, as in a real-world application, these lambda functions become hard to read without them.

 Besides providing a shorter way to define lambda functions, the capture operator can also be used with named functions. We'll explore this further in the next section.

Modules and Named Functions

In Elixir, modules group functions together, much like a namespace. Usually, functions that reside in the same module are related to one another. You create a module using the `defmodule` construct:

```
iex> defmodule StringHelper do
...>    def palindrome?(term) do
...>        String.reverse(term) == term
...>    end
...> end
{:module, StringHelper,
 <<70, 79, 82, 49, 0, 0, 4, 0, 66, 69, 65, 77, 65, 116, 85, 56, 0, 0, 0,
119, 0,
    0, 0, 11, 19, 69, 108, 105, 120, 105, 114, 46, 83, 116, 114, 105, 110,
103,
    72, 101, 108, 112, 101, 114, 8, 95, 95, ...>>, {:palindrome?, 1}}
iex> StringHelper.palindrome?("abcd")
false
iex> StringHelper.palindrome?("abba")
true
```

In the preceding example we're also creating a function inside the `StringHelper` module, using the `def` construct, that checks whether a given string is a palindrome. This is a named function, and contrary to the anonymous functions, must be created inside a module.

Function names, like variable names, start with a lowercase letter, and if they contain more than one word, they are separated by underscore(s). They may end in ! and ?. The convention in the Elixir community is that function names ending in ! denote that the function may raise an error, whereas function names ending in ? indicate that that function either returns `true` or `false`–which is the case of our `palindrome?` function.

Note that unlike anonymous functions, we don't need to put a dot between the function name and the parenthesis when calling named functions. This is deliberate and serves to explicitly differentiate calls to anonymous and named functions.

As the implementation of our `palindrome?` function is very small, we can inline it with the following syntax:

```
def palindrome?(term), do: String.reverse(term) == term
```

This works with other constructs that use the `do ... end` syntax, such as `defmodule` or `if`. We will explore `if` (and other classical control flow mechanisms) in the Control-flow section.

Before we go any further, as our examples are getting bigger, we must discuss how you can write Elixir code in files. As you can see in the previous example, you can define modules on an IEx session–however, any typo while writing them results in having to start from the beginning.

Put the contents of the last example in a file–let's call it `"string_helper.ex"` (we usually name the file with the name of the module we're defining in it). Elixir source code files may have two extensions: `.ex` or `.exs`. The difference between them is that the former is compiled to disk (creating `.beam` files), while the latter is compiled only in memory. We mostly use the `.ex` extension when working on a real application, except for the test files that use the `.exs` extension (as there's no point in compiling them to disk).

Having your file created, you can use the `elixirc` command in your terminal to compile it, passing the name of the file whose contents you want compiled. More interestingly, you can pass the filename to the `iex` command (`iex string_helper.ex` in our case). This will make Elixir compile your file, which will make our `StringHelper` module (and its functions) available in the IEx session. If you're already inside the IEx session and want to compile a new file, you can use the `c` command, passing the filename as a string:

```
iex> c("examples/string_helper.ex")
[StringHelper]
```

You can also nest modules:

```
$ cat examples/nesting_modules.ex
defmodule Helpers do
  defmodule StringHelper do
    # StringHelper code goes here
  end
end
```

 In the preceding example, the line starting with # is commented. That's the syntax to comment lines in Elixir. There's no syntax for multi-line comments–if you want to comment a block of code, prepend each line of that block with #.

However, during compilation, Elixir will prepend the outer module name to the inner module name, and separate them with a dot. This is just an amenity, as there is no relationship between these two modules. This syntax is equivalent to the following one, which is used much more in Elixir applications:

```
$ cat examples/nesting_modules_inline.ex
defmodule Helpers.StringHelper do
  # StringHelper code goes here
end
```

We'll now explain the concept of *arity*, with our `palindrome?` function as an example. Named functions in Elixir are identified by their module name, the function's own name, and their arity. The arity of a function is the number of arguments it receives. Taking this into account, our `palindrome?` function is identified as `Helpers.StringHelper.palindrome?/1`, where /1 represents the arity of the function. You'll be seeing this notation a lot when browsing through Elixir documentation.

This concept is important because functions with the same name but different arities are, in effect, two different functions. However, for a human, it wouldn't make much sense that two functions with the same name (but different arities) are unrelated. As such, only use the same name for different functions when they are related to one another.

The common pattern in Elixir is to have lower-arity functions being implemented as calls to functions of the same name but with a higher arity. Let's extend our module with an `emphasize` function:

```
$ cat examples/string_helper_emphasize.ex
defmodule StringHelper do
  def palindrome?(term) do
    String.reverse(term) == term
  end
```

```
def emphasize(phrase) do
  emphasize(phrase, 3)
end

def emphasize(phrase, number_of_marks) do
  upcased_phrase = String.upcase(phrase)
  exclamation_marks = String.duplicate("!", number_of_marks)
  "#{upcased_phrase}#{exclamation_marks}"
end
end
```

Here, we can observe it in action:

```
iex> StringHelper.emphasize("wow")
"WOW!!!"
iex> StringHelper.emphasize("wow", 1)
"WOW!"
```

 We've used the def construct to create functions. By using it, our functions are exported and can be called in other modules. If you want to change this behavior, and make a function only available within the module where it's defined, use the defp construct.

The function with an arity of 1 is implemented by simply calling emphasize/2. This is useful when you want to offer a broad interface on your module, which allows you to have some clients that simply want to call emphasize/1 and not have to specify the number of exclamation marks, but also have some other clients that want to call emphasize/2 and specify the number of exclamation marks.

When the code is as simple as in this example, this multitude of functions is not necessary, as you can achieve the same end result using *default arguments*. We do that by using the \\ operator in front of the argument name, and then the default value it should have:

```
$ cat examples/string_helper_emphasize_with_default_args.ex
def emphasize(phrase, number_of_marks \\ 3) do
  upcased_phrase = String.upcase(phrase)
  exclamation_marks = String.duplicate("!", number_of_marks)
  "#{upcased_phrase}#{exclamation_marks}"
end
```

This will generate two functions with the same name and different arities, as in the last snippet. If your function has multiple bodies, as in the next example, you must define a function header with the default arguments defined there:

```
$ cat examples/string_helper_emphasize_with_function_header.ex
def emphasize(phrase, number_of_marks \\ 3)
```

```
def emphasize(_phrase, 0) do
  "This isn't the module you're looking for"
end
def emphasize(phrase, number_of_marks) do
  upcased_phrase = String.upcase(phrase)
  exclamation_marks = String.duplicate("!", number_of_marks)
  "#{upcased_phrase}#{exclamation_marks}"
end
```

In this example, we're also seeing an example of how we can use pattern matching in named functions. Note that the order in which we define our functions matters. Elixir will search from top to bottom for a clause that matches. If we had put the clause where we're matching against 0 on the second argument at the end, that definition of the emphasize function would become unreachable, as the other definition is more general and always matches. Elixir will help you avoid these situations, as it will emit a warning during compilation, alerting you of this situation.

Apart from using pattern matching (as we've seen in this example and on anonymous functions), on named functions we can use *guard clauses,* which extend on the pattern matching mechanism and allow us to set broader expectations on our functions. To use a guard clause on a function, we use the when clause after the list of arguments.

To see an example of this, we will use a guard clause on our palindrome? function. Up to this point, we were accepting an argument of any type. If we passed an integer to this function, an error would be raised, as we would be trying to call String.reverse on an integer. Let's change that:

```
$ cat examples/string_helper_palindrome_with_guard_clause.ex
def palindrome?(term) when is_bitstring(term) do
  String.reverse(term) == term
end
def palindrome?(_term), do: {:error, :unsupported_type}
```

We now state that we're expecting bitstring as an argument. We've also created a new definition of our function, which runs when the match doesn't occur on the first definition. Here it is in action:

```
iex> StringHelper.palindrome?("abba")
true
iex> StringHelper.palindrome?(123)
{:error, :unsupported_type}
```

Using guard clauses in our functions can lead to a lot of duplication, since we may be repeating the same clause over and over again. To combat this, Elixir 1.6 introduced the defguard construct, which allows us to define clauses that can be reused.

Moreover, using this construct may improve the readability of your code, since we can extract complex guard clauses and give them descriptive names. Let's see the previous example implemented using `defguard`:

```
$ cat examples/string_helper_palindrome_with_defguard.ex
defguard is_string(term) when is_bitstring(term)

def palindrome?(term) when is_string(term) do
  String.reverse(term) == term
end
def palindrome?(_term), do: {:error, :unsupported_type}
```

In this simple example, there's no clear advantage to using this construct. However, as your modules, along with your guard clauses, grow more complex, this technique becomes incredibly useful. Note that you can use `defguardp` to define a guard clause that is not exported, and can only be used within the module where it's defined.

 You can use other type-checking functions in guard clauses, as well as comparison operators, and also some other functions. You can find the full list at `https://hexdocs.pm/elixir/guards.html`.

To end this section, we will now showcase one of the most eminent features of the language: the *pipe* (| >) operator. This operator allows you to chain function calls, making the flow of your functions easy to read and comprehend. This operator takes the term that's at its left, and injects it as the first argument on the function at its right. This seemingly insipid feature increases the readability of your code, which is amazing since code is read many more times than it is written. To see this operator in action, let's add some more logic to our `palindrome?` function: We will now remove leading or trailing whitespaces from the term we're checking, and we'll also make our comparisons case-insensitive. This is the result:

```
$ cat examples/string_helper_palindrome_with_pipe_operator.ex
def palindrome?(term) do
  formatted_term = term
    |> String.trim()
    |> String.downcase()

  formatted_term |> String.reverse() == formatted_term
end
```

While the impact may seem negligible in this simple example, you'll see the expressiveness this operator brings as we build our application throughout the book.

Module attributes, directives, and uses

Modules in Elixir may contain *attributes*. They're normally used where you'd use constants in other languages. You define a module attribute with the following syntax:

```
$ cat examples/string_helper_with_module_attribute.ex
defmodule StringHelper do
  @default_mark "!"

  # rest of the StringHelper code
end
```

Then, we can use the @default_mark module attribute inside the functions of this module. This attribute only exists at compile time, as it's replaced by its value during this process.

There are some other use cases for module attributes: you can register them, which makes them accessible at runtime. For instance, Elixir registers the @moduledoc and @doc attributes, which can be used to provide documentation for modules and functions, respectively. This documentation can then be accessed at runtime by other Elixir tools, as we'll explore in the *Tooling and ecosystems* section.

 We're now mentioning macros for the first time. Macros are Elixir's mechanism to do meta-programming–generating code that writes code. We will not touch macros in this introductory chapter, as they will be properly examined in Chapter 6, *Metaprogramming – Code that Writes Itself.*

Elixir provides three lexically scoped directives to manage modules, plus a macro called use. We'll describe them now:

- alias is used to create aliases for other modules. You use it as alias Helpers.StringHelper, as: StrHlp, and you can then refer to that module as StrHlp. The as: portion is optional, and if you don't provide it, the alias will be set to the last part of the module name.
- We use require when we want to invoke what's defined as macros in a given module. As stated in the official documentation, is_odd/1 from the Integer module is defined as a macro. To use it in another module, you have to require it: require Integer.

- When we want to access functions from other modules without having to use the fully-qualified name, we use `import`. When we import a given module, we're also automatically requiring it. If we're constantly using `String.reverse/1` for instance, we can import it: `import String, only: [reverse: 1]`. Now we can just use `reverse` directly in our module. Apart from `only:`, you can also use `except:` to import all but a given number of functions from a module. Besides function names, `only:` and `except:` also accept `:modules` and `:functions` (which are self explanatory). You can also just use `import` without any option, but this isn't recommended, as it pollutes the scope of your module–always try to pass the `only:` option when using `import`.

- Last, but not least, we have `use`, which is a macro. This is commonly used to bring extra functionality to our modules. Beneath the surface, `use` calls the `require` directive and then calls the `__using__/1` callback, which allows the module being used to inject code into our context.

For now, you don't need to know how all of this works. It is enough to know that you have these constructs to deal with modules. When we dive into macros later in this book, all of this will become much clearer.

Working with collections

Contrary to the most common programming languages, Elixir doesn't have `while` or `do ... while` constructs, which makes sense, given all data types are immutable. The way to iterate in Elixir is by using recursion, through functions that call themselves. Most of your needs when working with collections are covered by the high-level abstractions Elixir provides, meaning that you may barely use recursion when writing your Elixir applications.

Nevertheless, we'll begin this section by briefly describing recursion, and show an example of a recursive function in Elixir. Then, we'll see how we can process a collection using the `Enum` module, and finish the section by talking about the benefits of processing a collection lazily, and how to do it using the `Stream` module.

Looping through recursion

We'll show you how to create a recursive functions through two simple examples: doubling each element on a list, and multiplying consecutive elements of a list. As mentioned earlier, although you probably won't be using this in your day-to-day coding, it's still very important to understand how this work. This way, if the abstractions Elixir provides aren't enough for your use case, you can just create your own recursive functions to accomplish what you need.

Before jumping into the examples, let's explain generally how recursive functions work. In Elixir, they're usually implemented as a multi-clause function, using pattern matching to control its flow of execution. The first clause sets the condition that will stop the recursion, and is followed by other broader clauses that apply the recursion.

In the first example, we want to take a list of integers as input, and return a new list where each element is multiplied by two. Let's see the code for such a function:

```
$ cat examples/double.ex
defmodule Recursion do
  def double([]), do: []

  def double([head | tail]) do
  [head * 2 | double(tail)]
  end
end
```

Here are its results:

```
iex> Recursion.double([2, 4, 6])
[4, 8, 12]
```

Besides using multi-clause functions, we're also using pattern matching in two ways: to know when we've reached the end (and the empty list) and treat it accordingly; and to extract the head and the tail of a list, similar to what we've shown in the *pattern matching* section. The recursion happens when we call double(tail). As we're only passing the tail to the recursive call, we're essentially iterating through the list. When we reach an empty list, the first clause matches, we return an empty list, and all of the intermediate calls will unfold and create our new list.

What if, instead of returning a new list, we want to return a single value? We'll exemplify this by multiplying consecutive elements of a list. Here's the code to do it:

```
$ cat examples/multiply.ex
defmodule Recursion do
  def multiply([]), do: 1
```

```
    def multiply([head | tail]) do
      head * multiply(tail)
    end
  end
```

Here's its use on an IEx session:

```
iex> Recursion.multiply([1, 2, 3])
6
```

The strategy is similar to the one shown in the previous example, except, instead of adding an element to a list at each step, we're now using our `head` as an accumulator. Also, it's important to note that, since we're doing a multiplication, our stopping condition must return 1 (the neutral element of this operation). The definition of the stopping condition varies between different problems, and is, arguably, one of the most important steps of defining a function recursively.

A common concern when dealing with recursive functions is its memory usage, as we have multiple function calls that will get into the stack. The Erlang runtime employs *tail-call optimization* whenever it can, which means that a recursive call won't generate a new stack push. For the runtime to do this optimization, you have to ensure that the last thing our function does is call another function (including itself)–or, in other words, make a *tail call*. Here's our `multiply` function updated to make tail calls:

```
$ cat examples/multiply_with_tail_recursion.ex
def multiply(list, accum \\ 1)
def multiply([], accum), do: accum
def multiply([head | tail], accum) do
  multiply(tail, head * accum)
end
```

The usual strategy is to pass an accumulator around, which enables us to use the tail-call optimization. Note that there's a trade-off here: On one hand, this optimization is important when dealing with large collections (since function calls don't consume additional memory); on the other hand, code that doesn't use this optimization is usually easier to read and comprehend, as it's usually more concise. When doing recursion, consider the advantages and disadvantages of each solution.

Eager processing with the Enum module

Having seen how recursion works in Elixir, we'll now show some examples of the abstractions that are built on top of it. We'll explore the Enum module, which contains a set of functions to work on collections. We've already seen some examples of collections in the *Elixir's data types* section, such as lists or maps. More generally, we can use the Enum module on collections that implement the Enumerable protocol.

 We haven't yet covered protocols. We will do so in the *Protocols* section.

Taking the two examples from our *Recursion* section, let's see how they become incredibly simple to implement using the Enum module:

```
iex> Enum.map([2, 4, 6], &(&1 * 2))
[4, 8, 12]
iex> Enum.reduce([1, 2, 3], 1, &(&1 * &2))
6
```

The map function receives a collection and a lambda, and returns a new list where the lambda is applied to each element of the collection.

The reduce function receives a collection, an accumulator, and a lambda. The lambda receives the current element of the collection and the accumulator, and the result of this lambda is the accumulator for the following iteration. At the end of the iteration, reduce returns the final accumulator value.

 We're using the capture operator to define a lambda. As we've previously hinted, you can also use it to capture named functions. In the following example, we're using the Integer.is_even/1 function to check which numbers are even in a collection:

```
iex> require Integer
Integer
iex> Enum.map([1, 2, 3], &Integer.is_even/1)
[false, true, false]
```

You'll see the Enum module being used in the application that we'll build throughout the book. For further usage of the Enum module, check its documentation at https://hexdocs. pm/elixir/Enum.html.

Comprehensions

Elixir provides another construct to iterate collections: *comprehensions*. As with the functions from the Enum module, comprehensions work on anything that implements the Enumerable protocol. Let's see a simple example:

```
iex> for x <- [2, 4, 6], do: x * 2
[4, 8, 12]
```

While, in this simple example, it is similar to Enum.map/2, comprehensions bring some other interesting features. You can, for instance, iterate over multiple collections and also apply filters. Let's see these two being applied in the following example:

```
iex> for x <- [1, 2, 3], y <- [4, 5, 6], Integer.is_odd(x), do: x * y
[4, 5, 6, 12, 15, 18]
```

Here we're doing a nested iteration–for each element of the first enumerable (which is represented by x), we will iterate through all elements of the second enumerable (represented by y). Also, we're applying a filter, and the body of our comprehension only gets executed when x is odd.

We won't be using comprehensions in the application we'll build throughout this book. However, it's important to mention them, as there are cases where using a comprehension instead of functions from the Enum module renders more elegant and expressive code

In our example, all comprehensions are returning a list, which is the default behavior. We can change that by passing the into: option, as you can see in this example:

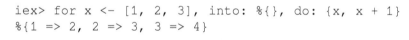

```
iex> for x <- [1, 2, 3], into: %{}, do: {x, x + 1}
%{1 => 2, 2 => 3, 3 => 4}
```

As you can see, now we're getting a map back. The into: option takes a collection that will receive the results of the comprehension. This collection must implement the Collectable protocol. This protocol can be seen as the opposite of the Enumerable protocol, and is used to create a new structure from the values of an existing collection. This also has usage outside of comprehensions–the Enum.into/2 function uses this protocol to create a new collection based on an enumerable.

Lazy processing with the stream module

We will now talk about a different way of processing collections, which, as functional programming, may require a shift in your mindset. Before talking about *lazy processing*, let's enumerate some of the shortcomings of working with the Enum module. The Enum module is referred to as being *eager*. This means that when processing a collection, this module will load the entire collection into memory. Furthermore, if you have a chain of functions you want to apply to a collection, the Enum module will iterate through your collection as many times as the functions are applying to it. Let's examine this further with an example:

```
iex> [1, 2, 3, 4, 5] \
...> |> Enum.map(&(&1 + 10)) \
...> |> Enum.zip(["a", "b", "c", "d", "e"])
[{11, "a"}, {12, "b"}, {13, "c"}, {14, "d"}, {15, "e"}]
```

 The \ on the end of the first two lines is to stop our Elixir console from evaluating this line right away, and wait for a new line instead. This way, we can write these operations with the pipe operator on multiple lines, which makes them more readable.

We take our initial collection and iterate it to add 10 to each element inside it. This generates a new list, which is passed to our next function. This function will zip the two lists together, which will produce a new list, which is returned to us. In this simple example, we need to traverse our list twice to build the desired result.

This is where the Stream module, and lazy processing, becomes advantageous. When working with lazy enumerables, the entire collection never gets loaded into memory, and contrary to what we're accustomed to, the computations aren't made right away. The results are produced as they are needed. Let's see this same example with the Stream module:

```
iex> [1, 2, 3, 4, 5] \
...> |> Stream.map(&(&1 + 1)) \
...> |> Stream.zip(["a", "b", "c", "d", "e"])
#Function<66.40091930/2 in Stream.zip/1>
```

As you can see, we're not getting our final list back. When we feed our list to Stream.map, the list is not iterated. Instead, the functions that will be applied on it are saved into a structure (along with the collection we're working on). We can then pass this structure into the next function, which will further save a new function to be applied to our list. This is really cool! But how do we make it return the result we're expecting? Just treat it as a regular (eager) enumerable, by applying a function from the Enum module, and it will start to produce results.

To exemplify this, we'll use the `Enum.take/2` function, which allows us to take a given number of items from an enumerable:

```
iex> [1, 2, 3, 4, 5] \
...> |> Stream.map(&(&1 + 10)) \
...> |> Stream.zip(["a", "b", "c", "d", "e"]) \
...> |> Enum.take(1)
[{11, "a"}]
```

As you can see, we're now getting the expected result back. Note that this is not a result of applying our computation to all the list and then just taking the first element. We've essentially only computed results for the first element, as that's all that was necessary. If you wanted to have the full list in the end, you could use the `Enum.to_list/1` function.

Streams are a really nimble way to process large, or even infinite, collections. Imagine that you're parsing values from a huge CSV file, and then running some functions on them. If you're running your application on the cloud, as most of us are these days, you probably have a short amount of memory. Using lazy processing, you can avoid having to load the whole file, processing it line by line. If you're processing an infinite collection, such as an RSS feed, lazy processing is also a great solution, as you can process each element of the collection incrementally, as they arrive.

Note that while the `Stream` module is amazing, it will not replace your usage of the `Enum` module. It's certainly great for very large collections, or even if you have a big chain of functions being applied to a collection and only want to traverse it once. However, for small or even medium collections, the `Stream` module will perform worse, as you're adding a lot of overhead, for instance, by having to save the functions you'll apply instead of applying them right away. Always analyze your situation carefully and take this into account when choosing to use the `Enum` or the `Stream` module for a given task.

We'll be using functions from the `Stream` module in the application we'll build in this book. You'll learn more about the `Stream` module in *Chapter 4, Powered by Erlang/OTP*.

Elixir provides some functions that wrap most of the complex parts of building streams. If you want to build your own lazy stream, check out these functions from the `Stream` module: `cycle`, `repeatedly`, `iterate`, `unfold`, and `resource`. The full documentation for the Stream can be found at `https://hexdocs.pm/elixir/Stream.html`.

Control flow

We're now introducing control-flow constructs. In Elixir, they aren't used as often as in traditional imperative languages, because we can fulfill our control-flow needs, using a mix of pattern matching, multi-clause functions, and guard clauses. Whenever you're about to use one of the constructs we're presenting in this section, stop and check whether it's possible to employ a more functional approach. Code without these traditional control-flow constructs is usually easier to understand and test. If you get to a point where you have nested conditionals, it's almost guaranteed you can simplify it by using one of the approaches I mentioned earlier. Either way, you'll occasionally use these constructs, so it's important to know they exist.

if and unless

These two constructs can be used with the following syntax:

```
if <expression> do
  # expression was truthy
else
  # expression was falsy
end

unless <expression> do
  # expression was falsy
else
  # expression was truthy
end
```

As with the `def` construct, they can be inlined. For `if`, you'd do this:

```
if <expression>, do: # expression was truthy, else: # expression was falsy
```

For both constructs, the `else` clause is optional. They will return `nil` if the main clause doesn't match and no `else` clause was provided.

cond

`cond` can be seen as a multi-way `if` statement, where the first *truthy* condition will run its associated code. This may substitute chains of `if ... else if` blocks. Let's see this with an example on IEx:

```
iex> x = 5
```

```
5
iex> cond do
...>    x * x == 9 -> "x was 3"
...>    x * x == 16 -> "x was 4"
...>    x * x == 25 -> "x was 5"
...>    true -> "none of the above matched"
...> end
"x was 5"
```

`true` in a condition will serve as a default condition, which will run when no other clause matches.

case

`case` accepts an expression, and one or more patterns, which will match against the return value of the expression. These patterns may include guard clauses. These patterns are matched (from top to bottom), and will run the code associated with the first expression that matches. Here is a simple example:

```
iex> case Enum.random(1..10) do
...>    2 -> "The lucky ball was 2"
...>    7 -> "The lucky ball was 7"
...>    _ -> "The lucky ball was not 2 nor 7"
...> end
"The lucky ball was not 2 nor 7"
```

Note that your output may differ when running this example, as we're matching against `Enum.random/1`. In here, the default condition is represented by using _ in the pattern, which will match anything. Although a bit more condensed, the `case` construct is similar to a multi-clause function.

with

This control-flow construct, introduced in Elixir 1.2, accepts one or more expressions, a `do` block, and optionally an `else` block. It allows you to use pattern matching on the return value of each expression, running the `do` block if every pattern matches. If one of the patterns doesn't match, two things may happen: If provided, the `else` block will be executed; otherwise, it will return the value that didn't match the expression. In practice, `with` allows you to replace a chain of nested instances of `case` or a group of multi-clause functions.

To demonstrate the usefulness of `with`, let's see an example:

```
iex> options = [x: [y: [z: "the value we're after!"]]]
[x: [y: [z: "the value we're after!"]]]
iex> case Keyword.fetch(options, :x) do
...>    {:ok, value} -> case Keyword.fetch(value, :y) do
...>      {:ok, inner_value} -> case Keyword.fetch(inner_value, :z) do
...>        {:ok, inner_inner_value} -> inner_inner_value
...>        _ -> "non-existing key"
...>      end
...>      _ -> "non-existing key"
...>    end
...>    _ -> "non-existing key"
...> end
"the value we're after!"
```

We're using the `Keyword.fetch/2` function to get the value of a key from a keyword list. This function returns `{:ok, value}` when the key exists, and `:error` otherwise. We want to retrieve the value that's nested on three keyword lists. However, let's say that if we try to fetch a key that doesn't exist on the keyword list, we have to return `"non-existing key"`. Let's achieve the same behavior using `with`, operating on the same `options` list as the preceding example:

```
iex> with {:ok, value} <- Keyword.fetch(options, :x),
...>      {:ok, inner_value} <- Keyword.fetch(value, :y),
...>      {:ok, inner_inner_value} <- Keyword.fetch(inner_value, :z),
...>      do: inner_inner_value
"the value we're after!"
```

Note that, since our expression is really small, we're using the shorthand `do:` syntax (but we can also use a regular `do ... end` block). As you can see, we're getting the same result back. Let's try to fetch a key that doesn't exist:

```
iex> with {:ok, value} <- Keyword.fetch(options, :missing_key),
...>      {:ok, inner_value} <- Keyword.fetch(value, :y),
...>      {:ok, inner_inner_value} <- Keyword.fetch(inner_value, :z),
...>      do: inner_inner_value
:error
```

Since we didn't provide an `else` block, we're getting back the value that didn't match, which is the return value of `Keyword.fetch/2` when a key doesn't exist in the keyword list provided. Let's do the same, but by providing an `else` block:

```
iex> with {:ok, value} <- Keyword.fetch(options, :missing_key),
...> {:ok, inner_value} <- Keyword.fetch(value, :y),
...> {:ok, inner_inner_value} <- Keyword.fetch(inner_value, :z) do
```

```
...> inner_inner_value
...> else
...> :error -> "non-existing key"
...> _ -> "some other error"
...> end
"non-existing key"
```

Since we're now providing an `else` block, we can now handle error cases accordingly. As you can see, `else` takes a list of patterns to match on. As you do with `case`, you can use _ as a default clause, which would run when the patterns above (if any) didn't match.

As you can see, `with` is a very helpful construct, which allows us to create very expressive code that is concise and easy to read. Moreover, you can control how to handle each error separately, using pattern matching inside the `else` block.

 The first expression provided to `with` has to be on the same line of `with` itself, you'll get a `SyntaxError` otherwise. If you do want to have `with` on its own line, wrap the expressions provided to it in parentheses.

Exceptions

Much like `if` and `else`, exceptions in Elixir aren't used as much as in other popular imperative languages. Exceptions aren't used for control flow, and are left for when truly exceptional things occur. When they do, your process is usually running under a supervision tree, and upon crashing, the supervisor of your process will be notified and (possibly, depending on the strategy) restart it. Then, upon being restarted, you're back to a known and stable state, and the effects of the exceptional event are no longer present. In the Elixir and Erlang communities, this is usually referred to as the "Let it crash!" philosophy. We'll be examining this in greater detail in `Chapter 3`, *Processes – The Bedrock for Concurrency and Fault Tolerance*, when we talk about processes, supervisors, and supervision trees.

For now, I'll list the traditional error-handling constructs. You can raise an error with the `raise` construct, which takes one or two arguments. If you provide only one argument, it will raise a `RuntimeError`, with the argument as the message. If you provide two arguments, the first argument is the type of error, while the second is a keyword list of attributes for that error (all errors must at least accept the `message:` attribute). Let's see this in action:

```
iex> raise "Something very strange occurred"
** (RuntimeError) Something very strange occurred
```

```
iex> raise ArithmeticError, message: "Some weird math going on here"
** (ArithmeticError) Some weird math going on here
```

You can rescue an error by using the `rescue` construct (you can rescue from a `try` block or from a whole function, pairing it with `def`). You define patterns on the rescue clause. You can use _ to match on anything. If none of the patterns match, the error will not be rescued and the program will behave as if no rescue clause was present:

```
iex> try do
...> 5 / 0
...> rescue
...> e in ArithmeticError -> "Tried to divide by 0."
...> _ -> "None of the above matched"
...> end
"Tried to divide by 0."
```

Since we're not doing anything with the error, and just returning a string, we could just use `ArithmeticError` in the pattern. Only use this syntax if you want to capture the error itself. When none of the patterns match, we get the error back in our console:

```
iex> try do
...>    5 / 0
...> rescue
...>    ArgumentError -> "ArgumentError was raised."
...> end
** (ArithmeticError) bad argument in arithmetic expression
```

Furthermore, you can also pass an `else` and/or an `after` block to the `try/rescue` block. The `else` block will match on the results of the `try` body when it finishes without raising any error. As for the `after` construct, it will always get executed, regardless of the errors that were raised. This is commonly used to clean up some resources (closing a file descriptor, for instance).

We've mentioned in this section that we don't use exceptions to control the flow of our programs, but in fact there's a special construct in Elixir for this. The syntax is similar to the one shown earlier, but you use `throw` instead of `raise`, and `catch` instead of `rescue`. As mentioned in the official *Getting Started guide* (http://elixir-lang.github.io/getting-started/try-catch-and-rescue.html) this should be used in *situations where it is not possible to retrieve a value unless by using throw and catch*. It's also mentioned that *those situations are quite uncommon in practice.*

Typespecs and behaviours

As already mentioned in the beginning of this chapter, Elixir is a dynamic programming language. As such, we don't declare the type of each variable, as it depends on the value each variable is bound to at each moment.

Usually dynamic programming languages yield higher productivity, as programmers don't need to declare types and can focus on developing the logic of an application. However, this comes at a cost: Certain errors, which in statically-typed languages would be caught at compile-time, may only be caught at runtime in dynamic languages. The time saved by using a dynamic language is then used (often in excess) on debugging in production.

We're not advocating for statically-typed languages–this book is about Elixir, after all. But what if you could have the best of both worlds?

It turns out you can! *Type specifications*, or *typespecs*, are a mechanism to annotate function signatures with the respective types (arguments and return values). Typespecs are also used to create custom data types. Let's explore them in more detail, before jumping into behaviours.

Typespecs

Typespecs are written using the `@spec` module directive, followed by `function_name(argument_type) :: return_type`. This module directive is placed right before the definition of the function we're annotating.

To demonstrate how to apply typespecs to a function, let's bring back our `palindrome?` function:

```
$ cat examples/string_helper.ex
defmodule StringHelper do
  def palindrome?(term) do
    String.reverse(term) == term
  end
end
```

Given that the module name is `StringHelper`, and that it's using functions from the `String` module, we can see that this function receives a string. As it uses the == operator, and also hinted at by the trailing ? on the function name, we know this function returns a Boolean. With this information, writing the typespec for this function is straightforward:

```
$ cat examples/string_helper_palindrome_with_typespec.ex
defmodule StringHelper do
```

```
    @spec palindrome?(String.t) :: boolean
    def palindrome?(term) do
      String.reverse(term) == term
    end
  end
```

You can also define your own types to use in typespecs, by using the `@type` directive within a module (usually the module where that type is used the most). Let's say that you frequently use a tuple in your module that contains the name of a country on the first element, and its population on the second, as in `{"Portugal, 10_309_573}`. You can create a type for this data structure with this:

```
@type country_with_population :: {String.t, integer}
```

Then, you could use `country_with_population` in typespecs as you'd use any other type.

Defining a type in a module will export it, making it available to all modules. If you want your type to be private to the module where it's defined, use the `@typep` directive. Similar to the `@moduledoc` and `@doc` directives (to document modules and functions, respectively), you can use the `@typedoc` directive to provide documentation for a certain type.

 In typespecs, the string type is usually represented by `String.t`. You can also use `string` but the Elixir community discourages this, with the goal of avoiding confusion with the `charlist` type, which represents strings in Erlang. If you use `string` in typespecs, the compiler will emit a warning.

Typespecs also provide great documentation, as we can quickly grasp what types this function accepts and returns. This example only shows a subset of the types you can use–please refer to the official documentation to get a full list, at

`https://hexdocs.pm/elixir/typespecs.html`

Dialyzer

Dialyzer (`http://erlang.org/doc/man/dialyzer.html`) is a tool that ships with Erlang and performs static analysis of code. It analyses compiled `.beam` files, making it available for all programming languages that run on the Erlang VM (such as Elixir!). While Dialyzer can be helpful on projects that don't have typespecs (as it can, for instance, find redundant code), its power is maximized on projects that have their functions annotated with typespecs. This way, Dialyzer is able to report on typing errors, which brings you closer to the security you can get on a statically-typed language.

Although we won't be exploring Dialyzer in this book, we highly recommend its usage, as it can be very helpful. Particularly, we feel that the `Dialyxir` library (`https://github.com/jeremyjh/dialyxir`), is a great way to integrate Dialyzer into Elixir projects, as it abstracts away part of the complexity of dealing with Dialyzer directly.

Behaviours

Behaviours provide a way to describe a set of functions that have to be implemented by a module, while also ensuring that the module implements the functions in that set. If you come from an object-oriented programming background, you can think of behaviours as abstract base classes that define interfaces. After declaring the behaviour, we can then create other modules that adopt this behaviour. A behaviour creates an explicit contract, which states what the modules that adopt the behaviour need to implement. This way, we can have our business logic tied to abstractions (the behaviour) instead of concrete implementations. We can swap two implementations of the same behaviour with very little and localized change in our application–the place where we define the implementation of the behaviour we're going to use.

Let's demonstrate this concept with an example. We'll define a behaviour, called `Presenter`, that has only one function: `present`. We'll then define a module that adopts this behaviour, called `CLIPresenter`. We could also have other modules that would adopt this behaviour, such as a `GraphicalPresenter`. A behaviour is created using the `@callback` directive inside a module, providing a typespec for each function this behaviour contains. Thus, to define our `Presenter` behaviour, we use the following:

```
$ cat examples/presenter.ex
defmodule Presenter do
  @callback present(String.t) :: atom
end
```

And now we define the module that will adopt this behaviour:

```
$ cat examples/cli_presenter.ex
defmodule CLIPresenter do
 @behaviour Presenter

 @impl true
 def present(text) do
 IO.puts(text)
 end
end
```

We can see this module working in the next snippet:

```
iex> CLIPresenter.present("printing text to the command line")
printing text to the command line
:ok
```

From Elixir 1.5 onwards, we may use the `@impl` directive to mark the functions that are implemented as callbacks for a behaviour. In our case, we'd put the `@impl` directive on top of the `present` function:

```
$ cat examples/cli_presenter_with_impl_annotation.ex
defmodule CLIPresenter do
  @behaviour Presenter

  @impl true
  def present(text) do
    IO.puts(text)
  end
end
```

We can be even more specific and use `@impl Presenter`, to state that this function is a callback from the `Presenter` behaviour. This brings two major advantages:

- Increased readability, as it's now explicit which functions make up part of our API and which functions are callback implementations.
- Greater consistency, as the Elixir compiler will check whether the functions you're marking with `@impl` are part of a behaviour your module is adopting.

Note that when you set `@impl` on a module, you must set it on all callback functions on that module, otherwise a warning will be issued. Furthermore, you can only use `@impl` on functions that are callbacks, otherwise a compilation warning will be issued as well.

> You can use `@optional_callbacks` to mark one or more functions as optional when adopting a certain behaviour. You need to provide a keyword list, with function names as keys, and arity as the value. If we wanted our `present/1` function to be optional in the `Presenter` behaviour, we would use:
>
> ```
> $ cat examples/presenter_with_optional_callbacks.ex
> defmodule Presenter do
>   @callback present(String.t) :: atom
>   @optional_callbacks present: 1
> end
> ```

If we didn't implement all of the functions declared in the `Presenter` behaviour (by commenting the `CLIPresenter.present/1` function, for instance), the Elixir compiler would emit the following warning:

```
warning: undefined behaviour function present/1 (for behaviour Presenter)
```

Behaviours help us follow the open/closed principle, since we can extend our system without modifying what we already have. If, in the future, we would need a new type of presenter, we'd just have to create a new module that adopts the `Presenter` behaviour, without having to change the behaviour or its current implementations. We'll be using behaviours in the application we'll build in this book, and you'll see them in action again in the next chapter.

Protocols

Throughout this introductory chapter, we've mentioned a couple of times that Elixir has protocols, with `Enumerable` being one of the examples. In this section, we'll dive into protocols and even define our own!

Protocols, like the behaviours we've seen in the last section, define a set of functions that have to be implemented. In that sense, both constructs serve as a way to achieve polymorphism in Elixir–being able to display multiple forms of behavior, but all linked to a single interface. While behaviours define a set of functions that a module needs to implement, and are thus tied to a module, protocols define a set of functions that a data type must implement. This means that, with protocols, we have data type polymorphism, and we're able to write functions that behave differently depending on the type of their arguments.

Let's now see how we can create a new protocol. We'll pick up, and extend, the example present in the official *Getting Started guide* (at `http://elixir-lang.github.io/getting-started/protocols.html`). We will define a `Size` protocol, which will be implemented by each data type. To define a new protocol, we use the `defprotocol` construct:

```
$ cat examples/size.ex
defprotocol Size do
  @doc "Calculates the size of a data structure"
  def size(data)
end
```

We're stating that our `Size` protocol expects the data types that will implement it must define a `size/1` function, where the argument is the data structure we want to know the size of.

You can use the `@doc` directive to add documentation to this function, as you normally do with named functions inside modules. We can now define the implementation of this protocol for the data types we're interested in, using the `defimpl` construct:

```
$ cat examples/size_implementations_basic_types.ex
defimpl Size, for: BitString do
  def size(string), do: byte_size(string)
end

defimpl Size, for: Map do
  def size(map), do: map_size(map)
end

defimpl Size, for: Tuple do
  def size(tuple), do: tuple_size(tuple)
end
```

We didn't define an implementation for the lists, as in Elixir, size is usually used for data structures that have their size precomputed. For types where we have to compute this on demand, such as lists, the length term is used instead of size. This is further observable by looking at the name of the function used to get the dimension of a list: `Kernel.length/1`.

With this defined, we can see our protocol in action:

```
iex> Size.size("a string")
8
iex> Size.size(%{a: "b", c: "d"})
2
iex> Size.size({1, 2, 3})
3
```

If we try to use our protocol on a type that doesn't have an implementation defined, an error is raised:

```
iex> Size.size([1, 2, 3, 4])
** (Protocol.UndefinedError) protocol Size not implemented for [1, 2, 3, 4]
```

You can define an implementation for a protocol on all Elixir data types: `Atom`, `BitString`, `Float`, `Function`, `Integer`, `Tuple`, `List`, `Map`, `PID`, `Port`, and `Reference`. Note that `BitString` is used for the binary type as well.

Having to implement a protocol for all types may quickly become monotonous and exhausting. You can define a fallback behavior for types that don't implement your protocol by implementing the protocol for `Any`. Let's do this for our `Size` protocol:

```
$ cat examples/size_implementation_any.ex
defimpl Size, for: Any do
  def size(_), do: 0
end
```

You have to define the desired behavior when a type doesn't implement your protocol. In this case, we're saying that it has a size of 0 (which might not make sense, since the data type may have a size different than 0, but let's ignore that detail).

We now have two options for this implementation to be used: Either mark the modules where we want this fallback behavior with `@derive [Size]` (the `List` module, for instance), or use `@fallback_to_any true` in the definition of our `Size` protocol. The former is more laborious as you have to annotate each module that you want to assume the behavior for `Any`, while the latter is simpler since you make it work on all data types just by changing the definition of your protocol. In the Elixir community, explicitness is usually preferred, and, as such, you're more likely to see the `@derive` approach in Elixir projects.

While implementing protocols for Elixir's data types already opens a world of possibilities, we can only fully utilize Elixir's extensibility when we mix them with *structs*. We haven't yet talked about structs, so we'll introduce them in the next section.

Structs

Structs are an abstraction built on top of maps. We define a struct inside a module, with the `defstruct` construct. The struct's name is the name of the module it's being defined in (which means you can only define one struct per module). To `defstruct`, we pass a keyword list, which contains the key-value pairs that define the fields that struct has, along with their default values. Let's define a `Folder` struct:

```
$ cat examples/folder.ex
defmodule Folder do
  defstruct name: "new folder", files_info: [], path: nil
end
```

We can now use it in our IEx session:

```
iex> %Folder{}
%Folder{files_info: [], name: "new folder", path: nil}
iex> %Folder{}.name
```

```
"new folder"
iex> %Folder{}.files_info
[]
```

Elixir already has a `File` module, which provides several functions to deal with files. One of them is the `File.stat/2`, which returns a `%File.Stat{}` struct with information about the provided path. The `files_info` field in our `%Folder{}` struct is a list, which will contain `%File.Stat{}` structs as elements. Let's initialize a folder with one file:

```
iex> folder = %Folder{files_info: [File.stat!("string_helper.ex")]}
%Folder{files_info: [%File.Stat{access: :read_write,
   atime: {{2017, 12, 31}, {16, 58, 56}}, ctime: {{2017, 12, 30}, {3, 40,
29}},
   gid: 100, inode: 3290229, links: 1, major_device: 65024, minor_device:
0,
   mode: 33188, mtime: {{2017, 12, 30}, {3, 40, 29}}, size: 509, type:
:regular,
   uid: 1000}], name: "new folder", path: nil}
```

Note that this example assumes you have a `"string_helper.ex"` file in the directory where you started `iex`. Also note that we're using `File.stat!`, which works similarly to `File.stat`, but, instead of returning a `{:ok, result}` tuple, it returns the result itself.

We now have our `%Folder{}` struct with one file. We can now show you the syntax to update a struct, which is similar to the one used in maps (or you can use the functions from the `Map` module). Assuming you also have a `"recursion.ex"` file on your current working directory, you can use this syntax to update the struct:

```
iex> folder = %Folder{ folder | files_info: [File.stat!("recursion.ex") |
folder.files_info]}
%Folder{files_info: [%File.Stat{access: :read_write,
   atime: {{2017, 12, 30}, {20, 8, 29}}, ctime: {{2017, 12, 30}, {20, 8,
25}},
   gid: 100, inode: 3278529, links: 1, major_device: 65024, minor_device:
0,
   mode: 33188, mtime: {{2017, 12, 30}, {20, 8, 25}}, size: 270, type:
:regular,
   uid: 1000},
  %File.Stat{access: :read_write, atime: {{2017, 12, 31}, {16, 58, 56}},
   ctime: {{2017, 12, 30}, {3, 40, 29}}, gid: 100, inode: 3290229, links:
1,
   major_device: 65024, minor_device: 0, mode: 33188,
   mtime: {{2017, 12, 30}, {3, 40, 29}}, size: 509, type: :regular, uid:
1000}],
 name: "new folder", path: nil}
iex> folder.files_info
```

```
[%File.Stat{access: :read_write, atime: {{2017, 12, 30}, {20, 8, 29}},
  ctime: {{2017, 12, 30}, {20, 8, 25}}, gid: 100, inode: 3278529, links: 1,
  major_device: 65024, minor_device: 0, mode: 33188,
  mtime: {{2017, 12, 30}, {20, 8, 25}}, size: 270, type: :regular, uid:
1000},
  %File.Stat{access: :read_write, atime: {{2017, 12, 31}, {16, 58, 56}},
  ctime: {{2017, 12, 30}, {3, 40, 29}}, gid: 100, inode: 3290229, links: 1,
  major_device: 65024, minor_device: 0, mode: 33188,
  mtime: {{2017, 12, 30}, {3, 40, 29}}, size: 509, type: :regular, uid:
1000}]
```

As you can see, we now have two files in our `%Folder{}` struct.

 Although structs are implemented on top of maps, they do not share protocol implementations with the `Map` module. This means that you can't, out of the box, iterate on a struct, as it doesn't implement the `Enumerable` protocol.

We'll end our little tour of structs with two more bits of information. First, if you don't provide a default value when defining the fields of a struct, `nil` will be assumed as its default value. Second, you can enforce that certain fields are required when creating your struct. You do that with the `@enforce_keys` module attribute. If we wanted to make sure `path` was provided when creating our `%Folder{}` struct, we would define it as following:

```
$ cat examples/folder_with_enforce_keys.ex
defmodule Folder do
  @enforce_keys :path

  defstruct name: "new folder", files_info: [], path: nil
end
```

If you don't provide `path` when creating this struct, `ArgumentError` will be raised:

```
iex> %Folder{}
** (ArgumentError) the following keys must also be given when building
struct Folder: [:path]
    expanding struct: Folder.__struct__/1
    iex:46: (file)
iex> %Folder{path: "/a/b/c/"}
%Folder{files_info: [], name: "new folder", path: "/a/b/c/"}
```

Bringing structs and protocols together

Now that we have the `%Folder{}` struct defined, we can define its implementation for the `Size` protocol.

We'll first define the implementation for the `%File.Stat{}` struct, as we can then use this to implement the protocol for `%Folder{}`. Here's the implementation for `%File.Stat{}`:

```
$ cat examples/size_implementations_file_stat_and_folder.ex
defimpl Size, for: File.Stat do
  def size(file_stat), do: file_stat.size
end

# ...
```

With this in place, our implementation for our `%Folder{}` struct is as follows:

```
$ cat examples/size_implementations_file_stat_and_folder.ex
# ...

defimpl Size, for: Folder do
  def size(folder) do
    folder.files_info
    |> Enum.map(&Size.size(&1))
    |> Enum.sum()
  end
end
```

To find out the size of a folder, we sum the size of each file it contains. As such, this implementation iterates through our `files_info` list, using the `Size` implementation for `%File.Stat{}` to get the size of each file, summing all the sizes in the end. In the following snippet, we can see this implementation being used on the `folder` variable we just defined:

```
iex> Size.size(folder)
779
```

With this, we can see the full power of mixing structs and protocols, which lets us have polymorphic functions based on the data type of their arguments. We now have a common interface, `Size.size(data)`, that allows us to find out the size of pretty much anything we want, provided that we implement the `Size` protocol for the data type we're interested in.

Tooling and ecosystems

The last section of this chapter is dedicated to one of the most renowned characteristics of Elixir: its incredible tooling. Also, since we can directly use Erlang libraries, we can take advantage of a very mature ecosystem that has been around for decades. First, let's begin with Elixir's interactive shell, IEx.

IEx

In the beginning of this chapter, we provided some instructions on how to start and stop an Elixir shell. You've seen it in use throughout this chapter. We'll now show you some other interesting things you can do inside IEx.

In this chapter, we've been giving you links to the official documentation of several Elixir modules. You can access this documentation right from IEx, using the h command. Let's say you want to know more about the Enum module:

```
iex> h Enum
Enum
#...,
```

The preceding code provides a set of algorithms that enumerate over enumerables according to the Enumerable protocol.

Note that, for brevity, the output of this command was cropped.

You can even pass a fully qualified function name, and get information about it. Let's say, for example, you don't remember the order of the arguments for the Enum.map/2 function:

```
iex> h Enum.map/2
def map(enumerable, fun)
@spec map(t(), (element() -> any())) :: list()

Returns a list where each item is the result of invoking fun on each
corresponding item of enumerable.
For maps, the function expects a key-value tuple.
## Examples

  iex> Enum.map([1, 2, 3], fn(x) -> x * 2 end)
  [2, 4, 6]

  iex> Enum.map([a: 1, b: 2], fn({k, v}) -> {k, -v} end)
  [a: -1, b: -2]
```

Another very interesting feature, which ships from Elixir 1.5 onwards, is the ability to set breakpoints from IEx. To showcase this, let's create a breakpoint on the StringHelper.palindrome?/1 function we've defined in the *Functions and modules* section, present in the "string_helper.ex" file:

```
iex> break! StringHelper.palindrome?/1
1
iex> StringHelper.palindrome?("abba")
Break reached: StringHelper.palindrome?/1 (string_helper.ex:2)
```

```
1: defmodule StringHelper do
2:   def palindrome?(term) when is_bitstring(term) do
3:     String.reverse(term) == term
4:   end

pry(1)> term
"abba"
pry(2)> whereami
Location: string_helper.ex:2

1: defmodule StringHelper do
2:   def palindrome?(term) when is_bitstring(term) do
3:     String.reverse(term) == term
4:   end
```

As you can see, you could access the argument passed to the function, `term`, and also use `whereami` to show the location where the breakpoint stopped the execution. To resume the execution, you use the `continue` command to go to the next breakpoint, or `respawn` to exit and start a new shell.

From Elixir 1.6 onward, you can also use pattern matching and guard clauses when setting a breakpoint. The breakpoint we defined earlier could also be set as `break! StringHelper.palindrome?("abba")`, which would make our breakpoint work when that function is called with `"abba"` as the argument.

> You can also use `IEx.pry` to set a breakpoint on the source-code file, instead of doing it via IEx. Use the method that's most appealing to you.

To finish this section, we'll show you a handy feature of IEx: the ability to access values from the history. Sometimes, you call a certain function and realize afterward that you wanted to bind the result of that function call to a variable. If this happens, you can use the `v/1` function. You pass it a number, which represents the position of the expression from which you want to retrieve the value (starting at 1). You can also pass a negative number, which makes the position relative to the current expression in the shell. You can call this function without providing an argument, which is the same as calling `v(-1)` –which means we're getting the value from the last expression. Let's see an example:

```
iex> 7 * 3
21
iex> a = v
21
iex> a * 2
42
```

```
iex> v(-3)
21
```

There are more things you can do with IEx, such as configuring it or connecting to remote shells. Please refer to the official documentation (at `https://hexdocs.pm/iex/IEx.html`) for further usage examples of IEx.

Mix

Mix is the Swiss-army knife of the Elixir tools. It's used to compile and run your application, manage your dependencies, run tests, and even for profiling your code. You can see which Mix tasks are available by typing `mix help` in your terminal. We won't explain its usage here, since the next chapter's purpose is to show you how you can use Mix to create and maintain an Elixir project.

ExUnit

Elixir comes with a fully fledged unit test framework: *ExUnit*. We'll use it to write tests for the application built in the course of this book. `Chapter 9`, *Finding Zen Through Testing*, is dedicated to testing, where we'll demonstrate how you can write tests for your application that let you sleep at night.

Erlang interoperability

As we stated at the beginning of this chapter, Elixir targets the Erlang runtime. Elixir is compiled to byte-code that can run on an Erlang VM (or BEAM), and Erlang libraries can be used in your Elixir projects (and vice versa). The philosophy in the Elixir community is to not reinvent the wheel and directly use Erlang libraries when appropriate. The creation of Elixir libraries that simply wrap an underlying Erlang library is discouraged, as you can directly call an Erlang library from your Elixir code.

We can take advantage not only of Erlang libraries, but also of their tooling. For instance, Erlang ships with a tool called Observer, which allows you to monitor your server and provides you with tons of useful information about the Erlang VM, such as the running processes or dynamic charts of load. We'll explore this tool in greater detail in `Chapter 11`, *Keeping an Eye on Your Processes*, when we talk about monitoring.

To utilize an Erlang library, you write its name as an atom and then call functions on it. Elixir doesn't have a `Math` module, so when more advanced mathematical operators are needed, it's common to call the `math` Erlang library. Let's use this library to calculate the natural logarithm of 10:

```
iex> :math.log(10)
2.302585092994046
```

 You can check out Erlang's standard libraries at `http://erlang.org/doc/apps/stdlib/index.html`.

When we introduced the data types in Elixir, we mentioned the `Port` type, which is a reference to a resource used by the Erlang VM to interact with external resources. Let's now see how we can use them to interact with an operating system process. To interact with ports, we use functions from the `Port` module. In the following example, we'll use the `whoami` UNIX command, which prints the username associated with the current user. To do that, we open a port and provide the name of the executable we want to run:

```
iex> port = Port.open({:spawn, "whoami"}, [:binary])
#Port<0.3730>
```

We passed the `[:binary]` option so that we get our result as a binary instead of a list of bytes. We now use the IEx `flush()` helper to print the messages received by the port:

```
iex> flush()
{#Port<0.3731>, {:data, "dcaixinha\n"}}
:ok
```

As our operating system process died after returning its result, the port is also closed. If this was not the case, we could use the `Port.close/1` function to explicitly close the port. Also note that this was a very simple example. You can have more complex interactions by using the `Kernel.send/2` function to dynamically send messages (that contain commands) to your port. In the official documentation for ports (which is available at `https://hexdocs.pm/elixir/Port.html`), you can see how this can be achieved.

If all we're interested in is running an operating-system command and getting its result back, we can use the `System.cmd/3` function, which is an abstraction on top of ports that allows us to achieve this effortlessly.

Summary

We've now reached the end of the first chapter, which contains a condensed introduction to Elixir. We didn't visit every aspect of the language, but provided several links that are worth exploring. Our goal is to provide the necessary knowledge for you to follow the next chapters, where we'll build a complex application. A lot of ground was covered in this chapter, so it's normal if you don't remember every concept we covered. Let's recap the most important points:

- Elixir is a dynamic language, and the type of a variable is determined by the value it holds.
- Every data type is immutable, which means that you never actually change the contents of a variable, you operate on copies of it. You can, however, rebind a variable, which will make it point to a new memory location, leaving its old contents untouched.
- Elixir code is organized in modules, which contain a set of functions.
- Functions are first-class citizens, as you can assign them to variables and pass them as arguments to other functions.
- Iteration in Elixir is always made through recursion. There are no `while` or `do ... while` constructs. Elixir provides a set of modules, such as `Enum` and `Stream`, that abstract the recursion and let you work with collections efficiently.
- The usual control-flow constructs, such as `if` and `else` statements, are less common in Elixir. You still use them occasionally, but you normally use a combination of pattern matching and multi-clause functions to control the flow of your programs.
- Exceptions aren't used for control-flow. Instead, they are used for truly exceptional events. We rely on supervision trees (which we'll discuss in `Chapter 3`, *Processes – The Bedrock for Concurrency and Fault Tolerance*) to recover from exceptions.
- You can annotate your functions with typespecs, or type specifications, bringing some of the safety of static-type languages into a dynamic language. These annotations also serve as a type of documentation for your functions.
- Elixir provides great mechanisms to have extensibility in your code, such as Behaviours and Protocols.
- Elixir comes bundled with amazing tooling, and you can also take advantage of all the libraries in the Erlang ecosystem.

In the next chapter, we'll learn how to use Mix to create a new project, while also describing the application we'll build throughout this book. This was the only chapter that contained ad hoc examples, and in the following chapters, we'll always use our application to exemplify the concepts that we want to explain.

Innards of an Elixir Project

2

After looking at the building blocks in the past chapter, we will now explore the fundamental aspects of any Elixir project. There are a few rules that need to be followed, but fortunately every one of them is simple to adopt and contributes to an understandable project structure. An application that doesn't get in the way of the evolution and maintenance tasks during all its years in production is a joy for the people who work with it, and this is exactly what we aim for.

We will start by learning what an Elixir application is and how we can structure an Elixir project, along with some of the existing good practices that you can leverage. We will introduce **Umbrella applications** and how they can help you to define more rigid boundaries between your project's components. When creating our umbrella project, we will use some common scaffolding mix tasks, which let you quickly create an Elixir project from scratch. Afterward, we'll talk about **ElixirDrip**, a polished web file server that we'll be developing along this journey. Since we are setting the foundations of our application, we will also establish some rules and best practices regarding code style, using Credo, and the new Elixir 1.6 code formatter.

In this chapter, you will learn the following topics:

- What an Elixir application is
- How to structure an Elixir project
- Different ways of specifying project dependencies
- What an umbrella project is and how it can help to structure your projects
- Using *mix new* to quickly get new projects up to speed
- Laying the foundations of ElixirDrip, the project we'll develop throughout this book
- Defining behaviours, to allow different behaviour implementations
- Using *xref* to understand the dependencies between your project files
- Establishing a consistent code style with Credo and the Elixir formatter

Elixir applications

Elixir inherits a lot of concepts from Erlang/OTP, and the **application's behaviour** is one of those concepts. For the Erlang VM, an application is a component that can be started and stopped as a single unit, and is described by an .app file (for example, hello_world.app) that defines, among other things, the **Application Module Callback**. This is a module that needs to implement a start/2 function that's responsible for kickstarting the application, usually by spawning its **top-level supervisor** (in the next chapter, you'll learn all about supervisors). In a way, you can think about the start/2 function as the common main entry point on applications developed with other programming languages.

Because we're using Elixir, we don't need to explicitly specify the .app file. The Elixir compiler will find the correct application module callback by looking for a module using the Application behaviour and will then generate the .app file for us.

Let's use mix to generate a sample project with a supervisor to see all these Application concepts applied in practice:

```
$ mix new sample_project --sup
* creating README.md
* creating .gitignore
* creating mix.exs
* creating config
* creating config/config.exs
* creating lib
* creating lib/sample_project.ex
* creating lib/sample_project/application.ex
* creating test
* creating test/test_helper.exs
* creating test/sample_project_test.exs

Your Mix project was created successfully.
You can use "mix" to compile it, test it, and more:

cd sample_project
  mix test
```

We just ran a Mix task named new and passed it two arguments, sample_project and --sup. Mix is a tool that comes with Elixir and helps you to create, organize and maintain your Elixir projects. For example, you can use Mix every time you need to fetch the project dependencies or run the application, by running mix <task> <arguments>. Since dependencies can also add their own Mix tasks, you will be able to run them in the exact same way.

We are defining the application `start/2` callback function in the following `SampleProject.Application` module. This function will be called during the project's initialization, because this module is using the `Application` behaviour. This callback strategy is a common pattern applied in other scenarios as well.

Being the entry point of your application, you should use this opportunity to start everything you will need afterwards. In our case, we created a sample project with a supervisor so we could see the `start/2` function starting a supervisor for us during the application's initialization:

```
$ cat lib/sample_project/application.ex
defmodule SampleProject.Application do
  use Application

  def start(_type, _args) do
    children = []

    opts = [strategy: :one_for_one, name: SampleProject.Supervisor]
    Supervisor.start_link(children, opts)
  end
end
```

If we hadn't created the project with an initial supervisor (by omitting the `--sup` flag), we would not have a `SampleProject.Application` module implementing the `start/2` callback, and therefore our project would not need to be started. This could be the case if you want to create a project to serve mainly as a bundle of modules and functions that may be included in other projects but does not need to be started per se.

The `mix.exs` file defines your Mix project and shows, among other things, which applications are started when you run your project. Looking at the `application/0` function inside `mix.exs` (which lives in the root of the project), you can see the `SampleProject.Application` being started alongside the `logger` application, which will be started as an extra application. This means that when your application starts, the `logger` application is already up and running. Every application referenced by the `mod` and `extra_applications` entries needs to implement the same `start/2` application module callback, so it can be properly started. Take a look at this code block:

```
$ cat mix.exs
defmodule SampleProject.Mixfile do
  use Mix.Project

  def project do
    [
```

```
      app: :sample_project,
      version: "0.1.0",
      elixir: "~> 1.4",
      start_permanent: Mix.env == :prod,
      deps: deps()
    ]
  end

  def application do
    [
      extra_applications: [:logger],
      mod: {SampleProject.Application, []}
    ]
  end

  defp deps do
    []
  end
end
```

We can also confirm this by starting the application with iex and calling the
Application.started_applications/0 function. We can observe that, along with
other applications started by Elixir, we have our sample_project and the logger extra
application. Take a look at this code:

```
$ iex -S mix
iex> Application.started_applications()
[{:sample_project, 'sample_project', '0.1.0'}, {:logger, 'logger',
'1.5.2'},
 {:mix, 'mix', '1.5.2'}, {:iex, 'iex', '1.5.2'}, {:elixir, 'elixir',
'1.5.2'},
 {:compiler, 'ERTS CXC 138 10', '7.1.3'},
 {:stdlib, 'ERTS CXC 138 10', '3.4.2'}, {:kernel, 'ERTS CXC 138 10',
'5.4'}]
```

In the previous snippet, we are running a script (due to the -S option), mix, inside an IEx
shell. When we run Mix without specifying any task, it will run the default run task,
responsible for starting and running the current application and its dependencies. Hence,
what we're doing here is equivalent to executing the run task with iex -S mix run.

If your application does not implement the aforementioned `start/2` callback function by using the `Application` module, you will still see it among the other started applications returned by the `Application.started_applications/0` function. However, since your application does not need to be started, you can call any of its functions even if you stop the application first with `Application.stop(:your_app)`.

After compiling the application with `mix compile`, take a peek inside the `_build/dev/lib/sample_project/ebin` folder. You will find the flat hierarchy of compiled modules and a `sample_project.app` file. This file defines your application using Erlang terms, and its goal is to let the Erlang VM know how to start your application. Mix automatically generates this file for us by looking at the `mix.exs` file. In the following snippet, you can see the `vsn`, `extra_applications`, and `mod` entries that were obtained from the values set by the `application/0` and the `project/0` functions of the `mix.exs` file. Take a look at this code block:

```
$ cat _build/dev/lib/sample_project/ebin/sample_project.app
{application, sample_project,
             [{applications, [kernel, stdlib, elixir, logger]},
              {description, "sample_project"},
              {modules, ['Elixir.SampleProject',
                         'Elixir.SampleProject.Application']},
              {registered, []},
              {vsn, "0.1.0"},
              {extra_applications, [logger]},
              {mod, {'Elixir.SampleProject.Application', []}}]}.
```

One of the compelling aspects of developing with Elixir is that, in the end, every module is compiled to its own BEAM bytecode file (using the full module name as its filename) and placed in the corresponding application's folder. Take a look at this code:

```
$ ls _build/dev/lib/sample_project/ebin
Elixir.SampleProject.Application.beam
Elixir.SampleProject.beam
sample_project.app
```

Moreover, there are no namespaces in Elixir. When you need to call a function from another module, you will have to use its full name or define an explicit alias, even if the module you're calling lives under the same application. In the same vein, there is no hidden magic behind the scenes loading modules for us based on some particular folder structure.

This inclination towards explicitness is a common aspect throughout Elixir, where nothing (or very little) is hidden from the developer. Another defining characteristic of Elixir is its relatively small set of language concepts and abstractions. This parsimony stems directly from the Elixir core team, *who believes there is a limited amount of features a language can provide without hindering its learning and without causing fragmentation in the community.* Everywhere you look, you will find explicitness and simplicity as two of the main drivers of the Elixir ecosystem.

Elixir project structure

In the previous section, we created a sample project with Mix, but we didn't explore it thoroughly. Despite not enforcing a rigid structure and looking really simple, the Elixir project structure sets the baseline of every project, enabling you to get up to speed when facing a new codebase.

Let's create a simpler project, using `mix new simple_project` to generate the initial folder structure for us. Besides creating the `.gitignore` and `README.md` files, it also created the `mix.exs` file and three separate folders: `config`, `lib` and `test`. Take a look at this:

```
$ mix new simple_project
* creating README.md
* creating .gitignore
* creating mix.exs
* creating config
* creating config/config.exs
* creating lib
* creating lib/simple_project.ex
* creating test
* creating test/test_helper.exs
* creating test/simple_project_test.exs

Your Mix project was created successfully.
You can use "mix" to compile it, test it, and more:

    cd simple_project
    mix test

Run "mix help" for more commands.
```

You can find the main configuration file, `config.exs`, inside the `config` folder. This is where you place your application configuration. The configuration file starts by using the `Mix.Config` module, so we can define configuration entries with the `config/2` macro.

This configuration file is only considered by the current application running. If your application is used by another application as a dependency, its configuration file won't be considered. If your application needs to fetch some configuration entries from the `config/config.exs` file, your documentation should be clear about that, because those configurations will need to be explicitly added to the configuration file of the main application.

The following code example shows a possible configuration for our `:simple_project` application. In the end, we are importing an environment specific configuration file, by interpolating the `Mix.env` value on the imported configuration file name. This is especially useful when we need different configuration values depending on the current Mix environment. Each configuration entry can then be retrieved with `Application.get_env(:simple_project, :configuration_key)`. If the following configuration syntax feels weird, remember that the last element of the configuration entry is a keyword list, consisting of a variable sized list of tuples with two elements each (that is to say: `[{:timeout_secs, 20}, {:max_number_of_processes, 1000}, {:max_upload_size_bytes, 10_000}]`). Take a look at this:

```
$ cat config/config.exs
use Mix.Config

config :simple_project,
  timeout_secs: 20,
  max_number_of_processes: 1000,
  max_upload_size_bytes: 10_000

import_config "#{Mix.env}.exs"
```

It is in the `lib` folder that you'll place your code. Mix created a `SimpleProject` empty module inside the `lib/simple_project.ex` file, and it's also in the `lib` folder that you will find the module implementing the `start/2` application module callback. It's important to notice that Elixir does not enforce any kind of `lib/` folder structure and how the actual files defining your modules are organized inside. You can have a `lib/foo.ex` file defining a `Xyz.SomeContext.My.Super.Module` that will be compiled into an `Elixir.Xyz.SomeContext.My.Super.Module.beam` file.

The last folder created for us is the `test` folder. All the tests you create should live here. Mix also created a `test_helper.exs` responsible for starting ExUnit, the testing framework that ships with Elixir. You may use this helper to configure your test runs.

Every test file on the `test` folder has to end with `_test.exs`. If not, your test cases won't run when you do `mix test`. Mix will only warn you if you have a test file in the `test` folder whose name ends in `_test` but does not have the expected extension; if the name does not match `*_test`, it proceeds without any warning, and your test file simply won't run.

Let's now check how we can define the dependencies of an Elixir project.

Project dependencies

We already analyzed the purpose of the `mix.exs` file. Its importance is paramount, since the information contained in it defines how the Erlang VM actually runs your Elixir project. However, we didn't examine how Mix actually uses this file to also know the dependencies of our application and how it should fetch and start them.

Mix looks for the application dependencies in the `deps` entry returned by the `project/0` function of the module defined by the `mix.exs` file. Each entry of this list is a tuple, pointing to the application our application depends on.

To help developers find libraries, the Elixir core team created Hex (https://github.com/hexpm/hex), a package manager for the Erlang VM that Mix uses by default. You can find all the public available libraries on `hex.pm` (https://hex.pm/), and there is also the possibility of uploading your libraries to private repositories hosted by `hex.pm`.

If you just set the dependency name and version in the `mix.exs` file (that is to say, `{:library, "~> 1.0.1"}`), it will be fetched from `hex.pm`. If your dependency lives in a private repository, you should add the `organization` option to its dependency entry in the `deps` list.

You can also pass additional options for each dependency. By using the `git` or `path` options, you can fetch the dependency from a Git repository or a local path, respectively. As you will see next, dependency management inside umbrella applications also leverage the same dependencies mechanism: if your dependency lives under the same umbrella project, you can use it by setting the `in_umbrella` option to `true`.

Elixir makes managing your dependencies a breeze: by default, Elixir will add your dependency to the so-called *runtime applications*. This ensures your dependencies are all running when your application starts and are included when you create your application release package.

In previous Elixir versions, dependencies were not always considered runtime applications, so the developer needed to add them manually to the `applications` entry returned by the `project` function in the `mix.exs` file. This was a source of confusion, since even library applications, which do not implement the application module callback (consisting of only a bundle of modules and functions), needed to be mentioned along with the other runtime applications, or else they would not be included in the package release. Due to this confusing behavior, since Elixir 1.4, applications are considered runtime applications by default.

Mix also allows you to settle on a particular package version with the `override` option. This is especially useful when a package in your `deps` list depends on a different version of a package you already depend on. If your code depends on a `http_client` dependency that uses Poison Version `~> 2.0`, but you also specify in your `deps` list that you need Poison Version `~> 3.0`, you will have a conflict. Adding the `override` option to your `poison` entry will force Mix to fetch and use version `3.*` of the package.

Throughout this book, you will see some `# ...` snippets in some of the code samples. This is used to signal we omitted the actual code since it wasn't relevant for our example and could hinder its comprehension.

Finally, you can also set dependencies that will only be used and fetched in specific Mix environments. Defining the `only` option as a list of `Mix.env` values such as `[:dev, :test]` will let you build and run your application, using that dependency only in those environments. You can use this approach to unclutter your release from development dependencies such as test-report formatters, benchmark tools, debuggers, and so on:

```
defmodule SimpleProject.Mixfile do
  use Mix.Project

  def project do
  [
  app: :simple_project,
  deps: deps(),
  # ...
  ]
  end
  # ...
  defp deps do
  [
  {:dep_from_hexpm, "~> 3.3.0"},
  {:private_dep_from_hexpm, "~> 0.2.0", organization: "coding_co"},
```

```
  {:dep_from_git, git: "https://github.com/elixir-lang/my_dep.git", tag:
  "2.1.0"},
  {:local_dep, path: "../packages/local_dep"},
  {:umbrella_dep, in_umbrella: true},
  {:specific_dep, "0.7.1", override: true},
  {:dev_test_dep, ">= 1.0", only: [:dev, :test]}
  ]
  end
end
```

In the following section, we will understand what an umbrella project is and how it can be used to lay the foundations of our application.

Umbrella projects

In the previous section, we started by defining and creating a sample Elixir application with Mix. By using the application's behaviour, we were able to start and stop it as a unit, and other applications could depend on it by pointing to this application in their dependencies.

As time passes, and your application gets bigger, you start thinking about how to divide it into smaller independent components with well-defined responsibilities. At this point, will you create a project from scratch for your recently extracted logic and add it as a dependency? Probably not, since, for now, those extracted components only make sense in the context of your original application.

An umbrella project helps you in this situation, because it allows you to have more than one application under the same Elixir project. Mix lets you achieve this by placing your individual applications under an apps folder in your umbrella project, while still allowing you to run each application separately inside the same project. In the future, if you want to extract one of these umbrella applications to its own project, it is just a matter of copying the respective application folder content to a new code repository.

One of the advantages of this approach is that you can manage separate Elixir applications living in the same code repository, with clear boundaries. And since it allows us not only to group OTP applications under the same umbrella but also to establish well-defined interfaces between those applications, umbrella projects are an invaluable tool to help you architect your projects. By decoupling your umbrella applications, you will be able to implement and even run them in isolation.

To simplify the nomenclature, throughout this book we will explicitly use the terms *umbrella project* and *umbrella application* to refer to the root project and each of its contained applications, respectively.

To illustrate how umbrella projects make our life easier, let's start by laying the foundation of the project we will build throughout this book. In the following snippet, we are creating a new `elixir_drip` umbrella project with an `ElixirDrip.Umbrella` top module. We are also naming the project OTP application as `elixir_drip_umbrella`:

```
$ mix new elixir_drip --module ElixirDrip.Umbrella --app
elixir_drip_umbrella --umbrella

* creating .gitignore
* creating README.md
* creating mix.exs
* creating apps
* creating config
* creating config/config.exs

Your umbrella project was created successfully.
Inside your project, you will find an apps/ directory
where you can create and host many apps:

    cd elixir_drip
    cd apps
    mix new my_app

Commands like "mix compile" and "mix test" when executed
in the umbrella project root will automatically run
for each application in the apps/ directory.
```

 Adding the *umbrella* reference to both module and application names makes it clearer this is in fact an umbrella project and will let us use, further ahead, the name `elixir_drip` for the umbrella application that will be responsible for the business logic.

We can now analyze the generated `mix.exs` file. As you can see, we have a new `apps_path` entry returned by the `project/0` function, and we have no dependencies at all. Mix uses this to know where the umbrella applications live. Also notice the module's name: the `--module ElixirDrip.Umbrella` option we passed with the `mix new` command set its prefix.

Otherwise, the module name prefix would be the camel-case version of the project name passed to the `mix new <project_name>` task (`ProjectName`, that is). Take a look at this code:

```
$ cat mix.exs
defmodule ElixirDrip.Umbrella.Mixfile do
  use Mix.Project

  def project do
    [
      apps_path: "apps",
      start_permanent: Mix.env == :prod,
      deps: deps()
    ]
  end

  # Dependencies listed here are available only for this
  # project and cannot be accessed from applications inside
  # the apps folder.
  #
  # Run "mix help deps" for examples and options.
  defp deps do
    []
  end
end
```

We now have our first umbrella project ready for action. Sadly, it does not have any umbrella applications yet:

```
$ tree
.
├────── apps
├────── config
│      └────── config.exs
├────── deps
├────── mix.exs
└────── README.md

3 directories, 3 files
```

If you try to run it using the `iex -S mix` command, nothing will happen; you will only get the idleness of the Elixir interactive shell waiting for your input. Let's fix this by creating the first umbrella application of our project.

We will now use Phoenix and its Mix tasks, which depend on Elixir and Erlang being installed. To have the Phoenix Mix tasks available, we need to install Phoenix first.

To install Phoenix globally run `mix archive.install https://github.com/phoenixframework/archives/raw/master/phx_new.ez`. If we follow this route, we can use Phoenix Mix tasks even in projects, such as our umbrella project, without Phoenix being explicitly set as a dependency.

An alternative way to enable the Phoenix Mix tasks in our project would be to add Phoenix as a dependency in the umbrella project `mix.exs` file, and then run `mix deps.get` to fetch it as part of the project dependencies.

Inside the `apps` folder, we will create an Elixir application that will be responsible for encapsulating both the business logic and all the data access processes. For that, we will leverage the Mix `phx.new.ecto` task, that will create a barebones application with a repository and everything needed to start interacting with our database using **Ecto** (we'll take a deeper look at Ecto in `Chapter 7, Persisting Data with Ecto`). Take a look at this:

```
$ cd apps
$ mix phx.new.ecto elixir_drip --database postgres
* creating elixir_drip/config/config.exs
* creating elixir_drip/config/dev.exs
* creating elixir_drip/config/prod.exs
* creating elixir_drip/config/prod.secret.exs
* creating elixir_drip/config/test.exs
* creating elixir_drip/lib/elixir_drip/application.ex
* creating elixir_drip/lib/elixir_drip.ex
* creating elixir_drip/test/test_helper.exs
* creating elixir_drip/README.md
* creating elixir_drip/mix.exs
* creating elixir_drip/.gitignore
* creating elixir_drip/lib/elixir_drip/repo.ex
* creating elixir_drip/priv/repo/seeds.exs
* creating elixir_drip/test/support/data_case.ex

Fetch and install dependencies? [Y/n] Y
* running mix deps.get
```

We are all set! We just created our first `elixir_drip` umbrella application.

Looking at the `mix.exs` file of the `elixir_drip` application we just created, you can see that Mix automatically set the correct values for the `build_path`, `config_path`, `deps_path` and `lockfile` by pointing to those places under the umbrella root.

After creating the `elixir_drip` application, the `mix new` task created a `mix.lock` file on the path pointed by the `lockfile` configuration entry. This file was created because we also ran `mix deps.get` during the application creation (check the command output above). This file stores the specific versions of every dependency our project depends on and should be placed under your version control system along the rest of the code. This way, we ensure that every execution of the code relies on the same dependency versions. The same dependency versions contained in the `mix.lock` file are also considered when creating the application release. As a result, your application will run in production with the exact same set of dependencies.

Note that the `lockfile` and `deps_path` entries point to a `mix.lock` file and a `deps` folder living in the root of the umbrella project. This allows us to group and manage all the dependencies of our umbrella applications in a single common folder and collect them in the same lock file:

```
$ cat apps/elixir_drip/mix.exs
defmodule ElixirDrip.Mixfile do
  use Mix.Project

  def project do
    [
      app: :elixir_drip,
      version: "0.0.1",
      build_path: "../../_build",
      config_path: "../../config/config.exs",
      deps_path: "../../deps",
      lockfile: "../../mix.lock",
      elixir: "~> 1.4",
      elixirc_paths: elixirc_paths(Mix.env),
      start_permanent: Mix.env == :prod,
      aliases: aliases(),
      deps: deps()
    ]
  end

  def application do
    [
      mod: {ElixirDrip.Application, []},
      extra_applications: [:logger, :runtime_tools]
    ]
  end

  defp elixirc_paths(:test), do: ["lib", "test/support"]
  defp elixirc_paths(_), do: ["lib"]

  defp deps do
```

```
    [
      {:postgrex, ">= 0.0.0"},
      {:ecto, "~> 2.1"}
    ]
  end

  defp aliases do
    [
      "ecto.setup": ["ecto.create", "ecto.migrate", "run
priv/repo/seeds.exs"],
      "ecto.reset": ["ecto.drop", "ecto.setup"],
      "test": ["ecto.create --quiet", "ecto.migrate", "test"]
    ]
  end
end
```

It is also worth noting two aspects of the previous mix.exs file: how the paths to compile are pointed out to the compiler depending on the Mix.env value (for example, the test/support path is only compiled in the test environment) and the task aliases that were created for us given that our application relies on Ecto. Regarding the latter, we can now use mix ecto.reset inside this application folder to drop the database and set it up again afterwards. These aliases are really useful to streamline frequent commands and you should use them liberally according to your needs.

Independently of the number of umbrella applications living in your umbrella project, starting your project, and consequently all its umbrella applications, is just a matter of running mix in the project root. Conversely, if you want to run the test suite of every umbrella application, you should run mix test instead. We now have one application living under our umbrella, so we will definitely see something happening if we run our project. Let's do it:

```
$ iex -S mix
Erlang/OTP 20 [erts-9.1.5] [source] [64-bit] [smp:4:4] [ds:4:4:10] [async-
threads:10] [hipe] [kernel-poll:false]

Interactive Elixir (1.5.2) - press Ctrl+C to exit (type h() ENTER for help)
iex(1)>
16:22:21.146 [error] Postgrex.Protocol (#PID<0.202.0>) failed to connect:
** (DBConnection.ConnectionError) tcp connect (localhost:5432): connection
refused - :econnrefused

BREAK: (a)bort (c)ontinue (p)roc info (i)nfo (l)oaded
       (v)ersion (k)ill (D)b-tables (d)istribution
a
```

The error we got means that the `elixir_drip` umbrella application started, but when it tried to connect to the database indicated by its `config/config.exs` file, it failed since no database is currently running on `port 5432`. This error was expected since we don't have a database running yet.

Let's now take care of the client-facing component of our project. Our project frontend will be a Phoenix web application; hence, we'll use the `phx.new.web` Mix task to generate our `elixir_drip_web` umbrella application (remember we are still inside the `apps` folder of the umbrella project):

```
$ mix phx.new.web elixir_drip_web
* creating elixir_drip_web/config/config.exs
* creating elixir_drip_web/config/dev.exs
* creating elixir_drip_web/config/prod.exs
* creating elixir_drip_web/config/prod.secret.exs
* creating elixir_drip_web/config/test.exs
* creating elixir_drip_web/lib/elixir_drip_web.ex
* creating elixir_drip_web/lib/elixir_drip_web/application.ex
* creating elixir_drip_web/lib/elixir_drip_web/channels/user_socket.ex
* creating elixir_drip_web/lib/elixir_drip_web/endpoint.ex
* creating elixir_drip_web/lib/elixir_drip_web/router.ex
* creating elixir_drip_web/lib/elixir_drip_web/views/error_helpers.ex
* creating elixir_drip_web/lib/elixir_drip_web/views/error_view.ex
* creating elixir_drip_web/mix.exs
* creating elixir_drip_web/README.md
* creating elixir_drip_web/test/test_helper.exs
* creating elixir_drip_web/test/support/channel_case.ex
* creating elixir_drip_web/test/support/conn_case.ex
* creating elixir_drip_web/test/elixir_drip_web/views/error_view_test.exs
* creating elixir_drip_web/lib/elixir_drip_web/gettext.ex
* creating elixir_drip_web/priv/gettext/en/LC_MESSAGES/errors.po
* creating elixir_drip_web/priv/gettext/errors.pot
* creating
elixir_drip_web/lib/elixir_drip_web/controllers/page_controller.ex
* creating
elixir_drip_web/lib/elixir_drip_web/templates/layout/app.html.eex
* creating
elixir_drip_web/lib/elixir_drip_web/templates/page/index.html.eex
* creating elixir_drip_web/lib/elixir_drip_web/views/layout_view.ex
* creating elixir_drip_web/lib/elixir_drip_web/views/page_view.ex
* creating
elixir_drip_web/test/elixir_drip_web/controllers/page_controller_test.exs
* creating elixir_drip_web/test/elixir_drip_web/views/layout_view_test.exs
* creating elixir_drip_web/test/elixir_drip_web/views/page_view_test.exs
* creating elixir_drip_web/.gitignore
* creating elixir_drip_web/assets/brunch-config.js
* creating elixir_drip_web/assets/css/app.css
```

```
* creating elixir_drip_web/assets/css/phoenix.css
* creating elixir_drip_web/assets/js/app.js
* creating elixir_drip_web/assets/js/socket.js
* creating elixir_drip_web/assets/package.json
* creating elixir_drip_web/assets/static/robots.txt
* creating elixir_drip_web/assets/static/images/phoenix.png
* creating elixir_drip_web/assets/static/favicon.ico

Fetch and install dependencies? [Yn] Y
* running mix deps.get
* running mix deps.compile
Phoenix uses an optional assets build tool called brunch.io
that requires node.js and npm. Installation instructions for
node.js, which includes npm, can be found at http://nodejs.org.
  # ...
```

This created a Phoenix application as the `elixir_drip_web` umbrella application, so we now have two umbrella applications in the `apps` folder. Our web interface will expose the business logic implemented by the `elixir_drip` application, so we have to add the latter to the `elixir_drip_web` dependencies by editing its `mix.exs` file.

To access modules defined by the `elixir_drip` application from the `elixir_drip_web` application, we just need to add `{:elixir_drip, in_umbrella: true}` as one of the web application dependencies:

```
$ cat apps/elixir_drip_web/mix.exs
defmodule ElixirDripWeb.Mixfile do
  use Mix.Project

  def project do
    [
      # ...
    ]
  end

  def application do
    [
      mod: {ElixirDripWeb.Application, []},
      extra_applications: [:logger, :runtime_tools]
    ]
  end
  # ...
  defp deps do
    [
      {:elixir_drip, in_umbrella: true},
      {:phoenix, "~> 1.3.0"},
      {:phoenix_pubsub, "~> 1.0"},
```

```
        {:phoenix_ecto, "~> 3.2"},
        {:phoenix_html, "~> 2.10"},
        {:phoenix_live_reload, "~> 1.0", only: :dev},
        {:gettext, "~> 0.11"},
        {:cowboy, "~> 1.0"}
    ]
  end
  # ...
end
```

 We could have used the `mix phx.new elixir_drip --umbrella` command to create an umbrella project with both the `elixir_drip` and `elixir_drip_web` applications in one fell swoop, with the first being able to interact with the database, using Ecto, and the latter being a Phoenix web app. But with that approach, we would miss all the fun. You now know what the `phx.new <project_name> --umbrella` task does behind the scenes.

By observing how easy it is to create an umbrella project with several applications, you may be tempted to use this strategy by default when bootstrapping your project. After all, it gives you a way to precisely define your project boundaries and the concerns of each application, while keeping your code under the same code repository.

However, when resorting to an umbrella project you should be aware that no circular dependencies between your applications may exist, and version conflicts between your dependencies may also arise. Remember that all dependencies, even the ones of the applications you depend on, are placed in a common `deps` folder in the umbrella root. If one of your umbrella applications depends on the version X of `utility` and the dependency `remote_dep`, fetched from Hex, depends on the version Y of the same `utility`, you have a version conflict and Mix won't be able to fix it for you. You can solve this type of conflict by using the already mentioned `override` option.

You could also find yourself creating a `common` or `core` umbrella application on which your other umbrella applications will depend. However, the newly created `common` application may not even need to live under the same umbrella project, since it is just a bundle of modules with utility functions that do not belong anywhere else. In this case, you may consider to create it as a completely separate project and import it as a "normal" dependency (from its Git repository, or, even better, a Hex repository). The first iteration of extracting that common logic from the project was to place all those modules inside the `common` umbrella application. You can now easily pull this umbrella application out of the project afterwards if you want to. If you remember, an umbrella application is an independent and fully working Elixir application in the first place.

At the end of the day, umbrella projects give you more flexibility when deciding your project architecture. One of the main benefits is that you don't need to change your code if you want to pull your application from the umbrella afterwards. You may also decide further down the road that having an umbrella project is overkill. In this case, you will have to merge all the umbrella application modules and their dependencies into a single Elixir project, being aware of how each application was previously started. For web-facing projects, our recommendation is to create an umbrella project similar to what we did here: one for the business logic and the other for the web interface. This way, we can achieve a really concise and thin web layer, since its responsibility is solely to call the service logic and present its results.

 Keep in mind that you should always be able to use every feature of your project without having to pass through the web layer. This will only be possible if your web interface is really thin. A good rule of thumb is to design your project in a way that lets you use every feature from the comfort of an IEx session.

With the creation of our `elixir_drip` umbrella, we now have two of the umbrella applications that will compose our project. In the next section, we will properly introduce the project and its aspirations, and how its features will exemplify the ideas demonstrated in the chapters ahead.

ElixirDrip – our showcase application

To clearly illustrate how you may incorporate the concepts and strategies in this book, we will develop a fully fledged web application named **ElixirDrip**, which was kick-started by the umbrella project we have just created.

ElixirDrip aims to be a fast and scalable web storage service, allowing the user to easily store and share their files living on the cloud. Our users will be able to upload files to their cloud storage and then share those files with other ElixirDrip users.

We will be adding features to the ElixirDrip umbrella application as we progress, taking it closer to our final goal with each chapter. The most important features of our application will be tackled in specific chapters throughout this book. Consider the following:

- The design and implementation of our domain model will be analyzed in `Chapter 7`, *Persisting Data Using Ecto*, when we talk about data persistence and the usage of Ecto to efficiently query and update our application data.

- User account management and user authentication, along with our web interface for files and folders, will be tackled in Chapter 8, *Phoenix – a Flying Web Development Framework*.
- The steps that apply to each processed file, whether it is being uploaded or downloaded to or from ElixirDrip, will be first defined with the **GenStage** behaviour in Chapter 5, *Demand-Driven Processing*. We will implement the steps responsible for the remote media storage and for the real-time notifications shown to the user.
- Afterward, we will improve on the previous steps definition by creating a **domain-specific language (DSL)** that will better express how we process each file before reaching the cloud or being downloaded. This will be done in Chapter 6, *Metaprogramming– Code That Writes Itself*.
- In Chapter 8, *Phoenix – a Flying Web Development Framework*, our notification mechanism will be implemented. Every notification pushed to our users will be delivered over Phoenix Channels, a fast and bi-directional way of communicating with a Phoenix backend.
- The correctness of our application will be put to test in Chapter 9, *Finding Zen through Testing*, when we talk about testing best practices, unit and integration testing.
- We will create the ElixirDrip release using **Distillery**, and then deploy and run it on the cloud with **Kubernetes**. Every Elixir node deployed by us will be connected to its peers, improving the performance of our application. We will discuss all of this and more in Chapter 10, *Deploying in the Cloud*.
- Our journey does not end with our application serving live requests. We also need to make sure it stays healthy and that everything runs smoothly. In Chapter 11, *Keeping an Eye on Your Processes*, we will implement some best practices for monitoring and metric collection, ensuring we always stay on top. Moreover, we will also learn how to profile and trace our application while it's running in production.

We will keep the two already-created umbrella applications, elixir_drip and elixir_drip_web. The first will be responsible for the business logic, and the latter will be responsible for the web interface. However, on the business logic side, we will create specific modules (let's call them *contexts*) to aggregate related functionalities under a public interface. One of those contexts is the ElixirDrip.Storage module, which will encapsulate all media operations. The other context is the ElixirDrip.Accounts context, which is responsible for user management and authentication.

The following diagram shows a macro perspective of how the ElixirDrip umbrella application will look:

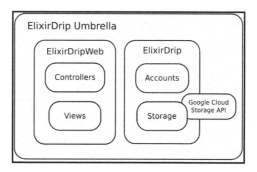

We already used the behaviour concept when we used the `Application` module to define the application module callback of the `elixir_drip` umbrella application. Let's now understand its purpose.

Using behaviours

One of the core parts of our project will be how we store and retrieve files on the cloud on behalf of our users. We decided not to place this component under its own umbrella application, because it is possible to define a clear boundary between the ElixirDrip business logic and its storage counterpart under the same umbrella application. To achieve this separation of concerns, we will encapsulate all the storage logic under an `ElixirDrip.Storage` module. This module will be the single entry point for every storage-related operation, while encapsulating the actual implementation details.

We will start by creating a `StorageProvider` behaviour, which defines two callbacks to be implemented and relies on typespecs to indicate, for each callback, its arguments and the possible return values. A behaviour allows us to establish the contract that every storage provider will have to comply to. Take a look at this:

```
$ cat apps/elixir_drip/lib/elixir_drip/behaviours/storage_provider.ex
defmodule ElixirDrip.Behaviours.StorageProvider do
  @type path :: binary()
  @type content :: bitstring()
  @type reason :: atom()
  @type details :: map()

  @callback upload(path, content) ::
              {:ok, :uploaded}
              | {:error, reason}
```

```
                    | {:error, reason, details}
    @callback download(path) ::
              {:ok, content}
              | {:error, reason}
              | {:error, reason, details}
    end
```

We will then implement this behaviour with two modules, a `Local` and a `Live` module, that will be used in local development and production, respectively. Using a behaviour ensures our modules always abide to the same contract, whether they are the previous two modules or the mock module that we'll use to fake the actual call to the provider when creating our tests in `Chapter 9`, *Finding Zen through Testing*.

Each implementation module only needs to annotate the behaviour it implements by using the `@behaviour` module attribute. From now on, for every module that materializes the behaviour, the compiler will check whether it implements the behaviour callbacks with the correct number of arguments:

```
$ cat
apps/elixir_drip/lib/elixir_drip/storage/providers/google_cloud_storage/loc
al.ex
defmodule ElixirDrip.Storage.Providers.GoogleCloudStorageLocal do
  @behaviour ElixirDrip.Behaviours.StorageProvider

  require Logger

  def upload(path, content) do
    Logger.debug("Uploading #{inspect(byte_size(content))} bytes to Google
Cloud Storage, path: #{path}")
    {:ok, :uploaded}
  end

  def download(path) do
    Logger.debug("Downloading #{path} from Google Cloud Storage")
    {:ok, "downloaded_content"}
  end
end
```

We selected Google Cloud Storage as the storage provider for ElixirDrip. Since its access logic is completely abstracted via a `StorageProvider` custom behaviour, it will be possible to easily switch in the future to other storage provider. This hypothetical new provider would only need to respect the same `StorageProvider` behaviour, hence it would need to implement both `upload/2` and `download/1` callbacks.

Deciding between the `Local` or `Live` implementation will be just a matter of adjusting the global or production configuration files. This is a common pattern applied when we want to inject different modules depending on the current Mix environment:

```
$ cat apps/elixir_drip/config/config.exs
use Mix.Config
  # ...
config :elixir_drip,
  storage_provider: ElixirDrip.Storage.Providers.GoogleCloudStorageLocal

import_config "#{Mix.env()}.exs"
```

As you can see from the following code, in the `prod.exs` configuration, we point to the `ElixirDrip.Storage.Providers.GoogleCloudStorageLive` module that will actually interact with the cloud storage provider. Since this configuration file is imported after the main `config.exs` configuration file, it will override the previous `storage_provider` configuration entry:

```
$ cat apps/elixir_drip/config/prod.exs
use Mix.Config
  # ...
config :elixir_drip,
  storage_provider: ElixirDrip.Storage.Providers.GoogleCloudStorageLive
```

The last piece of the puzzle is the creation of a generic `ElixirDrip.Storage.Provider` module that will delegate on the `StorageProvider` implementation designated by the `:storage_provider` configuration entry. This module hides the actual storage provider implementation from the caller, by delegating a `Provider.upload/2` or `Provider.download/1` call to the module returned by the `Application.get_env(elixir_drip, :storage_provider)` configuration.

Because we are using the `defdelegate/2` macro, Elixir expects the `@target` module to define the `upload/2` and `download/1` public functions, otherwise the delegation won't work:

```
$ cat apps/elixir_drip/lib/elixir_drip/storage/provider.ex
defmodule ElixirDrip.Storage.Provider do
  @moduledoc false

  @target Application.get_env(:elixir_drip, :storage_provider)

  defdelegate upload(path, content), to: @target
  defdelegate download(path), to: @target
end
```

Previously, we decided to expose every storage-related function via an
`ElixirDrip.Storage` module, which represents our `Storage` context. As such, this
context will rely on the previous `ElixirDrip.Storage.Provider` to interact with our
storage provider.

 If we don't want to have this
intermediary `ElixirDrip.Storage.Provider` module delegating to the
actual storage provider module, we could immediately fetch the `Local`
or `Live` module from the configuration (that is to say, using
`Application.get_env(:elixir_drip, :storage_provider)`) in the
consumer `ElixirDrip.Storage` module.

This context will do a lot more in a couple of chapters, but, for now, it only exposes two
functions, `store/2` and `retrieve/1`, both relying on the generic storage provider:

```
$ cat apps/elixir_drip/lib/elixir_drip/storage/storage.ex
defmodule ElixirDrip.Storage do
  alias ElixirDrip.Storage.Media
  alias ElixirDrip.Storage.Provider

  def store(%Media{} = media, content) do
    media
    |> generate_storage_key()
    |> Map.get(:storage_key)
    |> Provider.upload(content)
  end

  def retrieve(%Media{storage_key: storage_key}) do
    Provider.download(storage_key)
  end

  # ...
end
```

We will now look at our ElixirDrip application through the lens of the `xref` tool.

Viewing cross references with xref

Since Elixir 1.3, every time you compile your code, you are also using `xref` to find calls to
non-existent modules and functions. If the module we were pointing to in the ElixirDrip
application configuration (`config/config.exs`) had a typo, we would get the following
output:

```
$ mix clean && mix compile
==> elixir_drip
Compiling 10 files (.ex)
warning: function ElixirDrip.Storage.Providers.Typo.upload/2 is undefined
(module ElixirDrip.Storage.Providers.Typo is not available)
 lib/elixir_drip/storage/provider.ex:6

warning: function ElixirDrip.Storage.Providers.Typo.download/1 is undefined
(module ElixirDrip.Storage.Providers.Typo is not available)
 lib/elixir_drip/storage/provider.ex:7

Generated elixir_drip app
==> elixir_drip_web
Compiling 11 files (.ex)
Generated elixir_drip_web app
```

Behind the scenes, the compiler runs mix xref warnings, which results in those two warnings that let us know the generic provider is delegating the upload/2 and download/1 functions to a missing module.

Another useful functionality of xref is the graph mode is that it shows how the application files depend on one another by printing the application dependency graph. Let's generate the dependency graph of our umbrella project:

```
$ mix xref graph --format dot
==> elixir_drip
Generated "xref_graph.dot" in the current directory. To generate a PNG:

    dot -Tpng xref_graph.dot -o xref_graph.png

For more options see http://www.graphviz.org/.
==> elixir_drip_web
Generated "xref_graph.dot" in the current directory. To generate a PNG:

    dot -Tpng xref_graph.dot -o xref_graph.png

For more options see http://www.graphviz.org/.
```

xref detected we had an umbrella project, and so it generated the dependency graph for each umbrella application.

If we look at the following graph for our business logic application (here re-arranged for brevity), we can observe that the `application.ex` file references the `repo.ex` file, our local storage provider implementation points to the `StorageProvider` behaviour and our `Storage` context points to both the `Storage.Media` schema and the generic provider implementation:

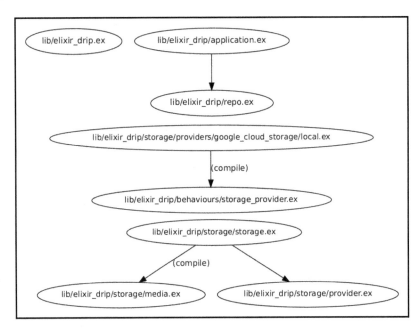

You can also leverage the `graph` mode to see all files referenced by a specific file or all files that reference the given file, using the `--source` or `--sink` option, respectively. This is especially convenient whenever you need to refactor an existing code base and want to know every module that depends on the soon-to-be changed file. The following are two examples of the `graph` mode applied to our umbrella project.

By encapsulating related logic and modules inside the same context, your dependency graphs will show a more or less self-contained hub for each context that connects to all the resources it encapsulates:

```
$ cd apps/elixir_drip
$ mix xref graph --format dot --source lib/elixir_drip/storage/storage.ex
Generated "xref_graph.dot" in the current directory. To generate a PNG:

    dot -Tpng xref_graph.dot -o xref_graph.png

For more options see http://www.graphviz.org/.
```

By running the mix xref graph command with the --source option, we get all the files that are referenced by the lib/elixir_drip/storage/storage.ex file. In our case, we find two files referenced by it, storage/media.ex and storage/provider.ex, which makes sense, since the modules defined by these two files live under the Storage context. The outcome of this last command can also be seen in the bottom of the previous diagram, where you can see the relationship between the storage.ex file and those two files.

Let's now find all the files that reference the media.ex file by passing the --sink option to mix xref:

```
$ cd apps/elixir_drip
$ mix xref graph --format dot --sink lib/elixir_drip/storage
/media.ex
Generated "xref_graph.dot" in the current directory. To generate a PNG:

    dot -Tpng xref_graph.dot -o xref_graph.png

For more options see http://www.graphviz.org/
```

By asking xref to show us every module that uses the media.ex file, we observe that, for now, only the Storage context file uses it. This confirms that our storage/media.ex file is only used inside the context it is supposed to to be used inside:

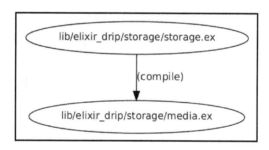

We haven't looked at the file dependency graph for the ElixirDripWeb application, since it was automatically created by the Phoenix generators. However, there is real value in using xref to get a quick glimpse of the codebase you're diving into. You will immediately identify modules that have common logic and are used by virtually every module, and modules that live strangely alone. In that case, consider whether you really want to keep them. For example, if you look at the graph for ElixirDrip, you will see the lib/elixir_drip.ex file disconnected from all the other files. Opening the file, you will find an empty module, so you can safely delete it.

Since version 1.6 of Elixir, the `xref` Mix task also accepts the `--include-siblings` option. When passed, this option considers all the umbrella dependencies of the project, so it will show the interdependencies between modules living in different umbrella applications as well.

We will now look at some of the tools one can use to ensure every Elixir codebase stays readable and respects the established best practices.

Adopting a consistent coding style

During your project inception, one of the most important steps is deciding on how to structure your project. The choices made here will, in the long term, affect how you maintain and evolve your application. The usage of static code analysis tools also contribute to the ease of maintenance of your project, letting you catch bugs, syntax errors and weird code style as soon as possible.

Here, we'll configure Credo to analyze our code, looking for possible refactors, common mistakes and inconsistencies and then use the Elixir 1.6 formatter to format all the code of our application.

We do not want to run our static analysis tools in production, so we will only add Credo as a dependency for the `dev` and `test` environments. We'll also make sure that Credo stays put when we run our project, by setting its `runtime` option as `false`. This way Mix knows that Credo is not a runtime application and as such it won't try to start it. Take a look at this:

```
$ cat mix.exs
defmodule ElixirDrip.Umbrella.Mixfile do
  use Mix.Project
  # ...
  defp deps do
    [
      {:credo, "~> 0.3", only: [:dev, :test], runtime: false}
    ]
  end
end
```

After fetching and compiling your dependencies with `mix do deps.get, deps.compile`, we may now run `mix credo` since its installation added a new Mix task:

```
$ mix credo
Checking 36 source files ...
```

```
   Code Readability
 │
 │  [R] → Modules should have a @moduledoc tag.
 │  apps/elixir_drip_web/lib/elixir_drip_web/application.ex:1:11
#(ElixirDripWeb.Application)

Please report incorrect results: https://github.com/rrrene/credo/issues

Analysis took 0.5 seconds (0.3s to load, 0.1s running checks)
54 mods/funs, found 1 code readability issue.
```

Credo tells us we are missing the documentation for the
`ElixirDripWeb.Application` module. For this last execution, we used the default
configuration shipped with Credo. However, it is recommended to have a configuration file
by project to ensure each project is checked against the same static analysis criteria,
independently of where the code is analyzed. We can generate a local configuration file by
using the `credo.gen.config` Mix task:

```
$ mix credo.gen.config
* creating .credo.exs

$ cat .credo.exs
%{
  configs: [
    %{
      checks: [
        {Credo.Check.Readability.ModuleDoc},
      ]
      # ...
```

In the generated configuration file, among several other checks, lives the `ModuleDoc` check,
which detects modules without documentation. If we disable this check by appending
`false` to its check tuple, Credo stops looking for modules without documentation and
consequently finds no issues within our project:

```
$ mix credo
Checking 36 source files ...

Please report incorrect results: https://github.com/rrrene/credo/issues

Analysis took 0.5 seconds (0.3s to load, 0.1s running checks)
54 mods/funs, found no issues.
```

For now, we'll keep the generated configuration file. To stop Credo from reporting issues due to non-existing module documentation, we need to set the `@moduledoc` attribute of the faulty module as `false`. With this approach we are saying the `ElixirDripWeb.Application` does not need to define module documentation and therefore ExDoc, the tool responsible for generating documentation for the project, won't look for it inside the module. This way, Credo also won't complain about the module missing documentation.

Not only do we want to keep away common mistakes and inconsistencies from our code base, we also want to keep a consistent style throughout our code. The objective here is to have code that looks as if it were written by a single person. Credo contains a style guide, so it can also check if the source code adopts a consistent code style by running it with the `--strict` option.

However, we will use instead the code formatter introduced in the 1.6 version of Elixir. This is mainly due to the fact that all the core Elixir codebases are already being formatted with this new tool (check `https://github.com/elixir-lang/elixir/issues/6643`), so it will quickly become the *de facto* standard.

The Elixir formatter can be used to format one or more Elixir files, for example, `mix format path/to/elixir/source1.ex path/to/source2.ex`. Alternatively, the project's root folder can have a `.formatter.exs` configuration file, indicating which files should be formatted. Here we'll follow the latter approach, by pointing to all the Elixir files:

```
$ cat .formatter.exs
[
  inputs: [
    "mix.exs",
    "apps/*/{config,lib,test}/**/*.{ex,exs}"
  ]
]
```

In the previous configuration, which lives in the root of the umbrella project, we are telling the formatter to format the `mix.exs` and all the Elixir files living in the `config`, `lib` and `test` folders inside each umbrella application we have.

After running `mix format` inside the umbrella project, we can see that files in both `elixir_drip` and `elixir_drip_web` umbrella applications were changed. Remember that we resorted to Mix tasks provided by Phoenix to generate our umbrella applications, so the code changed by the formatter had been automatically generated for us beforehand.

Here is a list of project files that were formatted when we ran `mix format`:

```
$ git status
  # ...
  modified: apps/elixir_drip/config/config.exs
  modified: apps/elixir_drip/lib/elixir_drip/application.ex
  modified: apps/elixir_drip/test/test_helper.exs
  modified: apps/elixir_drip_web/config/config.exs
  modified: apps/elixir_drip_web/config/dev.exs
  modified: apps/elixir_drip_web/lib/elixir_drip_web.ex
  modified: apps/elixir_drip_web/lib/elixir_drip_web/application.ex
  modified:
apps/elixir_drip_web/lib/elixir_drip_web/channels/user_socket.ex
  modified:
apps/elixir_drip_web/lib/elixir_drip_web/controllers/page_controller.ex
  modified: apps/elixir_drip_web/lib/elixir_drip_web/endpoint.ex
  modified: apps/elixir_drip_web/lib/elixir_drip_web/router.ex
  modified: apps/elixir_drip_web/lib/elixir_drip_web/views/error_helpers.ex
  modified: apps/elixir_drip_web/lib/elixir_drip_web/views/error_view.ex
  modified:
apps/elixir_drip_web/test/elixir_drip_web/controllers/page_controller_test.
exs
  modified:
apps/elixir_drip_web/test/elixir_drip_web/views/error_view_test.exs
  modified: apps/elixir_drip_web/test/support/channel_case.ex
  modified: apps/elixir_drip_web/test/support/conn_case.ex
  modified: apps/elixir_drip_web/test/test_helper.exs
  modified: mix.exs
```

 In the preceding snippet, and in the following paragraphs, we use `git` to check which files were changed by the formatter; feel free to use whatever tool suits you best.

The resulting code is guaranteed to be valid by the formatter, but nonetheless we can see many style changes. If we observe the change in the `config/config.exs` of the `elixir_drip` app, we can see the formatter added the empty parentheses to the `Mix.env` function call:

```
$ git diff apps/elixir_drip/config/config.exs
  # ...
 config :elixir_drip, ecto_repos: [ElixirDrip.Repo]

-import_config "#{Mix.env}.exs"
+import_config "#{Mix.env()}.exs"
```

In the same umbrella application, you can see the changes in the `application.ex` file that defines the application callback module. The formatter changed the indentation of the part of the code that starts the database repository supervisor. As you can see, the `Supervisor.start_link` call now spans seven lines, but it is arguably more intelligible than it was before:

```
$ git diff apps/elixir_drip/lib/elixir_drip/application.ex
  # ...
  def start(_type, _args) do
    import Supervisor.Spec, warn: false

-   Supervisor.start_link([
-     supervisor(ElixirDrip.Repo, []),
-   ], strategy: :one_for_one, name: ElixirDrip.Supervisor)
+   Supervisor.start_link(
+     [
+       supervisor(ElixirDrip.Repo, []),
+     ],
+     strategy: :one_for_one,
+     name: ElixirDrip.Supervisor
+   )
  end
end
```

These were just some specific examples of the work performed by the formatter. Automatic code formatting also has its role in many other languages (for example, the Go programming language). It aims to make the code easier to write, easier to learn, read and review and also easier to maintain.

Let's end this part by creating a `lint` Mix alias that runs the formatter and Credo in a single step when we execute `mix lint`.

 To enforce our static analysis rules, you could even create a way to automatically run `mix lint`. If you're using `git`, you can create a pre-commit hook that runs the formatter and only allows you to proceed if no files have been changed by the formatter and no issues were reported by Credo.

As you can see from this code, both `format` and `credo` tasks will be run when we execute `mix lint`. Be warned that these aliases don't appear in the list returned by `mix help`:

```
$ cat mix.exs
defmodule ElixirDrip.Umbrella.Mixfile do
  use Mix.Project

  def project do
    [
      # ...
      aliases: aliases()
    ]
  end

  defp deps do
    [
      # ...
    ]
  end

  defp aliases do
    [
      "lint": ["format", "credo"]
    ]
  end
end
```

This alias definition was just an example to show how easy it is to define your own aliases. If you need to create a Mix task from scratch, you can define a new module whose name starts with the `Mix.Tasks.` prefix. This module needs to use the `Mix.Task` module and define a `run/1` function:

```
defmodule Mix.Tasks.MyCustomTask do
  use Mix.Task

  def run(_args), do: IO.puts("Hello from custom task")
end
```

Later in the book, when we analyze project releases, we'll see how to create custom tasks that don't rely on Mix at all.

Summary

In this chapter, we looked at an Elixir project from different angles. Accompanied by the versatile Mix tool that comes with Elixir, we ended the chapter by kick-starting our ElixirDrip umbrella project with two umbrella applications. These were the key ideas we addressed here:

- An Elixir application defines an application callback function that is called when the VM starts any project, such as the `main` entry point of other languages. If you don't need to start your application, you don't need to implement the callback function. In this case, your code will amount to a simple bundle of modules and functions without any state.
- The Mix `compile` task compiles our code to BEAM bytecode and places every module under a flat folder structure, automatically creating an `.app` file for our project, so that the VM knows how to start every needed application.
- An Elixir project is composed of a `mix.exs` file and three folders, `config`, `lib` and `test`. After creating your project, you get an out-of-the-box a way to manage configuration values, to run your test suite, and to set and fetch your project dependencies.
- Independently of where your dependencies come from, Mix let's you fetch dependencies from Hex.pm, your code repository, a local path, or even another umbrella application.
- An umbrella project lets you easily have more than one application under the same Elixir project. We have used Mix tasks provided by Phoenix to generate our business logic and web-facing umbrella applications.
- ElixirDrip, a web storage service, will be developed as an umbrella project throughout this book. It will serve as an incubator for many of the concepts we'll explore.
- To avoid being stuck with a single storage provider, we used Elixir behaviours to abstract the implementation details of using a specific provider.
- Ease of maintenance and readability are essential qualities of any project. To keep ElixirDrip up to our standards, we used both Credo and the Elixir 1.6 formatter as static analysis tools.

In the next chapter, we will figure out how Elixir achieves its concurrency and fault-tolerance qualities by looking at the fundamental concepts borrowed from Erlang. Having a solid understanding of these ideas will pay dividends, since the conceptual model behind Elixir differs significantly from the world of imperative languages. You will never look at object-oriented languages the same way again!

3
Processes – The Bedrock of Concurrency and Fault Tolerance

Having learned how to create a new project in Elixir, we will now dive into one of the cornerstones of Elixir (inherited from Erlang): **processes**. Understanding how to work with them is paramount to creating concurrent and fault-tolerant applications in Elixir. Your typical application will easily contain hundreds, if not thousands, of processes running concurrently.

If this last sentence has raised some concerns over running thousands of processes in a single machine, note that we're referring to Erlang VM processes, which are much lighter than **Operating System** (**OS**) processes. Throughout this chapter, and the rest of the book, *process* refers to an Erlang VM process—unless we directly mention *OS process*.

In this chapter, we will cover the following topics:

- Erlang VM's inner workings and concurrency model
- Creating processes and passing messages between them
- Using processes to maintain state
- Building one of the components of our ElixirDrip application – the cache worker
- Using supervisors to make our applications fault tolerant
- Building supervision trees to have higher granularity in error recovery

Inside the BEAM

The Erlang VM is commonly known as **BEAM (Bogdan/Björn's Erlang Abstract Machine)**. It was designed to run highly-reliable systems that usually have many nines of availability, and are pretty much always able to respond to client requests. We will now look at some of the design decisions behind the BEAM, and how they enable the creation and deployment of such systems.

A process is the unit of concurrent execution inside the BEAM. As we will see throughout this chapter, they are the building block that enables the creation of scalable, robust, fault-tolerant systems. Before diving into some runtime considerations for using processes, let's explore how processes interact with one another.

There's much discussion about whether the BEAM is a legitimate implementation of the actor model, as described by Carl Hewitt in the 1970s. Robert Virding, a co-creator of Erlang, has repeatedly stated that, while developing Erlang, they arrived at an implementation that resembles the actor model by accident, only getting to know the actor model itself much later. Regardless, the term *actor* isn't widely used in the Elixir/Erlang community—we mostly just use the term *process*.

Each process in the BEAM maintains its own private state, which can never be shared with another process. Processes communicate via asynchronous message passing, and each one has its own mailbox, which stores the messages sent to that process. Upon receiving a message, a process can either just reply to it by performing a certain computation, sending messages to other processes, spawning new processes, or changing its own internal state. Queuing and dequeuing of messages from a mailbox are atomic, and a process handles them sequentially.

To send a message to a process, you must know its PID (a basic type, as we learned in `Chapter 1`, *Preparing for the Journey Ahead*) or its registered alias. A process can also send a message to itself, which will create a new message in its own mailbox, and will be handled in the future. Messages sent from one actor to another are guaranteed to maintain their order at the receiver's mailbox, but note that the interleaving of multiple messages sent by multiple processes is indeterminate on the receiver's end, and you should never rely on it.

To handle incoming messages, a process can use pattern matching. Empowered with this mechanism, we can build processes that either listen, or filter a certain kind of message, or just behave differently according to the message.

As previously stated, the message passing is asynchronous, but only from the sender perspective—when receiving a message, the process is blocked, waiting for a new message on its mailbox, as we will further explain in the next section.

While this isolated, share-nothing model of processes may raise some performance concerns, since every message exchanged has to be deep copied, it also brings some incredible benefits, such as these:

- It's easy to build concurrent applications. With no shared state, there's no need for mutexes or semaphores. Processes run concurrently (and possibly in parallel, if there are at least two CPU cores), allowing you to take full advantage of your hardware.
- Upon crashing, a process can instantly be replaced. As we will learn later in this chapter, we can have processes whose only job is to supervise other processes, and take a certain action when they go down. Again, since there's no shared state, the crash of a certain process can be resolved, in most cases, just by restarting it.
- There is no Stop-the-World garbage collection. Since each process maintains its own heap, garbage collection occurs at the process level. Moreover, when a process exits, its memory space can simply be reclaimed. Garbage collection doesn't stop the whole VM, which means that your processes may continue to reply to requests when a certain process is stopped for garbage collection.
- It is simple to distribute and scale horizontally. Given that processes are isolated, you can scale your application by adding more computing power, which in turn adds the ability to create more processes. With the incredible work done in the BEAM, communicating with a process on your own machine or some other machine in the cluster is virtually the same.

As we previously suggested, processes inside the BEAM are very lightweight, and can be spawned or destroyed with minimal overhead. Generally, it only takes a couple of microseconds to create a new process, while its initial memory usage is between 1 and 2 KB. To put this in perspective, by default, a thread uses 2 MB just for the stack on a Linux x86 system. This allows you to have millions of processes running in a single machine.

BEAM runs on a single OS process, and then spawns threads under that process, by default, based on the number of cores available. Each thread will run a scheduler that will preemptively manage the CPU time of each process. The BEAM is a soft real-time system, and this preemptive scheduling promotes fairness and liveness.

This way, a CPU-intensive process running for a long time will not influence the performance of other processes. Imagine that you're running an HTTP server in this model, where each request is handled by a different process. If a request from a certain client is taking more time to respond to, it will have no effect on other users of the HTTP server, keeping the system live for most users.

 We've stated that you can run millions of processes inside the BEAM, but that, by default, it's capped at around 256,000. You can increase this limit by passing options with the `--erl` flag when starting `elixir` or `iex`, as in: `iex --erl "+P 10000000"`. The +P option controls the maximum number of simultaneous processes inside the BEAM. You can check out other options at `http://erlang.org/doc/man/erl.html`.

Most programmers know that building a concurrent application is hard work. Frequently, making an application concurrent is not only delayed but sometimes the last resort, and is carried out when the performance requirements have no other solution. This probably happens because they know it is a source of some scary and hard-to-find bugs, and that generally this change makes programs harder to reason about.

While this is true with traditional concurrency primitives, such as threads, we want to make the case that this is not true for BEAM processes. Joe Armstrong, Erlang's co-creator, occasionally uses a very interesting expression when talking about Erlang: Concurrency-oriented programming. The philosophy is that concurrency should be baked into our programs right from the start, and that it's the basis for distribution and fault tolerance.

Well, that's enough theory! Let's now explore how to work with BEAM processes.

Working with processes

After seeing the conceptual model of how processes work inside the BEAM, we will now see how we can work with them. Namely, we will cover how to work with processes, how to pass messages between them, and, to showcase how we can use processes to maintain state, we will build a component of our ElixirDrip app, the cache worker.

Creating processes

You create a process by calling the `Kernel.spawn/1` function, which receives an anonymous function with no arguments:

```
iex> self()
#PID<0.85.0>
iex> spawn(fn ->
...>    :timer.sleep(2000)
...>    IO.puts "I'm running in process #{inspect(self())}"
...> end)
#PID<0.91.0>
I'm running in process #PID<0.91.0>
```

In this example, we're first calling `self()`, which returns the PID of the current process. In this case, it returned the PID of the shell process. Then, we use the `spawn` function to create a new process. As previously stated, it receives an anonymous function that will run in the newly created process. The anonymous function that we're passing to `spawn` uses the `timer` Erlang library to sleep for two seconds, and then uses the `puts` function from the `IO` module to print a string to the terminal. This string prints the PID of the current process. As we can see from the preceding output, when calling `self()` directly from IEx, we get its PID, `<0.85.0>`, but the string printed to the terminal shows the `<0.91.0>` PID–the PID of the process created by the `spawn` function. Note that the return value of this function is the PID of the process that was just created, which will be important later, when we start to pass messages between processes.

Another important aspect to point out is that the caller of the `spawn` function resumes its work as soon as the process is created. We've introduced sleep on the anonymous function so that this behavior is easily observed. If you run this example in your IEx session, you'll see that right after calling `spawn`, you get your shell back–meaning that the shell process has finished creating the new process and is ready to receive input. Then, about two seconds later, you see the string we talked about earlier being printed to the screen. This means that the sleep only occurred on the new process, and the caller of `spawn` was unblocked earlier.

Let's now look at something a bit more interesting. In the following example, we'll pass a variable defined in the outer scope to the newly created process:

```
iex> x = 4
4
iex> spawn(fn ->
...>    x = x * x
...>    IO.puts "The number squared is #{x}"
...> end)
```

```
The number squared is 16
#PID<0.109.0>
iex> x
4
```

We begin by creating a variable, x, which is bound to 4. Then, we use `spawn` as in the previous example, and create a new process that will take this variable and square it. Note, in this new process we're rebinding x, and then printing its new value. As x was 4, it makes sense that we see 16 printed to the console. However, note that, afterward, in the shell process, we print the value of x, and it's still 4. The variable from the outer scope is passed to the anonymous function that runs on the new process via the closure mechanism, which we saw in `Chapter 1`, *Preparing for the Journey Ahead*. Since processes do not share memory, the variable that the anonymous function is referencing is deep copied, and the rebinding of x on the new process doesn't affect the x defined in the shell process.

Often, we're not only interested in spawning a new process, but also in collecting its result at a later stage. Let's now look at message passing and see how we can achieve this.

Message passing between processes

After the initial contact with Elixir, when we start building applications with some degree of complexity, we frequently need our concurrent processes to cooperate with one another. As we've previously stated, processeses don't share memory–they communicate by passing messages back and forth. These messages contain Elixir terms–basically anything you can store in a variable can be sent in a message.

The sending of the message consists of storing it in the receiver's mailbox. The mailbox of a process is unbounded–however, in practice, it is bounded by the available memory. Let's now see this in action, by sending a message to ourselves in the shell process. To send a message, you use the `Kernel.send/2` function, providing the process ID as the first argument and the message itself as the second argument:

```
iex> send(self(), "hey, I'm messaging myself")
"hey, I'm messaging myself"
```

In this case, we're using the `Kernel.self/0` function to get our own PID, thus sending this message to our own mailbox. Remember that message passing is asynchronous, and the caller of `send` resumes its execution right after placing the message in the receiver's mailbox. Right now, the shell process has one message in its mailbox. To fetch it, we use the `receive` construct:

```
iex> receive do
...>    message -> IO.puts message
...> end
hey, I'm messaging myself
:ok
```

As you can see, `receive` was able to fetch from the mailbox the message we previously sent, and the message itself was printed to the shell. If you only want to process a certain kind of messages, you can use pattern-matching on the clauses provided to `receive`:

```
iex> send(self(), {:result, 2+2-1})
{:result, 3}
iex> receive do
...>    {:result, result} -> IO.puts "The result is #{result}"
...> end
The result is 3
:ok
```

This example is similar to the one shown before, but now we're only fetching from the mailbox messages that are two-element tuples, in which the first element is the `:result` atom. It's important to point out that if a message doesn't match any clause in the `receive` block, it will stay at the mailbox to be processed at a later stage. This means that if a process is frequently receiving messages that are never matched on `receive` blocks, its mailbox will grow indefinitely and this may ultimately cause the BEAM to crash, due to the excessive memory usage. To circumvent this problem, you can provide a clause that always matches, which will stop the mailbox from growing out of control:

```
iex> send(self(), {:other_result, 3+3-2})
{:other_result, 4}
iex> receive do
...>    {:result, result} -> IO.puts "The result is #{result}"
...>    _ -> {:error, :unexpected_message}
...> end
{:error, :unexpected_message}
```

This way, _ will match messages that didn't match on the clauses before it, having a response for this message and removing it from the mailbox. Then, we return an error tuple, which could also include reporting (either to logs or an error-tracking system), so that this can be analyzed later and also possibly track down the source of the unexpected messages.

When developing and/or debugging in an IEx session, it may be helpful to use the `IEx.Helpers.flush/0` function, which will remove all the messages from the mailbox of the shell process and print them out to the terminal.

As we've seen, `receive` will fetch a message from the mailbox of the process, and try to match it to the provided clauses. So far, we've called `receive` only after sending the messages to the shell process. If we call it with an empty mailbox, `receive` will block, waiting for a message:

```
iex> receive do
...>    message -> IO.puts "Message is #{message}"
...> end
```

The shell is now blocked and you have to manually terminate it (by pressing `Ctrl-\`, for instance). We would observe the same behavior if there were messages in the mailbox that didn't match any of the provided clauses. If we don't want `receive` to wait indefinitely for messages, we can provide an `after` clause, specifying the time we want `receive` to wait, in milliseconds:

```
iex> receive do
...> message -> IO.puts "Message is #{message}"
...> after
...> 2000 -> IO.puts "Timed out. No message received in 2 seconds."
...> end
Timed out. No message received in 2 seconds.
:ok
```

As you learned in the first chapter, everything in Elixir is an expression. Similar to what happens with the `case` construct, the return value of `receive` is the result of the last expression on the clause that was executed.

We'll end this section with a more elaborate example. Now that we know how to create processes, and also how to pass messages between them, let's tie all of this together, while also showcasing some advantages of having processes running concurrently.

First, let's define an anonymous function, which symbolizes a long-running computation by sleeping for half a second:

```
iex> long_running_computation = fn number ->
...>    :timer.sleep(500)
...>    "result for #{number}"
...> end
#Function<6.99386804/1 in :erl_eval.expr/5>
```

It takes a number as an argument, which represents the number to which the long-running computation would be applied. For a later comparison, let's create a list with integers from 1 to 50, and run this long computation on each element of that list. For now, we'll do this sequentially, using Enum.map/2:

```
iex> computation_results = fn ->
...>    (1..50)
...>    |> Enum.map(long_running_computation)
...> end
#Function<20.99386804/0 in :erl_eval.expr/5>
```

We're defining this inside an anonymous function so that we can check how long the execution takes, using the tc function from the timer Erlang module, as shown here:

```
iex(3)> :timer.tc(computation_results, [])
{25063563,
 ["result for 1", "result for 2", "result for 3", "result for 4",
  "result for 5", "result for 6", "result for 7", "result for 8", ...]}
```

This function returns a tuple with the execution time (in microseconds) on the first element, and the result of the function that was timed on the second element. Note that, for brevity, the result of the function was cropped, but it contains the result up to the 50th element. As we can see, the sequential version took around 25 seconds, which is easily explained by the 50 half-second sleeps that occurred, one for each element on the list.

Since we now know how to spawn and communicate with processes, let's perform this computation for each element of the list concurrently, spawning one process for each element, and aggregating the results afterward.

First, let's define the function that will receive the messages sent to the shell process:

```
iex> fetch_result = fn ->
...>    receive do
...>      {:computation_result, result} -> result
...>      _ -> {:error, :unexpected_message}
...>    end
...> end
#Function<20.99386804/0 in :erl_eval.expr/5>
```

This function will fetch a message from the mailbox. If this message is in the expected format, we return the result itself. For any other message that doesn't match the format we're expecting, we simply return an error tuple. Let's now use this anonymous function in our concurrent version:

```
iex> me = self()
#PID<0.85.0>
iex> concurrent_computation_results = fn ->
...>    (1..50)
...>    |> Enum.map(&(spawn(fn -> send(me, {:computation_result,
          long_running_computation.(&1)}) end)))
...>    |> Enum.map(fn _ -> fetch_result.() end)
...> end
#Function<20.99386804/0 in :erl_eval.expr/5>
```

Let's break down this example, as this code is very dense. We begin by binding the PID of the current process to me. This is important, because we'll later use it inside the spawn function, so that the new process knows the PID of its caller and sends a response back. We take our list of 50 integers, and create a process for each one. Each process will then send back a message to its caller (using the me variable), and the content of each message is a tuple with two elements: The first is just an atom that identifies the purpose of the message; the second is the result of executing the long-running computation, to which we pass the current element of our integers list. In the last two snippets, you can see the creation of processes and the message passing between them in action!

Let's now time the execution of this version:

```
iex> :timer.tc(concurrent_computation_results, [])
{513566,
 ["result for 1", "result for 2", "result for 3", "result for 9",
  "result for 4", "result for 10", "result for 5", "result for 6", ...]}
```

As we can see, the execution time dropped drastically, to nearly half a second. This result was obtained in a quad-core machine. This example is a bit synthetic (since the processes are just sleeping and returning a result), so the important takeaway is not from the absolute values, but the concept itself. Imagine that these processes are not sleeping but doing some sort of request to an external system (a third-party API, for instance). In this case, the process is idle for a long time as well, and you can reap great benefits from parallelizing its execution.

However, note that sometimes you can over-parallelize. For instance, if you want to calculate the square of each number in our integers list, you'd be better off doing it sequentially in one process. The overhead of creating the processes and then aggregating the results will make the parallel approach slower than the single-process one. The best solution depends on the computation we're aiming to parallelize, and this trade-off should be taken into account when architecting your program.

What we've achieved here is essentially a parallel map, and we can easily change its purpose by plugging in different anonymous functions. However, in practice, you don't have to create processes with `spawn` to parallelize your programs–you can use the abstractions Elixir provides, for instance the `Task` module, which will be covered in the next chapter. It's also noteworthy to point out that by running our computation concurrently, we have lost the original order when aggregating the results, as they arrive in a non-deterministic order. This is observable in the response from the preceding example, where the result for 9 comes in fourth place. If the order of the results matters, one possible solution would be to have some logic to sort the results properly when aggregating them.

Having seen how we can exchange messages between processes, it's now time to see how we can use processes to maintain state in our applications.

Building a cache worker

Processes in Elixir aren't solely used to run certain tasks concurrently. Often, they are also used as entities that maintain state. These processes frequently run for a long time (or possibly forever), and know how to handle a certain type of requests. Via message passing, other processes can query and/or modify the internal state of these processes. These types of processes are frequently called **Server Processes**.

As we stated at the beginning of this chapter, inside the BEAM, a process is the unit of concurrent execution. This means that multiple server processes may run concurrently, which is important for scalability and fault tolerance.

Let's remind you that there's no `loop` construct in Elixir. As we've depicted in Chapter 1, *Preparing for the Journey Ahead*, looping in Elixir is always done through recursion. The same holds true for making processes run in a loop–you use recursion. Particularly, we have to use endless-tail recursion, to ensure that no additional memory is consumed as a result of the process calling itself over and over again. If the last thing a function does is call another function, or itself, the usual stack push doesn't occur and instead a simple jump is performed. This means that using tail recursion won't consume any additional memory or cause a stack overflow.

When iterating through an enumerable, we don't need to code the recursion ourselves, we simply use abstractions provided by the language. Similar to this, most of the time we won't create server processes by coding the recursion by hand. We can use abstractions, which allow the removal of most boilerplate code. In the next chapter, you'll be introduced to the OTP framework, which, among other things, provides some abstractions to create server processes (namely, `GenServer`). However, we think it's important to show a lower-level view of how to work with processes, so that you understand how they work, which will empower you to create your own solutions when the abstractions, either provided by the language or a library, don't suit your needs.

To implement a server process, we have it executing an endless loop, waiting for a message on each iteration of the loop. Upon receiving a message, the process handles it and continues the loop. If you're concerned that having the process constantly running the loop may degrade performance, note that generally the loop isn't CPU intensive–most of the time, the process is waiting for a message (using the `receive` construct), which puts the process in a suspended state and doesn't consume CPU cycles.

We'll now see an example of a stateful server process. To avoid synthetic examples, we'll be implementing a component of the ElixirDrip application, presented in the previous chapter. The component is the cache worker, which is made up of the processes spawned by the cache supervisor to maintain the content that we want to cache. Whenever one of our users wants to download a certain file, our application will download it, and the cache supervisor process (further detailed in the next section) spawns a new process for this file, which will live for a certain amount of time (60 seconds, in the next example). This way, if the user wants to access this file again within this time frame, we won't have to fetch and decrypt the file again, and can just serve it from memory.

Note that this implementation is not the final one, as this worker will be implemented again in the next chapter using some abstractions. Let's now see the code for this server process:

```
$ cat examples/cache_worker.ex
defmodule CacheWorker do
  require Logger

  @expire_time 60_000

  def init(content) do
    spawn(fn ->
      timer = Process.send_after(self(), :expire, @expire_time)
      Logger.debug("#{inspect(self())}: CacheWorker started. Will
      expire in #
      {Process.read_timer(timer)} milliseconds.")
      loop(%{hits: 0, content: content, timer: timer})
    end)
  end

  defp loop(state) do
    new_state = receive do
      {:get_content, caller} -> get_content(state, caller)
      :refresh -> refresh_timer(state)
      :expire -> terminate(state)
      message -> unexpected_message(state, message)
    end

    loop(new_state)
  end

  defp get_content(%{content: content, hits: hits} = state, caller) do
    Logger.debug("Serving request for get_content. Content is #
    {content}")
    send(caller, {:response, content})
    new_state = refresh_timer(state)

    %{new_state | hits: hits + 1}
  end

  defp refresh_timer(%{timer: timer} = state) do
    Process.cancel_timer(timer)
    new_timer = Process.send_after(self(), :expire, @expire_time)
    expires_in = Process.read_timer(new_timer)
    Logger.debug("#{inspect(self())}: Canceled the previous expiration
    timer.
    Will now expire in {expires_in} milliseconds.")

    %{state | timer: new_timer}
```

```
    end

    defp terminate(%{hits: hits}) do
      Logger.debug("#{inspect(self())}: Terminating process... Served the
      cached
      content #{hits} times.")
      Process.exit(self(), :normal)
    end

    defp unexpected_message(state, message) do
      Logger.warn("#{inspect(self())}: Received unexpected message: #
      {inspect(message)}")
      state
    end
  end
```

The preceding code block is quite dense, so let's go through it, bit by bit.

First of all, we have the `init` function. This function is responsible for creating our process, and initializing its state. It uses the `send_after` function from the `Process` module to send a message to itself in the future–60 seconds after the creation in this case. The message itself is `:expire`, which will cause our process to exit. This is a very powerful and concise way of having a process alive for a certain amount of time, which is especially useful for caches. Then, this function calls the loop function with our initial state–the number of cache hits is set to `0`, the content we'll serve is the argument passed to `init`, and our timer is also kept in the state, so that we can manipulate it later.

Now we have our process running the `loop` recursive function. This function will fetch a message from the mailbox (or block here if the mailbox is empty, waiting for a message) and match it against the provided clauses. This server knows how to handle three types of messages:

- `:get_content`: Used to retrieve the content this process is holding
- `:refresh`: Used to refresh the timer of the current process, making it stay alive for at least another 60 seconds
- `:expire`: Used to signal the end of the current process, meaning that 60 seconds have passed without the timer being reset

Regardless of the message received, every clause must return the new state (which may be equal to the old one), as the return value of `receive` is bound to the `new_state` variable. This variable is then passed to the `loop` function, essentially setting the state for the next step of the loop. This is a common stateful server approach, computing the new state based on the message received, and looping recursively with the new state.

The `get_content` function sends a message back to the caller with the content that's present in the state. Then, it refreshes the timer for the current process, which is included in the new state, along with the updated number of hits that the current process has had.

The `refresh_timer` function is responsible for canceling the current timer (so that our process doesn't terminate earlier than expected), and creating a new one, which is added to the new state.

The `terminate` function is very straightforward, as it just uses the `Process.exit/2` function to terminate the current process. The second argument to this function is `:normal`, which is the exit reason. This exit reason can be any arbitrary term, but this one has a special meaning–it states that the process exited because it reached the end of its life cycle, and not because of a crash or a runtime error. We will talk about exit reasons again in the next section.

Lastly, we have the `unexpected_message` function, which just logs a warning stating that this process has received an unexpected message, and returns the state unchanged.

Let's now see this module in action:

```
iex> cache_worker_pid = CacheWorker.init("some binary content")
#PID<0.90.0>
03:36:07.427 [debug] #PID<0.90.0>: CacheWorker started. Will expire in
59997 milliseconds.
iex> send(cache_worker_pid, {:get_content, self()})
03:36:18.094 [debug] Serving request for get_content. Content is some
binary content
03:36:18.099 [debug] #PID<0.90.0>: Canceled the previous expiration timer.
Will now expire in 60000 milliseconds.
{:get_content, #PID<0.88.0>}
iex> send(cache_worker_pid, :refresh)
03:36:25.200 [debug] #PID<0.90.0>: Canceled the previous expiration timer.
Will now expire in 60000 milliseconds.
:refresh
iex> send(cache_worker_pid, {:get_content, self()})
03:36:26.750 [debug] Serving request for get_content. Content is some
binary content
03:36:26.750 [debug] #PID<0.90.0>: Canceled the previous expiration timer.
Will now expire in 60000 milliseconds.
```

```
{:get_content, #PID<0.88.0>}
iex> flush
{:response, "some binary content"}
{:response, "some binary content"}
:ok
iex> send(cache_worker_pid, :other_message)
03:36:35.178 [warn] #PID<0.90.0>: Received unexpected message:
:other_message
:other_message
iex>
03:37:26.755 [debug] #PID<0.90.0>: Terminating process... Served the cached
content 2 times.
```

We begin by calling the `init` function, which returns the PID of the newly created process. We bind it to a variable so that we can send messages to it. Then, we send the message that corresponds to getting the content. It's important to note that the request is handled asynchronously by the server. The server may have already responded to us with the result while we're issuing the next command (to refresh the timer), but we can resume our own execution and only collect the result when we need it. After sending the refresh message, we can see the debug message stating that the timer was updated. Then, we issue another request to get the content. Now, we use the `flush` function, which removes the messages from the mailbox of the shell process and prints them. As expected, we have two messages there. Lastly, we send a message that the server doesn't understand, and we can see that it logs such event. After waiting for a few seconds, we can also see the log message that informs us that the server process was terminated, as it didn't receive more messages to get the content or refresh the timer.

Our server process is working as expected, and at this point we already know how to use processes to maintain state. There's one final change to be made before wrapping up this section. Currently, the callers of our server process need to know the exact format of the message we can handle. This way, we're leaking the communication protocol, which may be a problem if we want to change it in the future. To circumvent this problem, usually, server processes have *interface* functions, which are wrappers that call the *implementation* functions (the ones we presented earlier). Let's extend our module with interface functions:

```
$ cat examples/cache_worker_with_interface_functions.ex
defmodule CacheWorker do
  # ...

  def get_content(server_pid) do
    send(server_pid, {:get_content, self()})

    receive do
      {:response, content} -> content
    after
```

```
      5000 -> {:error, :timeout}
    end
  end

  def refresh(server_pid) do
    send(server_pid, :refresh)
  end

  # ...
end
```

Note that we're not defining an interface function for the `:expire` message. Although our server knows how to interpret that message, it's for internal usage on the server, and in this case we don't want to expose it to our clients. Besides abstracting the communication protocol, interface functions allow us to create the illusion of a synchronous call–since we send the request message and block right after waiting for the response, it looks as though a synchronous call to the server just happened. We can also have different behaviors depending on the semantics of each function. For instance, for the `refresh` interface function, we just issue a fire-and-forget request, not caring about the response (note, however, that, in this case, we can't be sure that this message was actually delivered). Let's see these two functions in action:

```
iex> cache_worker_pid = CacheWorker.init("some binary content")
#PID<0.90.0>
04:07:40.574 [debug] #PID<0.90.0>: CacheWorker started.  Will expire in
59997 milliseconds.
iex> CacheWorker.get_content(cache_worker_pid)
04:07:49.738 [debug] Serving request for get_content. Content is some
binary content
04:07:49.738 [debug] #PID<0.90.0>: Canceled the previous expiration timer.
Will now expire in 60000 milliseconds.
"some binary content"
iex> CacheWorker.refresh(cache_worker_pid)
04:07:55.703 [debug] #PID<0.90.0>: Canceled the previous expiration timer.
Will now expire in 60000 milliseconds.
:refresh
iex>
04:08:55.704 [debug] #PID<0.90.0>: Terminating process... Served the cached
content 1 times.
```

As we can see, for the `get_content` function, the shell process only resumed after returning us the content we asked for, whereas for the `refresh` function, it returned right away. Note that we now have functions in the `CacheWorker` module that run in different processes. This is a common pattern in Elixir and Erlang applications, as there's no particular relationship between modules and processes. The functions present in a module can be called by any process.

We've now covered how to build stateful server processes that know how to handle a certain type of requests and may run for a long time. Let's now look at how we can link and monitor processes, a core component of fault tolerance in Elixir.

Detecting errors by linking and monitoring processes

So far, we've focused mostly on the concurrency aspect of processes. However, processes are also used to create fault-tolerant and reliable systems that can continue to operate even in the presence of errors.

To have fault-tolerant applications, you must first recognize the existence of failures, most of them being unexpected. These failures range from one of our dependencies being down (such as a database) to having hardware failures. Moreover, if you're running a distributed system, you can experience other issues, such as a remote machine becoming unavailable, or being in the presence of a network partition. Regardless of the cause, these failures must be detected, so that we can limit their impact and hopefully recover from it without human intervention.

It's virtually impossible to anticipate all the possible scenarios that may grind your application to a halt. It's far more efficient to accept that anything can fail, and design your system to react to it. When a certain component in your application does fail, you shouldn't need to take action on all the components of the system–the components that are completely unrelated to the failing component should resume their work, making the application provide as much service as possible to its clients. These are the characteristics of reliable and self-healing systems–they are able to recover from unforeseen errors as soon as possible.

As we saw throughout `Chapter 1`, *Preparing for the Journey Ahead*, an error can be raised in multiple situations. For instance, when a pattern-match fails or when we try to divide a number by 0. When these types of errors occur, the control of the execution is transferred up the call stack to the error-handling code. If this code is not present, the process where the error happened is terminated. Besides errors (for instance, created by calling `raise`) and throws (a last resort way of control-flow), which were both covered in the first chapter, an *exit* is also considered a runtime error in Elixir (which happens when a process is terminated with a reason other than `:normal`). Regardless of the type of runtime error, we've also seen how we can use the familiar `try` and `rescue` mechanisms to handle it.

Compared to more common, mainstream programming languges, the need to catch runtime errors in Elixir is far less frequent. A more pervasive idiom is to *let the process crash*, and do something about it afterwards (typically restart the process).

While this technique may seem controversial, there is reasoning behind it. When developing a system, most bugs are caught in either your unit or integration tests, or ultimately by the QA/acceptance team. The ones that do remain are the unpredictable bugs, that only happen erratically, and under certain circumstances, making them very hard to reproduce. The usual cause for this type of error lies in a certain form of inconsistent state. Thus, one possible solution is to let the process terminate, and start a new one afterward. It's commonly a good practice to log such errors, so that you can investigate their causes later on. Still, having your application designed this way allows you to recover from the error almost instantly, making it a reliable and robust application. In the Elixir and Erlang communities, this way of thinking and designing applications is often referred to as *let it crash*, since we don't explicitly catch the error and let the process crash. This kind of mindset encourages happy-path programming, in which we first focus on scenarios without any error conditions, allowing us to concentrate on the purpose of our application (and deal with the exception paths later).

It's interesting to note that the core tenet for fault tolerance is concurrency. As we explained in the beginning of this chapter, processes inside the BEAM are completely separated from one another–they don't share memory, and a crash of one process can't, by default, cause another process to crash. This process isolation allows us to constrain the negative effects that a runtime error may have on a process (or a group of related processes), which in most cases keep the majority of the system working as expected.

This isolation process by itself already provides some degree of resilience in our application. Using the cache worker defined in the last section, the crash of a worker that's holding certain content will not affect the execution flow of other workers, which will resume their work and continue to provide their service. However, this isolation is not enough to have fault-tolerant applications. We'll now learn about the mechanisms that Elixir provides to detect and react to the crash of a process.

Using links

One way to detect the crash of a process is through the use of *links*. When two processes are linked, and one exits, the other one will receive an *exit signal*, which notifies us that a process has crashed. One link always contains two processes, and the connection is bidirectional. One process may be linked to an arbitrary number of other processes, and there's no predefined limit in the system to the number of created links.

Besides the PID of the crashed process, the exit signal also contains the *exit reason*, which is an arbitrary term that describes the reason for the termination of the process. If the termination is a normal one, which means that the spawned process has finished its execution, the exit reason is `:normal`. By default, unless the exit reason is `:normal`, when a process receives an exit signal, it's also terminated, along with the linked process.

To create a link, we can use the `Process.link/1` function, which connects the calling process to the process with the PID that's provided as the argument. However, it's more common to create a link when a process is being spawned, through the `spawn_link/1` function, which atomically creates a new process and links it to the calling process. Let's see this in action by modifying our `CacheWorker.init/1` function to use `spawn_link/1`:

```
$ cat examples/cache_worker_with_spawn_link.ex
defmodule CacheWorker do
  # ...

  def init(content) do
    spawn_link(fn ->
      timer = Process.send_after(self(), :expire, @expire_time)
      Logger.debug("#{inspect(self())}: CacheWorker started.  Will expire
in #
      {Process.read_timer(timer)} milliseconds.")
      loop(%{hits: 0, content: content, timer: timer})
    end)
  end

  # ...
end
```

And now let's use it in an IEx session:

```
iex> cache_worker_pid = CacheWorker.init("some binary content")
#PID<0.90.0>
20:57:24.470 [debug] #PID<0.90.0>: CacheWorker started. Will expire in
59989 milliseconds.
iex> CacheWorker.get_content(cache_worker_pid)
20:57:35.401 [debug] Serving request for get_content. Content is some
binary content
20:57:35.401 [debug] #PID<0.90.0>: Canceled the previous expiration timer.
Will now expire in 60000 milliseconds.
"some binary content"
20:58:35.402 [debug] #PID<0.90.0>: Terminating process... Served the cached
content 1 times.
iex> cache_worker_pid = CacheWorker.init("some other binary content")
21:00:33.380 [debug] #PID<0.93.0>: CacheWorker started. Will expire in
60000 milliseconds.
#PID<0.93.0>
iex> CacheWorker.get_content(cache_worker_pid)
21:00:35.956 [debug] Serving request for get_content. Content is some
other binary content
21:00:35.956 [debug] #PID<0.93.0>: Canceled the previous expiration timer.
Will now expire in 60000 milliseconds.
"some other binary content"
iex> Process.exit(cache_worker_pid, :kill)
** (EXIT from #PID<0.88.0>) shell process exited with reason: killed
```

We begin by calling the `init` function, which will start a new process. Note that we're now using `spawn_link/1`, so this process is now linked with the shell process. We then issue a `get_content` request, which works as expected and returns the content. Then we wait for the timer of this process to expire, and we can see the log message stating that this process is terminating. Since this process terminated with the `:normal` reason, our shell process isn't affected. Then, we start a new process, issue a request to get its content, and manually kill it using the `Process.exit/2` function, providing `:kill` as the exit reason. The exit reason can be any term, but `:kill` is treated in a special way. When used as the exit reason, it ensures that the target process is unconditionally terminated, even if it's trapping exits (which we'll discuss soon). As we can see from the last message, the shell process was terminated as well, since it was linked to the process we just killed.

Links, in a way, break the process isolation we were talking about in the last section. However, this only happens when you explicitly link them. This technique is very powerful and may come in handy if, for instance, we want to always ensure that a certain group of related processes are killed as a whole, leaving no dangling processes behind.

What if we don't want our process to be terminated, and simply want to be notified of the crashes of our linked processes, so that we can act on them? That's where the concept of *trapping exits* becomes useful. When a process is trapping exits, it's not terminated upon receiving an exit signal. Instead, this exit signal is delivered, in the form of a message, to the mailbox of that process. That way, a trapping process can receive this message and act on it accordingly.

To set up an exit trap, you use `Process.flag(:trap_exit, true)`, which will make the current process trap exit signals. The message that is delivered to the process that's trapping exits has the following format: `{:EXIT, from_pid, exit_reason}`. In this message, `from_pid` is the PID of the process that crashed, whereas `exit_reason` is the exit reason that we described earlier. Let's now rerun the previous example, but now with the shell process trapping exists:

```
iex> Process.flag(:trap_exit, true)
false
iex> cache_worker_pid = CacheWorker.init("some binary content")
#PID<0.91.0>
21:41:38.453 [debug] #PID<0.91.0>: CacheWorker started. Will expire in
59995 milliseconds.
iex> CacheWorker.get_content(cache_worker_pid)
21:41:50.465 [debug] Serving request for get_content. Content is some
binary content
21:41:50.466 [debug] #PID<0.91.0>: Canceled the previous expiration timer.
Will now expire in 60000 milliseconds.
"some binary content"
iex> Process.exit(cache_worker_pid, :kill)
true
iex> flush
{:EXIT, #PID<0.91.0>, :killed}
:ok
```

First of all, we make the shell process trap exits. It returns `false` because this function returns the previous value for that flag. Then, the example is similar to what we have already seen. The interesting part is what happens when we call the `Process.exit/2` function. Now, after calling this, our shell process didn't terminate, and, as we can see (by using the `flush` function) it receives a message in its mailbox, notifying us of the crash of its linked process.

Let's now look at a different mechanism for detecting errors: monitors.

Using monitors

In certain scenarios, it is better to have errors being propagated in a single direction. This is the use case for *monitors*. A monitor is similar to a link, but while the latter is always bidirectional, the former is always unidirectional. Moreover, a process linked to others may terminate when one of them terminates (unless it's trapping exits), whereas monitors never cause the termination of the process that's monitoring others, and the default behavior is that it always receives a message in its mailbox. A single process may create multiple monitors.

To monitor a process, you call the `Process.monitor/1` function, providing as an argument the PID of the process you want to monitor. You may also provide the alias of a registered process, which we haven't covered yet. They will be covered in the next chapter. The result of calling this function is a reference (a basic type in Elixir) that identifies the newly-created monitor. In the event that the monitored process exits, the monitoring process receives a message with the following format: `{:DOWN, monitor_reference, :process, from_pid, exit_reason}`.

> In the event that you need to stop monitoring a certain process, you can use the `demonitor` function from the `Process` module, providing the monitor reference as an argument, returned by the call to `Process.monitor/1`.

Let's now see this in action, again using a `CacheWorker` process in our example:

```
iex> cache_worker_pid = CacheWorker.init("some binary content")
#PID<0.90.0>
22:13:41.448 [debug] #PID<0.90.0>: CacheWorker started. Will expire in
59996 milliseconds.
iex> CacheWorker.get_content(cache_worker_pid)
22:13:51.540 [debug] Serving request for get_content. Content is some
binary content
22:13:51.541 [debug] #PID<0.90.0>: Canceled the previous expiration timer.
Will now expire in 60000 milliseconds.
"some binary content"
iex> monitor_reference = Process.monitor(cache_worker_pid)
#Reference<0.3261553142.1274281985.104407>
22:14:51.552 [debug] #PID<0.90.0>: Terminating process... Served the cached
content 1 times.
iex> flush
{:DOWN, #Reference<0.3261553142.1274281985.104407>, :process, #PID<0.90.0>,
 :normal}
:ok
```

Note that we're using the `CacheWorker` version that uses `spawn` (and not `spawn_link`), which means that the shell process is not linked to the `CacheWorker` process. After spawning the `CacheWorker` process, and issuing a request to it, we use the `Process.monitor/1` function to monitor this process. In this example, we didn't need to use `Process.exit/2`, as we receive a message even if the exit reason is `:normal`. Therefore, we simply wait for the timer to finish, and then check the mailbox of the shell process, finding that we received the expected message. In a real-world application, we could then fetch this message from the mailbox and act accordingly.

The error-detection mechanisms presented in this section allows us to keep tabs on the processes we're interested in. In the next section, we'll look at supervisors, which use these mechanisms to detect errors, but also allow us to react when a process crashes, paving the way for error recovery.

Recovering from errors with supervisors and supervision trees

At the start of the previous section, we explained the *let it crash* philosophy, and why you should follow it to build reliable, fault-tolerant applications. Having learned about the mechanisms that Elixir provides to detect errors, we will now look at *supervisors*, which build on top of these mechanisms to provide us a way to recover from errors.

Before diving into supervisors, we want to point out an important aspect regarding error handling in applications that follow the *let it crash* philosophy. We've been discussing how this approach changes the way you handle errors, and that it provides fault tolerance because you can recover from errors by detecting them and taking some corrective action. However, this approach shouldn't be used with errors that you know beforehand may happen during the normal execution flow of your program, especially if you have a clean way of dealing with them. For instance, a process that's responsible for contacting an external dependency via its HTTP API shouldn't crash when it encounters the 404 status code in a response. This is a valid response, and you can handle this situation in your application by returning a `{:error, :not_found}` tuple back to the caller, for instance. The definition of an expected error varies greatly, as it depends on the domain of the application. Nevertheless, when building your application, consider taking some time to define the expected errors that may happen, and how your application will deal with them.

A supervisor is a process whose sole responsibility is to supervise other processes. Given that they have this confined purpose, usually supervisor code is very simple and straightforward. This is important because it lowers the likelihood of supervisors having a runtime error, making them highly unlikely to crash.

Supervisors are such a core component of Elixir and Erlang applications that they are an OTP behaviour. In the first chapter, we saw how to use behaviours to provide interfaces that other modules can adopt. Behaviours can also be used to extract generic code to a single place, and then another module may plug into it, implementing some specific callbacks that will contain the code that's specific to what we want to achieve in that module. This was a very simple explanation of how behaviours work, but it's just what you need to get to the end of this chapter. In the next chapter, we'll be taking a look at OTP and the behaviours it provides, and will explain this concept in greater detail.

Before getting into some examples, let's see the flow of a supervisor process. After having its process created, a supervisor will configure itself to trap exit signals. Then, it will create links between itself and each one of its children. With this in place, if a child crashes, the supervisor will receive an exit signal, allowing it to react to this event, according to the configuration that was provided when it started. Supervisors use links rather than monitors because the bidirectional communication means that if a supervisor crashes, all of its children will also be immediately terminated, which is useful to avoid dangling processes in a system.

Let's now see how to define and start a supervisor, and specifically how we can use a module to plug into the supervisor behaviour.

Defining and starting a supervisor

We'll now see an example of a supervisor. For now, we'll put the `CacheWorker` module to the side, as that will be used in the next section, where we'll be using dynamic supervisors. In this example, we'll be creating the upload pipeline supervisor. In our application, we'll create two pipelines, one for downloads and another for uploads, which will be used when a user of our application performs the respective action. These pipelines contain a set of steps that will be executed for every download or upload operation. One of these steps is the encryption/decryption step, which will encrypt the uploaded file before saving it on remote storage, and decrypt the downloaded file.

The modules we'll be showing in this example aren't the ones used in the final application. For instance, the `Encryption` module will be using `GenStage` (further explained in the next chapter), which would clutter our example. In fact, the `Encryption` module is so simplified that's merely a process running in a loop, waiting for messages, and printing the ones it receives to the terminal. This simplification will allows us to focus solely on the supervisor, which is the focus for this section. Note that you can always see all the source code by downloading it from the book's website.

To plug a module into the supervisor's behaviour, we only need to implement one callback: `init/1`. This callback will provide the specification of the processes that are started by this supervisor, along with some configuration. To interact with supervisors, we use the `Supervisor` module provided by Elixir. Let's see the code for the upload pipeline supervisor:

```
$ cat examples/upload_pipeline_supervisor.ex
defmodule ElixirDrip.Storage.Supervisors.Upload.Pipeline do
  use    Supervisor
  require Logger
  alias ElixirDrip.Storage.Pipeline.Encryption

  def start_link() do
    Supervisor.start_link(__MODULE__, :ok)
  end

  def init(:ok) do
    Logger.debug("#{inspect(self())} Starting the Upload Pipeline
Supervisor
      module...")

    Supervisor.init(
      [worker(Encryption, [], restart: :transient)],
      strategy: :one_for_one
    )
  end
end
```

Beginning with the `init` function, we can see that it receives one argument. In this case, we're pattern matching to `:ok`, as we won't be using it, but this argument could be used to pass a list of options from the caller process. Besides some logging that is helpful for debugging, the only thing this function does is call the `Supervisor.init/2`, which will start the children we pass as the argument. As we've stated earlier, we need to provide to the supervisor the specification of the processes that will be started under this supervisor–the list of child processes. This is the first argument passed to `Supervisor.init/2`.

In this case, the list only has one element, which is the result of calling the `worker` function. This function was imported from the `Supervisor.Spec` module when we called `use Supervisor` at the top of the module. This function will return the specification of a child process. The first argument is the name of the module that will be running in the child process, and the second argument is the list of arguments that will be provided to the `start_link` function of this module. Note that you didn't need to specify that you want to call this function in particular. This happens because the `start_link` name is the default one. You can override it and use a different one (by providing `:function` to the list of options), but we think it's better to adhere to the conventions used by the community, which will help other software developers understand your code. Lastly, the final argument to the `worker` function is a list of options. In this case, we're providing the restart value. `:transient` means that the child process will only be restarted if it terminates abnormally. We can also have `:temporary`, where the child process will never be restarted, or `:permanent`, where the child process will always be restarted, even if it terminates with the `:normal` exit reason.

The second argument passed to `Supervisor.init/2` is a list of options. In this case, we're providing the `:strategy` option, which defines how the supervisor will handle the crash of a child process. In our example, we're using `:one_for_one`, which means that when a child process is terminated, the supervisor will spawn a new process in its place. Other possible values are `:one_for_all`, which means that all children of this supervisor will be restarted when one child crashes, and also `:rest_for_one`, which will make the children that were started after the crashed process restart, in order (along with the crashed process itself, which is the first one). This means that when we use this strategy, the order in which we start the children of a supervisor matters. Note that up to Elixir 1.6, we also had the `:simple_one_for_one` strategy, which was used to have supervisors start children dynamically. However, in Elixir 1.6 this was deprecated, in favor of using the `DynamicSupervisor` module, which will be addressed in the next section.

The use of the `worker` function here means that this child is not a supervisor. We could also use the `supervisor` function, which would return the child specification for a supervisor. In this context, *worker* means anything that is not a supervisor. Having supervisors spawn other supervisors will lead to a *supervision tree*, which we'll cover in the last section of this chapter.

The way a supervisor terminates a child is also configurable through the :shutdown option. By default, if a child is a worker, the supervisor sends an exit signal to it and waits for five seconds, killing that child abruptly if it doesn't terminate in this interval. If the child is a supervisor, it'll by default wait forever. If you're interested in configuring this, check out the official Supervisor documentation at https://hexdocs.pm/elixir/Supervisor.html, which, as most of the Elixir documentation, is very thorough, and contains helpful examples.

In this section, we'll only be using module-based supervisors, as they are pedagogically more advantageous, since we have greater control on how the supervisor is initialized. However, know that you don't need to create a module for each supervisor you want to have. You can embed calls to functions from the Supervisor module in other modules, which may simplify your code once you become familiar with. Check out the Supervisor module documentation for examples on how to do this: https://hexdocs.pm/elixir/Supervisor.html.

Let's now focus on the start_link function. This function is just a wrapper to Supervisor.start_link/2, similar to what we did earlier when we introduced interface functions to our CacheWorker. Another noteworthy point is the use of __MODULE__, which is a special form that during compilation will be substituted by the name of the current module, which means that the first argument to Supervisor.start_link/2 is the name of the current module.

Let's now use this in an IEx session:

```
iex> c("examples/encryption.ex")
[ElixirDrip.Storage.Pipeline.Encryption]
iex> c("examples/upload_pipeline_supervisor.ex")
[ElixirDrip.Storage.Supervisors.Upload.Pipeline]
iex> {:ok, supervisor_pid} =
ElixirDrip.Storage.Supervisors.Upload.Pipeline.start_link()
19:37:33.693 [debug] #PID<0.97.0>: Starting the Upload Pipeline Supervisor
module...
19:37:33.695 [debug] #PID<0.98.0>: Starting the Encryption module...
{:ok, #PID<0.97.0>}
iex> send(pid(0, 98, 0), "some message")
#PID<0.98.0>: Encryption module received a message: some message
"some message"
iex> Process.exit(pid(0, 98, 0), :kill)
true
```

```
19:39:11.208 [debug] #PID<0.102.0>: Starting the Encryption module...
iex> send(pid(0, 102, 0), "some message")
#PID<0.102.0>: Encryption module received a message: some message
"some message"
```

First of all, we compile the needed files to run this example. In previous examples we omitted this, as they were using a single file. Since this example is a bit more complex, we're explicitly compiling them. Then, we call the start_link/0 function from our supervisor, which will start the supervisor itself and its single child, as we can observe from the debug messages. After that, we send a message to our encryption module, just to verify that it's working. In this case, it's just printing whatever we send to the terminal. Now that we're sure our worker process is running, we kill it using the Process.exit/2 function. We could also simulate a runtime error in our worker by putting raise somewhere in its code, but this approach makes the example more explicit. After killing the process, we can see a debug message stating that the Encryption module is starting again. This is the supervisor in action! It detected the crash of its child and started a new process in its place. Lastly, we issue a request to the new Encryption process, just to demonstrate that it's fully functional.

It's important to point out that if a child is constantly crashing, a supervisor won't keep restarting it forever—it relies on the maximum *restart frequency*. As we stated in the beginning of the previous section, the rationale for having supervisors is that there is a certain type of bugs that only happen under some circumstances. Restarting the process makes it start from scratch, with a clean state. If the process keeps on restarting, the issue is probably not caused by some intricate state. By default, a supervisor allows for three restarts in a five-second interval. If this limit is exceeded, the supervisor will terminate itself, along with all of its children. Having the supervisor terminate itself in these conditions is very important, as it allows the error to propagate in a supervision tree, as we'll see in the last section of this chapter. The number of errors in a timeframe and the time frame itself can be configured when starting the supervisor by passing the :max_restarts and :max_seconds options, respectively.

Streamlined child specs

Elixir 1.5 introduced streamlined child specs, which allow the child specifications to be defined in modules. Instead of relying on the worker and supervisor functions from the Supervisor.Spec module, supervisors now receive a list of modules as children, and will call the child_spec/1 function on each child module. This allows the child module to control how they are run under a supervisor.

Let's see the modules presented in the previous example now using streamlined child specs. In the supervisor, we only changed the init/1 function to the following:

```
$ cat examples/upload_pipeline_supervisor_with_streamlined_child_specs.ex
defmodule ElixirDrip.Storage.Supervisors.Upload.Pipeline do
  # ...

  def init(:ok) do
    Logger.debug("#{inspect(self())} Starting the Upload Pipeline
Supervisor module...")
    Supervisor.init([Encryption], strategy: :one_for_one)
  end
end
```

The code on the supervisor is now simpler, since part of the configuration has been moved to the child. In the Encryption module, we now have the following function:

```
def child_spec(_) do
  %{
    id: __MODULE__,
    start: {__MODULE__, :start_link, []},
    restart: :transient,
    shutdown: 10000,
    type: :worker
  }
end
```

This function has one argument, which we're not using, but could be used to allow the supervisor to configure certain options on this child. We now need to provide an id, which previously was implicitly the module name. Also, in the other version, shutdown (which is the time in milliseconds the supervisor waits for the child to terminate) by default set to 5,000 ms, and here we see an example of how to configure it. Another difference from the previous version is that child specifications are now just maps, instead of relying on the APIs of the worker and supervisor functions.

You may not have to define a child_spec/1 function on every occasion. For instance, the Agent and Task modules, explained in the next chapter, define a child_spec/1 function, allowing you to skip the creation of this function if you're using one of these modules. Note that in this case, you can always override it and provide your custom child specification.

This is currently the preferred way to define child specifications in the Elixir community. We wanted to show you both ways of defining a child specification, as you will probably encounter both when navigating through source code. However, when starting a project from scratch (or refactoring some code), opt for the option we're presenting now, as your code will be following the community conventions, making it easier for other people to grasp its contents.

Starting children at runtime using dynamic supervisors

We've now seen how we can work with supervisors to recover from errors, which will restart crashed processes according to the configuration we provide. However, so far we have to define the children of a supervisor up front, which will be started right after the supervisor starts. Sometimes this doesn't fit our needs, and we need a way to spawn a new child of a supervisor at runtime. This is where dynamic supervisors become useful.

Elixir Version 1.6 introduced the `DynamicSupervisor` module. As we've stated, this new module deprecates the `:simple_one_for_one` strategy of regular supervisors. There were many reasons for this extraction to happen, but two of the main ones are that the `:simple_one_for_one` strategy changed the semantics of the supervisor's initialization and shutdown, and also that some APIs from the Elixir standard library would be expecting different input (or even would not be available) depending on the supervision strategy.

To demonstrate this concept, we'll create a `CacheSupervisor` module, which will be responsible for the supervision of the `CacheWorker` processes we've been using throughout this chapter. However, the `CacheWorker` processes need to undergo some changes, because we need to have registered processes (under an alias) for our supervision to work properly. Note that, in the previous example, we were able to observe the supervisor reacting to the crash of an `Encryption` process, by starting a new one, but in a real application we would need to register the supervised processes, otherwise their clients could still be contacting an already terminated process.

The practice of keeping the PID of a previously created process becomes moot when we introduce supervisors, because the PIDs will change as processes crash and the supervisor creates new ones. We haven't yet covered the `GenServer` behaviour, and will do so in the beginning of the next chapter. You can still follow this example without any hassle, as the main focus will be on the supervisor–in fact, we won't show the code for the new `CacheWorker` here, as it's not relevant for the example. As always, if you're curious, you can find it in this chapter's source code.

Let's now see the code for the cache supervisor:

```
$ cat examples/cache_supervisor.ex
defmodule ElixirDrip.Storage.Supervisors.CacheSupervisor do
  use   DynamicSupervisor
  alias ElixirDrip.Storage.Workers.CacheWorker

  def start_link() do
    DynamicSupervisor.start_link(__MODULE__, [], name: __MODULE__)
  end

  def init(_) do
    DynamicSupervisor.init(strategy: :one_for_one, max_children: 100)
  end

  def put(id, content) when is_binary(id) and is_bitstring(content) do
    case find_cache(id) do
      nil -> start_worker(id, content)
      pid -> {:ok, pid}
    end
  end

  def get(id) when is_binary(id) do
    case find_cache(id) do
      nil -> {:error, :not_found}
      pid -> CacheWorker.get_media(pid)
    end
  end

  def refresh(id) when is_binary(id) do
    case find_cache(id) do
      nil -> {:error, :not_found}
      pid -> CacheWorker.refresh(pid)
    end
  end

  defp start_worker(id, content) when is_binary(id) and
is_bitstring(content),
    do: DynamicSupervisor.start_child(__MODULE__, cache_worker_spec(id,
content))

  defp find_cache(id) when is_binary(id) do
    GenServer.whereis(CacheWorker.name_for(id))
  end

  defp cache_worker_spec(id, content) do
    Supervisor.child_spec(
      CacheWorker,
```

```
    start: {CacheWorker, :start_link, [id, content]},
    restart: :transient
  )
end
end
```

Let's explore the differences we see here, comparing it to the previous example. Apart from the difference in the module name, now `init/1` doesn't declare any children. It simply starts the supervisor by providing some configuration. After the definition of the strategy, we can see the `:max_children` option, which is specific to the `DynamicSupervisor` module. This configures the maximum number of children that this process can spawn. You may use this to limit the concurrency, which will also limit the resource usage. In our example, if we let the cache process grow indefinitely, we could end up using all the available memory, crashing the BEAM.

This supervisor manages the `CacheWorker` processes we've already described. Note, however, that its interface changed a bit, as we're associating each content with an `id`. When trying to put or get something from the cache, it will use the `find_cache` function, which in turn uses the `GenServer.whereis/1` function.

By using this, we're checking whether a process for the `id` provided already exists. If it does, we simply return a tuple containing the PID of this process (when using `put`) or use the `CacheWorker.get_media/1` function to retrieve the content that corresponds to the given `id` (when using `get`). If it doesn't, we will create a new process that'll hold the content for this `id` (when using `put`) or return a tuple stating that the process wasn't found (when using `get`). When we call `put`, and a process for this `id` doesn't already exist, the supervisor kicks-in and dynamically creates a new child. This happens in the `start_worker` function, which in turn uses `DynamicSupervisor.start_child/2`.

Lastly, note how we're passing the child specification of this dynamic child. We could've just used what we mentioned earlier about streamlined child specs, having a `child_spec/1` function on the `CacheWorker` module. That would be totally correct. We just did it this way so that you can see how you can configure the child specification from the supervisor, allowing you to override any particular field you're interested in. Let's see this working in an IEx shell:

```
iex> c("examples/cache_worker_under_supervisor.ex")
[ElixirDrip.Storage.Workers.CacheWorker]
iex> c("examples/cache_supervisor.ex")
[ElixirDrip.Storage.Supervisors.CacheSupervisor]
iex> ElixirDrip.Storage.Supervisors.CacheSupervisor.start_link()
{:ok, #PID<0.97.0>}
iex> ElixirDrip.Storage.Supervisors.CacheSupervisor.put("abc", "def")
04:13:04.744 [debug] #PID<0.99.0>: CacheWorker started. Will expire in
```

```
60000 milliseconds.
{:ok, #PID<0.99.0>}
iex> ElixirDrip.Storage.Supervisors.CacheSupervisor.get("abc")
04:13:17.550 [debug] #PID<0.99.0>: Received :get_media and served 3
bytes 1 times.
04:13:17.550 [debug] #PID<0.99.0>: Canceled the previous expiration timer.
Will now expire in 60000 milliseconds.
{:ok, "def"}
iex> ElixirDrip.Storage.Supervisors.CacheSupervisor.get("xyz")
{:error, :not_found}
04:14:17.565 [debug] #PID<0.99.0>: Terminating process... Served the cached
content 1 times.
iex> ElixirDrip.Storage.Supervisors.CacheSupervisor.get("abc")
{:error, :not_found}
iex> ElixirDrip.Storage.Supervisors.CacheSupervisor.put("abc", "def")
04:14:25.386 [debug] #PID<0.104.0>: CacheWorker started.  Will expire in
60000 milliseconds.
{:ok, #PID<0.104.0>}
iex> Process.exit(pid(0, 104, 0), :kill)
true
04:14:42.485 [debug] #PID<0.106.0>: CacheWorker started.  Will expire in
60000 milliseconds.
iex> ElixirDrip.Storage.Supervisors.CacheSupervisor.get("abc")
04:14:46.674 [debug] #PID<0.106.0>: Received :get_media and served 3
bytes 1 times.
{:ok, "def"}
04:14:46.674 [debug] #PID<0.106.0>: Canceled the previous expiration timer.
Will now expire in 60000 milliseconds.
04:15:46.675 [debug] #PID<0.106.0>: Terminating process... Served the
cached
content 1 times.
```

After compiling the required files, we demonstrate the regular usage of this
CacheSupervisor. Then, we let the timer expire, and we can see that the supervisor didn't
restart the process. This happened because the restart strategy is :transient, and the
process exited normally. Then we start a new process, by putting some content into the
cache again. After that, we kill this newly created process, and immediately see a log
message stating that CacheWorker has started. This time, since the exit reason was :kill
(and not :normal) the supervisor intervened, starting a new process in the place of the
crashed one. As we can observe from the example, we can then access the content for our
id, even though our server process crashed.

We've now seen how to work with dynamic supervisors, and witnessed the flexibility they
can bring to our applications. Let's move to the final section of this chapter: supervision
trees.

Minimizing error effects with supervision trees

In the previous section, we worked with supervisors and observed how they enable error-recovery. They're crucial components when building fault-tolerant applications, and they significantly change the mindset from the prevalent error-recovery mechanisms, such as `try/catch`. Having seen how we can use supervisors to detect and recover from runtime errors, we'll now focus on how we can combine them, creating *supervision trees*, to have fine-grained error recovery in our applications, reducing the effect of an error on the overall system.

To build a supervision tree, you must consider the effects on the rest of the system when a certain processes terminates due to an error. This way, you'll group closely related processes together, which can be started and stopped as a whole, providing a consistent behavior. When building a supervision tree, you're implicitly encoding the dependencies between your processes. If designed properly, supervision trees allow you to minimize the effects of an error on a certain part of your system, allowing the rest to operate as usual. For instance, in our `ElixirDrip` example, an error in the upload pipeline for a certain file shouldn't impact the cache supervisor part, which may continue to serve cached content while the upload pipeline tries to recover from the error. The point of supervision trees is to first try to recover from the error locally, affecting only the truly required processes. If then this doesn't work, because the process being restarted keeps crashing, the supervisor itself will crash, moving up in the tree, and delegating the next action to be taken to the supervisor's supervisor.

It's common to see Elixir being advertised as a language that allows the development of realiable and fault-tolerant applications–including many times just in this book. While this is true, we think that's important to reinforce that the reliability and fault-tolerance properties are present when we design our application around them. Elixir provides you the tools to build such a system–these properties are not inherent to applications built with Elixir. Designing your supervision trees is an important step when building applications with these characteristics, and as such it should be given the proper importance. While this may look overwhelming when you're not used to creating applications in this way, note that the skill of designing with processes and supervisors will naturally grow over time–potentially even becoming your first approach when designing new systems. This step will force you to stop and think about the dependencies between the different parts of your system, which will lead to a cleaner, simpler design, which in turn improves the reliability of your application.

Let's now see a supervision tree in action. For this example, we'll be using the modules we developed throughout this chapter. However, they'll be used inside a new application, called `SimpleElixirDrip`, which was created with the `mix` tool, which you learned about in the last chapter (particularly, it was created with `mix new simple_elixir_drip --sup`). Instead of using the real `ElixirDrip` application, which would clutter the following examples, we'll just use this simpler version that only includes the modules we care about.

In the following diagram, we can see the supervision tree configured in the `SimpleElixirDrip` application:

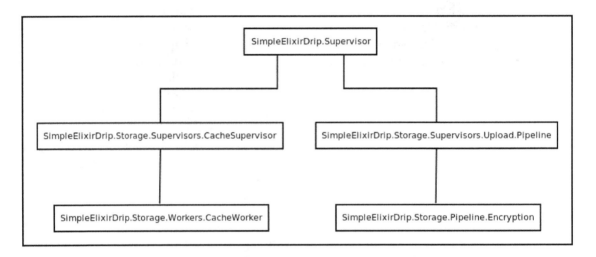

As we can see, we're using the modules we already discussed, with the cache worker as a child of the cache supervisor, and the encryption module as a child of the upload pipeline supervisor. The novelty in this example is that now both of these supervisors are now the child of a supervisor, called `SimpleElixirDrip.Supervisor`. In this application, this is the root supervisor. Usually, root supervisors are defined in the `application.ex` file, which is the starting point of our application. Note that if you use the `--sup` flag when creating a new project with Mix, this is automatically done by the generators.

We will now start our application. With the shell in the `simple_elixir_drip` directory, we use `iex -S mix` to start our application and to have an IEx session with all the modules of the application compiled and loaded. Before starting to use this IEx session to kill some processes and see the supervision tree working, let's use it to get a visualization of our supervision tree within the `observer` Erlang tool. First, in our IEx, issue the following commands:

```
iex> SimpleElixirDrip.Storage.Supervisors.CacheSupervisor.put("abc", "def")
23:30:15.139 [debug] #PID<0.118.0>: CacheWorker started. Will expire in
60000 milliseconds.
{:ok, #PID<0.118.0>}
iex> :observer.start()
:ok
```

First, we use the `put/2` function from our cache supervisor module, so that its process is supervising one child. Then, we call `:observer.start()`, which will start this tool. If you click on the **Applications** tab, you'll see the supervision tree we defined earlier, mapped inside `observer`, as we can see in the following screenshot:

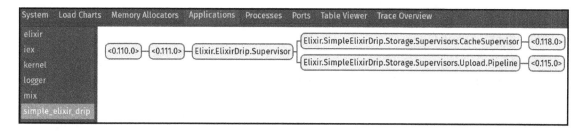

This can be a handy way to check your supervision trees as you're developing your application! Observer is an incredible tool, and its power goes far and beyond presenting process trees. We'll explore this tool further in `Chapter 11`, *Keeping an Eye on Your Processes*.

Now, let's go back to our IEx session and play with the supervision tree. As we've discussed in the previous sections, supervisors provide a way to recover from a failure in one of its children, by detecting the crash and starting a new process in the place of the old one. If a cache worker crashes, the cache supervisor will detect this and start a new cache worker in its place. We've also discussed that this won't happen forever if a child keeps crashing. The supervisor will tolerate a certain restart frequency, according to the configuration it has. If no configuration was provided (as is the case in our `SimpleElixirDrip` application), a supervisor will tolerate three restarts in a five-second window. If this limit is exceeded, the supervisor will terminate all of its children, and then terminate itself.

Let's now induce a high number of failures in a short period of time on a child of the cache supervisor, so that we can observe its behavior:

```
iex> SimpleElixirDrip.Storage.Supervisors.CacheSupervisor.put("ghj", "klm")
00:05:36.881 [debug] #PID<0.401.0>: CacheWorker started. Will expire in
60000 milliseconds.
{:ok, #PID<0.401.0>}
iex> SimpleElixirDrip.Storage.Supervisors.CacheSupervisor.get("ghj")
00:05:42.253 [debug] #PID<0.401.0>: Received :get_media and served 3
bytes 1 times.
{:ok, "klm"}
00:05:42.253 [debug] #PID<0.401.0>: Canceled the previous expiration timer.
Will now expire in 60000 milliseconds.
iex> (1..4) \
...> |> Enum.map(fn _ ->
...> SimpleElixirDrip.Storage.Workers.CacheWorker.name_for("ghj")
...> |> GenServer.whereis()
...> |> Process.exit(:kill)
...> :timer.sleep(500)
...> end)
00:05:50.641 [debug] #PID<0.411.0>: CacheWorker started. Will expire in
60000 milliseconds.
00:05:50.843 [debug] #PID<0.412.0>: CacheWorker started. Will expire in
60000 milliseconds.
00:05:51.044 [debug] #PID<0.413.0>: CacheWorker started. Will expire in
60000 milliseconds.
00:05:51.244 [debug] #PID<0.414.0> Starting the CacheSupervisor module...
[:ok, :ok, :ok, :ok]
```

We begin by putting some content in our cache, and fetch it right after, just to demonstrate the process is alive. After that, we kill the process that's responsible for the id we just created four times in a row. Since we're now using registered processes (that are referenced by an alias), we make use of it to find the process that we're interested in–again, note that registered processes will be covered in the next chapter. After having the PID of the process, we terminate it, by sending an exit signal. After that, we sleep for half a second, only to make sure that the new process has started, before we proceed to the next step of the iteration.

Take a look at the debug messages that appear after that. We can see a CacheWorker process being initialized for the first three crashes we've provoked. On the fourth one, the supervisor realizes that it has exceeded its restart frequency, and terminates all of its children, and also itself. The termination of the cache supervisor is detected by the root supervisor, SimpleElixirDrip.Supervisor, which tries to recover from this situation by spawning a new cache supervisor. This is the behavior we're looking for in supervision trees.

Note that the bubble up of the error could go on, and if the cache supervisor kept crashing at a rate that would exceed the restart frequency of the root supervisor, it would lead the root supervisor to terminate itself, which would stop our application.

As we've seen, supervision trees allow us to minimize the impact of errors, by trying to resolve an error as locally as possible. When this is not possible, the error bubbles up, and the next supervisor tries to solve it by restarting a wider part of the system.

Summary

In this chapter, we explored how processes are the key for concurrency and fault tolerance in Elixir applications. Let's wrap up this chapter by looking at the most important points:

- Inside the BEAM, processes are completely isolated from one another, and share no memory between them.
- A process is very lightweight in terms of resources, allowing the creation of millions of processes in a single machine.
- Processes communicate with each other via asynchronous message passing.
- A process may run in a loop by using endless recursion. Also, it can keep state by using arguments on the recursion.
- A process can detect the crash of another process using links or monitors. Links are always bidirectional, and, by default, upon receiving an exit signal, will cause all linked processes to terminate as well. Monitors are unidirectional, and the monitoring process will receive a message if the monitored process crashes.
- By trapping exits, a process is able to continue when one of its linked processes terminates. When a process is trapping exits, it will receive a message if one of its linked processes is terminated, allowing it to react to this event.
- A supervisor is a process whose single responsibility is to supervise other processes. When one of its children crashes, a supervisor takes some action, according to its configuration. Frequently, the supervisor will start a new process in place of the one that crashed.
- A dynamic supervisor allows us to start child processes at runtime. We can configure the maximum number of children that can be spawned under a dynamic supervisor.

- A supervisor may be supervising other supervisors, which generates a supervision tree. A supervision tree is an important component of fault-tolerant systems, since it allows us to minimize the effects of an error, for instance, when we're able to fix an error closer to the leaves of a tree. When this is not possible, the errors are bubbled up through the tree, making the application consistent so that it doesn't leave dangling processes.

This chapter contained some lower-level constructs that are very important to comprehend, such as `receive`, but they probably won't be used in your day-to-day coding. In the next chapter, we'll cover one of the most important topics in the Elixir and Erlang world: the abstractions that the OTP framework provides (along with other abstractions provided by Elixir).

4
Powered by Erlang/OTP

As we saw in the previous chapter, a common idiom, also seen in Erlang, is to spawn processes to keep state and concurrently perform computations whose side effects may be retrieved by some means afterwards. This approach gives you endless possibilities but is more verbose and prone to errors, given it requires you to build on top of the existing basic primitives from the get-go.

To help with the previous issue, the Erlang creators decided to create higher-level abstractions for some common use cases and collected the recommended design principles to apply when writing Erlang projects. Thus, a set of libraries named **Open Telecom Platform** (**OTP**) was born.

In this chapter, we will delve into some of those incredibly useful OTP behaviours that Elixir inherited from Erlang, such as GenServer, and some of the abstractions provided by Elixir on top of those, such as Agent, Task, and Registry. Besides these behaviours, we will analyze the **Erlang Term Storage** (**ETS**) and its disk counterpart, which provides a useful way to store data.

In this chapter, we'll be covering the following topics:

- How GenServer works and how can we use it to implement a `CacheWorker` process
- The Agent behaviour and how it facilitates using a process to keep state
- Running asynchronous and parallel tasks with the Task module
- Efficiently storing and retrieving data with the ETS and its disk-based version
- Naming processes with process registers and using the registry introduced by Elixir 1.4

GenServer

We know by now that the Erlang VM lets millions of processes live happily on their own, and communicating with them is only possible via message exchange, which is the process of enqueueing messages on each process mailbox.

This interaction between processes can be seen as a client-server interaction, in the sense that a process asks the other, by enqueuing a message on its mailbox, to do something on its behalf. To implement the service, the server process would have to devise its `receive` loop, passing around its internal state, handling unexpected messages, and so on. While implementing the server-side logic, one also has to think in advance of possible edge cases that may corrupt the server's internal state or place it in a deadlock situation, unable to process any more requests.

While tackling their telecommunication projects at Ericsson, and after implementing a lot of server processes, the fine folks at Ericsson found a common set of traits that were always ending up being implemented. These patterns were pervasive enough to justify creating abstractions for them, so they could be easily applied everywhere. Thus, OTP was born, defining the so-called OTP behaviours.

Independently of the side of the pond you are in, in Elixir parlance, you will see behaviours with an *u*, so we'll also adopt it here. Oddly enough, Erlang accepts both spellings.

If we implement a calculator server by using an OTP behaviour such as `GenServer` (the short form of **Generic Server**), we will only need to implement the calculator logic on specific callback functions, and the GenServer behaviour will take care of handling errors, keeping state, properly replying to synchronous calls or not replying at all to asynchronous ones, and so on, all of this while providing us the tranquility and peace of mind of serving our calculator functionality on top of battle-tested code that achieves nine "nines" of availability in production.

The nine "nines", or 99.9999999%, of availability, refers to the usage of Erlang on a telephony switch, serving 40 million calls per week, while being down only 31 milliseconds per year. You may check out this link for more information about Erlang from Joe Armstrong, one of its creators: `http://www.rabbitmq.com/resources/armstrong.pdf`.

Following the same approach, Elixir also provides some useful behaviours, allowing developers to focus themselves as much as possible on the specifics of the problems at hand, instead of having to also reason about the complexities of developing a concurrent system from scratch. We will look at some of the Elixir behaviours in the next chapter. For now, let's put the GenServer behaviour to good use.

GenServer at your service

As we briefly hinted at before, we can leverage the GenServer behaviour to implement a process that will provide some kind of service through a well-defined public interface. To do so, one only has to `use GenServer` in its module and implement the necessary callbacks:

```
iex> defmodule Calculator do
...>    use GenServer
...>
...>    def handle_call({:mult5, number}, _from, state) do
...>      {:reply, number*5, state}
...>    end
...> end

{:module, Calculator,
 <<70, 79, 82, 49, 0, 0, 12, 224, 66, 69, 65, 77, 65, 116,
 85, 56, 0, 0, 1, 138,
   0, 0, 0, 42, 17, 69, 108, 105, 120, 105, 114, 46, 67,
 97, 108, 99, 117, 108,
   97, 116, 111, 114, 8, 95, 95, 105, 110, ...>>,
   {:handle_call, 3}}

iex> {:ok, calc} = GenServer.start_link(Calculator, [])
{:ok, #PID<0.461.0>}

iex> GenServer.call(calc, {:mult5, 7})
35
```

In the preceding example, we are defining a simple `Calculator` module that only knows how to answer to a synchronous `{:mult5, number}` call. We know this because it only implements the `handle_call/3` callback function, pattern-matching on the mentioned tuple.

Remember that if you need to better understand a module function or a specific callback, the documentation is a joy to read and it is at the distance of an IEx shell. Use h `Module.function/arity` for functions and b `Module.callback/arity` for callbacks.

We are starting a `Calculator` process and calling it afterwards by using the `start_link/2` and `call/2` functions, both belonging to the `GenServer` module. To look at the actual message sent when we `call` the calculator process, let's create a dummy process that only echoes the message it receives to the *stdout*:

```
iex> defmodule Echo do
...>    def echoes() do
...>       receive do
...>          message ->
...>             IO.puts "Echo on #{inspect(self())}: #{inspect(message)}"
...>          end
...>
...>          echoes()
...>    end
...> end

{:module, Echo,
 <<70, 79, 82, 49, 0, 0, 5, 148, 66, 69, 65, 77, 65, 116,
   85, 56, 0, 0, 0, 145, 0, 0, 0, 16, 11, 69, 108, 105,
   120, 105, 114, 46, 69, 99, 104, 111, 8, 95, 95, 105,
   110, 102, 111, 95, 95, 9, 102, ...>>, {:echoes, 0}}

iex> echo = Process.spawn(&Echo.echoes/0 , [])
#PID<0.467.0>
```

If we now use `GenServer` to send the echo process a synchronous message with `call/2`, we can see the structure of the message being sent. The message has the format `{:"$gen_call", from, contents}`, where the second element of the tuple is a `{pid, reference}` tuple identifying the sender and the message, and the last element is the contents we passed on the call. We got a timeout because `GenServer.call/2` is synchronous and, as such, the caller expects a reply, respecting the `GenServer` protocol in the meantime. However, it got none:

```
iex> GenServer.call(echo, {:hello, :echo})
Echo on #PID<0.467.0>: {:"$gen_call", {#PID<0.448.0>,
#Reference<0.2270275367.1586495491.177847>}, {:hello, :echo}}

** (exit) exited in: GenServer.call(#PID<0.467.0>, {:hello, :echo}, 5000)
    ** (EXIT) time out
    (elixir) lib/gen_server.ex:774: GenServer.call/3
```

We will now send an asynchronous request with `GenServer.cast/2` so that we can observe its message structure. Compared to the previous synchronous message, it misses the second element of the tuple, identifying the sender and the message. This makes total sense, since the server handling the request doesn't need to reply to the message.

We also didn't get a timeout, since we didn't wait for any response from the server:

```
iex> GenServer.cast(echo, {:hi_again, :echo})
Echo on #PID<0.467.0>: {:"$gen_cast", {:hi_again, :echo}}
:ok
```

By using the `GenServer` behaviour, we get better error reporting for free when the process ends abnormally. We also get a default `child_spec` definition so that we can easily place our `GenServer` processes under a supervision tree. To look at the full list of callbacks, we can check the possible completions suggested by IEx, starting with the `Calculator` module:

```
iex> Calculator.<tab>
child_spec/1 code_change/3 handle_call/3 handle_cast/2
handle_info/2 init/1 terminate/2
```

As you can see in the following error output, besides the actual `FunctionClauseError`, we get to know the last message handled and its sender, the process's internal state at the time and information about the client, namely if it is still alive and from where the call originated from:

```
iex> {:ok, calc} = GenServer.start(Calculator, [])
{:ok, #PID<0.526.0>}

iex> GenServer.call(calc, :unexpected)
** (exit) exited in: GenServer.call(#PID<0.526.0>, :unexpected, 5000)
    ** (EXIT) an exception was raised:
        ** (FunctionClauseError) no function clause matching in
Calculator.handle_call/3
        # ...

16:50:40.976 [error] GenServer #PID<0.526.0> terminating
** (FunctionClauseError) no function clause matching in
Calculator.handle_call/3
    iex:14: Calculator.handle_call(:unexpected, {#PID<0.515.0>,
    #Reference<0.2270275367.1586495489.187163>}, [])
    (stdlib) gen_server.erl:636: :gen_server.try_handle_call/4
    (stdlib) gen_server.erl:665: :gen_server.handle_msg/6
    (stdlib) proc_lib.erl:247: :proc_lib.init_p_do_apply/3
Last message (from #PID<0.515.0>): :unexpected
State: []
Client #PID<0.515.0> is alive
    (stdlib) gen.erl:169: :gen.do_call/4
    (elixir) lib/gen_server.ex:771: GenServer.call/3
    (stdlib) erl_eval.erl:670: :erl_eval.do_apply/6
    (elixir) src/elixir.erl:239: :elixir.eval_forms/4
    (iex) lib/iex/evaluator.ex:231: IEx.Evaluator.handle_eval/5
```

```
(iex) lib/iex/evaluator.ex:212: IEx.Evaluator.do_eval/3
(iex) lib/iex/evaluator.ex:190: IEx.Evaluator.eval/3
(iex) lib/iex/evaluator.ex:89: IEx.Evaluator.loop/1
```

As we saw in this section, the GenServer behaviour does a lot of the heavy lifting for us. By using it, the developer doesn't need to implement the communication details between client and server and is able to exclusively develop the specific server logic. Let's use this behaviour on our ElixirDrip application.

Implementing a CacheWorker with GenServer

We will now implement a CacheWorker process on ElixirDrip, which we'll use to keep the most recent media in memory. By using this cache mechanism, we hope to reduce the time it takes for a file to be downloaded and also avoid having to run the full download pipeline for every download handled by ElixirDrip.

Our CacheWorker will keep some content in memory for a while, associated with a specific cache key. In our case, the cache key will be the id of the media. Since we don't want to spawn more than one cache process for the same media, we will also use the media id on the process name. This way, if someone tries to cache media that already lives in the cache, it will be informed that a process with the same name already exists:

```
iex> CacheWorker.start_link("1", "content")
{:ok, #PID<0.468.0>}

iex> CacheWorker.start_link("1", "other content")
{:error, {:already_started, #PID<0.468.0>}}
```

When we call the CacheWorker.start_link/2 function with the media id and the respective content, the GenServer.start_link/3 will be called with the CacheWorker module, the contents to be cached, and the :name option. The module passed to it has to implement the init/1 function callback, which will then be responsible for the server's initialization.

 We are using a {:global, {:cache, <media_id>}} tuple when registering the process to avoid the need to use an atom as the name for each process. With this approach, each cache process will be named {:cache, <media_id>}. Atoms should be avoided as process names because they aren't garbage collected and therefore, if we use them to identify dynamically spawned processes, we risk hitting the maximum number of atoms. You can find out all about registering processes near the end of this chapter.

It is important to note that the `GenServer.start_link/3` function call is still done by the process spawning the `GenServer`, whereas the `init/1` function already runs on the spawned server. The call to `GenServer.start_link/3` will be blocked until the `init/1` callback ends, so you should check whether your `init/1` function takes too long. The second argument passed to the `GenServer.start_link/3` function is always passed to the `init/1` function, even if the spawned server doesn't need initialization arguments. In our case, we need to pass the media content to the `init/1` function so that the spawned process can store it on its internal state.

If the initialization procedure on `init/1` takes too long, just send an asynchronous message to the current process during initialization, and then do the actual server initialization work afterwards, not blocking the spawning process at all.

This means doing `GenServer.cast(self(), {:initialize, some_args})` before returning from the `init/1` call, and then, on the `handle_cast({:initialize, some_args}, _state)` function, perform the actual slow initialization procedure, returning a `{:noreply, new_state}` tuple with the new process state.

We will also save the number of times it served the cached content on the cache process. You can see the current state of the `CacheWorker` in the following code snippet. It starts and keeps content in memory, but for now, we are still unable to access the process's internal state, including the cached content:

```
$ cat apps/elixir_drip/lib/elixir_drip/storage/workers/cache_worker.ex
defmodule ElixirDrip.Storage.Workers.CacheWorker do
  use GenServer

  def start_link(media_id, content) do
    GenServer.start_link(__MODULE__, content, name: name_for(media_id))
  end

  defp name_for(media_id), do: {:global, {:cache, media_id}}

  def init(content) do
    {:ok, %{hits: 0, content: content}}
  end
end
```

A cache should allow its clients to retrieve the content it stores, and ours currently does not.

Let's fix this by creating a `handle_call/3` function callback that knows how to reply to a `:get_media` message:

```
$ cat apps/elixir_drip/lib/elixir_drip/storage/workers/cache_worker.ex
defmodule ElixirDrip.Storage.Workers.CacheWorker do
  use GenServer

  def start_link(media_id, content) do
    GenServer.start_link(__MODULE__, content, name: name_for(media_id))
  end

  defp name_for(media_id), do: {:global, {:cache, media_id}}

  def init(content) do
    {:ok, %{hits: 0, content: content}}
  end

  def handle_call(:get_media, _from, %{hits: hits, content: content} =
state) do
    {:reply, {:ok, content}, %{state | hits: hits + 1}}
  end
end
```

We are now able to fetch the cached contents in the following way:

```
iex> {:ok, cache} = CacheWorker.start_link("3", "some content")
{:ok, #PID<0.516.0>}

iex> GenServer.call(cache, :get_media)
{:ok, "some content"}
```

Our current cache version lives forever in memory, instead of expiring after a while. It only stops if we explicitly terminate it. What we need is an expiration mechanism. Let's send a delayed `:expire` message to the process itself when it starts and then, when that message actually arrives, we will terminate the cache process normally:

```
iex> timer = Process.send_after(self(), :a_10min_delayed_message, 600_000)
#Reference<0.1448220797.3761766401.179853>

iex> Process.read_timer(timer)
574847

iex> Process.cancel_timer(timer)
554295

iex> Process.cancel_timer(timer)
false
```

If the media was accessed now, it may be accessed again right after. For that reason, we will also want to postpone the sending of the :expire message whenever a cache hit happens. We will follow a similar approach to the previous example, by saving the reference returned by Process.send_after/3 so that we can cancel it later and issue a new, delayed :expire message when a cache hit happens.

After we add the expiration mechanism, our cache looks like this:

```
$ cat apps/elixir_drip/lib/elixir_drip/storage/workers/cache_worker.ex
defmodule ElixirDrip.Storage.Workers.CacheWorker do
  use GenServer

  @expire_time 60_000

  def start_link(media_id, content) do
    GenServer.start_link(__MODULE__, content, name: name_for
    (media_id))
  end

  def name_for(media_id), do: {:global, {:cache, media_id}}

  def init(content) do
    timer = Process.send_after(self(), :expire, @expire_time)
    {:ok, %{hits: 0, content: content, timer: timer}}
  end

  def handle_info(:expire, %{hits: hits} = state) do
    IO.puts "#{inspect(self())}: Terminating cache,
    served #{hits} hits"
    {:stop, :normal, state}
  end

  def handle_info(msg, state), do: super(msg, state)

  def get_media(pid), do: GenServer.call(pid, :get_media)

  def handle_call(:get_media, _from, %{hits: hits, content:
  content, timer: timer} = state) do
    {:reply, {:ok, content}, %{state | hits: hits + 1, timer:
    refresh_timer(timer)}}
  end

  defp refresh_timer(timer) do
    Process.cancel_timer(timer)
    Process.send_after(self(), :expire, @expire_time)
  end
end
```

You may have noticed that we are using the `handle_info/2` function callback to handle the `:expire` message, instead of the `call` and `cast` callbacks we used until now. This is due to the fact that when we do a `Process.send_after/3`, we are sending a *plain* message instead of a message customized by the GenServer behaviour. All of those messages that don't follow the GenServer message protocol will be handled by the available `handle_info/2` callbacks, including our `:expire` message.

For all the other *plain* messages, we simply delegate on the default `handle_info/2` GenServer implementation. This is also important because message tuples such as `{:EXIT, _, _}` and `{:DOWN, _, _, _}` may be sent to your GenServer process. Your process will receive the first message when it is trapping exits and you try to end it with `Process.exit/2`. The `:DOWN` message will reach your process when it's monitoring another process, and the latter exits for any reason. If you don't want to explicitly handle these `:EXIT` and `:DOWN` messages yourself, let the default `handle_info/2` do it for you.

Let's see how our expiration mechanism now works:

```
iex> alias ElixirDrip.Storage.Workers.CacheWorker
ElixirDrip.Storage.Workers.CacheWorker

iex> CacheWorker.start_link("5", "some content")
{:ok, #PID<0.904.0>}

#PID<0.904.0>: Terminating cache, served 0 hits # after a minute

iex> {:ok, cache} = CacheWorker.start_link("6", "other content")
{:ok, #PID<0.906.0>}

iex> 1..3 |> Enum.map(fn _ -> GenServer.call(c, :get_media) end)
[ok: "other content", ok: "other content", ok: "other content"]

#PID<0.906.0>: Terminating cache, served 3 hits # after a minute
```

With this in place, we can also add a way to refresh the cache without retrieving its contents. This will allow us to refresh the cache by sending it an asynchronous `:refresh` message using `GenServer.cast(cache_pid, :refresh)`:

```
$ cat apps/elixir_drip/lib/elixir_drip/storage/workers/cache_worker.ex
defmodule ElixirDrip.Storage.Workers.CacheWorker do
  use GenServer
  # ...
  def handle_cast(:refresh, %{timer: timer} = state),
    do: {:noreply, %{state | timer: refresh_timer()}}
```

```
  # ...
end
```

We now have a proper cache worker ready to store everything we throw at it. We just didn't talk about a small detail: why do we call it a `worker` process? It's a common idiom to name supervised processes as `workers`. In our case, every cache process will be supervised by its own `CacheSupervisor`, hence the `CacheWorker` name. This will be an example of the dynamic supervision we talked about in the previous chapter, since no cache processes will exist when starting the application, and we'll gradually spawn processes as needed at runtime.

We'll now add two functions to our supervisor, `CacheSupervisor.put/2` and `CacheSupervisor.get/1`, that will spawn a new cache process (if there is none for the same media `id`) and retrieve the cached media contents from an existing cache process. The latter relies on the `CacheWorker.name_for/1` function we previously created and provides us with the name tuple we used for each process, given the media `id`:

```
$ cat apps/elixir_drip/lib/elixir_drip/storage/supervisors/
cache_supervisor.ex
defmodule ElixirDrip.Storage.Supervisors.CacheSupervisor do
  use DynamicSupervisor
  alias ElixirDrip.Storage.Workers.CacheWorker
  # ...
  def put(id, content)
    when is_binary(id) and is_bitstring(content) do
      DynamicSupervisor.start_child(
        __MODULE__,
        cache_worker_spec(id, content)
      )
  end

  def get(id) when is_binary(id) do
    case find_cache(id) do
      nil -> nil
      pid -> CacheWorker.get_media(pid)
    end
  end

  def find_cache(id) when is_binary(id) do
    GenServer.whereis(CacheWorker.name_for(id))
  end
end
```

Let's now analyze one of the abstractions introduced by Elixir to simplify the creation of servers whose single purpose is to keep an internal state.

Agent

As we saw in the previous section, `GenServer` lets you create a server process that can handle synchronous and asynchronous interactions with its clients, while also giving you a way to handle other kinds of *low-level* messages (sent using `Process.send/3`) with the `handle_info/2` callback.

However, there will be times when you don't want to control whether the communication is sync or asynchronous. You don't need to handle *out-of-band* messages, you just want to spawn a process that properly stores information in its internal state and shares it when needed. In this case, a `GenServer` feels overkill for the task at hand.

Instead, you can employ an `Agent` and get it over with. Think of it as a `GenServer` tailored to only perform internal state management. Let's try to implement our `CacheWorker` as an `Agent`, and see how it goes.

Our `AgentCacheWorker` will keep, as its previous `GenServer` version, a map with `hits` as a counter for the number of times it served the cached content and a `content` entry for the content itself. We will expose a `get_media/1` module function, similar to what we had for the `CacheWorker`, to allow our clients to easily retrieve the content from the agent state:

```
$ cat apps/elixir_drip/lib/elixir_drip/storage/workers/
agent_cache_worker.ex
defmodule ElixirDrip.Storage.Workers.AgentCacheWorker do
  use Agent
  alias ElixirDrip.Storage.Workers.CacheWorker

  def start_link(media_id, content) do
    Agent.start_link(fn ->
      %{hits: 0, content: content}
    end, name: CacheWorker.name_for(media_id))
  end

  def get_media(pid),
    do: Agent.get(pid,
                  fn (%{hits: hits, content: content}) ->
                    hits = hits+1
                    content
                  end)
end
```

If we now try our cache agent, it looks like it works flawlessly. But in the end, when we resort to `Agent.get/2` to look at the complete internal state of the agent, we see that the number of hits weren't updated after our three accesses:

```
iex> alias ElixirDrip.Storage.Workers.AgentCacheWorker, as: AgentCache
ElixirDrip.Storage.Workers.AgentCacheWorker

iex> {:ok, agent} = AgentCache.start_link("1", "content")
{:ok, #PID<0.473.0>}

iex> 1..3 |> Enum.map(fn _ -> AgentCache.get_media(agent) end)
["content", "content", "content"]

iex> Agent.get(agent, &(&1))
%{content: "content", hits: 0}
```

Let's fix the preceding problem by changing the Agent.get/2 function
to Agent.get_and_update/2, and changing the return value of the lambda to a tuple
with two elements, where the first is the value that will be returned to the client, and the
second the new state value, this time with the hits entry incremented:

```
defmodule ElixirDrip.Storage.Workers.AgentCacheWorker do
  use Agent
  alias ElixirDrip.Storage.Workers.CacheWorker
  # ...
  def get_media(pid),
    do: Agent.get_and_update(pid,
    fn (%{hits: hits, content: content} = state) ->
    {state.content, %{state | hits: hits + 1}}
  end)
end
```

If we now try to fetch the contents from a new agent using Agent.get_and_update/2,
we'll obtain the correct number of hits:

```
iex> {:ok, agent2} = AgentCache.start_link("2", "other content")
{:ok, #PID<0.539.0>}

iex> 1..3 |> Enum.map(fn _ -> AgentCache.get_media(agent2) end)
["other content", "other content", "other content"]

iex> Agent.get(agent, &(&1))
%{content: "other content", hits: 3}
```

One thing you should notice is that the lambda we pass as the second argument runs on the
Agent process and, as such, the agent will put any other request on hold during the lambda
execution. If you want the Agent state to be updated by more than one client, you should
always perform the state update on the server process (by doing it inside the lambda
function scope). This way, you avoid a race condition, where the agent state could be
updated by another client while you were busy determining the new state.

At first sight, and for all that matters, it seems that our `AgentCacheWorker` does the same as its `CacheWorker` counterpart. We are able to start it via `start_link/2`, passing it the media `id` and its contents, and we can fetch the cached content using the `AgentCacheWorker.get_media/1` function. However, our agent process will live forever because we haven't implemented an expiration mechanism. Any expiration mechanism we may devise will have to live outside the agent since, as we'll see, an `Agent` can't handle out-of-band messages with the `handle_info/2` callback. If we add a `handle_info/2` function to the `AgentCacheWorker` as we are doing ahead, it still won't handle a message that's sent with `Process.send/3`:

```
defmodule ElixirDrip.Storage.Workers.AgentCacheWorker do
  use Agent
  alias ElixirDrip.Storage.Workers.CacheWorker
  # ...
  def handle_info(message, state) do
    Logger.debug("#{inspect(self())} Just got an OOB message: #{message}")

    {:noreply, state}
  end
end
```

If we send an `:oob_message` to an `AgentCacheWorker` process, we will get an error message on the IEx shell, saying the message wasn't expected, even if the `handle_info/2` was defined on the module:

```
iex> {:ok, agent} = AgentCache.start_link("6", "alchemy for beginners")
{:ok, #PID<0.475.0>}

iex> Process.send(agent, :oob_message, [])
:ok

22:24:07.362 [error] Agent.Server #PID<0.475.0> received unexpected
message in handle_info/2: :oob_message
```

So, the elegant expiration mechanism we had using the `Process.send_after/3` and `handle_info/2` function callback won't work with `Agent` processes. A feasible but probably too intricate alternative would consist of spawning a linked process during the `Agent` initialization that would then rely on the `Process.send_after/3` function to send an `:expire` message to itself. Upon receiving this message, the process would do a `Process.exit(agent, :expired)`. Since the agent wasn't expecting an `:expired` exit signal and it isn't trapping exits, it would simply exit with the `:expired` reason.

We'll leave the previous suggestion as an exercise for the reader. Keep in mind that if the abstraction at hand doesn't provide you with the flexibility you need from the get-go, sometimes you're better avoiding it in the first place. Looking at our `Agent` example, since we want to expire cached contents after a while, it is simpler to choose the `GenServer` route instead.

> The less code you write, the smaller the probability of introducing a bug. In Elixir if you rely as much as possible in the OTP abstractions, you are in a good position to keep your code running for years to come with minimum interruptions.

We will now look at the `Task` module and how it allows us to perform one-off computations in parallel, allowing us to wait for the outcome of those if needed.

Task

As we saw earlier, processes are cheap to spawn in Elixir because we are always in the realm of the BEAM. This is the perfect setup for us to spawn a process whenever we need. If you need to do something in parallel, you can spawn a process. If you need to do many things in parallel, you can spawn many processes. The virtual machine won't break a sweat and you will have an army of processes in no time to accomplish whatever you need.

However, process communication is laborious, so if you need results from those parallel computations, you will have to receive the results via message passing and eventually terminate the processes afterwards.

In this situation, we can resort to the `Task` module, using its `Task.async/1` function to spawn tasks, and then use `Task.await/1` when you need the results from the tasks you previously spawned.

Imagine that we want to tell our users their rank relative to the disk space they currently use. Fetching the disk space of each and every user could be an expensive query to make, so we want to off-load it to a parallel task and only look at those values when they're really needed:

```
disk_space_by_user_task = Task.async(fn ->
  # expensive query
  [
    %{user_id: 4, disk_space: 600},
    %{user_id: 2, disk_space: 123},
    %{user_id: 1, disk_space: 1024},
    %{user_id: 5, disk_space: 50},
```

```
      %{user_id: 3, disk_space: 0.5}
  ]
end)

# performing other work here

{%{disk_space: disk_space}, user_rank} = disk_space_by_user_task
  |> Task.await(timeout)
  |> Enum.sort(&(&1.disk_space <= &2.disk_space))
  |> Enum.with_index(1)
  |> Enum.find(&(elem(&1, 0).user_id == current_user))

Notifications.send(current_user, "You're using #{disk_space} MB,
making you the \##{user_rank} user in terms of disk usage.")
```

In the previous example, we are delegating the expensive query on an asynchronous `Task`, hence the current process can continue its work until it really needs the task results. When the task results are needed to continue, the process tries to obtain them using `Task.await/2`. If the task doesn't return before the `timeout` expires, the current process exits, so in our case, we are sure it won't send a notification if the disk usage stats don't arrive.

Notice how the current process effectively stops to wait at the `Task.await/2` call. How could we spawn multiple tasks and then aggregate their results? Without further ado, let's delve into parallel tasks.

Parallel tasks

To help us understand how tasks work, we need a lazy cache mechanism. For this purpose, let's define a `SlowCacheSupervisor` process that delegates its `put/2` and `get/1` to the well-behaved `CacheSupervisor` already introduced, but before that, it sleeps for as many seconds as the media `id` it receives:

```
defmodule ElixirDrip.Storage.Supervisors.SlowCacheSupervisor do
  @behaviour ElixirDrip.Behaviours.CacheSupervisor

  alias ElixirDrip.Storage.Supervisors.CacheSupervisor, as: RealCache

  def put(id, content), do: RealCache.put(id, content)

  def get(id) do
    secs_to_nap = case Integer.parse(id) do
      {sleep_time, _} -> sleep_time
      _ -> 1
```

```
      end

    Process.sleep(secs_to_nap * 1000)
    RealCache.get(id)
  end
  # ...
end
```

We now want to create a parallel text search for our application. This `Search` module will expose a `search_for/2` function that will receive a list of media identifiers (or a single media `id`) and an expression, and will search each media contents for the given expression. We'll assume all the media we need already lives in the cache.

The smallest unit of work here is performed by the function that does the search on a single piece of media. It fetches the content from the cache, splits it into lines, and then uses `Stream.with_index/1` to pair each line with its line number. After this, we reduce the stream we just created, adding a tuple with the line number and contents to the results list if the expression was found on the current line:

```
defmodule ElixirDrip.Storage.Search do
  alias ElixirDrip.Storage.Supervisors.SlowCacheSupervisor, as: Cache
  # ...
  def search_for(media_id, expression) do
    raw_content_lines = media_id
                        |> Cache.get()
                        |> elem(1)
                        |> String.split("\n")

    result = raw_content_lines
    |> Stream.with_index()
    |> Enum.reduce(
      [],
      fn({content, line}, accum) ->
        case found?(expression, content) do
          nil -> accum
          _ -> accum ++ [{line + 1, content}]
        end
      end)

    {media_id, result}
  end

  defp found?(expression, content) do
    regex = ~r/#{expression}/
    Regex.run(regex, content, return: :index)
  end
end
```

We will now implement our first search, properly named `naive_search_for/2`, since it simply searches through each piece of media sequentially:

```elixir
defmodule ElixirDrip.Storage.Search do
  # ...
  def naive_search_for(media_ids, expression) when is_list(media_ids) do
    media_ids
    |> Enum.map(&search_for(&1, expression))
    |> Enum.into(%{})
  end
end
```

The preceding implementation doesn't leverage at all how easy is for Elixir to spawn millions of processes. Let's fill our cache with data so that we can implement an improved search:

```elixir
iex> alias ElixirDrip.Storage.Supervisors.SlowCacheSupervisor, as: Cache
ElixirDrip.Storage.Supervisors.SlowCacheSupervisor

iex> fill_cache = fn (how_many, offset) ->
...> offset..(offset + (how_many-1))
...> |> Enum.each(&Cache.put(to_string(&1), "Media content #{&1}."))
...> end
#Function<12.99386804/2 in :erl_eval.expr/5>

iex> fill_cache.(3, 6)
14:17:40.483 [debug] Spawning a slow cache for 6, content size: 16 bytes.
14:17:40.485 [debug] #PID<0.452.0>: CacheWorker started. Will expire in a while.
14:17:40.485 [debug] Spawning a slow cache for 7, content size: 16 bytes.
14:17:40.485 [debug] #PID<0.453.0>: CacheWorker started. Will expire in a while.
14:17:40.485 [debug] Spawning a slow cache for 8, content size: 16 bytes.
14:17:40.485 [debug] #PID<0.454.0>: CacheWorker started. Will expire in a while.
:ok
```

With the previous snippet, we stored three files with ids `"6"`, `"7"` and `"8"` in the cache. If we then retrieve those files from the cache in parallel, we will have to wait eight seconds before getting the contents of the three files.

Recall that the `SlowCacheSupervisor.get/1` function sleeps for the number of seconds indicated by the media id. If we are calling this function in parallel, the time it takes for all calls to return is equal to the time of the slowest call.

Our improved search will spawn a task for each search and then wait for all of them afterwards. Notice that we are using the `Task.async/3` function, which receives the module, function name, and arguments, instead of a lambda like we used previously:

```
defmodule ElixirDrip.Storage.Search do
  # ...
  def task_search_for(media_ids, expression, timeout \\ 10_000) when
is_list(media_ids) do
    media_ids
    |> Enum.map(&Task.async(__MODULE__, :search_for, [&1, expression]))
    |> Enum.map(&Task.await(&1, timeout))
  end
end
```

You can see how it performs in the following code. The complete call took eight seconds to return the results: 1 ms after it started, each task tried to fetch the cache contents and then the three cache workers responded in 6, 7, and 8 seconds afterwards:

```
iex> Logger.debug "#{inspect(self())} Start"; ElixirDrip.Utils.measure(fn
-> Search.task_search_for_verbose(["8", "7", "6"], "media") end)

09:57:04.368 #PID<0.613.0> Start

09:57:04.369 #PID<0.613.0> Spawned a search for 8, PID: #PID<0.740.0>
09:57:04.369 #PID<0.613.0> Spawned a search for 7, PID: #PID<0.741.0>
09:57:04.369 #PID<0.613.0> Spawned a search for 6, PID: #PID<0.742.0>

09:57:04.369 #PID<0.613.0> Will now wait for task PID: #PID<0.740.0>

09:57:04.369 Fetching cached content for 8...
09:57:04.369 Fetching cached content for 7...
09:57:04.369 Fetching cached content for 6...

09:57:10.370 #PID<0.560.0>: Received :get_media and served '"Content of
media 6."' bytes 1 times.
09:57:11.370 #PID<0.561.0>: Received :get_media and served '"Content of
media 7."' bytes 1 times.
09:57:12.370 #PID<0.562.0>: Received :get_media and served '"Content of
media 8."' bytes 1 times.

09:57:12.371 #PID<0.613.0> Task PID: #PID<0.740.0> returned with 1
result(s) for 8
09:57:12.371 #PID<0.613.0> Will now wait for task PID: #PID<0.741.0>

09:57:12.371 #PID<0.613.0> Task PID: #PID<0.741.0> returned with 1
result(s) for 7
09:57:12.371 #PID<0.613.0> Will now wait for task PID: #PID<0.742.0>
```

```
09:57:12.371 #PID<0.613.0> Task PID: #PID<0.742.0> returned with 1
result(s) for 6

09:57:12.372 Took: 8.002136 secs
```

It all looks good; just notice that we are sequentially waiting on each task to complete, so we will only run `Task.await/1` for the next task when the current `Task.await/1` call returns. That is the reason why we immediately see the shell process <0.613.0> waiting for the first task (with PID <0.740.0>), but then it only does the same for the remaining tasks eight seconds afterwards, after the first task returns.

> The `task_search_for_verbose/2` function called on the previous example is equivalent to the `task_search_for/2` function, adding only calls to `Logger.debug/1`, so we can observe what's happening under the hood.

Now, consider the following situation: we have to return after 10 seconds, no matter what, and we have a really big file in the cache with id "25", so it will take 25 seconds to be fetched from our slow cache. If we call `Search.task_search_for(["8", "25"], "media")`, it will terminate the current process, which spawned the two search tasks, because the second task doesn't end before the timeout (and we aren't trapping exits). However, as you can see in the following code, it ends after 18 seconds, because it waited eight seconds for the first task to complete, and then it blocks for another 10 seconds (the timeout passed on the `await/1` call) before returning from the `Task.await/1` for the second task:

```
iex> Logger.debug "#{inspect(self())} Start"; ElixirDrip.Utils.measure(fn
-> Search.task_search_for_verbose(["8", "25"], "media") end)

12:10:06.878 #PID<0.613.0> Start

12:10:06.878 #PID<0.613.0> Spawned a search for 8, PID: #PID<0.947.0>
12:10:06.878 #PID<0.613.0> Spawned a search for 25, PID: #PID<0.948.0>
12:10:06.878 #PID<0.613.0> Will now wait for task PID: #PID<0.947.0>
12:10:06.878 Fetching cached content for 8...
12:10:06.878 Fetching cached content for 25...

Seconds elapsed: 1 secs
# ...
Seconds elapsed: 7 secs

12:10:14.879 #PID<0.562.0>: Received :get_media and served '"Content
of media 8."' bytes 1 times.
12:10:14.882 #PID<0.613.0> Task PID: #PID<0.947.0> returned with 1
result(s) for 8
```

```
12:10:14.882 #PID<0.613.0> Will now wait for task PID: #PID<0.948.0>

Seconds elapsed: 8 secs
# ...
Seconds elapsed: 17 secs

** (exit) exited in: Task.await(%Task{owner: #PID<0.613.0>, pid:
#PID<0.948.0>, ref: #Reference<0.3922080717.158334979.65414>}, 10000)
    ** (EXIT) time out
    (elixir) lib/task.ex:493: Task.await/2
    (elixir_drip) lib/elixir_drip/storage/search.ex:34: anonymous fn/1 in
ElixirDrip.Storage.Search.task_search_for_verbose/2
    (elixir) lib/enum.ex:1294: Enum."-map/2-lists^map/1-0-"/2
    (elixir) lib/enum.ex:1294: Enum."-map/2-lists^map/1-0-"/2
    (elixir_drip) lib/elixir_drip/utils.ex:19: anonymous fn/1 in
ElixirDrip.Utils.safe_function/1
    (stdlib) timer.erl:166: :timer.tc/1
    (elixir_drip) lib/elixir_drip/utils.ex:11: ElixirDrip.Utils.measure/1
```

If we want to timeout after a while using the previous approach, we would need to keep track of the remaining time until timeout and only wait for each task accordingly. Fortunately, spawning parallel tasks is a really common pattern in concurrent programming, and therefore, Elixir 1.4 introduced the Task.async_stream functions, which let us, among other nice features, set a single timeout for all the tasks it spawns.

The Task.async_stream functions will spawn a new process, linked to the current one, and this intermediate process will then spawn all the required tasks, aggregating the task results as they conclude. We are still in Task territory, so the default behavior should be familiar: if a spawned task times out or unexpectedly dies, its exit signal will be sent to the intermediate process that will then terminate the remaining tasks and propagate the exit signal to the original process.

Let's now implement our text search feature using the Task.async_stream/5 function so that we can be sure it only waits 10 seconds for task results. This function gives us the semantics we associate with the Stream module, in the sense that each task will be lazily performed. By default, the number of running tasks at the same time is given by the numbers of schedulers in the VM. We can also control this via the :max_concurrency option. Compare this approach with the previous one, where we spawned all the tasks in advance, disregarding the number of available schedulers. If each task needs to use a finite resource, such as a database connection, the eager approach with many tasks could quickly deplete the pool of available resources:

```
defmodule ElixirDrip.Storage.Search do
  # ...
  def task_stream_search_for(media_ids, expression, concurrency
```

```
  \\ 4, timeout \\ 10_000) when is_list(media_ids) do
    options = [max_concurrency: concurrency, timeout: timeout]

    media_ids
    |> Task.async_stream(__MODULE__, :search_for, [expression],
    options)
    |> Enum.map(&elem(&1, 1))
    |> Enum.into(%{})
  end
end
```

The `Task.async_stream/5` function, besides the `:max_concurrency` and `:timeout` options, receives a collection and the module, function, and additional arguments that each task will process. Each element of the collection will be passed to the function as the first argument. In our case, the first argument of each call will be the media id and we will pass the search expression as the last argument. Each task will yield a `{:ok, result}` tuple, thus we are extracting the last element of each tuple from the result, before injecting it into a map:

```
iex> Logger.debug "#{inspect(self())} Start"; ElixirDrip.Utils.measure(fn
-> Search.task_stream_search_for(["6",
"7", "8"], "media") end)

07:04:42.859 #PID<0.883.0> Start

07:04:50.801 Took: 8.01131 secs
```

As we saw previously, the `Task.async_stream` functions have the same `Task` semantics, hence if any task times out, the exit signal is propagated to the process that spawned the tasks. Because we aren't trapping exits, this process will exit along with all the other tasks, which at this point may already be concluded. You can see in the following code that the results of spawning two tasks will take 25 and 8 seconds, respectively, with a 10 second timeout:

```
iex> Logger.debug "#{inspect(self())} Start"; ElixirDrip.Utils.measure(fn
-> Search.task_stream_search_for
(["25", "8"], "media") end)

07:23:00.315 #PID<0.883.0> Start

07:23:00.321 Fetching cached content for 25...
07:23:00.321 Fetching cached content for 8...

Seconds elapsed: 1 secs
# ...
Seconds elapsed: 7 secs
```

```
07:23:08.252 #PID<0.895.0>: Received :get_media and served
'"Content of media 8."' bytes 7 times.

Seconds elapsed: 8 secs
Seconds elapsed: 9 secs

** (exit) exited in: Task.Supervised.stream(10000)
    ** (EXIT) time out
    (elixir) lib/task/supervised.ex:269: Task.Supervised.stream_reduce/7
    (elixir) lib/enum.ex:1919: Enum.map/2
    (elixir_drip) lib/elixir_drip/storage/search.ex:44:
ElixirDrip.Storage.Search.task_stream_search_for/4
    (stdlib) timer.erl:166: :timer.tc/1
    (elixir_drip) lib/elixir_drip/utils.ex:13: ElixirDrip.Utils.measure/1

Seconds elapsed: 10 secs
```

What we want is to return after 10 seconds with the results we have, instead of not returning at all because one task didn't end before the bell. For situations like these, we have the `:on_timeout` option. Its value is `:exit` by default, meaning it will propagate the exit signal from the task, thus the process that spawned the tasks will exit too. This is the behavior we just observed. We can also pass it as `:kill_task`, and the task that took too long is simply ended. When a task is terminated like this, the result it yields will always be a `{:exit, :timeout}` tuple, instead of the successful `{:ok, result}`:

```
defmodule ElixirDrip.Storage.Search do
  # ...
  def safe_task_stream_search_for(media_ids, expression, concurrency
  \\ 4, timeout \\ 10_000) when is_list(media_ids) do
    options = [max_concurrency: concurrency, timeout: timeout,
    on_timeout: :kill_task]

    media_ids
    |> Task.async_stream(__MODULE__, :search_for, [expression],
    options)
    |> Enum.map(&elem(&1, 1))
    |> Enum.reject(&(&1 == :timeout))
    |> Enum.into(%{})
  end
end
```

Recall that the search task for media `"25"` timed out and therefore it yielded a `{:exit, :timeout}` tuple, that will be then filtered with the call to `Enum.reject/2` before returning the results. With this version, a search on media with ids `"25"`, `"8"`, `"6"`, and `"7"` yields the following after 10 seconds:

```
iex> Logger.debug "#{inspect(self())} Start";
Search.safe_task_stream_search_for(["25", "8", "6", "7"], "media")

10:14:06.861 #PID<0.463.0> Start

10:14:06.873 Fetching cached content for 25...
10:14:06.873 Fetching cached content for 8...
10:14:06.873 Fetching cached content for 6...
10:14:06.874 Fetching cached content for 7...

# ...
Seconds elapsed: 6 secs
10:14:12.874 #PID<0.473.0>: Received :get_media and served
'"Content of media 6."' bytes 1 times.

10:14:13.868 Seconds elapsed: 7 secs
10:14:13.874 #PID<0.474.0>: Received :get_media and served
'"Content of media 7."' bytes 1 times.

10:14:14.869 Seconds elapsed: 8 secs
10:14:14.874 #PID<0.475.0>: Received :get_media and served
'"Content of media 8."' bytes 1 times.

# ...
10:14:16.871 Seconds elapsed: 10 secs

%{
  "6" => [{1, "Content of media 6."}],
  "7" => [{1, "Content of media 7."}],
  "8" => [{1, "Content of media 8."}]
}
```

We can finally observe the results of our text search: for each media `id`, it returns a list with the number and the contents of the line that matched the search expression. It always returns in the time span we defined, so we can deliver snappier results to our users.

Let's now see how we can use the ETS tool that comes with Erlang/OTP to store the results of text searches performed on ElixirDrip.

Using (D)ETS

In the previous section, we implemented the ElixirDrip text search functionality by using `Task.async_stream/5` to search several text files at the same time. The text search function lived on the `ElixirDrip.Storage.Search` module and its last iteration could be used like this:

```
iex> alias ElixirDrip.Storage.Search

iex> media_ids = ["25", "8", "6", "7"]

iex> search_expression = "media"

iex> Search.safe_task_stream_search_for(media_ids,
search_expression)

%{
  "6" => [{1, "Content of media 6."}],
  "7" => [{1, "Content of media 7."}],
  "8" => [{1, "Content of media 8."}]
}
```

It returned a map with entries for every searched file whose search ended on the allotted time. For each media id, it yields a list of two-element tuples, where the first tuple element corresponds to the line where the expression was found and the second element contains the actual line's contents.

Remember that ElixirDrip spawns a CacheWorker to keep files in memory for a while to speed up consecutive downloads, but reaps those processes after a while in order to keep the memory usage in check. The Search.search_for/2 function that performs the actual file search assumes there is already a CacheWorker process for the file to be searched. Hence, if we want to search a specific text file, we will have to download it before actually searching through it.

The objective here is to implement a cache to store search results in order to improve subsequent searches. Instead of immediately downloading a file only to search through its contents, we will first take a look at the search results cache to find whether the same search had already been done.

We will implement this cache using the ETS, an Erlang OTP construct that allow us to efficiently store and query arbitrary Erlang terms in memory. We use the term *efficiently* here because an ETS table gives you constant access time, no matter the size of the data you store on it. Since ETS data lives in memory, it shouldn't strike as a surprise if we tell you that each ETS table belongs to a specific process. In a scenario where the ETS data should be kept, we have to cautiously handle the termination of the process holding the corresponding ETS table to ensure that the table doesn't get lost.

Let's create a module that's a GenServer based SearchCacheWorker module that will encapsulate the logic of our search results cache. Since we will have only one SearchCacheWorker, we are registering it under the ElixirDrip.Storage.Workers.SearchCacheWorker alias (its module name).

This way, we don't need to know the `SearchCacheWorker` PID to send messages to it:

```
$ cat apps/elixir_drip/lib/elixir_drip/storage/workers/
search_cache_worker.ex
defmodule ElixirDrip.Storage.Workers.SearchCacheWorker do
  @moduledoc false

  use GenServer
  require Logger

  @search_cache :search_cache

  def start_link() do
    GenServer.start_link(__MODULE__, [], name: __MODULE__)
  end

  def init(_) do
    Logger.debug("#{inspect(self())}: SearchCacheWorker started.")
    search_cache = :ets.new(@search_cache, [:named_table, :set,
    :protected])

    {:ok, search_cache}
  end
end
```

As we can observe, it's an ordinary `GenServer` that creates a new ETS table called `:search_cache` during its initialization and stores the table name on its state. If we didn't pass the `:named_table` option to the `:ets.new/2` function, we would get a `Reference` to the table instead of its name. The `:set` option makes the ETS table work as a standard map, where every key must be unique and each key only points to a single value. We are also setting the table access mode as `:protected`, which means only the process owner can write to the table, whereas other processes are able to read from it.

 Instead of a `:set`, an ETS table can also behave like an `:ordered_set`, a `:bag`, or a `:duplicate_bag`. The `:ordered_set` keeps your table ordered by key, whereas a `:bag` can have more than one unique value per key. The `:duplicate_bag` removes the uniqueness requirement from the latter. Regarding the table access mode, aside from `:protected`, you can also set it as `:private` or `:public`, meaning no-one except the process owner can access it, or everyone has read and write access, respectively.

In order to store text search results in our ETS table, we will implement a `cache_search_result/3` function that receives the `media_id`, the `search_expression`, and the associated search `result` we want to store.

Since the table can only be written by its process owner, this function will simply do a `GenServer.call/2` to the process owner that will then be responsible for updating the ETS table on the correspondent `handle_call/3` callback:

```
$ cat apps/elixir_drip/lib/elixir_drip/storage/workers/
search_cache_worker.ex
defmodule ElixirDrip.Storage.Workers.SearchCacheWorker do
  # ...
  def cache_search_result(media_id, search_expression, result) do
    GenServer.call(__MODULE__, {:put, media_id, search_expression,
    result})
  end

  def handle_call({:put, media_id, search_expression, result}, _from,
  search_cache) do
    created_at = :os.system_time(:seconds)

    result = :ets.insert_new(search_cache, {{media_id,
    search_expression}, {created_at, result}})

    {:reply, {:ok, result}, search_cache}
  end
end
```

To insert a new value into the ETS table, we pass the table name (stored on the process state) and the new entry to the `:ets.insert_new/2` function. This new entry has to always be a tuple with the key on the first element. In our case, we are passing `{{media_id, search_expression}, {created_at, result}}` as the second argument, so our key is the `{media_id, search_expression}` tuple, and its value is another tuple with the `created_at` timestamp and the actual text search result (towards the end of this section, you will understand why we are storing the timestamp as well). The `:ets.insert_new/2` call will return a boolean value, indicating the operation's success:

```
iex> SearchCacheWorker.cache_search_result("1", "media",
"lorem ipsum media 1 contents")
{:ok, true}

iex> SearchCacheWorker.cache_search_result("1", "media",
"this can't be cached")
{:ok, false}

iex> SearchCacheWorker.cache_search_result("1", "other",
"other phrase found on media 1 contents")
{:ok, true}
```

We set the table access mode as `:protected`, hence every process can read its contents.

In this scenario, we don't need to ask the owner process to fetch the data stored on the table for us, we can just interact directly with it. This is why we store the table name on the `@search_cache` module attribute: since every process is able to read from the table, the table name can't live solely on the state of the process owner.

To access a table entry, you can use the `:ets.lookup/2` function, which receives the table name or reference and the `key` we are looking for. This function returns a list of entries that have that key. In our case, every returned list will only have one element, because we're using a `:set` ETS table:

```
iex> :ets.lookup(:search_cache, {"1", "media"})
[{{"1", "media"}, {1518475143, "lorem ipsum media 1 contents"}}]

iex> :ets.lookup(:search_cache, {"1", "unknown"})
[]
```

As you just saw, we get a list with a `{key, value}` tuple when there is an entry for that key. To easily fetch the stored value, we encapsulated the `:ets.lookup/2` function in the `search_result_for/2` function:

```
$ cat apps/elixir_drip/lib/elixir_drip/storage/workers/
search_cache_worker.ex
defmodule ElixirDrip.Storage.Workers.SearchCacheWorker do
  # ...
  @search_cache :search_cache

  def search_result_for(media_id, search_expression) do
    case :ets.lookup(@search_cache, {media_id, search_expression}) do
      [] ->
        nil
      [{_key, {_created_at, search_result}}] ->
        search_result
    end
  end
end
```

With the previous function, we can't fetch all the text searches cached for a given `media_id`. If we want to implement it, we need our query to only look at the first element of the key tuple, which contains the `media_id`. The `:ets.match_object/2` function allows us to do exactly that: with it, you can pattern match on specific fields:

```
iex> :ets.match_object(:search_cache, {{"1", :"_"}, :"_"})
[
  {{"1", "other"}, {1518509888, "other phrase found on media 1
  contents"}},
  {{"1", "media"}, {1518475143, "lorem ipsum media 1 contents"}}
]
```

Let's create an `all_search_results_for/1` function that pattern matches on the `media_id` element of the key tuple, similar to what we just did. We've used the special form `:"_"` to indicate that, for our `{{media_id, search_expression} {created_at, result}}` entries, we don't care about the `search_expression` tuple element nor the last tuple corresponding to the value of each entry:

```
$ cat apps/elixir_drip/lib/elixir_drip/storage/workers/
search_cache_worker.ex
defmodule ElixirDrip.Storage.Workers.SearchCacheWorker do
  # ...
  @search_cache :search_cache

  def all_search_results_for(media_id) do
    case :ets.match_object(@search_cache, {{media_id, :"_"}, :"_"}) do
      [] ->
        nil
      all_objects ->
        all_objects
        |> Enum.map(fn {key, value} ->
          {elem(key, 1), elem(value, 1)}
        end)
    end
  end
end
```

`:ets.match_object/2` returns a list with every entry that matches our search criteria. In order to return only the `search_expression` and the `result` of each entry, we map the resulting list, respectively getting the first from the entry `key` and the latter from the `entry` value:

```
iex> SearchCacheWorker.all_search_results_for("1")
[{"other", "other phrase found on media 1 contents"}, {"media",
"lorem ipsum media 1 contents"}]
```

Finally, let's use the `created_at` timestamp that's stored every time we cache a search result. The idea here is to create a `SearchCacheWorker.expired_search_results/0` that will return all the search results keys that were created more than `@expiration_secs` ago. For this, we will have to use the `:ets.select/2` function. This construct allows us to apply a guard clause to each entry we are pattern matching, and this is exactly what we want here:

```
iex> expiration_secs = 60
60

iex> expiration_time = :os.system_time(:seconds) - expiration_secs
1518512436
```

```
iex> query = [
...> {
...> {:"$1", {:"$2", :"_"}},
...> [{:<, :"$2", {:const, expiration_time}}],
...> [:"$1"]
...> }
...> ]
[
  {{:"$1", {:"$2", :_}}, [{:<, :"$2", {:const, 1518512436}}], [:"$1"]}
]
```

The query structure isn't that friendly, but don't be wary of it just yet. An
:ets.select query is composed of one or more clauses, each clause being a three-element
tuple. Let's inspect our single clause query. The first element of the clause, {:"$1",
{:"$2", :"_"}}, is the pattern we will apply to every entry in our table. Here, we are
associating the :"$1" variable to the {media_id, search_expression} key and the
:"$2" to the created_at tuple element.

The second element, [{:<, :"$2", {:const, expiration_time}}], is the guard
clause, and tells us that we will only select entries whose :"$2" value is lower than the
expiration_time defined in this scope. The last element of the clause tuple, [:"$1"],
shows how we want to return the values of the query. If we wanted to return the full
entries stored on the table, we could use the :"$_" variable instead of :"$1".

With our query in place, let's use it to see which search results have expired. First, let's just
cache a new search result so that we can be sure the query is working properly:

```
iex> SearchCacheWorker.cache_search_result("7", "media", "really fresh
media 7 contents")
{:ok, true}

iex> :ets.select(:search_cache, query)
[{"1", "other"}, {"1", "media"}, {"5", "media"}]
```

The :ets.select/2 call didn't return the key of the search result we've just cached, so we
are good to go. We can now implement the
SearchCacheWorker.expired_search_results/0 function, which leverages the code
we just created. We encapsulated the query on the private
expired_search_results_query/1 just to tidy things up:

```
$ cat apps/elixir_drip/lib/elixir_drip/storage/workers/
search_cache_worker.ex
defmodule ElixirDrip.Storage.Workers.SearchCacheWorker do
  # ...
  @search_cache :search_cache
```

```
@expiration_secs 60

def expired_search_results(expiration_secs \\ @expiration_secs) do
  query = expired_search_results_query(expiration_secs)

  :ets.select(@search_cache, query)
end

defp expired_search_results_query(expiration_secs) do
  expiration_time = :os.system_time(:seconds) - expiration_secs

  [
    {
      {:"$1", {:"$2", :"_"}},
      [{:<, :"$2", {:const, expiration_time}}],
      [:"$1"]
    }
  ]
end
end
```

Even if we can now understand the syntax of these :ets.select/2 queries, their funky expressiveness means that in a month or two, we will probably need a moment to grasp what a query like this does. To help with this difficulty, the :ets Erlang module provides the :ets.fun2ms/1 function, which receives a lambda function and outputs a query with the proper syntax to be passed to the :ets.select/3 function. This is how we could obtain an equivalent query that gives us the entries that expired:

```
iex> query = :ets.fun2ms(
...> fn {key, {created_at, result}} when created_at < expiration_time ->
...>   key
...> end)

[
  {
    {:"$1", {:"$2", :"$3"}},
    [{:<, :"$2", {:const, 1518520114}}],
    [:"$1"]}
]
```

As you can see, the :ets.fun2ms/1 call is more intelligible than what we had. It receives a table entry as its single argument, it applies a guard to the created_at field to filter out still valid entries, and then returns the key of the expired ones. There is a catch, though: if you call :ets.fun2ms/1 inside a module of yours, you will get a :badarg error, saying the function we passed has to be a function generated in the shell, or needs to be transformed with an Erlang *parse transform* before it can be used.

The *parse transform* is a feature of Erlang that allows one to access the code tree representation, a sort of Erlang metaprogramming. The introduction of Elixir 1.5 deprecated the use of these *parse transform* constructs, so we are left with using :ets.fun2ms/1 with shell functions, like we just did previously.

If you still want to use an :ets.fun2ms/1-based approach, check the ex2ms package (https://hex.pm/packages/ex2ms), which allows you to accomplish the same using Elixir macros. For our specific use-case, it was enough to generate the select query inside an IEx shell with :ets.fun2ms/1 and then just copy the result to SearchCacheWorker.expired_search_results_query/1.

Let's now create a way to delete entries from our search results cache. Since this operation changes the ETS table, it will have to be performed by its processor owner, hence the use of the GenServer.call/2 function. We have two delete_cache_search functions, one that creates the tuple key with the received media_id and search_expression to then perform the GenServer.call/2, while the other just passes the received key list to it:

```
$ cat apps/elixir_drip/lib/elixir_drip/storage/workers/
search_cache_worker.ex
defmodule ElixirDrip.Storage.Workers.SearchCacheWorker do
  # ...
  def delete_cache_search(media_id, search_expression) do
    GenServer.call(__MODULE__, {:delete, [{media_id, search_expression}]})
  end

  def delete_cache_search(keys) when is_list(keys) and
  length(keys) > 0 do
    GenServer.call(__MODULE__, {:delete, keys})
  end

  def handle_call({:delete, keys}, _from, search_cache)
  when is_list(keys) do
    result = delete(keys)
             |> Enum.reduce(true, fn r, acc -> r && acc end)

    {:reply, {:ok, result}, search_cache}
  end

  defp delete([]), do: []
  defp delete([key|rest]),
    do: [delete(key)] ++ delete(rest)
  defp delete(key), do: :ets.delete(@search_cache, key)
```

The `delete_cache_search` calls are both handled by the same `handle_call/3` callback that pattern matches on `{:delete, keys}`. This handler relies on the `delete/1` private function to actually execute the `:ets.delete/2` call, recursively iterating on the list of keys it receives. Also note that we are reducing the results of all delete operations just for the sake of it, since `:ets.delete/2` always returns `true` no matter what.

We can now pipe the results of `SearchCacheWorker.expired_search_results/0` to `SearchCacheWorker.delete_cache_search/1` in order to sweep those older cached search results:

```
iex> SearchCacheWorker.expired_search_results
[{"1", "other"}, {"1", "media"}, {"5", "media"}]

iex> SearchCacheWorker.expired_search_results() |>
SearchCacheWorker.delete_cache_search()
{:ok, true}

iex> SearchCacheWorker.expired_search_results
[]
```

Considering we are using a `GenServer` as the ETS table guardian, we could implement the same approach we previously adopted on the `CacheWorker` to expire itself, but this time we would periodically sweep old cached results instead. We will leave this improvement as a suggestion for the reader.

Our `SearchCacheWorker` lives happily in memory and performs as expected, providing a constant access time to the millions of search results it stores. But as you can see in the following code, an ETS table lives in memory and it will go to `/dev/null` as soon as its process owner dies:

```
iex> :ets.info(:search_cache)
[
  read_concurrency: false,
  write_concurrency: false,
  compressed: false,
  memory: 331,
  owner: #PID<0.672.0>,
  heir: :none,
  name: :search_cache,
  size: 1,
  node: :nonode@nohost,
  named_table: true,
  type: :set,
  keypos: 1,
  protection: :protected
]
```

```
iex> guardian = pid("0.672.0")
#PID<0.672.0>

iex> Process.alive? guardian
true

iex> Process.exit guardian, :bye
true

iex> Process.alive? guardian
false

iex> :ets.info(:search_cache)
:undefined
```

Let's now check how can we persist an ETS table in disk.

Disk-based ETS

There may be scenarios where you want the information stored on the ETS table to be persisted in disk. You lose the performance of an in-memory data structure, but you get your information stored to disk if anything goes south. To cater for this case, Erlang provides DETS, a *disk-based* ETS solution that abides almost completely to the same ETS contract you already know and expect. You can't use it if you need an :ordered_set table since you're limited to 2 GB of data; instead, you will have to start it in a different way and properly close it, and that's essentially it.

Let's now implement a FlexibleSearchCacheWorker module that, depending on the argument passed to its start_link/1 function, uses a DETS or an ETS to store search results. This module will implement all the functions provided by SearchCacheWorker, but the changes we'll need to do are very small:

```
$ cat apps/elixir_drip/lib/elixir_drip/storage/workers/
flexible_search_cache_worker.ex
defmodule ElixirDrip.Storage.Workers.FlexibleSearchCacheWorker do
  use GenServer
  require Logger

  @search_cache :search_cache

  def start_link(storage \\ :ets) do
    GenServer.start_link(__MODULE__, storage, name: __MODULE__)
  end

  def init(storage) do
```

```
    Logger.debug("#{inspect(self())}: FlexibleSearchCacheWorker
    started with #{storage}.")
    search_cache = case storage do
      :ets -> :ets.new(@search_cache, [:named_table, :set,
      :protected])
      :dets ->
        {:ok, name} = :dets.open_file(@search_cache, [type: :set])
        name
    end

    {:ok, {storage, search_cache}}
  end
end
```

As you can see, depending on the `storage` value (one of `:ets` or `:dets`), we initialize an ETS or a DETS table. We then save both the `storage` and `search_cache` values on the process state. By default, the `:dets.open_file/2` function creates a file with the table name if it doesn't exist yet. The next time we start a DETS-based `FlexibleSearchCacheWorker` process, it will read from the file instead of creating a table from scratch.

 Recall that `ElixirDrip.Storage.Workers.FlexibleSearchCacheWorker` is actually a module alias that gets expanded to an atom (for example, `:"Elixir.ElixirDrip.Storage.Workers.FlexibleSearch CacheWorker"`). Likewise, all Erlang modules are represented as atoms. This is the reason why we use `:ets.new(...)` to call the `new/2` function of the `:ets` module and also why we can call functions like `storage.lookup(...)`.

Let's now see the changes we had to do for `FlexibleSearchCacheWorker` so that it also has a `search_result_for/2` function. Previously, instead of using a `GenServer.call/2`, we were directly doing a `lookup` on `SearchCacheWorker.search_result_for/2`. Here, we are using the `GenServer` approach because we need the `storage` value from the process state in order to know which Erlang module will handle our function call. The rest stays the same. This is only possible because the `:ets` and `:dets` APIs are interchangeable:

```
$ cat apps/elixir_drip/lib/elixir_drip/storage/workers/
flexible_search_cache_worker.ex
defmodule ElixirDrip.Storage.Workers.FlexibleSearchCacheWorker do
  # ...
  def search_result_for(media_id, search_expression) do
    GenServer.call(__MODULE__, {:search_result_for, media_id,
    search_expression})
```

```
    end

    def handle_call({:search_result_for, media_id, search_expression},
    _from, {storage, search_cache}) do
      result = case storage.lookup(search_cache, {media_id,
      search_expression}) do
        [] ->
          nil
        [{_key, {_created_at, search_result}}] ->
          search_result
      end

      {:reply, {:ok, result}, {storage, search_cache}}
    end
  end
```

All of the remaining `FlexibleSearchCacheWorker` functions will be implemented in the same way: using the atom stored on the `storage` variable instead of explicitly using `:ets` and converting each `SearchCacheWorker` function to a normal `GenServer.call/2` with the respective `handle_call/3` callback so that we can access the storage value in the first place.

 We won't analyze all the `SearchCacheWorker` functions here, but you can check the full implementation of the `FlexibleSearchCacheWorker` module on the ElixirDrip source code.

Since we created a file during initialization, we should be good citizens and close the file when the process exits. To do that, we will implement the `terminate/2` callback:

```
$ cat apps/elixir_drip/lib/elixir_drip/storage/workers/
flexible_search_cache_worker.ex
defmodule ElixirDrip.Storage.Workers.FlexibleSearchCacheWorker do
  # ...
  def terminate(reason, {storage, search_cache}) do
    Logger.debug("#{inspect(self())}: FlexibleSearchCacheWorker
    using #{storage} ending due to #{reason}.")

    case storage do
      :dets ->
        storage.close(search_cache)
      _ ->
        :noop
    end
  end
end
```

We pattern match on the `storage` value and only do something if the process was using a `:dets` table for storage. This callback won't be called if the process ends abruptly (for example, it receives a `:brutal_kill` from the supervisor or an exit signal other than `:normal`), thus, in some cases the DETS table may not be closed. If this happens, the next time the table is opened, it will be repaired by `:dets`. This reparation process is a costly operation and can take a while to repair large tables, so it's always better to properly close the table.

With the `FlexibleSearchCacheWorker`, we can now quickly change from an in-memory ETS table to a disk-based version of it, and vice-versa. This flexibility was only possible because the `:ets` and `:dets` modules have the same contract for most of the commonly used functions.

The next level of data storage provided by Erlang is Mnesia. We won't talk about it in this book, but you should know it gives you an abstraction closer to what one expects from a database, including a nicer query language and atomic transactions. It can be transparently replicated through different nodes, allowing you to query data without knowing where the data actually lives. It can also be persisted both in memory and in disk. Think of it as the child prodigy of the ETS and DETS modules (it is actually backed by them).

We will now end our ETS and DETS analysis and dive into the amazing world of process registers. Without them, we would have to know the PIDs of all the processes our applications spawn, and life would be much harder.

Registry

When we started our `GenServer`-based `CacheWorker`, you may recall that we used `{:global, {:cache, <media_id>}}` as the value for the `:name` option so that we could use the `{:cache, <media_id>}` tuple as its name. Behind the scenes, our cache processes were being registered using the `:global` Erlang module, which is started with every running application and serves as a single distributed process register when we have more than one node connected. At this stage, we are still running a single node, thus, as far as we can tell, we could be using `Registry`, an Elixir process register introduced in version 1.4.

A process register lets us associate a name to a given process. Let's query the `:global` registry after spawning two cache workers:

```
iex> alias ElixirDrip.Storage.Supervisors.CacheSupervisor, as: Cache
ElixirDrip.Storage.Supervisors.CacheSupervisor

iex> Cache.put("5", "something")
```

```
{:ok, #PID<0.685.0>}

iex> Cache.put("7", "something else")
{:ok, #PID<0.687.0>}

iex> :global.registered_names()
[{:cache, "5"}, {:cache, "7"}]
```

Since a register monitors the registered PIDs, when a registered process exits, the register updates its state accordingly. Let's terminate the {:cache, "5"} process and see what happens:

```
iex> :global.registered_names()
[{:cache, "5"}, {:cache, "7"}]

iex> cache5 = :global.whereis_name({:cache, "5"})
#PID<0.685.0>

iex> Process.exit(cache5, :some_reason)
true

iex> Process.alive?(cache5)
false

iex> :global.registered_names()
[{:cache, "7"}]

iex> :global.whereis_name({:cache, "5"})
:undefined
```

If we want to replace the use of :global by Registry for the CacheWorker processes, we would have to start a named registry instance, let's call it ElixirDrip.Registry, and then we would have to change the {:global, {:cache, <media_id>}} to {:via, Registry, {ElixirDrip.Registry, {:cache, <media_id>}}}. This :via tuple informs the GenServer.start_link/3 function how it should register the soon-to-be spawned process. In our case, it should register the process PID on an existing process named ElixirDrip.Registry, using the Registry module, which implements the register_name/2 function.

 Process registers should implement four functions, register_name/2, unregister_name/1, whereis_name/1, and send/2, in fact mimicking what the :global Erlang module does. All of this (and much more) can be found in the Erlang documentation (http://erlang.org/doc/man/gen_server.html#start_link-3).

Let's commence by starting the `ElixirDrip.Registry` as a worker under our main supervision tree, during our application's initialization:

```
$ cat apps/elixir_drip/lib/elixir_drip/application.ex
defmodule ElixirDrip.Application do
  use Application

  def start(_type, _args) do
    import Supervisor.Spec, warn: false

    Supervisor.start_link(
      [
        supervisor(ElixirDrip.Repo, []),
        supervisor(CacheSupervisor, [], name: CacheSupervisor),
        worker(Registry, [[keys: :unique, name: ElixirDrip.Registry]])
      ],
      strategy: :one_for_one,
      name: ElixirDrip.Supervisor
    )
  end
end
```

We now just need to change how we are generating the name for each `CacheWorker`. As we stated previously, the only difference is that we now return a `:via` tuple, instead of the previous `:global` tuple:

```
$ cat apps/elixir_drip/lib/elixir_drip/storage/workers/cache_worker.ex
defmodule ElixirDrip.Storage.Workers.CacheWorker do
  use GenServer
  # ...
  def start_link(media_id, content) do
    GenServer.start_link(__MODULE__, content, name: name_for(media_id))
  end

  def name_for(media_id), do: {:via, Registry, {ElixirDrip.Registry,
  {:cache, media_id}}}
  # ...
end
```

We can now interact with the `ElixirDrip.Registry` and every `CacheWorker` that was spawned will be registered on it. When we use `CacheSupervisor.put/2`, a `CacheWorker` is spawned and registered under the name returned by the `CacheWorker.name_for/1` function. If we try to spawn a process with the same name, we get an `:already_started` error tuple:

```
iex> alias ElixirDrip.Storage.Supervisors.CacheSupervisor
ElixirDrip.Storage.Supervisors.CacheSupervisor
```

```
iex> alias ElixirDrip.Storage.Workers.CacheWorker
ElixirDrip.Storage.Workers.CacheWorker

iex> CacheSupervisor.put("3", "2 + 2 is four, minus 1 is three.")
{:ok, #PID<0.452.0>}

iex> CacheSupervisor.put("3", "2 + 2 is four, minus 1 is three.")
{:error, {:already_started, #PID<0.452.0>}}

iex> Registry.lookup(ElixirDrip.Registry, {:cache, "3"})
[{#PID<0.452.0>, nil}]

iex> Registry.lookup(ElixirDrip.Registry, :nonexistent)
[]

iex> Registry.whereis_name({ElixirDrip.Registry, {:cache, "3"}})
#PID<0.452.0>

iex> name = CacheWorker.name_for("3")
{:via, Registry, {ElixirDrip.Registry, {:cache, "3"}}}

iex> pid = GenServer.whereis(name)
#PID<0.452.0>

iex> GenServer.call(pid, :get_media)
{:ok, "2 + 2 is four, minus 1 is three."}
```

In the preceding example, we obtained the PID using the `Registry.lookup/2`, the `Registry.whereis_name/1`, and finally the `GenServer.whereis/1`. In the first case, we pass the running registry (`ElixirDrip.Registry`) and the `{:cache, "3"}` key, and we use the specific `Registry` API to retrieve the PID.

We use the `whereis_name/1` callback in the second case. A module that wants to provide process registration using `:via` tuples needs to implement this callback and mimic its `:global` counterpart. Since it only receives one argument, the name of the running registry is passed as the first element of the name tuple. The value we pass to this callback matches the third element of the `:via` tuple.

In the last case, we use `GenServer.whereis/1`, which knows how to handle a `:via` tuple. As such, we can pass it the return value of `CacheWorker.name_for/1` and it will return us the PID of the respective `CacheWorker` process.

If you start an IEx shell and try to *Tab*-complete `Registry.`, you won't see the `register_name/2`, `unregister_name/1`, `whereis_name/1`, and `send/2` functions. You should find this weird; after all, the processes are being registered through those functions since we are using a `:via` tuple, even if it's a fancy one backed by Elixir `Registry`. The trick here is that those four functions are annotated with `@doc false`, and therefore they don't show up when you try to *Tab*-complete inside an IEx shell. You can confirm this yourself by checking the `Registry` source code at `https://github.com/elixir-lang/registry/blob/master/lib/registry.ex`.

If we wanted to implement our own process register, say, `ElixirDrip.ProcessRegister`, we could use a `GenServer` which keeps a map as state, using the name passed on each `register_name/2` call as keys. We would then need to start this `ProcessRegister` when our application starts and change the `CacheWorker.name_for/1` function to return `{:via, ElixirDrip.ProcessRegister, {:cache, <media_id>}}`. These changes would be enough to have our own process register up and running. You can find a possible implementation of this `ElixirDrip.ProcessRegister` on `./apps/elixir_drip/lib/elixir_drip/process_register.ex`.

We just saw how we can use a process register to manage process names instead of having to always use PIDs. Now, consider the following situation: if the register didn't monitor the processes it contains and it was just a plain map of names to PIDs, we could end up with registered PIDs for processes that already ended, and our register would need to be manually updated for each registered process that dies. Process registers overcome this situation by calling `Process.monitor/1` during process registration and implementing a `handle_info/2` callback to act upon the arrival of `:DOWN` tuples. This way, the register is informed whenever one of the registered processes dies and as such it can safely remove the corresponding entry from its internal state.

After this incursion into process registration and `:via` tuples, we will end this section, still using the `:global` tuples for our `CacheWorker` processes. Since we are only running a single Erlang node for now, using the global register or a local one (for example, `Registry`) feels like a minor decision. Nonetheless, this will be critical for our cache hit rate when we start more than one node for our `ElixirDrip` application.

Let's analyze what would happen if we had two running nodes connected to each other, both doing local process registration. In this case, each node can't possibly know which processes were spawned on the other one. If a request for media `"1"` arrives to the first node and no process exists with the name `{:cache, "1"}`, it will fetch the media contents and then spawn a new `CacheWorker` with that name. In this scenario with multiple nodes, our nodes live behind a load balancer and thus the same request could be routed to different nodes. If another request arrives for media `"1"` and it is routed to the other node, the node won't find any process named `{:cache, "1"}` (because we are doing local process registration) and will need to fetch the media contents again, not taking advantage of the warm cache on the other node.

To leverage the warm cache in the previous situation, we would only need to change the `CacheWorker.name_for/1` to return the `{:global, {:cache, <media_id>}}` tuple; everything else would stay the same. By globally registering the spawned `CacheWorker` processes, the node handling the second request for media `"1"` would be able to find a remote process named `{:cache, "1"}` living on the other node and would then dispatch the request to it. With the nodes connected and doing process registration with the `:global` module, we are sure the cached media only lives in a single node. Every request for media, independently of the node handling it, will be routed to the correct node if a `CacheWorker` process for that media already exists. We put a distributed cache on top of several nodes purely by changing the way we register a process. Pretty impressive, if you ask us.

Summary

In this chapter, we applied different OTP constructs to our ElixirDrip application and we are now able to tackle a broader array of problems armed with this new set of tools. These tools are not fully-fledged solutions or frameworks, but rather tools that help you build your applications, not getting in the way. Elixir also sports the mantra of *providing tools, not solutions*, an expression coined by Robert Virding, one of the creators of Erlang.

This chapter highlighted some of the great tools Elixir puts at your disposal. A lot has been said, and many different concepts were introduced:

- We started by implementing a `GenServer`-based cache worker to keep the most recent media in memory for faster access. To keep the memory usage in check, we decided to expire the cache process after a while, and we achieved this by sending a delayed `:expire` message to the process.

- We also analyzed the simpler, `GenServer`-based, `Agent` abstraction, for those cases when we just need to spawn a process to store state for us.

- With the `Task` module, we analyzed how multiple processors could be put to good use by running asynchronous tasks. Based on our comprehension of how tasks work, we implemented a `Search` module capable of searching through text files living on our cache. The first iteration of the search function worked sequentially, but by the end of this section, we had a robust parallel search returning all the available search results, even if some of those parallel tasks may have timed out.

- Later, we checked how the Erlang Term Storage and its disk-based counterpart provide a flexible key-value storage, letting us store, manage, and query arbitrary data through the `:ets` and `:dets` set of functions. We used many of these functions while building the `SearchCacheWorker`, a module responsible for caching the text search results.

- We ended this chapter by inspecting what happens when we register a process under a name. We analyzed the `:global` process register and we looked at `Registry`, an Elixir module introduced in version 1.4 that also performs process registration. We concluded by examining the motive behind our usage of global process registration and how we will leverage it to improve our cache hit rate.

In the next chapter, we will define a demand-driven media pipeline to handle all of our download and upload requests. You will see how easy it is to process events in different stages, without being worried that one of the stages could bring your pipeline to a halt.

Demand-Driven Processing

5

We have already seen how Elixir is especially suited to spawning million of processes. This capability lets the developer easily run simultaneous execution flows, only capped by the number of available processors on the machine.

Nevertheless, all this power may not be sufficient if a huge amount of data continuously flows to your application. If you don't process it fast enough, the message boxes of your processes will start to pile up and eventually use all your memory, bringing your application to a halt.

In this chapter we'll analyze how Elixir tackles this problem by controlling the rate at which data is processed with the recently introduced `GenStage` behaviour. Later on, we'll apply this behaviour to the ElixirDrip application to define the steps performed for each download and upload operation.

In the end, we will see how the `Flow` module sits on top of GenStage to provide its processing prowess in a streamlined fashion, with a set of functions comparable to what we expect to find on the `Enum` and `Stream` modules.

In this chapter, we will cover the following topics:

- GenStage and how it enables you to process data in a demand-driven way
- Implementing a download and upload pipeline with GenStage
- Using Flow to create a composable and lazy query

GenStage

GenStage is an Elixir behaviour that was in the making for a while. The plan was to include it in the Elixir standard library but it grew sufficiently enough to justify its own `:gen_stage` library.

Elixir lets you lazily process collections with the `Stream` module, and we previously saw how we can process a collection in parallel by spawning tasks for each element in the collection. However, if the process through which we are passing our collection has many steps, the usage of `Task.async_stream` isn't the best solution because, for each step, it will wait for all tasks to return or time out, before calling the next wave of `Task.async_stream`.

What we want is something that can spawn the needed processes to consume the collection in parallel, but without the need to synchronize at the end of each step. And since we are considering multiple steps, it's plausible that one of the steps will be slower. In this scenario, the processes performing this step will inevitably become the bottleneck of the whole *assembly line*. And if the data we are processing is big enough, we can jam our production line by filling up the mailboxes of the processes trying to cope with the data influx.

What the `GenStage` abstraction gives us is an elegant way to tackle this problem, by looking at it in a different way. Instead of each step working in isolation by simply executing its task and then passing the results to the next step, `GenStage` introduces a way for later steps to signal to the previous ones that they are ready to receive more input. This way, we are sure each step only processes what it is capable of, and no more. This strategy is called back-pressure and lets us churn through our input data as fast as possible without halting the *assembly line*. Instead of being controlled by the data producers, the rate at which data is processed is controlled by those who process it, thus the data processing is demand-driven.

Each step of our `GenStage` pipeline will be a `Producer`, `Consumer`, or `ProducerConsumer` process. These processes will communicate among themselves through message passing; in `GenStage` lingo, those messages are called `events`. The last step of your pipeline will be `Consumer`, characterized by only consuming `events` that arrive to it from the pipeline. Since there are no more stages after the `Consumer` stage, a `Consumer` process will never receive demand from a later stage.

In the beginning of any `GenStage` pipeline, we have a `Producer` process: the only responsibility of these processes is to handle demand from downstream processes, by introducing new events in the pipeline. Any `Producer` has to comply with the received demand, never producing more events than the current demand. This is the crucial aspect that allows `GenStage` to transform a lot of events in different phases, without ever halting the whole process.

A `GenStage` pipeline will have a `Producer` and a `Consumer` stage. If we want to have one or more intermediate stages, these will have to simultaneously consume events from upstream and push events downstream, such as a `Producer` and a `Consumer`, at the same time. These intermediate stages are `ProducerConsumer` stages that know how to handle a demand from later stages and how to send demands upstream:

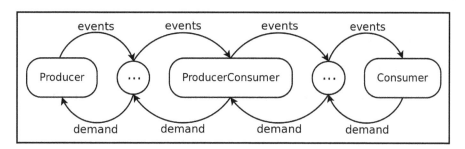

We are talking about an Elixir behaviour; hence creating the stages for the pipeline will be as simple as adding `use GenStage` and then implementing the appropriate function callbacks. Every `ProducerConsumer` and `Consumer` will need to subscribe to the previous `GenStage` process so it can receive events from the upstream. These subscription options dictate how a stage listens for events from a previous process and are usually passed during process initialization.

> You can also start stages in isolation (for example, `GenStage.start_link/3`) and only create the subscriptions afterward with `GenStage.sync_subscribe/2`. However, we will subscribe our stages on their `init/1` callbacks to ensure a stage always starts with a valid subscription, even if it crashed previously and was restarted by its supervisor.

`Consumer` will have to return a `{:consumer, state, subscription_options}` tuple on `init/1`, whereas `ProducerConsumer` will return a similar tuple but with `:producer_consumer` on the first element. As you may have guessed, given that `Producer` doesn't receive events from anyone, it doesn't need subscription options. Its `init/1` callback simply returns a `{:producer, state}` tuple.

The `:subscribe_to` option passed during the initialization of a `Consumer` or `ProducerConsumer` stage should point to the `GenStage` process we are subscribing to, and the `:min_demand` and `:max_demand` options will respectively define the minimum and maximum number of events passing through that pipeline stage.

You can observe an example of subscription options for a hypothetical Shipping stage in the following code snippet. This stage will subscribe to the Packaging stage and it will demand at most 10 events from the previous stage. This means that at any given time there will be no more than 10 events passing through this stage:

```
defmodule Shipping do
  use GenStage
  # ...
  @dummy_state []

  def start_link() do
    subscription_options = [
      subscribe_to: [{Packaging, min_demand: 3, max_demand: 10}]
    ]

    GenStage.start_link(__MODULE__, subscription_options, name:
    __MODULE__)
  end

  def init(subscription_options),
    do: {:consumer, @dummy_state, subscription_options}

  def handle_events(tasks, _from, _state) do
    Enum.each(tasks, &perform_step(&1))

    {:noreply, [], @dummy_state}
  end
end
```

Let's analyze how the Shipping stage demand would be managed in a GenStage pipeline:

- The :min_demand option defines the threshold that triggers a new demand. When it starts, the Shipping stage asks for 10 events (corresponding to the :max_demand value), since it doesn't have any events to process.
- The Packaging stage only had five events to send, thus the Shipping stage will only receive five events to process. Since the :min_demand threshold is three, the Shipping stage will wait for two more events to arrive before it demands more events from upstream.
- When those two events arrive, the Shipping stage has received seven events from the 10 it initially asked for and therefore reaches its :min_demand threshold of three. At this point, it will ask for seven more events, hence waiting for the :max_demand number of events again.

The `GenStage` behaviour builds up from `GenServer`, meaning you can also use the `handle_call/3` and `handle_cast/2` callbacks from it. However, these two callbacks let you emit events by returning `{:reply, reply, [events], new_state}` and `{:noreply, [event], new_state}`, respectively (notice the `[events]` element). You can think of a `GenStage` process as a customized `GenServer` process that also knows how to `handle_events/3` (in the case of `Consumer` or `ProducerConsumer`) or `handle_demand/2` (in the case of `Producer`).

Any `Consumer` stage will also have to implement the `handle_events/3` callback, through which it receives the events it needs to process. In the end, it needs to return a `{:noreply, [], state}` tuple, where the second element is the events to emit, and the last one the new state of the `GenStage` process. Since we are considering a `Consumer` stage, the second element will always be an empty list, since by definition a `Consumer` stage doesn't emit events.

A `ProducerConsumer` stage will also have to implement the same `handle_events/3` callback, but in contrast, it will need to emit new events. To emit events, this stage needs to return a similar `{:noreply, events, state}` tuple, where the `events` element contains the events to be passed downstream.

We just observed how we can start the `Consumer` and `ProducerConsumer` stages by passing their subscription options during initialization. A `Producer` stage is simpler to start in the sense that it doesn't subscribe to any previous stage. The `init/1` function of a `Producer` stage only needs to return a `{:producer, state}` tuple. Then, it needs to implement a different callback, `handle_demand/2`, so that it can react to new demands by producing new events, effectively starting the pipeline whenever it passes events downstream.

Our ElixirDrip application will have two pipelines composed of several steps. A file upload from our users will start a sequence of steps responsible for encrypting the file, storing it on the cloud, and finally, notifying the user that the upload was successfully completed. In the opposite direction, when the user clicks to download a file, a download process will commence, fetching the file from the cloud, decrypting it, and then finally notifying the user.

Let's start by thoroughly analyzing how the upload flow works.

The upload pipeline

Instead of manually starting each stage of our GenStage pipelines, we will be supervising the upload and download pipelines under a supervision tree. Each pipeline supervisor is responsible for starting and monitoring its child processes as usual, but in this case, it will also pass the subscription options to each stage it starts.

Each stage will be registered with a name, so that we can subscribe to stages by using the name of the stage it should receive events from. Given that, we will have stages used on both upload and download pipelines, we need a way to generate unique names for a stage based on the pipeline it belongs to. The following Common.stage_name/2 function receives a GenStage module and the pipeline direction (an :upload or :download atom) and returns a valid stage name. As an example, if we pass to it the ElixirDrip.Storage.Pipeline.Notifier and :upload arguments, it will return ElixirDrip.Storage.Pipeline.Notifier.Upload:

```
$ cat apps/elixir_drip/lib/elixir_drip/storage/pipeline/common.ex
defmodule ElixirDrip.Storage.Pipeline.Common do
  def stage_name(stage, direction) do
    direction = direction |> Atom.to_string() |> String.capitalize()

    Module.concat(stage, direction)
  end
end
```

The upload pipeline will be composed of four stages, Starter, Encryption, RemoteStorage, and Notifier, subscribed to each other. Our Notifier module will be the Consumer stage, we will have two ProducerConsumer stages, and the Starter module will be our Producer stage, responsible for introducing new events in the pipeline. Each stage is a worker to which we pass initialization arguments as usual. We will pass to every stage the name it should use and its subscription options. Since the Starter stage is our Producer, instead of subscription options it will receive the direction of the pipeline, allowing it to decide from which queue it should pull events:

```
$ cat apps/elixir_drip/lib/elixir_drip/storage/supervisors/
upload_pipeline_supervisor.ex
defmodule ElixirDrip.Storage.Supervisors.Upload.Pipeline do
  use Supervisor
  alias ElixirDrip.Storage.Pipeline.{
    Common,
    Starter,
    Encryption,
    RemoteStorage,
    Notifier
```

```
  }

  @direction :upload
  @starter_name Common.stage_name(Starter, @direction)
  @encryption_name Common.stage_name(Encryption, @direction)
  @storage_name Common.stage_name(RemoteStorage, @direction)
  @notifier_name Common.stage_name(Notifier, @direction)

  def start_link(),
    do: Supervisor.start_link(__MODULE__, [], name: __MODULE__)

  def init(_) do
    # defining the subscription options for each stage
    encryption_subscription = [subscribe_to: [{@starter_name,
    min_demand: 1, max_demand: 10}]]
    remote_storage_subscription = [subscribe_to: [{@encryption_name,
    min_demand: 1, max_demand: 10}]]
    notifier_subscription = [subscribe_to: [{@storage_name,
    min_demand: 1, max_demand: 10}]]

    # starting each stage as a worker
    # supervised by the current Supervisor module
    Supervisor.init([
      worker(Starter, [@starter_name, @direction], restart:
      :permanent),
      worker(Encryption, [@encryption_name, encryption_subscription],
      restart: :permanent),
      worker(RemoteStorage, [@storage_name,
      remote_storage_subscription], restart: :permanent),
      worker(Notifier, [@notifier_name, notifier_subscription],
      restart: :permanent)
    ],
    strategy: :rest_for_one,
    name: __MODULE__
    )
  end
end
```

Notice that we are using a generic supervisor, even if the child processes are GenStage processes, and this time we chose a :rest_for_one supervision strategy. This way we are sure that if, for example, a Starter process terminates unexpectedly, the supervisor will terminate all the other pipeline processes, given that they will now have nothing to consume. We are also defining the :restart option as :permanent, to ensure the pipeline supervisor always restarts its child processes (this is the default value of the child specification generated by GenStage).

The notifier stage

Let's now analyze our ElixirDrip upload stages by starting from the very end with our `Notifier` stage. As we just saw, when the pipeline-supervision tree starts, it passes a name and the subscription options to each stage. In this case, we start the process as a consumer with no relevant state:

```
$ cat apps/elixir_drip/lib/elixir_drip/storage/pipeline/notifier.ex
defmodule ElixirDrip.Storage.Pipeline.Notifier do
  use GenStage
  require Logger

  @dummy_state []

  def start_link(name, subscription_options),
    do: GenStage.start_link(__MODULE__, subscription_options, name: name)

  def init(subscription_options),
    do: {:consumer, @dummy_state, subscription_options}

  # implementing the GenStage.handle_events/3 callback
  # we delegate the event processing to the notify_step/1 function
  def handle_events(tasks, _from, _state) do
    Enum.each(tasks, &notify_step(&1))

    {:noreply, [], @dummy_state}
  end

  defp notify_step(%{media: media, content: content, type:
:upload}) do
    # Invoke the notifier instead!

    Logger.debug("#{inspect(self())}: NOTIFICATION! Uploaded
    media #{media.id} to #{media.storage_key} with size: #
    {byte_size(content)} bytes.")
  end
end
```

Since the `Notifier` module is a consumer, we had to implement the `handle_events/3` callback. This callback will be called whenever there are events for it to process. In our case, we will iterate over the received `tasks` using the `notify_step/1` function, responsible for sending a notification to the relevant users. We are returning an empty list as the second element of our callback return value because a consumer, by definition, doesn't emit events.

Each event processed by the `Notifier` stage is a map containing the `media` (the structure holding the information about all media stored in ElixirDrip), the actual media `content`, and the `type` of the event. As you can see, we are explicitly pattern-matching the `type` field of the map with the `:upload` value, to ensure this `notify_step/1` only processes `:upload` events.

The RemoteStorage stage

The `Notifier` stage will receive events emitted by the previous `RemoteStorage` stage. The only responsibility of the `RemoteStorage` stage is to store the content of each event it receives on the cloud. After a successful upload, it just stores the upload timestamp and updates the media structure. For each upload event it receives and executes, it will emit an event downstream.

We don't need to keep state on this stage as well, so we simply return a `{:producer_consumer, _, subscription_options}` tuple after initialization. Each event passes through the `remote_storage_step/1` function. This function relies on the `Storage.Provider.upload/2` function to upload the contents to the cloud with the specific media `storage_key` and uses the `Storage.set_upload_timestamp/1` function to update the upload timestamp:

```
$ cat apps/elixir_drip/lib/elixir_drip/storage/pipeline/
remote_storage.ex
defmodule ElixirDrip.Storage.Pipeline.RemoteStorage do
  use GenStage
  require Logger
  alias ElixirDrip.Storage
  alias Storage.Provider
  alias Storage.Supervisors.CacheSupervisor, as: Cache

  @dummy_state []

  def start_link(name, subscription_options),
    do: GenStage.start_link(__MODULE__, subscription_options,
    name: name)

  def init(subscription_options),
    do: {:producer_consumer, @dummy_state, subscription_options}
  # implementing the GenStage.handle_events/3 callback
  # we delegate the event processing to the remote_storage_step
  /1 function
  def handle_events(tasks, _from, _state) do
    processed = Enum.map(tasks, &remote_storage_step(&1))
```

```
      {:noreply, processed, @dummy_state}
    end

  defp remote_storage_step(%{media: %{id: id, storage_key:
  storage_key} = media, content: content, type: :upload} =
  task) do
    Process.sleep(2000)

    Logger.debug("#{inspect(self())}: Uploading media #{id} to
    #{storage_key}, size: #{byte_size(content)} bytes.")

    {:ok, :uploaded} = Provider.upload(storage_key, content)

    %{task | media: Storage.set_upload_timestamp(media)}
  end
end
```

Each file stored in ElixirDrip is encrypted before being uploaded to the cloud. Let's now check the `Encryption` stage that precedes the `RemoteStorage` stage we have just analyzed.

The Encryption stage

The `Encryption` module of the upload pipeline is also a `ProducerConsumer` stage, therefore it will implement the `handle_events/3` callback as well. Similar to the previous stage, it doesn't keep state and transforms each event it receives using its own `encryption_step/1` function:

```
$ cat apps/elixir_drip/lib/elixir_drip/storage/pipeline/encryption.ex
defmodule ElixirDrip.Storage.Pipeline.Encryption do
  @dummy_state []

  use GenStage
  require Logger
  alias ElixirDrip.Storage.Providers.Encryption.Simple, as: Provider
  alias ElixirDrip.Storage.Supervisors.CacheSupervisor, as: Cache

  def start_link(name, subscription_options),
    do: GenStage.start_link(__MODULE__, subscription_options, name: name)

  def init(subscription_options),
    do: {:producer_consumer, @dummy_state, subscription_options}

  # implementing the GenStage.handle_events/3 callback
  # we delegate the event processing to the encryption_step/1 function
  def handle_events(tasks, _from, _state) do
```

```
    encrypted = Enum.map(tasks, &encryption_step(&1))

    {:noreply, encrypted, @dummy_state}
  end

  defp encryption_step(%{media: %{id: id, encryption_key:
  encryption_key},
  content: content, type: :upload} = task) do
    Process.sleep(1000)

    Cache.put(id, content)

    %{task | content: Provider.encrypt(content, encryption_key)}
  end
end
```

However, this `encryption_step/1` function does more than its `RemoteStorage.remote_storage_step/1` counterpart. Before actually encrypting the media contents, this stage caches the clear contents by spawning a `CacheWorker` process with the `Cache.put/2` call. Without getting into too much detail, this will allow us to short-circuit a download pipeline if the media being downloaded is already present in memory. If we try to download media that was uploaded seconds before, the response will be much faster since no decryption will have to take place. The downside of this strategy is the additional memory that `CacheWorker` uses to keep the media contents in memory for a while.

Let's now look at the `Starter` stage, which, as its name hints, is the one that actually triggers the whole `Upload` pipeline.

The Starter stage

We've finally reached the first stage of this upload pipeline walk-through. As an event producer, our `Starter` stage will implement the `handle_demand/2` callback instead of the `handle_events/3` we've implemented so far for our `Consumer` and `ProducerConsumer` stages. This will also be the only stage that will keep state. As a `Producer` stage, the `Starter` stage needs to know at all times the queue from which it fetches new upload tasks and the outstanding demand it received and it has not yet fulfilled. Accordingly, its `init/1` callback will return a `{:producer, state}` tuple where the `state` contains the queue, the type of events this `Starter` stage will create, and the pending demand.

The call to `QueueWorker.queue_name/1` with `:upload` will return the `QueueWorker` process name that contains the upload queue, similar to how we used the `Pipeline.Common.stage_name/1` function to generate the process names for each stage of the pipeline.

The `Encryption` stage we just saw subscribes to the `Starter` stage. Demand is sent upstream when the `Encryption` stage starts, and consequently the `Starter` stage receives demand through the `handle_demand/2` callback. The first argument passed to the callback is an integer corresponding to the number of events the subscriber is able to receive, whereas the other argument is the process state.

Every time a new demand arrives, the `Starter` stage tries to produce as many events as possible to fulfill the total demand, since it considers not only the new demand it got but also the pending demands it had from previous calls. It then tries to pop up the required number of events from the queue, emitting all of those to start the upload process. If the events fetched from the queue aren't enough to fulfill the total demand, we keep the outstanding demand on the process state:

```
$ cat apps/elixir_drip/lib/elixir_drip/storage/pipeline/starter.ex
defmodule ElixirDrip.Storage.Pipeline.Starter do
  use GenStage
  require Logger
  alias ElixirDrip.Storage.Workers.QueueWorker

  @queue_polling 5000

  def start_link(name, type),
    do: GenStage.start_link(__MODULE__, type, name: name)

  def init(type) do
    {
      :producer,
      %{queue: QueueWorker.queue_name(type), type: type, pending: 0}
    }
  end

  # implementing the GenServer.handle_info/2 callback
  # to check if there are more events in the queue to fulfill
  pending demand
  def handle_info(:try_again, %{queue: queue, pending: demand} = state),
    do: send_events_from_queue(queue, demand, state)

  # implementing the GenStage.handle_demand/2 callback
  # we end up using the send_events_from_queue/1 function
  # to respond to the received demand
  def handle_demand(demand, %{queue: queue, pending: pending} = state)
```

```
  when demand > 0 do
    total_demand = demand + pending

    send_events_from_queue(queue, total_demand, state)
  end

  defp send_events_from_queue(queue, how_many, %{type: type} = state) do
    tasks = queue
            |> QueueWorker.dequeue(how_many)
            |> Enum.map(&Map.put(&1, :type, type))

    if length(tasks) < how_many do
      Process.send_after(self(), :try_again, @queue_polling)
    end

    {:noreply, tasks, %{state | pending: how_many - length(tasks)}}
  end
end
```

You may have noticed that we also implemented a `handle_info/2` callback to react to a `:try_again` message. When this message arrives, the process will try again to fulfill its pending demand. We are sending that message using the `Process.send_after/3` function in the `send_events_from_queue/3` function, after checking whether the events we got from the queue are enough to satisfy the current demand. Why is this needed?

If we didn't have this polling strategy in place, our `Starter` producer would never fulfill the pending demand on its own. Consider the following `NaiveStarter` module, similar to the `Starter` module except that it doesn't send any `:try_again` messages to itself:

```
defmodule Pipeline.NaiveStarter do
  # ...
  defp send_events_from_queue(queue, how_many, %{type: type} = state) do
    tasks = queue
            |> QueueWorker.dequeue(how_many)
            |> Enum.map(&Map.put(&1, :type, type))

    # Don't send any :try_again message
    # if length(tasks) < how_many do
    # Process.send_after(self(), :try_again, @queue_polling)
    # end

    {:noreply, tasks, %{state | pending: how_many - length(tasks)}}
  end
end
```

After initialization, the `Encryption` stage asks the `NaiveStarter` stage for 10 events and waits for new events. As a consequence, the `handle_demand/2` callback is called and the `NaiveStarter` producer tries to fetch events from the queue. Nonetheless, there were only four events available, so the `NaiveStarter` stage sends those four events downstream and updates its `pending` demand to six. The `Encryption` stage will then receive and process those four events. Given its `min_threshold` of three and the fact it only got four of the 10 events it previously asked for the `Encryption` stage won't send any new demands upstream. From the `NaiveStarter` stage perspective, things don't look good either: since it only reacts to new demands, it will never try to push new events to the queue if the `Encryption` stage doesn't ask for them. In this *deadlock* scenario, the `Encryption` stage will sit forever waiting for the remaining six events, and the `NaiveStarter` stage will sit forever waiting for new demand.

That is the reason why our `Starter` stage routinely checks whether the queue has enough events to fulfill the pending demand, and if there are any events, it immediately pushes them downstream. After all, if we registered the demand, we can be sure the subscriber is waiting for events. A corollary that follows is that subscribers only communicate their needs once, so your producers have to not only keep track of pending demands but also respond to them as soon as possible.

We will now perform the same walk-through for the download pipeline.

The download pipeline

Similar to the previous pipeline, the download pipeline is also composed by the same four stages: `Starter`, `RemoteStorage`, `Encryption`, and `Notifier`. However, this time the `Encryption` stage is performed after we obtain the actual encrypted contents stored on the cloud. This pipeline starts with a download request being enqueued. Then, the `Starter` stage fetches this request from the queue and produces an event from it, which will be processed by the `RemoteStorage` stage. This stage checks whether there is already a `CacheWorker` process for the requested media. If that's the case, it places the clear cached contents on the event and sets the event `status` to `:original`, informing the subsequent stages that the event already contains the *original* media contents. When the `:download` event reaches the `Encryption` stage, the content is only decrypted if the `:original` `status` isn't present on the event. In the end, the `Notifier` step tells the user that the media is now ready to be downloaded.

Compared to the upload pipeline supervisor, the download pipeline supervisor only differs on the subscription order between the different stages (now RemoteStorage stage is the second one instead of being the third) and the value of the @direction module attribute, which is now :download.

```
$ cat apps/elixir_drip/lib/elixir_drip/storage/supervisors/
download_pipeline_supervisor.ex
defmodule ElixirDrip.Storage.Supervisors.Download.Pipeline do
  use Supervisor
  # ...
  @direction :download
  # ...
  def init(_) do
    remote_storage_subscription = [subscribe_to: [{@starter_name,
    min_demand: 1, max_demand: 10}]]
    encryption_subscription = [subscribe_to: [{@storage_name,
    min_demand: 1, max_demand: 10}]]
    notifier_subscription = [subscribe_to: [{@encryption_name,
    min_demand: 1, max_demand: 10}]]

    Supervisor.init([
      # ...
    ],
    strategy: :rest_for_one,
    name: __MODULE__
    )
  end
end
```

Once more, let's start from the end of the download pipeline, by analyzing its consumer, the Notifier stage.

The Notifier stage

The Notifier stage of the download pipeline subscribes to the Encryption stage. This stage shares the same Notifier module that also serves the upload pipeline. The difference lies in the process alias given to the download Notifier process (ElixirDrip.Storage.Pipeline.Notifier.Download), and in the new implementation of the notify_step/1 function that now pattern-matches on the :download value for the event type key. Everything else remains untouched:

```
$ cat apps/elixir_drip/lib/elixir_drip/storage/pipeline/notifier.ex
defmodule ElixirDrip.Storage.Pipeline.Notifier do
  # ...
  def start_link(name, subscription_options),
```

```
        do: GenStage.start_link(__MODULE__, subscription_options, name: name)

    def init(subscription_options),
      do: {:consumer, @dummy_state, subscription_options}

    def handle_events(tasks, _from, _state) do
      Enum.each(tasks, &notify_step(&1))

      {:noreply, [], @dummy_state}
    end

    defp notify_step(%{media: %{id: id}, content: content, type:
    :download}) do
      # Invoke the notifier instead!

      Logger.debug("#{inspect(self())}: NOTIFICATION! Downloaded media
      #{id}, content: #{inspect(content)}, size: #{byte_size(content)}
      bytes.")
    end
  end
```

As you can see, the `notify_step/1` function, which handles download events, is currently identical to the one that handles upload events (the only thing that changes is the logged message). We are simply logging a message to the console using the `Logger.debug/1` function, but this will change once we actually implement the user notifications with Phoenix Channels.

Let's now check how the `Encryption` stage handles download events.

The Encryption stage

On the download pipeline, the `Encryption` stage subscribes to events coming from the `RemoteStorage` stage. Similarly to the `Notifier` stage, the function that handles download events for this stage lives side by side with the function that handles upload events.

This time, however, the `Encryption` module has two `encryption_step/1` functions to handle download events: one that pattern-matches on the `:original` value of the `status` event field and one that handles all the other download events, corresponding to those cases when the media contents are still encrypted:

```
$ cat apps/elixir_drip/lib/elixir_drip/storage/pipeline/encryption.ex
defmodule ElixirDrip.Storage.Pipeline.Encryption do
  # ...
  def start_link(name, subscription_options),
```

```
    do: GenStage.start_link(__MODULE__, subscription_options, name: name)

  def init(subscription_options),
    do: {:producer_consumer, @dummy_state, subscription_options}

  # the GenStage.handle_events/3 callback
  # delegates the processing of each event to another encryption_step
  /1 function
  # that pattern-matches on %{type: :download}
  def handle_events(tasks, _from, _state) do
    encrypted = Enum.map(tasks, &encryption_step(&1))

    {:noreply, encrypted, @dummy_state}
  end

  # the %{status: :original} indicates the content is ready to be
  delivered
  defp encryption_step(%{media: media, content: _content, status:
  :original, type: :download} = task),
    do: task

  # given there's no %{status: :original}, we need to decrypt the
  content
  defp encryption_step(%{media: %{id: id, encryption_key:
  encryption_key},
  content: content, type: :download} = task) do
    Process.sleep(1000)

    clear_content = Provider.decrypt(content, encryption_key)
    Cache.put(id, clear_content)

    %{task | content: clear_content}
  end
end
```

In the first case, the download event reaches the Encryption stage already with the original media contents (because the file was fetched from cache in a previous stage). As such, the encryption_step/1 function simply returns the same event it got. If the download event doesn't have the :original value on the status field, it means the media contents present on the event need to be decrypted with the media encryption_key before emitting a new event downstream. The media contents are cached after being decrypted to speed up further downloads.

The RemoteStorage stage

It's in the `remote_storage_step/1` function of the `RemoteStorage` stage that we try to find whether there is a `CacheWorker` for the media contained on the download event. This stage receives download events from the `Starter` event producer and emits events downstream with the media contents. If there was a `CacheWorker` for the media, the contents of the event emitted by this stage correspond to the media original contents, therefore, the event is *tagged* as `:original` using the `status` event field; if not, this stage simply fetches the media-encrypted contents from the cloud provider and passes them along:

```
$ cat apps/elixir_drip/lib/elixir_drip/storage/pipeline/
remote_storage.ex
defmodule ElixirDrip.Storage.Pipeline.RemoteStorage do
  # ...
  def start_link(name, subscription_options),
    do: GenStage.start_link(__MODULE__, subscription_options, name: name)

  def init(subscription_options),
    do: {:producer_consumer, @dummy_state, subscription_options}

  # the GenStage.handle_events/3 callback
  # delegates the processing of each event to another
  remote_storage_step/1 function
  # that pattern-matches on %{type: :download}
  def handle_events(tasks, _from, _state) do
    processed = Enum.map(tasks, &remote_storage_step(&1))

    {:noreply, processed, @dummy_state}
  end

  defp remote_storage_step(%{media: %{id: id, storage_key:
storage_key}, type: :download} = task) do
    Process.sleep(2000)

    result = case Cache.get(id) do
      nil ->
        {:ok, content} = Provider.download(storage_key)
        %{content: content}

      {:ok, content} ->
        %{content: content, status: :original}
    end

    Map.merge(task, result)
  end
end
```

Finally, let's observe how the `Starter` stage works for the download pipeline.

The Starter stage

When we previously analyzed how the `Starter` stage worked for the upload pipeline, we saw how we passed a `type` as an initialization parameter so that the upload `Starter` stage knew from which `QueueWorker` process it should fetch new upload requests. For the download `Starter` stage, the approach is exactly the same: we initialize the `Starter` process on the download pipeline supervisor with the `@starter_name` and `@direction` arguments, which in this case will have the `ElixirDrip.Storage.Pipeline.Starter.Download` and `:download` values. This will be enough for the `Starter` stage to commence producing events on the download pipeline:

```
iex> alias ElixirDrip.Storage.Pipeline.Common
ElixirDrip.Storage.Pipeline.Common

iex> alias ElixirDrip.Storage.Pipeline.Starter
ElixirDrip.Storage.Pipeline.Starter

iex> starter_name = Common.stage_name(Starter, :download)
ElixirDrip.Storage.Pipeline.Starter.Download

iex> starter_process = Process.whereis(starter_name)
#PID<0.426.0>

iex> Process.alive?(starter_process)
true
```

Since the logic for fetching new download requests from the `QueueWorker` process and injecting them on the download pipeline is exactly the same as the logic we already used on the upload pipeline, the implementation of the `send_events_from_queue/3` function used by the `Starter.handle_demand/2` and `Starter.handle_info/2` callbacks can be exactly the same. This function can serve both download and upload pipelines because, after retrieving the transfer request (be it an upload or download) from the queue, the call to `send_events_from_queue/3` also places the `type` entry on the event map:

```
$ cat apps/elixir_drip/lib/elixir_drip/storage/pipeline/starter.ex
defmodule ElixirDrip.Storage.Pipeline.Starter do
  # ...
  defp send_events_from_queue(queue, how_many, %{type: type} = state) do
    tasks = queue
            |> QueueWorker.dequeue(how_many)
            |> Enum.map(&Map.put(&1, :type, type))
```

```
    if length(tasks) < how_many do
      Process.send_after(self(), :try_again, @queue_polling)
    end

    {:noreply, tasks, %{state | pending: how_many - length(tasks)}}
  end
end
```

We covered a lot in this section about GenStage. However, there is still a bit more for us to do.

Final remarks

Despite being an impressive tool, `GenStage`, and its cousin `Flow`, are not silver bullets. By using these abstractions, one incurs some expense due to the initial setup. Remember that, under the hood, processes are being spawned and messages are being exchanged and potentially buffered. As such, consider whether you really need to apply `GenStage` or whether you simply want a multistep pipeline that processes events, without the need for a back-pressure mechanism. If it's parallel processing you're after, maybe the `Task.async_stream/1` we already talked about can do the job.

You can check the `:message_queue_len` entry of the `Process.info/1` result to know how many messages a process currently has in its mailbox. The following snippet shows the usage of `Process.info/1` with a process that simply waits forever:

```
iex> pid = spawn(fn -> Process.sleep(:infinity) end)
#PID<0.450.0>

iex> Process.info(pid)[:message_queue_len]
0

iex> Process.send(pid, :hi_there, [])
:ok

iex> Process.send(pid, :hows_the_weather, [])
:ok

iex> Process.info(pid)[:message_queue_len]
2

iex> Process.info(pid)
[
  current_function: {Process, :sleep, 1},
  initial_call: {:erlang, :apply, 2},
  status: :waiting,
```

```
    message_queue_len: 2,
    messages: [:hi_there, :hows_the_weather],
    # ...
]
```

In software engineering, we should avoid premature optimization. If you notice your processes getting slower and their message queues piling up, it is a sign that some of your processes aren't able to cope with the demand, and you may then consider GenStage to overcome the situation.

You should also avoid writing business logic on your `GenStage` modules. After all, their sole purpose is to control how events flow during runtime. Having your business-logic code on separate modules makes it easier for you to tinker with it, test it, and have a clear picture of what each step is doing. Applying `GenStage` is just a particular way of orchestrating how those steps will be performed.

Another aspect worth noting is that we started both GenStage pipelines with a single worker process per stage, thus we only spawned one process per step. This helped to illustrate how GenStage worked, but it doesn't mean you have to do the same. You can spawn multiple workers (that is, `Consumer` or `ProducerConsumers` stages) per step and then subscribe them all to one or more producers (that is, `Producer` or `ProducerConsumers` stages). This is the reason why the `:subscribe_to` option receives a list of tuples, each configuring a specific subscription. By adopting this approach, you can control how many parallel processes perform each step, allowing you to scale a particular stage that is becoming a bottleneck.

If you want to see an example of a GenStage pipeline with parallel steps, you can find one in the `examples/parallel_genstage` folder of our ElixirDrip umbrella project. It's being compiled with the `ElixirDrip` application, so to see it in action you just need to launch an IEx shell and run `ParallelGenStage.Supervisor.start_link`. You can also check the following chapter, where we implement a Domain-Specific Language to easily define new pipelines, with the option to define how many workers should be spawned for each stage.

We will now examine `Flow`, an Elixir library based on `GenStage` that allows us to easily process a collection in parallel.

Flow

Since the early days, Elixir has allowed us to easily process collections using the Enum and Stream modules. In the first case, the collection is traversed as soon as it reaches an Enum call, if we use the respective Stream function instead, we can delay the actual enumeration of the collection until the very last moment. This is why we say Stream functions are lazy and Enum functions are eager.

As a result, if we transform a collection by chaining Enum.map/2 calls, an intermediate collection will be created for each call to an Enum function. This behavior contrasts with the behavior we would get if we chained a bunch of Stream.map/2 calls. In the latter case, the entire collection would be traversed at most once, and only when the resulting stream reaches an Enum function (such as Enum.to_list/1), forcing each element of the stream to be evaluated.

The Enum and Stream modules provide an invaluable set of tools to work with collections, but do not leverage the Elixir capability to run multiple flows of execution in parallel. Before Flow was introduced, if someone wanted to process a collection in parallel, they would have had to implement the actual processing logic, spawn the needed processes responsible for executing it, and in the end define how to aggregate the results from those multiple flows of execution.

Flow was created to simplify this scenario. Instead of implementing parallel-processing the hard way, one can simply use a familiar set of functions, such as each/2, map/2, filter/2, or reduce/3, but provided by the Flow module instead. These functions are semantically equivalent to the functions with the same name that live on the Enum module, but with the parallel *factor* baked in.

Flow uses the same concepts of events, Producer and Consumer stages, and can have multiple intermediate stages, that is, ProducerConsumer stages, through which our events flow, so it should come as no surprise that Flow leverages all the incredible work done on the GenStage behaviour. Flow is even able to process events coming directly from other GenStage processes, turning those processes into Producers stages of the new Flow being created.

You should be aware that, by default, `Flow` processes an input collection in batches of 500 elements. If you don't see an improvement in your performance tests when compared with the naive eager solution, this may be the reason. Try to fine-tune the `:min_demand` and `:max_demand` parameters that effectively control how many elements are processed in parallel each time. Also, if you don't get better performance with `Flow`, this may be a hint you're better off without it for that kind of data and volume.

Even if, for the time being, we don't have a way to efficiently query the media stored in ElixirDrip, let's try to apply the `Flow` toolset to figure out the disk space used by each user.

Sample data

To execute a query, we need data. Let's create the `ElixirDrip.Search.SampleData` module to encapsulate all the methods responsible for data creation. We will start with the `users/0` function, which returns a list with nine users, associating each user's `id` with their `email`:

```
$ cat examples/sample_data.exs
defmodule ElixirDrip.Search.SampleData do
  @moduledoc false

  def users do
    [
      %{id: 1, email: "andre_albuquerque@elixir.pt"},
      %{id: 2, email: "daniel_caixinha@elixir.pt"},
      %{id: 3, email: "jose_valim@elixir.br"},
      %{id: 4, email: "joe_armstrong@erlang.uk"},
      %{id: 5, email: "robert_virding@erlang.se"},
      %{id: 6, email: "mike_williams@erlang.wls"},
      %{id: 7, email: "jose_lusquinos@panda.pt"},
      %{id: 8, email: "atenas@meow.cat"},
      %{id: 9, email: "billy_boy@woof.dog"},
    ]
  end
end
```

Our objective is to know the disk usage per user, but we also want the user information to be as comprehensible as possible so it can be displayed on a dashboard of some sort. Let's create some functions to improve the information we have about our users:

```
$ cat examples/sample_data.exs
defmodule ElixirDrip.Search.SampleData do
```

```
# ...
def set_name_domain(%{email: email} = user) do
{name, domain} = email
|> String.split("@")
|> List.to_tuple()

user
|> Map.put(:name, name)
|> Map.put(:domain, domain)
end

def set_full_name(%{name: name} = user) do
full_name = name
|> String.split("_")
|> Enum.map(&String.capitalize(&1))
|> Enum.join(" ")

Map.put(user, :full_name, full_name)
end

def set_country(%{domain: domain} = user) do
country = domain
|> String.split(".")
|> Enum.reverse()
|> Enum.at(0)
|> String.upcase()

Map.put(user, :country, country)
end

def set_preferences(%{domain: domain} = user) do
preferences = domain
|> String.split(".")
|> Enum.at(0)

Map.put(user, :preferences, preferences)
end
end
```

We will now use the previous sample data module on our `search.exs` script by using the `import_file/1` function provided by the `IEx.Helpers` module. As we'll see, if we pass our users through a data-transformation process composed by each one of these functions, we will get a prettier information set:

```
$ cat examples/search.exs
import_file("./examples/sample_data.exs")

alias ElixirDrip.Search.SampleData, as: Data
```

```
users = Data.users()

pretty_users = users
               |> Flow.from_enumerable(max_demand: 1)
               |> Flow.map(&Data.set_name_domain(&1))
               |> Flow.map(&Data.set_full_name(&1))
               |> Flow.map(&Data.set_country(&1))
               |> Flow.map(&Data.set_preferences(&1))
```

Due to its lazy nature, `Flow` doesn't immediately enumerate the collection. To force execution of the pending `Flow` operations, we will have to pass its result to an eager function, such as `Enum.to_list/1`. Notice how we are doing just that, by passing the value of the `pretty_users` variable of the preceding `search.exs` script to the `Enum.to_list/1` function:

```
iex> import_file("./examples/search.exs")
# ...

iex> pretty_users |> Enum.to_list()
[
  # ...

  %{
    country: "WLS",
    domain: "erlang.wls",
    email: "mike_williams@erlang.wls",
    full_name: "Mike Williams",
    id: 6,
    name: "mike_williams",
    preferences: "erlang"
  },
  %{
    country: "PT",
    domain: "panda.pt",
    email: "jose_lusquinos@panda.pt",
 full_name: "Jose Lusquinos",
 id: 7,
 name: "jose_lusquinos",
 preferences: "panda"
  },

  # ...
]
```

If we focus ourselves on the `pretty_users` value, we will see the `Flow` recipe that defines how that data pipeline will actually be processed. In our case, we can see four `map` operations, obtaining their input from an enumerable collection with our users in their initial form.

The `import_file/1` function runs the script as if it had been typed inside the current shell. We are able to access the `pretty_users` variable because the evaluation changed the current scope. If we didn't want to change the current scope, we could have used the `Code.eval_file/1` function, which returns a `{result, bindings}` tuple. If we'd used the latter, the `pretty_users` variable would only be accessible through the `bindings[:pretty_users]` variable.

Notice also the number of `stages` that were declared by default for us. These `stages` are the number of parallel execution flows that will process our data, and by default correspond to the number of available schedulers (given by `System.schedulers_online/0`). My laptop has an Intel i5 processor with two cores, each capable of running two threads, thus the four stages:

```
iex> pretty_users
%Flow{
 operations: [
 {:mapper, :map, [&ElixirDrip.Search.SampleData.set_preferences/1]},
 {:mapper, :map, [&ElixirDrip.Search.SampleData.set_country/1]},
 {:mapper, :map, [&ElixirDrip.Search.SampleData.set_full_name/1]},
 {:mapper, :map, [&ElixirDrip.Search.SampleData.set_name_domain/1]}
 ],
 options: [stages: 4, max_demand: 1],
 producers: {:enumerables,
 [
 [
 %{email: "andre_albuquerque@elixir.pt", id: 1},
 %{email: "daniel_caixinha@elixir.pt", id: 2},
 %{email: "jose_valim@elixir.br", id: 3},
 %{email: "joe_armstrong@erlang.uk", id: 4},
 %{email: "robert_virding@erlang.se", id: 5},
 %{email: "mike_williams@erlang.wls", id: 6},
 %{email: "jose_lusquinos@panda.pt", id: 7},
 %{email: "atenas@meow.cat", id: 8},
 %{email: "billy_boy@woof.dog", id: 9}
 ]
 ]},
 window: %Flow.Window.Global{periodically: [], trigger: nil}
 }
```

We now have a set of users, but still no media to query. Let's fix this by creating some auxiliary functions on the `SampleData` module to generate media:

```
$ cat examples/sample_data.exs
defmodule ElixirDrip.Search.SampleData do
  # ...
  def media_set do
    [
      generate_media_for_user(1, 3),
      generate_media_for_user(4, 3),
      generate_media_for_user(6, 3),
      generate_media_for_user(2, 2),
      generate_media_for_user(3, 1),
      generate_media_for_user(5, 4),
    ]
  end

  defp generate_media_for_user(id, user_id) do
    possible_extensions = [".bmp", ".jpg", ".png", ".mp3", ".md",
    ".doc", ".pdf"]

    file_name = 10
                |> :crypto.strong_rand_bytes()
                |> Base.encode32()
                |> String.downcase()

    %Media{
      id: id,
      user_id: user_id,
      file_name: file_name <> random_from(possible_extensions),
      file_size: :rand.uniform(10_000)
    }
  end

  defp random_from([]), do: nil
  defp random_from([item]), do: item
  defp random_from(collection) do
    index = :rand.uniform(length(collection) - 1)
    Enum.at(collection, index)
  end
end
```

The previous `SampleData.media_set/0` function will return a collection of six `Media` structures, three of them belonging to user 3, and the remaining items belonging to users 2, 1, and 4.

In this section, before every IEx shell output shown, we run `import_file("./examples/search.exs")`, similar to what we just did on the last IEx interaction example. This lets us run the current version of the `examples/search.exs` script before interacting with its results. We will indicate this by adding a `# 'search.exs' already evaluated` comment, instead of showing the previous snippet every time.

If we now generate a new media set, we'll obtain something similar to the following example. Those additional fields appeared because we are effectively creating `Storage.Media` structures backed by an Ecto schema. We will analyze this thoroughly when we create those schemas in Chapter 7, *Persisting Data Using Ecto*, but for now you can disregard those new fields:

```
iex> raw_media_set = SampleData.media_set()
[
  %ElixirDrip.Storage.Media{
    __meta__: #Ecto.Schema.Metadata<:built, "storage_media">,
    encryption_key: nil,
    file_name: "kignrrplwpcvtnsa.mp3",
    file_size: 4152,
    full_path: nil,
    id: 1,
    inserted_at: nil,
    metadata: %{},
    storage_key: nil,
    updated_at: nil,
    uploaded_at: nil,
    user_id: 3
  },
  %ElixirDrip.Storage.Media{
    __meta__: #Ecto.Schema.Metadata<:built, "storage_media">,
    encryption_key: nil,
    file_name: "b2zj7loja6ie4cnp.md",
    file_size: 285,
    full_path: nil,
    id: 2,
    inserted_at: nil,
    metadata: %{},
    storage_key: nil,
    updated_at: nil,
    uploaded_at: nil,
    user_id: 2
  },

  # ...
```

```
]

iex> raw_media_set |> Enum.count()
6
```

Let's filter the `raw_media_set` on our `search.exs` script so that we only keep the needed fields in the collection:

```
$ cat examples/search.exs
import_file("./examples/sample_data.exs")
# ...
media_set = raw_media_set
            |> Flow.from_enumerable()
            |> Flow.map(&Map.take(&1, [:id, :user_id, :file_name,
:file_size]))
            |> Enum.to_list()
```

By running the previous script, we now get a streamlined `media_set` list, with just the fields we need:

```
# 'search.exs' already evaluated

iex> media_set
[
  %{file_name: "ylcab53cvp5gauei.doc", file_size: 8915, id: 1, user_id: 3},
  %{file_name: "5clgulo2hg24layj.mp3", file_size: 7644, id: 4, user_id: 3},
  %{file_name: "ym5yj435shtlenih.png", file_size: 5309, id: 6, user_id: 3},
  %{file_name: "qvs3igorje7gc4ko.mp3", file_size: 540, id: 2, user_id: 2},
  %{file_name: "cgdsam3gqp56gzvk.mp3", file_size: 8695, id: 3, user_id: 1},
  %{file_name: "m4yijgulcijddvmp.mp3", file_size: 5922, id: 5, user_id: 4}
]
```

With the `media_set` prepared, we're now ready to start "flowing" it into our data query pipelines.

Lazy queries

The first thing we want is to use `Flow` to count how many files each user has currently stored on ElixirDrip. In practice, we want to `reduce` our `media_set`, by incrementing each user's counter for each file. The naive approach could be something like the following:

```
$ cat examples/search.exs
import_file("./examples/sample_data.exs")
# ...
files_by_user_v1 = media_set
            |> Flow.from_enumerable(max_demand: 1)
```

```
|> Flow.reduce(fn -> %{} end,
          fn media, accum ->
            Map.update(accum, media.user_id, 1, &(&1 + 1))
          end)
```

However, if we run the script and check the outcome of the `files_by_user_v1` flow, we will see a weird result:

```
# 'search.exs' already evaluated

iex> files_by_user_v1 |> Enum.to_list()
[{1, 1}, {3, 1}, {2, 1}, {3, 2}, {4, 1}]
```

The explanation for what's happening here lies in how the collection elements are being distributed among the different stages. Remember that, because our collection is processed in parallel with `Flow` and we have set the `max_demand` parameter to 1, it will be consumed in batches of a single element. We are reducing the collection in parallel, so with four stages, there are four concurrent `reduce` operations happening. Since we are passing the `from_enumerable/2` result directly to the `reduce/3` function, `Flow` is just sending the input batches emitted by the first step stages to the `reduce` stages in the end, without any concern for whether those messages sent downstream are being sent to the correct `reduce` stage.

In this scenario, we have six `media` elements being passed to four stages, so one of the files belonging to user 3 could reach one `reduce` stage, while the remaining two files go to other stages. This is exactly what's happening with the preceding output; on the resulting list, we have two tuples for user 3, {3, 1} and {3, 2}, revealing that one of the stages only processed one file, whereas another stage got the remaining files for the same user.

What we need is a way to control which elements are being passed to each `reduce` stage. `Flow` lets us route events to specific `reduce` stages with the `Flow.partition/2` function. This function creates an intermediate set of new `stages` according to a specific criteria on, thereby allowing us to direct files from the same user to the same `reduce` stage.

Let's do this by defining the hash function used by the `Flow.partition/2` function to create new stages:

```
$ cat examples/search.exs
import_file("./examples/sample_data.exs")
# ...
files_by_user_v2 = media_set
          |> Flow.from_enumerable(max_demand: 1)
          |> Flow.partition(hash: fn m -> {m, m.user_id-1} end)
          |> Flow.reduce(fn -> %{} end,
          fn media, accum ->
```

```
Map.update(accum, media.user_id, 1, &(&1 + 1))
end)
```

On the preceding function, we are passing a lambda function as the `:hash` option to the `Flow.partition/2` call. This lambda receives an element from the collection and has to yield a two-element tuple, which contains the resulting element that will be emitted and the value of the hashing function that will point to the right stage.

 We are subtracting one from the `user_id` value: each stage created by the `partition/2` call is 0-index based, hence for N users starting with `id=1`, we want N-1 hashing values starting at 0. If we incorrectly defined the `:hash` lambda as `fn m -> {m, m.user_id} end`, we would obtain something like `[{2, 1}, {1, 1}, {3, 3}]`. As you can see, the single file user 4 had wasn't considered, because it was allocated to stage 4, and we only had stages 0 to 3.

With this `:hash` function, we now get the expected result. You should also be aware that with `Flow`, results aren't sorted by default. We don't control how fast results are produced, so no order is guaranteed. We can now see that user 3 has three files on ElixirDrip, and the other three users only have one each:

```
# 'search.exs' already evaluated

iex> files_by_user_v2 |> Enum.to_list()
[{1, 1}, {2, 1}, {4, 1}, {3, 3}]
```

In situations where we want to distribute the collection items by stages and we have each item uniquely identified by a key, we could instead use the `:key` option of the `Flow.partition/2` function. This option allows you to not implement the hashing function at all. If you pass the `{:key, :user_id}` tuple as this option value, it assumes all items are maps in order to use the `:user_id` field of the item as the hashing value. If you pass `{:elem, 2}` instead, it assumes all items are tuples and it should use the third element (tuples are 0-index based) as the hashing value to route items to stages.

Let's iterate just one more time on the preceding version we already had working:

```
$ cat examples/search.exs
import_file("./examples/sample_data.exs")
# ...
files_by_user_v3 = media_set
            |> Flow.from_enumerable(max_demand: 1)
            |> Flow.partition(key: {:key, :user_id})
            |> Flow.reduce(fn -> %{} end,
            fn media, accum ->
```

```
Map.update(accum, media.user_id, 1, &(&1 + 1))
end)
```

Looking at the preceding query, one can easily discern its steps: we grab the `media_set`, create a new set of stages using the `:user_id` field to partition the items, and then we count the existing media files by user. When compared to the eager version of this query, the changes we made aren't that big and the actual `reduce` operation has the exact same semantics as the eager `reduce` operation. With minimal effort, we got a lazy parallel query that can leverage all the available resources of the machine. This is the delight of every programmer who wants to maximize the efficiency of their code.

Disk-usage rank query

In the previous section, we ended up getting the number of files per user. We will now iterate on the previous result to create a disk-usage ranking. Since we want the disk usage, we will have to update the previous `files_by_user_v3` flow so that it accumulates each file size per user `id` as well:

```
$ cat examples/search.exs
import_file("./examples/sample_data.exs")
# ...
disk_usage_by_user = media_set
            |> Flow.from_enumerable(max_demand: 1)
            |> Flow.partition(key: {:key, :user_id})
            |> Flow.reduce(fn -> %{} end,
            fn %{user_id: user_id, file_size: size}, accum ->
            Map.update(accum, user_id, size, &(&1 + size))
            end)
```

The previous `disk_usage_by_user` flow gives us the expected results, showing each user's disk usage. User 3 is clearly using much more space than the other users:

```
# 'search.exs' already evaluated

iex> disk_usage_by_user |> Enum.to_list()
[{2, 540}, {1, 8695}, {3, 21868}, {4, 5922}]
```

But who is this user 3? It would be nice to know the names of our users along with their disk usage, instead of only their ids. Since we have a flow on both the `disk_usage_by_user` and `pretty_users` variables, we can combine them to create a new lazy and parallel query so we know who our users actually are. This combination will be performed by the `Flow.bounded_join/6` function, which will receive the two flows and will combine them into a new, single flow, by matching the items of one flow to the items of the other.

Let's create our `disk_usage_ranking_v1` flow, based on the previous two flows we had. To join the existing flows, we have to point out to the `Flow.bounded_join/6` function how it should match the events flowing from each individual flow. The `& (&1.id)` lambda shows how the `id` is retrieved from each `pretty_users` item, whereas the `& (elem(&1, 0))` indicates how the `id` should be fetched from the `disk_usage_by_user` flow. The last lambda receives a single element from each flow through its two arguments and lets you emit new events. In this case, we are emitting a new map with `user` and `disk` fields, where the value of the first comes from the `pretty_users` flow and the value of the latter comes from the `disk_usage_by_user` one:

```
$ cat examples/search.exs
import_file("./examples/sample_data.exs")
# ...
disk_usage_ranking_v1 = Flow.bounded_join(
  :inner,
  pretty_users,
  disk_usage_by_user,
  &(&1.id),
  &(elem(&1, 0)),
  fn user, {_user_id, total_size} ->
    %{user: user.full_name, disk_usage: total_size/1000}
  end)
  |> Enum.sort(&(&1.disk_usage >= &2.disk_usage))
```

Since `Flow` doesn't ensure any order, in the end we sort the resulting list by descending order of `disk_usage` value. Let's now try our joint flow:

```
# 'search.exs' already evaluated

iex> disk_usage_ranking_v1 |> Enum.to_list()
[
  %{disk_usage: 21.868, user: "Jose Valim"},
  %{disk_usage: 8.695, user: "Andre Albuquerque"},
  %{disk_usage: 5.922, user: "Joe Armstrong"},
  %{disk_usage: 0.54, user: "Daniel Caixinha"}
]
```

We now get a much prettier result, and we can see how José is using almost 22 megabytes on ElixirDrip. However, we had nine users. Why are we seeing just a subset of users in our ranking? Similar to what `inner join` does on SQL, we are doing an `:inner` bounded join here (look at the first argument passed to the `Flow.bounded_join/6` function). This means the resulting flow will only have events if there were matching items on the left and right input flows. In our case, we were only emitting events for users on the `pretty_users` flow that also had files on the `disk_usage_by_user` flow.

What we really want is to have events on the resulting flow for all users, independently of each user having files or not. To achieve this, we simply need to change the bounded join mode from `:inner` to `:left`, since the `left` flow is the `pretty_users` flow. This way, it will emit new events for every item on the `left` flow, independently of having a corresponding item on the `right` flow or not:

```
$ cat examples/search.exs
import_file("./examples/sample_data.exs")
# ...
disk_usage_ranking_v2 = Flow.bounded_join(
  :left_outer,
  pretty_users,
  disk_usage_by_user,
  &(&1.id),
  &(elem(&1, 0)),
  fn user, right_elem ->
    disk_usage = case right_elem do
      nil -> 0
      {_user_id, total_size} -> total_size
    end

    %{user: user.full_name, disk_usage: disk_usage}
  end)
  |> Enum.sort(&(&1.disk_usage >= &2.disk_usage))
```

As you can see, we had to change the last lambda function, responsible for the emission of new events. Since we are now doing a `:left` bounded join, there will be times when a `user` has no entry on the `disk_usage_by_user` flow. When this happens, the function argument representing the element from the `right` flow is passed as `nil`, and our lambda function has to cater for it. In our case, if the `right_elem` parameter is `nil`, we know the user isn't using any disk space so we simply return `0` as the `disk_usage` value.

We now have a proper disk-usage ranking, showing each user's name:

```
# 'search.exs' already evaluated

iex> disk_usage_ranking_v2 |> Enum.to_list()
[
 %{disk_usage: 21868, user: "Jose Valim"},
 %{disk_usage: 8695, user: "Andre Albuquerque"},
 %{disk_usage: 5922, user: "Joe Armstrong"},
 %{disk_usage: 540, user: "Daniel Caixinha"},
 %{disk_usage: 0, user: "Mike Williams"},
 %{disk_usage: 0, user: "Atenas"},
 %{disk_usage: 0, user: "Robert Virding"},
 %{disk_usage: 0, user: "Jose Lusquinos"},
 %{disk_usage: 0, user: "Billy Boy"}
]
```

In all the previous examples, we used `Flow` with finite data sets. This means that after the work is done, the spawned processes are ended since they won't need to process any more events. However, one could also use `Flow` to process infinite streams of data. On the ElixirDrip sphere, imagine that we wanted a disk-usage ranking updated in realtime. In this case, we would have to decide when the ranking should be updated, since by definition we couldn't wait for every upload to be done to then update the ranking. This is where the concept of `window` comes in: `Flow` lets you create a pipeline that, for example, processes events every five minutes, buffering them in the meantime. There's much more to be said about processing infinite data with `Flow`, so do not consider it only as a possible tool to handle finite data sets.

As we observed throughout this section, when compared with `GenStage`, `Flow` allows us to work with events in a streamlined way. Since it sits on top of `GenStage`, by using `Flow`, one benefits from all the `GenStage` features but should also be aware of the associated process-spawning and message-passing overhead that comes with it. As any tool out there, `Flow` is not a silver bullet; it shines on contexts where the data to process spans gigabytes of data and/or the event-processing is CPU- or I/O-intensive, but ultimately one should rely on benchmarks to decide whether to use `Flow` or not.

Summary

In this chapter we learned how Elixir elegantly tackles the problem of processing events in stages by analyzing the `GenStage` and `Flow` abstractions:

- We implemented our media upload and download pipelines with `GenStage`, putting to good use its elegant back-pressure mechanism. To achieve this, we had to implement the needed callbacks on the different modules behind the pipeline stages and start each pipeline supervisor on the application initialization.
- We then examined `Flow`, an abstraction based on `GenStage` that lets you process collections in a lazy and concurrent fashion, while keeping much of the semantics one associates with the `Enum` and `Stream` modules.

The advantage of using `GenStage` is that no step in the media pipeline will ever be overwhelmed with requests coming from upstream. If you want to process large datasets or when the bulk of the processing is CPU- or I/O-bound, that's when `Flow` shines. In this day and age, where multi-core processors are the norm, having a tool like `Flow` is invaluable as it lets you use all the available cores in your machine.

In the next chapter, we will start by understanding how metaprogramming works in Elixir, and by the end of the chapter we will have a DSL to represent the download and upload pipelines we have implemented here. Let's jump right into it!

6
Metaprogramming – Code That Writes Itself

We will now analyze how we can develop code that writes code for us, before being finally transformed into BEAM bytecode. This will let us extend Elixir, inject new code into existing modules, and even write a domain-specific language to simplify our media pipeline definitions.

What you will see through this chapter is only possible due to the incredible tools Elixir gives us to manipulate the abstract syntax tree just before it is turned into bytecode. Let's jump right into it!

In this chapter, we'll cover the following:

- What is an abstract syntax tree and how to access it?
- Using the special forms `quote/2` and `unquote/1`
- Macro hygiene and the caller and macro contexts
- Applying `use` and its `__using__/1` function
- Using module attributes to collect information about the caller module
- Creating a domain-specific language with macros

The abstract syntax tree

You may have already heard about **Abstract Syntax Trees** (**AST**s) in other languages. As the name indicates, these are tree-like data structures that represent the code syntax. In Elixir, we call these representations *quoted expressions*.

If we try to obtain the quoted expression of simple expressions, such as single atoms, strings, integers or floats, lists or two element tuples, we'll see their quoted representation doesn't change when compared to their *normal* representation. These elements are called *literals* because we get the same value after quoting them. Take a look at the following code:

```
iex> quote do: :"Funky.Atom"
:"Funky.Atom"

iex> quote do: ["a", "b", "c", "z"]
["a", "b", "c", "z"]

iex> quote do: 1.88
1.88

iex> quote do: "really big string but still simple"
"really big string but still simple"

iex> {:elixir, :rocks} == quote do: {:elixir, :rocks}
true
```

The tree form of the quoted expressions is created by nesting three-element tuples and can be seen for complex snippets of code, which are composed by more than just Elixir literals:

```
iex> quoted_case = quote do
...> case 1 == 2 do
...> true -> "it seems 1 == 2 is true"
...> _ -> IO.puts "1 == 2 isn't true after all"
...> end
...> end
{:case, [],
  [
    {:==, [context: Elixir, import: Kernel], [1, 2]},
    [
      do: [
        {:->, [], [[true], "it seems 1 == 2 is true"]},
        {:->, [],
          [
            [{:_, [], Elixir}],
            {{:., [], [{:__aliases__, [alias: false], [:IO]}, :puts]}, [],
              ["1 == 2 isn't true after all"]}
          ]}
      ]
    ]
  ]}
```

In the preceding example, we are obtaining the quoted representation of a `case` statement. Each three-element tuple is usually composed by an atom (or another three-element tuple) for the function name, a list with metadata, and an arguments list. If the tuple represents a variable, the last element of the tuple will instead be an atom.

To evaluate a quoted expression, we can use the `Code.eval_quoted/3` function. If we evaluate the previous `quoted_case` representation, we will get a two-element tuple, with the evaluation result and the value of the passed bindings after evaluation (the `:ok` atom is the return value of calling `IO.puts/1`):

```
iex> Code.eval_quoted quoted_case
1 == 2 isn't true after all
{:ok, []}
```

Our quoted `case` expression didn't have any variables, so we weren't able to observe how *bindings* work. Let's now see what bindings are for with the following quoted expression using a variable x:

```
iex> quoted_case_with_vars = quote do
...>     case x == 2 do
...>       true -> "it seems x == 2"
...>       _ -> IO.puts "x == 2 isn't true after all"
...>     end
...> end
{:case, [],
  [
    {:==, [context: Elixir, import: Kernel], [{:x, [], Elixir}, 2]},
    [
      do: [
        {:->, [], [[true], "it seems x == 2"]},
        {:->, [],
          [
            [{:_, [], Elixir}],
            {{:., [], [{:__aliases__, [alias: false], [:IO]}, :puts]}, [],
              ["x == 2 isn't true after all"]}
          ]}
      ]
    ]
  ]}
```

If you compare this quoted expression with the previous one, besides the minimal changes to the strings we're using, you can observe that the only change is, instead of having the `1` on the `case` equality comparison, we have the quoted representation of getting the value of x.

However, if we evaluate the `quoted_case_with_vars` expression with an explicit `[x: 3]` binding, it won't yield the expected result:

```
iex> Code.eval_quoted quoted_case_with_vars, [x: 3]
warning: variable "x" does not exist and is being expanded to "x()", please
use parentheses to remove the ambiguity or change the variable name
  nofile:1

** (CompileError) nofile:1: undefined function x/0
    (stdlib) lists.erl:1354: :lists.mapfoldl/3
```

The behavior we're seeing here is deliberate, and the main reason for it is to spare ourselves from headaches further down the road; by default, these expressions are evaluated on a separate context and aren't able to access external variables (even if in this case we're passing x). If we want our expressions to access an outer value, like x, we have to wrap the x with a call to `var!/1`:

```
iex> quoted_case_with_external_vars = quote do
...> case var!(x) == 2 do
...> true -> "it seems x == 2"
...> _ -> IO.puts "x == 2 isn't true after all"
...> end
...> end
{:case, [],
 [
   {:==, [context: Elixir, import: Kernel],
    [{:var!, [context: Elixir, import: Kernel], [{:x, [], Elixir}]}, 2]},
    [
      do: [
        {:->, [], [[true], "it seems x == 2"]},
        {:->, [],
         [
           [{:_, [], Elixir}],
           {{:., [], [{:__aliases__, [alias: false], [:IO]}, :puts]}, [],
            ["x == 2 isn't true after all"]}
         ]}
      ]
    ]
 ]}
```

This way, our case expression finally has access to the bindings we set on the `Code.eval_quoted/2` call:

```
iex> Code.eval_quoted quoted_case_with_external_vars, [x: 2]
{"it seems x == 2", [x: 2]}
```

The previous examples highlighted a very important aspect of metaprogramming in Elixir: the final quoted expressions generated by us, are only able to access variables outside their context if we explicitly said so through `var!/1`.

This inability to access the outer context by default is called *macro hygiene* and is the safeguard that keeps things separate, without leaking into the context of the caller. The decision of accessing (and possibly changing) the outer context should be fully considered by the developer, and this *separation by default* rule helps keeps things sane.

After looking at the code representation before its actual compilation into bytecode, we will now understand how macros work and how we can leverage them to manipulate specific parts of the syntax tree.

Tinkering with macros

Despite all the *meta* hype, we can think about macros as normal functions that need to respect some constraints regarding their arguments and their output. Every argument passed to a macro is converted first into its quoted representation, and the value returned by a macro should also be a valid quoted representation. This is why you commonly see the last statement of a macro being a `quote` block. It's also worth recalling that macros, as functions, can only be defined inside a module.

Another aspect worth mentioning is that macros are expanded before compile time. Macro expansion is the name given to the compiler process of evaluating the macro code and then replacing the call to the macro by the outcome of evaluating the macro (remember that a macro needs to return a valid quoted expression). While compiling our application, the Elixir compiler will expand a macro whenever it finds one. This expansion process is recursive because the quoted expression returned by a macro may still include the usage of another macro. When the compiler finishes expanding all the user-defined macros, it will still have to expand the macros that come with Elixir, such as `alias` and `def`, for example. Some of these macros live on the `Kernel` module, whereas others live on the `Kernel.SpecialForms` module.

 If you need to see what happens on each expansion step, you can use the `Macro.expand_once/2` function. If you want to see the final quoted expression that will be compiled into BEAM bytecode, use the `Macro.expand/2` function instead.

Let's now define a `Demo` module that will contain our first `simple/1` macro:

```
iex> defmodule Demo do
...>   defmacro simple(param) do
...>     IO.puts "Inside the Demo.simple/1 macro"
...>     IO.inspect param
...>
...>     result = quote do
...>       IO.puts "This will be injected into the caller context"
...>       :os.system_time(:seconds)
...>     end
...>
...>     IO.puts "Demo.simple/1 result"
...>     IO.inspect result
...>
...>     result
...>   end
...> end
{:module, Demo, <<70, 79, ...>>, {:simple, 1}}
```

On the preceding `Demo` module, we log the `param` passed to our `simple/1` macro, and in the end we also log the macro result before returning it. Our macro returns a block composed by a call to `IO.puts/1` and a second call to `:os.system_time/1`. We are calling it from the `Playground.do_something/0` function ahead. The macro call will be replaced by the given code block on the syntax tree of the `Playground` module as soon as it is expanded.

By evaluating the `Playground` module, our macro will also be evaluated as soon the `Demo.simple/1` macro is expanded. This is the reason why we see the output generated by the `IO.inspect/1` calls for the `param` and the final macro `result` variables right after we define the module on the interactive shell:

```
iex> defmodule Playground do
...> import Demo
...>
...> def do_something do
...> IO.puts "Inside the Playground.do_something/0 function"
...>
...> simple(5 == (25/5))
...> end
...> end

Inside the Demo.simple/1 macro
{:==, [line: 9], [5, {:/, [line: 9], [25, 5]}]}

Demo.simple/1 result
```

```
{:__block__, [],
 [
  {{:., [], [{:__aliases__, [alias: false], [:IO]}, :puts]}, [],
  ["This will be injected into the caller context"]},
  {{:., [], [:os, :system_time]}, [], [:seconds]}
 ]}

{:module, Playground, <<70, 79, ...>>, {:do_something, 0}}
```

In the previous example, we can see the quoted representation of the passed argument as well as of the result returned by our `simple/1` macro. As we already expected, the `param` variable contains the quoted expression of `5 == 25/5`, and the result of our macro consists of a code block (look at the `__block__` tuple) with two entries: one for the `IO.puts/1` call and the other for the `:os.system_time/1` call.

Everything looks good, but let's be really sure that those two quoted expressions represent the code we expect. For this, we will use the `Macro.to_string/1` function, which receives a quoted expression and returns the equivalent Elixir code:

```
iex> IO.puts Macro.to_string {:==, [line: 9], [5, {:/, [line: 9], [25,
5]}]}
5 == 25 / 5
:ok

iex> IO.puts Macro.to_string {:__block__, [],
...> [
...> {{:., [], [{:__aliases__, [alias: false], [:IO]}, :puts]}, [],
...> ["This will be injected into the caller context"]},
...> {{:., [], [:os, :system_time]}, [], [:seconds]}
...> ]}
(
  IO.puts("This will be injected into the caller context")
  :os.system_time(:seconds)
)
:ok
```

As we can see, both quoted expressions return the Elixir code we expected. We can now continue exploring how macros work while being assured the world still makes sense.

 The `:ok` atom you see above, one for each `IO.puts Macro.to_string` ... call, is the outcome of doing `IO.puts/1`. We use it because `Macro.to_string/1` returns a pretty string for the resulting Elixir code, indented and with newline characters.

Let's now understand the rules that control how our macro code may access the outer context it lives in.

Hygienic accesses

Every time we are inside a quote block, Elixir is generating the quoted representation of that code block for us. If it finds an `inexisting_var` variable during this process, Elixir is happy to return its quoted representation, `{:inexisting_var, [], Elixir}`, on the quoted representation of the code block. However, if we inject this quoted expression on a caller module, we'll get an error because the `inexisting_var` doesn't exist at all on the context where the generated code will run.

 Even if the variable `inexisting_var` was defined in the caller context, the macro wouldn't be able to access it because we didn't use the `var!/1` wrapper around the `inexisting_var`. If we try to compile the `Playground` module, we would get a warning saying `variable "inexisting_var" does not exist and is being expanded to "inexisting_var()"` and finally we would get a `CompileError` saying `undefined function inexisting_var/0`.

If we add an `IO.puts inexisting_var` call on the quoted expression returned by the `Demo.simple/1` macro, we'll see it as an element of the `__block__` tuple (right before it fails the compilation):

```
# Demo.simple/1 result doing `IO.puts inexisting_var`

{:__block__, [],
 [
   {{:., [], [{:__aliases__, [alias: false], [:IO]}, :puts]}, [],
   [{:inexisting_var, [], Demo}]},
   {{:., [], [{:__aliases__, [alias: false], [:IO]}, :puts]}, [],
   ["This will be injected into the caller context"]},
   {{:., [], [:os, :system_time]}, [], [:seconds]}
 ]}
```

Compare the previous `__block__` tuple with the next one, where we do `IO.puts var!(inexisting_var)` instead. We can clearly see the `var!/1` usage so we are able to access the `inexisting_var` on the outer context, in this case the context of the caller. This will only work if the caller actually defined the `inexisting_var` variable in the first place:

```
# Demo.simple/1 result doing `IO.puts var!(inexisting_var)`

{:__block__, [],
 [
   {{:., [], [{:__aliases__, [alias: false], [:IO]}, :puts]}, [],
   [{:var!, [context: Demo, import: Kernel], [{:inexisting_var, [],
   Demo}]}]},
```

```
    {{:., [], [{:__aliases__, [alias: false], [:IO]}, :puts]}, [],
    ["This will be injected into the caller context"]},
    {{:., [], [:os, :system_time]}, [], [:seconds]}
  ]}
```

We say the quoted expression returned by a macro runs on the *caller context* because it is injected into the caller code's own quoted representation. In the end, the macro quoted representation is indistinguishable from all all the other code of the caller and ends up being executed at the same time.

All the statements of your macro that live outside the returned `quote` block are evaluated whenever the Elixir compiler finds your macro being used in the code and consequently expands it. When these statements run, they run when the macro code is evaluated, so we say they run on the *macro context*.

If you consider the `Demo.simple/1` macro we previously defined, the `IO.puts "This will be injected into the caller context"` statement executes on the caller context, whereas the `IO.puts "Inside the Demo.simple/1 macro"` statement is executed on the macro context.

Even if you define a variable inside the quoted expression returned by the macro, the place where the quoted expression is injected won't be able to access it because in Elixir macros are *hygienic*. We already saw this when we investigated how `quote/2` works, and here the behavior is the same: a variable defined or manipulated inside a macro `quote` block can only affect the caller context if it's wrapped inside a `var!/1` function call.

You may also pass to the `var!/2` function a second argument indicating in which context the given variable should live. This is useful when you want to define a variable inside your macro quoted block but don't want to pollute the caller context. Consider the following module:

```
iex> defmodule CleanAccess do
...>   defmacro start_counter(counter) do
...>     quote do
...>       var!(counter_var, CleanAccess) = unquote(counter)
...>     end
...>   end
...>
...>   defmacro get_counter() do
...>     quote do
...>       var!(counter_var, CleanAccess)
...>     end
...>   end
...>
...>   defmacro multiply_by(number) do
```

```
...>       quote do
...>          var!(counter_var, CleanAccess) =
unquote(number)*var!(counter_var, CleanAccess)
...>          end
...>      end
...> end
{:module, CleanAccess,
 <<70, 79, 82, ...>>, {:multiply_by, 1}}
```

Let's import the previous CleanAccess module into a new CleanAccessDemo module:

```
iex> defmodule CleanAccessDemo do
...>      import CleanAccess
...>
...>      def show_it() do
...>         IO.puts "Start with: #{start_counter(3)}"
...>         IO.puts "Counter: #{get_counter()}"
...>         IO.puts "Multiply by 5: #{multiply_by(5)}"
...>         IO.puts "Counter: #{get_counter()}"
...>         IO.puts "Start with: #{start_counter(1)}"
...>         IO.puts "Counter: #{get_counter()}"
...>         IO.puts "Binding on the CleanAccessDemo module:
#{inspect(binding(CleanAccessDemo))}"
...>      end
...> end

iex> CleanAccessDemo.show_it
Start with: 3
Counter: 3
Multiply by 5: 15
Counter: 15
Start with: 1
Counter: 1
Binding on the CleanAccessDemo module: []
:ok

iex> counter_var
** (CompileError) iex:117: undefined function counter_var/0
```

The macros inside the CleanAccess module manipulate the counter_var in the CleanAccess context, but, as we can observe, the counter_var never leaks to the caller context. When you are creating your own macros, consider whether you really need to access the caller context, or whether you are able to do as we did here, and simply define those variables in the context of the module defining the macros.

Famous (un)quotes

Let's now investigate what unquote does and see its role on the interaction of the quote and unquote dynamic duo. Until now we only injected quoted expressions on the caller module (recall the code block injected by the Demo.simple/1 macro injected on the Playground module).

As you will see, the unquote/1 macro will be extensively used, almost whenever we use a macro. The unquote/1 macro can only be used inside a quote block and lets us inject the value of a variable defined on an outer scope.

Let's continue with the previous Demo module, but this time we want the param variable to be used inside the quote block returned by the Demo.simple/1 macro:

```
iex> defmodule Demo do
...>   defmacro simple(param) do
...>     IO.puts "Inside the Demo.simple/1 macro"
...>     IO.inspect param
...>
...>     result = quote do
...>       param_value = unquote(param)
...>       IO.puts "(injected into the caller context) param value is
#{param_value}"
...>       :os.system_time(:seconds)
...>     end
...>
...>     IO.puts "Demo.simple/1 result with unquoted param"
...>     IO.inspect result
...>
...>     result
...>   end
...> end
{:module, Demo,
 <<70, 79, ...>>, {:simple, 1}}
```

As you can see, the only significant difference is that we are assigning the param_value variable inside the quote block with the unquoted param value. To convert the quote block into its properly quoted representation, Elixir will evaluate the code it contains. When it finds an unquote statement, Elixir stops the conversion into the quoted format and simply injects the value of what's inside the unquote statement. For this reason the return value of calling unquote/1 needs to be a valid quoted expression:

```
iex> defmodule Playground do
...>   import Demo
...>
```

```
...>     def do_something do
...>        IO.puts "Inside the Playground.do_something/0 function"
...>
...>        simple(5 == (25/5))
...>     end
...> end

Inside the Demo.simple/1 macro
{:==, [line: 8], [5, {:/, [line: 8], [25, 5]}]}

Demo.simple/1 result with unquoted param
{:__block__, [],
  [
    {:=, [],
     [{:param_value, [], Demo}, {:==, [line: 8], [5, {:/, [line: 8],
     [25, 5]}]}]},
    {{:., [], [{:__aliases__, [alias: false], [:IO]}, :puts]}, [],
    # ...
```

If we now import the macro into our Playground module again, we can observe that the first statement on the code block is binding to a param_value variable that is the exact same quoted value our Demo.simple/1 received via the param argument. To see this, check the last element of the :__block__ tuple to identify the block statements, and then consider the first tuple, which starts with :=, where the binding operation is being made. Recall that the {:==, [line: 8], [5, {:/, [line: 8], [25, 5]}]} expression is the quoted representation of 5 == (25/5) that was passed through the param macro argument in the first place.

Remember that the param argument is injected in its quoted representation form because that's how macros work: they pass the arguments already as quoted expressions. If we passed [1, 2, 3, 4, 5, "a big list whose quoted representation is the same"] as the param value, it would be injected exactly like that on the resulting quoted block because lists are literals.

Since the :== tuple contains the quoted representation of 5 == (25/5), if we bind a new other_param_value variable using the same unquote approach, an identical :== tuple will appear for the other_param_value assignment. This means the == comparison will be evaluated twice, one for the param_value and the other for the other_param_value assignments:

```
defmodule Demo do
  defmacro simple(param) do
    # ...
    result = quote do
```

```
        param_value = unquote(param)
        other_param_value = unquote(param)
        # ...
      end
    end
  end
```

This new binding will add another binding statement to the quoted block we are generating on the `Demo.simple/1` macro as expected, but, as we said, it also injects again the quoted representation of the `==` comparison. This is where things get trickier: since it injects the quoted representation of the comparison and not the result of the comparison (this is what `unquote/1` does; it injects into the quoted block the expression passed to it as argument), when the `Playground` module calls `do_something/0`, it will execute the same comparison twice to reach the conclusion that `25/5` compares positively with `5`. You can observe exactly this in the following snippet, where we can observe the two assignments (check the two `:=` tuples) and the corresponding two equality comparisons (check the two `:==` tuples):

```
# ...
Demo.simple/1 result
{:__block__, [],
  [
    {:=, [], # first assignment
    [
      {:param_value, [], Demo},
      {:==, [line: 31], [5, {:/, [line: 31], [25, 5]}]}]
    ]},
    {:=, [], # second assignment
    [
      {:other_param_value, [], Demo},
      {:==, [line: 31], [5, {:/, [line: 31], [25, 5]}]}]
    ]},
    {{:., [], [{:__aliases__, [alias: false], [:IO]}, :puts]}, [],

# ...
```

The duplicate execution scenario we just considered is usually what we don't want. Imagine if the expression being run twice had side effects–oops! We have just launched two probes to Pluto instead of the single one we planned. This is where the `bind_quoted` option of the `quote` macro comes in. Instead of doing `unquote` twice, we bind (as the name indicates) a quoted value to a variable that can then be used inside the `quote` block:

```
defmodule Demo do
  defmacro simple(param) do
    # ...
    result = quote bind_quoted: [evaluated_param: param] do
      param_value = evaluated_param
```

```
      other_param_value = evaluated_param
      IO.puts "(injected into the caller context) param value is
      #{param_value}"
      :os.system_time(:seconds)
    end
  end
end
```

The preceding `quote` block will do as many bindings as the entries on the `bind_quoted` keyword list at the beginning of the quoted block. In our case, it will start by assigning the `param` quoted value to the `evaluated_param` variable inside the `quoted` block (notice the first `:=` tuple):

```
# ...
Demo.simple/1 result
{:__block__, [],
  [
    {:=, [], # bind_quoted assignment
      [
        {:evaluated_param, [], Demo},
        {:==, [line: 38], [5, {:/, [line: 38], [25, 5]}]} # param quoted
        value
      ]},
    {:__block__, [],
      [
        {:=, [], [{:param_value, [], Demo}, {:evaluated_param, [],
        Demo}]},
        {:=, [], [{:other_param_value, [], Demo}, {:evaluated_param, [],
        Demo}]},
        {{:., [], [{:__aliases__, [alias: false], [:IO]}, :puts]}, [],
# ...
```

After all the bindings derived from the `bind_quoted` keyword list, the quoted block starts. However, this time the `param_value` and the `other_param_value` assignments both point to the `evaluated_param` value, instead of each using its own quoted representation of the `5 == 25/5` comparison. Notice how the `param` quoted value was only injected once during the initial bindings phase. Another advantage of this approach is that your quote blocks inside your macros become uncluttered from all the `unquote/1` calls.

 Inside a `quote` block with the `bind_quoted` option, the usage of `unquote/1` is disabled by default. This means that if you use the `unquote/1` macro in this scenario, for example, by doing `unquote(x)` inside the `quote` block, it will get expanded to `{:unquote, [], [{:x, [], Elixir}]}`, instead of injecting whatever `x` is into the current quoted expression.

This may be useful in situations where you want the `unquote` statements only to be evaluated at run time (recall that the macro expansion phase happens just before compile time).

Defining a function with your macro is a typical example of where you would apply this approach. To do this, you first pass the `[fun_name: :do_work]` keyword list as the value of the `bind_quoted` option of the `quote` block returned by your macro. By using `bind_quoted` we know `unquote` is disabled, so it won't immediately inject the value we pass to it on the current quoted representation. This means you would be able to then define a function inside the `quote` block returned by the macro like this: `def unquote(fun_name)(), do: "working!"`. The `unquote(fun_name)` would be evaluated on the caller context, where the `fun_name` variable exists (due to the `bind_quoted` usage).

You can think about using `unquote` as the analogous operation of interpolating strings. When you are composing a string, if your string has `#{some_var}`, the composition stops and the `some_var` value is injected in its place. When you define a `quote` block to be returned by your macro, wherever an `unquote(some_var)` call appears, the conversion into quoted representation halts and the `some_var` value is injected, without any transformation, into the current AST of the `quote` block.

Macros – a silver bullet?

After seeing how you can easily manipulate the quoted representation of your code and even create code that effortlessly generates code for you, it may be tempting to consider the usage of macros whenever you are tackling a new problem or implementing a new application. After all, even Elixir uses macros for many of its own constructs, such as `Kernel.is_nil/1` or `Kernel.if/3`.

Nonetheless, you should also bear in mind that macros deliberately hide some of the complexity of the code and therefore may hinder the comprehension of the code to its full extent. And, as you've seen, there are some important nuances that you should be aware of when using macros. The rule of thumb when writing code is that you should favor readability over cleverness. Therefore, you should always ask whether, by not using macros, you could accomplish the same using other constructs of the language that may increase the explicitness of the code.

Generally speaking, debugging code generated by macros is in many cases trickier. And, as Kernighan says, *debugging is twice as hard as writing code in the first place,* so you should definitely use macros with parsimony.

Despite having the potential to cause havoc, macros have their place in a modern language such as Elixir and allow you to solve problems that otherwise would be very tricky or really cumbersome to solve. Many Elixir libraries use macros to reduce the friction of using them in other projects. For example, by importing the `Ecto.Query` module of the `Ecto` library (we will talk about this in the next chapter), you can create a query such as this: `query = from m in Media, where: m.file_size > 500, select: m`. This is a valid Elixir expression and illustrates the expressiveness that macros can bring to your code.

A very wise Latin expression can be applied to macros, as it may also be applied to life: *abusus non tollit usum,* usually translated to *abuse doesn't take away use.* Despite the fact that macros can contribute to unneeded complexity, they are convenient tools that, when applied correctly, allow you to write better code. And, even if sometimes macros aren't used properly, they may be just what you need for your problem.

Regarding metaprogramming, achieving the right balance is key. Let's now apply what we've learned to create a macro that will allow us to measure the time it takes for a function to be executed.

Extending modules

After understanding how macros work, we will now apply the insights we just got to see how we can create macros that add functionality to the caller module. Our objective here is to create a macro, `ElixirDrip.Chronometer.defchrono/2`, equivalent to the existing `def/2` macro but with the additional feature that logs how long the function call took.

Let's start by looking at the end result. We want to be able to define functions such as `defchrono fun_name(arg1, arg2), do: ...` and when we call the `fun_name/2` function, it will tell us `Took 123 µs to run SomeModule.fun_name/2`. The following `MeasuredModule` will be our research subject:

```
$ cat examples/measured_module.exs
defmodule MeasuredModule do
  import ElixirDrip.Chronometer

  defchrono_vn slow_times(x, y) do
    Process.sleep(2000)
    x * y
  end
```

```
end
```

In the previous snippet, we are using the _vn suffix for the macro name because the
defchrono macro we are developing will have several iterations, starting with v0 and
ending in v5. Each time we introduce a new iteration, the previous MeasuredModule will
be updated to use the new defchrono macro version.

The single purpose of the first iteration of our defchrono macro is to analyze the
arguments passed to it. Since the function_definition and the body arguments are
already quoted (as any other macro argument), we can simply inject their values on the
quote block returned by the macro with unquote/1:

```
$ cat apps/elixir_drip/lib/elixir_drip/chronometer.ex
defmodule ElixirDrip.Chronometer do

  defmacro defchrono_v0(function_definition, do: body) do
    IO.puts "On defchrono_v0, function definition:"
    IO.inspect function_definition
    IO.puts "Body:"
    IO.inspect body

    quote do
      def unquote(function_definition) do
        unquote(body)
      end
    end
  end
end
```

Let's try this inside an IEx shell, so we can observe the values of our macro arguments:

```
iex> c "./examples/measured_module.exs"
On defchrono_v0, function definition:
{:slow_times, [line: 4], [{:x, [line: 4], nil}, {:y, [line: 4], nil}]}
Body:
{:__block__, [],
 [
   {{:., [line: 5], [{:__aliases__, [line: 5], [:Process]}, :sleep]},
   [line: 5],
    [2000]},
   {:*, [line: 6], [{:x, [line: 6], nil}, {:y, [line: 6], nil}]}
 ]}
[MeasuredModule]

iex> MeasuredModule.slow_times(2, 3)
6
```

According to what we're seeing here, the function definition is a normal three-element tuple where the last element is a list with the function arguments and the body of the function consists of a __block__ tuple whose last element is a list with the quoted representation of the two body statements, so there is also nothing new here.

We were able to call the slow_times/2 function because our macro returns itself a def macro with the same function_definition and body we pass as arguments. The next step now is to actually measure the time the function takes to execute. For this, we will use the :timer.tc/1 Erlang function that receives a lambda function and executes it, returning the time it took (in microseconds) and the lambda result.

We could do this right inside the quoted block returned by our macro, but it's better to do it on its own function inside the Chronometer module. This way, it's easier to test it, and we reduce the code we inject to the caller context. Let's create the Chronometer.run_and_measure/1 function:

```
$ cat apps/elixir_drip/lib/elixir_drip/chronometer.ex
defmodule ElixirDrip.Chronometer do
  # ...
  def run_and_measure(to_measure) do
    {time_µs, result} = :timer.tc(to_measure)
    IO.puts "Run in #{time_µs} µs"

    result
  end
end
```

This way, we can use this function even without resorting to any macro at all. If we call result = Chronometer.run_and_measure(fn -> Process.sleep(1000) end), we will see Run in 1000961 µs and result will get the :ok atom returned by the Process.sleep/1 call.

Let's now use the run_and_measure/1 on the next macro iteration, defchrono_v1:

```
$ cat apps/elixir_drip/lib/elixir_drip/chronometer.ex
defmodule ElixirDrip.Chronometer do
  # ...
  defmacro defchrono_v1(function_definition, do: body) do
    IO.puts "On defchrono_v1, function definition:"
    IO.inspect function_definition

    quote do
      def unquote(function_definition) do
        Chronometer.run_and_measure(fn -> unquote(body) end)
      end
```

```
      end
    end
  end
```

If we now call the `MeasuredModule.slow_times/2` function, we know it takes two seconds. But if we are using our macro to measure several functions, we will have a hard time figuring out which measured time corresponds to each function just by looking at the logs:

```
iex> c "./examples/measured_module.exs"
On defchrono_v1, function definition:
{:slow_times, [line: 4], [{:x, [line: 4], nil}, {:y, [line: 4], nil}]}
[MeasuredModule]

iex> MeasuredModule.slow_times(4, 5)
Run in 2000621 µs
20
```

To overcome the previous problem, let's create a `v2` macro that logs the name of the function besides the actual time it took to execute. Looking at the IEx output in the preceding code block, you can see that when we compile the `MeasuredModule`, we print the function definition. This function definition is a three-element tuple as expected, where the function name is present on the first element and the list of function arguments lives on the last one. We could pattern match on this tuple to extract the function name and arguments, but there is already the `Macro.decompose_call/1` function that does this for us. The following is how the `defchrono_v2` macro looks now:

```
$ cat apps/elixir_drip/lib/elixir_drip/chronometer.ex
defmodule ElixirDrip.Chronometer do
  # ...
  defmacro defchrono_v2(function_definition, do: body) do
    {function, args} = Macro.decompose_call(function_definition)
    IO.puts "On defchrono_v2, function definition:"
    IO.inspect function_definition
    IO.puts "Function"
    IO.inspect function
    IO.puts "Arguments"
    IO.inspect args

    quote do
      def unquote(function_definition) do
        Chronometer.run_and_measure(unquote(function), fn ->
        unquote(body) end)
      end
    end
  end
end
```

```
  end
```

For the previous iteration, we created a `run_and_measure/2` function that also receives the function name as argument, besides the lambda to run:

```
$ cat apps/elixir_drip/lib/elixir_drip/chronometer.ex
defmodule ElixirDrip.Chronometer do
  # ...
  def run_and_measure(to_run, to_measure) do
    {time_µs, result} = :timer.tc(to_measure)
    IO.puts "Took #{time_µs} µs to run #{to_run}"

    result
  end
end
```

By using the `defchrono_v2` macro on the `MeasuredModule` we now get a nicer result. It is also possible to observe the outcome of applying the `Macro.decompose_call/1` function:

```
iex> c "./examples/measured_module.exs"
On defchrono_v2, function definition:
{:slow_times, [line: 4], [{:x, [line: 4], nil}, {:y, [line: 4], nil}]}
Function
:slow_times
Arguments
[{:x, [line: 4], nil}, {:y, [line: 4], nil}]
[MeasuredModule]

iex> MeasuredModule.slow_times(6, 7)
Took 2000960 µs to run slow_times
42
```

But what if we have many `slow_times` functions, with different arity or they are living on different modules? The current output of our macro only shows the function name, so with more than one `slow_times` function, we wouldn't know which function had run by only looking at the macro output. Let's create a `Chronometer.pretty_signature/3` function that receives the module, function names and the list of arguments, and returns a string formatted as `Module.function/arity`:

```
$ cat apps/elixir_drip/lib/elixir_drip/chronometer.ex
defmodule ElixirDrip.Chronometer do
  # ...
  def pretty_signature(module, function, args) when is_list(args) do
    module = module
             |> Atom.to_string()
             |> String.replace_leading("Elixir.", "")
```

```
        "#{module}.#{function}/#{length(args)}"
    end
end
```

Let's use the `pretty_signature/3` function on the v3 macro iteration. This time, we are printing the `ast_to_return` generated by our `quote` block to see which values are being passed to the `pretty_signature/3` function that creates the function's full name:

```
$ cat apps/elixir_drip/lib/elixir_drip/chronometer.ex
defmodule ElixirDrip.Chronometer do
  # ...
  defmacro defchrono_v3(function_definition, do: body) do
    {function, args} = Macro.decompose_call(function_definition)
    IO.puts "On defchrono_v3"
    IO.inspect function_definition
    IO.puts "Function"
    IO.inspect function
    IO.puts "Arguments"
    IO.inspect args

    ast_to_return = quote do
      def unquote(function_definition) do
        signature =
          Chronometer.pretty_signature(__MODULE__, unquote(function),
          unquote(args))

        Chronometer.run_and_measure(signature, fn -> unquote(body) end)
      end
    end

    IO.puts "Returning"
    ast_to_return
    |> Macro.to_string()
    |> IO.puts()

    ast_to_return
  end
end
```

If we now compile our `MeasuredModule` and run its `slow_times/2` function again, we have no doubts regarding which function was measured:

```
iex> c "./examples/measured_module.exs"
On defchrono_v3
{:slow_times, [line: 4], [{:x, [line: 4], nil}, {:y, [line: 4], nil}]}
Function
:slow_times
Arguments
```

```
[{:x, [line: 4], nil}, {:y, [line: 4], nil}]
Returning
def(slow_times(x, y)) do
  signature = Chronometer.pretty_signature(__MODULE__, :slow_times, [x, y])
  Chronometer.run_and_measure(signature, fn ->
    Process.sleep(2000)
    x * y
  end)
end
[MeasuredModule]

iex> MeasuredModule.slow_times(8, 9)
Took 2001016 µs to run MeasuredModule.slow_times/2
72
```

You may have noticed that we call `unquote/1` for the `function` and `args` values that we pass to the `pretty_signature/3` function. In contrast, we don't do it for the `__MODULE__/0` call we are using to get the module of the function that's being measured. This makes sense because the `__MODULE__/0` is actually a macro, and we want it to be expanded on the caller context. This is why we see the `__MODULE__` expression on the text representation of the AST returned by our `defchrono_v3` macro. If we had instead used `pretty_signature(unquote(__MODULE__), ..., ...)`, the `__MODULE__` expression would have been evaluated in the macro context, resulting in `ElixirDrip.Chronometer`.

The `v3` iteration yields the result we were expecting, so all seems well. Let's now try to apply our macro to the `slow_square/1` function that defines a default argument:

```
$ cat examples/measured_module.exs
defmodule MeasuredModule do
  import ElixirDrip.Chronometer
  # ...
  defchrono_v3 slow_square(x \\ 3) do
    Process.sleep(2000)
    x * x
  end
end
```

As you can see from this code, if we compile the `MeasuredModule` again, we now get an error saying there is no `\\/2` function:

```
iex> c "./examples/measured_module.exs"
On defchrono_v3
{:slow_square, [line: 4], [{:\\, [line: 4], [{:x, [line: 4], nil}, 3]}]}
Function
:slow_square
Arguments
```

```
[{:\\, [line: 4], [{:x, [line: 4], nil}, 3]}]
Returning
def(slow_square(x \\ 3)) do
  signature = Chronometer.pretty_signature(__MODULE__, :slow_square,
  [x \\ 3])
  Chronometer.run_and_measure(signature, fn ->
    Process.sleep(2000)
    x * x
  end)
end

== Compilation error in file examples/measured_module.exs ==
** (CompileError) examples/measured_module.exs:4: undefined function \\/2
    (stdlib) lists.erl:1338: :lists.foreach/2
    (stdlib) erl_eval.erl:670: :erl_eval.do_apply/6
**
```

Why is the compiler complaining about the weird `\\/2` function? Since we are using a default argument, the `args` value is still a list but now contains a single `:\\` tuple, whose argument (third element of the tuple) is the x variable and the 3 default value. This makes total sense, and we are actually able to reproduce it using the good ol' `quote`:

```
iex> quote do: x \\ 3
{:\\, [], [{:x, [], Elixir}, 3]}

iex> quote do: [x, y]
[{:x, [], Elixir}, {:y, [], Elixir}]
```

Because we apply `unquote/1` to the `args` value that will be passed to the `pretty_signature/3` function, we are injecting the quoted representation of `[x \\ 3]` as the third argument of the `Chronometer.pretty_signature(...)` statement. When the compiler tries to compile this expression, it evaluates the `x \\ 3` part and breaks because there's no `\\/2` function.

We now know what the problem is. Let's fix it by calculating the arity right on the macro context and pass it directly to the updated `pretty_signature/3` function, which now receives the `arity` value instead of the `args` list as the last argument:

```
$ cat apps/elixir_drip/lib/elixir_drip/chronometer.ex
defmodule ElixirDrip.Chronometer do
  # ...
  defmacro defchrono_v4(function_definition, do: body) do
    {function, args} = Macro.decompose_call(function_definition)
    arity = length(args)
    IO.puts "On defchrono_v4"
    IO.inspect function_definition
```

```
      IO.puts "Function"
      IO.inspect function
      IO.puts "Arguments"
      IO.inspect args

      ast_to_return = quote do
        def unquote(function_definition) do
          signature =
            Chronometer.pretty_signature(__MODULE__, unquote(function),
            unquote(arity))

            Chronometer.run_and_measure(signature, fn -> unquote(body) end)
        end
      end

      IO.puts "Returning"
      ast_to_return
      |> Macro.to_string()
      |> IO.puts()

      ast_to_return
    end

    def pretty_signature(module, function, arity) do
      module = module
               |> Atom.to_string()
               |> String.replace_leading("Elixir.", "")

      "#{module}.#{function}/#{arity}"
    end
  end
```

It now works even when we use default arguments, given that we calculate the `arity` value in advance:

```
iex> c "./examples/measured_module.exs"
On defchrono_v4
{:slow_square, [line: 4], [{:\\, [line: 4], [{:x, [line: 4], nil},
3]}]}
Function
:slow_square
Arguments
[{:\\, [line: 4], [{:x, [line: 4], nil}, 3]}]
Returning
def(slow_square(x \\ 3)) do
  signature = Chronometer.pretty_signature(__MODULE__, :slow_square, 1)
  Chronometer.run_and_measure(signature, fn ->
    Process.sleep(2000)
```

```
    x * x
  end)
end
[MeasuredModule]

iex> MeasuredModule.slow_square()
Took 2000981 µs to run MeasuredModule.slow_square/1
9

iex> MeasuredModule.slow_square(5)
Took 2000324 µs to run MeasuredModule.slow_square/1
25
```

This poses as a valuable lesson that you should follow when using macros. Do as much as possible on the macro context to inject the smallest code chunk possible into the caller context. And when your macro receives arguments, try to think about every possible way those arguments may be passed to cater for all edge cases. Those who use your macro may not be as fluent as you with metaprogramming, and the errors that result from using macros are sometimes cryptic, in contrast to the detailed error messages we came to expect and appreciate from *normal* Elixir. This is one of the reasons why you should be doubly careful with your macros.

Our `defchrono_v4` macro is now working as expected. Let's take one step further and make this work using the `bind_quoted` option on the `quote` block. This is the trickiest part of our `defchrono` macro, due to the different moments when the macro is evaluated.

On this new macro iteration, we'll use for the first time the `Macro.escape/1` function. Let's just do a brief detour to understand how it works. You can think about this function as a cousin of the `quote/1` macro, since it also returns a quoted expression. However, instead of always returning the quoted representation of the code it receives, it evaluates the code it gets and only then returns its quoted representation. Check the following snippet that illustrates this difference:

```
iex> a = %{this: "is", a: "map"}
%{a: "map", this: "is"}

iex> quoted_a = quote do: a
{:a, [], Elixir}

iex> escaped_a = Macro.escape a
{:%{}, [], [a: "map", this: "is"]}
```

We will now analyze how the `defchrono_v5` macro works with the `bind_quoted` option. As we have already seen, the `bind_quoted` option let's you access the variables defined by it on the `quote` block because it defines for us as many assignments as there are entries on the `bind_quoted` keyword list. Its usage also disables `unquote/1` by default, so those `unquote/1` calls (for the `function_definition`, `function`, `arity`, and `body`) will appear in their AST form on the quoted representation returned by the macro:

```
$ cat apps/elixir_drip/lib/elixir_drip/chronometer.ex
defmodule ElixirDrip.Chronometer do
  # ...
  defmacro defchrono_v5(function_definition, do: body) do
    {function, args} = Macro.decompose_call(function_definition)
    arity = length(args)
    IO.puts "On defchrono_v5"
    IO.inspect function_definition
    IO.puts "Escaped function_definition"
    IO.inspect Macro.escape(function_definition)
    IO.puts "Function"
    IO.inspect function
    IO.puts "Arguments"
    IO.inspect args

    ast_to_return = quote bind_quoted: [
      function_definition: Macro.escape(function_definition),
      body: Macro.escape(body),
      function: function,
      arity: arity
    ] do
      def unquote(function_definition) do
        signature =
          Chronometer.pretty_signature(__MODULE__, unquote(function),
          unquote(arity))

        Chronometer.run_and_measure(signature, fn -> unquote(body) end)
      end
    end

    IO.puts "Returning"
    ast_to_return
    |> Macro.to_string()
    |> IO.puts()

    ast_to_return
  end
```

Since the `unquote/1` calls are now disabled, they will be injected into the caller context and their evaluation will be postponed, instead of being evaluated at compile time. When they are finally evaluated, it is expected that each variable being unquoted contains code already in its quoted representation, ready to be injected into the final AST. This is the reason we use `Macro.escape/1` for the `function_definition` and `body` arguments, which by definition, are already quoted (if you remember, both are macro arguments).

This is what we see when compiling the `MeasuredModule` using the `defchrono_v5` macro:

```
iex> c "./examples/measured_module.exs"
On defchrono_v5
{:slow_square, [line: 4], [{:\\, [line: 4], [{:x, [line: 4], nil}, 3]}]}
Escaped function_definition
{:{}, [],
 [
   :slow_square,
   [line: 4],
   [{:{}, [], [:\\, [line: 4], [{:{}, [], [:x, [line: 4], nil]}, 3]]}]
 ]}
Function
:slow_square
Arguments
[{:\\, [line: 4], [{:x, [line: 4], nil}, 3]}]
Returning
(
  function_definition = {:slow_square, [line: 4], [{:\\, [line: 4],
  [{:x, [line: 4], nil}, 3]}]}
  body = {:__block__, [], [{{:., [line: 5], [{:__aliases__, [line: 5],
  [:Process]}, :sleep]}, [line: 5], [2000]}, {:*, [line: 6], [{:x,
  [line: 6], nil}, {:x, [line: 6], nil}]}]}
  function = :slow_square
  arity = 1

  def(unquote(function_definition)) do
    signature = Chronometer.pretty_signature(__MODULE__,
    unquote(function), unquote(arity))
    Chronometer.run_and_measure(signature, fn -> unquote(body) end)
  end
)
[MeasuredModule]

iex> MeasuredModule.slow_square(9)
Took 2009285 µs to run MeasuredModule.slow_square/1
81
```

Notice the four assignments we are injecting into the caller module before the `def/2` call, one for each `bind_quoted` variable. Because we escape the `function_definition` before injecting it into the `quote` block via the `bind_quoted` option, we can see its expected quoted representation on the `function_definition` assignment:

```
    # ...
Returning
(
    function_definition = {:slow_square, [line: 4], [{:\\, [line: 4], [{:x,
[line: 4], nil}, 3]}]}
    # ...
```

If we forgot to escape the `function_definition` variable, we would see this assignment instead (before getting a compilation error due to an `undefined function slow_square/1`):

```
    # ...
Returning
(
    function_definition = slow_square(x \\ 3)
    # ...

== Compilation error in file examples/measured_module.exs ==
** (CompileError) examples/measured_module.exs:4: undefined function
slow_square/1
    (elixir_drip) expanding macro: ElixirDrip.Chronometer.defchrono_v5/2
    examples/measured_module.exs:4: MeasuredModule (module)
** (CompileError) compile error
    (iex) lib/iex/helpers.ex:183: IEx.Helpers.c/2
```

This error makes total sense, since without escaping the `function_definition` variable, the expression would reach the caller module as a *normal* and not a quoted expression, and the compiler would try to evaluate it as usual. Since at that point there's no `slow_square/1` function, it halts the compilation with the error we just saw.

You can also see we are using `Macro.escape/1` for both the `function_definition` and the `body` variables, but not for the `function` and `arity` variables. This happens because the latter variables are both literals, given they are always an atom and an integer. Since they are invariably represented in the same way, independently of being quoted or not, we decided not to apply the `Macro.escape/1` function.

Let's now focus ourselves on the code generated by the defchrono_v5 macro. We will create a MeasuredModuleExpanded that *manually* accomplishes what the macro does for us automatically. As you can see, we are defining the function_definition and body variables with valid quoted representations (the metadata part of each tuple is being set to [] to reduce the noise):

```
$ cat examples/measured_module_expanded.exs
defmodule MeasuredModuleExpanded do
  alias ElixirDrip.Chronometer

  function_definition = {:slow_square, [], [{:\\, [], [{:x, [], nil}, 3]}]}
  body = {:__block__, [], [{{:., [], [{:__aliases__, [], [:Process]},
:sleep]}, [], [2000]}, {:*, [], [{:x, [], nil}, {:x, [], nil}]}]}
  function = :slow_square
  arity = 1

  def (unquote(function_definition)) do
    signature =
      Chronometer.pretty_signature(__MODULE__, unquote(function),
unquote(arity))
    Chronometer.run_and_measure(signature, fn -> unquote(body) end)
  end
end
```

You may find it strange to see several unquote/1 calls without the enclosing quote block, given we've previously said the unquote/1 macro could only be used inside a quote block. But if you look closely enough, you will see two hidden quote blocks.

We are using the def/2 macro to define the function as usual. Since it is a macro, its arguments are always transformed into their quoted representation via quote/1. Hence, we are able to do unquote(function_definition) and unquote(function|arity|body) inside the first and second arguments of the def/2 macro, respectively because those unquote/1 calls are happening inside the quote block of each def/2 macro argument.

After compiling the MeasuredModuleExpanded, we are able to call the *manually* defined slow_square/1 function:

```
iex> c "./examples/measured_module_expanded.exs"
[MeasuredModuleExpanded]

iex> MeasuredModuleExpanded.slow_square 5
Took 2000906 µs to run MeasuredModuleExpanded.slow_square/1
25
```

```
iex> MeasuredModuleExpanded.slow_square
Took 2000317 µs to run MeasuredModuleExpanded.slow_square/1
9
```

We covered a lot of new concepts and techniques up to now, and it may seem daunting at first. But be rest assured that independently of what we do with macros, the only magic happening is that we are injecting code into the caller module. The injected code needs to be in a specific *quoted* format, and that's it.

Let's now check how we can pass options to macros and use this technique to choose which time unit should be used to display the execution time reported by our defchrono/2 macro.

Using the use and __using__/1 macros

Our objective is now to choose the time unit that will be used to time our functions. To achieve this we will employ the use macro, which you have probably seen a few times now (the CacheWorker module previously implemented by us used GenServer). Instead of importing the ElixirDrip.Chronometer module, we are now using it:

```
$ cat examples/measured_module.exs
defmodule MeasuredModule do
  use ElixirDrip.Chronometer, unit: :secs

  defchrono slow_times(x, y) do
    Process.sleep(2000)
    x * y
  end

  defchrono slow_square(x \\ 3) do
    Process.sleep(2000)
    x * x
  end
end
```

When the compiler finds the use statement on the MeasuredModule, it will run the __using__/1 macro of the ElixirDrip.Chronometer module. You will see this strategy a lot because it provides a standard way for the *used* module to be invoked, and most of the times injects whatever it needs into the caller module. Another extremely useful feature of use is that it lets us pass arguments to the invoked __using__/1 macro. In the preceding example, we are passing a keyword list with a single :unit entry.

Let's analyze what the `Chronometer.__using__/1` macro is doing for us. Given we are passing the `[unit: :secs]` keyword list to the macro (observe the `use Chronometer, unit: :secs` statement), we are able to store the `:secs` atom on a `time_unit` variable. Since `__using__/1` is a macro, it needs to abide by all the macro rules; namely, it needs to return a quoted expression.

On the quoted block injected into the caller module, we are importing the `ElixirDrip.Chronometer` module and then we register a `@time_unit` module attribute to store the chosen time unit. Notice that if no time unit is passed on the `use` statement as `:unit`, the `@time_unit` would be `nil`:

```
$ cat apps/elixir_drip/lib/elixir_drip/chronometer.ex
defmodule ElixirDrip.Chronometer do
  # ...
  defmacro __using__(options) do
    time_unit = options[:unit]

    quote do
      import unquote(__MODULE__)

      Module.register_attribute(__MODULE__, :time_unit, [])
      @time_unit unquote(time_unit)
    end
  end

  defmacro defchrono(function_definition, do: body) do
    {function, args} = Macro.decompose_call(function_definition)
    arity = length(args)

    quote bind_quoted: [
      function_definition: Macro.escape(function_definition),
      body: Macro.escape(body),
      function: function,
      arity: arity
    ] do
      def unquote(function_definition) do
        signature =
          pretty_signature(__MODULE__, unquote(function),
          unquote(arity))

        run_and_measure(@time_unit, signature, fn -> unquote(body) end)
      end
    end
  end
  # ...
end
```

The only way we changed the `defchrono/2` macro (besides cleaning up those debug `IO.puts/1` calls we had) was to call a new `run_and_measure/3` function that also receives the time unit to use. We then passed the `@time_unit` value to the new `run_and_measure/3` implementation that you can find as follows:

```
$ cat apps/elixir_drip/lib/elixir_drip/chronometer.ex
defmodule ElixirDrip.Chronometer do
  # ...
  def run_and_measure(time_unit, to_run, to_measure) do
    {time_µs, result} = :timer.tc(to_measure)

    {units, measured_time} = convert_time(time_unit, time_µs)
    IO.puts "Took #{measured_time} #{units} to run #{to_run}"

    result
  end

  defp convert_time(:hrs, time), do: {"hrs", time/(1_000_000*60*60)}
  defp convert_time(:mins, time), do: {"mins", time/(1_000_000*60)}
  defp convert_time(:secs, time), do: {"secs", time/1_000_000}
  defp convert_time(:millisecs, time), do: {"ms", time/1000}
  defp convert_time(:microsecs, time), do: {"µs", time}
  defp convert_time(_, time), do: {"µs", time}
end
```

By passing the time unit via the `use` mechanism, we are able to measure, using a variety of units, how long the `MeasuredModule` function calls take. If the `:unit` entry isn't passed as a `use` argument in the first place, the `@time_unit` would be passed to the `run_and_measure/3` function as `nil`, and we would default to showing the time in microseconds (notice the last catch-all `convert_time/2` function):

```
iex> c "./examples/measured_module.exs"
[MeasuredModule]

iex> MeasuredModule.slow_square
Took 2.001091 secs to run MeasuredModule.slow_square/1
9

iex> MeasuredModule.slow_times(9, 34)
Took 2.001472 secs to run MeasuredModule.slow_times/2
306
```

As you may have guessed by now, the importance of the `use` macro is paramount. Everywhere you look, be it Elixir itself or many third-party libraries, you will find the `use` macro as the common entry point to other modules. Given its pervasiveness, it may strike you as a *standard* way of injecting code into the caller module.

However, if you want to only *define* some new functions on the caller module, the `import/1` macro is more than enough.

Remember that the module calling `import ElixirDrip.Chronometer` will be able to call all the public macros and functions defined in the `Chronometer` module, without the need to specify the module first. You can even argue that to achieve the same outcome as we did with the previous `use` example, we could have changed the `defchrono/2` macro to also receive the `time_unit` as an argument, besides the function definition and the body of the measured function. Consider the following macro, which receives the `time_unit` parameter and doesn't change anything else:

```
$ cat apps/elixir_drip/lib/elixir_drip/chronometer.ex
defmodule ElixirDrip.Chronometer do
  # ...
  defmacro defchrono_with_units(time_unit, function_definition,
  do: body) do
    {function, args} = Macro.decompose_call(function_definition)
    arity = length(args)

    quote bind_quoted: [
      function_definition: Macro.escape(function_definition),
      body: Macro.escape(body),
      function: function,
      arity: arity,
      time_unit: time_unit
    ] do
      def unquote(function_definition) do
        signature =
          pretty_signature(__MODULE__, unquote(function),
          unquote(arity))

        run_and_measure(unquote(time_unit), signature, fn ->
        unquote(body) end)
      end
    end
  end
end
```

By using the `defchrono_with_units/3` macro, we wouldn't need the `use` mechanism because we wouldn't need to register a module attribute at all in the first place, and the `import` construct would be more than enough for our needs:

```
iex> defmodule SlowMath do
...> import ElixirDrip.Chronometer
...>
...> defchrono_with_units :mins, slow_sum(x, y) do
```

```
...> Process.sleep(1500)
...> IO.puts("slow sum: #{x + y}")
...> x+y
...> end
...> end

{:module, SlowMath,
  <<70, 79, 82, 49, 0, 0, 6, 248, 66, 69, 65, 77, 65, 116, 85, 56, 0,
    0, 1, 37,
    0, 0, 0, 27, 8, 69, 108, 105, 120, 105, 114, 46, 90, 8, 95, 95,
    105, 110,
    102, 111, 95, 95, 9, 102, 117, 110, 99, ...>>, {:slow_sum, 2}}

iex> SlowMath.slow_sum(33, 44)
slow sum: 77
Took 0.02501955 mins to run SlowMath.slow_sum/2
77
```

During our previous macro study, we started by directly *importing* the `Chronometer` module to the `MeasuredModule`, and in the last iteration we injected the `import` `Chronometer` statement with the help of the `__using__`/1 macro. In contrast with how *public* functions work, macros can't be used until you explicitly say you want to use them. Besides the `import`/1 macro, you can use the `require`/2 macro to access all the public macros of a module. However, this approach still expects that we prefix every macro call with the respective module. If we used `require` instead of `import` in our example, we would have to define all the `MeasuredModule` function calls with `ElixirDrip.Chronometer.defchrono`/2.

This is also the reason, even after doing `require Logger`, you still need to prefix your `debug`/1 macro calls with `Logger`:

```
iex> Logger.debug "hi there"
** (CompileError) iex:2: you must require Logger before invoking the macro
Logger.debug/1
    (elixir) src/elixir_dispatch.erl:97:
:elixir_dispatch.dispatch_require/6
iex> require Logger
Logger
iex> debug "still problematic"
** (CompileError) iex:3: undefined function debug/1

iex> Logger.debug "finally working"
08:28:53.657 [debug] finally working
:ok
```

We will now continue our trip into the world of macros. On the next stop, we'll have the opportunity to apply what we've learned up to this point and create a domain-specific language to help us define **GenStage Pipelines**. Let's get started!

Creating a domain-specific language

You may recall the chapter where we used `GenStage` to implement our upload and download pipelines. This enabled us to define each step role, and the `GenStage` behaviour would handle the subscription and message-passing logic between steps, ensuring that no step would get boggled with too many events.

We now want to improve on what we accomplished previously, by streamlining the pipeline and steps definition. To make this happen, we will create our very own **Domain-Specific Language** (**DSL**) to help define GenStage-based pipelines, with the help of some interesting macro tools. This will allow us to remove the *boilerplate* from our pipeline definitions and improve their expressiveness.

Given that, with macros, we are writing code that will generate code for us, it is a good tactic to, at least in the beginning, check the final generated code whenever you change the code-generation logic. Remember that `Macro.to_string/1` gives you the *pretty* string representation of any quoted expression, including the AST you're returning from your `__using__/1` macro.

Let's start by looking at the end result, so that we know what we are aiming for. Starting with a draft of how we want our pipeline definition gives us a clearer picture of what we need to implement:

```
$ cat apps/elixir_drip/lib/elixir_drip/storage/supervisors/
streamlined_upload_pipeline.ex
defmodule ElixirDrip.Storage.Supervisors.Upload.StreamlinedPipeline do
  alias ElixirDrip.Pipeliner
  alias ElixirDrip.Storage.Pipeline.{
    Starter,
    Encryption,
    RemoteStorage,
    Notifier
  }

  use Pipeliner,
    name: :upload_pipeline, min_demand: 1, max_demand: 10, count: 1

  start Starter, args: [:upload]
```

```
        step RemoteStorage
        step Encryption
        finish Notifier
    end
```

On this streamlined upload pipeline, we set the default `:min_demand`, `:max_demand` and `:count` options, which will be respected by every pipeline step, if they don't explicitly override them. Optionally, for each step, we can pass arguments that will be used to initialize the state of the `GenStage` process. We do exactly this on the `Starter` stage, to indicate from which queue it should fetch the upload tasks to create and emit the corresponding events. The other steps don't need any initialization arguments at all.

Now go back to the `ElixirDrip.Storage.Supervisors.Upload.Pipeline` and compare our streamlined version to the original upload pipeline. This version is arguably clearer, showing the sequence of stages without the additional statements for the subscription options. As we will see later, the subscription options are being inferred from the relative order of the pipeline stages.

Our plan is as follows:

- We will start by setting the default pipeline options as module attributes.
- Then, we'll collect a list with every stage of the pipeline.
- Afterward, we'll define the worker specs for each stage, so we can supervise each stage under the pipeline supervisor. It's here that we'll also create the logic to generate the subscription options for all the `ProducerConsumer` and `Consumer` steps.
- The last step will be to define the `start_link/0` and `init/1` functions of the pipeline, given that our pipelines are in fact regular supervisors.
- In the end, we will also take the opportunity to streamline our `Producer`, `ProducerConsumer`, and `Consumer` module definitions.

Let's get right into it!

Registering module attributes

Let's start by setting the default pipeline options. We want to register them as `@default_min_demand`, `@default_max_demand`, and `@default_count` on the caller module. If they aren't passed via the `use` parameters, we will set them as 1, 10, and 1, respectively.

Having the `count` as 1 means that each step will have a single process. This helps to debug and visualize things but doesn't leverage the Elixir capability of concurrently running thousands of processes. The `min_demand` and `max_demand` are also really small, and should be increased in a production scenario. For reference, and because these values also signal how suited to batch processing the `GenStage` constructs are, the default `max_demand` is set to `1000` and the `min_demand` to half that:

```
$ cat apps/elixir_drip/lib/elixir_drip/dsl/pipeliner.ex
defmodule ElixirDrip.Pipeliner do
  @pipeliner_default_count 1
  @pipeliner_default_min_demand 1
  @pipeliner_default_max_demand 10

  defmacro __using__(opts) do
    # defining the parameter values
    name = get_or_default(opts, :name, random_name(:pipeliner))
    default_count = get_or_default(opts, :count,
    @pipeliner_default_count)
    default_min_demand = get_or_default(opts, :min_demand,
    @pipeliner_default_min_demand)
    default_max_demand = get_or_default(opts, :max_demand,
    @pipeliner_default_max_demand)

    IO.puts "Building Pipeliner: #{name}"
    quote do
      use Supervisor
      import unquote(__MODULE__)

      # registering the needed module attributes
      Module.register_attribute(__MODULE__, :default_count, [])
      Module.register_attribute(__MODULE__, :default_min_demand, [])
      Module.register_attribute(__MODULE__, :default_max_demand, [])
      @default_count unquote(default_count)
      @default_min_demand unquote(default_min_demand)
      @default_max_demand unquote(default_max_demand)

      # helper function to see the pipeline default values
      def show_default_values do
        IO.puts "Defaults: count, min_demand, max_demand"
        [@default_count, @default_min_demand, @default_max_demand]
        |> Enum.map(&IO.inspect(&1))
      end
    end
  end

  # to get the parameter value from the `__using__/1` keyword options
  def get_or_default(options, _key, default \\ nil)
```

```
    def get_or_default([], _key, default), do: default
    def get_or_default(options, key, default) do
      case options[key] do
        nil -> default
        value -> value
      end
    end

    # to generate random names for each process and pipeline
    defp random_name(name), do: Module.concat(name, random_suffix())
    defp random_suffix, do: "P" <> (:crypto.strong_rand_bytes(4) |>
Base.encode16())
end
```

As you can see, we are employing the `use/2` and `__using__/1` macros to inject into the caller module the generated module attributes with the default `GenStage` parameters. We are temporarily injecting the `show_default_values/0` function only to assert that we are setting the expected values. In the following code snippet, we define two candidate modules, using the current version of the `ElixirDrip.Pipeliner`; the former is not defining any parameter and the latter is defining all the available parameters:

```
iex> defmodule Foo do
...> use ElixirDrip.Pipeliner
...> end
Building Pipeliner: Elixir.pipeliner.P95BE84C3

{:module, Foo,
 <<70, 79, 82, ...>>, {:show_default_values, 0}}

iex> Foo.show_default_values
Defaults: count=1, min_demand=1, max_demand=10
:ok

iex> defmodule Bar do
...> use ElixirDrip.Pipeliner, name: :bar, min_demand: 3, max_demand: 5,
count: 4
...> end
Building Pipeliner: bar

{:module, Bar,
 <<70, 79, 82, ...>>, {:show_default_values, 0}}

iex> Bar.show_default_values
Defaults: count=4, min_demand=3, max_demand=5
```

We were able to pass the pipeline parameters as expected. Let's now collect all pipeline steps in a list, so we can later create the subscription options and the worker definitions.

Collecting a list of pipeline steps

To collect the pipeline steps, we will register a @pipeline_steps module attribute. But, this time, we will pass the :accumulate option, meaning that every time this module attribute is used, it will append to its current value the value passed to it. When the compilation ends, the @pipeline_steps module attribute will contain a list with all those values, in our case all the pipeline steps:

```
$ cat apps/elixir_drip/lib/elixir_drip/dsl/pipeliner.ex
defmodule ElixirDrip.Pipeliner do
  # ...
  defmacro __using__(opts) do
    # ...
    IO.puts "Building Pipeliner: #{name}"
    quote do
      # ...
      Module.register_attribute(__MODULE__, :pipeline_steps,
      accumulate: true)

      @before_compile unquote(__MODULE__)

      def show_pipeline_steps do
        IO.puts "Trying to directly get the @pipeline_steps is a no-go:"
        IO.inspect(@pipeline_steps)

        IO.puts "Here are the pipeline steps:"
        get_pipeline_steps()
        |> IO.inspect()
      end
    end
  end

  defmacro __before_compile__(_environment) do
    quote do
      def get_pipeline_steps do
        Enum.reverse(@pipeline_steps)
      end
    end
  end
end
```

As you can see from the preceding snippet, we are also using the `@before_compile` module attribute. This module attribute indicates to the compiler that it should run the `__before_compile__/1` macro of the indicated module just before the compilation ends. In our case, we simply return the quoted representation of a `get_pipeline_steps/0` function that yields the reversed value of the `@pipeline_steps` module attribute.

If we simply try to access the `@pipeline_steps`, as we do in the first part of the `show_pipeline_steps/0` function, we won't get the collected steps we want. This happens because when the compiler expands the module attribute in that `IO.inspect/1` statement, the pipeline steps hadn't been collected yet. By defining a `get_pipeline_steps/0` function that returns the pipeline steps just before the compilation ends, we can be sure that all steps have been collected:

```
iex> defmodule Baz do
...> use ElixirDrip.Pipeliner
...> @pipeline_steps "a first step"
...> @pipeline_steps "a second step"
...> @pipeline_steps %{name: "a third step"}
...> @pipeline_steps 4.04
...> @pipeline_steps ["the", "last", "step"]
...> end
Building Pipeliner: Elixir.pipeliner.PC16BC9E5

{:module, Baz,
 <<70, 79, 82, ...>>, :ok}

iex> Baz.show_pipeline_steps
Trying to directly get the @pipeline_steps is a no-go:
[]
Here are the pipeline steps:
[
  "a first step",
  "a second step",
  %{name: "a third step"},
  4.04,
  ["the", "last", "step"]
]
```

In the previous example, we were defining the various steps manually to illustrate how they are collected into the `@pipeline_steps` list. Let's now create the `start/2`, `step/2` and `finish/2` macros that will actually create the *recipes* for each step, which later will be used to create the corresponding worker specs.

Let's focus ourselves on the `start/2` macro, given that all the mentioned macros are equivalent. The only difference lies in the first element of the returned keyword list: here, it has a `:producer` key, whereas on the `step/2` and `finish/2` macros, the key is a `:producer_consumer` and `:consumer` atom, respectively:

```
$ cat apps/elixir_drip/lib/elixir_drip/dsl/pipeliner.ex
defmodule ElixirDrip.Pipeliner do
  # ...
  defmacro start(producer, opts \\ []) do
    quote bind_quoted: [producer: producer, opts: opts] do
      options_and_args = get_options_and_args(opts, @default_count,
      @default_min_demand, @default_max_demand)

      @pipeline_steps [producer: producer] ++ options_and_args
      IO.puts "START: #{producer}, #{inspect(options_and_args)}"
    end
  end

  def get_options_and_args(opts, default_count, default_min_demand,
  default_max_demand) do
    options_and_args = fill_options_and_args(opts, default_count,
    default_min_demand, default_max_demand)

    options = Keyword.drop(options_and_args, [:args])
    [
      args: options_and_args[:args],
      options: options
    ]
  end

  def fill_options_and_args(options, default_count, default_min_demand,
  default_max_demand) do
    [{:args, []},
     {:count, default_count},
     {:min_demand, default_min_demand},
     {:max_demand, default_max_demand}]
    |> Enum.reduce([], fn {key, default}, result ->
      Keyword.put(result, key, get_or_default(options, key, default))
    end)
  end
end
```

On the `start/2` macro, after binding the `opts` variable, we rely on the `get_options_and_args/4` function to build the `options_and_args` value. This function receives a keyword list such as `[args: [:a, :b], min_demand: 3]` and returns a keyword list with `args` and `options` entries, for example, `[args: [:a, :b], options: [count: 1, min_demand: 3, max_demand: 10]]`. The arguments and options will be used as the internal state of the `GenStage` process and on the creation of the worker specs, respectively.

Let's now define the remaining `step/2` and `finish/2` macros:

```
$ cat apps/elixir_drip/lib/elixir_drip/dsl/pipeliner.ex
defmodule ElixirDrip.Pipeliner do
  # ...
  defmacro step(producer_consumer, opts \\ []) do
    quote bind_quoted: [producer_consumer: producer_consumer, opts:
    opts] do
      options_and_args = get_options_and_args(opts, @default_count,
      @default_min_demand, @default_max_demand)

      @pipeline_steps [producer_consumer: producer_consumer] ++
      options_and_args
      IO.puts "STEP: #{producer_consumer}, #
      {inspect(options_and_args)}"
    end
  end

  defmacro finish(consumer, opts \\ []) do
    quote bind_quoted: [consumer: consumer, opts: opts] do
      options_and_args = get_options_and_args(opts, @default_count,
      @default_min_demand, @default_max_demand)

      @pipeline_steps [consumer: consumer] ++ options_and_args
      IO.puts "CONSUMER: #{consumer}, #{inspect(options_and_args)}"
    end
  end
end
```

If we now define a pipeline, its pipeline steps with all the needed options will be initialized:

```
iex> defmodule Qaz do
...>    use ElixirDrip.Pipeliner
...>    start StartModule, args: [:start_arg1, :start_arg2], count: 2
...>    step Step1Module, min_demand: 4, max_demand: 6, count: 3,
...>    step Step2Module, count: 5
...>    finish FinishModule
...> end
Building Pipeliner: Elixir.pipeliner.P4B05D0B0
```

```
START: Elixir.StartModule, [args: [:start_arg1, :start_arg2], options:
[max_demand: 10, min_demand: 1, count: 2]]
STEP: Elixir.Step1Module, [args: [], options: [max_demand: 6, min_demand:
4, count: 3]]
STEP: Elixir.Step2Module, [args: [], options: [max_demand: 10, min_demand:
1, count: 5]]
CONSUMER: Elixir.FinishModule, [args: [], options: [max_demand: 10,
min_demand: 1, count: 1]]

{:module, Qaz,
 <<70, 79, 82, ...>>, :ok}
```

And we can use the `show_pipeline_steps/0` function to analyze those steps:

```
iex> Qaz.show_pipeline_steps
Trying to directly get the @pipeline_steps is a no-go:
[]
Here are the pipeline steps:
[
  [
    producer: StartModule,
    args: [:start_arg1, :start_arg2],
    options: [max_demand: 10, min_demand: 1, count: 2]
  ],
  [
    producer_consumer: Step1Module,
    args: [],
    options: [max_demand: 6, min_demand: 4, count: 3]
  ],
  [
    producer_consumer: Step2Module,
    args: [],
    options: [max_demand: 10, min_demand: 1, count: 5]
  ],
  [
    consumer: FinishModule,
    args: [],
    options: [max_demand: 10, min_demand: 1, count: 1]
  ]
]
```

Our next goal is to convert the previous pipeline steps into worker specs, so we can later initialize each worker with the respective subscription options.

Generating worker specs and subscription options

As we did previously, let's start with the logic that will convert a `start` step into a functional worker spec.

Producer stage

Given we are creating the pipeline `worker` specs, we need to import the `Supervisor.Spec` module so that we can use the `Supervisor.Spec.worker/3` function.

Since `GenStage` producers don't subscribe to any stage, we just need to create as many worker specs as the `count` option indicates. We concatenate the generated random `name` to the optional arguments to ensure that this name is passed when the `start_link` function is called during the producer process initialization. In the end, we return a tuple with two lists (created by *unzipping* the `{name, worker_spec}` tuples), one with the producer worker names, and the other with the corresponding worker specs:

```
$ cat apps/elixir_drip/lib/elixir_drip/dsl/pipeliner.ex
defmodule ElixirDrip.Pipeliner do
  import Supervisor.Spec
  # ...
  def get_worker_specs(producer: producer, args: args, options:
  options) do
    {count, _options} = Keyword.pop(options, :count)

    1..count
    |> Enum.map(fn _ ->
      name = random_name(producer)
      {name, worker(producer, args ++ [name], id: Atom.to_string(name))}
    end)
    |> Enum.unzip()
  end
end
```

If we call the `get_worker_specs/1` function with the first step of the `Qaz` pipeline, the following is what we get:

```
iex> producer_step = Qaz.show_pipeline_steps |> Enum.at(0)
[
  producer: StartModule,
  args: [:start_arg1, :start_arg2],
  options: [max_demand: 10, min_demand: 1, count: 2]
]
```

```
iex> ElixirDrip.Pipeliner.get_worker_specs(producer_step)
{
  [StartModule.P5EDD23C9, StartModule.P12858ABF], # worker names
  [ # worker specs
    {"Elixir.StartModule.P5EDD23C9",
     {StartModule, :start_link,
      [:start_arg1, :start_arg2, StartModule.P5EDD23C9]},
      :permanent, 5000, :worker, [StartModule]},
    {"Elixir.StartModule.P12858ABF",
     {StartModule, :start_link,
      [:start_arg1, :start_arg2, StartModule.P12858ABF]},
      :permanent, 5000, :worker, [StartModule]}
  ]
}
```

Notice the list of worker specs. When the supervisor initializes these workers, it will call the `StartModule.start_link/3` function, passing the `:start_arg1`, `:start_arg2` and the `StartModule.x` name as arguments. Given that we need to always pass the `name` argument, the `start_link` function of the producer module needs to receive `n+1` arguments, where `n` is the number of optional arguments.

Let's now see the slightly more complex case of the consumer stages, which also need subscription options to be started.

ProducerConsumer and Consumer stages

We now want to create an equivalent `get_worker_specs/1` function that also receives the subscription options that each worker should use. To illustrate this case, let's use the second stage of the previous `Qaz` pipeline:

```
iex> producer_consumer_step = Qaz.show_pipeline_steps |> Enum.at(1)
[
  producer_consumer: Step1Module,
  args: [],
  options: [max_demand: 6, min_demand: 4, count: 3]
]
```

We will spawn three `Step1Module` processes (given by the `count` option), and these processes will all subscribe to every process of the previous stage. The previous stage will have two processes (we already analyzed their worker specs); therefore, each of the three `Step1Module` processes will subscribe to the producer processes whose names were already generated. This is the reason we also return a list with all the process names for a given stage:

```
$ cat apps/elixir_drip/lib/elixir_drip/dsl/pipeliner.ex
```

```
defmodule ElixirDrip.Pipeliner do
  import Supervisor.Spec
  # ...
  def get_worker_specs(producer_consumer: producer_consumer,
  args: args, options: options, names_to_subscribe:
  names_to_subscribe),
    do: get_worker_specs_with_subscriptions(producer_consumer,
    args: args, options: options, names_to_subscribe:
    names_to_subscribe)

  defp get_worker_specs_with_subscriptions(consumer,
  args: args, options: options, names_to_subscribe: names_to_subscribe) do
    {count, options} = Keyword.pop(options, :count)

    subscriptions = names_to_subscribe
                    |> Enum.map(fn to_subscribe ->
                       {to_subscribe, options}
                    end)

    1..count
    |> Enum.map(fn _ ->
      name = random_name(consumer)
      args = args ++ [name, subscriptions]

      {name, worker(consumer, args, id: Atom.to_string(name))}
    end)
    |> Enum.unzip()
  end
end
```

As you can see, we have a `get_worker_specs/1` function that pattern-matches on a keyword list with a `:producer_consumer` and a `:names_to_subscribe` entries. This function delegates the work to the `get_worker_specs_with_subscriptions/2` function, which is very similar to the function we have for producer stages, but it adds the subscriptions as a *required* argument, besides with the existing `name`. We will use the last function for both `ProducerConsumer` and `Consumer` stages, since their respective processes need to subscribe to processes emitting events:

```
iex> ElixirDrip.Pipeliner.get_worker_specs(producer_consumer_step ++
[names_to_subscribe: [StartModule.P5EDD23C9, StartModule.P12858A
BF]])
{
 # worker names
 [Step1Module.P44712585, Step1Module.P68393018, Step1Module.P0F918D60],
  [ # worker specs
    {"Elixir.Step1Module.P44712585",
     {Step1Module, :start_link,
```

```
[
  Step1Module.P44712585, # name
  [ # subscriptions
    {StartModule.P5EDD23C9, [max_demand: 6, min_demand: 4]},
    {StartModule.P12858ABF, [max_demand: 6, min_demand: 4]}
  ]
]}, :permanent, 5000, :worker, [Step1Module]},
{"Elixir.Step1Module.P68393018", ...},
{"Elixir.Step1Module.P0F918D60", ...}
]
}
```

As you can see, the function returned three `Step1Module` worker specs named `Step1Module.P44712585`, `Step1Module.P68393018` and `Step1Module.P0F918D60`, each subscribing to the two `StartModule` processes passed via the `:names_to_subscribe` keyword. Given the `Step1Module` stage didn't define any arguments, only the `name` and `subscriptions` will be passed to the `Step1Module.start_link/2` function.

Before we move on, we need to create a similar `get_worker_specs/1` function that pattern-matches on the `:consumer` keyword entry instead:

```
$ cat apps/elixir_drip/lib/elixir_drip/dsl/pipeliner.ex
defmodule ElixirDrip.Pipeliner do
  import Supervisor.Spec
  # ...
  def get_worker_specs(producer_consumer: producer_consumer,
  args: args, options: options, names_to_subscribe:
  names_to_subscribe),
    do: get_worker_specs_with_subscriptions(producer_consumer,
    args: args, options: options, names_to_subscribe:
    names_to_subscribe)
  # ...
end
```

We are now able to tackle the following phase: how to collect the worker specs of each stage.

Collecting the pipeline worker specs

The goal is now to generate and aggregate the worker specs of each stage, while also passing them the process names of the previous stage (except on the first producer stage, which doesn't subscribe to any stage).

This is exactly what the following `pipeline_specs/1` function does: it starts by reducing all the `steps` it receives. When the resulting `worker_specs` is empty, it means we are looking at the first producer step, so we simply add the outcome of `get_worker_specs(step)` to the end result. If it isn't empty, it means we are processing a `ProducerConsumer` or a `Consumer` stage, so we need to add the `names_to_subscribe` keyword to the `step` before getting its worker specs:

```
$ cat apps/elixir_drip/lib/elixir_drip/dsl/pipeliner.ex
defmodule ElixirDrip.Pipeliner do
  import Supervisor.Spec
  # ...
  def pipeline_specs(steps) do
    steps
    |> Enum.reduce([], fn step, worker_specs ->
      step = case Enum.empty?(worker_specs) do
        true -> step
        _ ->
          {names_to_subscribe, _} = Enum.at(worker_specs, -1)
          step ++ [names_to_subscribe: names_to_subscribe]
      end
      worker_specs ++ [get_worker_specs(step)]
    end)
    |> Enum.unzip()
    |> elem(1)
    |> List.flatten()
  end
end
```

The `Enum.reduce/2` result is a list where each element is a tuple with the worker name and its spec, so we unzip it to get a tuple with a list of all the worker names in one element and a list of all the worker specs in the other, grab the list with the worker specs, and flatten it. We finally have the worker specs ready to be parsed by the pipeline supervisor! Take a look at the following:

```
iex> Qaz.show_pipeline_steps |> ElixirDrip.Pipeliner.pipeline_specs
[
  # two StartModule processes
  {"Elixir.StartModule.PB6AD0F42",
   {StartModule, :start_link, [:start_arg1, :start_arg2,
   StartModule.PB6AD0F42]},
   :permanent, 5000, :worker, [StartModule]},
  {"Elixir.StartModule.PDD3D519D", ...},

  # three Step1Module processes subscribing
  # to the two previous stage processes
  {"Elixir.Step1Module.PAEC81181",
```

```
  {Step1Module, :start_link,
   [
     Step1Module.PAEC81181,
     [ # two subscriptions for each process
       {StartModule.PB6AD0F42, [max_demand: 6, min_demand: 4]},
       {StartModule.PDD3D519D, [max_demand: 6, min_demand: 4]}
     ]
   ]}, :permanent, 5000, :worker, [Step1Module]},
{"Elixir.Step1Module.PAEC1AE45", ...},
{"Elixir.Step1Module.PAEC5EBB3", ...},

# five Step2Module processes subscribing
# to the previous three stage processes
{"Elixir.Step2Module.P08E72352",
 {Step2Module, :start_link,
  [
    Step2Module.P08E72352,
    [ # three subscriptions for each process
      {Step1Module.PAEC81181, [max_demand: 10, min_demand: 1]},
      {Step1Module.PAEC1AE45, [max_demand: 10, min_demand: 1]},
      {Step1Module.PAEC5EBB3, [max_demand: 10, min_demand: 1]}
    ]
  ]}, :permanent, 5000, :worker, [Step2Module]},
{"Elixir.Step2Module.P1470075A", ...},
{"Elixir.Step2Module.P9200FBE7", ...},
{"Elixir.Step2Module.PD4EB8A27", ...},
{"Elixir.Step2Module.P7A005C99", ...},

# one FinishModule process subscribing
# to the previous five stage processes
{"Elixir.FinishModule.PA2194E2F",
 {FinishModule, :start_link,
  [
    FinishModule.PA2194E2F,
    [
      {Step2Module.P08E72352, [max_demand: 10, min_demand: 1]},
      {Step2Module.P1470075A, [max_demand: 10, min_demand: 1]},
      {Step2Module.P9200FBE7, [max_demand: 10, min_demand: 1]},
      {Step2Module.PD4EB8A27, [max_demand: 10, min_demand: 1]},
      {Step2Module.P7A005C99, [max_demand: 10, min_demand: 1]}
    ]
  ]}, :permanent, 5000, :worker, [FinishModule]}
]
```

If we pass all the worker specs mentioned previously to a `Supervisor.init/2` function, it will happily start all the 11 pipeline processes, assuming the `StartModule`, `Step1Module`, `Step2Module`, and `FinishModule` modules exist and implement the needed `GenStage` callback functions; that is to say, `handle_demand/2` for a `Producer` stage and `handle_events/3` for a `ProducerConsumer` or `Consumer` stage.

Let's now define the pipeline supervisor functions, so we can have a fully functional DSL!

Defining the supervisor functions

Given that all the hard work has already been done in the previous sections, we just need to inject in the caller module the `start_link/0` and `init/1` functions, so it can be started as a normal supervisor:

```
$ cat apps/elixir_drip/lib/elixir_drip/dsl/pipeliner.ex
defmodule ElixirDrip.Pipeliner do
  import Supervisor.Spec
  # ...
  defmacro __using__(opts) do
    # ...
    IO.puts "Building Pipeliner: #{name}"
    quote do
      # ...
      Module.register_attribute(__MODULE__, :pipeline_steps,
      accumulate: true)

      @before_compile unquote(__MODULE__)

      def start_link(),
        do: Supervisor.start_link(__MODULE__, [], name: unquote(name))

      def init(_) do
        worker_specs_to_start = get_pipeline_steps()
                                |> pipeline_specs()

        Supervisor.init(
          worker_specs_to_start,
          strategy: :rest_for_one,
          name: __MODULE__
        )
      end

      def show_pipeline_steps do
        # ...
      end
```

```
      end
    end
  end
```

On the `start_link/0` function, we simply start the supervisor with the `name` we previously obtained. On the `init/1` function, we fetch the pipeline steps, convert them to worker specs, and then initialize the supervisor with the mentioned worker specs.

Notice that most of the functions used for the DSL aren't injected on the caller module. We opt instead to call the functions that live on the `ElixirDrip.Pipeliner` module (the caller module can access those because it imports the `Pipeliner` module). This is a good practice that aims to avoid cluttering the caller module with functions that are only needed in compile time for macro expansion.

 To see the full code of the `ElixirDrip.Pipeliner` module, check the `apps/elixir_drip/lib/elixir_drip/dsl/pipeliner.ex` file on the ElixirDrip umbrella project.

We could end here and call it a day; after all, the pipeline DSL is complete and working as expected. But wouldn't it be nice to have some mechanism that would simplify the definition of the pipeline stages as well? Check the next section for some more metaprogramming goodies.

Streamlining GenStage modules

For now, our pipeline modules (that is, `Starter`, `Encryption`, `RemoteStorage`, and `Notifier`) are still defining the needed `start_link` and `init/1` functions by themselves. Let's start by streamlining the pipeline producer modules.

Simpler pipeline producers

For the producer stage, we are currently passing the `name` and `type` via the `start_link/2` function:

```
$ cat apps/elixir_drip/lib/elixir_drip/storage/pipeline/starter.ex
defmodule ElixirDrip.Storage.Pipeline.Starter do
  use GenStage
  require Logger
  alias ElixirDrip.Storage.Workers.QueueWorker

  @queue_polling 5000
```

```
def start_link(name, type) do
  GenStage.start_link(__MODULE__, type, name: name)
end

def init(type) do
  Logger.debug("#{inspect(self())}: #{type} Pipeline Starter
  started.")

  {
    :producer,
    %{queue: QueueWorker.queue_name(type), type: type, pending: 0}
  }
end
# ...
end
```

We can see a pattern here: the `name` argument is only used by the `start_link/2` function to set the producer process name when we start it, whereas the `type` argument is simply passed to the `init/1` function via the `GenStage.start_link/3` call, and it's used to initialize the process state. In a sense, we can consider the `name` argument as required because the process start depends on it and the `type` argument as optional, since it only contributes for the initial state of the process. In the end, the `init/1` function returns a two element tuple with `:producer` and the initial process state.

Let's create a `Pipeliner.Producer` macro module that helps in the definition of the two previous functions. We will apply again the `use/__using__/1` construct to indicate what the optional arguments are. The preceding code snippet will be simplified into the following:

```
$ cat apps/elixir_drip/lib/elixir_drip/storage/pipeline/starter.ex
defmodule ElixirDrip.Storage.Pipeline.Starter do
  require Logger
  alias ElixirDrip.Storage.Workers.QueueWorker

  use ElixirDrip.Pipeliner.Producer, args: [:type]

  @impl ElixirDrip.Pipeliner.Producer
  def prepare_state([type]) do
    Logger.debug("#{inspect(self())}: #{type} Pipeline Starter
    started.")

    %{queue: QueueWorker.queue_name(type), type: type, pending: 0}
  end
  # ...
end
```

Looking at the end result, we can understand this module is a producer with one optional argument that needs to execute some additional steps to prepare the initial process state. Behind the scenes, a `start_link/2` function that sets a random name for the process and an `init/1` function that calls the `prepare_state/1` function are being set for us by the `Pipeliner.Producer` module.

We rely on the `Pipeliner.get_or_default/3` function to fetch the `args` passed via the `__using__/1` options, and we then create the optional and required arguments, using the `create_args/2` function. This function relies on the `Macro.var/2` function to generate the quoted representation of each variable.

Remember that every quoted representation is a, possibly nested, three-element tuple. Therefore, function variables are also represented in the same way. Doing `Macro.var(:name, __MODULE__)` will yield `{:name, [], __MODULE__}`, the variable quoted representation, ready to be injected into another AST.

Given that the generated `start_link` function will have to receive both optional and required arguments, we merge them into a new `function_args` variable. The number of arguments this function receives changes proportionally to the number of optional arguments we have. In this kind of situation, the `unquote_splicing/1` is really useful because it unquotes in place each element of the list it receives, making it the perfect aid when defining a function with variable arguments.

In this example, the `function_args` variable will contain `[{:type, [], __MODULE__}, {:name, [], __MODULE__}]`; that is to say, the quoted representation of the `type` and `name` variables.

When we define the `start_link` function with the `unquote_splicing(function_args)` arguments, the function arguments will effectively become `unquote(type), unquote(name)`. On the `start_link` function body, we use the `name` argument as the new process name and pass the `optional_args` list to the `init/1` function, via the second argument of the `GenStage.start_link/3` function:

```
$ cat apps/elixir_drip/lib/elixir_drip/dsl/pipeliner_producer.ex
defmodule ElixirDrip.Pipeliner.Producer do
  import ElixirDrip.Pipeliner
  # ...
  defmacro __using__(opts) do
    args = get_or_default(opts, :args, [])

    optional_args = create_args(__MODULE__, args)
    required_args = create_args(__MODULE__, [:name])
```

```
    function_args = optional_args ++ required_args

    quote do
      use GenStage
      # ...
      def start_link(unquote_splicing(function_args)) do
        GenStage.start_link(__MODULE__, unquote(optional_args), name: name)
      end
      # ...
    end
  end

  defp create_args(_, []), do: []
  defp create_args(module, arg_names),
    do: Enum.map(arg_names, &Macro.var(&1, module))
end
```

Let's now analyze how the `init/1` function is generated. As we previously saw, the `optional_args` list is passed to the `init/1` function (notice the enclosing `[...]` used to pattern-match on the single argument of the `init/1` function). As such, this function receives the list and then calls the default implementation of the `prepare_state/1` function, which is also injected into the caller module by the `Pipeliner.Producer` module. In the end, it returns the expected `{:producer, state}` tuple that the `GenStage` behaviour requires:

```
$ cat apps/elixir_drip/lib/elixir_drip/dsl/pipeliner_producer.ex
defmodule ElixirDrip.Pipeliner.Producer do
  import ElixirDrip.Pipeliner

  @callback prepare_state(list(any)) :: any

  defmacro __using__(opts) do
    # ... optional_args, required_args and function_args definition

    quote do
      use GenStage
      @behaviour unquote(__MODULE__)
      @behaviour GenStage
      # ...

      @impl GenStage
      def init([unquote_splicing(optional_args)]) do
        args = prepare_state(unquote(optional_args))

        {:producer, args}
      end
```

```
        @impl unquote(__MODULE__)
        def prepare_state(args), do: args

        defoverridable unquote(__MODULE__)
      end
    end
    # ...
end
```

The default implementation of the `prepare_state/1` function consists of an identity function because it returns exactly the arguments it receives. To allow the caller module to implement its own version of the `prepare_state/1` function and override the default version, we define the `prepare_state/1` function as a `@callback`, and we then say that it is possible to override the functions of the module being injected with `defoverridable` `Pipeliner.Producer`. By calling the `defoverridable/1` with a module, we are saying that every implemented callback function of the indicated module is *overridable*. In our case, given that the only callback is the `prepare_state/1` function, we could have designated the specific callback by using `defoverridable [prepare_state: 2]` instead.

We are using the `@impl Foo` annotations to indicate to the compiler that those functions are implementing a callback from the `Foo` module. One of the benefits of doing this is that, once the compiler sees one `@impl` annotation, it will check whether the function name and arity of *all* the overriding functions match the signature of the respective behaviour callbacks. Using the `@impl` mechanism once is enough for the compiler to check every behaviour the module implements. So if we omit the `@impl GenStage` from the `init/1` function we are injecting on the caller module, the following warning would be raised:

```
iex> recompile
==> elixir_drip
Compiling 12 files (.ex)

warning: module attribute @impl was not set for function init/1 callback
(specified in GenStage). This either means you forgot to add the "@impl
true" annotation before the definition or that you are accidentally
overriding this callback
    lib/elixir_drip/storage/pipeline/starter.ex:24
```

Let's now apply the same approach to simplify our pipeline consumers.

Simpler pipeline (producer) consumers

The approach we'll now adopt is really similar to the previous one for producer stages. Currently, this is what the `RemoteStorage` stage looks like:

```
$ cat apps/elixir_drip/lib/elixir_drip/storage/pipeline/
remote_storage.ex
defmodule ElixirDrip.Storage.Pipeline.RemoteStorage do
  use GenStage
  require Logger
  alias ElixirDrip.Storage
  alias Storage.Provider
  alias Storage.Supervisors.CacheSupervisor, as: Cache

  @dummy_state []

  def start_link(name, subscription_options),
    do: GenStage.start_link(__MODULE__, subscription_options, name: name)

  def init(subscription_options) do
    Logger.debug("#{inspect(self())}: Pipeline RemoteStorage started.
    Options: #{inspect(subscription_options)}")

    {:producer_consumer, @dummy_state, subscription_options}
  end
  # ...
end
```

Let's see the end result applied to the same `RemoteStorage` stage, which is a producer consumer. The main difference here lies in the additional `type` option passed via the `use` options (the module we'll create will be used by both producer consumers and consumers) and the new subscription options, both needed by the `init/1` callback:

```
$ cat apps/elixir_drip/lib/elixir_drip/storage/pipeline/
remote_storage.ex
defmodule ElixirDrip.Storage.Pipeline.RemoteStorage do
  require Logger
  alias ElixirDrip.Storage
  alias Storage.Provider
  alias Storage.Supervisors.CacheSupervisor, as: Cache

  use ElixirDrip.Pipeliner.Consumer, type: :producer_consumer

  @impl ElixirDrip.Pipeliner.Consumer
  def prepare_state(@dummy_state) do
    Logger.debug("#{inspect(self())}: Streamlined Pipeline
    RemoteStorage started.")
```

```
          @dummy_state
      end
      # ...
  end
```

In this scenario, we are overriding the default implementation of the `prepare_state/1` function only to log the debug message, given our implementation returns the same value initially passed as the function argument.

As we briefly hinted before, the `Pipeliner.Consumer` also needs to pass the subscription options to the `init/1` GenStage callback. Besides the optional arguments, the `start_link` function will receive the `name` and `sub_options` required arguments. Since the `name` argument is only used at this point, it isn't passed to the `init/1` function. Only the optional and `sub_options` arguments are passed to it. This is the reason why we use the `optional_and_subscription_args` on the `init/1` callback definition, instead of only passing the optional arguments as we did on the `Pipeliner.Producer` module:

```
$ cat apps/elixir_drip/lib/elixir_drip/dsl/pipeliner_consumer.ex
defmodule ElixirDrip.Pipeliner.Consumer do
  import ElixirDrip.Pipeliner

  @callback prepare_state(list(any)) :: any

  defmacro __using__(opts) do
    # validating the :type option
    type = get_or_default(opts, :type)
    if type not in [:producer_consumer, :consumer] do
      raise ArgumentError, ":type needs to be one of :producer_consumer
      or :consumer"
    end

    # creating the arguments passed to
    # the start_link and init/1 functions
    args = get_or_default(opts, :args, [])

    optional_args = create_args(__MODULE__, args)
    required_args = create_args(__MODULE__, [:name, :sub_options])

    # start_link arguments
    function_args = optional_args ++ required_args

    # init/1 arguments with the subscription options
    optional_and_subscription_args = optional_args ++
    create_args(__MODULE__, [:sub_options])

    quote do
```

```
        # returning the quoted block macro result
      end
    end
    # ...
end
```

In the previous code snippet, we started by validating the `type` option passed through the `use/2` options. Afterward, we will `unquote` the `type` option as the first element of the three-element tuple returned by the `init/1` callback, to indicate whether this stage is a `:producer_consumer` or a `:consumer` stage:

```
$ cat apps/elixir_drip/lib/elixir_drip/dsl/pipeliner_consumer.ex
defmodule ElixirDrip.Pipeliner.Consumer do
  import ElixirDrip.Pipeliner
  # ...
  defmacro __using__(opts) do
    # ...
    quote do
      use GenStage
      @behaviour unquote(__MODULE__)
      @behaviour GenStage

      # we are passing the optional_and_subscription_args
      # to the init/1 function via the GenStage.start_link/3 function
      def start_link(unquote_splicing(function_args)) do
        GenStage.start_link(
            __MODULE__, unquote(optional_and_subscription_args), name: name)
      end

      @impl GenStage
      def init([unquote_splicing(optional_and_subscription_args)]) do
        state = prepare_state(unquote(optional_args))

        # injecting the stage type
        {unquote(type), state, subscribe_to: sub_options}
      end

      @impl unquote(__MODULE__)
      def prepare_state(args), do: args

      defoverridable unquote(__MODULE__)
    end
  end
  # ...
end
```

To use the same module to streamline the `Notifier` stage definition, it will be just a matter of passing `:consumer` as the `type` option when we use the `Pipeliner.Consumer` module:

```
$ cat apps/elixir_drip/lib/elixir_drip/storage/pipeline/notifier.ex

defmodule ElixirDrip.Storage.Pipeline.Notifier do
  require Logger

  @dummy_state []

  use ElixirDrip.Pipeliner.Consumer, type: :consumer

  @impl ElixirDrip.Pipeliner.Consumer
  def prepare_state([]) do
    Logger.debug("#{inspect(self())}: Streamlined Pipeline Notifier
    started.")

    @dummy_state
  end
  # ...
end
```

We have not only created a DSL to better express a `GenStage` pipeline, but we also simplified each stage definition by using the recently created `Pipeliner.Producer` and `Pipeliner.Consumer` modules. By applying some neat macro patterns, we were able to remove a lot of the boilerplate we had.

We will now recap some of the constructs and tools we used.

Macros cheat sheet

Metaprogramming may feel daunting at first. We're doing a lot even before compilation starts, and the errors and warnings we get may seem cryptic sometimes. Having a clear end goal on your mind, and performing small iterations, will allow you to get comfortable with the `quote/2` and `unquote/1` dance and let you accomplish some neat macro-based features.

What follows is a brief compilation of the main concepts and tools we applied, which you can now incorporate in your tool belt:

- The abstract syntax tree of any expression, also called a *quoted representation,* is a nested structure of three element tuples that the compiler knows how to convert into BEAM bytecode. You can get this quoted representation by using the `quote/2` macro.

- Inside a `quote/1` block, the compiler is generating the quoted representation of each statement. When it finds an `unquote/1`, it stops the AST generation and evaluates and injects the value it gets.

- The `bind_quoted` option of the `quote/2` macro helps you to not only declutter your macros but also to avoid potential bugs because you only evaluate the *bind-quoted* variables once. By default, it disables the `unquote/1` calls inside the `quote` block. Given the `bind_quoted` option expects variables in their quoted form, you may need to use `Macro.escape/1` for not-literal variables.

- `Code.eval_quoted/3` receives a quoted expression and evaluates it, returning the result and the resulting bindings.

- `Macro.to_string/1` receives a quoted expression and returns the respective source code, indented and ready to be piped to the `IO.puts/1` function.

- Saving the `result` of a macro (in its quoted form) and doing a `Macro.to_string(result) |> IO.puts` before returning the macro `result`, helps you to see the code your macro is actually generating.

- When using `var!/2` to prevail over the macro hygiene, you should ideally pass the module where the macro lives as the variable context. This way, we only leak into the macro module, not into the caller module. Think thrice if you really need to pollute the caller module.

- Apply the `use/2` macro if you need to do something on `__using__/1`, such as creating module attributes on the caller module, and so on. If not, you can simply use `import/2` to get the macros and functions of your macro module accessible.

- Reduce as much as possible the code being injected into the caller module. By calling normal functions living on the macro module, you are able to test them more easily and this way you simplify as much as possible the actual code injected into the caller module.

- Compile-time hooks let you perform custom logic at different moments of the code's life cycle. Like the `@before_compile` applied by us that lets us access the accumulated values present on module attributes just before compilation starts, there are other hooks like `@after_compile`, `@on_definition`, and `@on_load`.

- If you want the caller module to be able to override some of the functions you're injecting, the `@behaviour`, `@impl`, and the `defoverridable/1` macro can help you to safely implement adopted behaviours and allow the caller module to redefine some of those default implementations.

You can now go out and explore, having all these new tools at your disposal. Metaprogramming begs you to tinker with it and to try new ways of applying it. At this stage, you aren't confined to the standard building blocks you're offered at the entrance, but you are now able to create your very own building blocks from scratch!

Summary

We accomplished a lot throughout this chapter. Let's look back at the main topics that we covered:

- The Elixir abstract syntax tree consists of a tree-like data structure composed of nested three-element tuples representing your code. This data structure can be manipulated using the `quote/2` and `unquote/1` constructs and is also called a *quoted expression*.
- By default, Elixir enforces a macro hygiene rule that doesn't allow us to impinge into the caller module, unless we specifically want to.
- Macros are functions whose arguments are quoted before reaching the function body and have to return valid quoted expressions as well. Macros are expanded right before compile time.
- The `use` and `__using__/1` macros let the macro module inject code into the caller module. We used these constructs to register a `@time_unit` module attribute in the caller module, so we could control the time units used by the `defchrono/2` macro.
- We created a domain-specific language to streamline the definition of parallel GenStage pipelines, and we also improved the pipeline stage definition, only requiring the `handle_demand/2` and `handle_events/2` callbacks to be implemented.

Here, we have understood how metaprogramming works. In the following chapter, we will delve into Ecto and how it helps us to persist and query our application data. Given the heavy metaprogramming usage by Ecto, you will feel right at home!

Persisting Data Using Ecto

Given the data storage nature of the application we're developing, it's crucial to ensure the persistence of all the media information stored in ElixirDrip works properly. To accomplish this, we will use PostgreSQL as our database, and Ecto as a tool that easily lets us interact with the database and access our application data.

As you will see, working with a database in Elixir is a joy, thanks to the well-crafted abstractions that make our code more expressive while, at the same time, ensuring the required performance in all the data-access operations.

A distinct feature of Ecto is that it never tries to hide the database from you or force you to use its abstractions. You have total flexibility, meaning that you can always overcome the abstraction layer by directly issuing SQL statements from your Elixir application, and Ecto will happily convert the results into plain Elixir data structures. After all, the database is there to help us!

In this chapter, we'll cover the following topics:

- Connecting to the database
- Creating database tables and their Elixir representation
- Using changesets to update our data
- Managing relationships between tables
- Ensuring data integrity with database constraints
- Composing expressive queries

Let's start by connecting to the ElixirDrip database.

Connecting to the database

In the introduction, we hinted at how we'll use Ecto to store our application data in a PostgreSQL database. Ecto is able to connect to many databases, but for each database it needs the respective driver to establish the connection, support queries, and so on.

In our case we'll use the `postgrex` library, which provides the PostgreSQL Elixir driver. But don't think Ecto is tied to PostgreSQL in any way, because Ecto supports other databases like MySQL, DynamoDB, and SQLite, among others.

Let's start by adding the `ecto` and `postgrex` libraries to our `elixir_drip` umbrella app dependencies:

```
$ cat apps/elixir_drip/mix.exs
defmodule ElixirDrip.Mixfile do
  use Mix.Project

  defp deps do
    [
      {:postgrex, "~> 0.13"},
      {:ecto, "~> 2.1"},
      # ...
    ]
  end
end
```

These two dependencies will be fetched by `mix` as soon as we run `mix deps.get`. The next step consists of defining and configuring the Ecto repository. Every database operation passes through it, and it's the responsibility of the repository to ask the underlying database driver to interact with the database on its behalf.

 The repository will use an Ecto adapter, in our case `Ecto.Adapters.Postgres`, and it's this adapter that will interact with the `postgrex` driver.

The following `ElixirDrip.Repo` module materializes our Ecto repository:

```
$ cat apps/elixir_drip/lib/elixir_drip/repo.ex
defmodule ElixirDrip.Repo do
  use Ecto.Repo, otp_app: :elixir_drip

  def init(_, opts) do
    {:ok, Keyword.put(opts, :url, System.get_env("DATABASE_URL"))}
  end
end
```

By using `Ecto.Repo`, we will be able to perform all the database operations through the `ElixirDrip.Repo` module. The `:otp_app` option is mandatory and indicates which application has the repository configuration; in our case, the repository configuration exists under the `elixir_drip` application configuration.

We are overriding the `Ecto.Repo.init/2` callback so we can dynamically set the database URL when the application starts. This may be useful because Elixir is a compiled language, and so the configuration values set during compile-time end up crystallized into your application. With this approach, you're able to connect your compiled ElixirDrip application to a different database by setting a given `DATABASE_URL` environment variable before running the application.

By analyzing the `elixir_drip` configuration file, we will find the `:ecto_repos` entry, which points to a list of Ecto repositories. These repositories are used when we run any Ecto Mix task, such as the `ecto.create` task responsible for database creation, which we'll look at in a minute:

```
$ cat apps/elixir_drip/config/config.exs
use Mix.Config

config :elixir_drip, ecto_repos: [ElixirDrip.Repo]
# ...
import_config "#{Mix.env()}.exs"
```

In the end, we're importing a `"#{Mix.env()}.exs"` configuration file (using the `Mix.Config.import_config/1` macro). As such, let's check the `dev.exs` configuration file used in development:

```
$ cat apps/elixir_drip/config/dev.exs
use Mix.Config

config :elixir_drip, ElixirDrip.Repo,
  adapter: Ecto.Adapters.Postgres,
  username: System.get_env("DB_USER"),
  password: System.get_env("DB_PASS"),
  database: System.get_env("DB_NAME"),
  hostname: System.get_env("DB_HOST"),
  port: System.get_env("DB_PORT"),
  pool_size: 10
```

In the previous snippet, we have `ElixirDrip.Repo` being configured in the scope of the `:elixir_drip` application (as we pointed out previously with the `:otp_app` option when we defined the repository). We are using the Ecto Postgres database adapter, and in development we obtain the `username`, `password`, `database`, `hostname`, and `port` values from the `DB_*` environment variables.

We're running a PostgreSQL database on port 5432 in our current development environment, so we've set the values of the DB_* environment variables as follows:

```
$ env | grep DB_
DB_PORT=5432
DB_NAME=elixir_drip_dev
DB_PASS=123456
DB_HOST=localhost
DB_USER=postgres
```

As we saw in the development configuration file, these environment variables are being used to set all the required configurations to start ElixirDrip.Repo.

With the previous configuration in place, we're just missing one last piece of the puzzle to get the repository up and running: we need to actually start the repository as a supervisor. To do this, we'll edit the ElixirDrip.Application module and add the ElixirDrip.Repo supervisor as one more child that will be started by the elixir_drip root supervisor:

```
$ cat apps/elixir_drip/lib/elixir_drip/application.ex
defmodule ElixirDrip.Application do
  use Application

  def start(_type, _args) do
    import Supervisor.Spec, warn: false

    Supervisor.start_link(
      [
        supervisor(ElixirDrip.Repo, []),
        # ...
      ],
      strategy: :one_for_one,
      name: ElixirDrip.Supervisor
    )
  end
end
```

We will now finally interact with the database! Let's start by creating the database with the ecto.create Mix task. This task will create the database given by the :database entry of the ElixirDrip.Repo configuration on the dev Mix environment:

```
$ echo $MIX_ENV
dev

$ mix ecto.create
The database for ElixirDrip.Repo has been created
```

```
$ mix ecto.create
The database for ElixirDrip.Repo has already been created
```

If you try to create the database again, Ecto tells you the database already exists. Let's now execute our first SQL query, by looking at the `pg_catalog.pg_tables` table that exists in every PostgreSQL database. For this, we will ask `ElixirDrip.Repo` to run a raw SQL query for us with the `Repo.query/1` function:

```
iex> {:ok, result} = ElixirDrip.Repo.query("select * from
pg_catalog.pg_tables")
16:29:16.295 [debug] QUERY OK db=3.4ms
select * from pg_catalog.pg_tables []

{:ok,
 %Postgrex.Result{
   columns: ["schemaname", "tablename", "tableowner", "tablespace",
    "hasindexes", "hasrules", "hastriggers", "rowsecurity"],
   command: :select,
   connection_id: 27527,
   num_rows: 62,
   rows: [
     ["pg_catalog", "pg_statistic", "postgres", nil, true, false,
     false, false],
     # ...
   ]
}}

iex> result.rows |> Enum.slice(0, 3)
[
  ["pg_catalog", "pg_statistic", "postgres", nil, true, false, false,
  false],
  ["pg_catalog", "pg_type", "postgres", nil, true, false, false, false],
  ["pg_catalog", "pg_authid", "postgres", "pg_global", true, false, false,
  false]
]
```

The `debug` log message shows us the query that was executed, and we got an `:ok` tuple with a `Postgrex.Result` with 62 rows retrieved. Each list in the `rows` field corresponds to a row in the query result.

We just ran a raw SQL query with the `ElixirDrip.Repo.query/1` function. As you'll see in the following sections, we will use the `Repo.one/2` and `Repo.all/2` callbacks to run a query that, respectively, retrieves one or more than one result.

Let's now use the `ElixirDrip.Repo.all/2` callback to run the previous query, but this time only obtaining the `tablename` column:

```
iex> ElixirDrip.Repo.all(from r in "pg_tables", select: [:tablename])
17:02:58.339 [debug] QUERY OK source="pg_tables" db=11.9ms decode=7.3ms
queue=0.1ms
SELECT p0."tablename" FROM "pg_tables" AS p0 []
[
 %{tablename: "pg_statistic"},
 %{tablename: "pg_type"},
 %{tablename: "pg_authid"},
 # ...
]
```

Don't worry too much about the query syntax we've used, we have a whole section dedicated to it at the end of this chapter. As you may have guessed, Ecto isn't only about reading data from the database. You have `Repo.update/2`, `Repo.insert/2`, `Repo.delete/2`, and many other callbacks that allow you to work with the database as you please. We will explore many of these throughout this chapter.

For now, we will start by defining the ElixirDrip Ecto schemas to simplify how we interact with the database and implement our application business logic.

Schemas and migrations

Given we are now connected to the database, we will set the data foundations of our project. In this section, we'll create the schemas that represent our users and their media, and the corresponding data migrations.

Schemas

Our ElixirDrip project allows users to safely store their media, and eventually share it with other users. Therefore, we need to have a way to represent users and media as database tables.

To help developers with this, Ecto has the *schema* construct. Its purpose is to establish a mapping between any information stored in the database and its representation in Elixir data structures.

Let's define the schema to represent the users' media:

```
$ cat apps/elixir_drip/lib/elixir_drip/storage/media.ex
defmodule ElixirDrip.Storage.Media do
  use Ecto.Schema

  schema "storage_media" do
    field :user_id, :id
    field :file_name, :string
    field :full_path, :string
    field :file_size, :integer
    field :metadata, :map, default: %{}
    field :encryption_key, :string
    field :storage_key, :string
    field :uploaded_at, :utc_datetime

    timestamps()
  end
end
```

We are defining this schema under the `Storage` context, because there may be more than one schema for the same database table. Imagine if we had an `Audit` context that only needed to know about the media creator (given by `user_id`), file path, name, and the respective storage key. In this case, an `Audit.Media` schema could be created and it would only expose the needed fields. This way, we can avoid having a single schema that needs to expose every table field, leading to unnecessary bloat and noise.

We start by *using* the `Ecto.Schema` module so we can leverage the `schema/2` macro. Its first argument identifies the source of the schema; in our case, it is the `storage_media` database table. Then, we have a list of fields, each with its name and type. Given we are omitting the `:id` field, Ecto adds an `:id` field of the `:integer` type to serve as primary key. We are also using the `timestamps/1` macro to generate the `:inserted_at` and `:updated_at` timestamp fields for us.

Integers as primary keys are given sequentially, thus we may end up with a *smart* user trying to find other files by their ID. Let's mitigate this by using a custom type for our identifiers.

Custom field types

Given the flexibility that Ecto aims for, it should come as no surprise if we tell you that, besides the field types supported out of the box such as :string, :integer, and :map, Ecto also allows you to define your own custom types.

To create a custom type module, you need to implement the Ecto.Type behaviour. We will create a custom Ksuid Ecto type to use as the primary key of all our schemas. KSUIDs, or *K-Sortable Unique IDentifiers*, are as safe and random as UUIDs, but have the cool property of being lexicographically sortable. These identifiers are 20 bytes long and their string representation is always 27 characters long.

We just need to add the ksuid library to our ElixirDrip dependencies declared on the elixir_drip umbrella app mix.exs file (that is, add {:ksuid, "~> 0.1.2"} to the list returned by the deps/0 function), and then create the following module:

```
$ cat apps/elixir_drip/lib/elixir_drip/ecto/ksuid.ex
defmodule ElixirDrip.Ecto.Ksuid do
  @behaviour Ecto.Type

  def type, do: :string

  def cast(ksuid)
  when is_binary(ksuid) and byte_size(ksuid) == 27, do: {:ok, ksuid}
  def cast(_), do: :error

  def load(ksuid), do: {:ok, ksuid}

  def dump(binary) when is_binary(binary), do: {:ok, binary}
  def dump(_), do: :error

  def autogenerate, do: Ksuid.generate()
end
```

To implement the Ecto.Type behaviour, our Ecto.Ksuid module needs to implement four functions: type/0, cast/1, load/1, and dump/1. The first function indicates the underlying schema type; in our case, the KSUID will be stored as :string. The cast/1 function is called when we check the parameters of a changeset; for any KSUID field, it's just a matter of keeping the KSUID as a binary.

The last two functions, load/1 and dump/1, are used to load data from the database and store it on the database, respectively. There's no need to apply any guard clause when we load the data from the database, because it enforces the type of data it stores in each field.

Since we are using the KSUID custom type as the primary key, we need to also implement the `autogenerate/0` function, which will be called by Ecto when persisting the schema if we pass the `:autogenerate` option on the schema primary-key definition.

 The random part of KSUIDs is 6 bits longer than UUIDs, so we can rest assured the collision probability is even smaller than UUIDs. You can find more information about KSUIDs at `https://github.com/segmentio/ksuid`.

Let's now adapt our `Storage.Media` schema to use the newly created `Ecto.Ksuid` custom type:

```
$ cat apps/elixir_drip/lib/elixir_drip/storage/media.ex
defmodule ElixirDrip.Storage.Media do
  use Ecto.Schema

  @primary_key {:id, ElixirDrip.Ecto.Ksuid, autogenerate: true}
  schema "storage_media" do
    field :user_id, ElixirDrip.Ecto.Ksuid
    # ...
  end
end
```

We use the `@primary_key` module attribute to configure the schema primary key. The first tuple element indicates the field that should be used as a key, the second element sets the field type, and the third is used to pass additional options. By having the `:autogenerate` option as `true`, we know the `Ecto.Ksuid.autogenerate/0` function will be called whenever a new primary key is needed.

 In the initial version of the `Storage.Media` schema, the `@primary_key` attribute was defined by default as `{:id, :id, autogenerate: true}`, because we hadn't defined it explicitly. If you don't want to set a primary key in your schema, set this `@primary_key` attribute as `false`.

Let's now create the schema that will represent our ElixirDrip users.

Users or media owners?

Our user-management functions aren't related to storage *per se*, so we will encapsulate them inside a new `ElixirDrip.Accounts` context. Naturally, the `User` schema that we'll create will also live there:

```
$ cat apps/elixir_drip/lib/elixir_drip/accounts/user.ex
defmodule ElixirDrip.Accounts.User do
```

```
use Ecto.Schema
import Ecto.Changeset

alias __MODULE__

@primary_key {:id, ElixirDrip.Ecto.Ksuid, autogenerate: true}
schema "users" do
  field :username, :string
  field :hashed_password, :string
  field :password, :string, virtual: true
  field :email, :string

  timestamps()
end
# ...
end
```

Pretty similarly to what we already did for the `Media` schema, the `User` schema is also identified by a KSUID. Besides `id`, this schema also has four string fields: `username`, `password`, `hashed_password`, and `email`. Notice that because we're setting the `password` field as `virtual`, it won't be persisted in the database. We will use this virtual field when we analyze how Ecto changesets work.

As you can see in the following code, the `ElixirDrip.Accounts` context is responsible for creating new users and validating the password submitted when someone tries to log in. For now, we will only analyze how the `Accounts` context relies on the `Comeonin.Bcrypt` module to verify passwords in a secure way (the creation and retrieval of Ecto schemas will be thoroughly examined in the following sections):

```
$ cat apps/elixir_drip/lib/elixir_drip/accounts/accounts.ex
defmodule ElixirDrip.Accounts do
  alias ElixirDrip.Repo
  alias ElixirDrip.Accounts.User

  def create_user(attrs \\ %{}), do: # ...

  def get_user_by_username(username), do: # ...

  def login_user_with_pw(username, password) do
    with %User{} = user <- get_user_by_username(username),
         true <- verify_user_password(user, password) do
      {:ok, user}
    else
      _ ->
        Comeonin.Bcrypt.dummy_checkpw()
        :error
```

```
      end
    end

    defp verify_user_password(%User{} = user, password) do
      Comeonin.Bcrypt.checkpw(password, user.hashed_password)
    end
  end
```

After we find the user with the given `username`, we call the `verify_user_password/2` function to check whether the password is valid or not. If the password doesn't match, we call the `Comeonin.Bcrypt.dummy_checkpw/0` function. The time it takes for this function to return isn't constant, hence an attacker won't be able to perform a timing attack against our login system.

Having the previous `User` schema in the `Accounts` context makes total sense but creates a problem that we need to solve. Because this schema lives in the `Accounts` context, the `Storage` context isn't allowed to interact with it. But we still need to have the concept of a *user* on the `Storage` side, since all media files are owned by one or more users.

To solve this, let's define a new `Owner` schema living on the `Storage` context, which is also backed by the same `users` table:

```
$ cat apps/elixir_drip/lib/elixir_drip/storage/owner.ex
defmodule ElixirDrip.Storage.Owner do
  use Ecto.Schema

  @primary_key {:id, ElixirDrip.Ecto.Ksuid, autogenerate: true}
  schema "users" do
    field :email, :string
  end
end
```

If you have experience with ORM tools, you may find it weird to have more than one schema backed by the same database table. However, this approach of having separate bounded contexts, with separate schemas that ultimately reflect the same database table, help us avoid having a single, enormous schema that needs to serve every purpose. This way, we can have a schema for user management, a schema for media ownership, and another for audit purposes, for example, each with its own perspective on what a user is.

Schemas are really useful, but they aren't mandatory. As such, how do you decide whether you need them or not?

Schema or not – that is the question

So far, we've talked about schemas as if they were obligatory when one considers implementing the database access with Ecto. Before Ecto 2.0, this was true to some extent, given that many database queries without schemas were more verbose than their schema-powered counterparts, and some database operations were only possible if you chose the schema way of doing things.

Fortunately, those days are over, and you can now perform all operations and queries without a schema in place. As an example, imagine we have a `users` database table with `:username` and `:email` fields. You could insert two new entries on this table by calling the `Repo.insert_all/2` function and passing a list of lists, such as `[[username: "andre", email: "aa@elixir.pt"], [username: "daniel", email: "dc@elixir.pt"]]`, representing the two new rows to insert.

The same happens when you want to retrieve data from the database, and your queries happen to join a lot of tables. Does it make sense to try to fit all the results into the different schemas involved in the query? Probably not. It would be better to simply map the result to an Elixir standard data structure (say, a map), and call it a day.

The key takeaway here is that you can have more than one schema for the same database table, or you can have none. It depends on your needs, and fortunately Elixir makes it easy for you to change it afterwards. Imagine you had no schema for a given table and a query of yours was returning a list of maps. If you decide to add a `Foo` schema, with a minimal change, your query can now return a list of `Foo` structures. The existing pattern-matches for the previous list of maps will probably continue to work, given that an Elixir struct is really just a special map.

The `Storage.Media` schema that we defined will be backed by a database table. Let's see how we can create it using Ecto *migrations*.

Migrations

As we've already seen, the purpose of our `Media` schema is to represent the data that we retrieve from the database in the Elixir world. Since we are using a relational database, data is persisted in database tables.

To create the tables, instead of executing a SQL script directly on the database, we will use Ecto migrations to apply every database schema change for us.

Migrations live on the `priv/repo/migrations` folder as Elixir scripts and their name should abide by the `<timestamp>_<snake_case_name>.exs` format, for example `20180112095312_create_media.exs`. To execute a migration or roll back an existing one, you should use `ecto.migrate` or `ecto.rollback`, respectively.

Here's the `CreateMedia` migration responsible for the creation of the `storage_media` database table:

```
$ cat apps/elixir_drip/priv/repo/migrations/
20180112095312_create_media.exs
defmodule ElixirDrip.Repo.Migrations.Storage.Media do
  use Ecto.Migration

  def change do
    create table(:storage_media, primary_key: false) do
      add :id, :string, primary_key: true, size: 27
      add :file_name, :string
      add :full_path, :string
      add :metadata, :map
      add :encryption_key, :string
      add :storage_key, :string
      add :uploaded_at, :utc_datetime

      timestamps(type: :utc_datetime)
    end
  end
end
```

As you can see, the migration consists of a normal module that *uses* the `Ecto.Migration` module. Here you can see we are using the `create/2` macro and the `table/2` function to create the `storage_media` table.

Because we're implementing the `change/0` function on the migration module, Ecto expects to be capable of automatically reverting the operation when we run the `ecto.rollback` Mix task, without the need for us to explicitly indicate the revert operation.

If you prefer, or if Ecto can't figure out automatically how to revert the migration, you can implement the `up/0` and `down/0` functions instead, which will be run when the `ecto.migrate` and `ecto.rollback` Mix tasks are executed, respectively.

We are passing the `:primary_key` option as `false` on the `table/2` call, because we want to explicitly define it as a 27-character `string` field afterwards. The `table/2` function will return a `Table` struct that represents the table that will be created, whereas the `create/2` macro will receive the `Table` struct and the list of fields, and will create the corresponding table.

Let's run the migration and then check its status with the `ecto.migrations` Mix task:

```
$ mix ecto.migrate
18:16:18.548 [info] == Running
ElixirDrip.Repo.Migrations.Storage.Media.change/0 forward
18:16:18.548 [info] create table storage_media
18:16:18.572 [info] == Migrated in 0.0s

$ mix ecto.migrations

Repo: ElixirDrip.Repo

  Status Migration ID Migration Name
  --------------------------------------------------
    up 20180112095312 create_media
```

As you can see, our `create_media` migration was correctly applied. We will now define the schemas and migrations that will materialize the relationship between our users and their media.

Relationships

Our objective here is to implement the relationship between the `Media` and `Owner` schemas. In the beginning, a media file will only have a single owner: the user who uploaded the media into the system. This user can then share it with other users. As such, a media file may be owned by more than one user, and it will certainly be owned by at least one.

On the opposite side of this relationship, we have the media owners. A recently-created user won't have any media files, but eventually it will have dozens of files:

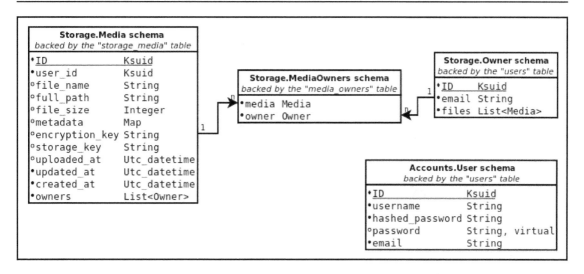

In database parlance, we have a classical many-to-many relation. As such, we need an additional association table, since we already have the `media` and `users` database tables. Let's create the `media_owners` table with a migration:

```
$ cat
apps/elixir_drip/priv/repo/migrations/20180408150211_create_media_owners.ex
s
defmodule ElixirDrip.Repo.Migrations.CreateMediaOwners do
  use Ecto.Migration

  def change do
    create table(:media_owners) do
      add :media_id, references(:storage_media, type: :string)
      add :user_id, references(:users, type: :string)

      timestamps(type: :utc_datetime)
    end
  end
end
```

This migration creates the `media_owners` table with two string columns, `media_id` and `user_id`. By using the `references/2` macro for both fields, they will be defined as foreign keys. Every value that we place on the `media_id` and `user_id` columns needs to exist on the `id` column of the `storage_media` and `users` tables, respectively. We didn't need to use the `name` option to indicate the primary key of the referenced tables because it defaults to `:id`, which is the name of our primary key fields on both tables.

Now we just need to run `mix ecto.migrate` for the media_owners table to be created. The next step is to create a `MediaOwners` schema, backed by the media_owners table, that will link the `Media` and `Owner` schemas.

Similar to what we already did with the other schemas, we say the new `MediaOwners` schema is backed by the `"media_owners"` table. Besides having the `inserted_at` and `updated_at` timestamps, this schema uses the `Schema.belongs_to/3` macro to define the `media` and `owner` fields.

By using the `belongs_to/3` macro, we indicate to Ecto that this schema may belong to the `Media` and `Owner` schemas, through the `media_id` and `user_id` foreign keys. Since we are using a custom type for our IDs, we need to indicate this to Ecto as well.

 We could have used `file` and `person` for the field names, because field names don't need to match the schemas they point to. We could also have omitted the name of the foreign key for the `media` field, since, by default, Ecto sets its name as `<field_name>_id`.

At this point, we already have the join table and schema in place. Let's now change the existing `Media` and `Owner` schemas to complete our many-to-many relationship. The following changes will let us easily access all `owners` of a certain media file and all `files` of a certain user:

```
$ cat apps/elixir_drip/lib/elixir_drip/storage/media.ex
defmodule ElixirDrip.Storage.Media do
  use Ecto.Schema
  # ...
  alias ElixirDrip.Storage.{
    Owner,
    MediaOwners
  }

  @primary_key {:id, ElixirDrip.Ecto.Ksuid, autogenerate: true}
  schema "storage_media" do
    # ...
    field :uploaded_at, :utc_datetime
    many_to_many :owners, Owner, join_through: MediaOwners,
    join_keys: [media_id: :id, user_id: :id]

    timestamps()
  end
  # ...
end
```

On the `Media` schema, we added a new `owners` field with the `many_to_many/3` macro. We indicate that each element will be backed by the `Owner` schema, and Ecto can find the information about which media owners to fetch on the `MediaOwners` schema (the `:join_through` option is required). We also pass the `:join_keys` option, indicating the foreign key names of the join schema. In our case, the `MediaOwners` schema has a `media_id` field pointing to the `id` field on the current `Media` schema, and a `user_id` field pointing to the `id` field on the associated `Owner` schema.

> You may omit the `:join_keys` option if the keys Ecto sets by default match the keys you have on the join schema. We are defining the association with the `Owner` schema on the `Media` schema, so Ecto will look at the schema names and set the join keys as `[media_id: :id, owner_id: :id]`. Also, the order of the entries in the `:join_keys` keyword list is important: the two entries should indicate how Ecto can reach the current and associated schema, respectively.

Now we just need to update the `Owner` schema to have our many-to-many relationship:

```
$ cat apps/elixir_drip/lib/elixir_drip/storage/owner.ex
defmodule ElixirDrip.Storage.Owner do
  use Ecto.Schema

  alias ElixirDrip.Storage.{
    Media,
    MediaOwners
  }

  @primary_key {:id, ElixirDrip.Ecto.Ksuid, autogenerate: true}
  schema "users" do
    field :email, :string
    many_to_many :files, Media, join_through: MediaOwners, join_keys:
    [user_id: :id, media_id: :id]
  end
end
```

Similar to the previous `Media` change, we add a new `files` field to the `Owner` schema with the `Schema.many_to_many/3` macro. This association is also mediated by the `MediaOwners` schema and Ecto can reach the current and associated `Media` schema by respectively using the `user_id` and the `media_id` fields of the join schema.

The last change to the `Owner` schema was the missing piece of the puzzle. With the database created and our data model now connected, we can start to persist media data. Let's check how can we leverage Ecto to validate the changes we want to apply to our stored data.

Changesets

Let's now analyze how can we update the information stored in the database. The way Ecto allows you to change this information may feel weird at first, since it asks you to always use a `changeset` that describes how the data manipulation should be accomplished. These changesets will help us to ensure the changes we are persisting are valid and don't break any of the constraints we have in place.

To understand how changesets can be helpful, let's imagine the following scenario, using an object-oriented language with an Object-Relational Mapping framework: you have a `media` object with dozens of fields, and you update a couple of them, then you perform a `media.save` and those two fields will be updated on the database row for that particular media. To compose the actual SQL `update` statement, the ORM needs to know how to identify the fields that changed, and issue the `update` statement only for those. The ORM will also do some validations for you and halt the execution of the SQL statement if something doesn't seem right.

There's some magic there that we usually don't control and don't want to, but in certain cases the outcome may not be what you were expecting. With Ecto, no one will identify the fields for you, and you need to explicitly specify the fields you want to validate and how you want to validate them.

All this work may strike you as too cumbersome, but Ecto allows you to do all of this in an elegant and sane way, giving you full control of every database operation. Since these changesets that represent a database operation are Elixir structs, you will manipulate them with normal data transformations by passing those structs through the functions provided by the `Ecto.Changeset` module. With each manipulation, you iterate on your changeset, allowing you to easily reason about what's happening under the hood.

Do not hesitate to `inspect/1` an Ecto changeset, it will show you really useful information, such as the `data` you're manipulating, the `changes` that will be applied to it, eventual validation `errors`, and the `action` that should be performed when the changeset is actually persisted in the database. The field that you probably will use the most is `valid?`, which lets you to know whether the changeset is good to be persisted or not.

We will now see how we can create a new `Media` schema to represent the media of our users.

Media

The changeset for the initial version of a `Media` schema will be created by the `create_initial_changeset/4` function exposed by the `Storage.Media` module.

Given that the database does not know what KSUIDs are, we generate a unique identifier at this stage. It will also be used to generate a `storage_key`, that is the actual name of the file stored on the cloud storage:

```
$ cat apps/elixir_drip/lib/elixir_drip/storage/media.ex
defmodule ElixirDrip.Storage.Media do
  use Ecto.Schema

  alias __MODULE__
  alias Ecto.Changeset
  # ...
  def create_initial_changeset(user_id, file_name, full_path,
  file_size) do
    id = Ksuid.generate()

    attrs = %{
      id: id,
      user_id: user_id,
      storage_key: generate_storage_key(id, file_name),
      encryption_key: Encryption.generate_key(),
      file_name: file_name,
      full_path: full_path,
      file_size: file_size,
    }

    %Media{}
    |> Changeset.cast(attrs, cast_attrs())
    |> Changeset.validate_required(required_attrs())
    |> validate_field(:full_path)
```

```
        |> validate_field(:file_name)
    end

    defp cast_attrs, do: [:id, :user_id, :file_name, :full_path,
    :file_size, :metadata, :encryption_key, :storage_key, :uploaded_at]

    defp required_attrs, do: [:id, :user_id, :file_name, :full_path,
    :file_size, :encryption_key, :storage_key]
end
```

The first step of the pipeline is to pass `%Media{}`, an empty `Media` struct, as the first argument to the `Changeset.cast/3` function, along with `attrs` and the list of attributes that should be *cast* on the last argument. Since we are creating a `Media` struct for the first time, we are casting all the attributes. Only the parameters included in the last argument list will be considered by Ecto when we actually apply the changeset.

For each attribute on the list, Ecto will check its field type on the `Media` schema and will cast the respective value on the `attrs` map as a result. As an example, imagine that the `attrs` map contains an integer `id`. When Ecto tries to convert it according to the `Media :id` field type, it will return an invalid changeset:

```
iex> %Media{} |> Ecto.Changeset.cast(%{id: 123}, [:id])
#Ecto.Changeset<
 action: nil,
 changes: %{},
 errors: [
 id: {"is invalid", [type: ElixirDrip.Ecto.Ksuid, validation:
 :cast]}
 ],
 data: #ElixirDrip.Storage.Media<>,
 valid?: false
>

iex> %Media{} |> Ecto.Changeset.cast(%{id: "13KyEPDoSJ5HbEfEEd30XPTMhW1"},
[:id])
#Ecto.Changeset<
 action: nil,
 changes: %{id: "13KyEPDoSJ5HbEfEEd30XPTMhW1"},
 errors: [],
 data: #ElixirDrip.Storage.Media<>,
 valid?: true
>
```

Validating changesets like this is especially useful, given that these new values could come directly from the end user, and therefore need to be considered unsafe.

As you can see, an invalid changeset contains useful information about which field is invalid, so you can use this changeset on the frontend to show a meaningful error message.

In the next pipeline step, we validate whether all the required fields are present on the changeset with the `Changeset.validate_required/2` function. If any of the `required_attrs` passed are `nil` or `empty`, this function will invalidate the changeset.

We use the `validate_field/1` function on the last two steps of the pipeline to validate the `:full_path` and `:file_name` fields. This is a `Storage.Media` function that relies on an Ecto custom field validation, applied using the `Changeset.validate_change/4` function:

```
$ cat apps/elixir_drip/lib/elixir_drip/storage/media.ex
defmodule ElixirDrip.Storage.Media do
  # ...
  @custom_validations [
    full_path: %{validator: &__MODULE__.is_valid_path?/1, error_msg:
    "Invalid full path"},
    file_name: %{validator: &__MODULE__.is_valid_name?/1, error_msg:
    "Invalid file name"},
  ]

  def validate_field(changeset, field) do
    validator = @custom_validations[field][:validator]
    error_msg = @custom_validations[field][:error_msg]

    Changeset.validate_change(changeset, field, fn _, value ->
      case validator.(value) do
        {:ok, :valid} -> []
        _ -> [{field, error_msg}]
      end
    end)
  end

  def is_valid_path?(path) when is_binary(path) do
    valid? = String.starts_with?(path, "$") && !String.ends_with?(path,
"/")

    case valid? do
      true -> {:ok, :valid}
      false -> {:error, :invalid_path}
    end
  end

  def is_valid_name?(name) when is_binary(name) do
    valid? = byte_size(name) > 0 && !String.contains?(name, "/")
```

```
            case valid? do
                true -> {:ok, :valid}
                false -> {:error, :invalid_name}
            end
        end
    end
```

As you can see, the last argument of `Changeset.validate_change/3` receives a lambda function that serves as the field validator, which will return a list with the eventual field errors. If no errors exist, it will simply return an empty list. Otherwise, it will return the field name and the error message. It's inside this lambda function that we are delegating the validation on the `Media.is_valid_path?/1` or `Media.is_valid_name?/1` functions, based on the field name.

 Because at this stage we are only focusing on the `Media` schema, the only database operation performed by our `Storage.store/3` function is an insertion of a new `Media` entry. The final version of the `Storage.store/3` function will be analyzed in the *Media ownership* section.

In the end, if the outcome of `Media.create_initial_changeset/4` is valid, we are able to insert a new `Media` in the database. It's the responsibility of the `Storage.store/4` function to create the initial changeset, so we can then insert the new `Media` in the database and enqueue an upload task to be processed by our pipeline:

```
$ cat apps/elixir_drip/lib/elixir_drip/storage/storage.ex
defmodule ElixirDrip.Storage do

    alias Ecto.Changeset
    alias ElixirDrip.Repo
    alias ElixirDrip.Storage.Media
    alias ElixirDrip.Storage.Workers.QueueWorker, as: Queue

    def store(user_id, file_name, full_path, content) do
        file_size = byte_size(content)
        with %Owner{} = owner <- get_owner(user_id),
             %Changeset{} = changeset <-
             Media.create_initial_changeset(owner.id, file_name, full_path,
             file_size),
             {:ok, %Media{} = media} <- Repo.insert(changeset)
        do
            upload_task = %{
                media: media,
                content: content,
                type: :upload
            }
```

```
      Queue.enqueue(Queue.Upload, upload_task)

        {:ok, :upload_enqueued, media}
      else
        error -> error
      end
    end
    # ...
  end
```

In the preceding function, we start by retrieving the `Owner` schema with the passed `user_id`, which will be persisted with the new `Media` as the media creator. After this, we are creating the changeset with the `Media.create_initial_changeset/4` function and passing its result to the `Repo.insert/1` function.

The `Repo.insert/1` function, like all the other `Ecto.Repo` callbacks, only proceeds with the operation when it's called with a valid changeset. If not, it will return a tuple error that we're handling on the `else` clause of the `with` construct. Here's an example of an update operation (using the `Repo.update/1` callback) that doesn't succeed because we had an invalid changeset:

```
iex> media
        |> Ecto.Changeset.cast(%{full_path: "an/invalid/path"},
        [:full_path])
        |> Media.validate_field(:full_path)
        |> ElixirDrip.Repo.update()

{:error,
 #Ecto.Changeset<
   action: :update,
   changes: %{full_path: "an/invalid/path"},
   errors: [full_path: {"Invalid full path", []}],
   data: #ElixirDrip.Storage.Media<>,
   valid?: false
 >}
```

The need to explicitly validate the information you're changing with changesets may feel weird at first, but this explicitness helps because you can now have different changesets. Since we always need to `cast` the parameters we want to consider, there's no way a field update can go unnoticed when you only want to update the `uploaded_at` timestamp, for example. By looking at the fields your data manipulation functions are *casting*, you immediately know which fields may be changed by that function.

Let's now see how we can create new ElixirDrip users.

Users

In the *Schemas* section, we defined the `Accounts.User` schema with a `virtual password` field. This is useful whenever you want your schema to have a field but you don't want it to be persisted.

We never want to store user passwords in plain text. The idea here is to temporarily place the plain text password on this `password` field, which will be then hashed and inserted as the value of the `hashed_password` field in the last step of our `User.create_changeset/2` function:

```
$ cat apps/elixir_drip/lib/elixir_drip/accounts/user.ex
defmodule ElixirDrip.Accounts.User do
  # ...
  @email_regex ~r/^[A-Z0-9._%+-]+@[A-Z0-9.-]+\.[A-Z]{2,}$/i

  def create_changeset(%User{} = user, attrs) do
    user
    |> cast(attrs, [:username, :password, :email])
    |> validate_required([:username, :password, :email])
    |> validate_length(:username, min: 1, max: 30)
    |> validate_length(:password, min: 8, max: 100)
    |> validate_format(:email, @email_regex)
    |> put_hashed_password()
  end

  defp put_hashed_password(%Ecto.Changeset{valid?: false} = changeset),
  do: changeset
  defp put_hashed_password(%Ecto.Changeset{valid?: true, changes: %
  {password: pw}} = changeset) do
    changeset
    |> put_change(:hashed_password, Comeonin.Bcrypt.hashpwsalt(pw))
  end
end
```

Besides the `validate_required/2` function that we have already used in the previous `User.create_changeset/2` function, we are also using the `validate_length/2` and `validate_format/2` functions of the `Changeset` module. As the name implies, the first lets us validate the string length of a certain field, while the latter function allows us to validate a string field against a regular expression.

We are using the `comeonin` library to securely generate the password hash. As such, we added the `{:comeonin, "~> 4.1"}` tuple to the `deps/0` function on the `elixir_drip` umbrella app Mix file.

In the last step in the pipeline, we call the `put_hashed_password/1` private function, which will use the `Changeset.put_change/3` function to update the changeset with the hashed password returned by the `Comeonin.BCrypt.hashpwsalt/1` function.

This `put_change/3` function receives the changeset, the field name to update, and the new value, and blindly adds a change to the changeset for the field in question. You should only use the `put_change/3` function when you want to update a changeset with data created by you or coming from other secure places, such as another component of your application:

```
iex> changeset = %User{} |> Changeset.cast(%{email: "abc@good.mail"},
[:email])
#Ecto.Changeset<
  action: nil,
  changes: %{email: "abc@good.mail"},
  errors: [],
  data: #ElixirDrip.Accounts.User<>,
  valid?: true
>

iex> changeset |> Changeset.cast(%{email: 123}, [:email])
#Ecto.Changeset<
  action: nil,
  changes: %{email: "abc@good.mail"},
  errors: [email: {"is invalid", [type: :string, validation: :cast]}],
  data: #ElixirDrip.Accounts.User<>,
  valid?: false
>

iex> changeset |> Changeset.put_change(:email, 123)
#Ecto.Changeset<
  action: nil,
  changes: %{email: 123},
  errors: [],
  data: #ElixirDrip.Accounts.User<>,
  valid?: true
>
```

In the preceding snippet, we aren't allowed to set the user email to `123` if we use `cast/3`, but Ecto happily lets us add an email change to `123` if we use the `put_change/3` function instead (notice how it returns a valid changeset). When you are sure the provided data is safe, the `put_change/3` function lets you skip any validations you may have. Keep this in mind when considering `put_change/3` over the `cast/3` function.

In the next section, we will learn how changesets can also be applied to associations between schemas. In our case, we will associate media files with their respective owners.

Media ownership

In the previous Media section, we simply inserted a new Media entry when we saved the media file for our users with the Storage.store/3 function. However, this was only a partial solution, since we have a many-to-many relationship between the Media and Owner schemas.

Our goal here is to create a new MediaOwners schema entry when we store a file for the first time with the Storage.store/3 function, effectively associating the user with the uploaded media:

```
$ cat apps/elixir_drip/lib/elixir_drip/storage/storage.ex
defmodule ElixirDrip.Storage do
  # ...
  def store(user_id, file_name, full_path, content) do
    file_size = byte_size(content)
    with %Owner{} = owner <- get_owner(user_id),
         %Changeset{} = changeset <- Media.create_initial_changeset
         (owner.id, file_name, full_path, file_size),
         %Changeset{} = changeset <- Changeset.put_assoc(changeset,
         :owners, [owner]),
         {:ok, %Media{} = media} <- Repo.insert(changeset)
    do
      # ... upload task enqueue

      {:ok, :upload_enqueued, media}
    else
      error -> error
    end
  end
  # ...
end
```

As you can see, the only change from the previous version of the store/3 function is the usage of Changeset.put_assoc/3 before we insert the changeset in the database. With it, we are adding to the changeset an association between the new Media entry and the Owner fetched from the database in the first with step:

```
iex> changeset = Media.create_initial_changeset(owner.id, fi
le_name, full_path, file_size)
#Ecto.Changeset<
  action: nil,
  changes: %{
    # ...
  },
  errors: [],
```

```
    data: #ElixirDrip.Storage.Media<>,
    valid?: true
>

iex> changeset = Changeset.put_assoc(changeset, :owners, [owner])
#Ecto.Changeset<
  action: nil,
  changes: %{
    # ...
    owners: [
      #Ecto.Changeset<action: :update, changes: %{}, errors: [],
       data: #ElixirDrip.Storage.Owner<>, valid?: true>
    ]
  },
  errors: [],
  data: #ElixirDrip.Storage.Media<>,
  valid?: true
>
```

By using the `Changeset.put_assoc/3` function, Ecto will update the `owners` field of the `Media` schema for us. This function expects that we pass it the entire association (in our case, *all* the owners of a given media), and it will then update it accordingly. Here we are creating a new media, thus we are sure it will only have a single owner (hence the list with a single `owner` element).

Now consider a media that was previously associated with a `prev_owner` user. If you had a changeset for it and tried to execute `put_assoc(changeset, :owners, [prev_owner, new_owner])`, you would get a valid changeset because we simply *added* a new owner. However, if we try to change the existing owners by passing `[new_owner]` as the new list of owners (we are trying to delete the existing association with `prev_owner`), by default Ecto will raise an error. The way Ecto reacts in this scenario is controlled by the `:on_replace` option, when we define a `many_to_many` field. If we want Ecto to delete the stale associations for us, we should set this option to `:delete`.

Let's now try the fully-fledged `Storage.store/3` function. As you can see here, after fetching the owner for the ID we're passing, Ecto inserts a new row on the `storage_media` and `media_owners` tables as expected. Notice how Ecto even wrapped both insertions on a single transaction, ensuring the consistency of our database no matter what:

```
iex> xpto_user = Accounts.get_user_by_username("xpto")
%ElixirDrip.Accounts.User{
  __meta__: #Ecto.Schema.Metadata<:loaded, "users">,
  id: "13ix90kpmblgJF4Ful762gqb6m2",
  # ...
}
```

```
iex)> Storage.store(xpto_user.id, "hello_world.txt", "$/hello/world", "Hi
there, this is a test.")

19:39:17.617 [debug] QUERY OK source="users" db=0.6ms
SELECT u0."id", u0."email" FROM "users" AS u0 WHERE (u0."id" = $1)
["13ix90kpmblgJF4Ful762gqb6m2"]

19:39:17.618 [debug] QUERY OK db=0.1ms queue=0.1ms
begin []

19:39:17.634 [debug] QUERY OK db=15.9ms
INSERT INTO "storage_media"
("encryption_key","file_name","file_size","full_path","id","metadata","stor
age_key","user_id","inserted_at","updated_at") VALUES
($1,$2,$3,$4,$5,$6,$7,$8,$9,$10) [...]

19:39:17.636 [debug] QUERY OK db=1.9ms
INSERT INTO "media_owners"
("media_id","user_id","inserted_at","updated_at") VALUES ($1,$2,$3,$4)
RETURNING "id" ["13j6fLDKPbkbbQ6Fo2Cuyb2MF4s",
"13ix90kpmblgJF4Ful762gqb6m2", ...]

19:39:17.640 [debug] QUERY OK db=3.2ms
commit []
# ...
```

Our ElixirDrip users will also be able to share their media with other users. Each time a file is shared, we will need to update the media-users association. This time however, we will directly manipulate the `MediaOwners` join schema:

```
$ cat apps/elixir_drip/lib/elixir_drip/storage/storage.ex
defmodule ElixirDrip.Storage do
  # ...
  def share(user_id, media_id, allowed_user_id) do
    with {:ok, :creator} <- is_creator?(user_id, media_id) do
      %MediaOwners{}
      |> Changeset.cast(%{user_id: allowed_user_id, media_id:
      media_id}, [:user_id, :media_id])
      |> Repo.insert()
    else
      error -> error
    end
  end

end
```

On the `Storage.share/3` function, we start by ensuring the user sharing the media is the one who uploaded it in the first place (the `is_creator?/2` function will be analyzed later in this chapter). If the user is the media creator, we then proceed to create and insert a changeset associating `media_id` with `allowed_user_id`, allowing a new user to view and download the media in question. By creating a new entry in the `MediaOwners` join schema, we are letting one more user access the given media file.

If we also wanted to use the `Changeset.put_assoc/3` approach here, we would have to first fetch a list with all the existing media owners, and then add the new allowed user to this list. Despite being a valid alternative, this approach would imply an additional database query to fetch the existing owners.

Some of the operations analyzed in this section use underlying database constraints to ensure the consistency of our data. In the next section, we'll understand how Ecto leverages database constraints and allows us to easily work with them.

Constraints

When we analyzed the `User.create_changeset/2` function, we didn't have any validation in place to check whether the username we are storing in the database already exists or not. For a system like ours, this could spell trouble. As such, let's create a unique index on the `users` table for the `username` column:

```
$ cat apps/elixir_drip/priv/repo/migrations/
20180320101722_unique_users_constraint.exs
defmodule ElixirDrip.Repo.Migrations.UniqueUsersConstraint do
  use Ecto.Migration

  def change do
    create unique_index(:users, [:username])
  end
end
```

After we apply this migration with `mix ecto.migrate`, the database will start to enforce username uniqueness on any operation on the `users` table. Let's see what happens if we try to update the `xpto_user` username to an already existing username:

```
iex> xpto_user
%ElixirDrip.Accounts.User{ ... }

iex> update_op = Changeset.cast(xpto_user, %{username: "jose"},
[:username])
#Ecto.Changeset<
```

```
    action: nil,
    changes: %{username: "jose"},
    errors: [],
    data: #ElixirDrip.Accounts.User<>,
    valid?: true
>

iex> Repo.update(update_op)
07:43:57.503 [debug] QUERY ERROR db=29.6ms queue=0.1ms
UPDATE "users" SET "username" = $1, "updated_at" = $2 WHERE "id" = $3
["jose", {{2018, 4, 26}, {7, 43, 57, 470077}},
"13ix90kpmblgJF4Ful762gqb6m2"]
** (Ecto.ConstraintError) constraint error when attempting to update
struct:

    * unique: users_username_index
# ...
```

As expected, the database didn't allow the update and Ecto raised a constraint error. Albeit correct, this behavior doesn't help us that much because we normally use the `valid?` and `errors` changeset fields to check whether an error occurred. To tackle this kind of situation, Ecto provides the `Changeset.unique_constraint/3` function, which checks the uniqueness constraint when we perform the database operation and returns an `{:error, changeset}` tuple if the operation violates the constraint in place.

Let's apply this `Changeset.unique_constraint/3` to the `User.create_changeset/2` function, which we use when creating new ElixirDrip users:

```
$ cat apps/elixir_drip/lib/elixir_drip/accounts/user.ex
defmodule ElixirDrip.Accounts.User do
  use Ecto.Schema
  import Ecto.Changeset
  # ...
  def create_changeset(%User{} = user, attrs) do
    user
    |> cast(attrs, [:username, :password, :email])
    |> validate_required([:username, :password, :email])
    |> validate_length(:username, min: 1, max: 30)
    |> validate_length(:password, min: 8, max: 100)
    |> validate_format(:email, @email_regex)
    |> unique_constraint(:username)
    |> put_hashed_password()
  end
end
```

If we now try to create a new user with the same `"jose"` username, we'll get the expected error tuple with the invalid changeset:

```
iex> Accounts.create_user(%{username: "jose", email: "abc@we
b.com", password: "secur3pwd"})

08:15:18.585 [debug] QUERY ERROR db=2.6ms
INSERT INTO "users"
("email","hashed_password","username","id","inserted_at","updated_at")
VALUES ($1,$2,$3,$4,$5,$6) ["abc@web.com",
"$2b$12$natqyxpFjE2zYxbroZf4h.xXUOPclcZh1lGxfOxapyi6BTF2uqRBm", "jose",
"13jOqf9qgZePNpSRNOChyPfHfP8", {{2018, 4, 26}, {8, 15, 18, 582405}},
{{2018, 4, 26}, {8, 15, 18, 582420}}]

{:error,
 #Ecto.Changeset<
   action: :insert,
   changes: %{
     email: "abc@web.com",
     hashed_password: "$2b$12$natqyxpFjE2zYxbroZf4h
     .xXUOPclcZh1lGxfOxapyi6BTF2uqRBm",
     password: "secur3pwd",
     username: "jose"
   },
   errors: [username: {"has already been taken", []}],
   data: #ElixirDrip.Accounts.User<>,
   valid?: false
 >}
```

Notice that, since we are relying on a database unique index, we only get the expected error when we actually hit the database with the `Repo.insert/2` (or `Repo.update/2`) function.

Let's now use the same approach to ensure that each media can only be shared once with the same user. We will also create a database unique index, but this time applied to the two foreign key fields on the `media_owners` table, `media_id` and `user_id`. If someone tries to share a file with a user and there is already a `MediaOwners` entry for that media and user ID pair, the operation should not be allowed:

```
$ cat
apps/elixir_drip/priv/repo/migrations/20180408161233_unique_shares_constrai
nt.exs
defmodule ElixirDrip.Repo.Migrations.UniqueSharesConstraint do
  use Ecto.Migration

  def change do
    create unique_index(:media_owners, [:media_id, :user_id], name:
    :single_share_index)
```

```
      end
   end
```

On this last migration, besides indicating the two `media_id` and `user_id` columns, we are also explicitly naming this unique constraint to `:single_share_index`. All constraints have names, so if we don't set it, Ecto will generate a name based on the table and field names for us. The default name in this case would be `:media_owners_media_id_user_id_index`, too verbose in my view.

We defined a constraint name because, as you can see here, we need to indicate it when calling `Changeset.unique_constraint/3` on the `Storage.share/3` function:

```
$ cat apps/elixir_drip/lib/elixir_drip/storage/storage.ex
defmodule ElixirDrip.Storage do
  # ...
  def share(user_id, media_id, allowed_user_id) do
    with {:ok, :creator} <- is_creator?(user_id, media_id) do
      %MediaOwners{}
      |> Changeset.cast(%{user_id: allowed_user_id, media_id:
      media_id}, [:user_id, :media_id])
      |> Changeset.unique_constraint(:existing_share, name:
      :single_share_index)
      |> Changeset.foreign_key_constraint(:user_id)
      |> Changeset.foreign_key_constraint(:media_id)
      |> Repo.insert()
    else
      error -> error
    end
  end
end
```

Let's now see what happens when we try to share a file again with the same user (`xpto_user` already had access to the given `file`):

```
iex> Storage.share(jose_user.id, file.id, xpto_user.id)
09:10:17.572 [debug] QUERY OK source="storage_media" db=2.5ms queue=0.1ms
SELECT s0."id", s0."user_id", s0."file_name", s0."full_path",
s0."file_size", s0."metadata", s0."encryption_key", s0."storage_key",
s0."uploaded_at", s0."inserted_at", s0."updated_at" FROM "storage_media" AS
s0 WHERE (s0."id" = $1) AND (s0."user_id" = $2)
["13Kvv5GQey9oPFWEAqqSFECYGag", "13KvtrMQ9uRB8MqkJpKSSQZxnBa"]

09:10:17.572 [debug] QUERY OK db=0.3ms queue=0.1ms
begin []

09:10:17.575 [debug] QUERY ERROR db=2.0ms
INSERT INTO "media_owners"
```

```
("media_id","user_id","inserted_at","updated_at") VALUES ($1,$2,$3,$4)
RETURNING "id" ["13Kvv5GQey9oPFWEAqqSFECYGag",
"13ix90kpmblgJF4Ful762gqb6m2", {{2018, 4, 26}, {9, 10, 17, 572987}},
{{2018, 4, 26}, {9, 10, 17, 573007}}]

09:10:17.575 [debug] QUERY OK db=0.2ms
rollback []

{:error,
 #Ecto.Changeset<
   action: :insert,
   changes: %{
     media_id: "13Kvv5GQey9oPFWEAqqSFECYGag",
     user_id: "13ix90kpmblgJF4Ful762gqb6m2"
   },
   errors: [existing_share: {"has already been taken", []}],
   data: #ElixirDrip.Storage.MediaOwners<>,
   valid?: false
 >}
```

As expected, the database rollbacks the insert operation and we get an error saying the
`existing_share` `"has already been taken"`. This message is the default error
message; if you want to change it, you can pass the `:message` option when we call the
`unique_constraint/3` function.

Notice how we also use the `Changeset.foreign_key_constraint/3` function to achieve
the same error-handling behavior, but this time for the two foreign keys we have in place. If
we didn't have these calls, Ecto would raise an error if a non-existing ID was used as one of
the foreign keys:

```
iex> Storage.share(jose_owner.id, file.id, "13Kvv5GQey9oPFWEAqqINVALID!")
# ...
{:error,
 #Ecto.Changeset<
   action: :insert,
   changes: %{
     media_id: "13Kvv86zvDHF6xJSZMNsfBZrN5o",
     user_id: "13Kvv5GQey9oPFWEAqqINVALID!"
   },
   errors: [user_id: {"does not exist", []}],
   data: #ElixirDrip.Storage.MediaOwners<>,
   valid?: false
 >}
```

Besides sharing, we also allow our users to delete their ElixirDrip media (as long as it was
uploaded by them). These files might have been shared with other users in the meantime,
so we also need to take care of the lingering media shares on the `MediaOwners` schema.

To elegantly solve this, we'll ask the database to do the heavy-lifting for us once more. We will recreate the `media_id` foreign key we have on the `media_owners` table, so that, when a `Media` entry is deleted from the database, all the existing media shares on `MediaOwners` referencing the deleted `Media` will also be deleted. To achieve this cascading behavior, we just need to create the foreign key again with the `:on_delete` option set to `:delete_all`:

```
$ cat apps/elixir_drip/priv/repo/migrations/
20180409214938_change_media_owners_on_delete_media.exs
defmodule ElixirDrip.Repo.Migrations.ChangeMediaOwnersOnDeleteMedia do
  use Ecto.Migration

  def change do
    drop constraint(:media_owners, :media_owners_media_id_fkey)

    alter table(:media_owners) do
      modify :media_id, references(:storage_media, type: :string,
      on_delete: :delete_all)
    end
  end
end
```

The previous migration makes our `Storage.delete/2` function as concise as possible, since the deletion of media shares will be automatically taken care of by the database. Since `Repo.delete/2` expects a struct, we'll pass it a `Media` struct only containing the media ID to delete:

```
$ cat apps/elixir_drip/lib/elixir_drip/storage/storage.ex
defmodule ElixirDrip.Storage do
  # ...
  def delete(user_id, media_id) do
  with {:ok, :creator} <- is_creator?(user_id, media_id) do
  %Media{id: media_id}
  |> Repo.delete()
  else
  error -> error
  end
  end
end
```

Now if `jose_user`, the owner of the `file` we are using, deletes it, we will see that the `xpto_user` number of files is reduced by 1. In the following example, we are using the `Repo.preload/3` callback to fetch the files associated with an owner. This is how we fetch, or *preload*, all associations of a given struct. Since we're passing the `:force` option to it, Ecto will try to fetch the associations again, even if they're already loaded on the struct:

```
iex> xpto_user_with_files = Storage.get_owner(xpto_user.id) |>
```

```
Repo.preload(:files)
# ...

iex> xpto_user_with_files.files |> Enum.count
2

iex> Storage.delete(jose_user.id, file.id)
08:55:04.018 [debug] QUERY OK db=3.3ms
DELETE FROM "storage_media" WHERE "id" = $1 ["13Kvv5GQey9oPFWEAqqSFECYGag"]
# ...

{:ok,
 %ElixirDrip.Storage.Media{
   __meta__: #Ecto.Schema.Metadata<:deleted, "storage_media">,
   id: "13Kvv5GQey9oPFWEAqqSFECYGag",
   # ...
 }}

iex> xpto_user_with_files = xpto_user_with_files |> Repo.preload(:files,
force: true)
# ...

iex> xpto_user_with_files.files |> Enum.count
1
```

In this section, we saw how Ecto allows us to easily put to good use the powerful tools provided by the database. In the next section, we'll continue to interact with the database, ranging from writing queries in Elixir syntax to using plain SQL when needed.

Queries

At the beginning of this chapter, we ran a SQL query with `Repo.query/3` as soon as we had a database connection, to verify that our connection was working as expected. Ultimately, Ecto is all about flexibility, so it lets you work with raw SQL as easily as you work with its query API.

 We need to import the `Ecto.Query` module so we can write Ecto queries without the need to always prefix the needed macros (for example, `where/3` and `group_by/3`).

If you're used to SQL, you will feel right at home with Ecto queries. Ecto uses the same SQL keywords (from, where, select, and so on) with the semantics you expect, so the following query, where we select a User with a specific username, won't catch you off-guard:

```
iex> query = from u in User,
...> where: u.username == "andre",
...> select: u
#Ecto.Query<from u in ElixirDrip.Accounts.User,
 where: u.username == "andre", select: u>

iex> Repo.one(query)
08:23:09.189 [debug] QUERY OK source="users" db=1.8ms queue=0.1ms
SELECT u0."id", u0."username", u0."hashed_password", u0."email",
u0."inserted_at", u0."updated_at" FROM "users" AS u0 WHERE (u0."username" =
'andre') []

%ElixirDrip.Accounts.User{
  username: "andre"
  # ...
}
```

As we discussed previously, schemas are optional. As such, the same query without a schema would need to specify the table name ("users") and the fields that should be selected from the database. This happens because, without a schema, Ecto doesn't know which fields belong to the table:

```
iex> query = from u in "users",
...> where: u.username == "andre",
...> select: [:id, :username]
#Ecto.Query<from u in "users", where: u.username == "andre",
 select: [:id, :username]>

iex> Repo.one(query)
08:29:34.550 [debug] QUERY OK source="users" db=1.6ms
SELECT u0."id", u0."username" FROM "users" AS u0 WHERE (u0."username" =
'andre') []

%{id: "13ucZ46LTdsfvezCPviNJ96gYqu", username: "andre"}
```

To understand how we can compose Ecto queries, we will see how ElixirDrip fetches all the media in a given folder for a specific user.

Media folder queries

Our Phoenix umbrella application will send us a `user_id` and a `folder_path` values and we will need to fetch all the `Media` entries on the given path. Paths in ElixirDrip always start with $, so `$`, `$/folder`, and `$/a/b/c/d/e/f/g` are all valid paths (notice that paths can't have a trailing slash).

Under the hood, we store the full path of each media file, but we store all the media in a single folder on Google Cloud Storage (given by each media `storage_key`). As such, typical file operations, such as `move` and `rename`, are just a matter of changing the media `full_path` and the `file_name` accordingly:

```
iex> Storage.list_all_media
         |> Enum.map(fn m -> %{user_id: m.user_id,
                             file_name: m.file_name,
                             path: m.full_path,
                             storage_key: m.storage_key}
                  end)
# ...
```

The following table shows the output of the previous IEx interaction (the outcome of the previous snippet is a list of maps, each with `file_name`, `path`, `storage_key`, and `user_id` fields):

file_name	path	storage_key	user_id
"test6.txt"	"$/this/is/the/full/path6"	"13uhI..._20180429T165535.txt"	"...Yqu"
"222.txt"	"$/second/folder"	"13Kvv8..._20180416T210715.txt"	"...nBa"
"README.md"	"$"	"13Kvvb..._20180416T210718.md"	"...nBa"
# ...			

We can see that currently ElixirDrip contains at least three files; the first belongs to the user ID ending in `Yqu` and the other two to the `nBa` user.

If the `nBa` user asks for his files on the `$` folder, he will get at least two entries: a `README.md` file and a `second` folder, since the root folder contains the markdown file and the nested `second/folder/222.txt` file. Our goal is to implement the following `Storage.media_by_folder/2` function:

```
iex> Storage.media_by_folder("13KvtrMQ9uRB8MqkJpKSSQZxnBa",
"$")
%{
  files: [
    %{
      full_path: "$",
```

```
        id: "13Kvvb4o0gzSYT2HcCGAhAkEZGt",
        name: "README.md",
        size: 14
      }
    ],
    folders: [ %{files: 1, name: "second", size: 19} ]
}

iex> Storage.media_by_folder("13KvtrMQ9uRB8MqkJpKSSQZxnBa",
"$/nowhere/to/be/found")
%{files: [], folders: []}
```

With the previous data structure, the ElixirDripWeb umbrella app will be able to render a pretty list of files and folders for any path.

We will compose the previous function step by step, reusing any *partial* queries that we may have along the way. We will start by implementing the `Storage.user_media_query/1` function, which returns all the media accessible by a given user:

```
$ cat apps/elixir_drip/lib/elixir_drip/storage/storage.ex
defmodule ElixirDrip.Storage do
  import Ecto.Query
  # ...
  defp user_media_query(user_id) do
    from media_owner in MediaOwners,
      join: media in Media,
      on: media_owner.media_id == media.id,
      where: media_owner.user_id == ^user_id,
      select: media
  end
end
```

This query joins the `MediaOwners` and `Media` schemas and returns all the media for that `user_id`. To use external values on the query, such as our `user_id`, we need to prepend them with `^`. Also notice how we are able to select only the `media` fields by indicating the `select: media` clause. If we omitted the `select` clause, the query would return both schemas with all the fields.

The previous query is used in different `Storage` functions, including in the following `user_media_on_folder/2` function:

```
$ cat apps/elixir_drip/lib/elixir_drip/storage/storage.ex
defmodule ElixirDrip.Storage do
  import Ecto.Query
  import ElixirDrip.Storage.Macros
```

```
# ...
defp user_media_on_folder(user_id, folder_path) do
folder_path_size = String.length(folder_path)
folder_path_size = -folder_path_size

user_media = user_media_query(user_id)
|> exclude(:select)

from [_mo, m] in user_media,
where: like(m.full_path, ^"#{folder_path}%"),
select: %{
id: m.id,
full_path: m.full_path,
file_name: m.file_name,
file_size: m.file_size,
remaining_path: remaining_path(^folder_path_size, m.full_path)
}
end
end
```

Before reusing the previous query, we reset the `select` clause of the `user_media` query, making it return both schemas again (the schemas that we join in the original query). We have to reset the query `select` clause because we need to redefine it, and a query can only have one `select` clause.

We are using the `Query.API.like/2` function to search for entries where the full path begins with the `folder_path` (for example, a `folder_path` of "$" would yield a "$%" search expression, matching every full path starting with $). Ecto will then translate this into the specific SQL LIKE query for the underlying database.

This time, we select the results into a new map, and we call the `remaining_path/2` macro for the last map entry. For a `folder_path` of $, the remaining path of a media file with $/second/folder as its full path would be /second/folder.

 When we used the `like/2` function, Ecto *translated* it into the corresponding SQL LIKE query. Given the number of heterogeneous databases that Ecto can work with (using the corresponding adapters), it's impracticable (or even impossible, when the database doesn't support it) to implement every operation for every database. Hence, Ecto lets us use the following fragment construct whenever we want to execute a given expression directly in the database, without its intervention.

The `remaining_path/2` macro lives on the `Storage.Macros` module and leverages the *fragment* construct provided by Ecto:

```
$ cat apps/elixir_drip/lib/elixir_drip/storage/macros.ex
defmodule ElixirDrip.Storage.Macros do
  defmacro remaining_path(pwd_size, full_path) do
    quote do
      fragment("RIGHT(?, ?)", unquote(full_path), unquote(pwd_size))
    end
  end
end
```

Our `remaining_path/2` macro uses a fragment to execute the `RIGHT` SQL function that returns the last n characters of a given string, or strips the first n characters if the n value is negative.

In the previous `user_media_on_folder/2` function, we could have directly used the `fragment/1` function on the query, but, this way, we get an arguably clearer query, without a glimpse of SQL. This `user_media_on_folder/2` function will return a query, but its results aren't yet in the expected format, as you can see in the following code snippet. You can also observe the `RIGHT` and `LIKE` SQL functions being called:

```
iex> Storage.user_media_on_folder("13KvtrMQ9uRB8MqkJpKSSQZxnBa", "$")
        |> Repo.all
08:55:04.570 [debug] QUERY OK source="media_owners" db=2.7ms
SELECT s1."id", s1."full_path", s1."file_name", s1."file_size",
right(s1."full_path", $1) FROM "media_owners" AS m0 INNER JOIN
"storage_media" AS s1 ON m0."media_id" = s1."id" WHERE (m0."user_id" = $2)
AND (s1."full_path" LIKE $3) [-1, "13KvtrMQ9uRB8MqkJpKSSQZxnBa", "$%"]

[
  %{
    file_name: "222.txt",
    file_size: 19,
    full_path: "$/second/folder",
    id: "13Kvv86zvDHF6xJSZMNsfBZrN5o",
    remaining_path: "/second/folder"
  },
  %{
    file_name: "README.md",
    file_size: 14,
    full_path: "$",
    id: "13Kvvb4o0gzSYT2HcCGAhAkEZGt",
    remaining_path: ""
  }
]
```

We then use the result of the previous `user_media_on_folder/2` function as a subquery in the following `_media_by_folder/2` function. Besides mapping some of the fields to a shorter name (that is, `file_name` to `name`, and `file_size` to `size`), we add a new `is_folder` entry to each resulting map using the `Storage.Macros.is_folder/1` fragment-based macro.

> By using the previous result as a subquery, we are able to select its output again, exactly the same behavior you expect from a regular SQL subquery. If you tried to select the previous result again without wrapping it in a `subquery/1` call, you would get an error saying you can't have more than one `select` clause per query.

The `is_folder/1` macro relies on the SQL `LENGTH` function to decide whether a file entry should be shown as a folder:

```
$ cat apps/elixir_drip/lib/elixir_drip/storage/macros.ex
defmodule ElixirDrip.Storage.Macros do
  defmacro is_folder(remaining_path) do
    quote do
      fragment("LENGTH(?) > 0", unquote(remaining_path))
    end
  end
end
```

Each entry returned by the previous function contained a `remaining_path` field. If this field is empty, it means the corresponding file exists in the given folder; otherwise, this file is nested inside one or more folders in the current folder, hence only its folder should be presented:

```
$ cat apps/elixir_drip/lib/elixir_drip/storage/storage.ex
defmodule ElixirDrip.Storage do
  import Ecto.Query
  import ElixirDrip.Storage.Macros
  # ...
  defp _media_by_folder(user_id, folder_path) do
    user_media_on_folder = user_media_on_folder(user_id, folder_path)

    folder_media = from e in subquery(user_media_on_folder),
      select: %{
        id: e.id,
        name: e.file_name,
        full_path: e.full_path,
        size: e.file_size,
        remaining_path: e.remaining_path,
        is_folder: is_folder(e.remaining_path)
      }
```

```
        folder_media
        |> Repo.all()
        |> files_and_folders_to_present()
    end
end
```

We then use the `Storage.files_and_folders_to_present/1` function to convert the `folder_media` entries with the `is_folder` field into a map with the `files` and `folders` entries that the ElixirDrip web controller expects. This function reduces those entries into the final map. Based on the `is_folder` value, it adds an entry to the correct field of the map (you may check the chapter source code for the full function definition).

The query logic we've just analyzed is exposed by the `Storage` module through the `media_by_folder/2` function, which simply validates `folder_path` before delegating the work to the previous `_media_by_folder/2` function:

```
$ cat apps/elixir_drip/lib/elixir_drip/storage/storage.ex
defmodule ElixirDrip.Storage do
  import Ecto.Query
  import ElixirDrip.Storage.Macros
  # ...
  def media_by_folder(user_id, folder_path) do
    with {:ok, :valid} <- Media.is_valid_path?(folder_path) do
      _media_by_folder(user_id, folder_path)
    else
      error -> error
    end
  end
end
```

We will now see how Ecto fetches schemas that are associated with other schemas.

Loading schemas and their associations

By default, Ecto doesn't load any associations for us. If we retrieve an `Owner` schema, Ecto will tell you that the `files` field isn't loaded yet:

```
iex> owner = Repo.get!(Owner, "13KvtrMQ9uRB8MqkJpKSSQZxnBa")
11:15:18.878 [debug] QUERY OK source="users" db=1.2ms decode=2.8ms
SELECT u0."id", u0."email" FROM "users" AS u0 WHERE (u0."id" = $1)
["13KvtrMQ9uRB8MqkJpKSSQZxnBa"]

%ElixirDrip.Storage.Owner{
  __meta__: #Ecto.Schema.Metadata<:loaded, "users">,
  email: "jose@hey.ho",
```

```
    files: #Ecto.Association.NotLoaded<association :files is not loaded>,
    id: "13KvtrMQ9uRB8MqkJpKSSQZxnBa"
}
```

If you want to access their files, you need to explicitly call the `Repo.preload/2` callback
with the schema and the field to load:

```
iex> Repo.preload(owner, :files)
11:18:06.335 [debug] QUERY OK source="storage_media" db=4.1ms decode=0.1ms
SELECT s0."id", s0."user_id", s0."file_name", s0."full_path",
s0."file_size", s0."metadata", s0."encryption_key", s0."storage_key",
s0."uploaded_at", s0."inserted_at", s0."updated_at", u1."id" FROM
"storage_media" AS s0 INNER JOIN "users" AS u1 ON u1."id" = ANY($1) INNER
JOIN "media_owners" AS m2 ON m2."user_id" = u1."id" WHERE (m2."media_id" =
s0."id") ORDER BY u1."id" [["13KvtrMQ9uRB8MqkJpKSSQZxnBa"]]

%ElixirDrip.Storage.Owner{
    __meta__: #Ecto.Schema.Metadata<:loaded, "users">,
    email: "jose@hey.ho",
    files: [
      %ElixirDrip.Storage.Media{ ... },
    ],
    id: "13KvtrMQ9uRB8MqkJpKSSQZxnBa"
}
```

Arguably, explicitness is always good. However, this approach implies an additional query
to retrieve the files (notice the additional SELECT statement after we called the
`Repo.preload/2` callback).

We can also use the `Query.preload/3` macro when composing an Ecto query. Hence, the
previous query could be rewritten as:

```
iex> query = from o in Owner,
...> where: o.id == "13KvtrMQ9uRB8MqkJpKSSQZxnBa",
...> preload: [:files]
#Ecto.Query<from o in ElixirDrip.Storage.Owner,
 where: o.id == "13KvtrMQ9uRB8MqkJpKSSQZxnBa",
 preload: [:files]>

iex> Repo.one(query)
14:23:22.140 [debug] QUERY OK source="users" db=1.5ms
# ...
14:23:22.143 [debug] QUERY OK source="storage_media" db=2.1ms decode=0.1ms
queue=0.2ms
# ...

%ElixirDrip.Storage.Owner{
```

```
  __meta__: #Ecto.Schema.Metadata<:loaded, "users">,
  email: "jose@hey.ho",
  files: [
    %ElixirDrip.Storage.Media{ ... }
  ]
}
```

However, we still observe that we also had to execute more than one SQL query to retrieve the `Owner` schema and its corresponding files. To fetch all the associated files in one fell swoop, we could do something like this:

```
iex> query = from o in Owner,
...> join: mo in MediaOwners,
...> on: o.id == mo.user_id,
...> join: f in Media,
...> on: mo.media_id == f.id,
...> where: o.id == "13KvtrMQ9uRB8MqkJpKSSQZxnBa",
...> preload: [files: f]
#Ecto.Query<from o in ElixirDrip.Storage.Owner,
 join: m0 in ElixirDrip.Storage.MediaOwners,
 on: o.id == m0.user_id, join: m1 in ElixirDrip.Storage.Media,
 on: m0.media_id == m1.id,
 where: o.id == "13KvtrMQ9uRB8MqkJpKSSQZxnBa",
 preload: [files: m1]>

iex> Repo.one(query)
14:53:45.680 [debug] QUERY OK source="users" db=2.9ms decode=0.4ms
SELECT ...

%ElixirDrip.Storage.Owner{
  __meta__: #Ecto.Schema.Metadata<:loaded, "users">,
  email: "jose@hey.ho",
  files: [
  %ElixirDrip.Storage.Media{ ... }
  ]
}
```

In the previous query, we had to manually join the `Owner`, `MediaOwners`, and `Media` schemas, before telling Ecto to `preload` the `files` field with the associated `Media` rows. We will now create the exact same query, but using the `Ecto.assoc/2` construct, which will handle the inner join for us.

The `Ecto.assoc/2` function receives an existing struct, such as the `owner` we have been using, and the association we want to fill, and returns the corresponding query. In the following example, we pass the `owner` and the `:files` field to it, and we get a query that associates the `Owner` and `Media` schemas (via the `MediaOwners` schema):

```
iex> Ecto.assoc(owner, :files)
#Ecto.Query<from m0 in ElixirDrip.Storage.Media,
 join: o in ElixirDrip.Storage.Owner,
 on: o.id in ^["13KvtrMQ9uRB8MqkJpKSSQZxnBa"],
 join: m1 in ElixirDrip.Storage.MediaOwners,
 on: m1.user_id == o.id, where: m1.media_id == m0.id>
```

In the next query, we use the same `assoc/2` function to join the `o` struct from the `Owner` schema to the association given by `assoc(o, :files)`. We then tell Ecto to `preload` the `files` field with the `f` struct as we did before:

```
iex> query = from o in Owner,
...> join: f in assoc(o, :files),
...> where: o.id == "13KvtrMQ9uRB8MqkJpKSSQZxnBa",
...> preload: [files: f]
#Ecto.Query<from o in ElixirDrip.Storage.Owner,
 join: f in assoc(o, :files),
 where: o.id == "13KvtrMQ9uRB8MqkJpKSSQZxnBa",
 preload: [files: f]>

iex> owner = Repo.one(query)
14:39:33.862 [debug] QUERY OK source="users" db=3.7ms decode=0.1ms
SELECT u0."id", u0."email", s1."id", s1."user_id", s1."file_name",
s1."full_path", s1."file_size", s1."metadata", s1."encryption_key",
s1."storage_key", s1."uploaded_at", s1."inserted_at", s1."updated_at" FROM
"users" AS u0 INNER JOIN "media_owners" AS m2 ON m2."user_id" = u0."id"
INNER JOIN "storage_media" AS s1 ON m2."media_id" = s1."id" WHERE (u0."id"
= '13KvtrMQ9uRB8MqkJpKSSQZxnBa') []

%ElixirDrip.Storage.Owner{
    __meta__: #Ecto.Schema.Metadata<:loaded, "users">,
    email: "jose@hey.ho",
    files: [
      %ElixirDrip.Storage.Media{ ... }
    ]
}
```

Now imagine that one of the `owner` files was renamed in the meantime, after we'd already loaded its files. Say, instead of `222.txt`, its name was changed to `proper_name.txt` with the `Storage.rename/3` function. However, if we try to `preload` the `owner` files again, we will still see the file with the old name. This happens because, by default, `Repo.preload/2` will only fetch the associated records from the database if the association isn't loaded yet. To force it, we need to pass the `:force` option as `true`:

```
iex> Repo.preload(owner_with_files, :files, force: true)
17:27:10.174 [debug] QUERY OK source="storage_media" db=0.9ms
SELECT ...
```

```
%ElixirDrip.Storage.Owner{
  __meta__: #Ecto.Schema.Metadata<:loaded, "users">,
  email: "jose@hey.ho",
  files: [
    %ElixirDrip.Storage.Media{
      file_name: "proper_name.txt",
      # ...
    },
  ]
}
```

In the next section, we will learn how can we validate before doing a move or rename operation if a file already exists.

Queries with raw SQL

Both the move/3 and rename/3 functions rely on the private _move/4 function, which is able to change simultaneously the full path and filename of a media file:

```
$ cat apps/elixir_drip/lib/elixir_drip/storage/storage.ex
defmodule ElixirDrip.Storage do
  # ...
  def move(user_id, media_id, new_path),
    do: _move(user_id, media_id, new_path, nil)

  def rename(user_id, media_id, new_name),
    do: _move(user_id, media_id, nil, new_name)

  defp _move(user_id, media_id, new_path, new_name), do: ...
  # ...
end
```

This _move/4 function only allows the media file creator to change its folder or its filename. Then, it gets the media file, the new path, and filename, and checks whether a file on the new path exists with the new name. If everything went well, it creates the changeset, validates the new full_path and file_name fields, and updates the Media schema:

```
defp _move(user_id, media_id, new_path, new_name) do
  with {:ok, :creator} <- is_creator?(user_id, media_id),
       %Media{} = media <- get_media(media_id),
       new_path <- new_path(media, new_path),
       new_name <- new_name(media, new_name),
       {:ok, :nonexistent} <- media_already_exists?(user_id, new_path,
       new_name)
  do
    media
```

```
   |> Changeset.cast(%{full_path: new_path, file_name: new_name},
   [:full_path, :file_name])
   |> Media.validate_field(:full_path)
   |> Media.validate_field(:file_name)
   |> Repo.update()
 else
   error -> error
 end
end
```

We will now analyze how the `media_already_exists?/3` function works. The idea here is to utilize the `user_media_query/1` function and search for a media file with the given `full_path` and `file_name`.

We could run this query through `Repo.all/1` and, if we had one or more rows, we would know that a file already exists with the given `full_path` and `file_name`. However, this approach is highly inefficient because, in our case, the database can stop the query as soon as it finds one result.

What we want here is to apply the SQL `EXISTS` operator to the query we composed. This way, a single row matching the criteria is enough for the database to return the expected results.

To accomplish this, we will get the raw SQL query with the `Repo.to_sql/2` function and then wrap the resulting query string in a `SELECT TRUE WHERE EXISTS (...)` SQL statement. The `vars` element of the tuple we get contains the list of values that we are interpolating on the query, namely the `user_id`, `full_path`, and `file_name` we're searching for:

```
def media_already_exists?(user_id, full_path, file_name) do
  user_media = user_media_query(user_id)

  query = from [_mo, m] in user_media,
  where: m.full_path == ^full_path,
  where: m.file_name == ^file_name

  {query, vars} = Repo.to_sql(:all, query)
  query = "SELECT TRUE WHERE EXISTS (#{query})"

  Repo.query!(query, vars).rows
  |> Enum.empty?()
  |> case do
  true -> {:ok, :nonexistent}
  _ -> {:error, :already_exists}
  end
end
```

We then pass the SQL query string and the `vars` that we got to the `Repo.query!/2` function, so we can finally get the results from the database. The query only returns `TRUE` if the subquery yields any row, hence we check whether the `rows` field is empty to return the result tuple.

As you can see here, `Repo.query!/2` returns a `Postgrex.Result` struct that, among other fields, also contains the `rows` field that we used. The rows field consists of a list of lists, corresponding to each row fetched from the database:

```
iex> Repo.query!("SELECT * FROM users", [])
06:46:24.907 [debug] QUERY OK db=11.9ms
SELECT * FROM users []
%Postgrex.Result{
  columns: ["id", "username", "hashed_password", "inserted_at",
   "updated_at", "email"],
  command: :select,
  connection_id: 15974,
  num_rows: 4,
  rows: [
    [
      "13KvtrMQ9uRB8MqkJpKSSQZxnBa",
      # ...
    ],
    # ...
  ]
}
```

In this scenario, we didn't use a `fragment` because we needed to inject a whole subquery and not a simpler Ecto expression (Ecto only lets us use subqueries in the `from` and `join` clauses). We are now able to efficiently detect whether media with a specific path and name already exists.

In the next section, we will answer the question: Who are the top users of our ElixirDrip application?

Finding top users with aggregates

In the current ElixirDrip application, there are four users, `jose`, `xpto`, `daniel`, and `andre`:

```
iex> Repo.all(from u in User, select: map(u, [:id, :username, :email]))

10:48:41.609 [debug] QUERY OK source="users" db=7.4ms queue=0.1ms
SELECT u0."id", u0."username", u0."email" FROM "users" AS u0 []
[
```

```
%{email: "jose@hey.ho", id: "13KvtrMQ9uRB8MqkJpKSSQZxnBa", username:
"jose"},
%{email: "xp@to.foo", id: "13ix90kpmblgJF4Ful762gqb6m2", username:
"xpto"},
%{email: "daniel@right.here", id: "13ucVBdFw40QqbYjwm65jEml7P9",
username: "daniel"},
%{email: "andre@somewhere.com", id: "13ucZ46LTdsfvezCPviNJ96gYqu",
username: "andre"}
]
```

Notice how we are using the `Query.API.map/2` function for Ecto to select the results into a map with only the `id`, `username`, and `email` fields, instead of defining the map *manually* by `%{id: u.id, ...}`. We could have defined the query as `from User, select: [:id, :username, :email]`, but this would get us a list of `User` schemas, each with only those three fields filled.

Since we are storing each `Media` with the ID of the user who uploaded it (the `media.user_id` field), we can count the number of files and the disk usage per user just by looking at this schema:

```
iex> user_stats = from m in Media,
...> group_by: m.user_id,
...> select: %{
...> media_count: count(m.id),
...> disk_usage: sum(m.file_size),
...> user_id: m.user_id
...> }

#Ecto.Query<from m in ElixirDrip.Storage.Media,
 group_by: [m.user_id],
 select: %{media_count: count(m.id), disk_usage: sum(m.file_size), user_id:
m.user_id}>

iex> Repo.all(user_stats)

10:42:26.430 [debug] QUERY OK source="storage_media" db=18.8ms decode=8.4ms
queue=0.3ms
SELECT count(s0."id"), sum(s0."file_size"), s0."user_id" FROM
"storage_media" AS s0 GROUP BY s0."user_id" []
[
  %{disk_usage: 25, media_count: 1, user_id:
"13ix90kpmblgJF4Ful762gqb6m2"},
  %{disk_usage: 161, media_count: 7, user_id:
"13ucZ46LTdsfvezCPviNJ96gYqu"},
```

```
    %{disk_usage: 103, media_count: 8, user_id:
  "13KvtrMQ9uRB8MqkJpKSSQZxnBa"}
  ]
```

In the previous query, we use two aggregate functions, `Query.API.count/1` and `Query.API.sum/1`, and then group the results by `User.user_id`. In the query shown on the `debug` log message, you can see those aggregate functions being translated into the respective SQL functions when the query is finally executed.

The result we obtained is valid, but doesn't show us the users that may exist without their first media upload. To accomplish this, we will query the database in a *schemaless* fashion, by directly joining the `storage_media` and `users` tables, but this time using `left_join`, which will show us an entry even if no media exists for a given user:

```
iex> schemaless_users_media = from u in "users",
...> left_join: m in "storage_media",
...> on: u.id == m.user_id,
...> group_by: u.id,
...> select: %{
...> media_count: count(m.id),
...> disk_usage: sum(m.file_size),
...> username: u.username
...> }

#Ecto.Query<from u in "users", left_join: s in "storage_media",
 on: u.id == s.user_id, group_by: [u.id],
 select: %{media_count: count(s.id), disk_usage: sum(s.file_size),
 username: u.username}>

iex> Repo.all(schemaless_users_media)

13:53:27.429 [debug] QUERY OK source="users" db=0.4ms
SELECT count(s1."id"), sum(s1."file_size"), u0."username" FROM "users" AS
u0 LEFT OUTER JOIN "storage_media" AS s1 ON u0."id" = s1."user_id" GROUP BY
u0."id" []
[
  %{disk_usage: 103, media_count: 8, username: "jose"},
  %{disk_usage: 25, media_count: 1, username: "xpto"},
  %{disk_usage: 161, media_count: 7, username: "andre"},
  %{disk_usage: nil, media_count: 0, username: "daniel"}
]
```

We got the desired four entries, one by each user, and we can now see that `daniel` hasn't uploaded any media to ElixirDrip. Moreover, albeit correct, these results aren't ordered.

The following query orders the results in descending order, by number of uploaded files. As you can see, it only adds the `order_by` clause to the `schemaless_users_media` query:

```
iex> schemaless_ordered_users_media = from [u,m] in schemaless_users_media,
...> order_by: [desc: 1]

#Ecto.Query<from u in "users", left_join: s in "storage_media",
 on: u.id == s.user_id, group_by: [u.id], order_by: [desc: 1],
 select: %{media_count: count(s.id), disk_usage: sum(s.file_size),
username: u.username}>

iex> Repo.all(schemaless_ordered_users_media)

13:54:24.179 [debug] QUERY OK source="users" db=1.5ms queue=0.1ms
SELECT count(s1."id"), sum(s1."file_size"), u0."username" FROM "users" AS
u0 LEFT OUTER JOIN "storage_media" AS s1 ON u0."id" = s1."user_id" GROUP BY
u0."id" ORDER BY 1 DESC []
[
   %{disk_usage: 103, media_count: 8, username: "jose"},
   %{disk_usage: 161, media_count: 7, username: "andre"},
   %{disk_usage: 25, media_count: 1, username: "xpto"},
   %{disk_usage: nil, media_count: 0, username: "daniel"}
]
```

Ecto orders the results in descending-number-of-files order, because we passed the `[desc: 1]` keyword list to the `order_by/2` macro. The `1` indicates we want the results ordered by the *first* query column—in our case, the database column with the `count` result.

Despite the `media_count` entry appearing as the second entry of every map in the query outcome (that is, `[%{disk_usage: 103, media_count: 8, username: "jose"}, ...]`), the file tally appears on the first column of the query (that is, `SELECT count(s1."id"), sum(s1."file_size"), u0."username" ...`), hence the `desc: 1` order criterion pointing to the first column of the results.

Despite ordering as expected, indicating the column number isn't intuitive, and relies on the column order. Let's use the previous query as a subquery, and see how can we dynamically define both the sorting column and direction, instead of relying on an arbitrary integer:

```
iex> sort_order = :desc
:desc

iex> dynamic_order_schemaless_users_media = from e in
subquery(schemaless_users_media),
...> order_by: [{^sort_order, e.media_count}]
```

```
#Ecto.Query<from u in subquery(from u in "users",
  left_join: s in "storage_media",
  on: u.id == s.user_id,
  group_by: [u.id],
  select: %{media_count: count(s.id), disk_usage: sum(s.file_size),
  username: u.username}),
 order_by: [desc: u.media_count]>

iex> Repo.all(dynamic_order_schemaless_users_media)
14:11:59.452 [debug] QUERY OK db=1.8ms queue=0.2ms
SELECT s0."media_count", s0."disk_usage", s0."username" FROM (SELECT
count(s1."id") AS "media_count", sum(s1."file_size") AS "disk_usage",
u0."username" AS "username" FROM "users" AS u0 LEFT OUTER JOIN
"storage_media" AS s1 ON u0."id" = s1."user_id" GROUP BY u0."id") AS s0
ORDER BY s0."media_count" DESC []
[
  %{disk_usage: 103, media_count: 8, username: "jose"},
  %{disk_usage: 161, media_count: 7, username: "andre"},
  %{disk_usage: 25, media_count: 1, username: "xpto"},
  %{disk_usage: nil, media_count: 0, username: "daniel"}
]
```

Given that the order_by clause expects a keyword list, we inject the sort_order value as the first element of the {^sort_order, e.media_count} tuple, turning it into the :asc or :desc key. We can also point to the media_count field of the schemaless_users_media query, instead of relying on the column number, because we're now using it as a subquery.

The last iteration of this query will also allow the sorting field to be dynamically set. To accomplish this, we need to make use of the Query.API.field/2 function, which lets us dynamically access a struct field:

```
$ cat apps/elixir_drip/lib/elixir_drip/storage/storage.ex
defmodule ElixirDrip.Storage do
  # ...
  def get_top_users_by_usage(sort_field \\ :media_count, sort_order \\
  :desc, top \\ 10) do
    schemaless_users_media = from u in "users",
      # same query we previously defined ...

    dynamic_schemaless_users_media = from e in subquery
    (schemaless_users_media),
      order_by: [{^sort_order, field(e, ^sort_field)}],
      limit: ^top

    Repo.all(dynamic_schemaless_users_media)
  end
```

```
end
```

By passing the `top` variable to the `limit/2` clause, the previous `get_top_users_by_usage/3` function limits the results returned by the database. In practice, this sets the maximum number of users we want on our ElixirDrip top rank:

```
iex> Storage.get_top_users_by_usage(:media_count, :desc, 2)
15:14:21.644 [debug] QUERY OK db=3.3ms queue=0.1ms
SELECT s0."media_count", s0."disk_usage", s0."username" FROM (SELECT
count(s1."id") AS "media_count", sum(s1."file_size") AS "disk_usage",
u0."username" AS "username" FROM "users" AS u0 LEFT OUTER JOIN
"storage_media" AS s1 ON u0."id" = s1."user_id" GROUP BY u0."id") AS s0
ORDER BY s0."media_count" DESC LIMIT $1 [2]
[
  %{disk_usage: 103, media_count: 8, username: "jose"},
  %{disk_usage: 161, media_count: 7, username: "andre"}
]
```

To calculate simple aggregates, you can also rely on the `Repo.aggregate/3` callback. It receives a *queryable*, the aggregate operation, and the field, and computes the given aggregate:

```
iex> Repo.aggregate(Media, :avg, :file_size)
15:24:44.901 [debug] QUERY OK source="storage_media" db=1.6ms
SELECT avg(s0."file_size") FROM "storage_media" AS s0 []
#Decimal<18.0625000000000000>
```

The previous example tells us the average file size in the local ElixirDrip instance is 18 bytes. Imagine that we now want to calculate the average number of files for each user. Since we still have access to the `schemaless_users_media` query, it would be nice if we could simply pass it to the `Repo.aggregate(:avg, :media_count)` function. However, when we do this we get an error saying Ecto doesn't allow us to aggregate a query that already has a `group_by` clause:

```
iex> schemaless_users_media |> Repo.aggregate(:avg, :media_count)
** (Ecto.QueryError) cannot aggregate on query with group_by in query:
# ...
```

If we consider that Ecto relies on available SQL functions to calculate the aggregate, this makes total sense. After all, in standard SQL, a query with more than one GROUP BY clause isn't valid. As such, we will wrap the `schemaless_users_media` in a `subquery/2`, thus fixing the `Repo.aggregate/3` call. By using `subquery`, the outermost query ends up without any GROUP BY clause, allowing `Repo.aggregate/3` to add its own GROUP BY clause:

```
iex> subquery(schemaless_users_media) |> Repo.aggregate(:av
g, :media_count)
15:40:50.854 [debug] QUERY OK db=4.5ms queue=0.1ms
SELECT avg(s0."media_count") FROM (SELECT count(s1."id") AS "media_count",
sum(s1."file_size") AS "disk_usage", u0."username" AS "username" FROM
"users" AS u0 LEFT OUTER JOIN "storage_media" AS s1 ON u0."id" =
s1."user_id" GROUP BY u0."id") AS s0 []
#Decimal<4.0000000000000000>
```

We now know that each user stores an average of four files in ElixirDrip.

As we saw in this section, Ecto provides us with some terrific query tools that give us a lot of power and flexibility. You can query your data by relying on the schemas you've defined, or you can simply interact with the database tables and hand-pick the fields you want to retrieve. If Ecto doesn't provide an abstraction for a specific SQL function you need, you can directly invoke the SQL function from your queries, no questions asked.

It is worth noting that we aren't tied at all to Ecto schemas. For queries that calculate aggregates and/or span many tables, going *schemaless* is often the simplest solution, and lets you avoid the pain of trying to adapt your query output to the existing schemas you may have.

Summary

In this chapter, we not only understood what Ecto is, but also applied its four main concepts–Repository, Schemas, Changesets, and Queries–to our ElixirDrip umbrella project:

- We configured the application repository so we could connect (with the help of the Ecto adapter and the database driver) to our PostgreSQL database
- We defined the schemas that represent our database tables
- We learned how to use changesets to validate the changes made to information stored in the database

- We queried our data in many different ways, from schemaless queries to aggregate ones, using SQL functions abstracted by Ecto and others that need to be run through Ecto fragments

During this journey, we introduced, and later ran, migrations that allowed us to mould the structure of our database by creating the tables and constraints we needed. Among these changes were the foreign key constraints that shaped the relationship between the ElixirDrip schemas. We implemented a many-to-many relationship between users and media, using an intermediate schema that also illustrated how a one-to-many relationship works.

As evidence of how flexible Ecto is, we defined more than one schema backed by the same users database table, so we could work with users in the Accounts and Storage contexts. This possibility helps the developer avoid the so-called *fat model* anti-pattern, and it contrasts with other common database mappers that favor a one-to-one mapping between each database table and the respective code representation.

In the next chapter, you will see all this work on the backend being wonderfully presented with Phoenix – an Elixir web framework.

8
Phoenix – A Flying Web Framework

Having looked at Ecto and how we can use it to add a persistence layer to our application, we will now delve into Phoenix, the most popular web framework in Elixir. Phoenix is often characterized as being a productive, reliable, and fast framework.

Productive because it removes as much boilerplate code as possible, without impacting the explicitness cherished by the Elixir community. This way, you can move fast and take advantage of the macros and abstractions provided by Phoenix, without having to decrease the maintainability of your application. Moreover, Phoenix is great for building interactive applications, as it provides channels—permanent connections between the clients and the server. Instead of being tied to the traditional request-response model, you can use channels to keep a stateful conversation with your clients, which fundamentally changes the way you build interactive applications. Towards the end of this chapter, we'll add channels to our application, which will demonstrate the productivity gains that Phoenix brings for interactive applications.

Reliable as standing on the shoulders of battle-tested technologies such as Erlang/OTP, which is known to be used in some of the most reliable applications in the world. This is one of the most important factors in any application, regardless of the type of application or industry: we always want to maximize the uptime. This is where Phoenix soars, setting itself apart from most web frameworks. By taking advantage of the characteristics of the Erlang runtime, requests in Phoenix are completely isolated from each other, as they are handled in separate processes. As processes share nothing between them, a long-running request that's waiting on the database will not slow down other simpler requests that don't communicate with the database, hence maximizing the overall throughput of the system. Furthermore, Phoenix uses supervisors and supervision trees in order to create self-healing components, as we've seen throughout Chapter 3, *Processes – The Bedrock for Concurrency and Fault-Tolerance*.

Fast as a result of optimizing the most critical parts of the request-response flow, such as routing requests or rendering responses. Additionally, as each request is handled in a separate process, they will all run concurrently and utilize all the available CPU cores. Phoenix is known for, in certain scenarios, having response times measured in microseconds. In this chapter we'll point out some aspects of Phoenix that enable this blazingly fast performance.

By the end of the last chapter, the core of our application was completely built. From this point forward, the business logic inside ElixirDrip will not change. The purpose of this chapter is to add a presentation layer to our application, particularly a web layer using the Phoenix framework.

This may seem a minor detail, but it has been a topic frequently discussed in the Elixir community, which generally states that there should be a clear separation between your domain logic and your presentation layer. If, for instance, besides a web interface you also want a **Command Line Interface** (**CLI**) for your application, you shouldn't need to change your application. The CLI presenter should just call the API your application exposes, and transform the data to present it in a different way. Phoenix is *not* your application, but rather a framework to add a web presentation layer to it.

This is why in `Chapter 2`, *Innards of an Elixir Project*, we separated out Phoenix to a different umbrella application called `elixir_drip_web`. We're drawing a clear line that separates what is the core of our application from what is related to how we present it. With this separation in place, the `elixir_drip_web` application will only call functions from the public API of the `elixir_drip` application.

Even if we hadn't split our application under an umbrella, Phoenix encourages the separation of concerns even inside a single application. Although Phoenix is a traditional MVC web framework, the word *model* is barely used in the Phoenix community, and from Phoenix 1.3 onward the generators won't create a `models/` directory. The rationale is that everything inside your application domain is a model, and having a bunch of files inside a `models/` directory doesn't convey any meaning. Instead, Phoenix encourages you to design with intent and create your models around contexts, borrowing some concepts from the domain-driven design approach. An example of this was shown in the last chapter, where the `user` model is inside an `accounts` context, and the rest of the application interacts with the `user` always through this `accounts` context. Note, however, that there may be another `user` model inside a different context, which could have a different schema, adapted to the context it's inserted in. With this approach, we can get a lot of insights into the application we're exploring just by looking at the directory structure, without reading any source code. This also tells us how each model is relevant to the domain of our application, instead of just reflecting the underlying database structure, as was the case with the `models/` directory.

Before diving into Phoenix, we'll take a look at Plug, the underlying library that Phoenix builds upon.

This chapter will cover the following:

- The Plug specification
- Routing requests
- Handling requests in a controller
- Rendering views
- Authenticating users
- Implementing a JSON API
- Building interactive applications using channels

The Plug specification

Plug is a very central component of Phoenix, and as is stated in the documentation, *lives at the heart of Phoenix's HTTP layer*. The plug specification allows us to compose modules in web applications, abstracting the concept of a connection. Plug embraces the functional nature of Elixir and handles web requests by making a series of transformations on the connection, which eventually will be used to render the response.

There are two types of plugs: function plugs and module plugs. Regardless of the type, Plug's specification is very simple: a Plug must accept a connection and return a (possibly) modified connection. Later in this section, we'll explore what a connection is. Reading this elementary description, it's hard to imagine that Plug is at the heart of Phoenix. However, this simple concept is incredibly powerful, which becomes evident when you start to chain plugs together to achieve sophisticated functionality. Many of Phoenix's powerful constructs, such as routers and controllers, internally are just plugs, which further demonstrates their power. Furthermore, Plug is also an abstraction layer for the connection adapters of different web servers, and currently ships with an adapter for the `cowboy` web server.

We will build a plug for our ElixirDrip application later in this chapter, when we add authentication to it. For now, we will see a simple example of how to build module and function plugs, and also how we can chain them so that the connection transformation of the first plug is available to the second one.

Creating a module plug

A module plug has to export two functions: init and call. The init function is called at compile time, receives one argument, and its purpose is to prepare the options that will be passed to call. The call function is called at runtime and receives two arguments: the connection and the options returned by init. This function is where we'll transform the connection according to our needs. Having init allows you to prepare some of the work of your plug, which will be done during compilation. This way, call can be more performant, as its focus is solely on handling the request. Let's see an example:

```
$ cat my_module_plug.ex

defmodule MyModulePlug do
  import Plug.Conn

  def init(options), do: options

  def call(conn, _options) do
    conn
    |> assign(:username, "Gabriel")
  end
end
```

In init, we are not doing anything and simply return the options that were passed to us. Then, in the call function, we call assign, which is available in this context because we imported Plug.Conn at the top of the module. This function will ensure the provided key/value pair is saved in the connection, so that subsequent plugs may access it. These key/value pairs will be available in the assigns field of the connection. Let's now see how a function plug works, and how we can create a pipeline for our two plugs.

Creating a function plug

Function plugs are similar to module plugs, but they are contained in a function instead of a module. This means that we don't have to call the init to arrange the options. However, function plugs receive two arguments, exactly like the call function in module plugs: the connection and the options. The following function is a function plug:

```
def my_function_plug(conn, _options) do
  conn
  |> put_resp_content_type("text/plain")
  |> send_resp(200, "Hello #{conn.assigns.username}")
end
```

In this function, we take the connection and pass it through to `put_resp_content_type`, which will modify the connection to set the content type of the response. Then, we take this modified connection to send a response, setting 200 as the status code and returning a simple string. Note that we're interpolating `conn.assigns.username` into this string, which was filled by our module plug earlier. Both `put_resp_content_type` and `send_resp` are functions imported from `Plug.Conn`. This module, besides defining some handy functions to deal with connections, also defines a struct, `%Plug.Conn{}`, which is the representation of the connection we have been talking about. This will hold information about the request and the response, containing fields such as the request method, the headers for the request and the response, or the request parameters. For a full list of the fields present in this struct, look at the official documentation at `https://hexdocs.pm/plug/Plug.Conn.html`.

How do you choose between module and function plugs? If you want to share a plug across different modules, than you need to create a module plug. If your plug needs some heavy groundwork regarding the options you may pass to it, you're also better off with a module plug, as your plug may be more performant this way. If your requirements don't match any previous conditions, you can simply use a function plug, which can be created inside any other module. Let's now see how to chain our two plugs together:

```
$ cat my_plug_pipeline.ex

defmodule MyPlugPipeline do
  use Plug.Builder

  plug MyModulePlug
  plug :my_function_plug

  def my_function_plug(conn, _options) do
    conn
    |> put_resp_content_type("text/plain")
    |> send_resp(200, "Hello #{conn.assigns.username}!")
  end
end
```

Besides the `my_function_plug` function that we discussed before, this module contains our pipeline. The `plug` macro (exported by `Plug.Builder`) allows us to define the plugs that will be part of our pipeline. The first one is our module plug, `MyModulePlug`, and the second one is our function plug, `my_function_plug`. As you can see, when using a module plug we pass the name of the module, whereas with a function plug we provide the name of the function as an atom.

If a plug halts the Plug pipeline by calling the `Plug.Conn.halt/1` function, subsequent plugs will no longer be called. For instance, if `MyModulePlug` called the `halt/1` function, then `my_function_plug` would not be invoked. We'll see an example of this later in this chapter, when we implement authentication.

We'll now take our pipeline for a spin. Start an IEx session at the root of ElixirDrip with `iex -S mix`:

```
iex> c("my_module_plug.ex")
[MyModulePlug]
iex> c("my_plug_pipeline.ex")
[MyPlugPipeline]
iex> {:ok, _pid} = Plug.Adapters.Cowboy.http(MyPlugPipeline, [])
{:ok, #PID<0.481.0>}
```

After compiling our two modules, we start the `cowboy` web server, passing our Plug pipeline as the entry point. The `cowboy` adapter will take care of interacting with the web server, creating the connection, and then calling our Plug pipeline. The second argument for `http` is a set of options, which are not relevant for this example. With the server running, go to `http://localhost:4000` in your browser, and you will see the text **Hello Gabriel!** This demonstrates our two plugs working together, with the first one putting information into the connection and the second one consuming it.

We have now finished our tour around Plug. As you can see, it's both simple and powerful, and serves as the foundation for Phoenix. Speaking of Phoenix, it's about time we started exploring it! We'll start by seeing how requests are routed in Phoenix.

Routing requests

We'll now explore the flow of a traditional HTTP request, analyzing each step of the process up to when a response is rendered. As we've seen in the last section, Plug provides an adapter for the Cowboy web server, which we've used to demonstrate the two plugs we've created. Phoenix also uses this adapter to interact with the Cowboy web server. When a requests hits the server, this adapter handles it, creates a new conn (a `%Plug.Conn{}` struct), and calls the endpoint configured in your application. By default, the endpoint is called `<name_of_your_app>.Endpoint`. The endpoint is the boundary between the web server and our application code, so essentially the endpoint is the beginning of a request. Let's see the configuration for the endpoint:

```
$ cat apps/elixir_drip_web/config/config.exs

config :elixir_drip_web, ElixirDripWeb.Endpoint,
```

```
url: [host: "localhost"],
secret_key_base: "ez09 ...9cbq",
render_errors: [view: ElixirDripWeb.ErrorView, accepts: ~w(html json)],
pubsub: [name: ElixirDripWeb.PubSub, adapter: Phoenix.PubSub.PG2]
```

This is the default configuration for the endpoint. The `url` option configures the URL generation throughout the application. In this case, the host name is set to `localhost`. The `secret_key_base` is the key used as a base to generate secrets for encrypting or signing data, such as cookies or tokens. The `render_errors` option configures the module that is called when there's a failure in our application. We'll explore this further later in this chapter, when we talk about views. Lastly, there's the `pubsub` configuration, which configures the pubsub layer of Phoenix Channels, which we'll talk about near the end of this chapter, use this pubsub layer to broadcast messages.

Having seen how to configure the endpoint, let's take a look at a snippet from its module:

```
$ cat apps/elixir_drip_web/lib/elixir_drip_web/endpoint.ex

defmodule ElixirDripWeb.Endpoint do
  use Phoenix.Endpoint, otp_app: :elixir_drip_web

  # ...

  plug(Plug.RequestId)
  plug(Plug.Logger)

  # ...

  plug(ElixirDripWeb.Router)
end
```

The endpoint itself is a plug, which consists of a plug pipeline. As we've already seen in the beginning of this chapter, plugs are just functions that take a connection and return a (possibly modified) connection. The endpoint pipeline contains plugs that perform typical operations in a production web server, such as logging the request, dealing with static content or parsing the parameters. In the previous snippet, we're just showing a subset of the plugs present in the Endpoint. The first one, `Plug.RequestId`, is responsible for taking the request ID from the request headers (`x-request-id` by default) or generating a new request ID, and placing it in the response headers (again with `x-request-id` as the default). The second plug, `Plug.Logger`, is responsible for logging each request.

We're now beginning to see that, in Phoenix, handling a request is done by applying a series of functions that will transform the connection, eventually resulting in the creation of a response.

You can be productive, move fast, and just use the defaults, or easily fine-tune the framework to your needs, since these are just composable small functions. For instance, if you don't want to log any requests in your application, just remove the `plug(Plug.Logger)` line from your endpoint, and that's it. This modular design of Phoenix (also borrowed from Plug) is really important in the long run, as your application evolves and the requirements for it change.

 Although in `ElixirDripWeb` we're only using one endpoint, it's possible to have one application running more than one endpoint. For instance, you could have an endpoint with a different pipeline of plugs, with specific security policies enforced. However, this is not very common, as you can also achieve this by running those endpoints in separate umbrella applications.

In the previous example, we can see that the last plug in the endpoint is `ElixirDripWeb.Router`, which is the router of our application. Let's take a look at it now:

```
$ cat apps/elixir_drip_web/lib/elixir_drip_web/router.ex

defmodule ElixirDripWeb.Router do
  use ElixirDripWeb, :router

  pipeline :browser do
    plug(:accepts, ["html"])
    plug(:fetch_session)
    plug(:fetch_flash)
    plug(:protect_from_forgery)
    plug(:put_secure_browser_headers)
  end

  pipe_through(:browser)

  get("/files", ElixirDripWeb.FileController, :index)
  get("/files/:id", ElixirDripWeb.FileController, :show)
  get("/files/new", ElixirDripWeb.FileController, :new)
  post("/files", ElixirDripWeb.FileController, :create)

  get("/", PageController, :index)
end
```

The first line inside the module is `use ElixirDripWeb, :router`. This line will run the `router` function from the `ElixirDripWeb` module, which can be found at `apps/elixir_drip_web/lib/elixir_drip_web.ex`. This function will call `use Phoenix.Router` and import some modules, such as `Plug.Conn`. The same strategy is applied for controllers, views, and channels.

You may edit this file, but be careful—for instance, changes made on the `controller` function will be applied to every controller in the application.

As we can see, our router has one pipeline, called `:browser`. Before talking about pipelines, let's discuss the most important part of the router, the routes. Our first route is this one:

```
get("/files", ElixirDripWeb.FileController, :index)
```

The route is created by `get`, which is a Phoenix macro that corresponds to the HTTP verb GET. There's one Phoenix macro for each HTTP verb, with the name always corresponding to the verb. The first argument passed to this macro is the path that we want to match on, while the second and third arguments are the controller and the action inside it that will handle this request. When the `get` macro is expanded, it will generate a clause for the `Phoenix.Router.match/5` function. In our example, that clause would be:

```
def match(:get, "/files", ElixirDripWeb.FileController, :index, [])
```

The same thing would happen for the macros corresponding to the other HTTP verbs. In the beginning of this chapter, we stated that one of the reasons for Phoenix's incredible performance is that it optimizes some core parts of the traditional request-response flow. Here, we have our first evidence of this. While the router looks very sleek and readable, beneath the surface it's powered by pattern matching, particularly on the `Phoenix.Router.match/5` function. This makes our routing layer very performant, since pattern matching can be further optimized by the Erlang VM.

Let's now look at all the routes related to the `"/files"` path:

```
get("/files", ElixirDripWeb.FileController, :index)
get("/files/:id", ElixirDripWeb.FileController, :show)
get("/files/new", ElixirDripWeb.FileController, :new)
post("/files", ElixirDripWeb.FileController, :create)
```

This pattern is so common in Phoenix applications that it provides a `resources` macro, which allows us to express those four routes in a single line:

```
resources("/files", ElixirDripWeb.FileController, only: [:index, :show,
:new, :create])
```

By default, the `resources` macro generates routes for eight HTTP verbs, including PATCH and PUT. Since in this application we're not interested in all of those, we pass the `only` option, so that it only generates routes for those actions. We could instead pass the `except` option, which would work inversely. The `resources` macro can also be nested inside other `resources` macros.

This will generate nested routes according to the hierarchy of resources. We'll not explore this option in the ElixirDrip application, but this may come in handy when building a more complex system.

 Phoenix creates a mix task called `mix phx.routes`, which allows you to see the routes for your application. This task is very helpful when building the routing layer of an application, as it allows you to see which routes exist and debug potential issues.

Let's now take a look at the `:browser` pipeline in our router:

```
pipeline :browser do
  plug(:accepts, ["html"])
  plug(:fetch_session)
  plug(:fetch_flash)
  plug(:protect_from_forgery)
  plug(:put_secure_browser_headers)
end
```

The pipeline, much like the endpoint, is a list of plugs. These plugs are called sequentially, unless one of them halts the pipeline. As the name suggests, this pipeline is used for requests issued by a browser. The first plug will respect the Accept headers, defining the request format(s) that is (are) accepted. Then, the `fetch_session` plug will fetch the session and add it to the connection. The following plug, `fetch_flash`, fetches any flash messages that may have been present when the current request was made. Then, we have two plugs related to security, which protect form posts from attacks such as **Cross-Site Request Forgery (CSRF)**.

The `pipe_through` function configures which pipeline(s) will be called for a certain route. Given that for now we simply have `pipe_through(:browser)` at the root level of our router, the `:browser` pipeline will be called regardless of the route that matches. For now, we don't need to introduce scopes, since we're only serving browser requests. When we build a JSON API later in this chapter, you'll see the router being updated to use scopes, which will allow us to run different pipelines according to the path of the request. Note that the Phoenix generator creates a scope (for the root path, `"/"`) and puts the `pipe_through` inside that scope. For now, we're simplifying and removing that scope, since it's not needed for now—we'll talk about scopes once they're necessary in our application.

Before jumping into the controller, let's do a quick recap of the flow of a request:

- The endpoint receives a request from the adapter and calls the plugs in its pipeline, with the router being the last one
- The router will try to find a route for the path of the request

- Once it does, it saves the name of the controller module, as well as the action that will be invoked on it
- Before calling the controller, the router will run the Plug pipeline defined in the `pipe_through` call(s), if any
- After executing all the plugs in the pipeline(s), the router calls the action on the controller, both of which were configured in the route

Having arrived at this point, the job of the router is finished. Let's now take a look at what happens inside a controller.

Handling requests in a controller

At this point, the request is in the controller, which was called by the router according to the logic we described. We'll build the `FileController` that we saw in the router, and go through the four actions we've created routes for: index, show, new. and create. Let's begin with the index action:

```
$ cat apps/elixir_drip_web/lib/elixir_drip_web/controllers/
file_controller.ex

defmodule ElixirDripWeb.FileController do
  use ElixirDripWeb, :controller

  alias ElixirDrip.Storage

  def index(conn, %{"path" => path}) do
    with {:ok, media} <- Storage.media_by_folder("hardcoded_user_id",
    path) do
      render(conn, "index.html", files: media.files, folders:
      media.folders, current_path: path)
    else
      {:error, :invalid_path} ->
        conn
        |> put_flash(:error, "The path provided is invalid.")
        |> redirect(to: file_path(conn, :index, "path": "$"))
      _ ->
        conn
        |> put_flash(:error, "Unexpected error.")
        |> redirect(to: file_path(conn, :index, "path": "$"))
    end
  end
end
```

```
    def index(conn, _params), do: redirect(conn, to: file_path(conn,
    :index, "path": "$"))
end
```

Similar to what happens in the router, the `use` macro will require and import the necessary modules for the controller to work properly. Functions on the controller receive two parameters: the first is the connection, while the second is the parameters. Our `index` function is called when the action is index, which means that we'll list the files and folders for a specific path. We have two clauses for the `index` function. In the first one, we're pattern matching on the parameters for a `"path"` key and saving its value in the `path` variable. The path is a query parameter, and it contains the path of the folder that the user wants to view. When this key is present, we call the `Storage.media_by_folder/2` function, which resides in the `elixir_drip` umbrella application. This example shows one of the advantages of having split our ElixirDrip application into two umbrella applications. As you can see, our presentation layer is really thin, only calling functions from the public API of the core application.

 As you can see in the first `index` function clause, the parameters map has string keys. This is intentional, as we can't safely convert external data to atoms because we may pass the Erlang VM limit for the number of atoms, which would cause the VM to crash. At the boundaries of our application, we may then convert these strings to atoms, in a controlled manner, and then just use atom keys throughout our application.

For now, we're calling this function with a hardcoded user ID, as we don't yet have a way for users to log in to our application. We'll follow this path and make the functions from the `Storage` module return a static list of folders and files when this ID is provided. We're wrapping the call to this function in a `with` block so that we can pattern-match on its return value. When the call is successful, we call the `Phoenix.Controller.render/3` function. The first argument to this function is the connection, the second the name of the template we want to render, and the third is a keyword list, generally called **assigns**, which will be passed to the view. In the next section, we'll see how they are used in the view and the template. The second argument to the `render` function, `"index.html"`, was not necessary in this case. When it's not provided, Phoenix will use the name of the action and the format of the request to find the template to render. Since in this case we're following the convention, we can just drop it.

TIP

Although in this chapter we'll only use the `render` function to generate a response, there are other possibilities to render responses. We can use `text/2` to send a text response, `json/2` to send a JSON response, or `html/2` to send an HTML response. These functions are all in the `Phoenix.Controller` module, and don't require a view to return a response.

When the `media_by_folder` function returns an `{:error, :invalid_path}` tuple, meaning that the provided path is not valid, we handle the error first by calling the `put_flash` function, so that the user gets feedback on what happened, and then do a redirect to the root path (`"$"`), which is a path we know is valid. Let's break this down even further, since in these two lines there is so much happening.

First, the `put_flash` function will place a flash message in the connection. This will then get displayed in the browser because there's a `get_flash` function call on the application layout. We'll talk about layouts in the next section. For now, and because a picture is worth a thousand words, see how flash messages look on the following screenshot:

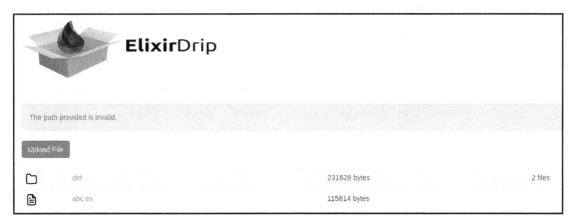

Second, we're using the `redirect/2` function to redirect the user to the root path. This function is really useful as it makes redirection really easy. The first argument to this function is, as usual, the connection, and the second argument is the path to redirect to. For this, we're using the `file_path` function, which in this case will generate the path for the index action of the file controller, passing the path as a query parameter. This function is dynamically generated by Phoenix and is usually called a **path helper**. As you can guess, the names for these dynamic functions are derived from the name of the controller used in the route definition. Instead of having the paths hardcoded, we generate them using the path helpers.

This way, as we update our routes, we don't need to update the paths across our application—we just need to update the routes themselves. As the path helpers are generated dynamically based on the routes, our application will keep working even when the routes change.

> For enhanced security, the :to option of the redirect function only accepts paths. If you want to redirect to any URL, use the :external option.

When a different kind of error happens, we catch it using the _ pattern and simply put a flash message stating that an unexpected error occurred and redirect to the root path, as we did for the invalid path error.

Finally, when the index action is called without the path parameter, we redirect the user to the root path, which will call the first clause of the index function. Let's now move on to the show action, whose purpose is to present the details for a certain file:

```
def show(conn, %{"id" => id}) do
  with {:ok, file} <- Storage.get_file_info("hardoced_user_id", id) do
    render(conn, file: file)
  else
    {:error, :not_found} ->
      conn
      |> put_flash(:error, "File not found.")
      |> redirect(to: file_path(conn, :index, "path": "$"))
    _ ->
      conn
      |> put_flash(:error, "Unexpected error.")
      |> redirect(to: file_path(conn, :index, "path": "$"))
  end
end
```

The logic in this action is very similar to the one for index. We extract the id from the query parameters by pattern matching on the second argument, and then call a function from the Storage module of the elixir_drip umbrella application. We pattern- match on the result of that function call to treat each case accordingly. So, there isn't much to talk about in this action. However, let's take this opportunity to demonstrate a very powerful Phoenix feature: action fallbacks.

As we can see, the catch all pattern is exactly the same as the one present in the index action. For the sake of this example, let's say that the blocks for {:error, :not_found} and {:error, :invalid_path} are also repeated in other actions. We'll now see how an action fallback allows us to remove this duplication and unify how we handle errors in this controller.

First of all, we need to add the following line before the index function:

```
action_fallback(ElixirDripWeb.FallbackController)
```

The Phoenix.Controller.action_fallback/1 function will register the plug you pass as an argument as a fallback for the action being performed by the controller. This fallback is used when the controller action fails to return a valid %Plug.Conn{} struct. When this happens, the fallback plug will receive two arguments: the connection as it was before the action was called and the return value of the controller action.

Let's now see the code for the module we're passing as an argument, the fallback controller:

```
$ cat apps/elixir_drip_web/lib/elixir_drip_web/controllers/
fallback_controller.ex

defmodule ElixirDripWeb.FallbackController do
  use Phoenix.Controller
  import ElixirDripWeb.Router.Helpers, only: [file_path: 3]

  def call(conn, {:error, :invalid_path}) do
    conn
    |> put_flash(:error, "The path provided is invalid.")
    |> redirect(to: file_path(conn, :index, "path": "$"))
  end

  def call(conn, {:error, :not_found}) do
    conn
    |> put_flash(:error, "File not found.")
    |> redirect(to: file_path(conn, :index, "path": "$"))
  end

  def call(conn, _error) do
    conn
    |> put_flash(:error, "Unexpected error.")
    |> redirect(to: file_path(conn, :index, "path": "$"))
  end
end
```

Essentially, we have copied the error handling logic to this controller, and we're pattern matching on the tuple returned by the controller action to handle each error appropriately. This is highly beneficial, since error handling logic is usually scattered across our application. For instance, the match all clause was already duplicated in the index and show actions. Note that it's not very common to handle unexpected errors in Elixir, as we're commonly more focused on the happy path.

However, you may want to ensure that your clients always get a valid response,which in our case involves getting redirected to the root path. In a real production deployment, we likely would flag this error to an error tracking system, so that its causes could be investigated later.

Another great advantage of using the fallback controller is the increased readability of your controllers. Let's check the code for the show action after this change:

```
def show(conn, %{"id" => id}) do
  with {:ok, file} <- Storage.get_file_info("hardcoded_user_id", id) do
    render(conn, file: file)
  end
end
```

Now, our code is solely focused on the happy path, resulting in a function that's much easier to grasp. This function is so simple that there's nothing more to add to the show action. Let's close this section by going through our last two actions, new and create. We'll discuss them together because these two actions are coupled: new is the action used to render the form that allows a user to upload a new file, and the create action is the one used to handle the form submission. In the next section, when we talk about views and templates, we'll see how this form is created and submitted. For now, let's look at the code for the new action:

```
def new(conn, %{"path" => path}) do
  render(conn, changeset: Storage.Media.create_changeset(%Storage.Media{}),
path: path)
end

def new(conn, _params) do
  render(conn, changeset: Storage.Media.create_changeset(%Storage.Media{}),
path: "$")
end
```

As we can see, the code for this action is really simple. When this action is called, we simply want to render the `"new.html"` template. As we'll see in the next section, this template needs a changeset. As such, we're generating an empty changeset and passing it on to the template. We have two function clauses, as we did for the index action: one to cater for the case when the `"path"` parameter is provided, and the other for when it's not. The code for this action is merely a way to glue the request from the router to the correct view and template. Let's now analyze the code for the create action:

```elixir
def create(conn, %{"file" => file_params}) do
  file_content =
    file_params
    |> Map.get("file")
    |> Map.get(:path)
    |> File.read!()

  with {:ok, :upload_enqueued, _changeset} <- Storage.store
  ("hardcoded_user_id", file_params["file_name"],
  file_params["full_path"], file_content) do
    conn
    |> put_flash(:info, "Your file upload is enqueued. A confirmation
    will appear shortly.")
    |> redirect(to: file_path(conn, :index, "path":
    file_params["full_path"]))
  else
    {:error, changeset} ->
      conn
      |> put_flash(:error, "Unable to upload file. Please check the
      errors below.")
      |> render(:new, changeset: changeset, path:
      file_params["full_path"])
  end
end
```

This action is a bit more complex, so let's go through it bit by bit. We bind the `file_params` to the data that was submitted through the form. In this case, it'll be a map containing information about the file being uploaded, as well as the file itself. We begin by getting the binary content of the file. We're using `File.read!/1` because Phoenix created a temporary file for the file submitted through the form. We bind the binary content of the file to `file_content`, which will then be passed to `Storage.store/4`. Besides the content itself, this function also receives the user ID of the owner of the file, as well as the name and path of the file.

When the file is stored correctly, we put up a flash message to give feedback to the user, and redirect him to the path of the file that was just uploaded. Note that this operation only enqueues an upload on the pipeline. We'll work on delivering a notification confirming that the file was successfully uploaded near the end of this chapter, when we talk about Phoenix Channels.

When the `store` function returns an error, we put up a flash message stating that some errors occurred, and rendering `"new.html"` template with the changeset containing the errors. This detail will allow us to render the errors directly from the changeset. We'll see how this works in greater detail in the next section. For now, we just need to take note that it's important to pass the failing changeset to the template. It's also worth pointing out that in this case, we need to pass the name of the template to the `render` function, since if we omitted it, Phoenix would try to render a template called `"create.html"`, which doesn't exist. In this case, we're only passing an atom (`:new`), instead of the string `"new.html"`. We can do this because when passing an atom to render, Phoenix will use the format of the current request (HTML in our case) to build the full name of the template.

We've now finished the controller section! Next, we'll look at what happens once the controller has done all the processing and starts to render a view.

Rendering views

Having explored how controllers work in Phoenix, we'll now look at the next step: rendering views. A view is a module that contains rendering functions, whose purpose is to convert data to a format that end users will consume. Continuing the example we gave in the two previous sections, we'll look at files and how they're rendered in our application. We'll create a file view module, named `ElixirDripWeb.FileView`. Here's the code for it:

```
$ cat apps/elixir_drip_web/lib/elixir_drip_web/views/file_view.ex

defmodule ElixirDripWeb.FileView do
  use ElixirDripWeb, :view

  def parent_directory(path) do
    Path.dirname(path)
  end
end
```

First of all, the name we're giving to this module is important. As we've seen in the previous section, the file controller never mentioned the view module when rendering a response. We were able to do this because Phoenix infers the name of the view module from the name of the controller module. To avoid confusion on this matter, Phoenix always uses singular names across your module names. If for some reason you can't follow these rules, and want to specify the name of the view you're calling, you only have to pass the name of the module view when calling `render` in the controller. This is yet another example of Phoenix letting you be productive and removing boilerplate code from your application, but at the same time giving you the options to adapt the framework to your needs.

Inside this view module, we only see a single function, `parent_directory`, which will be used inside a template, as we'll see in a bit. First we need to clarify what views and templates in Phoenix are. Whereas in many other frameworks, these two words are used interchangeably, in this framework they are two different concepts. A view, as we described previously, is a module that incorporates rendering functions. Those rendering functions can either be a `render` function in the module itself (as any other Elixir function), or can be defined from templates. A template is compiled from a file containing markup language mixed with EEx code, which allows us to substitute variables and loop through them in the template. The compilation of this file results in a function inside the corresponding view module. This separation of concerns between the view and the template enables us to render data in any form we need, either from a conventional Elixir function, a template engine (as EEx), or any other form. For now, we'll just use templates to render our views, but when we build a JSON API later in this chapter, we'll see an example of using a `render` function directly in the view module.

We've seen how controllers pass to the view the name of the template to be rendered (or how they infer it based on the action name). But how is the view able to find the template? The answer lies in a convention used by Phoenix. It looks for templates in a directory, which by default is `lib/elixir_drip_web/templates`. The name of the next directory is inferred from the name of the view module; in our example, our view module is named `FileView`, so it looks for templates inside the `file` directory. This directory contains files named after the current action (or the argument passed by the controller). For instance, the template for the index action on files is located at `apps/elixir_drip_web/lib/elixir_drip_web/templates/file/index.html.eex`. We'll look at it now. Since there's quite a bit of code in there, we'll go through it piece by piece. You can always take a look at the complete file in the path we mentioned. The first thing we do when indexing the files for a user is render a link to upload a new file:

```
<%= link("Upload File", to: file_path(@conn, :new, "path": @current_path),
class: "btn btn-primary") %>
```

The first thing to point out is the use of `<%= %>`. The code inside these tags is executed by the EEx engine, and the result is injected into the template. We may also put code inside `<% %>`, which will also be executed by the EEx engine, but in this case the result is not injected back into the template. As you'll see in the rest of the book, we'll mostly use the `<%= %>` form.

Then, inside these tags, we're calling the `link` function, which is from the `Phoenix.HTML.Link` module. This function, along with other HTML helpers we'll use in the following templates, is imported when we call `use ElixirDripWeb, :view`. These helpers are very useful and allow us to create common HTML structures in our templates. The link function will create an anchor element. The first argument is the text that will appear on the anchor, while the second argument is a keyword list. The `to:` key specifies the target of the link. We're using the path helpers we've seen before to create a link to the `:new` action of the file resource. Notice how we're passing the current path to this function. EEx allows us to reference the assigns that were passed to the template by prepending their name with a `@`. This syntax will generate an exception in the event that the `@current_path` isn't passed to the template. To avoid raising an exception in this case, we could use `assigns[:current_path]`. Lastly, we're passing the `class:` key, which allows us to define the class of the anchor being created—in this case, we're using that to stylize our link as a button. These classes are available because the Phoenix generators import the Bootstrap CSS library (and by default, are placed at `apps/elixir_drip_web/assets/css/phoenix.css`).

Let's now move on to the next piece:

```
<%= if Enum.empty?(@folders) && Enum.empty?(@files) do %>
  <p class="lead">This folder is empty!</p>
<% else %>
  # ...
<% end %>
```

Now, we're using a conditional expression to check whether the folders and files provided in the assigns are both empty. If they are, we insert a paragraph stating this. Otherwise, we execute what's in the `else` block, which we'll see next. Before going there, it's important to note that even with an `if`, we're using the `<%= %>` notation. As we saw in the first chapter, everything in Elixir is an expression, so if we want the result of an `if` injected into the template, we should use an appropriate notation. Let's now see what's in the else block:

```
<table class="table table-striped">
  <%= if @current_path != "$" do %>
    <tr>
      <td><img src="<%= static_path(@conn, "/images/folder.svg") %>"></td>
      <td colspan="3"><%= link("..", to: file_path(@conn, :index, "path":
```

```
       parent_directory(@current_path))) %></td>
    </tr>
<% end %>
```

This is where we'll start to render our folders and files. We begin by opening a table element, where we'll insert each folder and file. Before going through it, we're checking whether the current path is not the root path. If not, we want to render a virtual folder, pointing to the parent directory of the current one. Before the link, we're rendering an image, which shows you how to point to files inside your `static` folder: using the `static_path` path helper, passing the relative path of the file as argument. After the image, we render a link with the text "`..`", pointing to the parent of the current directory. Observe how we're passing the `path` query parameter: by calling the `parent_directory` function, defined on the `FileView` module. This function takes the current path as an argument and returns the path for the parent directory. Note that we didn't need to prepend the function name with its module. Guess why? Because this template will be compiled to a function inside that module, which means that we can call functions from that module just as if we were writing a regular Elixir function inside it. Let's move on to the next piece:

```
<%= for folder <- @folders do %>
  <tr>
    <td><img src="<%= static_path(@conn, "/images/folder.svg") %>"></td>
    <td><%= link(folder.name, to: file_path(@conn, :index, "path":
    @current_path <> "/" <> folder.name)) %></td>
    <td><%= folder.size %> bytes</td>
    <td><%= folder.files %> files</td>
  </tr>
<% end %>
```

Here, we see our first example of a loop in our template. Namely, we're using a comprehension to go through each folder in the folders list that was passed as an argument. Apart from this, the logic is very similar to the example we've seen already. First, we render an image, and then a link, this one allowing the user to enter the current folder. Finally, instead of injecting two empty columns, we populate them with the size of the current folder (the sum of the size of files and folders beneath it) and the number of files the current folder has. Let's move on to the final piece of this template:

```
<%= for file <- @files do %>
  <tr>
    <td><img src="<%= static_path(@conn, "/images/file.svg") %>"></td>
    <td><%= link(file.name, to: file_path(@conn, :show, file.id)) %></td>
    <td colspan="2"><%= file.size %> bytes</td>
  </tr>
<% end %>
</table>
```

This example is very similar to the last one. Instead of looping through the folders, we're now looping through the files. We render a different image, and the link we're creating points to a specific file (using its ID).

As we've mentioned previously, templates will compile down to functions inside their respective view module. This means that at runtime, the templates are already in memory, and there will be no disk reads or template engine computations to do. Moreover, Phoenix builds templates using linked lists and not concatenating huge strings (as many other frameworks do). This way, Phoenix will not be copying strings back and forth when rendering a template. As data types in Elixir are immutable, Phoenix can share the static parts of a response, as they'll never be modified. This efficiency when rendering templates is a very important part of Phoenix, enabling it to achieve the incredible performance we described in the beginning of this chapter.

Before moving on to the next template, let's see a screenshot of this template in action:

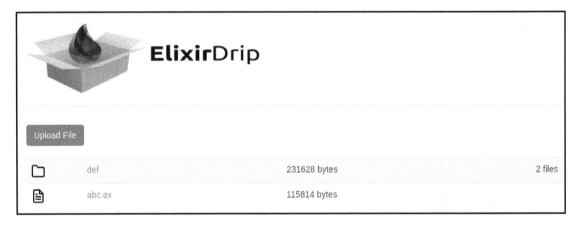

We'll now explore the template for the show action, which is located in `apps/elixir_drip_web/lib/elixir_drip_web/templates/file/show.html.eex`. In the template for the show action, we might copy what we have in the index template to render a file, but we would be duplicating that logic. In this example, we'll see how to nest templates, removing duplication along the way. First of all, we'll create a new template:

```
$ cat apps/elixir_drip_web/lib/elixir_drip_web/templates/file/
file.html.eex

<tr>
  <td><img src="<%= static_path(@conn, "/images/file.svg") %>"></td>
  <td><%= link(@file.name, to: file_path(@conn, :show, @file.id)) %></td>
  <td><%= @file.size %> bytes</td>
```

```
        <td/>
    </tr>
```

This is a copy of what we showed in the last piece of the index template, except that where we read `file`, we now see `@file`, since the file now comes from the assigns and not from the loop. Now, let's use this in the show template:

```
$ cat apps/elixir_drip_web/lib/elixir_drip_web/templates/file/show.html.eex

<div>
  <table class="table table-striped">
    <%= render("file.html", conn: @conn, file: @file) %>
    <tr>
      <td> Full path: </td>
      <td colspan="3"><%= @file.full_path %></td>
    </tr>
    <tr>
      <td> Uploaded at: </td>
      <td colspan="3"><%= @file.uploaded_at %></td>
    </tr>
  </table>
  <%= link("Back to folder", to: file_path(@conn, :index, "path":
@file.full_path), class: "btn btn-default") %>
</div>
```

In order for us to use the file template, we simply call `render`, passing the template name as an attribute (along with the necessary assigns). This way, we have a single way throughout our application to render a file, which not only removes duplication but also promotes visual consistency. We've also updated our index action to use the file template. Since this is the show action, besides rendering the general information about the file, we also show the full path of the file and when it was uploaded. Lastly, we render a link, which allows the user to go back to the folder where this file belongs. We do this using the same techniques we saw in the index template.

We'll now explore our last template, where we'll learn how we can generate forms in Phoenix. This is the template for the new action:

```
$ cat apps/elixir_drip_web/lib/elixir_drip_web/templates/file/
new.html.eex

<h1>Upload a File</h1>
<%= form_for @changeset, file_path(@conn, :create), [multipart: true, as:
:file], fn f -> %>
  <div class="form-group">
    <%= text_input f, :file_name, placeholder: "File Name", class:
    "form-control" %>
    <%= error_tag f, :file_name %>
```

```
    </div>
    <div class="form-group">
      <%= text_input f, :full_path, value: @path, placeholder: "Full Path",
      class: "form-control" %>
      <%= error_tag f, :full_path %>
    </div>
    <div class="form-group">
      <label>File</label>
      <%= file_input f, :file, class: "form-control" %>
    </div>
    <%= submit("Upload", class: "btn btn-primary") %>
  <% end %>
```

The core piece of this template is the `Phoenix.HTML.Form.form_for/4` function. The first argument for this function can either be a a changeset (as in our template), or a connection—in fact, it can be anything that implements the `Phoenix.HTML.FormData` protocol. These are then used to populate the form with data, such as default values or error messages. Remember that we passed our changeset to the template when calling `render` in the controller. The second argument is the action being called when the form is submitted—in our case, the create action on the file controller. The third argument is a keyword list, which allows us to configure how the form behaves. In this case, we're passing two options: `multipart: true`, which sets the `enctype` of the form to `multipart/form-data`, allowing us to upload files in this form; and `as: :file`, which defines the server side parameter in which all the parameters of the form are collected. This is why, in the `create` action of the file controller, we were pattern matching on the `file` parameter. Lastly, the final argument to `form_for` is a lambda that receives the form as an argument. The `form_for` function converts the first argument (the changeset in our case) to a form, and passes it on to the aforementioned lambda.

Now, we use helper functions from the `Phoenix.HTML.Form` module to generate the input fields we want. These functions receive the form (`f`) as an argument. Using the form, these functions may also fetch data from the changeset and pre-populate the fields. For instance, if our changeset had a default value for the filename, it would automatically show up in the form. Moreover, the integration between Phoenix forms and the Ecto change set allows us to render the errors from the changeset directly in the form. This is why we're calling the `error_tag` for both of our inputs. The `error_tag` function was generated by Phoenix, and by default is located in the `ErrorHelpers` module of your application (`ElixirDripWeb.ErrorHelpers` in our case).

Let's see this in action by intentionally generating an error in the form:

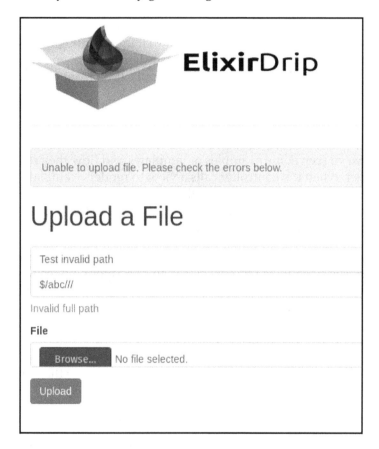

We've inserted an invalid path into the form. The backend detected this path is not valid, and returned a changeset with the errors. As we can see in the screenshot, the form was able to fetch the error from the changeset and displayed it next to the corresponding field. If no action was applied to the changeset (or the action is `:ignore`), the errors are not displayed, even if the changeset contains errors in the `:errors` field. Normally, the form is created with an empty changeset, which may carry errors (for instance, due to required fields being missing). However, we don't want to show errors to the user until he/she performs an action on the form.

To foster HTML safety in your application, Phoenix templates do not directly convert data types to strings. Instead, Phoenix implements `Phoenix.HTML.Safe` for most data types, guaranteeing that a safe HTML representation is returned.

The last piece of the form is the call to the `submit` function, which generates a button to submit the form. The first argument is the text displayed on the button, with the second argument being a keyword list of options, which are forwarded to the underlying button tag. As a final note on forms, we want to point out that in Phoenix, forms automatically generate a CSRF token. By default, Phoenix will also check this token (through the `:protect_from_forgery` plug), protecting your application from CSRF attacks.

Layouts

Up to this point, we've seen some examples of templates and how they're used to render responses. However, when the controller calls a view to render a template, that view is not rendered directly; the controller first renders the layout view, which then renders the template itself. This way, we can have a consistent style across the application (such as setting headers and footers), without duplicating them across templates.

However, layouts are regular templates. Everything you've learned for templates is also applied to layouts. The Phoenix generators create an `app` layout, which in our case is available at `apps/elixir_drip_web/lib/elixir_drip_web/templates/layout/app.html.eex`. This layout will be compiled into a function on `ElixirDripWeb.LayoutView` (which is located at `apps/elixir_drip_web/lib/elixir_drip_web/views/layout_view.ex`).

To render the template that you set in the controller, Phoenix nests that template inside the `app` layout. This is the particular line responsible for doing it:

```
<%= render(@view_module, @view_template, assigns) %>
```

Similar to what we did for the `file` template, we're calling the `render` function to render another template inside the current layout (which is a template). The `@view_module` and `@view_template` variables are assigned from Phoenix, and will contain the module name of the view being rendered and the template name inside that view, respectively. If for some reason you want to change the layout being rendered, you have several options: passing the `layout:` option when calling `render` in a controller; calling the `put_layout/2` plug in your controller; or calling the `put_layout/2` plug in your router pipeline, making this change effective for every request that goes through that pipeline.

Before wrapping up this section, we want to talk about `ErrorView`. This view was generated by Phoenix, and is a centralized place to have the logic to render errors in our application.

Phoenix detects any 400 or 500 status level errors and will use the `render/2` functions in this view to render an error message. Here are the two clauses that Phoenix generated:

```
$ cat apps/elixir_drip_web/lib/elixir_drip_web/views/error_view.ex

defmodule ElixirDripWeb.ErrorView do
  use ElixirDripWeb, :view

  def render("404.html", _assigns) do
    "Page not found"
  end

  def render("500.html", _assigns) do
    "Internal server error"
  end

  # ...
end
```

This will just return text to the browser, but in a real application you could customize it to render the appropriate 404 and 500 pages you want. If Phoenix doesn't find any `render/2` function clause matching the current error, the `template_not_found/2` function will be executed:

```
$ cat apps/elixir_drip_web/lib/elixir_drip_web/views/error_view.ex

defmodule ElixirDripWeb.ErrorView do
  # ...

  def template_not_found(_template, assigns) do
    render("500.html", assigns)
  end
end
```

As we can see, by default it'll just call the `"500.html"` template. We'll be touching on this module again later in this chapter, when we implement a JSON API for our application.

We've now reached the end of the view section. At this point, we've covered the basics of how Phoenix works, going all the way from the endpoint, through the router, going over a controller, and finally ending in a view. Taking all the knowledge we gained in these sections, we'll now apply it to adding authentication to our ElixirDrip application.

Authenticating users

In the last chapter, we saw how we handle user passwords in the `Accounts` context, using the `comeonin` library to sign and verify them. In this chapter, our focus is on extending our web interface to allow users to sign up and log in to our application, and also to restrict certain pages to logged in users. There's a myriad of libraries in the Elixir ecosystem that would allow us to achieve this in only a few lines of code. However, implementing our own authentication solution is beneficial for two reasons: it will give us the opportunity to explore Phoenix in greater depth and it will give us more freedom in how the authentication is made, allowing us to adapt it to fit our needs.

In order to have users authenticated, we first need to have the ability to create users in our application. We'll do this part from the bottom up, building the logic around the authentication of a user, and when that part is done, we'll work on allowing a user to sign up and log in.

As we hinted in the beginning of this chapter, we'll implement authentication using plugs. We'll create two plugs: the first is responsible for extracting the user ID from the session and loading the corresponding user into the connection, and the second is responsible for validating that a current user is present in the connection and restricting access to certain content when there isn't one. Let's begin with the first plug, called `FetchUser`:

```
$ cat apps/elixir_drip_web/lib/elixir_drip_web/plugs/fetch_user.ex

defmodule ElixirDripWeb.Plugs.FetchUser do
  import Plug.Conn

  alias ElixirDrip.Accounts

  def init(options), do: options

  def call(conn, _options) do
    user_id = get_session(conn, :user_id)
    find_user(conn, user_id)
  end

  defp find_user(conn, nil), do: conn
  defp find_user(conn, user_id) do
    user = Accounts.find_user(user_id)
    assign_current_user(conn, user)
  end

  defp assign_current_user(conn, nil), do: conn
  defp assign_current_user(conn, user) do
    conn
```

```
    |> assign(:current_user, user)
    |> assign(:user_id, user.id)
  end
end
```

We saw how plugs work at the beginning of this chapter: they take a connection and return a connection, possibly modifying it. Here, we have the first example of a plug inside our application. The init/1 function just returns the options that were passed, and these won't be used on the call/2 function. Inside the call/2 function, we begin by getting the value for the :user_id key from the session. We then take that value and pass it to the find_user/2 function. We then use pattern matching on the function clause to check whether that variable is nil. If it is, we simply return the connection, unmodified. If it isn't, we try to find the user corresponding to that user_id. We're again using pattern matching on the assign_current_user function. If we can't find a user with that ID, we just return the connection. If we can find a user, we assign it to the :current_user key (and its ID to the :user_id key), which will be stored inside the connection. The assign/3 function was imported from the Plug.Conn module, and is used to set key/value pairs in the assigns field of the connection. In the next plug, we'll see how we can access pairs inside this field. Let's now update our :browser pipeline in the router to call this plug:

```
$ cat apps/elixir_drip_web/lib/elixir_drip_web/router.ex

defmodule ElixirDripWeb.Router do
  use ElixirDripWeb, :router

  alias ElixirDripWeb.Plugs.FetchUser

  pipeline :browser do
    plug(:accepts, ["html"])
    plug(:fetch_session)
    plug(:fetch_flash)
    plug(:protect_from_forgery)
    plug(:put_secure_browser_headers)
    plug(FetchUser)
  end

  # ...

end
```

Now, the FetchUser plug will run for all requests that call the :browser pipeline, which for now is all of them. As we've seen, this plug will try to load a :user_id from the session and, if it finds one, put the corresponding user inside the assigns field of the connection, which will be available to subsequent plugs. Let's see how our next plug, called Auth, queries this field:

```
$ cat apps/elixir_drip_web/lib/elixir_drip_web/plugs/auth.ex

defmodule ElixirDripWeb.Plugs.Auth do
  import Plug.Conn
  import Phoenix.Controller, only: [put_flash: 3, redirect: 2]
  import ElixirDripWeb.Router.Helpers, only: [page_path: 2]

  def init(options), do: options

  def call(conn, _options) do
    case conn.assigns[:current_user] do
      nil ->
        conn
        |> put_flash(:error, "You need to be logged in to view this
        content.")
        |> halt()
        |> redirect(to: page_path(conn, :index))
      _ ->
        conn
    end
  end
end
```

Besides some necessary setup, such as importing modules and defining the required init/2 function, this plug checks whether there's a :current_user in the assigns field of the connection, which was potentially filled by the FetchUser plug. We then pattern-match on the result of the access to conn.assigns[:current_user]. If it's nil, it means that there wasn't a :user_id in the session (or there was one that didn't correspond to any user), and as such the :current_user wasn't loaded onto the connection. In this case, we put up a flash message informing the user he needs to be logged in, call the halt/1 function, and redirect the user to the landing page of our application, which doesn't require the user to be logged in. Note that the halt/1 function merely sets the :halted field of the connection to true, meaning that subsequent plugs will not be called, while our redirect is still performed.

So, where should we put a call to this plug? Anywhere we need to check whether a user is logged in. To exemplify, we'll restrict any action provided by the `FileController` to logged in users. There's more than one way to achieve this. For instance, we could create a new scope and pipeline in our router, where we would call this plug just for certain paths. However, we haven't addressed scopes yet, and we'll see an example of this in the next section. We'll take this opportunity to demonstrate a different way to achieve this: by calling a plug inside the controller. Let's update our file controller with the following:

```
$ cat apps/elixir_drip_web/lib/elixir_drip_web/controllers/
file_controller.ex

defmodule ElixirDripWeb.FileController do
  use ElixirDripWeb, :controller

  alias ElixirDrip.Storage

  plug ElixirDripWeb.Plugs.Auth

  # ...

end
```

Besides the pipeline(s) defined in the router, controllers may also have a pipeline of plugs inside them. In this case, this pipeline only contains a single element, and it will be called before any action performed on the controller. If we only wanted to authenticate users on certain actions, we could use the following:

```
plug ElixirDripWeb.Plugs.Auth when action in [:index]
```

This would result in calling the plug only when the action is index. Since we already have the plumbing in place to have the logged in user on the `conn.assigns` map, we may now replace our references to "`hardcoded_user_id`" with the ID of the current user. For instance, let's see the updated index action of the file controller:

```
$ cat apps/elixir_drip_web/lib/elixir_drip_web/controllers/
file_controller.ex

defmodule ElixirDripWeb.FileController do

  # ...

  def index(conn, %{"path" => path}) do
    user = conn.assigns.current_user

    with {:ok, media} <- Storage.media_by_folder(user.id, path) do
```

```
      #  ...
    end

    #  ...

  end
```

With this in place, our application now loads the files and folders for the user that is currently logged in. We've also updated other references to "hardcoded_user_id" in other actions of the controller. Let's now try to access our list of files before logging in to check that we're not allowed to:

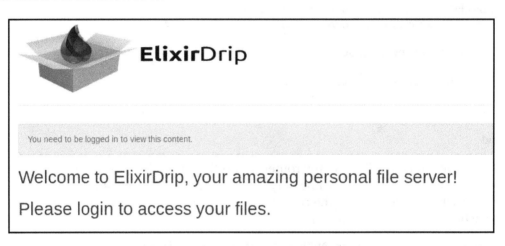

As you can see, we're now able to restrict parts of the application to logged in users. The only thing missing is allowing users to register or log in to our application. To allow users to register, we'll create modules very similar to the ones for files, shown throughout this chapter. We start by adding the following to the router:

```
resources("/users", ElixirDripWeb.UserController, only: [:new, :create])
```

This line will create the GET /users/new and POST /users routes. We'll not show here the code for the user controller, view, and templates, as it's similar to what we did for the file resources. You can find the code for the controller at lib/elixir_drip_web/controllers/user_controller.ex, for the view at lib/elixir_drip_web/views/user_view.ex, and for the templates in the lib/elixir_drip_web/templates/user folder, inside the elixir_drip_web umbrella application folder.

In a few paragraphs, we'll see where we use user-related resources in our application. For now, let's focus on the authentication part. Now that we have a way for users to register, we need to add a way for registered users to log in. To accomplish this, we'll create a session controller, which will render and process the login form and also take care of logouts. First of all, we add the following to our router:

```
resources("/sessions", ElixirDripWeb.SessionController, only: [:new,
:create])
delete("/sessions", ElixirDripWeb.SessionController, :delete)
```

The new and create actions are, as is the case with files and users, related to rendering a form and handling its submissions, respectively. The delete action is called when a user wants to log out of the system. Let's now move on to the session controller:

```
$ cat apps/elixir_drip_web/lib/elixir_drip_web/controllers/
session_controller.ex

defmodule ElixirDripWeb.SessionController do
  use ElixirDripWeb, :controller

  alias ElixirDrip.Accounts
  alias ElixirDripWeb.Plugs.Auth

  def new(conn, _params), do: render(conn)

  def create(conn, %{"username" => username, "password" => password}) do
    with {:ok, user} <- Accounts.login_user_with_pw(username, password) do
      conn
      |> Auth.login(user)
      |> put_flash(:info, "#{user.username}, you're now logged in.
      Welcome back!")
      |> redirect(to: file_path(conn, :index))
    else
      :error ->
        conn
        |> put_flash(:error, "Invalid username/password combination.")
        |> render(:new)
    end
  end

  def delete(conn, _params) do
    conn
    |> Auth.logout()
    |> redirect(to: page_path(conn, :index))
  end
end
```

By now, you're probably already familiar with this kind of code. Either way, let's go through it, function by function. The `new/2` function is very simple, as we're just calling `render(conn)`. This code is here just to glue together the request to the appropriate template and render it in the session view module. The only point worth emphasizing in this function is that, contrary to the new action for files and users, here we're not passing a changeset to the template. We just pass the connection, and the form will be created based on the information present in the connection, as we'll soon see.

Then we have the `create/2` function, used to process the login form submission. We call `login_user_with_pw/2` from the `Accounts` module to check whether the provided username/password pair is valid. If it is, we call the `Auth.login/2` function, put up a flash message welcoming the user, and perform a redirect to the files root directory. If either the username or the password is wrong, we put up a flash message indicating the login was unsuccessful, and render the form again. Finally, we have the `delete/2` function, which calls the `Auth.logout/1` function and redirects the user to the root path of our application.

At this point we're missing the `login/2` and `logout/1` functions from the `Auth` module. Before moving on to implement these functions, let's look at the session view and the template for the new action:

```
$ cat apps/elixir_drip_web/lib/elixir_drip_web/views/session_view.ex

defmodule ElixirDripWeb.SessionView do
  use ElixirDripWeb, :view
end
```

As you can see, this module is almost empty, merely calling `use ElixirDripWeb, :view`. Even in these cases, you have to create a view module for your resource, since the templates associated with it will be compiled into a function inside this module. Let's now check the template for the new action:

```
$ cat apps/elixir_drip_web/lib/elixir_drip_web/templates/session/new.html.eex

<h1>Login</h1>
<%= form_for @conn, session_path(@conn, :create), fn f -> %>
  <div class="form-group">
    <%= text_input f, :username, placeholder: "Username", class:
    "form-control" %>
  </div>
  <div class="form-group">
    <%= password_input f, :password, placeholder: "Password", class:
    "form-control" %>
  </div>
```

```
  <%= submit("Login", class: "btn btn-primary") %>
<% end %>
```

As we've mentioned before, we're now passing the connection to the `form_for/4` function, instead of a changeset. This means that the form will be, when possible, filled with information from the connection. For instance, when we fail to log in, the form will be re-rendered with the connection. In this case, the connection will contain the username under `conn.params["username"]`, which will make the form auto-fill the `username` input with this information. This form uses a function we haven't seen yet: `password_input/3`. This function is similar to the `text_input/3` one, with the difference that the text introduced in this input will be masked (and is never auto-filled based on connection information).

At this point, we're almost done with the authentication work. Let's now extend our `Auth` module with the functions we need:

```
$ cat apps/elixir_drip_web/lib/elixir_drip_web/plugs/auth.ex

defmodule ElixirDripWeb.Plugs.Auth do

  # ...

  def login(conn, user) do
    conn
    |> put_session(:user_id, user.id)
    |> assign(:current_user, user)
    |> configure_session(renew: true)
  end

  def logout(conn), do: configure_session(conn, drop: true)

  # ...

end
```

The `login/2` function receives a connection and a user, and updates the connection in three steps:

1. First, it puts the ID of the provided user in the session, under the `:user_id` key. This way, further requests will have access to this `:user_id`, and the `FetchUser` plug we've seen before will be able to find the user corresponding to this ID.
2. Second, it assigns the provided user to the `:current_user` key. As we've seen from the two plugs created in this chapter, we check whether a user is logged in by looking at the `:current_user` assign and checking whether it's empty. Since we're now logging in, we want to fill this assign as well.

3. Third, it calls `configure_session/2` with the `:renew` option set to `true`. This tells Phoenix to send back a response to the client with a different session cookie identifier, which allows us to protect our application against session fixation attacks.

In order for a user to be automatically logged in upon signing up, we've added a call to `Auth.login/2` to the create action of the user controller. You can check this piece of code at `lib/elixir_drip_web/controllers/user_controller.ex` (on the `elixir_drip_web` umbrella app)..

The `logout/1` function is a one-liner, as it's simply calling the `configure_session/2` function with the `:drop` option set to `true`. This means that a session cookie will not be included in the response, essentially deleting the session at the end of the request.

Having finished these two functions, we're now ready to glue it all together and add a way for users to sign up and log in to ElixirDrip. To accomplish that, we'll slightly modify the application layout to include links to these operations in the header, as in most websites. We'll update the `<header>` tag to include the following:

```
$ cat apps/elixir_drip_web/lib/elixir_drip_web/templates/layout/
app.html.eex

<!-- ... -->

<ul class="breadcrumb text-right">
  <%= if assigns[:current_user] do %>
    <li>Hi, <%= assigns[:current_user].username %>!</li>
    <li><%= link("Logout", to: session_path(@conn, :delete), method:
    "delete") %></li>
  <% else %>
    <li><%= link("Sign Up", to: user_path(@conn, :new)) %></li>
    <li><%= link("Login", to: session_path(@conn, :new)) %></li>
  <% end %>
</ul>

<!-- ... -->
```

We begin by checking whether a `:current_user` is assigned in the connection. If it is, we say *hi* to the user and present a logout link. If it isn't, we render two links: one to sign up and another one to log in. Note that we're generating all these links with the path helpers. Before wrapping up this section, let's see a few screenshots that show what have we done until now.

First, when we access the main page of the application, we see two links in the top-right corner, allowing a user to either sign up or log in:

Assuming we've already signed up with a user, this is how the login form looks when the authentication fails:

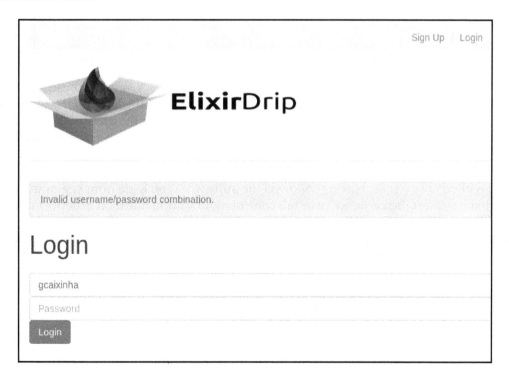

As we can see, we get a flash message informing us that the username/password combination is invalid. Upon entering the correct credentials, we see the following:

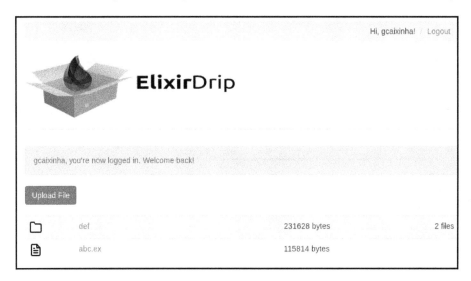

Upon logging in, we see a flash message welcoming the user back, and we present a list of folders and files for the logged in user. We can also observe that the links on the top-right have changed, and now we only have a single link, which allows the user to log out. If we click there, we're presented with the same page we saw in the first screenshot of this list.

We've now added authentication to our ElixirDrip application, implementing it from scratch without any hassle. Having followed the authentication logic from beginning to end through the request life cycle, we're in full control of how authentication is performed in our application. We could easily extend this implementation to accommodate specific security requirements for our application. Let's now move on to see how we can add a JSON API to our application.

Implementing a JSON API

Up to this point, we've been focusing on serving browser requests and returning HTML responses. In this section, we'll see how to extend the ElixirDrip application with a JSON API, giving our users the ability to interact with their files outside the browser. To demonstrate how to accomplish this, we'll implement the index action of the file controller, along with the ability to log in via the API. As usual, let's begin by looking at our updated router:

```
$ cat apps/elixir_drip_web/lib/elixir_drip_web/router.ex

defmodule ElixirDripWeb.Router do
  use ElixirDripWeb, :router

  # ...

  pipeline :api do
    plug(:accepts, ["json"])
  end

  scope "/", ElixirDripWeb do
    pipe_through(:browser)

    resources("/files", FileController, only: [:index, :new, :create,
    :show])

    # ...
  end

  scope "/api", ElixirDripWeb.Api as: :api do
    pipe_through(:api)

    get("/files", FileController, :index)
  end
end
```

We've created a new pipeline, named :api, which for now simply accepts JSON requests. We'll update this pipeline once we add authentication to our API later in this section. Next, we can see how to define scopes in a Phoenix router. Scopes provide a way to group routes under a common prefix path and run pipeline(s) on routes under that prefix path. In our case, we've put the routes we defined previously in this chapter under the first scope, in which the prefix path is the root path, "/". This is usually called the application scope. For routes inside this scope, the :browser pipeline will be called, as in the previous version of the router. It's also important to note that we're giving a second argument to the scope function, which is optional. This argument is the module name prefix, which will be prepended to the module name of the controller. Whereas in the first version of our router, we had to provide a fully qualified name for the controller name, we now just write the controller name, as we have ElixirDripWeb as the module name prefix for this scope. For example, whereas we previously had ElixirDripWeb.FileController in the file route, we now can simply write FileController. Lastly, the :as option we've provided is the named helper scope. Without it, the path helpers for this scope would collide with the ones from the application scope; for instance, for the GET "/files" route they'd both be called using file_path(conn, :index), which is wrong.

By passing this option, we can use this path helper as `api_file_path(conn, :index)`, with the one in the application scope being called in the same way.

Looking now at the next scope, we can see that the path prefix is `"api"`. It's in this scope that we'll have all the routes related to our API, and each one will call the `:api` pipeline we described before. Note that we're passing a different module name prefix in this scope, `ElixirDripWeb.Api`. This way, we'll have a different controller to handle API requests. There are different ways to implement this. We could, for instance, have the same controller handle both types of request, and then use the `Phoenix.Controller.get_format/1` function to know whether the incoming request is HTML or JSON.

We've opted to have separate controllers because we have code very specific to the HTML requests in our file controller, such as the `put_flash` function. We feel that the code is easier to read and comprehend if we have the logic for each type of request in its own module. Let's now look at the file controller for the API request:

```
$ cat apps/elixir_drip_web/lib/elixir_drip_web/api/controllers/
file_controller.ex

defmodule ElixirDripWeb.Api.FileController do
  use ElixirDripWeb, :controller

  alias ElixirDrip.Storage

  def index(conn, %{"path" => path}) do
    with {:ok, media} <- Storage.media_by_folder("hardcoded_user_id",
    path) do
      render(conn, files: media.files, folders: media.folders)
    else
      {:error, :invalid_path} ->
        render(conn, ElixirDripWeb.ErrorView, "400.json", message: "The
        path provided is invalid.")
    end
  end

  def index(conn, _params), do: render(conn, ElixirDripWeb.ErrorView,
  "400.json", message: "Missing 'path' query parameter")
end
```

For now, we don't have authentication via the API, so we're just passing a hardcoded user ID to the `media_by_folder/2` function. This code is very similar to the one for the index action in the HTML controller. When `media_by_function/2` returns the expected result, we call the `render` function, passing the `files` and `folders` assigns as we did in the HTML controller.

Note that we're not passing the name of the template to render, as it's inferred by Phoenix from the action name and the format of the request. Since this is the index action and the format of the request is JSON, the inferred name is "index.json".

When the provided path is invalid, the media_by_folder/2 function returns an error, which we're treating in the else block. We're not using an action fallback controller here, but we could use it in the same way as we did in the HTML controller if the handling of this error is shared across different actions or even controllers. When handling this error, we can also see that we're passing the module name when calling render. This allows us to centralize JSON error views in one module, which will be used across all controllers that are part of the API. Besides the view and the name of the error ("400.json" in this case, meaning Bad Request), we also pass a :message option in the assigns, which allows us to give some details about the cause of this error. Before taking a look at the ErrorView module, note that we have a second clause of the index function, for when the path query parameter isn't provided. In this case, we're also calling ErrorView with "400.json", but this time passing a different message:

```
$ cat apps/elixir_drip_web/lib/elixir_drip_web/views/error_view.ex

defmodule ElixirDripWeb.ErrorView do
  use ElixirDripWeb, :view

  def render("400.json", %{message: message}) do
    %{
      error: "bad request",
      details: message
    }
  end

  # ...

end
```

We're defining a function clause for the render function, using pattern matching on the first argument to set the error type, and on the second argument to extract the message passed in the controller. We then format it, returning a response to the client that informs the user that this was an invalid request and providing some details on why this error happened. Let's now see the code for the API file view:

```
cat $ apps/elixir_drip_web/lib/elixir_drip_web/api/views/file_view.ex

defmodule ElixirDripWeb.Api.FileView do
  use ElixirDripWeb, :view

  def render("index.json", %{files: files, folders: folders}) do
```

```
      %{
        response: %{
          files: render_many(files, __MODULE__, "file.json"),
          folders: render_many(folders, __MODULE__, "folder.json", as:
          :folder)
        }
      }
    end

    def render("file.json", %{file: file}) do
      %{id: file.id, name: file.name, full_path: file.full_path, size:
      file.size}
    end

    def render("folder.json", %{folder: folder}) do
      %{name: folder.name, size: folder.size, files: folder.files}
    end
  end
```

Whereas in the HTML we always used templates to render our responses, here we see an example of how to build a response with a `render` function directly in the view module. As in the error view, we use pattern matching on the action name and also to extract the assigns. Then, we build our response using the `Phoenix.View.render_many/4` function. The `files` and `folders` variables contain lists of maps, which means that we could simply use `files: files` instead of calling the `render_many` function. However, this way we're defining the way to represent either a file or a folder for JSON requests, which would remove duplication once we had more actions in this view module. Besides these lists, the `render_many` function receives a module name, which in both cases we set to `__MODULE__` because the render functions for files and folders are defined in the current module. The next argument is the name of the template, which we're setting accordingly for files and folders. Lastly, the final argument is the assigns map, which is optional. For the folders, we're passing the `:as` option with `:folder`, which defines the name of the assign provided to the render function (which we're pattern matching on in the `render` function of the `"file.json"` and `"folder.json"` templates). By default, Phoenix infers the name from the current view module name. We didn't need to specify the name as we're inside the `FileView` module and Phoenix infers it for us. However, for folders this is necessary.

Analyzing now the last two functions, we can see that they are being used to define the representation of either a file or a folder. We're simply building a map with the keys that we're interested in showing and fetching the corresponding information from each resource. Since this is the index action, we're using the `render_many` function to iterate through these resources and present each one of them.

To implement the show action, where we want to show a single resource, we can use the `render_one` function, which is very similar to the `render_many` function but instead of taking a list and rendering each element inside it, it simply renders one resource.

At this point, for the index action of the file controller, our JSON API is fully working! We could now make a request to the API, which would render the files and folders for our hardcoded user ID. We don't yet have a way for users to authenticate in the API, which is exactly what we'll tackle in the next section.

Authenticating users in the API

We'll now see how we can add authentication to the API we've created in this section. We'll be implementing session-based authentication, which probably isn't the most common way of authenticating users in an API—what is most widely seen is token-based authentication. However, we wanted to show how to port what we've already built for HTML requests. Moreover, we'll demonstrate how to authenticate with tokens in Phoenix in the next section, when we add authentication for channel joins. As usual, let's begin by looking at the updated router:

```
$ cat apps/elixir_drip_web/lib/elixir_drip_web/router.ex

defmodule ElixirDripWeb.Router do

  # ...

  pipeline :api do
    plug(:accepts, ["json"])
    plug(:fetch_session)
    plug(FetchUser)
  end

  # ...

  scope "/api", ElixirDripWeb.Api, as: :api do
    pipe_through(:api)

    get("/files", FileController, :index)

    post("/sessions", SessionController, :create)
    delete("/sessions", SessionController, :delete)
  end
end
```

First of all, we've updated the :api pipeline, which now, besides accepting JSON requests, also fetches the session and cookies (using the :fetch_session plug) and finally calls the FetchUser plug we've created, which loads the current user into the connection if there's a valid :user_id in the session.

We've also added two routes to the API scope, one to allow users to log in (the post one) and the other to allow users to log out (the delete one). Let's move on and see the code for the API session controller:

```
$ cat apps/elixir_drip_web/lib/elixir_drip_web/api/controllers/
session_controller.ex

defmodule ElixirDripWeb.Api.SessionController do
  use ElixirDripWeb, :controller

  alias ElixirDrip.Accounts
  alias ElixirDripWeb.Plugs.Auth

  def create(conn, %{"username" => username, "password" => password})  do
    with {:ok, user} <- Accounts.login_user_with_pw(username, password) do
      conn
      |> Auth.login(user)
      |> render("login.json", user: user)
    else
      _ ->
        conn
        |> put_status(:unauthorized)
        |> render(ElixirDripWeb.ErrorView, "401.json", message:
        "Invalid username/password combination.")
        |> halt()
    end
  end

  def delete(conn, _params) do
    conn
    |> Auth.logout()
    |> render("logout.json")
  end
end
```

The logic in this module is very similar to the one in the session controller we created before. To log in, we use the Accounts.login_user_with_pw/2 function and then call the Auth.login/2 function we've seen before in this chapter, which will put the current user in the session. Finally, we render the "login.json" template, passing the current user as an assign. If the login is unsuccessful, we render the "401.json" template from the ErrorView module, in the same way we explained before for the "400.json" template.

The logout is handled in the delete action, which merely calls the `Auth.logout/1` function, which in turn drops the current session and then renders the `"logout.json"` template.

Let's now see the code for the view that pairs with this controller:

```
$ cat apps/elixir_drip_web/lib/elixir_drip_web/api/views/
session_view.ex

defmodule ElixirDripWeb.Api.SessionView do
  use ElixirDripWeb, :view

  def render("login.json", %{user: user}) do
    %{response: "Logged in as #{user.username}"}
  end

  def render("logout.json", _assigns) do
    %{response: "Logged out"}
  end
end
```

This module contains the render functions that are called from the controller we saw before. As we did in the API file view, we're just using maps to build the responses that will be returned to our users. We've now finished the logic to handle login and logout in our API. At this point, we're just missing one thing: a way to restrict content to logged in users. We'll follow the same approach of the browser-based authentication, and call our `Auth` plug in the file controller. Here is the updated code for the API file controller:

```
defmodule ElixirDripWeb.Api.FileController do
  # ...

  plug ElixirDripWeb.Plugs.Auth, :json

  # ...
end
```

As in the HTML file controller, we're calling our `Auth` plug before executing any action of this controller, essentially requiring a logged in user for all the actions. However, there's one difference, we're passing an argument to our plug, `:json`. This update is required because we've updated our `Auth` plug to deal with both HTML and JSON requests. As such, we need to provide this option when calling it. The corresponding update was made in the HTML file controller, passing `:html` to the `Auth` plug. Let's check the updated version of this plug:

```
$ cat apps/elixir_drip_web/lib/elixir_drip_web/plugs/auth.ex

defmodule ElixirDripWeb.Plugs.Auth do
```

```
# ...

def init(format), do: format

def call(conn, format) do
  case conn.assigns[:current_user] do
    nil -> logged_out(conn, format)
    _ -> conn
  end
end

# ...

defp logged_out(conn, :html) do
  conn
  |> put_flash(:error, "You need to be logged in to view this
  content.")
  |> halt()
  |> redirect(to: page_path(conn, :index))
end

defp logged_out(conn, :json) do
  conn
  |> put_status(:unauthorized)
  |> halt()
  |> render(ElixirDripWeb.ErrorView, "401.json", message:
  "Unauthenticated user.")
  end
end
```

The logic to handle logged in users hasn't changed. If there's a current user in
`conn.assigns`, we simply return the connection, unmodified. It's when we need to handle
logged out users that the format of the request is necessary. As we've seen in the beginning
of this chapter, the options passed to module plugs are then served as the second argument
of the `call/2` function. Now, we make use of that argument and pass it to the
`logged_out/2` function. We use pattern-matching to handle each request format
accordingly. Handling logged out users for HTML requests is something we already had in
this module; we've merely extracted it to this function. The new part is the handling of
logged out users for JSON requests. In this case, we're putting the correct status code for the
response, halting the Plug pipeline, and then rendering the error view, passing
`"Unauthenticated user."` as the message assign.

We'll wrap up this section by seeing all of this work in action. First, we make a request to list the files at the root path ($) for the current user (a GET request to `api/files?path=$`). Since we haven't logged in yet, we receive the following response:

```
{"error": "Unauthenticated user."}
```

Let's now log in by doing a POST request to `api/sessions`, passing the username and password in the body of the request. To this request, we receive the following response:

```
{"response": "Logged in as gcaixinha"}
```

If we repeat the request to list the files, we now see:

```
{
  "response": {
    "folders": [
      {"size": 1034634, "name": "def", "files": 2}
    ],
    "files": [
      {"size": 115814, "name": "abc.ex", "id": "14...PZ", "full_path": "$"}
    ]
  }
}
```

This is a list of files for our user, rendered in JSON! If we want to log out, we merely have to make a DELETE request to `api/sessions`. With this, we've finished our tour around the JSON APIs in Phoenix. We'll now step into the last section of this chapter, where we'll use the renowned Phoenix Channels to add interactivity to our application.

Interactive applications using channels

Up to this point, we've been exploring how to use Phoenix to build traditional web applications, where the server receives a request and returns a response. Requests are isolated from one another, and it is the responsibility of the server to keep the state of the conversation with each client. This has been the way most web applications are built because it allows us to scale them easily. Since each request is stateless, the server can always treat them as a new one, giving us the ability to horizontally scale our applications.

In this section, we'll focus on adding channels to our application, which, as we'll see during this chapter, significantly simplifies the implementation of interactive applications. Instead of the traditional request/response flow we've already described (seen throughout this chapter), when using channels we have a permanent connection between the client and the server, which is only closed when either one exits or crashes. Upon opening a web page, the browser will connect to a channel on the server, which will maintain a separate process for each client.

This connection is then kept open, allowing the client and the server to send messages back and forth. The messages are usually called *events*. As the connection is kept open, we have a stateful conversation between the client and the server.

Fundamentally, a Phoenix channel is a conversation between two parties. As we've said, communication is bidirectional, so the senders and receivers of messages can switch roles at any time. A conversation is always about a topic, with the senders broadcasting messages on that topic and receivers subscribing to that topic to get those messages. Both senders and receivers may be involved in any number of topics. The bidirectional communication gives great flexibility to our applications. Whereas in the traditional request/response flow, the client had to make a request to have something rendered, now the server may simply emit an event in the channel, which upon delivery allows the client to act accordingly. We'll see some examples of this in this section.

This type of solution is not widely adopted because most web servers simply can't hold one connection open for each client. Phoenix, taking advantage of all the Erlang runtime features we've described throughout this book, allows us to do this. The Phoenix core team carried out some benchmarks, and eventually was able have two million channels open on a single server (more details on this is available here: `http://phoenixframework.org/blog/the-road-to-2-million-websocket-connections`). This benchmark is not very recent, with the blog post being published in November 2015. Nonetheless, this astonishing number shows that Phoenix provides a foundation that enables this type of architecture.

In this section, we'll apply all this to our ElixirDrip application, using channels to deliver a notification to the user that his/her download is ready, providing a link to download the file. As we've seen when building the pipeline to upload and download files, these operations are asynchronous. The last step in each pipeline is to call the `Notifier` module, which is responsible for letting the corresponding user know that the operation (either an upload or download) is completed. To demonstrate this, we've implemented the `enqueue_download` and `download` actions on the file controller, similar to what we showed earlier in this chapter. Let's now jump in and begin by preparing the server for the channels.

Preparing the server

We'll now adapt our server to allow clients to connect using Phoenix Channels. Just as with traditional web applications, our journey begins in the endpoint. When Phoenix generated the endpoint module, it included the following line:

```
$ cat apps/elixir_drip_web/lib/elixir_drip_web/endpoint.ex

defmodule ElixirDripWeb.Endpoint do
  # ...

  socket("/socket", ElixirDripWeb.UserSocket)

  # ...
end
```

`Phoenix.Endpoint.socket/2` defines a mount point for a socket handler, which will contain channel definitions. In this case, we're saying that clients that want to connect to a channel may connect to the `/socket` path, which will be handled by the module we're passing as the second argument. Let's now see the code for that module:

```
$ cat apps/elixir_drip_web/lib/elixir_drip_web/channels/user_socket.ex

defmodule ElixirDripWeb.UserSocket do
  use Phoenix.Socket

  ## Channels
  channel "users:*", ElixirDripWeb.UserChannel

  ## Transports
  transport(:websocket, Phoenix.Transports.WebSocket)
  # transport :longpoll, Phoenix.Transports.LongPoll

  def connect(_params, socket) do
    {:ok, socket}
  end

  def id(_socket), do: nil
end
```

First of all, this module defines the channels our application is exposing. The first argument passed to the `channel` function (which is imported from the `Phoenix.Socket` module) is the topic match pattern. By convention, topics usually take the form of some application concept, then a colon, followed by the ID of that same concept. In our case, since we'll have each user connected to the server in its own channel, we're creating the `"users:*"` match topic. This is just a convention though; your topics may just be plain strings, and each client subscribed to a topic will receive the broadcasts happening in that topic. The second argument to the `channel` function is the module that will handle the life cycle of events related to this topic. In a way, this module is the router for the channels, mapping each topic to the corresponding handler, which in this analogy is the controller.

The `channel` function has a :via option, which defines the transport adapters that are accepted on this channel. The default value is `[:websocket, :longpoll]`. For instance, if you only want to allow connections using the WebSocket protocol for a certain channel, you can pass `via: [:websocket]` as the last argument to the `Phoenix.Socket.channel/3` function.

The Phoenix generator has created the following two lines, related with the `Transports`. These define the transport protocols, which will be used when exchanging events on the channels. By default, it comes with the `WebSocket` transport active, and with the long poll commented out. Regardless of the transport mechanism, the end result is the same. The code for our channels won't need to change as we add or remove transport protocols from our application. The transports merely provide a way for clients to connect, and aren't related with the logic of our channels. Nowadays, most web browsers support WebSockets, but you might remove the comment from the long poll transport to support older browsers, connected via a different mechanism—but still operating through the channels we've defined.

If you find yourself with an exotic need, you can build your own transport mechanism by implementing the `Phoenix.Socket.Transport` behaviour.

Then, we have two functions in this module: `connect/2` and `id/1`. The `connect` function decides whether it should allow a client to connect or not. For now, we simply return `{:ok, socket}`, essentially allowing every connection to go through. Later in this section, we'll tackle authentication, and we'll be updating this function. The `id` function receives the socket returned by `connect` and is used to identify the socket based on some information stored in the socket itself, usually tying the connection to a particular user.

For now, we're just returning `nil`, as we don't have authentication in place. As with the `connect` function, we'll revisit this later, when we tackle authentication. Let's now move on to look at the user channel module, which is the handler for the `"users:*"` topic:

```
$ cat apps/elixir_drip_web/lib/elixir_drip_web/channels/user_channel.ex

defmodule ElixirDripWeb.UserChannel do
  use ElixirDripWeb, :channel

  def join("users:" <> user_id, _params, socket) do
    {:ok, assign(socket, :user_id, user_id)}
  end
end
```

We see the first callback for our channel: `join/3`. This functions gets called when the user wants to join the topic we're pattern matching on, and may be used to decide whether to allow the client to join or not. Again, we're simply letting everybody in. Note how we're using binary pattern matching on the function clause to extract the `user_id`. Then, we call the `Phoenix.Socket.assign/3` function to save some state inside the socket. This works in a similar way to what we've seen with the connection. The `assign` function will return the updated socket, which means that we're in fact returning `{:ok, socket}`, which allows the client to join this topic. Contrary to what happened with the connections in the traditional request/response flow, which were transformed in a pipeline and destroyed when the response was returned, the socket is transformed in a loop; the state of the socket is available as long as the connection is available. This way, each event being handled has access to the updated state of the socket, making the conversation between the client and the server stateful.

Besides the `join` callback, Phoenix Channels must also implement `terminate/2`, `handle_in/3`, and `handle_out/3`. The `terminate/2` callback is invoked when the connection is terminated, receiving the error reason and the socket. This can happen for many reasons, for instance the client leaving or the connection being closed. If necessary, you can use this callback to do some cleanup. We'll explore the other two callbacks later in this section. With this in place, our server is ready to accept connections and let users join channels. Let's now look at what we need to do on the client side.

Joining channels on the client

Having prepared the server, we'll now explore the client side of Phoenix Channels. First, we'll quickly go through the structure that Phoenix has generated for us, and then see how we can update it. The last line in our application layout, before closing the body, is:

```
<script src="<%= static_path(@conn, "/js/app.js") %>"></script>
```

This requires the `app.js` file, which is stored in `apps/elixir_drip_web/assets/js/app.js`. This is the entry point for our JavaScript code. Let's analyze its contents now:

```
$ cat apps/elixir_drip_web/assets/js/app.js

import "phoenix_html"
import socket from "./socket"

import Notification from "./notification"
Notification.init(socket, window.userId)
```

The first two lines were generated by Phoenix, while the last two lines were created by us. Besides importing some common helper functions to handle HTML, we're importing the socket object. We can see its code here:

```
$ cat apps/elixir_drip_web/assets/js/socket.js

import {Socket} from "phoenix"

let socket = new Socket("/socket", {
  params: {token: window.userToken},
  logger: (type, message, data) => { console.log(`${type}: ${message}`,
data) }
})

export default socket
```

Phoenix ships with a socket implementation, and we're importing it on the first line. Then, we're instantiating it, passing the path that accepts socket connections (the one we've defined on the server). We're also passing an object as the second argument. The `logger` key just defines a helpful debug message, which will be printed to the browser console. The `params` key contains what will be passed to the server as parameters. We're already passing the token to the server, but it'll be ignored for now. It's included here because Phoenix generated this piece of code, and it'll be exactly what we use to perform authentication. As we can see, the socket definition, using the Phoenix JavaScript channel client, is very simple.

Let's see our last JavaScript file, where we have logic related to notifications:

```
$ cat apps/elixir_drip_web/assets/js/notification.js

let Notification = {
  init(socket, userId) {
    socket.connect()

    let userChannel = socket.channel("users:" + userId)

    userChannel.join()
      .receive("ok", resp => { console.log("Joined successfully", resp) })
      .receive("error", reason => { console.log("Unable to join", reason)
})
  }
}

export default Notification
```

Here, we're creating the `Notification` object, whose responsibility is to receive events from the Phoenix Channels and present them in the page. For now, we'll focus on connecting to the socket and joining a channel. As we have already seen, the `init` function receives two arguments: the socket and the ID of the user. The socket is the object we analyzed before this one. The user ID, as we saw in `app.js`, is being passed as `window.userId`. This is available because we've added the following line to the application layout, just before requiring the `app.js` file:

```
<script>window.userId = "<%= assigns[:user_id] %>"</script>
```

This line fetches the `:user_id` from the assigns of the connection, which was set by the plugs we've already created in this chapter. We need the ID of the user because it will be used to identify the topic, allowing us to join the channel. This way, we'll have a separate channel for each user of our application. Resuming our analysis of the `Notification` object, after connecting to the socket we define the user channel, passing the topic for the channel as an argument. Finally, we try to join the channel with the topic specified in the previous line, calling `join` on the user channel. We then print some helpful debugging messages with the outcome of this operation.

With this code in place, if you open your browser console and access a page in our application, you'll see output similar to the following:

```
transport: connected to
ws://localhost:4000/socket/websocket?token=&vsn=2.0.0
Joined successfully
```

We're now connected to the server through a Phoenix channel, using the WebSocket protocol. With the connection step behind us, we're now ready to start exchanging events in the channel.

Exchanging events

With the channel connection established, we can now focus on sending and receiving events on the channel. The last step for both the upload and download pipelines is the notifier, which is responsible for letting the user know that their upload/download has finished. Now, we need to modify this step to call the `ElixirDripWeb` umbrella application, so that we emit the event that notifies the user that their operation is done. Here's the updated code for the notifier step:

```
$ cat apps/elixir_drip/lib/elixir_drip/storage/pipeline/notifier.ex

defmodule ElixirDrip.Storage.Pipeline.Notifier do
  # ...

  defp notify_step(%{media: %{id: id}, user_id: user_id, type: :download})
do
    ElixirDripWeb.Notifications.notify(:download, id, user_id)
  end

  # ...
end
```

When we reach the end of the pipeline for a download, we now call the `ElixirDripWeb.Notifications.notify/3` function. Let's now see the code for this newly created module:

```
$ cat apps/elixir_drip_web/lib/elixir_drip_web/notifications/
notifications.ex

defmodule ElixirDripWeb.Notifications do
  use GenServer
  import ElixirDripWeb.Router.Helpers, only: [file_path: 3]
  alias ElixirDripWeb.Endpoint

  def start_link do
    GenServer.start_link(__MODULE__, :ok, name: __MODULE__)
  end

  def init(:ok) do
    {:ok, []}
  end
```

```
  def notify(:download, id, user_id) do
    GenServer.cast(__MODULE__, {:download, id, user_id})
  end

  def handle_cast({:download, id, user_id}, state) do
    link = file_path(Endpoint, :show, id) <> "/download"
    Endpoint.broadcast("users:#{user_id}", "download", %{link: link,
    message: "Your download is ready. Start it by clicking here."})
    {:noreply, state}
  end
end
```

This is a regular GenServer, where the `notify` function calls `GenServer.cast`, which in turn will be handled by the `handle_cast` function callback next to it. Inside this callback, we first build the link for the file download, using its ID. Then, we call `Endpoint.broadcast`, passing as arguments the topic, the event, and a message (which has to be a serializable map). In this case, the event is `"download"`, with a message that informs the user that the download is ready.

In this case, we need to pass the topic because we're broadcasting a message outside the channel module, which means that we don't have a reference to the socket. For these cases, the `Phoenix.Endpoint` module provides the `broadcast` callback, which allows us to broadcast a message, giving a topic without needing to pass the socket. Soon, we'll see an example of broadcasting an event from the user channel module.

When we broadcast a message, it'll go to all clients connected to our server that are interested in this topic. Before this is actually completed, we may intercept an event before it's sent, allowing us to customize the payload or even not send it at all. This is done by calling the `Phoenix.Channel.intercept/1` function on the channel module, and implementing the corresponding `handle_out/3` callback. While this gives you greater flexibility when handling events, be warned that this may severely impact the performance of your application. When intercepting messages, the broadcast will be encoded as many times as there are subscribers to this topic, instead of just a single encoding when we don't intercept the event.

Lastly, we want to point out that, if our application was deployed across multiple connected nodes, the clients linked to other nodes would also receive the broadcast event, as Phoenix uses `Phoenix.PubSub` to relay events between nodes in the same cluster. Since we now have the event being emitted on the server, let's check out the changes necessary in the client to receive this event:

```
$ cat apps/elixir_drip_web/assets/js/notification.js

let Notification = {
```

```
init(socket, userId) {

  // ...

  let infoArea = document.getElementById("notify_info")
  let successArea = document.getElementById("notify_success")

  userChannel.on("download", ({link, message}) =>
  this.renderDownloadNotifcation(infoArea, successArea, message,
  link))
},

renderDownloadNotifcation(infoArea, successArea, message, link) {
  infoArea.innerHTML = ""
  successArea.innerHTML = `<a href="${link}">${message}</a>`
  }
}

export default Notification
```

We've changed the application layout to add an ID to the flash message elements so that we can get them in the init function. After getting those elements, we can see how to define a handler for events on our user channel. We're calling the on function on it, passing the name of the event we will handle and a lambda, which will be called whenever we receive this type of event. Note that the lambda will receive as arguments the values of the keys we've defined on the broadcast message—link and message in this example. Inside the lambda, we're simply calling the renderDownloadNotifcation function, which will display a link in the successArea element. Before that, we're blanking the infoArea element, so that previous flash messages disappear and we just show the notification we're rendering now.

Let's now see all this in action with some screenshots. When we click the "Download File" button, a flash message is displayed, informing us that the download is enqueued and a link will appear soon:

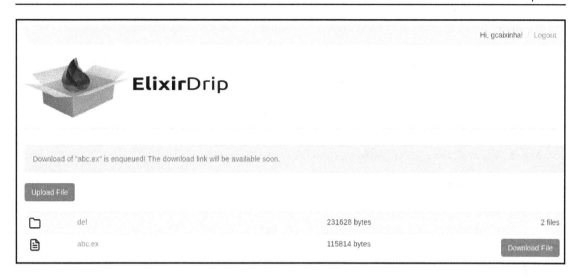

This will trigger the download pipeline, which entails downloading the file from Google Cloud Storage, decrypting it, and storing its contents in memory. The final step is the notifier, which will call the GenServer module we've seen before. This module will in turn broadcast the `"download"` event to the channel of the current user, providing the link to download the file. The following screenshot shows how this notification is displayed, providing the link for the user to download the file:

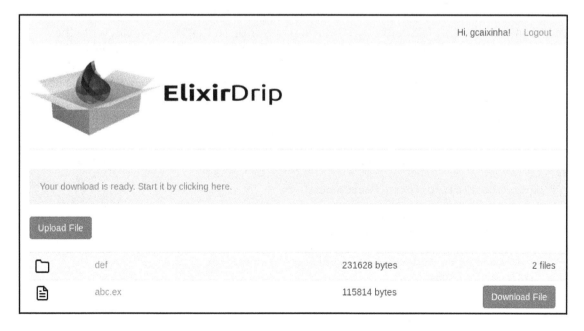

Before closing this section and moving on to authenticating socket connections, let's see how we can send events from the client side. To demonstrate this, we'll create the functionality that allows users to share a file with other users. This will be entirely driven by channels, without any change on the router or the controllers.

We've added a button to the show action of a file, and defined the callback of that button to be the following function:

```
$ cat apps/elixir_drip_web/assets/js/notification.js

let Notification = {
  // ...
  sharePopUp(userChannel) {
    let username = prompt("Share file with:", "username")
    if (username != null && username != "") {
      let splitUrl = window.location.href.split('/')
      let fileId = splitUrl.pop() || splitUrl.pop()

      userChannel.push("share", {username: username, file_id: fileId})
    }
  }
}

export default Notification
```

This function receives a `userChannel` argument, which is the channel we created previously on this file. We begin by rendering a prompt, so that the user can write the username of the user we're going to share this file with. Then, we have a couple of lines to extract the file ID from the current path. This is just preparation for the function call that matters: in the end, we `push` a `share` message to the `userChannel`. We provide the name of the event, along with the necessary parameters for the share to occur. This will emit the event on the current user's channel. Let's now see how to handle this event on the server. We need to adapt the user channel module:

```
$ cat apps/elixir_drip_web/lib/elixir_drip_web/channels/user_channel.ex

defmodule ElixirDripWeb.UserChannel do
  # ...
  alias ElixirDripWeb.Endpoint
  alias ElixirDrip.{Accounts, Storage}

  def handle_in("share", %{"username" => username, "file_id" =>
  file_id}, socket) do
    sharee = Accounts.get_user_by_username(username)
    case sharee do
      nil -> broadcast_sharee_not_found(socket, username)
```

```
        _ -> share_file(socket, socket.assigns.user_id, file_id, sharee)
      end

    {:noreply, socket}
  end

  defp share_file(socket, owner_id, file_id, sharee) do
    case Storage.share(owner_id, file_id, sharee.id) do
      {:ok, _media_owners} ->
        broadcast_to_owner(socket, sharee.username)
        broadcast_to_sharee(sharee.id, socket.assigns.user_id)
      {:error, _reason} ->
        broadcast_error_to_owner(socket, sharee.username)
    end
  end

  defp broadcast_to_owner(socket, sharee_username) do
    broadcast(socket, "share", %{message: "Successfully shared the file
    with #{sharee_username}."})
  end

  defp broadcast_to_sharee(sharee_user_id, owner_user_id) do
    owner = Accounts.find_user(owner_user_id)
    Endpoint.broadcast("users:#{sharee_user_id}", "share", %{message:
    "#{owner.username} has just shared a file with you!"})
  end

  defp broadcast_sharee_not_found(socket, username) do
    broadcast(socket, "share", %{message: "Couldn't find a user with #
    {username} username."})
  end

  defp broadcast_error_to_owner(socket, username) do
    broadcast(socket, "share", %{message: "Couldn't share the file with
    #{username}."})
  end
end
```

We use the `handle_in` callback to process events on the server (which may be sent from a client or even another server). We're pattern matching on the event name, and also on the parameters we need to perform this operation. Note that this example has a considerable size, but the channel-related code is really small. We have code to handle usernames that don't exist in the database, and also to handle errors that may occur when sharing the file (for instance, the file is already being shared with that user).

Let's go through the high-level logic of this example. We try to find a user with the provided username, and when we succeed, we try to share the file with that user. If this operation is also successful, we emit two events: one for the owner user, to notify that the file was shared with success; and a second one for the user that we shared the file with (the shared), to notify that someone has shared a file with him/her. Whenever there's an error while trying to share the file, we emit an event only to the owner user, to notify that the sharing of the file didn't happen. In this screenshot, we can see the result of a successful share between two users, and also the notifications they've received:

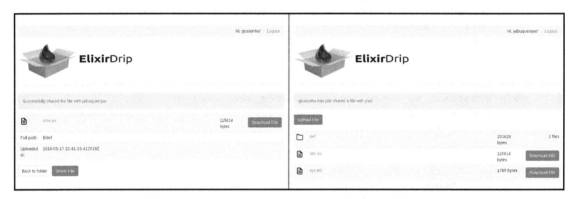

The result of a successful share between two users

We've now covered how to exchange events in a Phoenix channel. The plumbing and logic that we did for downloads in this section was also applied to uploads. You can check it out in the final version of the ElixirDrip application, which is shipped with this book.

Before wrapping up this section and moving on to adding authentication to the socket connections, we want to explore some considerations for using channels in a live environment. While we don't cover how to handle network splits and channels crashing in this book, it's important to consider it when deploying a real application. These events will eventually happen and you're better off designing your application taking them into account. The good news is that Phoenix already comes with some helpful behaviors. For instance, if a channel crashes, the Phoenix JavaScript client will try to reconnect to the server using an exponential backoff strategy, and if it's able to reconnect, it will try to rejoin the topics it was subscribed to before the crash. Besides this, you should also consider the message delivery guarantees (both for the client and server) in the event of network errors. The official Phoenix Channels guide, available at `https://hexdocs.pm/phoenix/channels.html`, contains some helpful tips to deal with these cases.

Authenticating socket connections

So far, we have been allowing any user of our application to connect to the socket, even if they weren't authenticated. In this case, since `:user_id` is `nil`, they were all connecting to the `users:` topic. We must update our application, so that only logged-in users can connect to the socket and join a channel. Whereas in the previous sections we implemented session-based authentication, this time we'll implement token-based authentication. This means that we'll assign a token for each authenticated user, and then validate that token when the user wants to connect to the socket.

When we explored the code in `apps/elixir_drip_web/assets/js/socket.js`, we saw that we're already passing the token to the server, using `window.userToken`. Let's begin by adding the following script tag to the application layout, similar to what we did for `window.userId`:

```
<script>window.userToken = "<%= assigns[:user_token] %>"</script>
```

We've added this line right after the one for `window.userId`. Now, `window.userToken` will hold whatever is in `assigns[:user_token]`. Let's now take care of filling this assign whenever we have a logged in user. To accomplish this, we'll update the `FetchUser` plug we created earlier in this chapter with the following:

```
$ cat apps/elixir_drip_web/lib/elixir_drip_web/plugs/fetch_user.ex

defmodule ElixirDripWeb.Plugs.FetchUser do
  # ...

  defp assign_current_user(conn, user) do
    token = generate_token(conn, user.id)

    conn
    |> assign(:current_user, user)
    |> assign(:user_id, user.id)
    |> assign(:user_token, token)
  end

  defp generate_token(conn, user_id) do
    Phoenix.Token.sign(conn, "user socket auth", user_id)
  end
end
```

Before assigning the current user, which means the user is logged in, we call the
`generate_token/2` function. This function uses the `sign` function from the
`Phoenix.Token` module. This function receives the connection, a salt, and the data to be
encoded, and it will create a signed token, which we're binding to the `token` variable. Then,
after assigning the `:current_user` and `:user_id` keys, we also assign the `:user_token`
key with the token we've just created. We're passing the connection as the first argument to
the `Phoenix.Token.sign/4` function, which will make this module sign the token with
the `:secret_key_base` that's configured in the endpoint, that lives inside the connection.
We could've just as easily pass the endpoint, or a secret key base string directly.

With this in place, all that remains is verifying this token when a user is trying to connect to
the socket. Let's see the updated `UserSocket` module:

```
$ cat apps/elixir_drip_web/lib/elixir_drip_web/channels/user_socket.ex

defmodule ElixirDripWeb.UserSocket do
  # ...

  @one_week_seconds 7 * 24 * 60 * 60

  def connect(%{"token" => token}, socket) do
    case Phoenix.Token.verify(socket, "user socket auth", token,
    max_age: @one_week_seconds) do
      {:ok, user_id} -> {:ok, assign(socket, :user_id, user_id)}
      {:error, _reason} -> :error
    end
  end

  def id(socket), do: "users_socket:#{socket.assigns.user_id}"
end
```

The first difference is that now we're using pattern matching on the first argument, extracting the value of the "token" parameter. Then, we're verifying the token the user provided using the `Phoenix.Token.verify/4` function. We're passing the socket as the first argument, which will be used to get the secret key base—this will be the same as the one used when signing, since the endpoint is the same. The next important part to note is that this function may receive a `:max_age` option (in seconds), allowing us to expire tokens after a certain amount of time. In this example, we don't accept a token that's older than a week, meaning that, if the user hasn't logged in during the past week, they won't be able to connect to the socket. We then use pattern matching inside the `case` block to handle each case accordingly. If the `verify` function returns `{:ok, user_id}`, we accept the connection, returning `{:ok, socket}`. We've moved the `assign` of `:user_id` in the socket to here, deleting it from the `UserChannel` module. When there's an error, we simply return `:error`, blocking this user from connecting to the socket. Lastly, we've also updated the `id/1` function, making it return a topic string identifying the user that connected to this socket. This way, we can identify all the sockets belonging to a user that may be used, for instance, to send a broadcast message to this topic to terminate all socket connections for a given user.

Now, if you open your browser console while being logged out, you'll see some error messages because the connection to the socket is failing. If you're using Firefox, you'll see an error message similar to this one:

```
Firefox can't establish a connection to the server at
ws://localhost:4000/socket/websocket?token=&vsn=2.0.0.
```

This error means that we've fulfilled our goal, and only logged in users are able to connect to the socket. Let's move on to the last section of this chapter, where we'll incorporate `Phoenix.Presence` in our ElixirDrip application.

Tracking users statuses using Presence

To finish this chapter, we'll take a quick look at how we can add a list of online users to our application, and in the process demonstrate how easy it is to accomplish this using Phoenix Presence. This feature was released in Phoenix 1.2 and is built on top of Phoenix PubSub and Channels. Phoenix Presence allows us to register process information on a topic, which is replicated transparently inside a cluster.

One of the special feature of Presence is that there's no single point of truth, and consequently there's no single point of failure. Whereas, in other programming languages, you'd likely use a database (or some other central component) to store the status of each user, Phoenix Presence implements a distributed gossip protocol that uses **Conflict-Free Replicated Data Types** (**CRDT**) to synchronize the state across the nodes in your cluster. This approach brings two main advantages over a central datastore: you're able to scale the system by adding more servers, and since there's no single server holding the data, the system is able to self-heal when there are failures (a server crashing or a network split). As Chris McCord likes to say, Phoenix puts cutting-edge computer science research into practice!

Although Presence is commonly used to track the status of users in an application, which is also our example, the abstraction that it gives is generic, making it possible to use this library in other scenarios. For instance, Presence could be used for service discovery. Much like Channels, Presence is a combination of a server-side and a client-side library. We'll now look at the code for this feature, beginning with the changes in the server. The first step is to use a Phoenix generator, which we're running in the directory for the `elixir_drip_web` umbrella application:

```
apps/elixir_drip_web/$ mix phx.gen.presence
```

This task will create a file in `apps/elixir_drip_web/lib/elixir_drip_web/channels/presence.ex` and the output instructs us to add the newly generated module to the supervision tree of our application. So, we added `supervisor(ElixirDripWeb.Presence, [])` to the `children` variable, which is defined in `apps/elixir_drip_web/lib/elixir_drip_web/application.ex`. Let's see the code for the `Presence` module that we just generated:

```
$ cat apps/elixir_drip_web/lib/elixir_drip_web/channels/presence.ex

defmodule ElixirDripWeb.Presence do
  use Phoenix.Presence, otp_app: :elixir_drip_web,
                        pubsub_server: ElixirDripWeb.PubSub
end
```

By calling `use Phoenix.Presence`, we're setting up this module to have the functions required to track the presence of our users. We're passing the necessary configuration, which is the name of our OTP application and also the PubSub server that will be used by Presence.

The next change is on the user channel module:

```
$ cat apps/elixir_drip_web/lib/elixir_drip_web/channels/user_channel.ex

defmodule ElixirDripWeb.UserChannel do
  # ...

  alias ElixirDripWeb.Presence

  def join("users:lobby", _auth_message, socket) do
    send(self(), :after_join)
    {:ok, socket}
  end

  def handle_info(:after_join, socket) do
    push(socket, "presence_state", Presence.list(socket))

    user = ElixirDrip.Accounts.find_user(socket.assigns.user_id)

    {:ok, _} =
      Presence.track(socket, socket.assigns.user_id, %{
        username: user.username
      })

    {:noreply, socket}
  end
end
```

We're defining a new `join` callback because we have a new topic, named `"users:lobby"`. Up to this point, we had one channel per user. Since we now want to track the presence of each user, we need a common topic, where the users of the channel will be notified of the joins and leaves happening on that channel. Before accepting the connection, by returning `{:ok, socket}`, we send a message to the current process, which will be handled by the `handle_info` callback defined later. This allows us to maintain a low execution time on the `join` function, as it'll just send a message and accept the connection while the Presence initialization is handled asynchronously.

In the `handle_info` callback, we begin by sending an event to the user that just joined, sending him the current state of the `presences` variable (which is generated by the `Presence.list/1` function). After that, we're calling a function from the `Accounts` context to get the user for the `user_id` present in the socket, which will be used later to pass the username to the `Presence.track/3` function. This function tells the Presence module to start tracking the current user.

Besides the socket, the `track` function receives a key that identifies the client that we're tracking (`user_id` in our case), and also a map containing additional information that we may want to track for this connection. In our example, we're passing the username for this user, so that we can later use it on the client side to display the username in the online users list. Note that this information doesn't need to be related to the user schema. For instance, we could also use this map to keep a timestamp of when the user was last seen online.

This is all it takes on the server side to add Presence to our application. Let's now see the client side. Since this logic is not really related to the notifications we've seen previously, and is even using a different channel topic, the online users list is in a different object. We can see its code here:

```
$ cat apps/elixir_drip_web/assets/js/online_users.js

import {Presence} from "phoenix"

let OnlineUsers = {
  init(socket) {
    let lobbyChannel = socket.channel("users:lobby")
    let presences = {}

    lobbyChannel.join()
      .receive("ok", resp => { console.log("Joined successfully", resp) })
      .receive("error", reason => { console.log("Unable to join",
      reason) })

    lobbyChannel.on("presence_state", state => {
      presences = Presence.syncState(presences, state)
      this.renderOnlineUsers(presences)
    })

    lobbyChannel.on("presence_diff", diff => {
      presences = Presence.syncDiff(presences, diff)
      this.renderOnlineUsers(presences)
    })
  },

  renderOnlineUsers(presences) {
    let response = ""

    Presence.list(presences, (id, {metas: [user, ...rest]}) => {
      let count = rest.length + 1
      response += `<li>${user.username} (count: ${count})</li>`
    })
```

```
    document.getElementById("online_users").innerHTML =
    `<ul>${response}</ul>`
  }
}

export default OnlineUsers
```

We begin by importing the Presence library provided by Phoenix. Then, the first part of this code is very similar to what we already saw in the previous section: we join the `"users:lobby"` topic we mentioned before and define handlers for events happening on this channel. Particularly, we're interested in two events: `"presence_state"` and `"presence_diff"`.

The `"presence_state"` event will contain the initial state, and is triggered when the user joins the channel. The `"presence_diff"` event gets triggered whenever another user joins or leaves the channel. The Presence library contains two functions to handle both of these events easily, called `Presence.syncState` and `Presence.syncDiff`. These functions will maintain the `presences` variable up to date.

After synchronizing the event payload with the `presences` variable, in both cases we're calling the `renderOnlineUsers` function to display the updated state in the browser. This function takes the `presences` and iterates through them to build a list of online users. We can iterate on the `presences` easily using the `Presence.list` function. Besides a Presences object, this function takes a callback function, which will be called for each Presence with two arguments: the ID of the Presence and a list of `metas`. This list will contain as many items as there are Presences with the same Presence ID. Since our Presence ID is `user_id`, we can use this to find out on how many devices a user is online. Each element in the `metas` list is an object, containing the additional information we passed as the last argument to the `track` function, on the user channel module. In this case, we're using the additional information to display a list of online users with their usernames (by calling `user.username`). Lastly, we update the `online_users` element to render our list, which is a `div` element we've added to the application layout.

With only a few snippets of code, we have an online users list working in our application, which will scale along with the number of servers our application runs on, and will also self-heal whenever there's a failure. Let's look at a screenshot of this in action:

Three different browser section

In this scenario, we have the `gcaixinha` user logged in to two different browser sessions, and the `jalbuquerque` user logged in to a third browser session. As you can see by the screenshot, each user gets the correct list of online users, also showing a count of 2 for the `gcaixinha` user, since he has two sessions open. If we logged out any of these users (or logged in with different ones), we'd see the online users list adjust accordingly. With the list of online users working, we've reached the end of this section. Let's now wrap up, recapping the most relevant points of this chapter.

Summary

In the process of adding a web layer to our application, we covered a lot of ground in this chapter. Let's run through the most important points in this chapter:

- Phoenix builds upon the Plug specification, which has two forms: module and function plugs. Both of them take a connection and return a connection, possibly modifying it before returning.
- An endpoint is the boundary where all requests to our web application start, and by default it contains a list of plugs that run for every request.
- Using macros, routers in Phoenix compile down to efficient pattern matching. Besides defining routes, we can create pipelines in the router, which are a group of plugs that run sequentially.

- Controller actions are functions that receive two arguments: the connection and the parameters of the request. Usually, we aim to keep our controller code as small as possible, calling some other module and rendering a view based on its response.

- Views are plain modules with rendering functions. Templates are compiled from a file containing markup language mixed with EEx code into a rendering function on a view. This separation between the view and the module allows us to render data in any form we want, either from a regular Elixir function or from a template engine.

- Session-based authentication can be done using the `:fetch_session` plug that ships with Phoenix, which we can use to load the session for each request.

- The assigns of a connection give us great flexibility, as this feature allows us to save the state during the life of a request, which will be available to subsequent modules. We saw some examples of how to use this, such as when adding authentication to our application.

- Scopes in a Phoenix router are a way to group routes under a common prefix path. Moreover, we are able to specify the module prefix name, allowing us to have a different set of controllers, views, and templates for a certain group of routes, as we did when implementing a JSON API.

- Phoenix channels are a game changer in the way we build our applications, as they provide a simple abstraction that's easy to work with. After a user connects to our socket, the connection remains open, which enables stateful conversations between the clients and the server. You don't need to work hard to figure out the context of a request, as it's kept in the socket. In this model, you just need to send and receive events on the channel, and react accordingly to each one of them.

In the next chapter, we'll tackle a very important topic that's so often overlooked: testing. With the ElixirDrip application finished, we'll now see how to properly test it from diverse perspectives.

Finding Zen through Testing

9

At this point, in terms of functionality, our ElixirDrip application is finished. However, we don't have any tests yet, so it's not really ready to be deployed to a live environment. Although we've left out testing to the end, we want to point out that this isn't the way we normally develop applications. We're big supporters of creating your tests incrementally, as you build the features of your application. However, we think that such an approach would be confusing, bringing more harm than good to the readability of this book.

Hence, we've condensed in this chapter all the types of testing we'll explore. We won't cover every module and function of ElixirDrip, but we'll go through all the concepts necessary to test everything in this application. We will not cover every type of testing there is—for instance, end-to-end testing—as we'll focus on the types of testing more commonly used when building an Elixir application.

There are some testing principles that are shared across languages and frameworks. We won't dive into the merits and disadvantages of each one, as it's out of the scope of this book. Nevertheless, let's briefly go through some of the principles that apply to every type of testing we'll dive into later:

- Tests should have the right level of isolation. In some type of tests, we want to have mocks in place whereas in other types, we want to test all of the real components interacting with each other.
- Test results should be repeatable. The result of our test suite should be deterministic, hence it should not depend on any external factors. Having flaky tests in our suite reduces the confidence we have in it, which is the main reason we started to write tests in the first place.
- Running the whole test suite should be fast. The definition of *fast* is very relative, but nonetheless you shouldn't need to think about whether you should run it or not. It should be so fast that you're constantly running it, and getting a very short feedback loop.

In this chapter, we'll cover the following topics:

- Creating unit tests, with and without mocks
- Having separate repository tests, which will test the interaction with the database
- Using `doctest` to embed tests inside a function's documentation
- Writing integration tests, which verify that the application is working as a whole
- Creating tests for our Phoenix Channels, which verify the connection to the socket and exchange of events work as expected
- Testing macros in a maintainable way
- Creating property-based tests, and some considerations on how to integrate them into an application

Let's now write the first type of tests in our application: unit tests.

Unit testing

In this section, we'll explore how to create tests in Elixir, using ExUnit. We'll split it between tests that exercise functions with and without side-effects, since we have different approaches for each type of function. Let's begin by the simpler case: testing functions that don't have side-effects.

Testing functions without side-effects

A unit test exercises a function from a certain module of the application. We might have more than one test exercising the same function (with different inputs, for instance). Let's begin by creating a simple test, which will allow us to analyze ExUnit in detail. We'll be creating the tests for the `is_valid_path?` function, which belongs to the `ElixirDrip.Storage.Media` module. For context, we present its implementation as follows:

```
$ cat apps/elixir_drip/lib/elixir_drip/storage/media.ex
defmodule ElixirDrip.Storage.Media do
  # ...

  def is_valid_path?(path) when is_binary(path) do
    valid? = String.starts_with?(path, "$") && !String.ends_with?
    (path, "/")

    case valid? do
      true -> {:ok, :valid}
```

```
      false -> {:error, :invalid_path}
    end
  end

  # ...
end
```

The logic in this function is very straightforward: to validate a path, it checks if the provided string starts with a $ and doesn't end with a /. Let's now see our first test for this function:

```
$ cat apps/elixir_drip/test/elixir_drip/storage/media_test.exs
defmodule ElixirDrip.Storage.MediaTest do
  use ExUnit.Case, async: true

  @subject ElixirDrip.Storage.Media

  test "is_valid_path?/1 returns {:ok, :valid} for a valid path" do
    path = "$/abc"

    assert {:ok, :valid} == @subject.is_valid_path?(path)
  end
end
```

We begin by calling use ExUnit.Case, which will make some macros available in our test module. We're passing the async: true option, which will make the tests in this module run concurrently. By default, the tests don't run concurrently. Since in Elixir we generally try to write code that's side-effect free, most of our tests will be able to run concurrently. Then we define a module attribute, named @subject, which contains the module that we're testing. This way, it's very clear which module is being tested, and also brings the benefit of only needing to change one line in the event that we rename the module.

Let's now analyze the test macro, imported from ExUnit.Case. This macro receives a string with the description for the test, and a block for the test code. In this case, we're testing for when the path is valid. We then use the assert macro, also from ExUnit.Case, to validate that the return value of the is_valid_path? function is the expected one. Let's now run our test. Since we have an umbrella application, running the tests in the root folder will target every application inside the umbrella.

For now, we're only interested in the `elixir_drip` application, so we change the working directory to `apps/elixir_drip`:

```
$ cd apps/elixir_drip
$ MIX_ENV=test mix test
.

Finished in 0.02 seconds
1 test, 0 failures

Randomized with seed 69987
```

As you can see, we run our tests with the `mix test` task. Without any argument, it will run every test in our suite. You provide the path to a test file to run the tests of a certain file, or even a path of a test file with a colon and a line number suffixed, which will just run the test on that line.

It's not mandatory to use the `assert` macro to check the outcome of each test. We might as well just use plain old pattern matching to validate the return values of our functions. However, we recommend the usage of the `assert` macro in test cases, mainly because it'll yield better error messages when the tests fail, allowing you to quickly understand what's going on. For instance, we've intentionally made the previous test fail, by matching on `{:ok, :validddd}`. Running the test with this change yields:

```
$ cd apps/elixir_drip
$ MIX_ENV=test mix test
  1) test is_valid_path?/1 returns {:ok, :valid} for a
     valid path (ElixirDrip.Storage.MediaTest)
     test/elixir_drip/storage/media_test.exs:6
     Assertion with == failed
     code:  assert {:ok, :validddd} ==
     @subject.is_valid_path?(path)
     left:  {:ok, :validddd}
     right: {:ok, :valid}
     stacktrace:
        test/elixir_drip/storage/media_test.exs:9: (test)
Finished in 0.02 seconds
1 test, 1 failure
Randomized with seed 69303
```

We get both sides of the match we passed to `assert`, making it easy to understand why the match failed.

To end this section, we'll test a different function from the same module, which will allow us to explore ExUnit even further. We'll test the `create_initial_changeset/4` function, which is responsible for creating the `%Media{} changeset` based on the provided attributes. Whereas in other frameworks, you have the validation logic tightly coupled with the database, in Ecto, we're able to test our validation logic as pure unit tests, which we're able to run concurrently. This is possible because Ecto has a modular design, decoupling the underlying database schema from the repository. Later in this chapter, we'll talk about repository tests that will actually hit the database. For now, we'll just focus on testing `changesets`.

In the previous test, the input data was created inside the test itself. Now, we'll see how to use the `setup` macro to inject context into our tests:

```
$ cat apps/elixir_drip/test/elixir_drip/storage/media_test.exs
defmodule ElixirDrip.Storage.MediaTest do
  use ExUnit.Case, async: true

  @subject ElixirDrip.Storage.Media

  setup do
    user_id = "0ujsswThIGTUYm2K8FjOOfXtY1K"
    file_name = "test.txt"
    full_path = "$/abc"
    file_size = 123

    {:ok, user_id: user_id, file_name: file_name, full_path: full_path,
    file_size: file_size}
  end

  test "create_initial_changeset/4 returns a valid changeset", context do
    changeset = @subject.create_initial_changeset(context.user_id,
    context.file_name, context.full_path, context.file_size)

    assert changeset.valid? == true
  end

  #  ...
end
```

Inside the `setup` block, we're creating the variables we need and returning them in the block's response. This will be injected into each `test`, and we can access it by binding it to a variable before the `test` block. We could even use pattern matching here to extract a certain field from the context map. Then, inside the `test`, we create a `changeset` with the context data and use the `assert` macro to make sure the `changeset` is valid. This approach allows us to define test data in only one place, which will then be shared by all the tests in this module. The `setup` macro runs before each test. If you want to run a certain block just once, for instance to initialize something that is shared between the tests, you can use the `setup_all` macro.

When creating unit tests, we usually don't just cover the happy path, and also test the error cases. Let's now create a test to check that a `changeset` isn't valid when we provide incorrect data:

```
$ cat apps/elixir_drip/test/elixir_drip/storage/media_test.exs
defmodule ElixirDrip.Storage.MediaTest do
  # ...

  describe "when the file name is invalid" do
    setup :invalid_file_name

    test "the changeset isn't valid", context do
      changeset = @subject.create_initial_changeset(context.user_id,
        context.file_name, context.full_path, context.file_size)

      assert changeset.valid? == false
    end

    test "the changeset contains the expected error message", context do
      changeset = @subject.create_initial_changeset(context.user_id,
        context.file_name, context.full_path, context.file_size)

      assert changeset.errors == [file_name: {"Invalid file name", []}]
    end
  end

  # ...

  defp invalid_file_name(_context) do
    {:ok, file_name: "a/bc" }
  end
end
```

We're using the `describe` function to group tests that have the same context. In this case, we're creating two tests for when the `file_name` parameter isn't valid. Inside a `describe` block, we can use `setup` once again to prepare the context for this test case. In this example, we're also seeing a different way of using the `setup` macro. Instead of providing a block as we did in the previous example, we can also provide an atom with the name of a function in this module which will set the desired context. The functions passed to `setup` always receive one argument, the context map, and return a possibly modified context back. As in the previous example, this context will then be injected into each test inside the `describe` block.

Besides the difference in using the `setup` macro, this example is very similar to the previous one. We create a `changeset` with the data from the context, and then assert on what's expected for each test. In this example, this is checking that the `changeset` isn't valid, and also that it contains the expected error message.

We want to point out a specific aspect of `describe` blocks that may surprise you: there can only be one level of them. Putting it in a different way, it's not allowed to nest `describe` blocks inside of other `describe` blocks. While this may seem strange at first, particularly if you're used to do this in other testing libraries, this brings a great benefit: it becomes really clear what's the purpose and context of each test. This is an intentional decision from the Elixir core team, and the rationale is that having too much nesting in these blocks will hinder the readability of the tests. You have to navigate to the outermost block, put that context in your brain, and then progressively move down until you find the desired test. By not allowing this nesting, ExUnit forces us to be descriptive in our tests, while keeping them intelligible for other people (or our future selves).

You can pass the `--trace` option to the `mix test` task to get the description of each test printed to the Terminal as they are run. Besides the description, you also get the time it took for each test to complete.

We've now reached the end of this section. As you saw, by separating the data validation from the repository, we're able to run tests that interact with the `changeset` functions in parallel, since those functions don't have side-effects. However, eventually our applications will contain some functions that have side-effects. Let's now explore how to write tests for these functions.

Testing functions with side-effects

While we aim to write pure functions in our applications, this isn't always possible. In this section, we'll explore how to test functions that have side-effects. In most other programming languages, this is done by creating mocks that verify the correct side-effect is being produced. However, in Elixir, these kind of mocks are avoided as much as possible, since they typically rely on changing a certain module or function globally. This change makes us run our tests sequentially, which will increase the time to run them and hence make us less productive in the long run.

We will still explore how to create mocks in Elixir, but beware that they aren't used as often as in testing frameworks of other programming languages. If the module you're testing has a dependency for a simple pure function from another module of your application, what's the added benefit of adding a mock for it? This is obviously a trade-off that each one of us has to manage, and taking this to the other extreme will probably lead to redundant coverage and all the issues associated with it.

Regardless of the approach you're taking, there are some cases where having mocks is probably necessary. For instance, we probably want to create a mock when our application is contacting an external entity, so that our tests don't depend on actual requests being made. We'll now see how to create mocks in Elixir that don't change the global state and therefore allow us to run our tests concurrently.

Creating mocks with Mox

As mentioned, we usually try to avoid mocks in Elixir, and especially dynamic mocks (also known as *ad-hoc* mocks). They're called this because they're usually created dynamically within each test, just to verify that a certain expectation was met on that test. Besides changing the global behavior and not allowing us to run our tests concurrently, this type of mocks have another disadvantage: they have no connection to the real implementation they're standing in for, which makes it possible for the mock and the real implementation to drift away, possibly resulting in having all the tests passing while your application is broken in production.

For all these reasons, we'll be creating mocks with the **Mox** library, created by José Valim, which tries to solve the issues described earlier. There are other options for creating mocks in Elixir, but we feel that this is the way that is most aligned with Elixir's philosophy.

Before moving on to the test itself, let's first see which function we'll be testing. In `Chapter 6`, *Metaprogramming – Code that Writes Itself*, we've built an upload and a download pipeline, which allow us to move files to and from Google Cloud Storage. One of the steps of these pipelines is the `:remote_storage` step, where the actual upload/download takes place. To demonstrate the usage of a mock, we'll be creating a test for the upload portion of this pipeline step. Let's see its implementation:

```
$ cat apps/elixir_drip/lib/elixir_drip/storage/pipeline/
remote_storage.ex
defmodule ElixirDrip.Storage.Pipeline.RemoteStorage do
  alias ElixirDrip.Storage.Providers.GoogleCloudStorageLive

  # ...

  @impl GenStage
  def handle_events(tasks, _from, _state) do
    processed = Enum.map(tasks, &remote_storage_step(&1))
    {:noreply, processed, @dummy_state}
  end

  defp remote_storage_step(%{media: %{id: id, storage_key: storage_key}
= media, content: content, type: :upload} = task) do
    Logger.debug("#{inspect(self())}: Uploading media #{id} to #
    {storage_key}, size: #{byte_size(content)} bytes.")
    {:ok, :uploaded} = GoogleCloudStorageLive.upload(storage_key,
    content)
    task
  end
end
```

We're testing the `handle_events/3` function, particularly when the task's type is `:upload`. The mock we want to introduce is for the `GoogleCloudStorageLive` module, since we don't want to actually contact Google's API in our tests. We'll now see how to accomplish this using the Mox library. First of all, we need to inject the dependency, so that we can swap it according to the environment we're running on. Here's our updated module:

```
$ cat apps/elixir_drip/lib/elixir_drip/storage/pipeline/remote_storage.ex
defmodule ElixirDrip.Storage.Pipeline.RemoteStorage do
  @storage_provider Application.get_env(:elixir_drip, :storage_provider)

  # ...

  defp remote_storage_step(%{media: %{id: id, storage_key: storage_key}
= media, content: content, type: :upload} = task) do
    Logger.debug("#{inspect(self())}: Uploading media #{id} to #
```

```
      {storage_key}, size: #{byte_size(content)} bytes.")
      {:ok, :uploaded} = @storage_provider.upload(storage_key, content)
      task
   end
end
```

Now we need to update the configuration of our application. First, we add this entry to the main configuration file:

```
$ cat apps/elixir_drip/config/config.exs
use Mix.Config

# ...

config :elixir_drip, storage_provider:
ElixirDrip.Storage.Providers.GoogleCloudStorageLive

import_config "#{Mix.env()}.exs"
```

This way, the actual implementation is the default one, which can then be overridden per environment. This is achieved by the last line of config.exs, where we're importing a new config file based on the MIX_ENV environment variable. Now, we update the configuration file for the test environment:

```
$ cat apps/elixir_drip/config/test.exs
use Mix.Config

# ...

config :elixir_drip, storage_provider:
ElixirDrip.Storage.Providers.GoogleCloudStorageMock
```

At this stage we have a different module being injected as the storage provider, depending on the environment. Before moving on to the test code, let's first set up Mox. First, we need to add it as a dependency in our Mix file:

```
$ cat apps/elixir_drip/mix.exs

defmodule ElixirDrip.Mixfile do
   # ...
   defp deps do
      [
         # ...
         {:mox, "~> 0.3", only: :test}
      ]
   end
```

```
  # ...
end
```

Note that after changing this, we'll need to run `mix deps.get` to fetch this new dependency. The last step on setting up Mox is to define the mocks that we'll have across our tests. Unlike other testing frameworks, using Mox you need to do this in one place instead of per test. The rationale is that you shouldn't be generating dynamic modules in your tests to serve as a mock, but instead define them in one central place; for instance, in `test_helper.exs` or in a `setup_all` block, if for some reason you need to do it in the test module. In this example, we'll do it in `test_helper.exs`:

```
$ cat apps/elixir_drip/test/test_helper.exs
ExUnit.start()

Mox.defmock(ElixirDrip.Storage.Providers.GoogleCloudStorageMock, for:
ElixirDrip.Behaviours.StorageProvider)
```

We're using `Mox.defmock/2` to define a mock with the name given as the first argument, which is based on the behaviour passed in the `:for` option of the second argument. Mox doesn't allow the creation of mocks without linking them to a behaviour. While this may feel like unnecessary work at first, remember that this will ensure the API of the mock and the real implementation don't drift away. Picking up on the explicitness that's present across Elixir's design and philosophy, Mox wants you to define explicit contracts, which both your actual implementation and your mock will have to abide to. This way, you'll not get to the point where your tests are all passing but your application is not working, which usually happens because your tests are abusing mocks and live in a different reality than your actual application.

 We have already created the `ElixirDrip.Behaviours.StorageProvider` behaviour in `Chapter 2`, *Innards of an Elixir Project*.

If we hadn't already done this, we would need to create the behaviour, make the real implementation adopt that behaviour, and only then make this change in `test_helper.exs`. We're done with the groundwork. Let's now check the test itself:

```
$ cat apps/elixir_drip/test/elixir_drip/storage/pipeline/
remote_storage_test.exs
defmodule ElixirDrip.Storage.Pipeline.RemoteStorageTest do
  use ExUnit.Case, async: true
  import Mox

  alias ElixirDrip.Storage.Providers.GoogleCloudStorageMock
```

```
@subject ElixirDrip.Storage.Pipeline.RemoteStorage

setup :verify_on_exit!

test "on upload it calls the GoogleCloudStorage client with the right
arguments" do
  expect(GoogleCloudStorageMock, :upload, fn "test_key",
  "test_content" -> {:ok, :uploaded} end)

  task = %{type: :upload, media: %{id: "test_id", storage_key:
  "test_key"}, content: "test_content"}
  @subject.handle_events([task], nil, nil)
end
end
```

The aim of this test is to check that our dependency is called with the right arguments. It's then the responsibility of the unit tests of that other module to check that it behaves correctly when given the right arguments. First of all, we're importing Mox, and then calling setup :verify_on_exit!. This setup call will make Mox verify that all the expectations defined in the current process were met, right before the process exits. Then, on the test itself, we're using the expect function (imported from Mox) to set an expectation on the mock we've created earlier. The first argument is the module we're setting the expectation on, the second argument is the name of the function, and the last argument is a lambda, which will be invoked once the mock receives this function call.

 If you want to set an expectation where your mock will receive that function call more than once, you can provide another argument to the expect function, defining how many times this function will be called on the mock. For instance, extending our last example, if we expected the :upload function to be called three times in our mock, we would use: expect(GoogleCloudStorageMock, :upload, 3, fn "test_key", "test_content" -> {:ok, :uploaded} end)

We're using pattern matching on the lambda's arguments to verify that the mock is being called with the right arguments. If the mock is called with different arguments, the match will fail, which in turn will make the test fail. If the mock is called with the right arguments, it'll return whatever is the result of the lambda. In this case, we're simply returning {:ok, :uploaded}, so that the pattern match works in the module being tested, making the test pass.

After setting this expectation, we're simply creating the necessary test data, where we define that this is an upload task, and then passing it on to the function we're testing on the subject. Looking at this test, it's very clear what are the expectations set on this test, hence making it easy to understand its purpose. If instead of setting an expectation you just wanted to stub that function call, you can just call the `Mox.stub/3` function. To check this and other functions available on Mox, please take a look at its documentation, available at `https://hexdocs.pm/mox/Mox.html`.

Note that we still have `async: true` at the top of the file, meaning that, although we're using mocks, this test will still run concurrently. However, this may not always be the case. Particularly, if the code you're testing is spawning new processes (for instance, spawning a GenServer), you won't be able to set expectations on function calls made by these processes. In these cases, you can configure Mox to work in global mode, where every process can access the expectation set by a different process (and stop running the tests concurrently with `async: false`), or make an explicit allowance for a certain process to access the expectations (allowing the tests to still run concurrently). Check the documentation mentioned earlier for details on how to use these modes.

We've now seen how to create functional mocks in Elixir, using Mox. Before wrapping up this section of testing functions with side-effects, let's talk about testing functions that interact with a repository.

Testing interactions with the repository separately

We'll now explore how to run the tests that interact with the application's repository separately. At the beginning of this chapter, we created some tests for the `%Media{}` struct, and seen how we can test the `changeset` logic without ever touching the database. Now, we'll see how to actually run the tests that hit the database.

A common question that's asked every once in a while is how to create a mock for the repository, so that we can test the functions that interact with it independently. While the repository is indeed another dependency, we think that creating a mock for it makes no sense, because in the repository tests, we want to verify that our commands and queries work as expected. We have already tested our business logic in `changeset` tests, so now we want to make sure everything is glued together as it should be. If we were to mock the repository, we would then still need to create integration tests that would verify this, so what's the advantage of creating the mock in this scenario?

One of the main reasons people want to avoid hitting the database in their tests is that it slows down the test suite, creating a slower, and hence less productive, feedback cycle. However, we're able to run tests that interact with the database concurrently, greatly removing the reason for this concern. Let's now see how we can run tests that hit the database concurrently. First, we need to configure our database pool in the test environment to use a special sandbox adapter:

```
$ cat apps/elixir_drip/config/test.exs
use Mix.Config

# ...

config :elixir_drip, ElixirDrip.Repo,
  pool: Ecto.Adapters.SQL.Sandbox
```

This adapter will wrap each connection to the database in a transaction, hence creating a safe mechanism to run concurrent tests against the database. Although the name of the adapter contains SQL, the concurrent mode can't be used for all SQL databases. For now, it can only be used with PostgreSQL, as using it with MySQL may lead to deadlocks, creating a brittle test suite. Now, we need to update our test_helper.exs, to configure the pool mode:

```
$ cat apps/elixir_drip/test/test_helper.exs
# ...
Ecto.Adapters.SQL.Sandbox.mode(ElixirDrip.Repo, :manual)
```

This will configure the pool mode to :manual, which means that in each test we will be explicitly checking out a connection. Let's now see the test itself. Although we will test queries against the %Media{} schema, due to our design being based on bounded contexts, the repository interactions for this schema live in the Storage context. Hence, our test will be against the Storage module. Also, note that we're separating the repository tests into a different file, allowing us to clearly see which tests are interacting with the repository (and the database) and which tests are plain unit tests. Let's check the code for this test:

```
$ cat apps/elixir_drip/test/elixir_drip/storage/storage_repo_test.exs
defmodule ElixirDrip.StorageRepoTest do
  use ExUnit.Case, async: true

  @subject ElixirDrip.Storage

  setup do
    :ok = Ecto.Adapters.SQL.Sandbox.checkout(ElixirDrip.Repo)
  end

  describe "when the user already uploaded some media" do
```

```
    setup [:create_user, :create_media]

    @tag :repository
    test "finds the media by ID", %{user: user, media: media} do
      {:ok, :download_enqueued, retrieved_media} =
      @subject.retrieve(user.id, media.id)

      expected_media_id = media.id
      assert %{full_path: "$", id: ^expected_media_id, name:
      "test.txt"} = retrieved_media
    end
  end

  defp create_user(_context) do
    {:ok, user} =
      ElixirDrip.Accounts.create_user(%{
        username: "test",
        password: "12345678",
        email: "test@test.com"
      })

    {:ok, user: user}
  end

  defp create_media(%{user: user}) do
    {:ok, :upload_enqueued, media} = @subject.store(user.id,
    "test.txt", "$", "some cool content")
    {:ok, media: media}
  end
end
```

First of all, we have the setup block, where we're checking out a connection from the pool, as we've discussed earlier. This way our current process will be the owner of this connection to the database. In the rest of the test, we're using the techniques we've already learned throughout this chapter to create descriptive tests. We use a describe block to set the context for a certain test (or group of tests), and then use setup inside it to arrange the necessary state for the test to run. In this case, that means creating a new user in the database, and then a new media entry associated with that user. Then, the test itself is verifying that we're able to fetch a media entry based on its ID and the associated user ID. Lastly, we use the assert macro to verify that the record we've just got out of the database is the one we're expecting.

Similar to what happens with Mox, there's extra work to be done when your tests (or the code you're testing) are spawning new processes. In that case, the adapter can be changed from `:manual` to `:shared` mode, or by setting an explicit allowance on a certain process. Please refer to the adapters documentation, available at `https://hexdocs.pm/ecto/Ecto.Adapters.SQL.Sandbox.html`, for more information on how to configure the adapter for these cases.

The last noteworthy part of this test is the usage of `@tag` attributes. Tags allow us to add metadata to each test (or a group of tests), which can then be used to only run (or stop from running) a certain group of tests. In this case, we're tagging this test with `:repository`, since it interacts with the repository. With this in place we can, for instance, configure our local development to run all but the repository tests, and only run the full test suite in a CI (continuous integration) environment. We can run all tests except the repository tests with:

```
$ MIX_ENV=test mix test --exclude repository:true
Excluding tags: [repository: "true"]
......
Finished in 0.1 seconds
7 tests, 0 failures, 1 skipped
```

As we can see, we had one test skipped, which is the repository test we just created. Conversely, if we just wanted to run the repository tests, we could pass the option `--only repository:true`. At this point, we're placing the `:repository` tag on the test itself. When the test module starts to contain more tests, we also want those tests to be tagged as well. To this end, we can use the `@moduletag` directive, which will place the given tag in all tests of the current module:

```
$ cat apps/elixir_drip/test/elixir_drip/storage/storage_repo_test.exs
defmodule ElixirDrip.StorageRepoTest do
  use ExUnit.Case, async: true

  @moduletag :repository

  # ...
end
```

With this we reach the end of the section dedicated to functions with side-effects. Let's now explore a very neat feature of Elixir: testing the documentation.

Testing the documentation

Throughout this book we've been saying how documentation is a first-class citizen of Elixir, which is a great help when onboarding new people to the language (or even for experienced developers being introduced to an application). One of the key enablers for this is the ability to embed tests within the documentation for a function, which will then ensure that the documentation is kept up to date with the code.

Pretty much every developer recognizes the value of concise and descriptive documentation, as it greatly helps the understanding of a function or a module without having to jump all over a project. The problem with documentation is that it's difficult to maintain, as the code may be updated without doing the corresponding change to the documentation, which creates outdated and misleading documentation. This caused certain communities to just stop writing documentation, as it's better having none than having deceitful documentation. To tackle this issue, but still keep the great value added by proper documentation, Elixir and ExUnit allow us to embed snippets of code in the documentation, which will get executed and compared against the expected output you define in the documentation as well. The name of this feature is `doctest`.

To exemplify the creation of `doctest`, we'll add documentation to the function we've tested previously, `ElixirDrip.Storage.Media.is_valid_path?/1`:

```
$ cat apps/elixir_drip/lib/elixir_drip/storage/media.ex
defmodule ElixirDrip.Storage.Media do
  # ...

  @doc"""
  Verifies if the provided `path` is valid or not.

  ## Examples

      iex> ElixirDrip.Storage.Media.is_valid_path?("$/abc")
      {:ok, :valid}

  When we provide an invalid path (that either doesn't start with `$`
  or ends with `/`), it returns {:error, :invalid_path}

      iex> ElixirDrip.Storage.Media.is_valid_path?("$/abc/")
      {:error, :invalid_path}

      iex> ElixirDrip.Storage.Media.is_valid_path?("/abc")
      {:error, :invalid_path}
  """
  def is_valid_path?(path) when is_binary(path) do
    # ...
```

```
    end

    # ...
  end
```

In here we're writing documentation with the @doc module attribute, as usual. Then, inside it we introduce some lines that begin with iex>, on which we append the code that we want to test. The line right after this one contains the expected output. ExUnit will then extract the code that's after iex>, run it, and compare it with what's written in the next line. To have these tests running as part of our test suite, we need to add the following to this module's test file:

```
$ cat apps/elixir_drip/test/elixir_drip/storage/media_test.exs
defmodule ElixirDrip.Storage.MediaTest do
  # ...

  doctest @subject

  # ...
end
```

The @subject module attribute was already defined previously, and contains the name of the module that we're testing. By adding this line, ExUnit will run the doctest snippets we've just created as part of our test suite. Let's run them now:

```
$ MIX_ENV=test mix test
. . . . . . . . . .

Finished in 12.6 seconds
3 doctests, 7 tests, 0 failures
```

As we can see, we now have 3 doctests as part of our test suite. Let's now intentionally make the test fail, so that we can observe its output in that case. We modified the documentation to expect a return value of {:ok, :other_atom}. Let's check its output:

```
$ MIX_ENV=test mix test
. . . . . . .

  1) doctest ElixirDrip.Storage.Media.is_valid_path?/1 (1)
  (ElixirDrip.Storage.MediaTest)
     test/elixir_drip/storage/media_test.exs:5
     Doctest failed
     code: ElixirDrip.Storage.Media.is_valid_path?("$/abc") === {:ok,
     :other_atom}
     left: {:ok, :valid}
     stacktrace:
       lib/elixir_drip/storage/media.ex:74: ElixirDrip.Storage.Media
```

```
(module)
```

```
. .
```

```
Finished in 0.3 seconds
3 doctests, 7 tests, 1 failure
```

In this case, the test fails, and we get back a nice error message, making it easy to understand what's going on and correct what's necessary. With this we've finished this subsection on `doctest`, and also the broader section on unit tests. Let's now move on to the next section, where we'll learn how to write integration tests.

Integration testing

Having covered unit tests, let's now move on to integration tests. In this type of testing, we're interested in asserting that all the different layers of our application are working together as expected. This is usually done by testing at the edges of your system, letting all the components in your application interact with each other, and then validating that the response is the anticipated one.

There are other types of testing, such as end-to-end testing, which go even a step further and test the system from the perspective of the end user. In our case, this would be through a browser, clicking through the buttons and links inside our application, and then asserting that the user sees the expected information. While we don't cover this type of testing in this book, much of what we'll talk about in this section also apply to end-to-end testing.

In this kind of test, where we're observing the application from the outside, we don't want to test every possible state combination that may occur. That should be done at the unit test level, checking every possible branch for the subject under test. At the integration level, we test the main paths that the user may take.

As stated previously, these tests will be done at the boundary of our system. This means that we will hit the endpoints just as the browser would, which will then go through the Phoenix pipelines and controllers, interact with the `elixir_drip` umbrella application, and finally return a response by rendering a view. As an example of an integration test, we will be creating a test with a `GET /files` request, which will go to the index action of the file controller. Let's check it now:

```
$ cat apps/elixir_drip_web/test/elixir_drip_web/controllers/
file_controller_test.exs
defmodule ElixirDripWeb.FileControllerTest do
  use ElixirDripWeb.ConnCase, async: true
```

```
setup [:create_user, :login_user, :create_media]

test "GET /files lists the files for the current user", %{conn: conn,
media: media} do
  response = get(conn, "/files?path=$")

  assert html_response(response, 200) =~ "test.txt"
  assert html_response(response, 200) =~ "/files/#
  {media.id}/download"
end

defp create_user(_context) do
  {:ok, user} =
    ElixirDrip.Accounts.create_user(%{
      username: "test",
      password: "12345678",
      email: "test@test.com"
    })

  {:ok, user: user}
end

defp login_user(%{conn: conn, user: user}) do
  conn = Plug.Test.init_test_session(conn, user_id: user.id)
  {:ok, conn: conn}
end

defp create_media(%{user: user}) do
  {:ok, :upload_enqueued, media} =
    ElixirDrip.Storage.store(user.id, "test.txt", "$", "some cool
    content")

  {:ok, media: media}
end
end
```

We begin by calling use `ElixirDripWeb.ConnCase`, which will import some
convenience modules to create and use connections in tests. If you want to check its
contents, it's available at `apps/elixir_drip_web/test/support/conn_case.ex`. We
then have a setup with three functions, which will create and log in a user, and then create
a media file for this user. The creation of the user and its media work the same way as in
the `StorageRepoTest` we've seen earlier. The new part here is the `login_user` function.
This setup function uses the `Plug.Test.init_test_session/2` function to initialize a
session, essentially logging in the previously created user. This way, our test requests will
run just as a real one would, including going through the authentication Plugs we created
in the last chapter.

With the setup for the test taken care of, we can now analyze the test itself. As we've seen previously, we use pattern match on the test header to fetch the `conn` and `media` that were created during the setup. We then use the `get` function to make a request, specifying the path we're testing. Note that we're not hitting the controller directly, but are instead going through the router and pipelines (if applicable), making our request very similar to a real one.

We then bind the response to this GET request to `response`. Now, we need to make assertions on the content of this response, to ensure that our application behaved as expected. To this end, we're using the `html_response` function, which is a Phoenix helper that allows us to keep our tests concise and clean. Using this helper, we're asserting that the status code of the response was `200`, and also that it contains the binaries we're specifying in the test. In this case, we're checking that the name of the file, `test.txt`, gets displayed in the response, and also that the link to download this media is present.

Having tested for the happy path, let's now test that the system behaves as expected when it receives a request from a user that's not logged in. Using what we've learned, we'll create two contexts: one for when the user is logged in, which will contain the test we have just seen, and another for when the user isn't logged in. Let's check the updated test file:

```
$ cat apps/elixir_drip_web/test/elixir_drip_web/controllers/
file_controller_test.exs
defmodule ElixirDripWeb.FileControllerTest do
  use ElixirDripWeb.ConnCase, async: true

  describe "when the user is authenticated" do
    # ...
  end

  describe "when the user is NOT authenticated" do
    setup [:create_user, :create_media]

    test "GET /files redirects the user to '/'", %{conn: conn} do
      response = get(conn, "/files?path=$")

      assert html_response(response, 302) =~ "You are being <a
      href=\"/\">redirected</a>"
    end
  end

  # ...
end
```

This test is very similar to the one we saw before. The difference is that we now don't call the `login_user` function in our setup, and hence our assertion is different. We now assert that the status code is `302`, and also that we're being redirected to `/`, which will return a page that asks the user to log in.

At this point, you may be wondering how this approach will be manageable, as the test cases grow and grow. It's highly likely that there will be more tests needing a logged in user. To this end, we can abstract the private functions that we have in this test to a `Case`, the same way Phoenix generators automatically give us the `ConnCase`. To create a new case we merely need to create a new module, call `use ExUnit.CaseTemplate`, and then provide a `setup` block, on which we inject the created user and the modified connection with the user already logged in. Then each test that would need a logged in user would simply call `use` with the name of the newly created module.

Another frequent way to reduce duplication across your tests is to use factory libraries, which automatically generate test data for us. We feel that adopting such libraries should only be done when you really feel the need for it. For the most part, you're fine with just functions that generate the test data. This might introduce some duplication between tests of modules with similar inputs, but we think that the explicitness and enhanced readability of knowing what your test requires right away outweighs the cost of duplication. This is a delicate trade-off, and as in most decisions for your application, you should re-evaluate it periodically.

To conclude this section, we want to talk about testing directly controllers and views. We will test them directly in our application, as the integration tests we've just wrote already cover them. As generally we aim to avoid having too much logic in our controllers and views, the integration tests are enough. We don't want to write tests specifically for controllers and views, as that will lead to redundant coverage. However, due to the functional nature of Elixir and Phoenix, actions in controllers and the views themselves are just functions. If for some reason you ever feel the need to test a controller or a view directly, you can do so using the techniques we've explored in this chapter.

Now we have our first integration tests. The principles used in the tests for GET `/files` can be used to test other features of our application. Remember that we don't want to test every possible scenario here; we just want to test as much as is necessary to deploy our application with confidence. Let's now move on to create tests for our Phoenix Channels.

Testing Phoenix Channels

At this point, we've covered unit and integration testing. Now, we'll explore how to create tests for the Phoenix Channels we created in the last chapter. This is not a type of testing *per se*, but it's still important to explore on its own, as it comes bundled with its own set of helpers.

As we've seen in the last chapter, connecting to a channel is a two-step procedure: we first connect to the socket (through the `UserSocket` module, in our case) to establish a connection with the server; then, after having a socket connected to the server, we use it to join the channels we're interested in. Therefore, we will have two test cases in this section: one for the `UserSocket` module, where we'll test that this module handles the authentication properly, and another for the `UserChannel` module, where we'll test that the channel reacts as expected to the events we'll create. Let's begin with the `UserSocket` tests:

```
$ cat apps/elixir_drip_web/test/elixir_drip_web/channels/
user_socket_test.exs
defmodule ElixirDripWeb.UserSocketTest do
  use ElixirDripWeb.ChannelCase, async: true

  @subject ElixirDripWeb.UserSocket

  describe "with a valid token" do
    test "it connects to the socket" do
      token = Phoenix.Token.sign(@endpoint, "user socket auth", "13")

      assert {:ok, socket} = connect(@subject, %{"token" => token})
      assert socket.assigns.user_id == "13"
    end
  end

  describe "with an invalid token" do
    test "it doesn't connect to the socket" do
      assert :error == connect(@subject, %{"token" => "010101"})
    end
  end

  describe "without providing a token" do
    test "it doesn't connect to the socket" do
      assert :error == connect(@subject, %{})
    end
  end
end
```

In the same way that we have `ConnCase` to provide helpers for using connections in tests, we have `ChannelCase` to provide helpers to work with channels inside our tests. In this test case, we'll use the `connect` function, which allows us to create a transport connection for the socket handler, to test its authentication mechanism. The `ChannelCase` module was generated by Phoenix and it's available at `apps/elixir_drip_web/test/support/channel_case.ex`.

In the first test, we provide a valid token, and then assert that both the connection to the socket was successful and that the `user_id` in the `socket.assigns` is the one we're expecting (the one we provided when signing the token). We then test two negative conditions: when the user provides an invalid token, and when the user doesn't provide any token at all. The two tests are very similar, because we're checking that we receive back an `:error` atom in both tests, meaning that the connection to the socket wasn't established. Since these tests don't generate side-effects, we can run them concurrently, which is why we've put `async: true` as an option to the `ChannelCase`.

With these tests in place we can carry on and test the `UserChannel` module. Let's check the code for it now:

```
$ cat apps/elixir_drip_web/test/elixir_drip_web/channels/
user_channel_test.exs
defmodule ElixirDripWeb.UserChannelTest do
  use ElixirDripWeb.ChannelCase

  setup [:create_users, :create_media, :connect_to_socket]

  test "join users:lobby pushes a 'presence_state' event to the
joiner", %{socket: socket} do
    {:ok, _reply, _socket} = subscribe_and_join(socket, "users:lobby")

    assert_push "presence_state", %{}
  end

  test "'share' events are emitted to the owner and sharee", %{socket:
socket, user: user, sharee: sharee, media: media} do
    {:ok, _reply, socket} = subscribe_and_join(socket, "users:#
{user.id}")
    ElixirDripWeb.Endpoint.subscribe(self(), "users:#{sharee.id}")

    push(socket, "share", %{"username" => "other_user", "file_id" =>
media.id})

    assert_broadcast "share", %{message: "Successfully shared the file
with other_user."}
    assert_receive %Phoenix.Socket.Broadcast{
```

```
        payload: %{message: "test has just shared a file with you!"}
    }
  end

  # ...
end
```

Before diving into the tests, let's first recap the channels we have in our application, as it will make the test easier to follow. First, we have the `"users:lobby"` topic, which all users connect to. This is used to track who's online at the current moment, and is powered by `Phoenix.Presence`. We then have a different topic for each user. The topic is of the format `"users:<user_id>"`, where `<user_id>` represents the ID of the user that's connecting to the socket. This channel is used to deliver notifications only to a single user, such as when a download or upload has been completed.

To unclutter the explanation, we're hiding the setup functions, as they're similar to what we've already seen. We're starting to see a pattern, and we could already be benefiting from having our own Case, where users and media are created. However, note that in this case the requirements are a bit different. We now need to create two users: one named `test`, which is the owner of the created media, and another user named `other_user`, which is the user we'll share the media with. If we had prematurely abstracted the creation of users to a Case, we'd now need to stop and try to adapt it to this new requirement. Our advice on this is to delay as much as possible this type of extraction, and first establish the bulk of the tests your application will have. Once you have them, the patterns will naturally emerge and you'll be able to see where you can remove duplication, without hindering the readability of the tests. As for the `connect_to_socket` function, it's just using the `connect` function to establish a connection, just like we did in the `UserSocket` tests.

In our first test, we're checking that joining the `"users:lobby"` channel works as expected. In this case, we want to validate that a `"presence_state"` event is pushed back to the user who just joined, as this is the only event emitted when joining this channel. We're using the `assert_push` helper, which will ensure that the channel has pushed a message for the given event back to the user.

The next test is a bit more complex. We now want to test that when a `"share"` event is received in the server, it will call the necessary functions to share the file with another user, but will also emit the events to the owner of the file and the sharee, informing that the sharing was successful. To test this, we need to subscribe to two channels: the one for the owner of the file, using the `subscribe_and_join` function, as we did previously, and the one for the sharee user, which we do using the `ElixirDripWeb.Endpoint.subscribe` function.

With this setup done, we then push a "share" event, containing the username of the sharee and the ID of the media we want to share. Now, we want to assert that the proper events were emitted. First, we use the `assert_broadcast` to ensure that the owner of the file received the confirmation message. Second, we use the plain old `assert_receive` to check that the test process has received the message that's destined to the sharee. The test process works as a regular client of each channel, which allows us to make the assertions we've been talking about.

Notice how the helpers provided by `ElixirDripWeb.ChannelCase` make our tests succinct and descriptive. They do a lot of work behind the scenes, simplifying our tests and allowing them to be clear and to the point.

Another important part to notice is that we don't have the `async: true` in this test case. The process that's interacting with the database in this test is the channel process, which is dynamically spawned when we join the channel. When running the tests concurrently, this newly created process isn't aware of the checked out connection to the database we have in the test process. Hence, in this case, we need to make this test run sequentially, so that the `SQL.Sandbox` adapter runs in shared mode, allowing the processes to share the connections to the database. However, we don't think this is worth worrying about. If we have most of our tests already running concurrently, probably all of the CPU cores will be used when running the test suite. If, for certain conditions, you need to make a test run serially, that shouldn't have a noticeable affect on your test suite runtime.

In some cases, it's not necessary to make the test run serially, because we can define an explicit allowance to share the database connection. In this test that wasn't possible to do because when we have access to the newly created process ID (after the join), that same process is already trying to query the database, when handling the `:after_join` message it has sent to itself. Please refer to Ecto's documentation to see how you can use the explicit allowance, at `https://hexdocs.pm/ecto/Ecto.Adapters.SQL.Sandbox.html`.

We've now seen how to create tests for Phoenix Channels, hence reaching the end of this section. Let's now learn how to create tests for macros.

Testing macros

In this section, we'll be checking out how to create tests for macros. Particularly, we'll be adding a test for the `defchrono` macro that we created in Chapter 6, *Metaprogramming – Code that Writes Itself*. Like the last section, where we added tests for our Phoenix Channels, this section isn't related to a type of testing, but rather related with showing how to test a particular component we've created.

The most common and effective approach to test macros is to assert on the behavior of the code generated by the macro, and not on the code generation itself. Testing the generated AST directly often leads to brittle and unmanageable tests. These tests can be seen as unit tests for macros, because they're testing the macro expansion itself. Our focus should be on integration tests for macros. This means that we'll create a test module, with the sole purpose of calling use on our macro, and then place assertions on this test module. Let's check the code for this test:

```
$ cat apps/elixir_drip/test/chronometer_test.exs
defmodule ElixirDrip.ChronometerTest do
  use ExUnit.Case, async: true

  import ExUnit.CaptureIO

  defmodule Factorial do
    use ElixirDrip.Chronometer, unit: :secs

    defchrono calculate(x) do
      _calc_factorial(x)
    end

    defp _calc_factorial(0), do: 1
    defp _calc_factorial(x) do
      x * _calc_factorial(x - 1)
    end
  end

  test "defchrono measures and prints the function execution time" do
    assert capture_io(fn ->
      Factorial.calculate(10000)
    end) =~ ~r/Took \d+\.\d+ secs to run
    ElixirDrip.ChronometerTest.Factorial.calculate\/1/
  end
end
```

Inside our test we're creating a module called Factorial. This module has one function, calculate/1, which calculates the factorial for the provided number. Inside this module, we're calling use on the macro we're testing, and then utilizing the defchrono macro for the calculate/1 function. Because we're using the defchrono macro, whenever this function is called it writes to the standard output its execution time.

Given that this is the behavior of the macro, our test then needs to focus on asserting that this message gets printed to the standard output when the `calculate/1` function is called. To achieve this, we're using a helper function from ExUnit, called `capture_io`. We use this function to assert that when we call `Factorial.calculate(10000)`, the expected message is sent to the standard output. We're using a regular expression because the runtime of this function call is variable, and we're only interested in knowing that the right message was printed, not on knowing exactly how long it took.

With this test in place, we verify that the macro is working correctly, without having to give up maintainability of our test suite for it. Since this test exercises the macro as a real module would, we can be confident that the macro is behaving as expected, which enables us to update and improve it without fearing the introduction of regressions. If, for a certain, reason you find yourself needing to create unit tests for your macros, you can use the `Macro.to_string/2` function, converting your macro from AST into an Elixir string. Then, you can compare this string to check that the macro is expanding the way you expect it to. However, as we advised before, when using this approach, be mindful that you might be creating brittle tests, and check if you couldn't test the same behavior without checking the macro expansion.

We've now reached the end of our short section on testing macros. Next up, we'll be talking about a very different kind of approach to testing: creating tests based on properties of our source code.

Property-based testing

We will conclude this chapter by talking about an exciting *new* way of testing: **property-based testing**. We say *new* because this type of testing has been used for a long time in the Erlang and Haskell communities (and possibly others), and is now making its way into the Elixir community. At the time of this writing, there are strong indications that property-based testing will be part of the core of Elixir, supposedly shipping with Elixir in version 1.7. Particularly, the library that we'll be using in our examples later on (`stream_data`) will be merged to Elixir itself. It's still unclear how this will be done, and if the API of the library will change. Nevertheless, by reading this and checking out the examples, you'll already be capable of entering this new way of testing, even if in the future things are done differently.

Before moving on to the examples, we need to discuss the purpose and characteristics of property-based tests. Contrary to unit tests where we, the developers, manually define the input condition for each test, in property-based tests, we simply define properties that the function we're testing possesses. In unit tests, we define ahead of time the conditions we'll be testing, and check the boundary conditions we feel are important. In property-based tests, after having the properties defined, we use data generators to create a vast collection of input data, which will then be fed to the function we're testing. We then assert that the property we've defined is respected for every input generated by the property-based testing framework.

When talking about property-based testing, the unit tests are commonly referred to as *example-based tests*. They're called this way because we need to come up with examples to test each function. One disadvantage of handcrafting the examples is that, because we were the ones writing the code, we're biased. Those biases will find their way to the examples we create, which will result in a less than ideal test suite. If, on the other hand, we define the properties of our functions, and let the testing framework come up with the input data, we're less likely to run into the same drawback.

Although harder, it's still possible to create biased or inaccurate properties. But what is a property? To be able to create good properties, we first need to answer this question. A property is a characteristic behavior of our code, that holds true for a certain set of data. Properties vary according to the function being tested, and in the beginning it is very hard to define them. We're so used to the traditional unit tests that stopping to think about the properties of our code is very hard. While in the beginning this practice will be painful, over time you'll feel more and more confident about defining the properties of the code you write. Besides providing a better coverage, by testing our functions with a vast input space, thinking about the properties of your code will also yield benefits in the design of your applications. When we stop to think about the properties of a certain function, which conditions always hold true for a certain input space, we frequently discover a new scope we weren't aware of, or start to think about the interactions happening with other functions or modules.

Enough theory! Let's check out the code for our first property test:

```
$ cat apps/elixir_drip/test/elixir_drip/storage/pipeline/
media_property_test.exs
defmodule ElixirDrip.Storage.MediaPropertyTest do
  use ExUnit.Case, async: true
  use ExUnitProperties

  @subject ElixirDrip.Storage.Media

  property "is_valid_path?/1 with valid paths returns {:ok, :valid}" do
    check all path <- string(:ascii),
```

```
            String.last(path) != "/" do
        assert @subject.is_valid_path?("$" <> path) == {:ok, :valid}
      end
    end
  end
```

We'll be adding property tests to the same function we created unit tests for: `is_valid_path?/1`. We've separated out the property tests to its own file just to make the example clearer, but we could just as well create these property tests inside the already existing test module for the `%Media{}` schema. The first difference to point out is that we're calling `use ExUnitProperties`. This will make available some necessary functions for the property-based test, such as `property/3` and `check/1`.

Then, we define the property for the valid input range, and the `is_valid_path?/1` will return `{:ok, :valid}`. To define the valid input range, we're using the data generators provided by the property-based testing framework. First, we generate a string with ASCII characters. The next step is to reject generations where the `path` ends with a `"/"`, as that's an invalid path. Finally, before calling the function we're testing that a `"$"` is prepended to the path, to ensure that it starts with this character. Finally, our assertion is a really simple one, matching that for this input range the function always returns `{:ok, :valid}`.

Let's now run these tests. Since we're using the `property` function, we already have a tag set up for us. This way, to only run the property tests, we can do the following:

```
$ MIX_ENV=test mix test --only property
Including tags: [:property]
Excluding tags: [:test]

.

Finished in 0.1 seconds
3 doctests, 1 property, 8 tests, 0 failures, 11 skipped
```

All green! The only test that has run was the property test. This property test only took 0.1 seconds to run. Since it was so fast, let's bump the number of runs a bit to see how it can be done. To configure the number of runs in this library, we do the following:

```
$ cat apps/elixir_drip/config/test.exs
use Mix.Config

# ...

config :stream_data, max_runs: 500
```

The default is 100. Having it increased to 500, let's run our test again:

```
$ MIX_ENV=test mix test --only property
Including tags: [:property]
Excluding tags: [:test]


.


Finished in 0.1 seconds
3 doctests, 1 property, 8 tests, 0 failures, 11 skipped
```

We now have a broader input space, and our property still took 0.1 seconds to run. In local development, we want a short execution time to have a short feedback loop. However, in CI the execution time is not as important, allowing us to increase this number a bit and checking for a greater input range, possibly finding out about edge cases we weren't aware of. Let's now add a new property-based test to the `is_valid_path?/1` function:

```
$ cat apps/elixir_drip/test/elixir_drip/storage/pipeline/
media_property_test.exs
defmodule ElixirDrip.Storage.MediaPropertyTest do
  # ...

  property "is_valid_path?/1 with invalid paths returns {:error,
  :invalid_path}" do
    check all path <- string(:ascii),
              String.first(path) != "$" do
      assert @subject.is_valid_path?(path) == {:error, :invalid_path}
    end

    check all path <- string(:ascii) do
      assert @subject.is_valid_path?(path <> "/") == {:error,
      :invalid_path}
    end
  end
end
```

This new property states that for all invalid paths, our function returns `{:error, :invalid_path}`. To check that this property holds true for all types of invalid paths, we have two generators inside it. One generator checks that for all paths that don't start with `"$"` the function returns the expected value. The other generator checks that for all paths that end with `"/"` the function also returns the expected value. Let's now run our property-based tests again:

```
$ MIX_ENV=test mix test --only property
Including tags: [:property]
Excluding tags: [:test]
```

```
. .

Finished in 0.3 seconds
3 doctests, 2 properties, 8 tests, 0 failures, 11 skipped
```

Once again, everything is green! The testing framework has generated a huge set of input data, and for all those inputs the `is_valid_path?/1` function behaved as expected. Note that this doesn't mean that our function is bug free, as property-based testing isn't a form of formal verification of software. However, we do have a great deal of confidence that this function is correctly written. We weren't able to make these tests fail when writing this book, but if we had come across a failure, the testing framework would shrink the input to the smallest possible input that breaks the property. This is very helpful because it makes the boundary condition easier to understand, as usually the input is shrunk to the point where we immediately see where we've made a mistake. To keep the shrinkability on the property-based tests, note that you have to use functions from the `StreamData` library.

But how do property-based tests integrate with the other types of testing in an application? As with most aspects related to testing, this will depend on the preferences of your team. Generally, they're not supposed to replace unit nor integration tests. Both of these types of testing continue to have their strengths. For instance, unit tests are well suited for situations where you want to test a cumbersome corner case directly. Moreover, because property-based tests usually take some time to run (because they're generating a huge amount of test executions), we don't think you should write them for every function in your application. That will lead to a slow and unmanageable test suite. Alternatively, you can pick a number of functions or modules that are critical to keep your application running, and create property-based tests for these functions or modules. This will increase the level of confidence you have in these critical components, which in turn will also increase the robustness of your application.

As we've seen during this section, property-based tests bring several benefits to your test suite. They allow us to ship our code with more confidence, which is the purpose of all types of testing. Since these tests generate different input data on each run, you're testing even further as time goes by. Besides the extra execution time, the only disadvantage when adopting this type of testing is the steep learning curve. To create and define properties for our functions requires a change of mindset, which in the beginning feels very hard. As with any craft, experience will make you better and better, and over time you'll see that creating properties for your functions is second nature. There are some patterns that you may use when starting out this journey. For instance, if the function you're testing has an inverse function, you can create a property stating that the inverse function reverts the action performed by original function.

Another useful trick is to use an already existing implementation as a way to assert the behavior of the function you're testing. For instance, if you're testing a function that's available in the Erlang standard library, it is possible that the output of your function is the same as the one from the Erlang standard library. With experience, other patterns will emerge and become part of your toolbox.

We've now reached the end of this exciting section. Let's conclude this chapter by recapping what we've covered in it.

Summary

In this chapter about testing, we went through a broad range of topics. Let's review the most important ones:

- Testing in Elixir is powered by the thorough ExUnit framework, which enables us to create descriptive and concise tests that are able to run concurrently.
- We can create function mocks in Elixir using the Mox library, allowing our tests to still run concurrently. Mocks have to be created based on a behaviour, so that the API of the mock and the real implementation don't diverge.
- Ecto's modular design allows us to separate changeset tests (which verify our business logic) from repository tests (which verify our queries and the interaction with the database). In either case, we're able to run the tests concurrently.
- Elixir provides a neat feature, called `doctest`, which enables us to embed tests inside the documentation that we write. These embedded tests ensure that the documentation is kept up to date, which is a key enabler for the first-class status of documentation in the Elixir community.
- Integration tests are done by testing our application from the edges. In our case, the edge is the web interface. Phoenix provides a set of useful helpers that simplify the assertions we need to make on our integration tests.
- Similar to what happens with integration tests, Phoenix provides a set of helpers to test Channels. Particularly, it exposes functions that not only allow us to connect to a socket, but also verify that a broadcast for a certain event has happened, or that the server has pushed a certain event to the Channel.

- The focus on testing macros should be on testing the code that the macro expands to, and not the code expansion itself. Testing the expansion itself should generally be avoided, since it may lead to brittle tests.
- Property-based tests are a very different approach to testing, where instead of coming up with examples for each test, we define properties that the function we're testing has, and then let the testing framework generate input data. Then, the framework checks that for every input provided to the function the properties were respected.

With the testing part finished, our application is ready to be deployed to a live environment. That's exactly what we'll do in the next chapter, where we'll learn how to deploy our ElixirDrip application in the cloud.

10
Deploying to the Cloud

At this point, we are able to provide all the media-server features that we envisioned at the beginning of this journey, but we still have ElixirDrip running locally. This will all change in this chapter; by the end of it, we'll have a streamlined version of ElixirDrip running in a hosted Kubernetes environment, with multiple connected nodes running the application.

We'll follow some of the existing best practices to ship ElixirDrip to production. While we're at it, we will delve into releases, containerization, Kubernetes, and continuous integration. It will be an eventful trip!

This chapter will cover the following topics:

- Releasing with Distillery
- Containerizing our application
- Deploying to Kubernetes
- Continuous deployment with Travis CI
- Connecting deployed Elixir nodes

Releasing with Distillery

So far, we have been running the application with `mix` or `mix phx.server`, and our code was being compiled on the fly before running. This way, only files changed after the last compilation are recompiled before running the application, contributing to a fast development experience.

If you're inside an IEx shell (that is, you started the application with `iex -S mix`), you can also call the `recompile/0` function whenever you want to compile the changes you just made, instead of having to quit and start the application again. This only works if you're inside a Mix project.

The code we're running is perfectly capable of performing its duties in production, but we don't want to deploy it like this. If we copy the umbrella project folder to production and then run it with `mix phx.server`, we would also be deploying the development and test dependencies and the entire source code of the application, resulting in an inefficient and unsafe production environment.

Because of its Erlang inheritance, Elixir applications can also be deployed like Erlang/OTP *releases*. The concept of a release is nothing more than a standard way of bundling all the things needed to run one or more applications, optionally including the **Erlang Runtime (ERTS)**, thus making this bundle self-sufficient.

Instead of using an Erlang tool to create a release for our ElixirDrip umbrella and deal with the Erlang-specific bits and bobs, we will rely on a library called Distillery to create a self-contained release. Distillery grabs any Mix project and produces a compliant Erlang/OTP release, with the runtime dependencies you choose, ready to be deployed.

 It is expected that Elixir 1.7 will bring release tooling to Mix. However, the initial version of this feature won't cover all the features Distillery currently has (such as hot upgrades). Thus, we can expect Distillery to be deprecated only when the release tooling in Mix implements all its features.

Since Distillery is a library, we'll install it by adding it as a dependency to our project (we don't need the library at runtime so we set its `:runtime` option accordingly):

```
$ cat mix.exs
# ...
  defp deps do
    [
      {:distillery, "~> 1.5", runtime: false},
      {:credo, "~> 0.3", only: [:dev, :test], runtime: false}
    ]
  end
# ...
```

Now, we just need to run `mix do deps.get, compile` to be able to execute the Distillery Mix tasks.

In the following sections, we'll configure and build the release of our ElixirDrip umbrella project.

Configuring the release

Distillery looks for a `rel` folder in the project root to find out how it should build the release. In its simplest form, this folder only needs to have a `config.exs` file.

To create a typical release configuration, we will run the Mix `release.init` task in the project root:

```
$ mix release.init
An example config file has been placed in rel/config.exs, review it,
make edits as needed/desired, and then run `mix release` to build the
release
```

The generated configuration file starts by loading any plugin that we may have in the `rel/plugins` folder and then uses the `Mix.Releases.Config` module so it can use its macros. Because we're setting `:default_release` as `:default`, if we just do `mix release` (that is, we didn't choose any `:release` configuration), it will use the first release defined in the `rel/config.exs` file. We also set `:default_environment` as `Mix.env()`, meaning that it will grab one of the release environments defined in this file based on the current Mix environment.

In the following snippet, the default configuration also defines a `:dev` environment. By setting `:dev_mode` as `true`, Distillery won't copy any BEAM code files to the release folder; instead, it will just symlink them, hence improving the release speed in `:dev`. By setting `:include_erts` as `false`, a copy of the Erlang runtime won't be placed in the release, so when the `:dev` release runs, it will use the available runtime.

Distillery also generated an Erlang *magic cookie* for us, which will be used as an authentication token when we want to connect different Erlang nodes. Since whoever has this token may be able to connect to our running nodes, you shouldn't store it in clear text in your codebase:

```
$ cat rel/config.exs
Path.join(["rel", "plugins", "*.exs"])
|> Path.wildcard()
|> Enum.map(&Code.eval_file(&1))

use Mix.Releases.Config,
    default_release: :default,
    default_environment: Mix.env()

environment :dev do
  set dev_mode: true
  set include_erts: false
  set cookie: :"c{E|>.dCI>YT>M7v@1iF&VNHs)^1M^?*e?=3dcD..."
```

```
end
# ...
```

We won't be using a release in development, so let's analyze the rest of the configuration file that configures the :prod release environment and a single :elixir_drip release. The :prod environment includes the Erlang runtime and removes the source from the release by setting the :include_src option to false. By bundling the runtime in the release, we make sure our application is able to run without Erlang or Elixir being available. The cookie we're setting here won't be used, because as we'll see in a moment, we will set it via a custom vm.args file.

In the following snippet, you can find the changes applied after the initial values set by Distillery with mix release.init:

```
$ cat rel/config.exs
# ...
environment :prod do
  set include_erts: true
  set include_src: false
  set cookie: :"won't be used, we set it via a custom vm.args file
(rel/custom.vm.args)"
end

release :elixir_drip do
  set vm_args: "rel/custom.vm.args"
  set version: current_version(:elixir_drip)
  set applications: [
    :runtime_tools,
    elixir_drip: :permanent,
    elixir_drip_web: :permanent
  ]
end
```

Our rel/config.exs file only defines a single :elixir_drip release, with the :applications instances that it will include. Besides the required :runtime_tools, Distillery added to the list both the :elixir_drip and :elixir_drip_web umbrella apps. It also sets the start type of each application as :permanent, meaning that if one of the applications terminates, all the other applications and the entire Erlang node will be terminated as well.

We are using the current_version/1 macro to set the release version as the version of the elixir_drip umbrella app. We could have set a simple "0.1.0" string instead.

By setting the :vm_args value, we're telling Distillery that we want to use our own vm.args file, living in rel/custom.vm.args.

A vm.args file lets us define which arguments are passed to the Erlang VM. If we don't specify any custom vm.args, this is the one Distillery would generate for us by default:

```
# Name of the node
-name elixir_drip@127.0.0.1

# Cookie for distributed erlang
-setcookie a_random_big_and_complex_cookie_value

# Enable SMP automatically based on availability
-smp auto
```

As you can see, by default, Distillery passes three parameters to the VM: the first one, name, sets the name of the Erlang node with the <name>@<host> format; the second one, setcookie, sets the cookie you need to use if you want to connect to the Erlang node; the third parameter, smp, controls whether the Erlang runtime should be started with the Symmetric Multiprocessing feature enabled or not.

 You can check all the available Erlang VM parameters in the Erlang documentation at http://erlang.org/doc/man/erl.html#init_flags. Here, we will only use the parameters that Distillery sets by default.

Because we are pointing to a custom vm.args file in the :elixir_drip release configuration, Distillery will, instead of generating a vm.args file from scratch, generate vm.args based on the rel/custom.vm.args file:

```
$ cat rel/custom.vm.args
-name <%= release_name %>@${POD_IP}

-setcookie ${ERLANG_COOKIE}

-smp auto
```

The previous file will be interpreted as an **Embedded Elixir (EEx)** template, so <%= release_name> will become elixir_drip, the name of the release configuration. The other difference lies in the way we are setting the host and cookie values. Instead of the actual values, we're using ${POD_IP} and ${ERLANG_COOKIE} as placeholders for the real values.

We're using this ${...} construct because we want to set these values only at runtime. For the host value, this is a hard requirement, since we only know the application host IP when the application is about to start. Regarding the cookie value, we would be perfectly able to set it in compile time, when the release is being created. Nonetheless, given its security importance, we prefer to set it only in the last possible moment.

In the following section, we'll learn the reason behind the ${...} construct.

Interpolating environment variables

Let's start by looking at the way we set the database configuration in the elixir_drip umbrella app while developing locally:

```
$ cat apps/elixir_drip/config/dev.exs
use Mix.Config

config :elixir_drip, ElixirDrip.Repo,
  adapter: Ecto.Adapters.Postgres,
  username: System.get_env("DB_USER"),
  password: System.get_env("DB_PASS"),
  database: System.get_env("DB_NAME"),
  hostname: System.get_env("DB_HOST"),
  port: System.get_env("DB_PORT"),
  pool_size: 10
```

All these Mix configuration entries are evaluated at runtime, so when we run the application with mix or mix phx.server, we know all those entries will be set according to the existing DB_* environment variables. If one of those environment variables doesn't exist, Mix will still be able to run the project, but the configuration entry in question will be set as nil.

When we build a release, these configuration files (such as config/config.exs and config/dev.exs) are evaluated and consequently set in stone in the sys.config release file. Look at what happens if we set a weird database hostname value before building the release:

```
$ MIX_ENV=dev DB_HOST=weird_value_crystallized_forever mix release
  # ...
==> Release successfully built!

$ cat _build/dev/rel/elixir_drip/releases/0.0.8/sys.config
  # ...
 {elixir_drip,
     [{ecto_repos, ['Elixir.ElixirDrip.Repo']},
```

```
{storage_provider,
'Elixir.ElixirDrip.Storage.Providers.GoogleCloudStorageLocal'},
{'Elixir.ElixirDrip.Repo',
    [{adapter,'Elixir.Ecto.Adapters.Postgres'},
    {username,<<"postgres">>},
    {password,<<"123456">>},
    {database,<<"elixir_drip_dev">>},
    {hostname,<<"weird_value_crystallized_forever">>},
    {port,<<"5432">>},
    {pool_size,10}]}]},
# ...
```

Even if we later run the release with the `DB_HOST` environment variable set, the `hostname` configuration will always be `"weird_value_crystallized_forever"`.

To overcome this, Distillery lets you set configuration values wrapped in `${...}` (such as `"${DB_HOST}"`), which will then be replaced at runtime by the corresponding environment variables. With this approach, we don't need to access all the configuration values when building the release. Production credentials or the host IP are examples of values that, for a multitude of reasons, are only available when running the application. This is especially useful in a case such as ours where the release will be built by Travis CI, an external continuous integration service.

This is the reason why our `config/prod.exs` configuration file, used by the `:prod` Mix environment looks, like this:

```
$ cat apps/elixir_drip/config/prod.exs
use Mix.Config

config :elixir_drip, ElixirDrip.Repo,
  adapter: Ecto.Adapters.Postgres,
  username: "${DB_USER}",
  password: "${DB_PASS}",
  database: "${DB_NAME}",
  hostname: "${DB_HOST}",
  port: "${DB_PORT}",
  pool_size: 15
  # ...
```

After building the `prod` release, this is what you will find in `sys.config`:

```
$ cat _build/prod/rel/elixir_drip/releases/0.0.8/sys.config
  # ...
{elixir_drip,
    [{ecto_repos,['Elixir.ElixirDrip.Repo']},
     {storage_provider,
         'Elixir.ElixirDrip.Storage.Providers.GoogleCloudStorageLive'},
```

```
            {'Elixir.ElixirDrip.Repo',
                [{adapter,'Elixir.Ecto.Adapters.Postgres'},
                {username,<<"${DB_USER}">>},
                {password,<<"${DB_PASS}">>},
                {database,<<"${DB_NAME}">>},
                {hostname,<<"${DB_HOST}">>},
                {port,<<"${DB_PORT}">>},
                {pool_size,15}]}]},
    # ...
```

If we now run the release with the REPLACE_OS_VARS environment variable set to true, Distillery will replace all the "${...}" values in the sys.config file that have a corresponding environment variable set.

A common pitfall related with this duality between runtime and build time (especially for those coming from interpreted languages such as Ruby), is to define module attributes whose values come from environment variables.

Imagine that our application had to send information to an external API using a unique URL. Since this URL is sensitive information, we can't store it with the rest of our code base, so we decide to fetch it from an environment variable, like this:

```
defmodule ExternalApi do
  @url System.get_env("EXTERNAL_API_URL")

  def send_information(payload),
    do: HTTPoison.post(@url, payload)
end
```

Everything works locally, so we decide to release this feature. When it reaches the live environment, a cryptic error starts to appear, and we can't find what's happening. We double-check the environment variables set in production, and we can see EXTERNAL_API_URL being correctly set there.

Are you able to spot what's wrong? Elixir is a compiled language; therefore, our ExternalApi module was compiled with the rest of the application when we built the release. At compile time, the EXTERNAL_API_URL environment variable wasn't set, hence the @url module attribute becomes nil, causing the error to happen.

Even if we set the `@url` value to `"${EXTERNAL_API_URL}"`, the error would still happen, because this value would never be replaced by the actual URL value (the `@url` value would always be `"${EXTERNAL_API_URL}"`). Only the `config.exs` configuration entries are placed in the `sys.config` file by Distillery. At runtime, when Distillery detects the `REPLACE_OS_VARS` flag, it replaces all the `${...}` placeholders that exist in the `sys.config` file with the values of the actual environment variables.

After understanding how we can safely use environment variables to configure the application at runtime, let's actually build and run the release!

Creating the release

To build the release, we need to simply run the release Mix task with `mix release`. Since in our `rel/config.exs` file we set `default_environment: Mix.env()`, the release default environment is given by the `MIX_ENV` environment variable.

In the following snippet, we are building the release. We're setting the `elixir_drip` umbrella app version in its `mix.exs` file as `0.0.8`, so the release becomes `elixir_drip:0.0.8` (`elixir_drip` is the release name and `0.0.8` results from setting the release version as `current_version(:elixir_drip)` in the `rel/config.exs` file):

```
$ MIX_ENV=prod mix release
==> elixir_drip
  # ...
Generated elixir_drip app
==> elixir_drip_web
Compiling 12 files (.ex)
Generated elixir_drip_web app

==> Assembling release..
==> Building release elixir_drip:0.0.8 using environment prod
==> Including ERTS 9.3.1 from /usr/local/lib/erlang/erts-9.3.1
==> Packaging release..
==> Release successfully built!
   You can run it in one of the following ways:
     Interactive: _build/prod/rel/elixir_drip/bin/elixir_drip console
     Foreground: _build/prod/rel/elixir_drip/bin/elixir_drip foreground
     Daemon: _build/prod/rel/elixir_drip/bin/elixir_drip start
```

If you look inside the resulting `*.tar.gz` release archive, you will find four folders (three if you don't include the ERTS): `bin`, `erts-<version>`, `lib`, and `releases/<app-version>`.

In the `bin` folder, you will find the Shell script that we will use to start the application, and in the `lib` folder, you will find all the compiled dependencies.

The `releases/<app-version>` folder contains a release resource file, `*.rel`, a `*.script` file, and a `*.boot` file. So, `elixir_drip.rel` contains a tuple with all the applications and respective versions contained in this release. Now, `elixir_drip.script` is an Erlang script that will start the Erlang node and then run the release. The Erlang runtime will use the binary format of this script, the `elixir_drip.boot` file, also present in this folder.

To run the release, we first need to set the expected environment variables for Distillery to interpolate them at runtime, and then we can interactively run the release with `_build/prod/rel/elixir_drip/bin/elixir_drip console`:

```
$ export REPLACE_OS_VARS=true POD_IP=127.0.0.1 ERLANG_COOKIE=cookie
DB_HOST=postgres DB_PORT=5432 DB_NAME=elixir_drip_dev DB_USER=postgres
DB_PASS=123456

$ env $(cat secrets/credentials.dev.env | xargs)
_build/prod/rel/elixir_drip/bin/elixir_drip console

Erlang/OTP 20 [erts-9.3.1] [source] [64-bit] [smp:4:4] [ds:4:4:10] [async-
threads:10] [hipe] [kernel-poll:false]

04:29:37.923 [info] Running ElixirDripWeb.Endpoint with Cowboy using
http://:::4000
Interactive Elixir (1.6.4) - press Ctrl+C to exit (type h() ENTER for help)
iex(elixir_drip@127.0.0.1)1>
```

Remember the `${POD_IP}` and `${ERLANG_COOKIE}` placeholders we set in our custom `vm.args` file before? We need to define them as environment variables before running the release, along with every other environment variable that should be interpolated by Distillery and is mentioned in the `elixir_drip` and `elixir_drip_web` `config/prod.exs` configuration files.

By doing `env $(cat secrets/credentials.dev.env | xargs)` before running the release, we are able to temporarily set two environment variables that will only exist for the current release run. This way, we avoid permanently setting the `SECRET_KEY_BASE` and `GOOGLE_STORAGE_CREDENTIALS` environment variables with sensitive information:

```
$ cat secrets/credentials.dev.env
SECRET_KEY_BASE=vh1pO...
GOOGLE_STORAGE_CREDENTIALS=ewogI...
```

In the next section, we'll see how we can implement a custom release task, which will allow us to run the database migrations.

Creating a custom release task

When we create a release with Distillery, our Elixir application is converted into an Erlang/OTP release, indistinguishable from any other Erlang application bundle. There's no Mix project, ideally no Elixir source code either, only files with BEAM bytecode and the specific release files needed to start the release.

However, this frugality poses a problem: given we don't have Mix, it's impossible to run the database migrations using the `ecto.migrate` Mix task with the release. And we are determined to not send the whole Elixir project to production, so we need to find a way without depending on Mix tasks.

To overcome this, we will implement a custom release task that delegates the migration execution to the `ElixirDrip.ReleaseTasks` module, which only depends on the `:ecto` and `:postgrex` applications:

```
$ cat apps/elixir_drip/lib/elixir_drip/release_tasks.ex
defmodule ElixirDrip.ReleaseTasks do
  alias Ecto.Migrator

  @start_apps [:postgrex, :ecto]

  def migrate_up, do: migrate(:up)
  def migrate_down, do: migrate(:down)

  defp migrate(direction) do
    options = case direction do
      :up -> [all: true]
      :down -> [step: 1]
    end

    IO.puts("Loading ElixirDrip umbrella app...")
    :ok = Application.load(:elixir_drip)

    IO.puts("Starting dependencies...")
    Enum.each(@start_apps, &Application.ensure_all_started/1)

    IO.puts("Starting ElixirDrip repo...")
    ElixirDrip.Repo.start_link(pool_size: 1)

    IO.puts("Running migrations for ElixirDrip...")
    run_migrations(direction, options)

    IO.puts("Success!")
    :init.stop()
  end
```

```
  defp priv_dir(app), do: "#{:code.priv_dir(app)}"

  defp run_migrations(direction, options) do
    Migrator.run(ElixirDrip.Repo, migrations_path(:elixir_drip), direction,
options)
  end

  defp migrations_path(app), do: Path.join([priv_dir(app), "repo",
"migrations"])
end
```

In this snippet, the bulk of the work is performed by the `migrate/1` private function. Depending on the migration direction, it applies all the migrations not yet run (the `:up` direction) or reverts the last applied migration (the `:down` direction). Before relying on `Ecto.Migrator` to run the migrations, it loads the `:elixir_drip` applications and waits for the `:ecto` and `:postgrex` applications to start, since we need them up and running for the migrations to be correctly applied/reverted.

After rebuilding the release, we're able to run the `ReleaseTasks.migrate_up/0` function by relying on the `command` utility provided by Distillery:

```
$ ERLANG_COOKIE=cookie REPLACE_OS_VARS=true
_build/prod/rel/elixir_drip/bin/elixir_drip command
Elixir.ElixirDrip.ReleaseTasks migrate_up
Loading ElixirDrip umbrella app...
Starting dependencies...
Starting ElixirDrip repo...
Running migrations for ElixirDrip...
Success!
17:12:06.169 [info] Already up
```

Recall that every Elixir module has an `Elixir.` prefix (`ElixirDrip.ReleaseTasks ==` `Elixir.ElixirDrip.ReleaseTasks` evaluates to `true`). We had to prefix `ElixirDrip.ReleaseTasks` in the previous snippet because we're in Erlang's turf, hence there's no IEx to automatically add the `Elixir.` prefix for us.

Instead of using the Distillery `command` utility, we will create two shell scripts in the `rel/commands` folder, `migrate_up.sh` and `migrate_down.sh`, which will help us to run these custom tasks. As you can see here, the `migrate_up.sh` script simply mimics what we did in the previous snippet:

```
$ cat rel/commands/migrate_up.sh
#!/bin/sh
$RELEASE_ROOT_DIR/bin/elixir_drip command Elixir.ElixirDrip.ReleaseTasks
migrate_up
```

The last step is to define two custom commands in the :elixir_drip release, migrate_up and migrate_down, which will respectively run the previous two shell scripts:

```
$ cat rel/config.exs
  # ...
release :elixir_drip do
  set vm_args: "rel/custom.vm.args"
  set version: current_version(:elixir_drip)
  set applications: [
    :runtime_tools,
    elixir_drip: :permanent,
    elixir_drip_web: :permanent
  ]
  set commands: [
    "migrate_up": "rel/commands/migrate_up.sh",
    "migrate_down": "rel/commands/migrate_down.sh"
  ]
end
```

If we now run the elixir_drip release with no arguments, it shows the two custom commands we've just created:

```
$ _build/prod/rel/elixir_drip/bin/elixir_drip
Usage: elixir_drip <task>

Service Control
=======================
  # ...
Custom Commands
=======================
/opt/app/elixir_drip/_build/prod/rel/elixir_drip/releases/0.0.8/commands/mi
grate_down.sh
/opt/app/elixir_drip/_build/prod/rel/elixir_drip/releases/0.0.8/commands/mi
grate_up.sh
```

We can now run the new custom commands as follows:

```
$ ERLANG_COOKIE=cookie REPLACE_OS_VARS=true
_build/prod/rel/elixir_drip/bin/elixir_drip migrate_up
Loading ElixirDrip umbrella app...
Starting dependencies...
Starting ElixirDrip repo...
Running migrations for elixir_drip...
Success!
15:13:25.946 [info] Already up
```

We're well on our way to having our application running on the cloud. In the next section, we'll use Docker to *containerize* our application.

Containerizing our application

Before we start laying the foundation of how we deploy our application to the cloud, we need to have our application running inside containers. To introduce containers, let's first analyze the problem they try to solve.

To build and run our ElixirDrip project, we need Erlang, Elixir, and Node.js correctly installed and available in the current $PATH, ready to be used. To deploy the application in production, we need to make sure those dependencies have the exact same version and are installed in production in the exact same way, because only then we can be sure the application behavior will be the same.

Doing things like this is cumbersome and time-consuming, but not an impossible endeavor. If only we had a cleaner way of building the environment and then saving it, so we could reuse it at a later time, wherever we needed it. This is exactly what containers allow us to do.

Containers are lightweight wrappers for applications, which not only contain the applications themselves, but also everything needed to successfully run them. Each container has its own processes, memory, and network interfaces, and runs in a secure way, isolated from other containers and the host operating system.

Since a containerized application is self-contained, it can be deployed to different environments as is. Because containers are lightweight, their deployment is fast and requires a fewer resources than fully fledged virtual machines.

Containers are instantiated from *images*, which are nothing more than snapshots of applications in their habitats. These images are created from *recipes* that describe how the application code, its configuration, and dependencies are set up inside the container. When we want to run a container, we indicate from which image the container will be instantiated.

An application running inside a container is able to write to the filesystem as it normally would, but it will never change the underlying image. Images are read only, so you can be sure that if an application runs locally with a given image, it will also run in other environments with the same image.

So far, we have talked about generic container concepts. From this point forward, we will analyze Docker examples, since this is the tool we'll use to create, manage, and run our application containers. All the examples in this chapter could also be achieved with other equivalent tools, such as rkt.

When you want to use an image you've just built locally on a remote machine, you can push it to a Docker registry and then fetch it from there. Since the image will be the same in both places, you can be sure the containers instantiated from it will be identical, with no more unpleasant surprises after deploying.

```
$ cat examples/Dockerfile.simple
FROM elixir:1.6.4-alpine

EXPOSE 4001

CMD while true; do echo "Hello World!" | nc -l -p 4001; done
```

In the previous snippet, you can find Dockerfile, a simple image *recipe*, based on an elixir:1.6.4-alpine image that already exists in the Docker public registry. After fetching this image, Docker exposes port 4001 and in the end runs a shell script forever that uses Netcat to deliver a Hello World! message.

To build the previous image, we are specifying the image tag (with -t) and indicating a specific examples/Dockerfile.simple (with -f). The last argument is the context in which the image is created; in our case, it's the examples folder:

```
$ docker build -t hello_world -f examples/Dockerfile.simple examples
Sending build context to Docker daemon 53.25kB
Step 1/3 : FROM elixir:1.6.4-alpine
 ---> cb08ed0e151a
Step 2/3 : EXPOSE 4001
 ---> Using cache
 ---> 43710db729b1
Step 3/3 : CMD while true; do echo "Hello World!" | nc -l -p 4001; done
 ---> Using cache
 ---> 9d2c59bb56f7
Successfully built 9d2c59bb56f7
Successfully tagged hello_world:latest
```

We can now see the image labeled as hello_world:latest with docker images:

```
$ docker images
REPOSITORY TAG IMAGE ID CREATED SIZE
hello_world latest 9d2c59bb56f7 12 minutes ago 84.1MB
```

We can now run the image with `docker run -p 4001:4001 hello_world:latest`. The `-p` option binds port `4001` in the container to port `4001` in the host. If we now open another terminal, we can interact with the container by sending requests to local port 4001:

```
$ curl localhost:4001
Hello World!
```

We can observe our running container with `docker ps`. Since we are executing an infinite loop, the container will never end on its own if we don't stop it:

```
$ docker ps
CONTAINER ID IMAGE COMMAND STATUS PORTS NAMES
eefca9fe7d54 hello_world:latest "/bin/sh -c 'while..." Up 4 minutes
0.0.0.0:4001->4001/tcp determined_shtern
```

Docker named our container `determined_shtern`, so we can do all container operations with this name, instead of using the unmemorable `eefca9fe7d54` container ID. If we want to set the container name, we can use the `--name` option when we do `docker run`. To stop the container we've just started, it is just a matter of running `docker stop <container name|id>`.

After this crash course on Docker, we can now run our application inside a Docker container.

Creating a development container

To create our container, we need to define the recipe describing how the image is assembled. Docker *recipes* are called `Dockerfiles`, and are nothing more than text files describing the operations needed to build the images.

The following snippet shows our `Dockerfile.dev`, since this is the `Dockerfile` that we'll use while developing:

```
$ cat Dockerfile.dev
FROM elixir:1.6.4-alpine

ENV TERM xterm
ENV LANG en_US.UTF-8
ENV LANGUAGE en_US:en
ENV LC_ALL en_US.UTF-8

ENV REFRESHED_AT 2018-06-05

ENV APP_PATH /opt/app
```

```
ENV APP_NAME elixir_drip
ENV HTTP_PORT 4000
ENV MIX_ENV dev

RUN apk add --no-cache build-base git inotify-tools nodejs nodejs-npm
RUN mix archive.install
https://github.com/phoenixframework/archives/raw/master/phx_new.ez --force
RUN mix local.hex --force && mix local.rebar --force

COPY . $APP_PATH/$APP_NAME

WORKDIR $APP_PATH/$APP_NAME

EXPOSE $HTTP_PORT

CMD ["mix run --no-halt"]
```

In this `Dockerfile`, the first lines starting with `FROM` indicate the parent image that we'll use; in our case, it will be the `elixir:1.6.4-alpine` image, which already comes with Elixir and Erlang installed in a compact Linux distribution called Alpine. We then set some environment variables (using the `ENV` instructions), such as the application path, name, the port it will use, and the `MIX_ENV` that controls the Mix environment.

Afterward, we use the `RUN` Docker instruction to install some dependencies in our container: `git`, `nodejs`, and the accompanying `npm` are installed with `apk` (the package management tool of Alpine Linux, on which our image is based). We then use `mix` to install Phoenix, Hex, and `rebar3` (an Erlang tool to create Erlang releases, used by many library dependencies).

The last portion of the `Dockerfile` copies the current directory (the root of the umbrella project) to the `/opt/app/elixir_drip` container path, sets the current directory inside the container, exposes the port, and ends by running the project with `mix run --no-halt`.

 We could have run the application with `CMD mix run --no-halt` (without the command being inside an array, that is, in *shell form*), but in this situation Docker prefixes the command with `/bin/sh -c '<command>'`, which may bring some funky behavior (in this case, your command wouldn't be running as PID 1, among other shell subtleties). Hence, it's usually better to run the command as we do in the `Dockerfile` with the array, also called **exec form**.

We've just created our first `Dockerfile`. Let's see how can we run it alongside other containers that we'll need.

Orchestrating more than one container

Every time we start ElixirDrip, it will try to connect to a running Postgres database. If we run it in our local development environment inside a container, it will be no different. In this case, we may install Postgres locally, we can set the application to connect to a remote database provided as a service, or we can spin up a new container running a Postgres database. Since this is only for local development purposes, the container option suits us well. Because we don't care about the data that we'll temporarily store, it can be deleted as soon as the container stops.

The next steps now could be writing the `Dockerfile` for the database container and then creating the Docker network plumbing to connect the ElixirDrip and database containers. While this approach works, there's a tool called Docker Compose that exists to help in this kind of situation.

Similarly to what we did for the ElixirDrip Docker image, we will now create the recipe that states how to run and connect multiple containers. The `docker-compose` tool will then process this recipe, a normal YAML file, and spin up the containers and all the other declared Docker resources.

 By default, the `docker-compose` input file is called `docker-compose.yml`. We'll call ours `docker-compose.dev.yml` because we'll have more than one `docker-compose` file (the other one will be responsible for running the application test suite and creating the application release).

Let's start by analyzing how `docker-compose.dev.yml` starts the `ElixirDrip` application:

```
$ cat docker-compose.dev.yml
version: '2.1'
services:
  app:
    image: elixir_drip:dev
    build:
      context: .
      dockerfile: Dockerfile.dev
    env_file: ./env/dev.env
    environment:
      SECRET_KEY_BASE:
      GOOGLE_STORAGE_CREDENTIALS:
    ports:
      - 4000:4000
    command: sh /opt/app/elixir_drip/script/start.sh
    depends_on:
```

```
    postgres:
      condition: service_healthy
  networks:
    - default
  volumes:
    - .:/opt/app/elixir_drip
# ...
```

In the previous snippet, we are declaring one `service` named `app`, which will use an image built from the `Dockerfile.dev` file (this image will be tagged as `elixir_drip:dev`). Besides the environment variables set in the `Dockerfile`, it will also set new variables present in the `env/dev.env` file (each line of this file has the `<name>=<value>` format).

We are also setting the `SECRET_KEY_BASE` and `GOOGLE_STORAGE_CREDENTIALS` environment variables in the `environment` section, without defining any values for those. Because this is sensitive information, we don't store them in the `env/dev.env` file. Since we haven't set a value for these variables, when we start the containers, `docker-compose` will look for those two environment variables in the host machine environment and set their values inside the container.

Then, we bind the host port 4000 to the same container port, and we override the initial command set in `Dockerfile.dev` by running the `script/start.sh` shell script. In the `depends_on` section, we state that the `app` service depends on the `postgres` service running in a *healthy* state (we'll define what *healthy* means in a second) and that it should join a network named `default`.

We wrap up the `app` service definition by mounting a volume, meaning that every change in the current directory (that is, `.`, the umbrella project root) will be reflected in the `/opt/app/elixir_drip` folder inside the container (and vice versa).

As we saw, the `app` service depends on the `postgres` service, but we haven't defined it yet. Let's fix this:

```
$ cat docker-compose.dev.yml
version: '2.1'
services:
  app:
    # ...
  postgres:
    environment:
      POSTGRES_USER: postgres
      POSTGRES_PASSWORD: "123456"
      PSQL_TRUST_LOCALNET: 'true'
      ENCODING: UTF8
```

```
image: postgres:9.6
healthcheck:
  test: ["CMD", "pg_isready", "-d", "postgres", "-U", "postgres"]
  interval: 10s
  timeout: 3s
  retries: 10
ports:
  - 5000:5432
networks:
  - default
```

This `postgres` service is simpler, in the sense that it doesn't have a `Dockerfile` or its own `env_file`. We declare its environment variables, the image that should be used to spin up the container, and we then define how the health check should be performed. In this case, if the `pg_isready -d postgres -U postgres` shell command returns successfully, Docker Compose deems the `postgres` service healthy and consequently starts the `app` service. We then map the ports as we did previously and we make sure the `postgres` service joins the same `default` network.

As you can see here, when the `app` service starts, the `script/start.sh` shell script fetches all the Mix dependencies, creates and migrates the database, and then starts the Phoenix server:

```
$ cat script/start.sh
mix deps.get
mix ecto.create && mix ecto.migrate
mix phx.server
```

Before running the compose file for the first time, we just need to set the secret environment variables in the current shell. Since we're in development, we can simply use the fake test values with `export $(cat secrets/credentials.test.env | xargs)`.

We are now able to run the `docker-compose.dev.yml` compose file with `docker-compose -f docker-compose.dev.yml up`. If you're running it for the first time, you will see Docker building the `Dockerfile.dev` image, fetching the `postgres:9.6` image, starting the `postgres` service, and then starting the `app` service.

Pass the -d option when you start all the containers with docker-compose (that is, docker-compose -f docker-compose.dev.yml up -d) to start them in *detached* mode, meaning that they won't grab the current STDOUT shell, and will continue in the background. If you still want to see the logs for all the containers started by the docker-compose.dev.yml file, run docker-compose -f docker-compose.dev.yml logs -ft, where the -f option indicates that we want to follow the log output of all the containers, and the -t option indicates that we want to see the timestamp of each log message.

We can also see both containers running with docker ps (both container names have the umbrella_ prefix because of the umbrella project folder name):

```
$ docker ps
CONTAINER ID IMAGE COMMAND CREATED STATUS PORTS NAMES
a1935721c401 elixir_drip:dev "sh /opt/app/elixir_..." 8 minutes ago Up 5
minutes 0.0.0.0:4000->4000/tcp umbrella_app_1
a895dda2e1cd postgres:9.6 "docker-entrypoint.s..." 8 minutes ago Up 5 minutes
(healthy) 0.0.0.0:5000->5432/tcp umbrella_postgres_1
```

You should now be able to reach the ElixirDrip application running inside the container from the host machine:

```
$ curl http://localhost:4000
<!DOCTYPE html>
<html lang="en">
  <head>
    <meta charset="utf-8">
  # ...
```

If you want to run a shell inside the umbrella_app_1 container, it is just a matter of doing docker exec -it umbrella_app_1 sh. We need both the -i and -t options to be able to interact with the shell process running inside the container.

In the following code snippet, we can see all the processes running inside the container. The start script is the PID 1 process, which spawned other processes that are running our application on top of the Erlang VM:

```
$ docker exec -i -t umbrella_app_1 sh

/opt/app/elixir_drip> ps aux
PID USER TIME COMMAND
    1 root 0:00 sh /opt/app/elixir_drip/script/start.sh
  152 root 0:02 /usr/local/lib/erlang/erts-9.3.1/bin/beam.smp -- -root
/usr/local/lib/erlang -progname erl -- -home /root -- -pa
```

```
173 root 0:00 erl_child_setup 1048576
197 root 0:00 inet_gethost 4
198 root 0:00 inet_gethost 4
199 root 0:00 sh
204 root 0:00 ps aux
```

Because the application is already running and listening to port 4000, we aren't able to start our application again and attach an IEx shell to it (that is, `iex -S mix phx.server`).

> If you want to force the build of the images present in the `docker-compose.yml` file, while starting your containers with `docker-compose up`, pass the `--build` option, as in `docker-compose -f docker-compose.dev.yml up --build -d`.

To overcome this, you can temporarily replace the `mix phx.server` line in the `start.sh` script with `tail -f /dev/null` and start the containers again in the same way. Since `tail -f /dev/null` will never end, it will keep the `app` service container running indefinitely. When you run a shell again inside the container, this is what you'll find:

```
$ docker exec -i -t umbrella_app_1 sh

/opt/app/elixir_drip> ps aux
PID USER TIME COMMAND
    1 root 0:00 sh /opt/app/elixir_drip/script/start.sh
  153 root 0:00 tail -f /dev/null
  154 root 0:00 sh
  160 root 0:00 ps aux
```

Since no application is running, we are now able to *manually* start the application with `iex -S mix phx.server` or simply `mix phx.server`, if we don't need an IEx shell.

> If you don't want to change the `start.sh` script, you can instead override the command set in the `docker-compose.dev.yml` file by running the `app` service with `docker-compose -f docker-compose.dev.yml run -d app tail -f /dev/null`. Because we don't run the `start.sh` script, we'll still need to run the `mix deps.get` and `mix ecto.create && mix ecto.migrate` commands inside a container shell before being able to run the application.

We now have a containerized development environment, which we can easily spin up and tinker with. Our deployment will also rely heavily on containers, so in the next section, we'll learn how our solution will change to accommodate the deployment requirements.

Composing the deployment containers

Our goal here is to have an automated way to run the project test suite, and if everything goes well, to build a new image that only contains the release and push it to the production environment.

For this, we'll use a specific compose file, `docker-compose.test.yml`, which performs two steps: first, it spins up the `release` service that builds the release, runs the tests, and tags the image as `release_prepared:latest`. Then, it spins up the `app` service that creates the final image by copying the release from the previous image:

```
$ cat umbrella/docker-compose.test.yml
version: '2.3'
services:
  app:
    # ...
  release:
    image: release_prepared:latest
    build:
      context: .
      dockerfile: Dockerfile
    env_file:
      - ./env/test.env
    working_dir: /opt/app/elixir_drip
    command: ["/bin/sh", "script/test.sh"]
    ports:
      - 4000:4000
    depends_on:
      postgres:
        condition: service_healthy
  postgres:
    # ...
```

As you can see in the following code, the `Dockerfile` used by the Compose `release` service does the bulk of the work needed for the release. It starts by fetching the dependencies, compiling the application and the Phoenix assets, and then building the release. In the end, it copies `elixir_drip.tar.gz` to the `/tmp/elixir_drip` folder.

```
$ cat Dockerfile
FROM elixir:1.6.4-alpine

# Setting the needed environment variables
ENV APP_PATH /opt/app
ENV APP_NAME elixir_drip
ENV APP_VERSION 0.0.8
ENV HTTP_PORT 4000
ENV HTTPS_PORT 4040
ENV MIX_ENV prod

# Installing the dependencies
RUN apk add --no-cache build-base git nodejs nodejs-npm
RUN mix archive.install
https://github.com/phoenixframework/archives/raw/master/phx_new.ez --force
RUN mix local.hex --force && mix local.rebar --force

# Copying the host current folder to the container
COPY . $APP_PATH/$APP_NAME
WORKDIR $APP_PATH/$APP_NAME

# Compiling the project and the Phoenix static assets
RUN MIX_ENV=$MIX_ENV mix do clean, deps.get, compile
RUN cd apps/elixir_drip_web/assets \
    && npm install \
    && ./node_modules/brunch/bin/brunch b -p

# Building the release
RUN cd $APP_PATH/$APP_NAME \
    && MIX_ENV=$MIX_ENV mix phx.digest \
    && MIX_ENV=$MIX_ENV mix release --env=$MIX_ENV

# Setting up the release to be copied
RUN mkdir -p /tmp/$APP_NAME
RUN cp
$APP_PATH/$APP_NAME/_build/$MIX_ENV/rel/$APP_NAME/releases/$APP_VERSION/$AP
P_NAME.tar.gz /tmp/$APP_NAME

WORKDIR /tmp/$APP_NAME
RUN tar -xzf $APP_NAME.tar.gz
RUN rm -rf $APP_NAME.tar.gz
```

```
RUN echo "Release in place, ready to be copied."

EXPOSE $HTTP_PORT $HTTPS_PORT

CMD ["sh", "-c", "bin/$APP_NAME foreground"]
```

Compared to the previous `release` service, the `app` service is slightly simpler. This service builds an image based on the `Dockerfile.deploy` recipe and tags it as `gcr.io/${PROJECT_ID}/elixir-drip-prod:${BUILD_TAG}`. Because it depends on the `release` service, the `app` service will only start when `release` has already started.

In the next section, we'll learn the reason behind the image tag we're setting, but for now, just notice how this tag needs the `PROJECT_ID` and `BUILD_TAG` environment variables to be set before the Compose `docker-compose.test.yml` file starts:

```
$ cat umbrella/docker-compose.test.yml
version: '2.3'
services:
  app:
    image: gcr.io/${PROJECT_ID}/elixir-drip-prod:${BUILD_TAG}
    build:
      context: .
      dockerfile: Dockerfile.deploy
    depends_on:
        - release
    command: ["echo", "Release image ready to be deployed."]
  release:
    # ...
  postgres:
    # ...
```

The main purpose of the `Dockerfile.deploy` file is to copy the release folder from the `release_prepared:latest` image built by the Compose `release` service to the image that will be deployed to production. To achieve this, the source image is aliased as `builder` in the first `FROM` command, and then is used as the source of the `COPY` command with the `--from` option:

```
$ cat Dockerfile.deploy
FROM release_prepared:latest as builder

RUN ls -la /tmp/elixir_drip \
  && echo "Found the release, will copy it to the final image."

FROM elixir:1.6.4-alpine as runner
  # ...
ENV APP_PATH /opt/app
```

```
ENV APP_NAME elixir_drip
ENV HTTP_PORT 4000
ENV HTTPS_PORT 4040
ENV REPLACE_OS_VARS true

RUN apk add --no-cache bash

COPY --from=builder /tmp/$APP_NAME $APP_PATH/$APP_NAME

WORKDIR $APP_PATH/$APP_NAME

EXPOSE $HTTP_PORT $HTTPS_PORT

CMD ["sh", "-c", "bin/$APP_NAME foreground"]
```

With this approach, we're able to deploy an image that contains just the release and the dependencies that it needs to run (namely, `bash`), reducing the size of the deployed image from 575 MB to 122 MB:

```
$ docker images
REPOSITORY TAG IMAGE ID CREATED SIZE
gcr.io/<project_id>/elixir-drip-prod v0.0.8 c8b38f6bbdb2 7 hours ago 122MB
release_prepared latest 7f7043ed9ac8 7 hours ago 575MB
  # ...
```

Besides the smaller size, the deployed image doesn't include any source code, hence reducing the impact a malicious user could have if they gained access to one of the production servers.

If we now run `PROJECT_ID=<project_id> BUILD_TAG=<build_tag> docker-compose -f docker-compose.test.yml run app`, we will trigger the process that we've just analyzed, and in the end, an image tagged `<project_id>:<build_tag>` will exist, ready to be deployed.

In the next section, we'll learn how the production environment of ElixirDrip works and which steps are needed to get the application up and running on the cloud.

Deploying to Kubernetes

We will now deploy the ElixirDrip application to the **Google Kubernetes Engine** (**GKE**), a hosted **Kubernetes** (**K8s**) solution provided by Google. Kubernetes is an open source tool that lets us configure, orchestrate, and scale a great number of containers by relying on configuration files and providing a unified way of automating every operation.

Google provides a free trial period of 12 months with a $300 credit to try the services that compose Google Cloud Platform, including the Google Kubernetes Engine (check out `https://cloud.google.com/free/`). This allows our readers to try a hosted K8s solution without any cost. As an alternative, all the examples in this and the following sections also work with `minikube`, a tool that lets you run a K8s cluster on your local machine (check out `https://kubernetes.io/docs/getting-started-guides/minikube/`).

Before diving into the deployment tasks, we need to clarify some of the concepts and nomenclature that Kubernetes uses. A **cluster** groups one or more **nodes**, and each of these nodes provides computational resources, such as CPU, memory, and disk. If you want to separate the resources of a cluster, you can create **namespaces** that work like virtual clusters.

Because these computational resources are clustered, when you deploy something, you just say how much CPU and memory it needs, and Kubernetes makes sure the application has everything it needs to work. Notice that you don't specify which node runs the application; you just specify the application requirements and Kubernetes handles the load distribution for you. If a node suddenly breaks, the load will be transparently shifted to other available nodes.

In the previous sections, we have containerized our application, but we won't directly deploy containers to Kubernetes. Instead, K8s has the concept of **pods**, which is nothing more than a group of one or more containers. Because of the way pods are created, containers in the same pod share the same IP address and port space.

To deploy our ElixirDrip application, we will appropriately use a **deployment** controller, which describes how to create the pods that will serve our application. After deploying a pod, it will happily run as long as its resource requirements are fulfilled.

By default, no pod is accessible from outside the cluster, so we will have to expose it somehow if we want to serve client requests with it. At any given moment, pods may be started to face a surge in requests, so how do we route requests to pods that are transient in nature? This is achieved by creating a **service** that maps a port accessible from the outside to a specific group of pods, identified by their labels, not by their IP.

It's also important to note that all these Kubernetes objects, such as pods, services, and deployments, are all represented using similar YAML configuration files. This is a crucial aspect, because it effectively enables you to have the infrastructure stored as code in your code repository. Also, all your interactions with Kubernetes clusters, including applying infrastructure changes, can be done with the kubectl tool. Using a single, common interface for everything Kubernetes-related significantly simplifies the user experience.

After creating your account on Google Cloud Platform, install and run the Google Cloud SDK tool (gcloud init) to log in and create a new project. You can now create a cluster with gcloud container clusters create <cluster-name>.

If you don't have kubectl installed, install it with gcloud (that is, gcloud components install kubectl) and it will be automatically configured to access the cluster. If you already have kubectl installed, run gcloud container clusters get-credentials <cluster-name> to update your kubectl configuration with the cluster credentials.

At this point, you should have a Google Cloud Platform project created and a Kubernetes cluster up and running:

```
$ gcloud projects list
PROJECT_ID NAME PROJECT_NUMBER
intense-talent-188323 My First Project 5338223468

$ gcloud container clusters list
NAME LOCATION MASTER_VERSION MASTER_IP MACHINE_TYPE NODE_VERSION NUM_NODES
STATUS
elixir-drip-prod-cluster europe-west1-b 1.8.8-gke.0 35.205.44.153 n1-
standard-1 1.8.8-gke.0 1 RUNNING

$ kubectl cluster-info
Kubernetes master is running at https://35.205.44.153
GLBCDefaultBackend is running at
https://35.205.44.153/api/v1/namespaces/kube-system/services/default-http-b
ackend:http/proxy
Heapster is running at
https://35.205.44.153/api/v1/namespaces/kube-system/services/heapster/proxy
KubeDNS is running at
https://35.205.44.153/api/v1/namespaces/kube-system/services/kube-dns:dns/p
roxy
kubernetes-dashboard is running at
https://35.205.44.153/api/v1/namespaces/kube-system/services/https:kubernet
es-dashboard:/proxy
```

Most of the Google Cloud Platform services that we'll use need to be associated with a billing account. Go to `https://console.cloud.google.com`, choose `Billing` on the left-hand side, and then `New billing account` to create and enable a billing account. After creating the account, use its billing account ID to link the current project to it:

```
$ gcloud beta billing projects link intense-talent-188323 --billing-
account=012345-6789AB-CDEF01
billingAccountName: billingAccounts/012345-6789AB-CDEF01
billingEnabled: true
name: projects/intense-talent-188323/billingInfo
projectId: intense-talent-188323

$ gcloud beta billing projects list --billing-account=012345-6789AB-CDEF01
PROJECT_ID BILLING_ACCOUNT_ID BILLING_ENABLED
intense-talent-188323 012345-6789AB-CDEF01 True
```

We will also need to activate the following Google APIs on our project: the Kubernetes Engine API (`container.googleapis.com`), the Container Registry API (`containerregistry.googleapis.com`), Cloud SQL (`sql-component.googleapis.com`), the Cloud SQL API (`sqladmin.googleapis.com`), Cloud Storage (`storage-component.googleapis.com`), and the Cloud Storage JSON API (`storage-api.googleapis.com`). To activate these services, run the `gcloud services enable <API>` command for each API URL, as we do here:

```
$ gcloud services enable container.googleapis.com
Waiting for async operation operations/tmo-acf.b1897824-... to complete...
Operation finished successfully.
```

Because of the credit you have, you won't be billed during the free trial. Nonetheless, remember to stop all the Google Cloud Platform services and delete all the Kubernetes objects after you've finished, to avoid spending all the free credit with just idle computation. A quick way to stop everything is to close the billing account associated with the project.

Let's now configure the database that will be used by our application when deployed on the cloud.

Configuring the cloud database

In the local development environment, we were spinning up a Postgres database every time we started our application with `docker-compose up`. This won't be our approach when we deploy the application to the Kubernetes cluster because we'll use the Cloud SQL database solution provided by Google.

Use `gcloud sql` to create a new database instance (it will take a few minutes):

```
$ gcloud sql instances create elixir-drip-production --database-
version=POSTGRES_9_6
# ...

$ gcloud sql instances list
NAME DATABASE_VERSION LOCATION TIER ADDRESS STATUS
elixir-drip-production POSTGRES_9_6 europe-west1-b db-custom-1-3840
35.195.47.137 RUNNABLE
```

Let's now create the `postgres` database user that our application will use:

```
$ gcloud sql users create postgres % --instance=elixir-drip-production --
password=a-really-c0mplex-password
Creating Cloud SQL user...done.
Created user [exampleuser].

$ gcloud sql users list --instance=elixir-drip-production
NAME HOST
postgres
```

Because of the way Cloud SQL works, no application should be able to directly connect to the database. Instead, the application should connect itself to a Cloud SQL proxy, which will then securely handle the database connection. To cater for this, we will deploy pods with two containers, one with our application and the other running the SQL proxy.

Every time an external application needs to access Google Cloud resources, we need to create a *service account* for it. We can then restrict the external application access by defining the roles assigned to the service account. In this case, the service account will need to access the database, so we will assign it `roles/cloudsql.client`:

```
$ gcloud iam service-accounts create elixirdrip-prod-sql-client --display-
name "ElixirDrip Prod SQL client"
Created service account [elixirdrip-prod-sql-client].

$ gcloud projects add-iam-policy-binding intense-talent-188323 --member
serviceAccount:elixirdrip-prod-sql-client@intense-
talent-188323.iam.gserviceaccount.com --role roles/cloudsql.client
```

```
bindings:
  # ...
- members:
  - serviceAccount:elixirdrip-prod-sql-client@intense-
talent-188323.iam.gserviceaccount.com
  role: roles/cloudsql.client
  # ...

$ gcloud iam service-accounts keys create secrets/elixirdrip-prod-sql.json
--iam-account elixirdrip-prod-sql-client@intense-
talent-188323.iam.gserviceaccount.com
created key [6fbdb...] of type [json] as [secrets/elixirdrip-prod-sql.json]
for [elixirdrip-prod-sql-client@intense-
talent-188323.iam.gserviceaccount.com]
$ cat secrets/elixirdrip-prod-sql.json
{
  "type": "service_account",
  "project_id": "intense-talent-188323",
  "private_key_id": "6fbdb...",
  "private_key": "abcdef..."
  # ...
}
```

In the previous snippet, we've created the `elixirdrip-prod-sql-client` service account, assigned it the `cloudsql.client` role, and then created a service account key that will be used by the Cloud SQL proxy to connect to the database.

> The generated key grants anyone the power to update the database, so we have to store it securely. Do not store the key with the rest of your application code!

When our application pod is deployed, the Cloud SQL proxy container will need to use this key to connect to the database. To enable pods to securely access sensitive information such as this, Kubernetes provides a type of object called a **secret**.

Secrets are also isolated per namespace, so let's create the `production` namespace before creating all the secrets.

Creating a namespace

Since we're using a single cluster, we will create two namespaces, staging and production, to isolate the resources dedicated to each environment. In a real scenario, you would instead have two separate clusters, to mitigate the risk of a staging hiccup affecting the production application:

```
$ kubectl create namespace production
namespace "production" created

$ kubectl create namespace staging
namespace "staging" created

$ kubectl get namespaces
NAME STATUS AGE
default Active 31d
kube-public Active 31d
kube-system Active 31d
production Active 45s
staging Active 52s
```

This time, we only used the kubectl command-line syntax to create the namespaces, because the only thing we had to configure was the namespace name. Nonetheless, we could have done the same thing by running kubectl apply -f deploy/elixir-drip-namespace-prod.yml. As you can see here, the equivalent YAML configuration file simply declares a resource of the Namespace kind with a production name:

```
$ cat deploy/elixir-drip-namespace-prod.yml
apiVersion: v1
kind: Namespace
metadata:
  name: production
```

In the next section, we'll create all the application secrets. Notice how we're always passing the -n production option to kubectl, hence creating every secret in the production namespace.

Creating secrets

We already have the Cloud SQL proxy credentials in `secrets/elixirdrip-prod-sql.json`, so we now just have to create a secret based on this file. In the following snippet, we're creating a `cloudsql-proxy-credentials` secret that contains a file-based value named `credentials.json`, hence the `--from-file` option:

```
$ kubectl -n production create secret generic cloudsql-proxy-credentials --
from-file=credentials.json=secrets/elixirdrip-prod-sql.json
secret "cloudsql-proxy-credentials" created
```

We will also need to pass the database user credentials to the application container. The following `cloudsql-postgres-credentials` secret has two literal values, named `username` and `password`:

```
$ kubectl -n production create secret generic cloudsql-postgres-credentials
--from-literal=username=postgres --from-literal=password=a-really-cOmplex-
password
secret "cloudsql-postgres-credentials" created
```

We will set the Erlang cookie value, used to connect the Erlang nodes running the application, as the `erlang-cookie` secret, and the key, used by Phoenix to encrypt and sign data (such as cookies and token), as the `secret-key-base` secret:

```
$ kubectl -n production create secret generic erlang-cookie --from-
literal=cookie=a-really-long-big-and-difficult-to-memorize-string
secret "erlang-cookie" created
```

```
$ kubectl -n production create secret generic secret-key-base --from-
literal=value=complex-random-and-high-entropy-char-string
secret "secret-key-base" created
```

We are using the Google Cloud Storage service to store the uploaded files, so our application needs a service account associated with the `roles/storage.objectAdmin` role. Similar to what we did for the SQL proxy service account, to configure the Cloud Storage service account, we need to create the service account, assign it to the correct role, and then generate and download the key file.

 Creating a Cloud Storage service account is similar to what we did for the SQL proxy service account, so we'll leave it as an exercise for the reader.

This time, however, the Elixir library we're using expects the credentials to be available as a Base64-encoded string, so we will convert the `secrets/elixirdrip-prod-storage.json` file to Base64 before creating the `google-storage-credentials` secret:

```
$ export STORAGE_CREDENTIALS=$(cat secrets/elixirdrip-prod-storage.json |
base64 -w 0)

$ kubectl -n production create secret generic google-storage-credentials --
from-literal=base64-credentials=$STORAGE_CREDENTIALS
secret "google-storage-credentials" created
```

With every secret created, we can now create the remaining Kubernetes objects needed to have the ElixirDrip application up and running in Kubernetes.

Publishing the production image

Before we deploy our first pod, we need to build the Docker production image and push it to the Docker registry. Our pod definition will then point to the pushed image.

We first need to configure `docker` to use `gcloud` when pushing images to `gcr.io`, Google's private Docker registry. To add `gcloud` as a Docker credentials helper, simply run `gcloud auth configure-docker` and follow the instructions.

To build the image, we will run the `docker-compose.test.yml` compose file and in the end, we'll have the `gcr.io/intense-talent-188323/elixir-drip-prod:manual_build` image ready to be published:

```
$ PROJECT_ID=intense-talent-188323 BUILD_TAG=manual_build docker-compose -f
docker-compose.test.yml run app
Building release
Step 1/30 : FROM elixir:1.6.4-alpine
 ---> 707fdc843c25
 # ...
Successfully built ca929a3cf856
Successfully tagged gcr.io/intense-talent-188323/elixir-drip-
prod:manual_build
Release image ready to be deployed.

$ docker images
REPOSITORY TAG IMAGE ID CREATED SIZE
gcr.io/intense-talent-188323/elixir-drip-prod manual_build ca929a3cf856 12
minutes ago 122MB
release_prepared latest e3094176e0a7 12 minutes ago 493MB
 # ...
```

To push the image, we'll use the standard Docker `push` command, which will use `gcloud` as a credentials helper, given that the image name starts with `gcr.io`:

```
$ docker push gcr.io/intense-talent-188323/elixir-drip-prod:manual_build
The push refers to repository [gcr.io/intense-talent-188323/elixir-drip-
prod]
3e0c1e866df3: Pushed
768e7e3dd3aa: Pushed
8d66bb10e0bf: Pushed
121882a60274: Pushed
cd7100a72410: Layer already exists
manual_build: digest:
sha256:18d5b7b44c7ac87b347af3022069a959bef289320f28037f7b27b16dd07f90e9
size: 1373
```

And we can now see the image in the Cloud Container registry, patiently waiting to be published:

```
$ gcloud container images list
NAME
gcr.io/intense-talent-188323/elixir-drip-prod

$ gcloud container images list-tags gcr.io/intense-talent-188323/elixir-
drip-prod
DIGEST TAGS TIMESTAMP
18d5b7b44c7a manual_build 2018-06-13T17:02:14
   # ...
```

After all the configuration and build steps, we'll finally deploy our first pod!

Deploying your first pod

To deploy our first pod, we will define a Kubernetes `Deployment` configuration file. This file will declare the deployment strategy (`spec.strategy`), how many pods we want to have at any given moment (`spec.replicas`), the volumes that will be provided to the pod (`spec.template.spec.volumes`), and the recipe that should be used to spin up the pod containers (`spec.template.spec.containers`):

```
$ cat deploy/elixir-drip-deployment-prod.yml
apiVersion: extensions/v1beta1
kind: Deployment
metadata:
  name: elixir-drip
  namespace: production
  labels:
```

```
      app: elixir-drip
      env: production
  spec:
    replicas: 3
    strategy:
      type: RollingUpdate
      rollingUpdate:
        maxUnavailable: 1
        maxSurge: 2
    template:
      metadata:
        labels:
          app: elixir-drip
          env: production
      spec:
        volumes:
          - name: cloudsql-proxy-creds-volume
            secret:
              secretName: cloudsql-proxy-credentials
        containers:
          # ...
```

Besides defining two labels (app and env), we name the deployment elixir-drip and set the namespace to production. We then specify that we want three pods running, and whenever there is an update, we allow, at most, one pod to be unavailable, and, at most, five pods running at the same time (one pod already terminated and three new pods running).

In the spec.template section, we declare the pod recipe: each pod will have the same app and env labels, and will have a volume based on the previously created cloudsql-proxy-credentials secret. In the spec.template.spec.containers section, we define the pod containers:

```
$ cat deploy/elixir-drip-deployment-prod.yml
apiVersion: extensions/v1beta1
kind: Deployment
  # ...
  template:
    # ...
    spec:
      # ...
      containers:
        - image: gcr.io/intense-talent-188323/elixir-drip-
          prod:manual_build
          name: elixir-drip-prod
          livenessProbe:
            httpGet:
```

```
          path: /health
          port: 4000
        initialDelaySeconds: 60
        timeoutSeconds: 15
      readinessProbe:
        httpGet:
          path: /health
          port: 4000
        initialDelaySeconds: 60
        timeoutSeconds: 15
      ports:
        - name: http
          containerPort: 4000
      env:
        # ...
```

The first container, `elixir-drip-prod`, will be based on the image we've just built and pushed to the Docker registry. It defines two probes, a *liveness* one and a *readiness* one, and exposes port 4000, before defining all the environment variables needed to spin up the application. As the name suggests, the readiness probe will be used by Kubernetes to detect whether a container is ready to accept requests right after it's deployed, whereas the liveness probe is used to decide whether Kubernetes should restart the container or not.

Here you can find some of the environment variables we're setting inside the container. Some environment variables, such as `DB_HOST` and `DB_PORT`, don't contain sensitive information, so we pass their value in clear text. Others, such as `GOOGLE_STORAGE_CREDENTIALS` and `DB_PASS`, fetch their values from the secrets we previously created.

```
$ cat deploy/elixir-drip-deployment-prod.yml
apiVersion: extensions/v1beta1
kind: Deployment
  # ...
  template:
    # ...
    spec:
      # ...
      containers:
        - image: gcr.io/intense-talent-188323/elixir-drip-
          prod:manual_build
          name: elixir-drip-prod
          env:
            # ...
            - name: DB_HOST
              value: 127.0.0.1
            - name: DB_PORT
              value: "5432"
```

```
            - name: GOOGLE_STORAGE_CREDENTIALS
              valueFrom:
                secretKeyRef:
                  name: google-storage-credentials
                  key: base64-credentials
            - name: DB_USER
              valueFrom:
                secretKeyRef:
                  name: cloudsql-postgres-credentials
                  key: username
            - name: DB_PASS
              valueFrom:
                secretKeyRef:
                  name: cloudsql-postgres-credentials
                  key: password
```

Remember when we said that containers in the same pod share the same IP and port space? That's the reason why we tell the ElixirDrip application running in the `elixir-drip-prod` container to connect itself to the database running *locally* on port 5432, despite this being the Cloud SQL proxy running in another container inside the same pod:

```
$ cat deploy/elixir-drip-deployment-prod.yml
apiVersion: extensions/v1beta1
kind: Deployment
  # ...
  template:
    # ...
    spec:
      volumes:
        - name: cloudsql-proxy-creds-volume
          secret:
            secretName: cloudsql-proxy-credentials
      containers:
        - image: gcr.io/cloudsql-docker/gce-proxy:1.11
          name: cloudsql-proxy
          command: ["/cloud_sql_proxy",
                    "-instances=intense-talent-188323:europe-
                      west1:elixir-drip-production=tcp:5432",
                    "-credential_file=/secrets/cloudsql/
                      credentials.json"]
          ports:
            - name: postgres
              containerPort: 5432
          volumeMounts:
            - name: cloudsql-proxy-creds-volume
              mountPath: /secrets/cloudsql
              readOnly: true
```

The Cloud SQL proxy container uses a Docker image provided by Google and starts the proxy by passing it to the `/secrets/cloudsql/credentials.json` credentials file. This file exists because we mount the `cloudsql-proxy-creds-volume` inside the container in the `/secrets/cloudsql` path, and we said the `cloudsql-proxy-credentials` secret had a single `credentials.json` file when we created the secret.

Before we are able to deploy the pod, we need to run the database migrations of our project in the production database. If we don't run them, the ElixirDrip application will fail when the container starts because it expects to find a database with specific tables and relations.

To overcome this, we will define and later create a Kubernetes job called `elixir-drip-migrations`, responsible for running the migrations.

Creating a Kubernetes job

Our `elixir-drip-migrations` job configuration file will be really similar to the previous `Deployment` configuration, but instead of running the container default command (that is, `sh -c bin/$APP_NAME foreground` set on `Dockerfile.deploy`), we override the command that will be run when the application container starts (that is, `sh -c bin/$APP_NAME migrate_up`). We also tell Kubernetes to never restart jobs like these, and that it should terminate the job after 300 seconds, no matter what:

```
$ cat deploy/elixir-drip-migrations-prod.yml
apiVersion: batch/v1
kind: Job
metadata:
  generateName: elixir-drip-migrations
  namespace: production
  labels:
    env: production
spec:
  activeDeadlineSeconds: 300
  template:
    metadata:
      labels:
        env: production
    spec:
      restartPolicy: Never
      volumes:
        # ...
      containers:
        - image: gcr.io/intense-talent-188323/elixir-drip-
          prod:manual_build
          name: elixir-drip-migrations
```

```
command: ["sh", "-c", "bin/$APP_NAME migrate_up"]
env:
  # ...
```

Normally, jobs end whenever Kubernetes detects the respective pod containers have ended. After running the migrations for us, the elixir-drip-migrations container will return an exit code (hopefully 0), hence terminating as expected. The problem here lies in the Cloud SQL proxy container, which will run indefinitely, even after the other container ends. Because of this, we're relying on activeDeadlineSeconds to terminate the pod.

Because we're using the metadata.generateName field, Kubernetes will append a random suffix to the elixir-drip-migrations name of the job. With this approach, we're sure there will never be two jobs with the same name.

The rest of the configuration file is exactly the same, since we're running the exact same release to run the database migrations (recall that the migrate_up task is the custom release task we've previously implemented). Let's run the migrations:

```
$ kubectl -n production create -f deploy/elixir-drip-migrations-prod.yml
job.batch "elixir-drip-migrationskv6tm" created

$ kubectl -n production get jobs
NAME DESIRED SUCCESSFUL AGE
elixir-drip-migrationskv6tm 1 0 4s

$ kubectl -n production get pods
NAME READY STATUS RESTARTS AGE
elixir-drip-646fb5cc94-7d2fs 2/2 Running 0 1d
elixir-drip-646fb5cc94-dmt2c 2/2 Running 0 1d
elixir-drip-646fb5cc94-pwgsq 2/2 Running 0 1d
elixir-drip-migrationskv6tm-lzx2n 2/2 Running 0 7s
```

And after a while, we see that one of the pod containers completed:

```
$ kubectl -n production get pods
NAME READY STATUS RESTARTS AGE
  # ...
elixir-drip-migrationskv6tm-lzx2n 1/2 Completed 0 56s

$ kubectl -n production logs elixir-drip-migrationskv6tm-lzx2n elixir-drip-
migrations
Loading ElixirDrip umbrella app...
Starting dependencies...
Starting ElixirDrip repo...
Running migrations for ElixirDrip...
Success!
18:08:46.048 [info] Already up
```

We're now finally able to deploy our pod to production:

```
$ kubectl -n production apply -f deploy/elixir-drip-deployment-prod.yml
deployment.extensions "elixir-drip" configured
$ kubectl -n production get pods
NAME READY STATUS RESTARTS AGE
elixir-drip-646fb5cc94-7d2fs 2/2 Terminating 0 1d
elixir-drip-646fb5cc94-dmt2c 2/2 Running 0 1d
elixir-drip-646fb5cc94-pwgsq 2/2 Running 0 1d
elixir-drip-68b7944c95-c4nhd 0/2 ContainerCreating 0 5s
elixir-drip-68b7944c95-ct6k7 0/2 ContainerCreating 0 5s
elixir-drip-68b7944c95-kqqcv 0/2 ContainerCreating 0 5s
```

Here, we're using the `kubectl` command because it updates a Kubernetes object with the same name if it already exists, and that's exactly what we want. After a bit, only the new pods are running:

```
$ kubectl -n production get pods
NAME READY STATUS RESTARTS AGE
elixir-drip-68b7944c95-c4nhd 2/2 Running 0 3m
elixir-drip-68b7944c95-ct6k7 2/2 Running 0 3m
elixir-drip-68b7944c95-kqqcv 2/2 Running 0 3m
```

To access our application, we just need to expose it to the world with the help of a Kubernetes service.

Exposing your pods to the world

In this section, we'll create a Kubernetes service, which will be responsible for exposing the pods we've just created. A service routes the requests to specific pods based on the label values of the `selector` section:

```
$ cat deploy/elixir-drip-loadbalancer-prod.yml
apiVersion: v1
kind: Service
metadata:
  name: elixir-drip-loadbalancer
  namespace: production
    env: production
spec:
  type: LoadBalancer
  selector:
    app: elixir-drip
    env: production
```

```
ports:
  - port: 80
    targetPort: 4000
```

We are routing requests arriving through port 80 of the load-balancer to port 4000 of a pod with the `app=elixir-drip` and `env=production` labels. Creating a `LoadBalancer` service like ours exposes the service using a load balancer from the cloud provider. This means a TCP load balancer, outside of Kubernetes and with its own IP, will be running and routing the requests to our pods.

 When using a `LoadBalancer` service, Kubernetes will automatically create the objects needed to route the requests to the pods, namely `NodePort` and `ClusterIP`. How the load-balancer works depends on the cloud provider, but each deployed service will always have its own load balancer, hence relying on just load balancers may be costly. A better alternative is to use a Kubernetes `Ingress`, which is able to do SSL termination, HTTP routing, and so on, and can be shared between services. In this book, we will just use the `LoadBalancer` service.

If we now check the existing services, this is what we'll see (we're using the `--watch` option, hence `kubectl` will update its output whenever one of the objects is updated):

```
$ kubectl create -f deploy/elixir-drip-loadbalancer-prod.yml
service "elixir-drip-loadbalancer" created

$ kubectl -n production get service --watch
NAME TYPE CLUSTER-IP EXTERNAL-IP PORT(S) AGE
elixir-drip-loadbalancer LoadBalancer 10.43.254.164 <pending> 80:32153/TCP
9s
elixir-drip-loadbalancer LoadBalancer 10.43.254.164 35.205.152.228
80:32153/TCP 1m
```

In the beginning, the load balancer IP was pending (probably because it wasn't provisioned yet), but after a minute, we finally got an external IP. We can now reach our application from the outside as shown here:

```
$ curl http://35.205.152.228
<!DOCTYPE html>
<html lang="en">
  <head>
    <meta charset="utf-8">
    <meta http-equiv="X-UA-Compatible" content="IE=edge">
    <meta name="viewport" content="width=device-width, initial-scale=1">
    <meta name="description" content="">
    <meta name="author" content="">
```

```
<title>Welcome to ElixirDrip!!!</title>
<link rel="stylesheet" href="/css/app-ddf53b1....css?vsn=d">
</head>
# ...
```

We started this section with the application running in the local development environment, and concluded with it being live and running in a hosted Kubernetes solution, being served by three redundant pods.

 At this point, we have the Kubernetes `production` environment set up and hosting our ElixirDrip application. We should now do the exact same thing, but for the `staging` environment, so we can preview the features we want to release before actually releasing them. You can create the environment by creating a new Kubernetes `staging` namespace and going from there, or you can go the extra mile and create a new cluster from the get-go. Once more, a new cluster implies using more resources, so keep an eye on your Google Cloud free credit.

However, instead of interacting with Kubernetes every time, we want to have the application redeployed with every change, ensuring the most up-to-date version is always the one serving live requests. We'll achieve this with the help of Travis CI.

Continuous deployment with Travis CI

Instead of relying on the previous `kubectl` commands and Kubernetes configuration files to update our application every time, we want to automate this process. Doing it manually is tedious, error prone, and not deterministic.

To automate this process, we will use Travis CI (`https://travis-ci.org/`), a continuous-integration service that is free for open source projects. To use it, we need to have our source code living in a GitHub repository (`https://github.com/`) and give Travis CI access to our GitHub project. Whenever a new change reaches the code repository, Travis CI detects it and tries to build the project, according to a recipe file that also belongs to the project source code (`.travis.yml`).

After pushing your code to GitHub, add the Travis CI GitHub app in the code repository. You now need to sign in to Travis CI with your GitHub credentials and activate the Travis CI automatic builds for the repository. You can find more information at `https://docs.travis-ci.com/user/getting-started/`. Because we want to trigger a build whenever a commit reaches a specific branch, activate the *Build pushed branches* option in Travis CI.

In our case, we will ask Travis CI to build the release image (the project tests also run in this phase), run the Kubernetes migrations job, and then apply a new Kubernetes deployment configuration file using the release image that was just built.

We will now create a `.travis.yml` file in the project root directory, establishing the build steps that Travis CI will perform for us:

```
$ cat .travis.yml
sudo: required

services:
  - docker

env:
  global:
    - PROJECT_ID=intense-talent-188323

before_install:
  # update Docker and install Docker Compose
  # ...

script:
  - BUILD_TAG=$TRAVIS_COMMIT docker-compose -f docker-compose.test.yml run
app

before_deploy:
  # install gcloud and kubectl
  # ...

deploy:
  - provider: script
    script: bash deploy/travis_deploy.sh $TRAVIS_COMMIT production
    skip_cleanup: true
    on:
      branch: master

after_script:
  - BUILD_TAG=$TRAVIS_COMMIT docker-compose -f docker-compose.test.yml down
```

In the previous snippet, we are telling Travis to do different things based on the build phase it is in. In the `before_install` phase, it updates Docker and installs Docker Compose. Then, in the `script` phase, it spins up the `docker-compose.test.yml` compose file to build the image release. If the previous step succeeds, it installs the needed `gcloud` and `kubectl` tools in the `before_deploy` phase. It's in the `deploy` phase that Travis will run the `deploy/travis_deploy.sh` script that actually deploys the application to Kubernetes. The last `after_script` step stops and removes the containers that were started in the previous `script` phase.

> Because we're using the `sudo: required` option, Travis spins up an Ubuntu machine for the build process. The `before_install` and `before_deploy` phases were omitted for brevity, but you can find the full `.travis.yml` file in this book's code.

When Travis detects a new commit in the `master` Git branch, it will start a temporary virtual machine, fetch the specific code version from the GitHub repository, and start the previously described steps. In the `.travis.yml` file, we are setting the `PROJECT_ID` environment variable, but Travis also sets the `TRAVIS_COMMIT` variable (among others) for us, which we'll use to tag the release image.

Remember the `app` service in the `docker-compose.test.yml` compose file tagging the resulting Docker image as `gcr.io/${PROJECT_ID}/elixir-drip-prod:${BUILD_TAG}`? This is why we need to set the `PROJECT_ID` and `BUILD_TAG` environment variables before starting the compose file (we use the Git commit as the `BUILD_TAG` value).

Before we delve into the `deploy/travis_deploy.sh` script, we need to create a Google Cloud service account, which will be used by Travis CI to push the new release image and apply the Kubernetes migrations job and deployment configuration files:

```
$ gcloud iam service-accounts create travis-ci-k8s-deployment-prod --
display-name "Travis CI K8s Prod Account"
Created service account [travis-ci-k8s-deployment-prod].

$ gcloud projects add-iam-policy-binding intense-talent-188323 --member
serviceAccount:travis-ci-k8s-deployment-prod@intense-
talent-188323.iam.gserviceaccount.com --role roles/container.developer

$ gcloud projects add-iam-policy-binding intense-talent-188323 --member
serviceAccount:travis-ci-k8s-deployment-prod@intense-
talent-188323.iam.gserviceaccount.com --role
roles/cloudbuild.builds.builder
  # ...
```

```
$ gcloud iam service-accounts keys create secrets/travis-ci-k8s-prod.json -
-iam-account travis-ci-k8s-deployment-prod@intense-
talent-188323.iam.gserviceaccount.com
created key [ca400...] of type [json] as [secrets/travis-ci-k8s-prod.json]
for [travis-ci-k8s-deployment-prod@intense-
talent-188323.iam.gserviceaccount.com]
```

We assigned the `container.developer` and `cloudbuild.builds.builder` roles to this new `travis-ci-k8s-deployment-prod` service account and generated a secret key. We will now use the `travis` Ruby gem to encrypt the service account key. We first need to log in, and then it's just a matter of running `travis encrypt-file`:

```
$ travis login
We need your GitHub login to identify you.
This information will not be sent to Travis CI, only to api.github.com.
The password will not be displayed.
Try running with --github-token or --auto if you don't want to enter your
password anyway.
Username: <username>
Password for <username>: ************
Successfully logged in as <username>!

$ travis encrypt-file secrets/travis-ci-k8s-prod.json secrets/travis-ci-
k8s-prod.json.enc --pro
encrypting secrets/travis-ci-k8s-prod.json for elixirdrip/ElixirDrip
storing result as secrets/travis-ci-k8s-prod.json.enc
storing secure env variables for decryption

Please add the following to your build script (before_install stage in your
.travis.yml, for instance):

    openssl aes-256-cbc -K $encrypted_69f31b87e2af_key -iv
$encrypted_69f31b87e2af_iv -in secrets/travis-ci-k8s-prod.json.enc -out
secrets/travis-ci-k8s-prod.json -d

Pro Tip: You can add it automatically by running with --add.

Make sure to add secrets/travis-ci-k8s-prod.json.enc to the git repository.
Make sure not to add secrets/travis-ci-k8s-prod.json to the git repository.
Commit all changes to your .travis.yml.
```

We now just need to add the suggested `openssl` command as a `before_install` step to the `.travis.yml` file:

```
$ cat .travis.yml
  # ...
before_install:
  # ...
  - openssl aes-256-cbc -K $encrypted_69f31b87e2af_key -iv
$encrypted_69f31b87e2af_iv -in secrets/travis-ci-k8s-prod.json.enc -out
secrets/travis-ci-k8s-prod.json -d
```

When Travis runs the `before_install` phase, it will decrypt the `secrets/travis-ci-k8s-prod.json.enc` present in the code repository and temporarily create a `secrets/travis-ci-k8s-prod.json` key for the deployment.

We need to set the `skip_cleanup` option in the `deploy` phase, because by default Travis will clean every artifact created during the previous phases, including the service account key we decrypted in the `before_install` phase.

Let's now analyze what the `deploy/travis_deploy.sh` script does. As you may have noticed in the `deploy` phase, this script is called with two arguments, the commit ID and the environment we're deploying to. As we discussed previously, we're using Kubernetes namespaces to separate the `staging` and `production` environments, hence we're using the last script argument as the namespace value whenever we use `kubectl`:

```bash
$ cat deploy/travis_deploy.sh
#!/bin/bash

COMMIT="$1"
ENVIRONMENT="$2"
echo "Deploying ${COMMIT} to ${ENVIRONMENT}"

gcloud auth activate-service-account --key-file secrets/travis-ci-k8s-
prod.json

ZONE=europe-west1-b
PROJECT_ID=intense-talent-188323
CLUSTER=elixir-drip-prod-cluster

gcloud --quiet config set compute/zone ${ZONE}
gcloud --quiet config set project ${PROJECT_ID}
gcloud --quiet config set container/cluster ${CLUSTER}
```

```
gcloud --quiet container clusters get-credentials ${CLUSTER}

yes | gcloud auth configure-docker

docker push gcr.io/${PROJECT_ID}/elixir-drip-prod:${COMMIT}

cat deploy/elixir-drip-migrations-prod.yml | sed
"s/\${BUILD_TAG}/${COMMIT}/g" > travis-migrations-prod.yml

kubectl -n ${ENVIRONMENT} create -f travis-migrations-prod.yml

cat deploy/elixir-drip-deployment-prod.yml | sed
"s/\${BUILD_TAG}/${COMMIT}/g" > travis-deployment-prod.yml

kubectl -n ${ENVIRONMENT} apply -f travis-deployment-prod.yml

echo "[SCRIPT] Success!"
```

The script starts by configuring `gcloud` to use the service account key, project, and cluster we have been using so far. It then configures `docker` to use `gcloud` and pushes the release image to the project Docker registry.

 To find your project zone, project ID, and cluster, look at the output of `gcloud projects list` and `gcloud container clusters list`.

Before running the migrations job and performing the deployment, we're generating the `travis-migrations-prod.yml` and `travis-deployment-prod.yml` configuration files from the `elixir-drip-migrations-prod.yml` and `elixir-drip-deployment-prod.yml` templates. Because `kubectl` doesn't replace any `${VAR}` entries with the respective `VAR` environment variables, we're passing both templates through `sed`, to replace any instances of `${BUILD_TAG}` with the value of the `COMMIT` variable set in the beginning of the script.

If in the previous section we used the `manual_build` tag in both the Kubernetes job and deployment configuration files, this time we're using the `${BUILD_TAG}` placeholder to indicate that the image tag will be set afterward:

```
$ cat deploy/elixir-drip-deployment-prod.yml
apiVersion: extensions/v1beta1
kind: Deployment
  # ...
  template:
    # ...
```

```
    spec:
      # ...
      containers:
        - image: gcr.io/intense-talent-188323/elixir-drip-
          prod:${BUILD_TAG}
```

With this Travis CI setup, every time we push a commit to the *master* branch, Travis CI will perform all these steps for us. In the end, we'll have an updated version of ElixirDrip up and running on the cloud. In the next section, we'll connect the deployed Elixir nodes so we can better use the media cache we've previously implemented.

Connecting the deployed Elixir nodes

Our objective in this section is to connect every ElixirDrip node running in Kubernetes. With the current setup, each Elixir node is running on its own pod, without even trying to connect to other pods.

When we introduced the Kubernetes deployment template, we briefly talked about the /health endpoint used by the readiness and liveness probe. Let's use this endpoint to get information about the node that replies to our HTTP GET requests. Here you can find the Phoenix controller that will handle the requests to /health:

```
$ cat apps/elixir_drip_web/lib/elixir_drip_web/controllers/
health_controller.ex
defmodule ElixirDripWeb.HealthController do
  @moduledoc false

  use ElixirDripWeb, :controller

  def health(conn, _params) do
    {_, timestamp} = Timex.format(DateTime.utc_now, "%FT%T%:z",
    :strftime)

    {:ok, hostname} = :inet.gethostname

    json(conn, %{
      ok: timestamp,
      hostname: to_string(hostname),
      node: Node.self(),
      connected_to: Node.list()
    })
  end
end
```

Besides the timestamp, the JSON response will get us the host name, the node name, and the list of nodes the current node is connected to. A controller needs a route to handle requests, so let's implement ours:

```
$ cat apps/elixir_drip_web/lib/elixir_drip_web/router.ex
defmodule ElixirDripWeb.Router do
  use ElixirDripWeb, :router
  # ...

  get("/health", ElixirDripWeb.HealthController, :health)

  # ...
end
```

We are routing /health GET requests to the :health action in HealthController. Notice that we aren't associating any pipeline (such as :api or :logger) to this route entry because we don't need any authentication or logging logic to be performed before we respond to the request. This endpoint will be used constantly by Kubernetes to assess how healthy the pod container running the application is.

Before trying the new endpoint, let's check which pods are currently running our application:

```
$ kubectl -n production get pods
NAME READY STATUS RESTARTS AGE
elixir-drip-6c4d8d64dc-28vjc 2/2 Running 0 7h
elixir-drip-6c4d8d64dc-n5x29 2/2 Running 0 7h
elixir-drip-6c4d8d64dc-rrvfg 2/2 Running 0 7h
```

If we now send a GET request to the load-balancer external IP with the /health path, this is what we'll get:

```
$ curl http://35.205.152.228/health
{"ok":"2018-06-16T16:09:16+00:00","node":"elixir_drip@10.40.2.70","hostname":"elixir-drip-6c4d8d64dc-n5x29","connected_to":[]}

$ curl http://35.205.152.228/health
{"ok":"2018-06-16T16:09:19+00:00","node":"elixir_drip@10.40.2.68","hostname":"elixir-drip-6c4d8d64dc-28vjc","connected_to":[]}
```

Notice how different requests end up being handled by different pods. Since we now know the IP of two pods, let's manually run our application inside the n5x29 pod and try to connect to the other 28vjc pod:

```
$ kubectl -n production exec -it elixir-drip-6c4d8d64dc-n5x29 -c elixir-
drip-prod sh

# sed -i.bak "s/elixir_drip/console/g" releases/0.0.8/vm.args
# PORT=5555 ./bin/elixir_drip console
Erlang/OTP 20 [erts-9.3.1] [source] [64-bit] [smp:1:1] [ds:1:1:10] [async-
threads:10] [hipe] [kernel-poll:false]

16:26:35.319 [info] Running ElixirDripWeb.Endpoint with Cowboy using
http://:::5555
Interactive Elixir (1.6.4) - press Ctrl+C to exit (type h() ENTER for help)
iex(console@10.40.2.70)1> # ...
```

We start the previous snippet by opening a shell inside the n5x29 container with kubectl exec -it (notice the similarities with the docker exec syntax). We then run the ElixirDrip release inside an interactive IEx shell with the console option.

We first had to change the name inside vm.args from elixir_drip to console (with the help of the sed tool), because there is already an ElixirDrip application running inside the container. This is also the reason why we had to start the application listening to another port, rather than 4000.

As we can see, this console node isn't connected to any node in the beginning, but we can easily connect it to the node running in the 28vjc pod:

```
iex(console@10.40.2.70)> Node.list()
[]

iex(console@10.40.2.70)> Node.connect(:"elixir_drip@10.40.2.68")
true

iex(console@10.40.2.70)> Node.list()
[:"elixir_drip@10.40.2.68"]
```

To automatically connect the nodes when they start, we'll use the libcluster library. With this library, each node is able to fetch the ElixirDrip pod IPs by querying the Kubernetes API and then connect to the other existing pods. This library will also periodically query the API to detect whether the number of pods changed, ensuring the node is always connected to active nodes.

We were able to connect to the other node because both nodes share the same Erlang cookie. If it wasn't the case, we could have updated the cookie in the console by using the `Node.set_cookie/2` function.

Besides adding the `{:libcluster, "~> 2.5"}` entry to the `mix.exs` file, we need to configure it. This is how we do it:

```
$ cat apps/elixir_drip/config/prod.exs
use Mix.Config
  # ...
config :libcluster,
  topologies: [
    elixir_drip_topology: [
      strategy: Cluster.Strategy.Kubernetes,
      config: [
        kubernetes_selector: "app=elixir-drip,env=production",
        kubernetes_node_basename: "elixir_drip"]]]
```

With the previous configuration, we are saying that we want to use the `Kubernetes` strategy to find other nodes to connect to, and we then specify the endpoint labels that `libcluster` will search for. The `kubernetes_node_basename` value defines the base name of each node. In our case, each node is named `elixir_drip@<pod-ip>` (remember the custom `vm.args` we set with Distillery), so `libcluster` will fetch the pod IPs from the Kubernetes API, say `ip-a`, `ip-b`, and `ip-c`, and then connect to two of these three Erlang nodes, named `elixir_drip@ip-a`, `elixir_drip@ip-b`, and `elixir_drip@ip-c`.

Because we're using a Kubernetes load balancer, an endpoint was automatically created for each pod. We can observe the endpoint labels with the `kubectl describe` command (also notice how we are fetching the endpoints by label in the first case; this is analogous to what the `libcluster` query does):

```
$ kubectl -n production get endpoints -l app=elixir-drip,env=production
NAME ENDPOINTS AGE
elixir-drip-loadbalancer 10.40.2.68:4000,10.40.2.69:4000,10.40.2.70:4000
32d

$ kubectl -n production describe endpoints elixir-drip-loadbalancer
Name: elixir-drip-loadbalancer
Namespace: production
Labels: app=elixir-drip
            env=production
Annotations: <none>
Subsets:
  Addresses: 10.40.2.68,10.40.2.69,10.40.2.70
```

```
NotReadyAddresses: <none>
Ports:
  Name Port Protocol
  ---- ---- --------
  <unset> 4000 TCP

Events: <none>
```

Code-wise, we don't need to change anything else. However, before redeploying the application with the nodes connected with the help of `libcluster`, we need to do one last change. By default, the service account that `libcluster` will use to query the Kubernetes API isn't allowed to query the endpoints. As such, we will create a custom `list-endpoints` role and then we'll bind this new role to the default production service account:

```
$ cat deploy/elixir-drip-role-list-endpoints.yml
apiVersion: rbac.authorization.k8s.io/v1
kind: Role
metadata:
  name: list-endpoints
  namespace: production
rules:
- apiGroups: [""]
  resources: ["endpoints"]
  verbs: ["get", "list", "watch"]
```

To associate the previous role with the default service account, we'll need to create the following `RoleBinding` object:

```
$ cat deploy/elixir-drip-role-binding-default-service-account.yml
apiVersion: rbac.authorization.k8s.io/v1
kind: RoleBinding
metadata:
  name: default-service-account-lists-endpoints
  namespace: production
subjects:
- kind: ServiceAccount
  name: default
  namespace: production
roleRef:
  kind: Role
  name: list-endpoints
  apiGroup: rbac.authorization.k8s.io
```

By default, only the admin user (not the one we've been using) has the permissions needed to create roles and bind them. As such, we need to get the admin credentials from the current cluster (run `gcloud container clusters list` to obtain the cluster name):

```
$ gcloud container clusters list --format="table(name,zone)"
NAME LOCATION
elixir-drip-prod-cluster europe-west1-b

$ gcloud container clusters describe elixir-drip-prod-cluster --zone
europe-west1-b | grep -A 1 password
  password: <admin-password>
  username: admin
```

And now we have everything we need to create the `list-endpoints` role and the respective role binding with the cluster admin credentials:

```
$ kubectl -n production --username=admin --password=<admin-password> create
-f deploy/elixir-drip-role-list-endpoints.yml
role.rbac.authorization.k8s.io "list-endpoints" created

$ kubectl -n production --username=admin --password=<admin-password> create
-f deploy/elixir-drip-role-binding-default-service-account.yml
rolebinding.rbac.authorization.k8s.io "default-service-account-lists-
endpoints" created
```

After redeploying the application, `libcluster` will now be able to query the existing endpoints with the desired `app` and `env` labels. If we hit the `/health` endpoint again, this is what we'll get:

```
$ curl http://35.205.152.228/health
{"ok":"2018-06-17T00:19:33+00:00","node":"elixir_drip@10.40.2.68","hostname
":"elixir-
drip-6c4d8d64dc-28vjc","connected_to":["elixir_drip@10.40.2.69","elixir_dri
p@10.40.2.70"]}

$ curl http://35.205.152.228/health
{"ok":"2018-06-17T00:19:36+00:00","node":"elixir_drip@10.40.2.69","hostname
":"elixir-drip-6c4d8d64dc-
rrvfg","connected_to":["elixir_drip@10.40.2.68","elixir_drip@10.40.2.70"]}
```

Hooray, we now have all the nodes connected! Pretty impressive if you ask us, given it was just a matter of configuring a new library and allowing the service account to query the Kubernetes API.

Let's now see how can we put the connected nodes to the test.

Testing the connected nodes

Remember how we started this section by logging into a pod and running an ElixirDrip console so we could manually connect to another Erlang node living in a different pod? This is exactly what we'll do, but this time we just need to run an ElixirDrip console in two different pods, since the nodes are already connected.

I'm running an ElixirDrip console in the `n5x29` and `28vjc` pods, and this time when I start the console in the `28vjc` pod (IP ending in `.68`), we immediately see `libcluster` telling us that it was able to connect to three Erlang nodes:

```
# PORT=6666 ./bin/elixir_drip console
Erlang/OTP 20 [erts-9.3.1] [source] [64-bit] [smp:1:1] [ds:1:1:10] [async-
threads:10] [hipe] [kernel-poll:false]

00:39:34.130 [info] [libcluster:elixir_drip_topology] connected to
:"elixir_drip@10.40.2.68"
00:39:34.132 [info] [libcluster:elixir_drip_topology] connected to
:"elixir_drip@10.40.2.69"
00:39:34.135 [info] [libcluster:elixir_drip_topology] connected to
:"elixir_drip@10.40.2.70"
00:39:34.167 [info] Running ElixirDripWeb.Endpoint with Cowboy using
http://:::6666
Interactive Elixir (1.6.4) - press Ctrl+C to exit (type h() ENTER for help)
iex(console@10.40.2.68)1> Node.list()
[:"elixir_drip@10.40.2.68", :"elixir_drip@10.40.2.69",
 :"elixir_drip@10.40.2.70", :"console@10.40.2.70"]
```

When I started the ElixirDrip console, it only connected to the existing `elixir_drip@<pod-ip>` nodes with the help of `libcluster`. However, because Erlang connections are by default transitive, both consoles end up being connected to each other, as the `Node.list/0` output shows.

We will now upload a file in one of the consoles (pod `n5x29` with an IP ending in `.70`):

```
iex(console@10.40.2.70)> user = Accounts.get_user_by_username("jose")
%ElixirDrip.Accounts.User{
  id: "167fsqnimMuu0pkSpBcuwiK3K7h",
  # ...
}

iex(console@10.40.2.70)> Storage.store(user.id,
"distributed_cache_test.txt", "$/distributed_test",
"(｡◕‿◕｡)(｡◕‿◕｡)(｡◕‿◕｡) ¯\_(ツ)_/¯ (-■_■)")

{:ok, :upload_enqueued, %ElixirDrip.Storage.Media{ ... }}
```

```
iex(console@10.40.2.70)10>
CacheSupervisor.find_cache("168isa6wYsW6sz5CaX5be30YbLp")
#PID<0.2037.0>
```

As soon as the previous file is cached, the other console (pod `28vjc`) is able to immediately retrieve the file from the cache as well:

```
iex(console@10.40.2.68)> user_id = "167fsqnimMuu0pkSpBcuwiK3K7h"
"167fsqnimMuu0pkSpBcuwiK3K7h"

iex(console@10.40.2.68)>
CacheSupervisor.find_cache("168isa6wYsW6sz5CaX5be30YbLp")
#PID<37846.2037.0>

iex(console@10.40.2.68)> Storage.retrieve_content(user_id,
"168isa6wYsW6sz5CaX5be30YbLp")
09:53:23.491 [info] Found cached content for 168isa6wYsW6sz5CaX5be30YbLp!
{:ok,
 %ElixirDrip.Storage.Media{ ... },
 "(｡◕‿◕｡)(｡◕‿◕｡)(｡◕‿◕｡) ¯\_(ツ)_/¯ (-■_■)"}
```

This is only possible because we are globally registering the `CacheWorker` processes by naming them as `{:global, {:cache, <media_id>}}`. When we connect the Erlang nodes, the global name servers running in each node are able to work together and provide a common process register. Because of this, the console running in the `28vjc` pod is able to find and interact with the remote `CacheWorker` process (`#PID<37846.2037.0>`) as if it was a local process. Instead of having to download the file from cloud storage, it can simply retrieve the file from the remote process.

With this approach, it doesn't matter which pod you send download requests to; if the media is cached somewhere, it will be retrieved from the cache!

Summary

We concluded this chapter with the distributed and cloud-hosted up-and-running version of ElixirDrip. From our humble beginning, where we delved into how releases work with Distillery, until the very end, with the application running in Kubernetes and being automatically deployed by Travis CI, we applied many interesting concepts and tools. We also containerized our application and applied some of the main Kubernetes building blocks, such as pods, services, and secrets.

You should also be aware that security wasn't a primary concern of this chapter's examples, so don't consider these exhaustive examples ready to be applied in a production environment, but instead as possible starting points for common aspects of nearly every Elixir application:

- Configuring a Distillery release with custom release tasks
- Containerizing an application with the end goal of building a streamlined release image and simplifying development in the local environment
- Interacting with a Kubernetes cluster by using `kubectl` and by applying Kubernetes configuration files
- Using a continuous integration tool, such as Travis CI, to automate the deployment process
- Connecting Erlang nodes running in different Kubernetes pods

Security in a cloud environment, building releases, containerization, Kubernetes, and continuous deployments are all complex topics, each deserving its own book. This chapter serves as an introduction to many of these concepts, and shows how a single person armed with a laptop can serve their application to the world in a robust and scalable way, by relying on the amazing cloud tools that exist today.

In the next chapter, we will learn how to collect application metrics and easily check, profile, and trace running processes, expanding our visibility about what's happening with our application in the production environment.

11
Keeping an Eye on Your Processes

With our application running on the cloud, we should have constant visibility at any given moment about what's happening. To accomplish this, we'll configure two different mechanisms to obtain information about the running ElixirDrip instances:

- A Prometheus server constantly collecting metrics about the running application and exposing them through a Grafana dashboard
- A way to run the Erlang observer tool while connected to the running Erlang nodes, in order to analyze the Erlang VM's overall status and the existing running processes
- Two ways to tap into what's happening with our production system: Profiling and tracing functions from our application

Let's start by understanding how Prometheus works and how it is a good fit for the established ElixirDrip architecture.

Collecting metrics

Prometheus is an open source monitoring tool that works in a pull fashion: instead of each individual application sending its collected metrics to the server, each application exposes an endpoint and the Prometheus server constantly scrapes the available metrics. It is also able to dynamically discover metric sources to scrape, and it comes with support out of the box for different sources, such as AWS EC2, Azure VM, and Google Container Engine instances.

On top of this, Prometheus provides a powerful query language and is also able to send alerts based on the collected data. These are the types of metrics Prometheus is able to collect:

- **Counter**: This allows you to count whenever something happens. By definition, counters can only increase.
- **Gauge**: This lets you track quantities that vary over time, such as CPU time or number of Elixir processes running in the BEAM. Each data point captures the value of the gauge metric at a specific moment in time.
- **Histogram**: This lets you sample observations, such as request duration or response sizes, and counts each observation in a predefined bucket. For each histogram, Prometheus also collects the number of observations and the sum of the observed values (with these, you can calculate the average of the observed values as well). With the data collected by histograms, you are able to calculate the distribution percentiles. Histograms are invaluable for understanding what's happening with any application, because they can tell you that a percentage of requests, say 99%, were handled in less than x milliseconds.
- **Summary**: This is similar to histograms, in the sense that this type of metric also samples observations and has associated sum and count metrics, but percentiles need to be configured *a priori* and are calculated on the client side. It reduces the Prometheus server's load because of this, but doesn't allow us to calculate different percentiles afterward.

 There is also the possibility of directly pushing metrics from a short-lived application, such as a batch job, but by default Prometheus will fetch the metrics from the monitored applications.

Regardless of the metric type, all Prometheus time series data has the following format:

```
<metric_name>{<lbl1>=<lbl1_val>,<lbl2>=<lbl2_val>,...} <value> <timestamp>
```

Histogram observations always have a `le` label with the bucket value; summary observations have a `quantile` label instead, and the measured value of counter metrics always goes up. Despite their individual characteristics, Prometheus observations share a common format.

Our first step is to configure the ElixirDrip application to collect the Prometheus metrics and expose them via the `/metrics` endpoint. Then, we will start a Prometheus server alongside ElixirDrip that will hit the ElixirDrip `/metrics` endpoint of the application from time to time to collect all the available metrics.

Exposing Prometheus metrics

To expose the Prometheus metrics, we will use a set of Elixir libraries that let us emit new metrics and also introduce out-of-the-box Phoenix, Plug, and Ecto metrics:

```
$ cat apps/elixir_drip/mix.exs
  # ...
  defp deps do
    [
      # ...
      {:prometheus, "~> 4.0", override: true},
      {:prometheus_ex, "~> 3.0", override: true},
      {:prometheus_ecto, "~> 1.0"},
    ]
  end
  # ...

$ cat apps/elixir_drip_web/mix.exs
  # ...
  defp deps do
    [
      # ...
      {:prometheus_phoenix, "~> 1.2"},
      {:prometheus_plugs, "~> 1.1"},
    ]
  end
  # ...
```

Let's now start with the Phoenix metrics. We need to define a simple EndpointInstrumenter module, which will use the PhoenixInstrumenter module:

```
$ cat apps/elixir_drip_web/lib/elixir_drip_web/prometheus/
endpoint_instrumenter.ex
defmodule ElixirDripWeb.EndpointInstrumenter do
  use Prometheus.PhoenixInstrumenter
end
```

We need to call the setup/0 function of this new module when the application starts:

```
$ cat apps/elixir_drip_web/lib/elixir_drip_web/application.ex
  # ...
  def start(_type, _args) do
    # ...
    ElixirDripWeb.EndpointInstrumenter.setup()
    # ...
  end
```

And finally, we should add our `EndpointInstrumenter` to the `instrumenters` list in the endpoint configuration:

```
$ cat apps/elixir_drip_web/config/config.exs
  # ...
config :elixir_drip_web, ElixirDripWeb.Endpoint,
  # ...
  instrumenters: [ElixirDripWeb.EndpointInstrumenter]
```

It's a really similar process for the Plug and Ecto libraries: we define a simple module using the respective Prometheus module, we configure it when the application starts, and then we configure the application to use it. In the case of Plug, the module will be called in the request pipeline, as a normal plug; in the case of Ecto, it will be configured as a logger. You can check the application code for the full details.

Besides defining `PlugInstrumenter` in the exact same way we did for `EndpointInstrumenter`, we've added a `label_value/2` function to define custom metrics, based on the `conn` plug passed to the : `def label_value(:request_path, conn), do:` `conn.request_path`function. This way, all the metrics collected by `PlugInstrumenter` will contain a custom `request_path` label with the `conn.request_path` value.

In the end, we need to expose the collected metrics. This is done in a similar way by defining a `MetricsExporter` module:

```
$ cat apps/elixir_drip_web/lib/elixir_drip_web/prometheus/
metrics_exporter.ex
defmodule ElixirDripWeb.MetricsExporter do
  use Prometheus.PlugExporter
end
```

Configure it when the application starts:

```
$ cat apps/elixir_drip_web/lib/elixir_drip_web/application.ex
  # ...
  def start(_type, _args) do
    # ...
    ElixirDripWeb.MetricsExporter.setup()
    # ...
  end
```

Then, add it like any other plug to the request pipeline, as shown here:

```
$ cat apps/elixir_drip_web/lib/elixir_drip_web/endpoint.ex
  # ...
```

```
      plug(ElixirDripWeb.MetricsExporter)
      plug(ElixirDripWeb.Router)
   end
```

We can now hit the `/metrics` endpoint. It's this wall of text that Prometheus knows how to parse and transform into time series data, ready to be queried:

```
$ curl http://localhost:4000/metrics
# TYPE http_requests_total counter
# HELP http_requests_total Total number of HTTP requests made.
http_requests_total{status_class="client-
error",method="GET",host="...",scheme="http",request_path="/index.action"}
1
http_requests_total{status_class="success",method="GET",host="10.40.0.10",s
cheme="http",request_path="/health"} 3785
http_requests_total{status_class="success",method="GET",host="10.40.0.10",s
cheme="http",request_path="/metrics"} 633
http_requests_total{status_class="success",method="GET",host="...",scheme="
http",request_path="/"} 3
# TYPE elixir_drip_cache_worker_hit_count counter
# HELP elixir_drip_cache_worker_hit_count Counter for each download served
by the CacheWorker instead of relying on the Cloud provider
elixir_drip_cache_worker_hit_count 1427
# ...
```

With the current Elixir `prometheus` libraries, we have multiple perspectives about the actual state of our application. But what if we want to measure the time a function takes? Or if want to send a custom counter whenever something happens? In these scenarios, the `prometheus_ex` library lets us emit any custom metric as long as it uses one of the four metric types supported by Prometheus.

Let's implement a custom metric to measure the time it takes the `Storage.store/4` function to execute.

Creating custom Prometheus metrics

To implement a custom metric, we will follow the same steps as we did previously: we will first configure our custom metric and then we will create a new `Chronometer.defmeasured/2` macro that not only defines a new function, but also emits a histogram metric based on the function name and module.

This time, however, the module that exposes the setup/0 function will be more complex, since it needs to register the metrics and also expose the count/1, observe/2, and observe_duration/2 functions:

```
$ cat apps/elixir_drip/lib/elixir_drip/prometheus/instrumenter.ex
defmodule ElixirDrip.Instrumenter do
  use Prometheus

  @histograms %{"storage_store" => "Time histogram for the Storage.store/
  4 function"}

  @counters %{"cache_worker_hit" => "Counter for each download served by
  the CacheWorker instead of relying on the Cloud provider"}

  @default_buckets :prometheus_http.microseconds_duration_buckets()

  def setup do
    @histograms
    |> Enum.map(&__MODULE__.histogram_config(&1, @default_buckets))
    |> Enum.each(&Histogram.new(&1))

    @counters
    |> Enum.map(&__MODULE__.counter_config(&1))
    |> Enum.each(&Counter.new(&1))
  end

  def counter_config({name, help}), do: [name: counter_name(name), help:
  help]
  def histogram_config({name, help}, buckets), do: [name:
  histogram_name(name), help: help, buckets: buckets]

  def counter_name(name),
    do: "elixir_drip_" <> to_string(name) <> "_count" |> String.to_atom()
  def histogram_name(name),
    do: "elixir_drip_" <> to_string(name) <> "_microseconds" |>
    String.to_atom()
  # ...
end
```

In the previous snippet, the setup/0 function iterates over the @histograms and @counters module attributes and calls the Histogram.new/1 and Counter.new/1 macros to configure the custom histograms and counters we want to set, respectively.

To generate the metric names, we prefix them with elixir_drip_ and then we add a suffix depending on the type of metric.

It's important to note that we need to explicitly add the time units of the histogram metric as a suffix (that is, `_microseconds`), otherwise the library doesn't know how to convert the measured time before emitting it (the alternative would be to set the `duration_units` keyword in the metric spec, but it is good practice to interpolate the metric units on its name).

To complete this `Instrumenter` module, we just need to define the `count` and `observe` functions for the new counter and histogram metrics:

```
$ cat apps/elixir_drip/lib/elixir_drip/prometheus/instrumenter.ex
defmodule ElixirDrip.Instrumenter do
  # ...
  @counters
  |> Enum.map(&elem(&1, 0))
  |> Enum.map(&String.to_atom(&1))
  |> Enum.map(fn counter ->
    def count(unquote(counter)), do: count(unquote(counter), 1)
    def count(unquote(counter), count), do: Counter.count([name:
    __MODULE__.counter_name(unquote(counter))], count)
  end)

  @histograms
  |> Enum.map(&elem(&1, 0))
  |> Enum.map(&String.to_atom(&1))
  |> Enum.map(fn histogram ->
    def observe(unquote(histogram), value), do:  Histogram.observe
    ([name: __MODULE__.histogram_name(unquote(histogram))], value)

    def observe_duration(unquote(histogram), body), do:
    Histogram.observe_duration([name: __MODULE__.histogram_name
    (unquote(histogram))], body.())
  end)
end
```

Whenever we call `Instrumenter.count(:cache_worker_hit, 2)`, we'll have the respective `elixir_drip_cache_worker_hit_count` metric emitted. If we call `Instrumenter.observe(:storage_store, 3_000_000)` instead, the `elixir_drip_storage_store_microseconds_bucket` metric plus the `_count` and `_sum` histogram metrics will be emitted and available on the `/metrics` endpoint.

Since in the previous *chapter 6*, *Metaprogramming–Code That Writes Itself* we implemented a `defchrono/2` macro to measure the time a function takes to execute, let's iterate on it to create a `defmeasured/2` macro that does the same, but instead of printing the time the function took, it emits a Prometheus histogram metric using the `Instrumenter.observe_duration/2` function:

```
$ cat apps/elixir_drip/lib/elixir_drip/chronometer.ex
# ...
defmacro defmeasured(function_definition, do: body) do
  {function, args} = Macro.decompose_call(function_definition)
  arity = length(args)

  quote bind_quoted: [
    function_definition: Macro.escape(function_definition),
    body: Macro.escape(body),
    function: function,
    arity: arity
  ] do
    require Prometheus.Metric.Histogram, as: Histogram

    def unquote(function_definition) do
      module_name = __MODULE__
                    |> Atom.to_string()
                    |> String.split(".")
                    |> Enum.at(-1)
                    |> String.downcase()

      function_name = Atom.to_string(unquote(function))

      histogram = String.to_atom("#{module_name}_#{function_name}")

      Instrumenter.observe_duration(histogram, fn -> unquote(body)
      end)
    end
  end
end
```

This `defmeasured/2` macro is really similar to what we did before, so we will just focus on the metrics part. We start by obtaining the module and function name to get the ElixirDrip metric alias (for example, `:storage_store`). This alias needs to match the keys of the `@histograms` map of the `Instrumenter` module, otherwise it won't pattern match any of the `observe_duration/2` function signatures. Then, it's just a matter of calling the `Instrumenter.observe_duration/2` function, which will rely on the function with the same name in the `Prometheus.Metric.Histogram` module.

We left the simpler counter metric to the end. To increase the cache hits counter whenever a `CacheWorker` serves its cached media, it's just a matter of calling the `Instrumenter.count/1` function on the `:get_media` handler:

```
$ cat apps/elixir_drip/lib/elixir_drip/storage/workers/cache_worker.ex
# ...
def handle_call(:get_media, _from, %{hits: hits, content: content,
```

```
    timer: timer} = state) do
      ElixirDrip.Instrumenter.count(:cache_worker_hit)
      # ...
    end
  end
```

We now just need to call `Instrumenter.setup/0` when the application starts, and we're golden:

```
$ cat apps/elixir_drip/lib/elixir_drip/application.ex
  # ...
  def start(_type, _args) do
    # ...
    ElixirDrip.Instrumenter.setup()
    # ...
  end
```

Now that we have the ElixirDrip application configured to collect and expose Prometheus metrics, we will update our local development environment to have a running Prometheus server.

Local Prometheus server

To test Prometheus locally, we will use Docker Compose to spin up a Prometheus container alongside the Postgres and ElixirDrip container we already have. The Prometheus container will also expose its port, and will hit the `/metrics` endpoint to scrape the application metrics. The Prometheus server knows about its *targets* through a configuration file. Let's create ours:

```
$ cat monitoring/prometheus.dev.yml
global:
  scrape_interval: 15s

scrape_configs:
  - job_name: 'prometheus'
    static_configs:
      - targets: ['localhost:9090']

  - job_name: 'elixir-drip'
    static_configs:
      - targets: ['app:4000']
```

As you can see, it is a YAML file that points to the available Prometheus targets. Our configuration is really simple, but you can configure every aspect with it. Remember that we said Prometheus is able to dynamically find other targets?

This is called *service discovery* and it's here that you can configure it.

In our case, we have two *jobs* (the `job` label will be added to every metric with the `job_name` value): the first tells Prometheus to scrape metrics from itself, and the second one tells it to fetch them from the `app` host running on port 4000. Because we're exposing the ElixirDrip metrics on the default `/metrics` endpoint expected by Prometheus, we don't need anything else (to change it, we should use the `metrics_path` configuration field).

 Recall that the Prometheus server running in its container is able to reach the ElixirDrip application by using the `app:4000` address, because the container running the application is called `app` in the `docker-compose.dev.yml` file that we use for local development.

If you run the `prom/prometheus` Docker image without changing anything, you'll be able to access Prometheus on port `9090`, but only its own metrics will be available. We have to copy the configuration file we've just defined to a custom Docker image created by us:

```
$ cat monitoring/Dockerfile.prometheus
FROM prom/prometheus

COPY monitoring/prometheus.dev.yml /etc/prometheus/

CMD ["--config.file=/etc/prometheus/prometheus.dev.yml"]
```

Besides copying the configuration file, we also override the run command when the container starts. We now just need to update the `docker-compose.dev.yml` file to also spin up a `prometheus` container, based on the `Dockerfile` we've just defined:

```
$ cat docker-compose.dev.yml
 version: '2.3'
 services:
  prometheus:
    build:
      context: .
      dockerfile: monitoring/Dockerfile.prometheus
    depends_on:
      app:
        condition: service_started
    ports:
      - 9090:9090
  app:
    image: elixir_drip:dev
    build:
 # ...
```

Now, if you start the application as usual with `docker-compose -f docker-compose.dev.yml up`, you can go to `http://localhost:9090/graph` and look for some metrics:

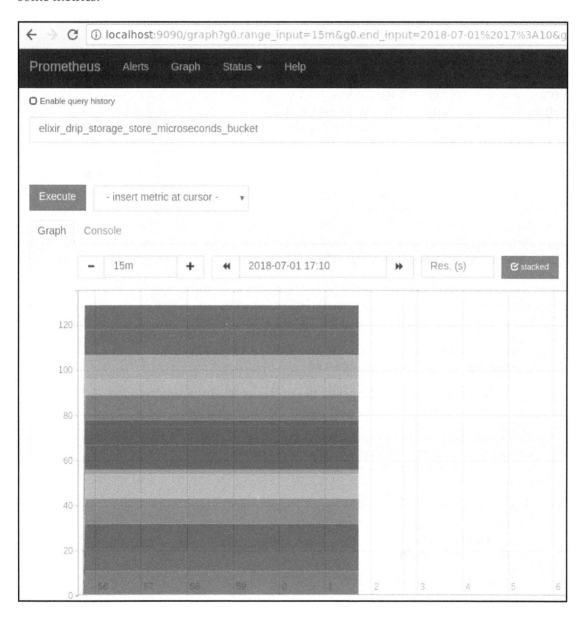

With the local environment up and running, let's configure our cloud to also host a Prometheus server (and some other goodies).

Deploying Prometheus in Kubernetes

As we did with our application in the previous chapter, we could configure a pod based on the Prometheus Docker image and call it a day. It would work, but whenever the Prometheus pod rotated, we would lose all the metrics because pods are ephemeral by nature. To have a proper monitoring solution in place, we should deploy Prometheus as the stateful application that it is, and utilize the abstractions that Kubernetes provides, such as `StatefulSets` and `PersistentVolumes`, among others.

However, doing this is not so trivial, so we will instead use Helm to install a chart that will take care of correctly deploying and configuring Prometheus and its companions in our Kubernetes cluster for us. You can think of Helm as a package manager (such as `apt`, `chocolatey`, or `homebrew`) for Kubernetes. A chart is nothing more than a bundle of Kubernetes templates (a sort of Kubernetes recipe) that Helm lets us install in our cluster. To use Helm, we also need its server-side counterpart: Tiller.

Tiller will run on the cluster and will install the charts according to the instructions provided by Helm running on your machine. Let's start by creating a `tiller-sa ServiceAccount` that will be used by Tiller:

```
$ kubectl -n kube-system create serviceaccount tiller-sa
serviceaccount "tiller-sa" created
```

Here's the role binding that will associate the previous service account to the `cluster-admin` role, so that Tiller has all the permissions it may need:

```
$ cat monitoring/tiller-sa-role-binding.yml
apiVersion: rbac.authorization.k8s.io/v1beta1
kind: ClusterRoleBinding
metadata:
  name: tiller-role-binding
roleRef:
  apiGroup: rbac.authorization.k8s.io
  kind: ClusterRole
  name: cluster-admin
subjects:
  - kind: ServiceAccount
    name: tiller-sa
    namespace: kube-system
```

Now, we just need to apply the previous `ClusterRoleBinding` resource:

```
$ kubectl create -f monitoring/tiller-sa-role-binding.yml
clusterrolebinding.rbac.authorization.k8s.io "tiller-role-binding" created
```

With the `tiller-sa` service account created, we can move on and install Helm and its brother, Tiller. Follow the instructions at `https://docs.helm.sh/using_helm/ #installing-helm` and you should end up with the `helm` binary somewhere in your path. Because we have the `kubectl` context configured to access our GKE cluster, `helm` will utilize this context to interact with the cluster and install its server-side component in one fell swoop:

```
$ helm init --service-account tiller-sa
Creating /home/andre/.helm
Creating /home/andre/.helm/repository
Creating /home/andre/.helm/repository/cache
Creating /home/andre/.helm/repository/local
Creating /home/andre/.helm/plugins
Creating /home/andre/.helm/starters
Creating /home/andre/.helm/cache/archive
Creating /home/andre/.helm/repository/repositories.yaml
Adding stable repo with URL:
https://kubernetes-charts.storage.googleapis.com
Adding local repo with URL: http://127.0.0.1:8879/charts
$HELM_HOME has been configured at /home/andre/.helm.

Tiller (the Helm server-side component) has been installed into your
Kubernetes Cluster.
```

After this, we can see the `tiller-deploy` pod running in the `kube-system` namespace:

```
$ kubectl get pods --all-namespaces
NAMESPACE NAME READY STATUS RESTARTS AGE
# ...
kube-system tiller-deploy-75d774db4f-fbxch 1/1 Running 5 3d
```

We will install two Helm charts: `prometheus-operator` and `kube-prometheus`. These two charts are provided by CoreOS and are being actively developed. The `kube-prometheus` chart uses the Kubernetes resources introduced by the `prometheus-operator` one, and simplifies the management of Prometheus and Grafana (among other tools) in a Kubernetes cluster (for example, the configuration of persistent storage, safe coordination of application upgrades, disaster recovery, and so on).

Besides Prometheus, we will also use Grafana. Grafana is an open source data visualization tool that is able to consume Prometheus metrics (among other data sources) and use them to create graphs and dashboards.

We first need to install the CoreOS repository, so that `helm` can then find the charts we need:

```
$ helm repo add coreos
https://s3-eu-west-1.amazonaws.com/coreos-charts/stable/
"coreos" has been added to your repositories
```

Now, it is just a matter of installing both charts on a specific `monitoring` namespace. We're using a different namespace to keep everything tidy, but the Prometheus server will still be able to monitor our ElixirDrip pods running in their `production` namespace:

```
$ helm install coreos/prometheus-operator --name prometheus-operator --
namespace monitoring
NAME: prometheus-operator
LAST DEPLOYED: Wed Jun 27 19:51:49 2018
NAMESPACE: monitoring
STATUS: DEPLOYED
  # ...

$ helm install coreos/kube-prometheus --name kube-prometheus --namespace
monitoring
NAME: kube-prometheus
LAST DEPLOYED: Wed Jun 27 20:04:00 2018
NAMESPACE: monitoring
STATUS: DEPLOYED
  # ...

$ kubectl -n monitoring get pods
NAME READY STATUS RESTARTS AGE
alertmanager-kube-prometheus-0 2/2 Running 4 2h
kube-prometheus-exporter-kube-state-5ffd856844-m6wbj 2/2 Running 0 1h
kube-prometheus-exporter-node-4d4t6 1/1 Running 2 2h
kube-prometheus-exporter-node-ppj2g 1/1 Running 0 1h
kube-prometheus-grafana-6c9496d766-q7278 2/2 Running 4 2h
prometheus-kube-prometheus-0 3/3 Running 1 2h
prometheus-operator-f454cb555-htqxx 1/1 Running 2 2h
```

After a while, you will be able to see all pods created by both charts running in the `monitoring` namespace.

> When I tried to deploy the two Helm charts on a GKE cluster with a single `n1-standard-1` node (1 vCPU and 3.75 GB of RAM), some of the pods weren't able to start, and an unschedulable pods notification appeared in the Google Cloud console. After activating the cluster autoscaler and setting its `maximum size` to 2, Kubernetes automatically scaled the cluster up to make room for the new pods.

If we forward port `9090` of the `prometheus-kube-prometheus-0` pod, we will be able to access the Prometheus server we've just deployed:

```
$ kubectl -n monitoring port-forward prometheus-kube-prometheus-0
49090:9090
Forwarding from 127.0.0.1:49090 -> 9090
Forwarding from [::1]:49090 -> 9090
# ...
```

If you now go to `http://localhost:9090/graph`, you will see the same Prometheus page that we accessed locally before. However, we still don't have any ElixirDrip metrics, because we haven't yet configured Prometheus to scrape the metrics exposed by the application's `/metrics` endpoint.

To scrape metrics from our application, we don't need to directly update the Prometheus configuration file, because `prometheus-operator` introduces a custom Kubernetes resource called `ServiceMonitor`, whose sole purpose is to configure how Prometheus should find available targets.

Before configuring our own `ServiceMonitor`, let's see the `ServiceMonitors` created by the operator for us:

```
$ kubectl -n monitoring get servicemonitors
NAME AGE
kube-prometheus 3h
kube-prometheus-alertmanager 3h
kube-prometheus-exporter-kube-controller-manager 3h
kube-prometheus-exporter-kube-dns 3h
kube-prometheus-exporter-kube-etcd 3h
kube-prometheus-exporter-kube-scheduler 3h
kube-prometheus-exporter-kube-state 3h
kube-prometheus-exporter-kubelets 3h
kube-prometheus-exporter-kubernetes 3h
kube-prometheus-exporter-node 3h
kube-prometheus-grafana 3h
prometheus-operator 3h
```

It's the `kube-prometheus-exporter-kubelets` service monitor that tells Prometheus how to scrape metrics from Kubernetes. By default, Prometheus fetches Kubernetes metrics in a secure way. However, due to how Google Kubernetes Engine works, we need to change the service monitor for this target:

```
$ kubectl -n monitoring get servicemonitor kube-prometheus-exporter-
kubelets -o yaml | sed 's/https/http/' | kubectl replace -f -
servicemonitor.monitoring.coreos.com "kube-prometheus-exporter-kubelets"
replaced
```

In the previous snippet, we get the YAML definition of `kube-prometheus-exporter-kubelets` ServiceMonitor, replace its `https` occurrences with `http`, and then replace its resource with the new HTTP-only version. With this change, Prometheus is able to scrape all the targets configured by the operator that came out of the box.

The `ServiceMonitor` resource we've just updated is a custom resource introduced by `prometheus-operator`. It enables us to configure Prometheus targets, without actually having to update any Prometheus configuration, by relying on similar Kubernetes concepts, such as label selectors. Here's the `ServiceMonitor` definition that we'll create to set ElixirDrip as a Prometheus target:

```
$ cat monitoring/elixir-drip-service-monitor-prod.yml
apiVersion: monitoring.coreos.com/v1
kind: ServiceMonitor
metadata:
  labels:
    app: prometheus
  name: elixir-drip-monitor
  namespace: monitoring
spec:
  jobLabel: elixir-drip
  endpoints:
  - interval: 30s
    port: web
  namespaceSelector:
    matchNames:
    - production
  selector:
    matchLabels:
      app: elixir-drip
```

We are setting the `app=prometheus` label in our custom `ServiceMonitor` because the `kube-prometheus` resource (of the `Prometheus` kind, also a custom resource introduced by the Prometheus operator) by default searches for `ServiceMonitors` with specific `app` label values (`alertmanager`, `grafana`, `prometheus`, and so on):

```
$ kubectl -n monitoring get prometheus kube-prometheus -o yaml
apiVersion: monitoring.coreos.com/v1
kind: Prometheus
metadata:
  # ...
  name: kube-prometheus
  namespace: monitoring
  # ...
  serviceMonitorSelector:
    matchExpressions:
    - key: app
      operator: In
      values:
      - alertmanager
      - exporter-coredns
      - exporter-kube-controller-manager
      - exporter-kube-dns
      - exporter-kube-etcd
      - exporter-kube-scheduler
      - exporter-kube-state
      - exporter-kubelets
      - exporter-kubernetes
      - exporter-node
      - grafana
      - prometheus
      - prometheus-operator
```

The `elixir-drip-monitor` we've just defined will search for endpoints with the `app=elixir-drip` label in the `production` namespace, and then configure Prometheus to scrape metrics through the `web` port of those endpoints. We didn't specify a custom metrics path since, by default, `ServiceMonitor` gets its metrics through the `/metrics` path:

```
$ kubectl create -f monitoring/elixir-drip-service-monitor-prod.yml
servicemonitor.monitoring.coreos.com "elixir-drip-monitor" created

$ kubectl -n monitoring get servicemonitors
NAME AGE
elixir-drip-monitor 16s
# ...
```

After creating `elixir-drip-monitor`, we are able to find an `elixir-drip-loadbalancer` entry among the other Prometheus targets exposed by the `http://localhost:49090/targets` URL:

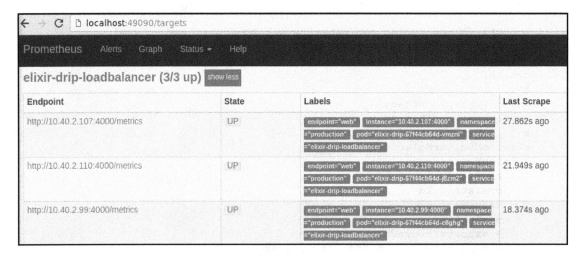

This means we can now query the ElixirDrip metrics with Prometheus. Despite Prometheus being able to graph our metrics, we'll use Grafana, an open source data visualization tool, which is able to use Prometheus as a data source. Luckily, the `prometheus-operator` we previously deployed also deploys a `grafana` pod, so it's just a matter of exposing port `3000` of the `kube-prometheus-grafana-6c9496d766-q7278` pod:

```
$ kubectl -n monitoring get pods -l app=kube-prometheus-grafana
NAME READY STATUS RESTARTS AGE
kube-prometheus-grafana-6c9496d766-q7278 2/2 Running 4 5d

$ kubectl -n monitoring port-forward kube-prometheus-grafana-6c9496d766-
q7278 43000:3000
Forwarding from 127.0.0.1:43000 -> 3000
Forwarding from [::1]:43000 -> 3000
```

If you now go to `http://localhost:43000`, you will be greeted by the Grafana home page. You can already find some Kubernetes dashboards if you click on **Home** and then open the **General** folder. This is the aspect of the **Kubernetes Capacity Planning** dashboard:

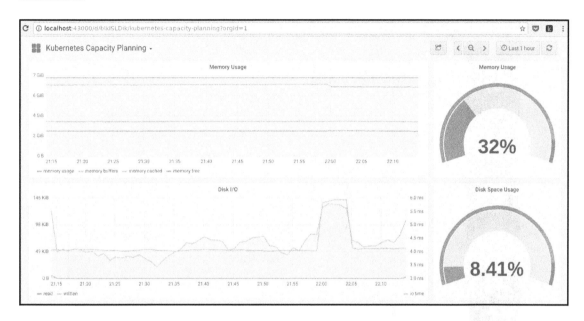

Sign in as `admin`/`admin` in the bottom-left corner so we can create our very first dashboard. By clicking on the plus sign and selecting **Create dashboard**, we can create our ElixirDrip dashboard. Before adding any panels, save it by pressing *Ctrl + S* after giving it a name.

We'll now add a panel that will show the response times histogram of the `/health` endpoint used by Kubernetes to assess whether our ElixirDrip pods are working as expected. Inside the **New panel** section, select `Graph` and a new graph with dummy data (actually a random walk) will appear:

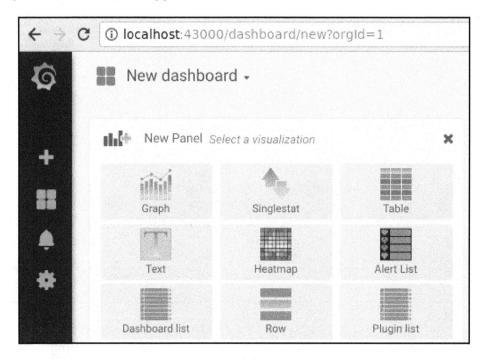

By clicking on the panel title, we can edit it. It's here that we can change the panel title (see the **General** tab), and it's also here that we'll configure everything related to our graph. Let's start with the `Metrics` tab and select the relevant metrics.

Because we used `prometheus-operator`, Grafana already has Prometheus configured as a data source, so it's just a matter of selecting it. If you start typing the metric name, Grafana will suggest metrics based on the available Prometheus data. Type `http_request_duration_microseconds_bucket{request_path="/health"}` as the first metric, and the graph will show you the `http_request_duration_microseconds_bucket` metric for every observation that has the custom label `request_path="/health"`.

By default, each legend key will show the full set of labels, including the `pod` and `le` labels (the latter gives you the metric bucket, a short form of *lower than or equal to*). To simplify, you can set each legend to only have the `pod` and `le` labels by writing the `{{pod}}` `{{le}}` expression in the `Legend format` field. However, we will still see 60 data series, because we currently have 20 buckets and three ElixirDrip pods (almost half of the data series don't even appear in the following screenshot):

If we don't care about specific pod response times, we may average the value of each bucket by using the `avg` aggregate operator:

```
avg(http_request_duration_microseconds_bucket{request_path="/health"}) by
(le)
```

With this approach, we don't want to know which pod emitted the data point, so we should remove the `{{pod}}` part from the legend format. Because the HTTP response times are being measured in microseconds, let's add the µs units to the legend (`{{le}}` µs).

Let's also change the `Left Y axis` by setting `No. of requests` as its label and its unit as `none`, so we can see the complete legend values.

To improve the readability of our graph, change the draw mode of the graph to `points` in the `Display` tab:

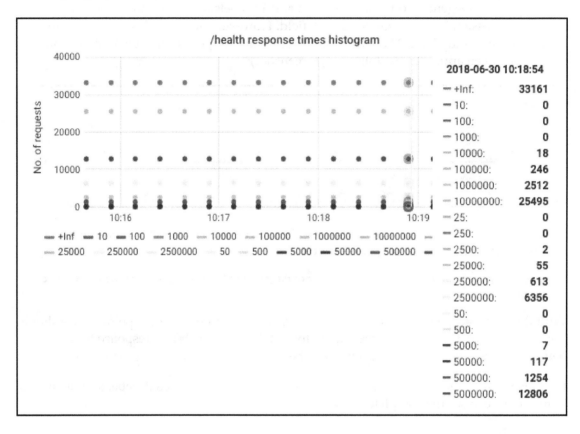

By looking at a specific point in time in our graph, we can conclude that most of the observations belong to the `+Inf`, 10 seconds (`10000000`), 5 seconds (`5000000`), 2.5 seconds (`2500000`), 1 second (`1000000`), and 0.5 seconds (`500000`) buckets. So, let's just consider these buckets by selecting them with the following metric expression:

```
avg(http_request_duration_microseconds_bucket{
request_path="/health",
le=~"\\+Inf|10000000|5000000|2500000|1000000|500000"}) by (le)
```

We now have a tidier graph, showing us the `/health` average response time split between our six buckets:

Still, this graph doesn't tell us at a glance what's happening with our application. Let's try to see the whole picture with percentiles.

Calculating percentiles

Instead of looking at the frequency of observations by bucket, let's use the `histogram_quantile()` query function to calculate some percentiles. This way, we'll better understand the distribution of our `/health` response times. We'll start by calculating the 50th percentile, replacing the previous metric with the following expression:

```
histogram_quantile(0.5,
  rate(
    http_request_duration_microseconds_bucket{request_path="/health",
    pod=~"elixir-drip.*"}[5m]
))
```

We are using the `rate(...)[5m]` function to take the 5-minute average rate of the samples in each histogram bucket. Because the histogram quantile is calculated for each combination of labels the metric has, we see three different graphs for each of our pods. We also need to change the `Legend format` to `50th percentile {{pod}}` and the unit of the `Left Y` axis to `microseconds (μs)`.

We can now observe that 50% of the `/health` requests in this time period took less than 8 seconds and the `8lts4` pod was the fastest pod:

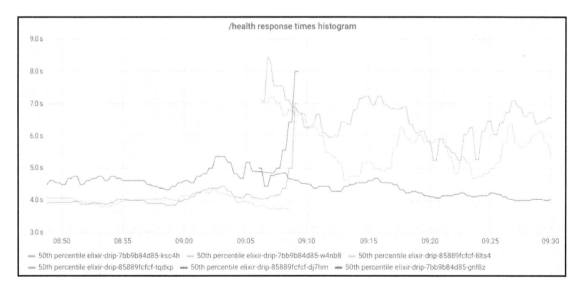

Having three graphs for each percentile we draw will soon get messy, so let's aggregate this percentile to only have a single data series:

```
histogram_quantile(0.5,
  sum without(instance, pod, host)(
    rate(http_request_duration_microseconds_bucket{request_path="/health",
pod=~"elixir-drip.*"}[5m]))
  )
```

We are using `sum without(...)` to remove the labels that vary from pod to pod, so that the pod aggregation works as expected. However, with this approach we end up losing the information about each individual pod. What we would like is to have a way to easily select the value of the `pod` label expression. Fortunately, Grafana allows us to define variables that can then be used in our graphs.

Setting Grafana variables

If you go to `Settings` (in the upper-right corner) and select `Variables`, we can add a new `pod` variable:

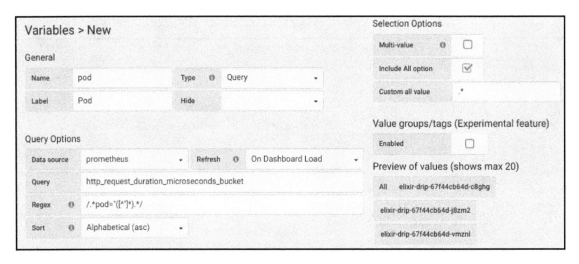

Besides the name of the variable, we set its type as `query` to obtain its values from a Prometheus `http_request_duration_microseconds_bucket` query. We then set `/.*pod="([^"]*).*/` as the regex that will extract the `pod` label value from each observation.

Recall that each Prometheus observation has the format
`<metric_name>{<lbl1>=<lbl1_val>,<lbl2>=<lbl2_val>,...}`
`<value> <timestamp>`.

The `pod` variable can assume distinct values of the `pod` label, but because we also selected the **Include All option**, we may say that the **All** value will insert a custom value; in our case, the **All** value will be `.*`. This will allow us to see the percentiles of one of the pods whose names were obtained from the variable query, or the aggregate percentile from all of them.

If we now set the `pod` label value to `$pod` in the previous 50th percentile metric expression, we are able to control its graph by changing the `Pod` dropdown in our dashboard. You can also use variables in any legend, so it's just a matter of updating the metric legend to `50th percentile {{$pod}}`:

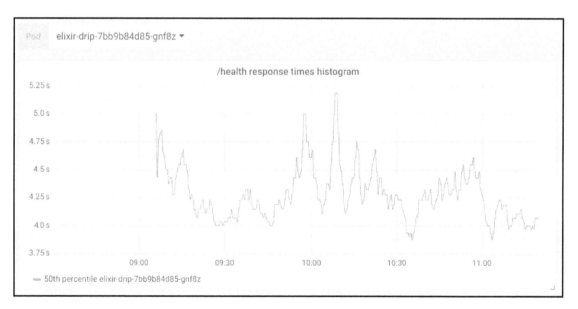

We now need to define the other percentiles in the same way, so let's define the following metrics for the 90th, 95th, 99th, and max percentiles, where `<percentile>` is $0.9, 0.95, 0.99$, and 1, respectively:

```
histogram_quantile(<percentile>, sum without(instance, pod, host) (
   rate(http_request_duration_microseconds_bucket{request_path="/health",
pod=~"$pod"}[5m])))
```

If we now look at the graph, you may find it weird that we can only see two data series, given that we've just defined five percentiles:

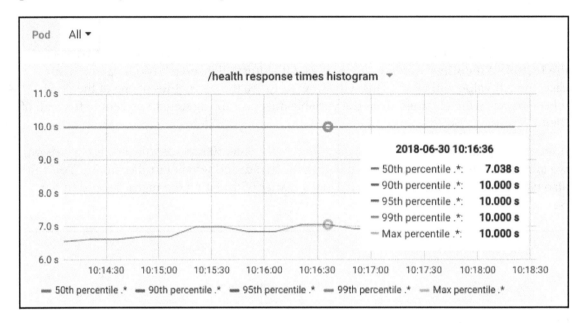

This is a common error that may happen when you use Prometheus histograms. Because you need to specify the bucket intervals up front, you may end up defining buckets where the vast majority of your observations fall into the top buckets. This results in the flat line we see at the 10 seconds line, where all percentiles with the exception of the 50th show the same values.

In our case, because we haven't overridden the default HTTP buckets set by the :prometheus_phoenix library, we are using the default 20 buckets (the 19 buckets shown next, plus the +Inf one) given by the :prometheus_http.microseconds_duration_buckets/0 function:

```
iex> :prometheus_http.microseconds_duration_buckets
[10, 25, 50, 100, 250, 500, 1000, 2500, 5000, 10000, 25000, 50000,
 100000, 250000, 500000, 1000000, 2500000, 5000000, 10000000]
```

To overcome this problem, we will override the default
`ElixirDripWeb.EndpointInstrumenter` configuration by setting new buckets from 500
microseconds to 25 seconds:

```
$ cat apps/elixir_drip_web/config/config.exs
# ...
config :prometheus, ElixirDripWeb.EndpointInstrumenter,
  duration_buckets: [500, 1000, 2500, 5000, 10_000, 25_000, 50_000,
    100_000, 250_000, 500_000, 1_000_000, 2_500_000, 5_000_000,
    10_000_000, 12_500_000, 15_000_000, 17_500_000, 20_000_000]
```

However, Phoenix isn't that slow, especially when we consider the `/health` route is being
served by the `HealthController.health/2` function, which simply generates a
timestamp and returns the list of nodes the current node is connected to. If you think
something fishy is going on, you're right: I've added a random sleep (that
is, `Process.sleep(:rand.uniform(13_000))`) between 1 and 13,000 milliseconds to the
`health/2` function so we could have more disparate response times.

Nonetheless, the principle still holds; it is likely that you will have to adjust your buckets
later on, after getting enough production data. In our case, we will remove the random
sleep and also add more buckets accordingly. This is how the same graph looks after these
changes were deployed:

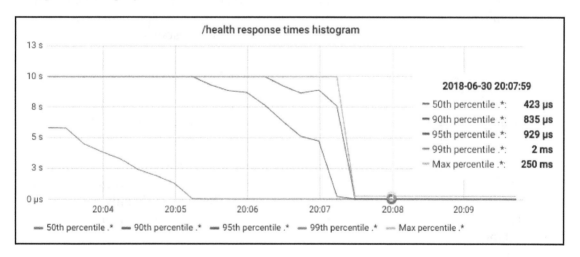

If we now zoom in, we'll find all the responses below 2.5 ms, and the 99th percentile below 1 ms, instead of the previous weird response times:

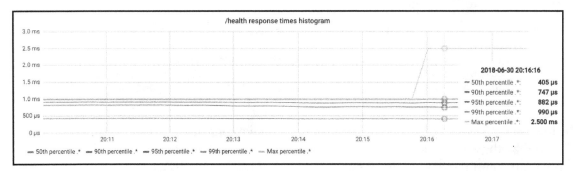

Response times are now much faster and in line with the expected Phoenix snappiness when handling requests backed by a function as simple as our `HealthController.health/2`. Let's check the other two metrics created by Prometheus histograms.

Because we've used a histogram for the HTTP response times, the `_sum` and `_count` metrics are also being collected. These metrics allow us to calculate the average HTTP request duration. As the name suggests, the `_sum` metric is a counter that accumulates the observed values, whereas the `_count` metric counts the number of observations. Armed with these two metrics, we can calculate the average `/health` response time in a given period:

```
rate(http_request_duration_microseconds_sum{request_path="/health",
pod=~"$pod"}[5m])
/
rate(http_request_duration_microseconds_count{request_path="/health",
pod=~"$pod"}[5m])
```

This will give us the average response time per pod. However, if we set the `pod` variable as `All`, we will get as many `Average` data series as the number of pods. To overcome this, we can aggregate the previous expression by taking its `max`. This way, we'll only have one `Average` data series that corresponds at any given time to the maximum average response time of all the existing pods:

```
max(rate(http_request_duration_microseconds_sum{request_path="/health",
pod=~"$pod"}[5m])
/
rate(http_request_duration_microseconds_count{request_path="/health",
pod=~"$pod"}[5m]))
```

When the average response time is presented in the same graph as the rest of the percentiles, it seems it almost doesn't change due to the graph's time axis catering for the percentiles times (the average response time stays consistently below 1 ms). To solve this, we can draw it using a new *y* axis on the right.

In any Grafana graph, you can click on the colored line in the graph legend and set **Y Axis** to **Right**. In our case, it's a bit trickier: because we have as many average response time data series as we have distinct `pod` variable values, we want to use **Series specific overrides** to affect all the data series in one go. Go to the **Display** tab, add a new override, and set its regex field as `/Average/`. Then, click on the + sign and choose the **Y-axis: 2** override, as shown in the following screenshot:

This will plot every graph data series that has `Average` in its name on the right *y* axis. We now just need to set the unit of the right *y* axis to `microseconds` (µs) in the `Axes` tab.

The average response times can now be seen in much more detail:

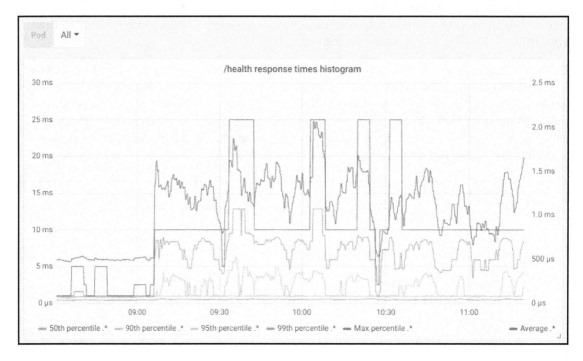

Armed with this knowledge, you can now create the graphs for the custom `Storage.store/4` histogram and the cache hit counter metrics that we set up previously.

A window to your nodes

Before we devise a way to look at and interact with our remote application, let's analyze how Elixir, given its Erlang heritage, works in a distributed environment. When you run an IEx shell or the ElixirDrip release, an Erlang VM starts. Each VM is called a *node*, and you can have many nodes running on the same computer.

To start a node, you define its `name` and *magic* `cookie`, and the node then tries to register itself on the local **Erlang Port Mapper Daemon (EPMD)**. This EPMD is a kind of name server that by default runs on port `4369` and registers which nodes are running in each host.

The `cookie` is indeed described as *magic*; check out the Erlang documentation at http://erlang.org/doc/reference_manual/distributed.html. Whoever knows the `cookie` value is able to connect to the nodes using it, no questions asked, so it's really important it is long and stored in a secure way. By default, Erlang forms clusters of nodes in clear, because it is assumed the cluster runs on a trusted network; anyone on the network is therefore able to intercept data exchanged between nodes.

In the following example, we start a node that sleeps for 20 seconds, and we then query the local EPMD about which nodes are currently running:

```
$ elixir --name simple@localhost --cookie yummy -e "Process.sleep(20000)" &

$ epmd -names
epmd: up and running on port 4369 with data:
name simple at port 35351
```

As you can see, port `35351` was assigned to the `simple` node. EPMD assigns a random high-number port to each node. If a remote node wants to connect to our `simple` node, it needs to set the same `yummy` cookie and then execute `Node.connect(:"simple@<local-hostname>")`, where `<local-hostname>` is the local host name. This would send a query to the `<local-hostname>` EPMD running on port `4369` about the `simple` node, which would reply successfully with port `35351`. With this information, the remote node is able to connect to the `simple` node via port `35351`.

Our first step is to connect to an ElixirDrip node running in a local Docker container, so we can then see what's happening inside the node.

Connecting to a containerized node

Before we connect to the node, we have to expose the container ports that will be used to connect the nodes. Edit your `docker-compose.dev.yml` file and add the following:

```
$ cat docker-compose.dev.yml
  # ...
  app:
    image: elixir_drip:dev
    # ...
    ports:
      - 4000:4000
```

```
                    - 4369
                    - 9001-9004
              #  . . .
```

The `9001-9004` port range is the range on which EPMD will assign ports to new nodes. We will tell EPMD to respect this range by passing the `inet_dist_listen_min` and `inet_dist_listen_max` parameters when running Elixir, and also when starting the application release. To pass these parameters when running the release, we need to set the `erl_opts` option in the release configuration:

```
$ cat rel/config.exs
  #  . . .
environment :prod do
  set include_erts: true
  set include_src: false
  set cookie: :"won't be used, we set it via a custom vm.args file
  (rel/custom.vm.args)"
  set erl_opts: "-kernel inet_dist_listen_min 9001 inet_dist_listen_max
  9004"
end
  #  . . .
```

If we set the same value for both the `inet_dist_listen_min` and `inet_dist_listen_max` parameters, we would only be able to run a single node in each host, because there can only be as many nodes as ports in this range. This would stop us from running any other node inside the pod, such as a console, for example (that is, running the release with `elixir_drip console`), as we did in the last chapter. This is why we set a range of four ports instead.

With the exposed ports in place, start the containers locally with `docker-compose -f docker-compose.dev.yml up -d` (`-d` means *detached* and hence containers will run in the background), run a shell inside the `app` container, and then start EPMD in debug mode with `epmd -d`, so we can see every interaction with it:

```
$ docker-compose -f docker-compose.dev.yml up -d
umbrella_postgres_1
umbrella_app_1
umbrella_prometheus_1

$ docker exec -i -t umbrella_app_1 bash

# epmd -d
epmd: Sun Jul 8 11:01:00 2018: epmd running - daemon = 0
```

Now, find the IP of the `app` container by running `docker inspect` on a host shell:

```
$ docker inspect umbrella_app_1 | grep "IPAddress"
            "SecondaryIPAddresses": null,
            "IPAddress": "",
                    "IPAddress": "172.21.0.3",
```

On another container shell, run the application while setting its name, cookie, and available port range:

```
$ docker exec -i -t umbrella_app_1 bash

# iex --name inside@172.21.0.3 --cookie testing --erl "-kernel
inet_dist_listen_min 9001 inet_dist_listen_max 9004" -S mix phx.server
  # ...
Interactive Elixir (1.6.4) - press Ctrl+C to exit (type h() ENTER for help)
iex(inside@172.21.0.3)1>
```

You will immediately see EPMD registering the `inside` node:

```
epmd: Sun Jul 8 11:19:42 2018: epmd running - daemon = 0
epmd: Sun Jul 8 11:20:45 2018: ** got ALIVE2_REQ
epmd: Sun Jul 8 11:20:45 2018: registering 'inside:1', port 9001
epmd: Sun Jul 8 11:20:45 2018: type 77 proto 0 highvsn 5 lowvsn 5
epmd: Sun Jul 8 11:20:45 2018: ** sent ALIVE2_RESP for "inside"
```

We can now connect to the node running inside the container. Let's spin up a node named `outside` on the host and then start the `observer` tool:

```
$ iex --name outside@0.0.0.0 --cookie testing --erl "-kernel
inet_dist_listen_min 9001 inet_dist_listen_max 9004"
Interactive Elixir (1.6.4) - press Ctrl+C to exit (type h() ENTER for help)
iex(outside@0.0.0.0)1> :observer.start
:ok
```

The `observer` interface will appear and we can go to `Nodes` `->` `Connect` `Node` to insert the node name running inside the container:

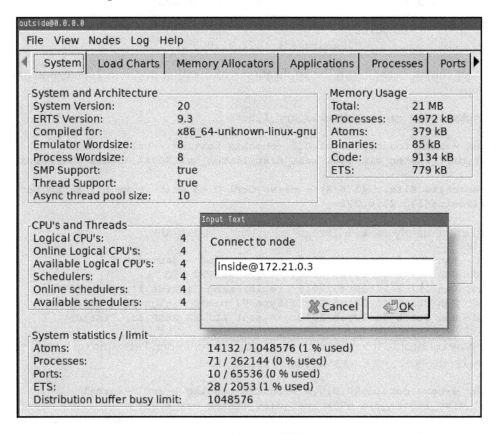

We can now select the `inside@172.21.0.3` node from the **Nodes** menu and see all the information about it, including the existing supervision trees for each running application; pry into the state of any processes; observe the CPU, memory, and IO load of the node; and much more:

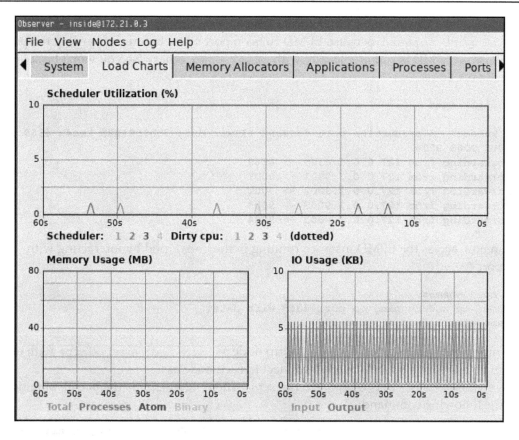

Let's now apply a similar strategy to connect to our ElixirDrip remote nodes.

Connecting to an Erlang node running in Kubernetes

In the previous section, we exposed a range of container ports that allow us to connect to Erlang nodes running inside the container from the outside. However, this time we don't want to expose the `4369` and `9001-9004` ports of the deployed pods by updating our Kubernetes `elixir-drip-loadbalancer` service because EPMD connections are not safe, even if you connect your nodes with TLS.

As such, we will forward the EPMD ports to the local environment with the help of `kubectl port-forward`. Because EPMD runs on port `4369`, before forwarding the ports make sure no EPMD is running locally with `pkill epmd`, otherwise you won't be able to forward port `4369`:

```
$ pkill epmd

$ kubectl -n production port-forward elixir-drip-7bb9b84d85-ksc4h 4369 9001
9002 9003 9004
Forwarding from 127.0.0.1:4369 -> 4369
Forwarding from 127.0.0.1:9001 -> 9001
Forwarding from 127.0.0.1:9002 -> 9002
Forwarding from 127.0.0.1:9003 -> 9003
Forwarding from 127.0.0.1:9003 -> 9004
```

We can now access the EPMD instance running in the `ksc4h` pod by interacting with local port `4369`:

```
$ epmd -names
epmd: up and running on port 4369 with data:
name elixir_drip at port 9001
```

Remember that we've named each ElixirDrip node as `elixir_drip@<pod-ip>` with our custom `vm.args` file, so we'll need to connect to each node as `Node.connect(:"elixir_drip@<pod-ip>")`, where `<pod-ip>` is the pod IP obtained with the following command:

```
$ kubectl -n production exec -t elixir-drip-7bb9b84d85-ksc4h -c elixir-
drip-prod -- env | grep POD_IP
POD_IP=10.40.0.41
```

By running `env | grep POD_IP` inside the `ksc4h` pod, we know the pod IP. However, the IP `10.40.0.41` is a Kubernetes internal IP with no meaningful value in our local environment. If we tried to connect to `elixir_drip@10.40.0.41` using the `Node.connect/1` function, the subsequent query to the EPMD running at the `10.40.0.41` address wouldn't work, since from the local point of view, there is no way to reach this address.

To overcome this, we will forward the `10.40.0.41` pod IP to the `localhost` address. First, ensure that you have the `net.ipv4.ip_forward=1` line uncommented in the `/etc/sysctl.conf` configuration file, so that we can set IPv4 forwarding rules. Then, forward the IP with the following command:

```
$ sudo iptables -t nat -A OUTPUT -d 10.40.0.41 -j DNAT --to-destination
127.0.0.1
```

```
$ ping 10.40.0.41
PING 10.40.0.41 (10.40.0.41) 56(84) bytes of data.
64 bytes from 10.40.0.41: icmp_seq=1 ttl=64 time=0.079 ms
64 bytes from 10.40.0.41: icmp_seq=2 ttl=64 time=0.086 ms
^C
```

We can now `ping` the pod IP, even if in reality it's the `localhost` replying. Let's now start a local IEx shell, similar to what we've done before, but this time we will name it `console@10.40.0.41`:

```
$ iex --name console@10.40.0.41 --cookie <cookie>
Erlang/OTP 20 [erts-9.3] [source] [64-bit] [smp:4:4] [ds:4:4:10] [async-
threads:10] [hipe] [kernel-poll:false]

Interactive Elixir (1.6.4) - press Ctrl+C to exit (type h() ENTER for help)
iex(console@10.40.0.41)>
```

The cookie value we're passing now (`<cookie>`) was set as a Kubernetes secret in the last chapter. We now have to set the same cookie value when running the `console@10.40.0.41` node to allow the latter to connect to the node running in the pod.

> If you don't remember the cookie you set on your Kubernetes secrets, you can always run an ElixirDrip console (`PORT=5678 ./bin/elixir_drip console`) inside the pod container and check the `Node.get_cookie/0` value. In our case, this is simpler because we're setting the cookie from an environment variable named `ERLANG_COOKIE`, so `kubectl exec -t <pod-name> -c <container-name> - env | grep ERLANG_COOKIE` should suffice.

After the previous port and IP forwarding setup, if we run `epmd -names`, we'll see two nodes (`console` and `elixir_drip`) registered. Remember we're querying the EPMD running on local port `4369`, which forwards to the same port on the `ksc4h` pod, so we're in fact querying the EPMD running in the remote pod:

```
$ epmd -names
epmd: up and running on port 4369 with data:
name console at port 43323
name elixir_drip at port 9001
```

We can now connect to the node running in the pod and start the `observer` tool:

```
iex(console@10.40.0.41)> Node.connect(:"elixir_drip@10.40.0.41")
true

iex(console@10.40.0.41)> :observer.start
:ok
```

Because we connected to the node before, it already shows up in the `Nodes` menu. We started `observer` from a running IEx shell again, but we can also immediately start the `observer` tool with Erlang:

```
$ erl -name console@10.40.0.41 -setcookie <cookie> -hidden -run observer
```

Using the Erlang approach, we aren't connected to any node from the get-go, so you still need to connect to the `elixir_drip@10.40.0.41` node with the `Nodes -> Connect Node` option.

Also, notice the `-hidden` flag that we're passing this time. By starting the local `console` node as hidden, it will only connect to a single node, instead of trying to connect by default to all the connected nodes available (due to the transitive nature of distributed Erlang):

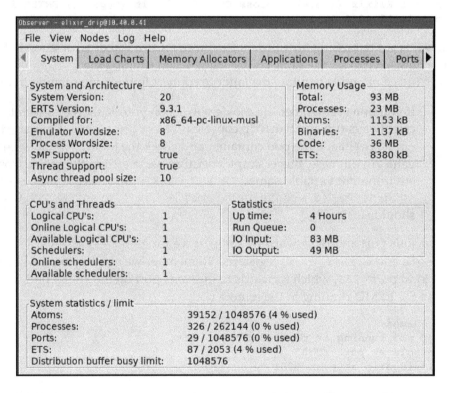

Let's now understand how can we run an IEx shell inside of a remote node.

Using a remote shell

If the information provided by the `observer` isn't enough, with this setup you can also run a remote shell from the comfort of your local shell:

```
$ iex --name console@10.40.0.41 --cookie $COOKIE --remsh
"elixir_drip@10.40.0.41"
Erlang/OTP 20 [erts-9.3] [source] [64-bit] [smp:4:4] [ds:4:4:10] [async-
threads:10] [hipe] [kernel-poll:false]

Interactive Elixir (1.6.4) - press Ctrl+C to exit (type h() ENTER for help)
iex(elixir_drip@10.40.0.41)> node()
:"elixir_drip@10.40.0.41"
iex(elixir_drip@10.40.0.41)> Node.list
[:"elixir_drip@10.40.2.143", :"elixir_drip@10.40.0.42",
:"console@10.40.0.41"]
```

As you can see, the current node (given by the `Kernel.node/0` function) is the remote one (`elixir_drip@10.40.0.41`), so whatever you run will be run on the remote node. Because we have the ElixirDrip nodes connected with the `libcluster` library, we see three nodes returned by the `Node.list/0` function.

Let's put the remote shell and `observer` tools to work for us by storing a file through remote shell and then looking at its contents with `observer`:

```
iex(elixir_drip@10.40.0.41)> jose_user =
ElixirDrip.Accounts.get_user_by_username("jose")
%ElixirDrip.Accounts.User{
  # ...
  username: "jose"
}

iex(elixir_drip@10.40.0.41)> ElixirDrip.Storage.store(jose_user.id,
"remote_shell_test.txt", "$/foo/bar", "ʕ•ᴥ•ʔ Vᴥ•V ᴀ^•ᴗ•^ᴀ (^_^) (^_^) Hello
from Remote Shell")
{:ok, :upload_enqueued,
 %ElixirDrip.Storage.Media{
   file_name: "remote_shell_test.txt",
   file_size: 95,
   full_path: "$/foo/bar",
   id: "173aBUSCM8nVJKPUDBe6EondStn",
   # ...
 }}
```

In the **Observer** that we've just started, go to the **Applications** tab and select the
`elixir_drip` application in the left-hand pane. Then, search for a `CacheWorker` process in
the supervision tree, whose parent is the `Supervisors.CacheSupervisor` process:

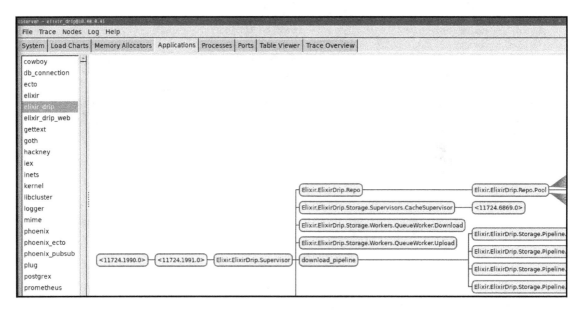

In our case, the `CacheWorker` process has the PID `11724.6869.0`. If you right-click on it
and select **Process info**, you can look at the process state:

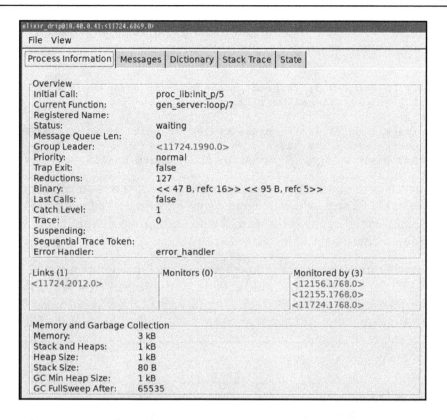

In the **State** tab, we can see the `CacheWorker` state:

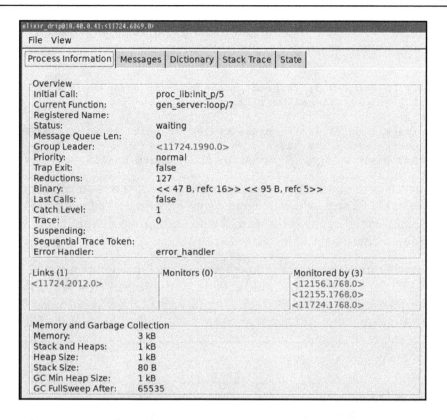

If you copy the binary content from the process state to an IEx shell and print it, you'll find, as expected, the file contents that we've just uploaded:

```
$ iex
Erlang/OTP 20 [erts-9.3] [source] [64-bit] [smp:4:4] [ds:4:4:10] [async-
threads:10] [hipe] [kernel-poll:false]

Interactive Elixir (1.6.4) - press Ctrl+C to exit (type h() ENTER for help)
iex> content = <<202,149,226, ...>>
"ʕ•ℒ•ʔ V•ℒ•V ₳^•ₐ•^₳ (^_^) (^_^) Hello from Remote Shell"
```

If you think the steps to connect the observer tool to a remote node are too cumbersome, check the `wobserver` library, which integrates with Phoenix and allows you to access all the information provided by the observer tool with your browser. You can find an example of how to configure this library in the book's source code.

The `wobserver` library also exposes Prometheus metrics (by default on the `/wobserver/metrics` path), so we could even set a new Kubernetes `ServiceMonitor` to scrape the metrics exposed by the `Wobserver` library about the VM (memory used and IO bytes), allowing us to create new Grafana graphs. Let's now move on to the last section of this chapter, where we'll explore how to investigate what's happening with our application running in production.

Inspecting application behavior

At the beginning of this chapter, we learned how to collect metrics throughout our application. That's the first step to successfully maintaining an application that is running smoothly in production. By collecting metrics and periodically analyzing them, we're aware of how well our application is performing. During this analysis, we will surely spot outliers or some odd behavior from a certain function or module, which will drive us to analyze its cause.

Besides learning how to collect metrics, we've also seen how to run a remote shell that's connected to our application in production. We'll also use a remote shell to run our experiments. Note that running them in production is dangerous. Since we're using our live environment, we risk bringing the service down for our clients, either due to a careless experiment or just from the added load to the system.

While this is true, and we do recommend the greatest of care when carrying out this sort of task, we also believe that this is the only way to get meaningful results. The weird behavior we've observed in production may only manifest itself in those exact conditions.

If you try to replicate it on your local machine, you may just get insignificant data and never get to the bottom of the issue you're trying to solve.

Elixir, standing on the shoulders of Erlang, has great support for profiling and tracing your applications safely in production. As we've said before, a great deal of care is necessary when doing this sort of operation in a live environment. Nevertheless, it's incredibly useful to have such great support from the Erlang VM to carry out profiling and/or tracing in your application.

It's important to note that, contrary to other systems, we won't pry into our production application by setting breakpoints and going step by step to try to analyze the context. All the observations that we will make are indirect and will never stop any process that's running in production. In the first chapter of this book, we saw how to use IEx helpers to set breakpoints from the shell. That's a helpful technique to debug your application when developing it locally, but it's not suitable for inspecting your application in production.

This section is divided into two sub-sections: in the first, we explore the use of one of the profilers built into Mix to understand what's happening with a certain function in our application, whereas in the latter, we use Erlang's `:dbg` module to trace how live requests are handled.

Profiling with the fprof profiler

We're now going to learn how to use one of the profilers that ships with Mix to analyze the performance of a certain function in our application. The profiler we're going to use is based on Erlang's `fprof` profiler. Mix exposes this profiler through a Mix task, which is how we're going to interact with it.

We're going to profile the `ElixirDrip.Storage.store/4` function, which is responsible for creating a new `Media` entry on the database and triggering an upload task. To simulate that this function is taking way longer than expected to complete, we're going to insert a `Process.sleep/1` call into the `ElixirDrip.Storage.Media.create_initial_changeset` function, which is one of the functions called by the `store` function.

The fascinating and intriguing cases to profile only come to life when an application is deployed in a live environment, is used by actual users, and generates unpredictable workloads. Nonetheless, using a `Process.sleep/1` call allows us to demonstrate the important aspects, which will enable you to carry out your own profiling whenever you have the need.

To profile our application we'll use the `mix profile.fprof` task:

```
$ mix profile.fprof -e
'ElixirDrip.Storage.store("177VXwhSuI7vjzkZOU7uvowAZzO", "test.txt", "$",
"some file content")'

Warmup...
Reading trace data...
End of trace!
Processing data...
Creating output...
Done!
```

			CNT	ACC
(ms)	OWN (ms)			
Total			4023	
2047.954	28.076			
:fprof.apply_start_stop/4			0	
2047.954	0.015			
anonymous fn/0 in :elixir_compiler_1.__FILE__/1			1	
2047.935	0.004			
ElixirDrip.Storage.store/4			1	
2047.931	0.016			
ElixirDrip.Instrumenter.observe_duration/2			1	
2047.837	0.010			
anonymous fn/4 in ElixirDrip.Storage.store/4			1	
2047.658	0.020			
:suspend			14	
2019.878	0.000			
ElixirDrip.Storage.Media.create_initial_changeset/4			1	
2006.250	0.038			
Process.sleep/1			1	
2000.888	0.020			
DBConnection.run/3			4	
38.715	0.047			
DBConnection.run_begin/3			2	
37.645	0.017			
ElixirDrip.Repo.insert/1			1	
35.661	0.004			
ElixirDrip.Repo.insert/2			2	
35.657	0.008			
Ecto.Repo.Schema.insert/4			2	
35.653	0.009			
# ...				

We've cropped the output of this command to make it easier to read. For instance, running this task will actually create an upload task, since we're running the profiled code in production.

To profile the `store` function, we're passing the `-e` argument, which contains the code that will be evaluated.

The profiler starts by doing a warmup, followed by the profiling itself, and finishes with an analysis of the generated data, which is printed to the terminal.

The profiler does a warm-up to ensure the generated data is as close to real requests as possible. During this phase, the profiler runs the code without measuring anything. This is important because this first run may need to perform some initial setup, such as connecting to the database, allowing for the second run (which is the one measured) to use the setup made by the first run.

Let's now analyze the most important part of the previous code block: the output of the profiler. The output consists of a table, where the first column contains the name of the function being measured and the remaining columns contain data corresponding to this function. The first data column, called `CNT`, contains the number of times this function was called during profiling. Then, we have two columns related to time measurements: `ACC` and `OWN`, both in milliseconds. The `ACC` column contains the total time spent in that function, whereas the `OWN` column contains the time spent in that function without taking into account the time of the functions called by it.

 By default, the output of the `profile.fprof` task is sorted by the `ACC` time, but we can also sort it by the `OWN` time, passing `--sort own` as an option to the `Mix` task.

Looking at this table, it's very clear where the problem resides: we have a huge jump from around 20 ms to around 38 ms. This is a by-product of having a synthetic example, as in the real world we probably wouldn't see such a clear divide in the time spent between two functions. Another clue that indicates this is a synthetic example is the huge difference between the `ACC` and `OWN` times. Since we've just made the process sleep on the `create_initial_changeset` function, which puts the process in a suspended state, we don't see it as having a big `OWN` timespan. In a real-world example though, you should also keep an eye on the times presented in the `OWN` column, which will promptly indicate which functions are internally taking the most time (without accounting for calls to other functions).

Let's run the profiler again, but now passing the `--callers` option. This will give us a more detailed view of where time is spent (at the cost of extra load on our production system). Let's analyze the output of this second run:

```
$ mix profile.fprof --callers -e
'ElixirDrip.Storage.store("177VXwhSuI7vjzkZOU7uvowAZzO", "test.txt", "$",
```

```
"some file content")'

Warmup...

# ...

ElixirDrip.Instrumenter.observe_duration/2                    1      2024.454
0.016
  anonymous fn/4 in ElixirDrip.Storage.store/                 1      2024.454
0.016  <--
    ElixirDrip.Storage.Media.create_initial_changeset/4       1      2004.626
0.027
    ElixirDrip.Repo.insert/1                                  1        14.972
0.005
    ElixirDrip.Storage.get_owner/1                            1         4.518
0.002
    Ecto.Changeset.put_assoc/3                                1         0.312
0.004
    ElixirDrip.Storage.Workers.QueueWorker.enqueue/2          1         0.010
0.001

anonymous fn/4 in ElixirDrip.Storage.store/4                 1      2004.626
0.027
  ElixirDrip.Storage.Media.create_initial_changeset/4        1      2004.626
0.027  <--
    Process.sleep/1                                          1      2000.753
0.033
    ElixirDrip.Storage.Media.create_changeset/2              1         1.870
0.024
    Ksuid.generate/0                                         1         1.141
0.043
    ElixirDrip.Storage.Media.generate_storage_key/2          1         0.572
0.012
    ElixirDrip.Storage.Providers.Encryption.Simple.generate_ 1         0.263
0.003

# ...
```

As we did in the first run, we've cropped the output of this command. When passing this option, we get a block dedicated to each profiled function we saw in the first run. On the right side, we can see an arrow on each of these blocks, which indicates the marked function for the current block. All of the numbers in the rest of the block are relative to the line with the arrow. For instance, in the first block, we can see that the marked function is `ElixirDrip.Storage.store`. In this profiler, we only have one caller, so all the time spent in the `store` function was from that single caller.

More interestingly, in the functions called by the `store` function, we can see in great detail where the time was spent. We can observe that the call to `ElixirDrip.Storage.Media.create_initial_changeset` took around two seconds, whereas the next longest call was to `ElixirDrip.Repo.insert`, which took around 15 milliseconds.

Again, as in the first example, there is a huge gap and it's unlikely that you will find this huge difference in a real profiling session. Nevertheless, we can see that the problem must reside within `ElixirDrip.Storage.Media.create_initial_changeset`. Since we're now using the `--callers` option, we can now move on to analyze the block dedicated to this function, which we're displaying right after the first block. In this second block, we can see that for the functions called by the `create_initial_changeset` function, most of the time (again, around two seconds) was spent calling the `Process.sleep` function. After this function call, the longest entry in this block belongs to the `ElixirDrip.Storage.Media.create_changeset` function, which took around 2 milliseconds. Thus, we've found our culprit! The next step would be to fix this and then closely monitor it to try and assess whether the problem has indeed been solved. If not, the investigation would start all over again, but now with a different system in place, which would lead to different profiling results.

We've now gone through a profiling session and learned how we can use the `fprof` profiler to analyze the behavior of our code. However, `fprof` isn't the only profiler that's shipped with Mix. We also have `eprof` and `cprof`, which, just like `fprof`, are Erlang profilers. You should use the one that's best suited for the type of profiling you'll be carrying out. The `eprof` profiler is a time-based profiler (such as `fprof`), but presents information in a different way. Besides the total call count for each function, it shows the percentage of time spent on each function, and also shows the number of microseconds per function call for each function. The `cprof` profiler only shows the number of function calls for each profiled function, which is essentially the first column we've seen on the output of `fprof`. If you're only interested in this metric, using `cprof` over `fprof` is advantageous because it'll have a lower impact on your production system. We recommend that you check out the official documentation for these Mix tasks, in order to find out all the available options.

 The documentation for `fprof` is available at `https://hexdocs.pm/mix/Mix.Tasks.Profile.Fprof.html`, for `eprof` at `https://hexdocs.pm/mix/master/Mix.Tasks.Profile.Eprof.html`, and for `cprof` at `https://hexdocs.pm/mix/Mix.Tasks.Profile.Cprof.html`.

We've reached the end of the profiling section. Let's now move on to the next topic, where we'll learn how to trace our live application.

Tracing with the :dbg module

Having seen how to profile the modules and functions of our application, let's now explore how to do tracing in a live environment. While in the previous section, we had to provide the data for the function we wanted to profile as input, in this section we'll follow a different approach. We will tell the VM the functions that we want to see traced, and then we'll observe the live calls that our users are making in production. This is really interesting because we're analyzing the behavior of our application with real data, which usually allows us to draw better conclusions. Moreover, as we discussed previously, there are certain bugs that only manifest themselves in a live environment. In such cases, we need to be able to tap into the live requests and try to figure out what's happening with them.

To carry out the tracing, we'll be using Erlang's :dbg module. There are some lower-level constructs to carry out tracing experiments, such as the :erlang.trace function. We think that dealing directly with these constructs brings no added value over just using :dbg, which provides a useful abstraction layer to carry out tracing experiments without having to worry about too many details. Moreover, we feel that using :dbg directly is already dangerous enough, since if misused, it can cause great damage to your production environment. The lower-level commands are usually more error-prone, and as such using them directly increases the likelihood of inadvertent side effects in production.

Let's check how a tracing experiment usually takes place. We begin by calling the following command in our IEx session:

```
iex> :dbg.tracer
{:ok, #PID<0.661.0>}
```

Calling the tracer function will spawn a new process, called a *tracer process*, which will be responsible for collecting the events associated with this tracing experiment. This process will receive messages in its mailbox according to the tracing patterns we define. In the following examples, we'll just print the tracing events to the console, but it's possible to configure :dbg to save the trace output to a file, which is handy when you want to analyze it later on.

To choose which functions we want to trace we'll use the :dbg.tp function:

```
iex> :dbg.tp(ElixirDrip.Storage, :store, 4, [])
{:ok, [{:matched, :elixir_drip@10.40.0.41, 1}]}
```

Using the tp function, we specify the module, function, and arity we want to trace. We may omit the arity of the function, which will result in tracing all the arities of that function name. In the same way, we may omit the function name, which will result in all of the functions of that module being traced.

The last argument, an empty list, is a match specification. It allows us to further refine the types of function calls we want to trace, and we'll explore it in a bit.

With the tracing pattern defined, there's one final step to start our tracing experiment:

```
iex> :dbg.p(:new, :c)
{:ok, [{:matched, :elixir_drip@10.40.0.41, 0}]}
```

Calling the p function this way will instruct the VM to trace function calls on new processes and ports that don't exist when this function is called, according to the tracing pattern we previously defined. There are some different options we could've used here. In the first argument, instead of :new, we could have used :all, which would trace all the processes in the VM. Another option would be to use self(), which would only trace function calls from the shell process—in certain conditions, this may be just what we need. As for the second argument, instead of tracing function calls, we might want to trace messages sent and received by a certain process. In that case, you can use :m in the second argument, which will trace the sent and received messages for the process with the PID of the first argument.

 Do not try to trace messages when you're covering all processes in the VM. In other words, don't use the :all and the :m options together when calling the :dbg.p function, as that will likely cause trouble in your production environment.

With this in place, we're ready to start tracing the calls to the store function. Since our application doesn't have real users, we simulated a user interacting with the system and uploaded a new file through our web application. Upon doing that, we observed the following entry in our IEx session:

```
(<0.769.0>) call
'Elixir.ElixirDrip.Storage':store(<<"17fVtjzyIYW4aKmfKXUG754u4AI">>,<<"test
ing_tracing.txt">>,<<"$">>,<<some live content\n>>)
```

We can see that the store function was called, and with which arguments. This by itself may not answer all the questions we have, but we can iterate and try to put more probes into the system, which will give us more information to grasp what's going on. For instance, let's say we've analyzed the code for the storage function and we suspect there's an issue when enqueing a new upload task. We'd begin by tracing that function as well:

```
iex> :dbg.tp(ElixirDrip.Storage.Workers.QueueWorker, :enqueue, 2, [])
{:ok, [{:matched, :elixir_drip@10.40.0.41, 1}]}
```

Now, after triggering a new file upload in our application, we see the following:

```
(<0.935.0>) call
'Elixir.ElixirDrip.Storage':store(<<"17fVtjzyIYW4aKmfKXUG754u4AI">>,<<"test
ing_tracing_with_queue.txt">>,<<"$">>,<<"some live content\n">>)
(<0.935.0>) call
'Elixir.ElixirDrip.Storage.Workers.QueueWorker':enqueue('Elixir.ElixirDrip.
Storage.Workers.QueueWorker.Upload',#{content => <<"some live content\n">>,
  media =>
    file_name => <<"testing_tracing_with_queue.txt">>,file_size => 6,
  full_path => <<"$">>,id => <<"17fXKLprLRYyN9E5xfzsOz7KCw0">>,
  storage_key => <<"17fXKLprLRYyN9E5xfzsOz7KCw0_20180720T232423.txt">>,
  inserted_at =>
  #{'__struct__' => 'Elixir.NaiveDateTime',
  calendar => 'Elixir.Calendar.ISO', day => 20, hour => 23,
  microsecond => {844068,6},
  minute => 24, month => 7, second => 23, year => 2018},
  updated_at =>
  #{'__struct__' => 'Elixir.NaiveDateTime',
  calendar => 'Elixir.Calendar.ISO', day => 20 ,hour => 23,
  microsecond => {844088,6},
  minute => 24, month => 7, second => 23, year => 2018},
  uploaded_at => nil,user_id => <<"17fVtjzyIYW4aKmfKXUG754u4AI">>},
  type => upload,
  # ...
  user_id => <<"17fVtjzyIYW4aKmfKXUG754u4AI">>})
```

We now see the `enqueue` function being traced, and we can inspect its arguments. In this case, we can check the `%Media{}` struct that was passed to it, which provides us some valuable information that would help to debug a real situation. If we still couldn't find anything, we'd repeat the process and try to narrow down the issue we're trying to solve. Just ensure you don't trace too many functions at once, as that may put too much load on the Erlang VM.

Let's now briefly explore match specifications and how they can help us to narrow down our traces. For the purpose of this example, let's say that we have reasons to believe that the issue we're trying to sort out only occurs when users are uploading files to the root path (`"$"`). In this case, we can set our trace pattern to only catch files being uploaded to this path. Here's the function call that creates this pattern:

```
iex> :dbg.tp(ElixirDrip.Storage, :store, 4, [{[:_, :_, "$", :_], [], []}])
{:ok, [{:matched, :elixir_drip@10.40.0.41, 1}, {:saved, 1}]}
```

This is similar to what we saw earlier, with the only difference in the last argument. As we've said before, the last argument is a match specification, which is composed of three parts: head, conditions, and body. Here, we're only making use of the head. Conceptually, what we're doing here is similar to pattern matching on a function clause. In this case, our `store` function has four arguments, and we're saying we only care about the third and want to match it against "`$`". This is a very complex topic in the Erlang world, and we won't dive into details in this book. If you want to further explore this topic, please check out the official documentation at `http://erlang.org/doc/apps/erts/match_spec.html`.

With this match specification in place, we'll only get traces from file uploads to that path, similar to the ones we've seen already. You can generalize this technique and apply it whenever you need to need to filter your traces based on a certain argument value.

To close this section, we'll learn how to change the match specification to get the return value of the traced functions in the trace output. In certain cases, having access to the arguments that a traced function received isn't enough, and we need access to its return value to figure out what's going on. For these cases, we can adapt the match specification as follows:

```
iex> :dbg.tp(ElixirDrip.Storage, :store, 4, [{[:_, :_, "$", :_], [],
[{:return_trace}]}])
{:ok, [{:matched, :elixir_drip@10.40.0.41, 1}, {:saved, 2}]}
```

In order to see the return value of the function we're tracing, we need to insert `{:return_trace}` into the body of the match specification (its last argument). With our trace pattern updated, we can now make a new file upload on the web interface, which will generate the following output in our IEx session:

```
(<0.784.0>) call
'Elixir.ElixirDrip.Storage':store(<<"17fVtjzyIYW4aKmfKXUG754u4AI">>,<<"test
ing_tracing_return_value.txt">>,<<"$">>,<<"some live content\n">>)
(<0.784.0>) returned from 'Elixir.ElixirDrip.Storage':store/4 ->
   {ok, upload_enqueued, file_name =>
<<"testing_tracing_return_value.txt">>,
                        file_size => 6,
                        full_path => <<"$">>,
                        id => <<"17fwfSOqxQnKxp2OhjB1eebDWrd">>,
                        storage_key =>
<<"17fwfSOqxQnKxp2OhjB1eebDWrd_20180721T025245">>,
                        # ...
                        user_id => <<"17fVtjzyIYW4aKmfKXUG754u4AI">>}}
```

As we can observe from the previous snippet, we now get the return value of the `store` function, a `{:ok, :upload_enqueued, %Media{}}` tuple.

Now for the last step of any tracing session: stopping all traces. To accomplish that, we just need to call the following function:

```
iex> :dbg.stop_clear
:ok
```

This is a very simple step. Nevertheless, it's a very important one, as skipping its execution may cause some unpleasant surprises.

Throughout this section, we've learned several techniques to trace our application as needed, depending on the task at hand. Note that these techniques don't have to be used in isolation; it's when combining them that obtain better insights about what's happening with our

Lastly, we want to point out that the tools we've described in this chapter aren't the only useful tools to profile/trace applications. Particularly, we want to mention the XProf (`https://github.com/Appliscale/xprof`) and Tracer (`https://github.com/gabiz/tracer`) libraries. We've chosen to demonstrate how to use the `:dbg` module because we think that it helps to better understand how tracing works on the Erlang VM. However, in your day-to-day work you may resort to using higher-level abstractions, such as the two libraries we've just mentioned. Let's now wrap up this chapter and recap the most important concepts we've explored in it.

Summary

Throughout this chapter, we analyzed different ways of understanding what's happening under the hood of an Elixir project running in its production environment. Permanently feeding your dashboards with collected metrics allows you to quickly assess your application's current state.

With Prometheus and Grafana, you can then take a deep dive into your metrics data and understand behaviors and patterns that may fly under the radar at first sight. We also learned how to emit custom Prometheus metrics by enriching our Elixir code with instrumentation calls, when the metrics provided out of the box by the Prometheus suite of libraries weren't enough.

Sometimes, it is imperative to have an updated and informed view of the deployed code that is running. In these cases, you can connect to your application and look at it armed with the powerful Observer tool. After deploying the application on the cloud, connecting to it is more difficult, but not impossible, thanks to the incredible distributed tools inherited from Erlang.

Another important aspect to ensure you're always up to date regarding your application health is alerting. We didn't cover it, but both Prometheus and Grafana are capable of triggering alerts based on a set of rules that are then delivered through different channels, ranging from the usual email to a custom solution catering to your requirements.

Configuring your monitoring architecture is an ongoing process, where you create new graphs and update existing dashboards based on the problems and bottlenecks that you find in your day-to-day operations. Similar to the majority of topics in software engineering, there's no cookie-cutter solution here either. Strive to have a few alerts and try to instrument as much as possible so you can have a general idea of every part of your system, and then fine-tune as you go.

We've seen several ways to tap into what's happening in our application running in production, by seeing how to profile and trace functions in it. The techniques we've explored aim to minimize the impact on the production system, without the need to ever stop a process to debug it. Much like our Elixir applications, the debugging and tracing techniques are based on asynchronous message passing between processes.

In this chapter, we covered the following topics:

- Prometheus, a popular open source monitoring solution heavily used for many projects in production
- Installing and configuring the `prometheus` suite of Elixir libraries to collect metrics about our ElixirDrip application
- Emitting custom histogram and counter metrics to measure the time a function takes to execute and to count the number of cache hits
- Using Prometheus locally and deploying a Prometheus and Grafana bundled solution to Kubernetes with the help of `helm` charts
- Configuring the Prometheus instance deployed in Kubernetes to automatically discover and scrape the metrics emitted by new ElixirDrip pods
- Using Grafana to create beautiful and expressive dashboards, representing the multitude of collected metrics in a meaningful way
- Distributed Erlang and how it allows us to run and connect multiple Elixir nodes
- Using Observer to peer into your running application, be it on the cloud or simply running in a local container

- Running a shell in a remote node living inside a Kubernetes pod
- Using the `mix profile.fprof` task to profile a certain function, alongwith some possible options we can pass to it
- Using Erlang's `:dbg` module to trace function calls and messages being exchanged in a running application

This is the last chapter of this book! We sincerely hope that you've enjoyed reading it as much as we've enjoyed writing it. Although we've reached the end of the book, the journey we've started together isn't over—it never will be.

While covering the broad range of topics we've presented in this book, along the way we left links to either documentation or interesting projects, so that you can continue the journey we started together and take your Elixir learning even further. We are fortunate to be part of such an energetic and vigorous community, and we can only imagine the amazing things that will come from this incredible group of people.

Other Books You May Enjoy

If you enjoyed this book, you may be interested in these other books by Packt:

Learning Functional Data Structures and Algorithms
Atul Khot, Raju Kumar Mishra

ISBN: 9781785888731

- Learn to think in the functional paradigm
- Understand common data structures and the associated algorithms, as well as the context in which they are commonly used
- Take a look at the runtime and space complexities with the O notation
- See how ADTs are implemented in a functional setting
- Explore the basic theme of immutability and persistent data structures
- Find out how the internal algorithms are redesigned to exploit structural sharing, so that the persistent data structures perform well, avoiding needless copying.
- Get to know functional features like lazy evaluation and recursion used to implement efficient algorithms
- Gain Scala best practices and idioms

Learning Functional Programming in Go
Lex Sheehan

ISBN: 9781787281394

- Learn how to compose reliable applications using high-order functions
- Explore techniques to eliminate side-effects using FP techniques such as currying
- Use first-class functions to implement pure functions
- Understand how to implement a lambda expression in Go
- Compose a working application using the decorator pattern
- Create faster programs using lazy evaluation
- Use Go concurrency constructs to compose a functionality pipeline
- Understand category theory and what it has to do with FP

Leave a review - let other readers know what you think

Please share your thoughts on this book with others by leaving a review on the site that you bought it from. If you purchased the book from Amazon, please leave us an honest review on this book's Amazon page. This is vital so that other potential readers can see and use your unbiased opinion to make purchasing decisions, we can understand what our customers think about our products, and our authors can see your feedback on the title that they have worked with Packt to create. It will only take a few minutes of your time, but is valuable to other potential customers, our authors, and Packt. Thank you!

Index

www.ingramcontent.com/pod-product-compliance
Lightning Source LLC
Chambersburg PA
CBHW060636060326
40690CB00020B/4423